Multi–User Virtual Environments for the Classroom:

Practical Approaches to Teaching in Virtual Worlds

Giovanni Vincenti
Towson University, USA

James Braman
Towson University, USA

Senior Editorial Director:	Kristin Klinger
Director of Book Publications:	Julia Mosemann
Editorial Director:	Lindsay Johnston
Acquisitions Editor:	Erika Carter
Development Editor:	Joel Gamon
Production Editor:	Sean Woznicki
Typesetters:	Milan Vracarich
Print Coordinator:	Jamie Snavely
Cover Design:	Nick Newcomer

Published in the United States of America by
Information Science Reference (an imprint of IGI Global)
701 E. Chocolate Avenue
Hershey PA 17033
Tel: 717-533-8845
Fax: 717-533-8661
E-mail: cust@igi-global.com
Web site: http://www.igi-global.com/reference

Library of Congress Cataloging-in-Publication Data

Multi-User Virtual Environments for the Classroom : Practical Approaches to Teaching in Virtual Worlds / Giovanni Vincenti and James Braman, editors.
    p. cm.
  Includes bibliographical references and index.
  Summary: "This book highlights cutting-edge teaching ideas using theoretical discussions, case studies, and experiments pertaining to virtual environments, including learning foreign languages in virtual environments and examples that encourage educators to design and develop new worlds of learning inside and outside the university"--Provided by publisher.
  ISBN 978-1-60960-545-2 (hardcover) -- ISBN 978-1-60960-546-9 (ebook) 1. Virtual reality in education. 2. Shared virtual environments. I. Vincenti, Giovanni, 1970- II. Braman, James, 1981-
  LB1044.87.M85 2011
  371.33'468--dc22
                                    2011008140

British Cataloguing in Publication Data
A Cataloguing in Publication record for this book is available from the British Library.

All work contributed to this book is new, previously-unpublished material. The views expressed in this book are those of the authors, but not necessarily of the publisher.

Table of Contents

Section 1
Pedagogy and MUVEs: A Necessary Intersection

Section 3
MUVEs in the Classroom: Experiences, Lessons and Applications

Detailed Table of Contents

Section 1
Pedagogy and MUVEs: A Necessary Intersection

In this chapter, DeMers argues that the major impediment to the adoption of multi-user virtual environments is a misperception that their use is more a function of their exotic nature than their ability to deliver a quality learning experience. The connection between best educational practices and the use of MUVEs as educational venues shows a mix of strong and weaker linkages parallels that of traditional education. MUVEs are extremely adept at providing active learning experiences, providing scenarios for students to examine their preconceptions, creating real-world settings for learning, and for developing collaborative environments and student-faculty interactions. There is evidence that, when well designed, educational environments support different learning styles, although this is poorly studied. The remaining best educational practices demonstrate either loose associations, or lack demonstrable examples for their support. These practices revolve around feedback both to students and to the instructor, and course assessment. Despite substantial research on these practices, there seems ample opportunity for virtual worlds to provide not only comparable, but often-superior examples of best practices when applied properly.

Chapter 2

The authors of this chapter examine current methods of pedagogical teaching in higher education and explore the possible mapping into a multi-user virtual environment. They consider the teaching process of construction and delivery for a module of student education. A discussion of the transition of delivery methods from the established, slow changing traditional media, to the modern flexibly of open-source driven, community-based methods which are the foundation of virtual environments are presented.

Chapter 3

Jim Barrett, Umeå University, Sweden
Stefan Gelfgren, Umeå University, Sweden

This chapter, based on a set of developed teaching scenarios, discusses how Second Life, can be used in student-centered pedagogy. Drawing upon experiences from traditional education, Web 2.0 tools, and problem-based pedagogy grounded in project work, social media, engineering, and digital humanities, this chapter presents a pedagogy based upon the concepts of participatory culture, and co-creation on the part of students in the learning process. The authors have been involved in developing the core curriculum for a term-long course for Museum Studies. Based upon the practical experience of conducting course work, the authors critically discuss ICT and problem oriented learning on a general level, including the benefits and disadvantages for the student and for the teachers.

Chapter 4

David M. Antonacci, University of Kansas Medical Center, USA
Nellie Modaress, University of Kansas Medical Center, USA
Edward Lee Lamoureux, Bradley University, USA
David Thomas, University of Colorado Denver, USA
Timothy Allen, Wharton Research Data Services, USA

User-created virtual worlds are emerging technologies with rapidly growing acceptance in education. The focus of this chapter is on virtual worlds for constructivist learning activities, because their use has application to many real-life courses and has the potential to transform teaching and learning. To assist educators with recognizing and understanding virtual world learning activities, the chapter discusses the Interaction-Combinations Integration model. Using a case study method, the authors examine the usefulness of this model to organize and describe actual virtual world learning activities, provide additional learning activity examples, and describe what was needed to implement and conduct these learning activities.

Chapter 5

Mitzi P. Trahan, University of Louisiana at Lafayette, USA
Nan B. Adams, Southeastern Louisiana University, USA
Susan Dupre, University of Louisiana at Lafayette, USA

The authors of this chapter present an overview of research related to Second Life, and demonstrate that practical applications of MUVEs in education and professional development can be merged with an existing model for learning in virtual learning environments. While the three-dimensional environment of online worlds often exhibit game-like ambiance, there is serious business going on "in-world.". In particular, Second Life is being used as a vehicle for university course delivery, conference sessions, informal meetings, collaborative projects, and creative products. The growing experimentation with multi-user virtual environments for educational purposes demands rigorous examination of all aspects of these digital worlds. While their use appears to enhance and expand traditional distance learning, educators acknowledge that barriers to access remain, including a steep learning curve for orienting users to MUVE navigation and functionality. The application of Adams's Knowledge Development Model for Virtual Learning Environments provides a framework for the design of in-world learning opportunities and activities, many of which tend to mirror pedagogical best-practices in real life.

Chapter 6

Carol M. Shepherd, National University, USA
Madelon Alpert, National University, USA

Greater teacher efficacy in online teaching and teaching in virtual worlds appears to be positively correlated with certain exhibited dispositions and practices. Inferential measures of dispositions such as friendliness, enthusiasm, active involvement, patience, and tolerance, among others, exhibited by professors in online instruction, lead to greater student participation and satisfaction. In this chapter, the authors discuss the analysis of four professors' teaching practices in a virtual environment and how certain teacher dispositions and practices emerged. Three areas were studied: instructor participation with students; the tone of communication with students; and the creation of a community of learners in a virtual world. The creation of a community of learners in a virtual environment helps to foster a sense of belonging, and was measured by activities such as informal course announcements, media, emails, and student and professor biographies, indicating that the instructor is interested in each student. There are two perspectives to online instruction discussed: that of the student, as well as that of the instructor.

Chapter 7

Keysha I. Gamor, ICF International, USA

Experiential learning has long been touted as critical to deep understanding, learning, and ownership of knowledge. Virtual worlds are one such category of technological tools that enhance the way in which we may engage in a learning experience. Using a virtual world for instruction does not, and should not, be an "all or nothing" proposition. Virtual worlds are flexible, rich, collaborative environments which can be used in a variety of ways to augment a traditional, instructor-led course, Web-based courses, and other types of courseware, in addition to serving as a 'stand-alone' solution. Grounded in experiential learning and constructivist theory, this chapter explores ways in which one may exploit the flexibility of a virtual world to meet the real-life demands of traditional courses.

Section 2
Roadmaps from Theory to Practice

Chapter 8

Andreas Konstantinidis, Aristotle University of Thessaloniki, Greece
Thrasyvoulos Tsiatsos, Aristotle University of Thessaloniki, Greece
Stavros Demetriadis, Aristotle University of Thessaloniki, Greece
Andreas Pomportsis, Aristotle University of Thessaloniki, Greece

A comparison of the potential of Learning Management Systems (LMS) and Multi-User Virtual Environments (MUVE) to facilitate the implementation of traditional face to face collaborative learning techniques in an online environment is discussed, as well as the benefits and challenges of an integrated approach. The chapter examines the combination of these two technological approaches to the collaborative learning pedagogy which can both diminish their weaknesses and amplify their strengths. Concluding the chapter is a discussion on an integrated approach, which merges two open source solutions: the popular LMS Moodle with the MUVE OpenSim.

Chapter 9

Alberto Bucciero, University of Salento, Italy
Nicoletta Di Blas Polytechnics of Milan , Italy
Luca Mainetti, University of Salento ,Italy
Paolo Paolini, Polytechnics of Milan, Italy
Caterina Poggi, Polytechnics of Milan, Italy

Here, the authors discuss how to make an effective use of Multi-User Virtual Environments in formal education. It draws on the authors' experience with four different programs deployed from 2002, involving more than 9,000 students from 18 European countries, including Israel and the USA. This chapter is intended as a set of "lessons learned" on all of the relevant aspects of this kind of enterprise, from design to implementation and actual deployment. It is therefore meant as a short "user's guide" for building effective and engaging edutainment experiences in virtual worlds.

Chapter 10

Hugh Denard, King's College, UK
Enrica Salvatori, Università di Pisa, Italy
Maria Simi, Università di Pisa, Italy

In this chapter, the authors evaluate the outcome of a two year-long experimental educational project using Second Life as a teaching and learning platform. The project's main goal was to investigate the added value of a multi-user environment in a multi-disciplinary and international context for learning about history, archaeology, acquiring a scientific approach and methodology to historical reconstruction and 3D visualization, as well as the skills to use different media technologies for communication and collaboration. The chapter describes educational facilities and resources as well as heritage visualization projects built in the Digital Humanities Island in Second Life, where the collaboration between King's College London and the University of Pisa took place.

A Faculty Innovator Grant allowed the Old Dominion University Career Management Center to develop the capability and protocol to take a group of students to an employer site in Second Life within the context of a one-credit-hour career course. This chapter describes the development process and the challenges encountered in preparing a class to visit and productively interact with employers in Second Life. It also discusses minimizing development costs and the amount of faculty time and effort necessary to incorporate trips to virtual worlds in their class syllabi. This chapter provides an interesting example of a "how to" for those interested in taking groups into Second Life rather than an academic study of the effects of a visit on the students.

Chapter 12

When educators started to use virtual worlds such as Second Life to create learning exercises, the natural approach was to script these exercises using in-world tools. However, experience with this approach highlighted a number of significant issues, including the high level of skill required to create and maintain the exercises and problems of scaling. As part of the PREVIEW project, the authors of this chapter had the opportunity to consider a new approach, where all the non-3D elements of the exercise were defined and managed on the Web. This chapter starts with a description of the "traditional" approach to MUVE exercise design, followed by an assessment of the problems inherent in this approach, and then goes on to describe the PIVOTE system itself from a technical, author, and user point of view, followed by expectations on how it could be developed in the future. The authors present two case studies of how PIVOTE has been used by different institutions.

Chapter 13

This chapter presents a case study of the use of a Virtual World environment in UK Higher Education. It reports on the activities carried out as part of the SIMiLLE (System for an Immersive and Mixed reality Language Learning) project to create a culturally sensitive virtual world to support language learning. The aim of the SIMiLLE project was to investigate the technical feasibility and pedagogical value of using virtual environments to provide a realistic socio-cultural setting for language learning interaction. The authors provide related background and provide information on the framework used for the evaluation of the system, followed by a summary of results and lessons learned.

Chapter 14

Various advantages of Multi-User Virtual Environments have been identified and discussed in related literature. MUVEs, however, have not been widely adopted in educational settings due to technical and pedagogical challenges. This chapter discusses a qualitative case study that examines how Second Life, was diffused on a University campus. Both instructor and student perspectives were examined using interviews, observations, and a survey as a data collection methods. The theory of diffusion of innovation was used as a theoretical framework in both the design of the study and the analysis of the data. The findings from the study indicate although the future application of MUVEs can be promising, various challenges exist for instructors to adopt these technologies in their classroom instruction.

Section 3
MUVEs in the Classroom: Experiences, Lessons and Applications

Science through Second Life focuses on the opportunities and challenges encountered by educators in the creation and realization of a series of virtual learning environments in Teen Second Life on the topic of environmental sustainability. Specific examples of learning activities, supportive instructional materials, and the pedagogical reasoning are woven into a larger narrative detailing a semester-long, 9th grade science class. By reporting our design and development process and the subsequent course of implementation of instructional activities, this chapter provides pre- and in-service teachers and instructional designers with a model of instructional design and practical considerations for developing MUVEs in a blended instructional environment.

Chapter 16

This chapter considers the effectiveness of virtual worlds as environments in which disaffected or "failed" learners can be reengaged with education. The premise is that virtual worlds allow learners to "play" with their identity and potentially reinvent themselves as better learners. In this chapter, this idea is supported by research which shows virtual worlds as engaging, motivating, fun places to learn. The topics of identity in virtual worlds, identity and learning, and education in virtual worlds are examined. One hundred 13 to 17 year old, students were observed working in the Second Life teen grid, which is a virtual world restricted to young people between 13 and 17 years old. Written feedback from students is analyzed and discussed in the chapter.

Melissa Gresalfi, Indiana University, USA
Jacqueline Barnes, Indiana University, USA
Patrick Pettyjohn, Indiana University, USA

This chapter considers the crucial role the teacher plays in supporting the successful use of immersive technology in the classroom, focusing particularly on the use of an interactive, online, multiplayer videogame called Quest Atlantis. This chapter presents an account of successful strategies for integrating immersive technologies into teaching practice, such that the game does not replace the teacher, nor the teacher replace the game, but rather the two are integrated in their mutual support of student learning. Specifically, the focus is on two distinct roles that teachers can play in leading whole-class discussions: attuning students to important concepts and connections in the game, and deepening opportunities to learn beyond what is afforded in game design. For each role, the authors present two contrasting cases with the goal of illuminating the central role that a teacher can play when integrating complex technologies into the classroom.

Mary Ann Mengel, Pennsylvania State University, USA

In this chapter, the author presents how undergraduate students in an environmental science course learned to make environmentally-conscious decisions by visiting a virtual green home in Second Life. One group of learners was immersed in a virtual field trip experience where they viewed evidence of green decisions in a virtual home. Another group studied the same content through a static Website. Pre-test and post-test results for both groups demonstrate significant differences in scores after instruction. Results suggest a virtual world can provide an instructionally effective medium if instructors allow ample time and training for students to become familiar with the environment. Feedback from Second Life participants suggests that learners felt they had participated in an "experience." Instructional design considerations which focus on creating an educational experience involving active tasks and social interactions might best maximize the educational usage of a virtual world.

Chapter 19

Marc Conrad, University of Bedfordshire, UK

Project Management is a field of intellectual and pragmatic enquiry that is inherently inter-disciplinary. It typically involves the integration of areas such as: project scoping, time, cost, and human resource management, while the management of effective inter-team communication, project risk, and procurement aspects are all central to the discipline. To try to cover all of these areas within a single university assignment presents somewhat of a challenge. This chapter demonstrates that the deployment of a Multi-User Virtual Environment can indeed encompass these areas in an effective manner, both from learning objectives, realism, and assessment points of view. This chapter has emerged from the author's experience of three years deployment of Second Life as an integral part of a unit on Project Management, offered as part of both undergraduate and postgraduate courses within the Department of Computer Science and Technology at the University of Bedfordshire.

Chapter 20

Bjoern Jaeger, Molde University College, Norway, & Curtin University, Australia
Berit Helgheim, Molde University College, Norway

Working in a virtual world creates new opportunities for both students and teachers. In particular, virtual team role playing provides excellent support for collaborative learning approaches in a cost efficient manner. This chapter describes the authors' experiences in developing a virtual team role play learning environment in Second Life® over a period of three years. Theoretical justification for bringing role playing into the virtual world is provided. Outlined in this chapter is role playing, its setup in both the real and virtual world, and a description of how it has evolved at one university, to a distributed case involving several locations. The author's experiences from role playing sessions are presented for each year in this chapter.

Chapter 21

Anne P. Massey, Indiana University, USA
Mitzi M. Montoya, Arizona State University, USA
Valerie Bartelt, Indiana University, USA

The authors Massey, Montoya, and Bartelt discuss how over the last two decades, communication and collaboration tools to support student project work have evolved significantly, with an expanding array of options. This chapter explores the use of collaborative tools in a cross-university course where virtual student teams engaged in a multi-week project. The project teams had access to a collaborative toolkit that included Web 1.0 and Web 2.0 tools, as well as collaboration spaces in a virtual world. Findings suggest that more successful student teams were better able to match Web 2.0 and virtual world collaborative technologies to project activities, while other, lower performing teams defaulted to more familiar Web 1.0 technologies. The virtual worlds played a key role in facilitating relationship building in the collaborative learning process. The findings presented in this chapter are particularly relevant to instructors seeking to integrate and use virtual worlds in the classroom for collaborative project work and distance learning.

The ubiquity of digital technology and the pervasiveness of the Web have led to a paradigm shift in how we live and work. The Object Design program at Towson University engages the network effect of emergent technologies developing pedagogy to keep pace with global developments. Students learn 21st century skills as they engage virtual immersive environments as a digital design tool, for iterative prototyping, as a virtual presence augmenting traditional studio practice, to engage new economic platforms, and as a virtual learning environment for global dialogue and collaboration. Steady growth in virtual immersive environments supports a burgeoning virtual goods market and further exploration for learning, training and innovation across social sectors: enterprise, education, and government in the evolution of society.

This chapter examines the instructional design of, and reports on research conducted within, a multiuser virtual environment created for a distributed collaborative engineering design course. The course's Advanced Interactive Discovery Environment provided a variety of synchronous online tools and communication devices to support SameTime virtual team collaborations and problem-solving within the course. Several research elements are examined, including how different team social communication patterns may be related to the patterns of team technology use. Relevant theoretical frameworks including social learning, media stickiness, and cognitive imprinting, and recommendations on how different tools can be effectively integrated into multiuser virtual environments to facilitate learning are discussed.

This chapter investigates whether an educational virtual environment can be developed to practice listening comprehension skills that meets second language student needs, complies with usability criteria, and is motivating to use. The authors investigate whether the usability of virtual reality technology positively affects language learning listening comprehension. The chapter provides background research and information in computer assisted language learning (CALL), VR, and second language methodology. Also presented are technical and qualitative descriptions of Realtown, a virtual environment designed to promote listening comprehension. Student errors, motivation, and ease of use, among other features, were measured on listening comprehension activities in Realtown. A further discussion in the chapter includes a longitudinal study on learning issues, first-person, and collaborative experiences in VR, including impacts of VR on learning and knowledge transfer when combined with traditional instruction.

Paulo Frias, University of Porto, Portugal
Ricardo N. Fernandes, University of Porto, Portugal
Ricardo Cruz, University of Porto, Portugal

Frias, Fernandes, and Cruz present a proposal for a case study that aims to describe and understand communicative and pedagogical processes involved in Second Life in the context of second language learning, by modeling in-world lessons of Portuguese as a second language for ERASMUS students arriving in Portugal. The purpose is to provide examples of situated e-learning driven activities and to perceive how an immersive environment stimulates learning by involving students in a virtual reality situation. Advantages of this platform compared to physical life teaching and learning contexts, through the inherent characteristics of this medium, such as the synchronous and simultaneous use of voice and text are discussed.

Regina Kaplan-Rakowski, Southern Illinois University, USA

The author uses her teaching experience, gained both in the real world and through virtual worlds, to convey several potential foreign language activities that can be conducted in a virtual environment. This chapter presents lesson plans to take advantage of several affordances of virtual worlds and presents activities that are difficult or even impossible in a traditional classroom. Teachers are encouraged to use the lessons as examples of possible activities, which they can modify accordingly to their needs and to the needs of their students, their experience, and their preferences.

Preface

As educators, we are often faced with the monumental task of imparting knowledge to many students. It is, by far, not a simple or trivial task. We spend our time dedicated to our students and experimenting with various pedagogical approaches in order to accomplish this goal in the best way possible. Each student is unique, and in combination, from these differences emerges distinct characteristics for each section of every class every time it is taught. Add to this again, the changes in the student body over time by way of differences in culture, technology, and progress. It is these changes, however, that spark the creative nature of educators, as we aim to meet the needs of new generations of learners over and over again.

Multi-User Virtual Environments, like the name implies, are environments designed to be able to host and let interact many users at once through some technological artifact. While there are many potential uses across many domains, our focus and interest relates to how educators can best use these types of spaces. There are many that may argue against the use of virtual environments, virtual reality, augmented reality, and even Web-based educational technology for that matter. On the flip side of the coin, there exist many who stand in opposition of this and advocate the usage of these types of technology. Even in our own experiences in promoting various educational techniques and tools, we have certainly run into those not willing to embrace change or experimentation of any kind. Teaching merely through books and lectures is quickly becoming overpowered by learning through the many forms of multimedia and Web based content that students are exposed to every day. Obtaining information and multitasking through these many types of media is not simply a skill, but it is a way of life for many students and teachers. Education is changing. For this very reason, we should be proactive towards reaching out to students through non-traditional means to enhance teaching and learning. Our particular focus is teaching and learning through multi-user virtual environments (MUVEs). The educational community has certainly seen an increase in interest for teaching in MUVEs like Second Life, Twinity, There, and World of Warcraft, just to name a few.

Virtual worlds in general have been a hot topic in the educational arena for some time. While many are avid supporters for a particular world or technology, some are quick to try out many of these new realms. While many of the authors of the chapters in this book focus on particular technologies, the ideas and concepts can certainly be ported to other and similar environments. While the particular features of one virtual world, when compared to another may be useful in some contexts, the similarities of these technologies are often astounding. No matter the particular environment or "world" in some cases, porting traditional ideas and lectures into these spaces are not always straight-forward. Many even consider these tools as too technical for present students with significant barriers of entry. We see these barriers as something that can be overcome though learning about best practices and learning through our students the best approaches to teaching. The plasticity of these environments allows us many venues to create simulations that truly immerse students in a particular subject and can also serve as another platform for online education. Through the use of innovative technology, we can reach a new generation of learners in profound ways.

The concept of this particular book was born out of yet another text. While working on a similar book on the general use of multi-user virtual environments for education, coupled with the number of responses and interest in the topic, we wanted to then create a book that would lend itself to case studies, best practices, lesson plans, and experimentation. With this book, we also wanted to open the idea to all types of education, including high-schools and other forms of learning. This book, *Multi-User Virtual Environments for the Classroom: Practical Approaches to Teaching in Virtual Worlds,* meets that goal by providing an open forum for the many contributors to present their lesson plans, experimental results, knowledge, and experiences in one volume.

It is important to understand that the idea of virtual environments should not be limited to the interaction of multiple users through computer software in the traditional view of Web 2.0 technologies. These kinds of environments are utilized for many different purposes daily. This means that the applications of MUVEs should not be limited to what is already available. The flexibility of space and environment offered by these technologies is unparalleled in the real world, thus effectively breaking many physical barriers of reality involving space and time, allowing us to find ourselves in the middle of a simulation of a historical city that is physically set on the other side of the globe. These environments not only allow us the flexibility to be other places, but to be other people, and to interact with people in multiple time zones around the world.

When we introduce the idea of a virtual environment, we are really discussing a simulation that displays characteristics with which we can interact. Such characteristics can be as tied to reality as the realization of a physics engine that governs the world. In this particular case, we can see that fields such as Computer-Aided Design or Engineering have been operating within virtual environments since its origins. The idea that the majority of modern airplanes operated by commercial and private airlines have been designed through the use of computers and programs that simulate a physical environment should set a parameter of reference for any further discussion about how virtual environments are not just games and fun.

Another significant endeavor that needs to be attributed to virtual environments is the utilization of simulations in overcoming personal barriers. Such barriers can be represented by fears such as agoraphobia (the fear of being in places where it may be difficult to get out quickly), arachnophobia (the fear of spiders), or acrophobia (fear of heights). Patients can easily face their fears through virtual environments that recreate the situation that provokes anxiety in a safe manner. Through exposure therapy, patients may show some habituation to the environment, thus overcoming their fear also in real life. To this end, many simulations, through MUVEs, games, and standalone programs have been breaking ground in terms of the realism that they can simulate. Ever increasing advancements are being made through both hardware and software, making these spaces more like life and engaging. Some are even beginning to simulate various sensations bring these to our physical bodies. Of course, skeptics may quickly rebut that we can live with minor fears, without the need of virtual environments to help the progression towards a phobia-free life. We should then look into other ways in which virtual environments help people carry on with their lives by observing the devastating effects that a post-traumatic stress disorder (PTSD) may have on someone. With the current situation of global unrest, we probably know someone who has fought in a war or been exposed to extremely stressful situations. Virtual environments have also been utilized in helping with the desensitization to traumatic events to which the patient was exposed, thus effectively working as rehabilitation therapy towards regaining a normal handle on life.

It is also important that we do not relegate the idea of MUVEs to desktops and laptops. The power of computing is increasing drastically every year as the size and the format of computers changes and often shrinks. This means that we often hold in our hands small computers that are as powerful as the ones that until a few years ago were managing the flight of spacecrafts or the operations of small- and medium-sized companies.

The latest and most important paradigm shift comes from a line of computers that is often regarded as the lost child for which there is no hope: gaming consoles. Such computers not only offer an unbelievable amount of processing power, they have also become a platform on which users interact for multiple purposes. If we go back a few years, we can probably remember Italian plumbers fighting turtles and crawling into green tubes. Although the success of gaming is undisputed, we can easily observe how even this once monolithic feat is now open to influences from other domains. It should be enough to realize that a good set of today's games offer an online experience that we can share with others, thus offering an alternative form of multi-user virtual environment. The second significant change is observed when we look at some of the most successful franchises in gaming; education has finally started utilizing the entertainment medium through games.

A next step that is likely to take place involves the blending of real and virtual life. We already witnessed a slight shift towards augmented reality, which refers to the injection of real-life environments into computer programs that are able to interact with the inputs and in some way integrate what we can see with the naked eye with digital extras. As this revolution is just beginning, we cannot yet state that there exist ways in which we can interact with others (thus leveraging the multi-user concept) while blending reality and virtuality. This reality is still in the making, but it will be here shortly. And the step to making sure that such augmented reality is integrated in an educational setting is also just a few steps away from the milestone we just mentioned. In beginning to set the stage for many such uses of MUVEs and similar technologies, are those in the educational forefront that have the foresight on innovative uses. In this book, many educators discuss their ideas and experiences through their chapters.

Section 1: Pedagogy and MUVEs: A Necessary Intersection, starts off the book by highlighting the intersection of MUVEs and the indispensible pedagogical experiences of educators working with these tools. The first chapter by Michael DeMers, *Linking MUVE Education and Best Educational Practices,* argues that the major impediment to the adoption of these tools is a misperception that their use is more a function of their exotic nature than their ability to deliver a quality learning experience. There is indeed quite a bit of educational merit to these environments as discussed in this chapter and throughout the book. In the next chapter by Capanni and Doolan, *Mapping Current Teaching and Learning Practices to Multi-User Virtual Environments,* the authors examine teaching in higher education and explore the mapping of content and delivery into MUVEs while discussing the transition from various media for education. Chapter 3, *Learning Places: A Case Study of Collaborative Pedagogy Using Online Virtual Worlds* by Jim Barrett and Stefan Gelfgren focuses on student centered pedagogy through teaching scenarios in Second Life based upon the concepts of participatory culture and co-creation. The next chapter is *Using the Interaction-Combination Integration Model to Explore Real-Life Learning in User-Created Virtual Worlds* by Antonacci, Modaress, Lamoureux, Thomas and Allen. The authors use a case study methodology to describe the Interaction-Combinations Integration Model in relation to constructivist learning activities relating to virtual worlds. Tranhan, Adams and Dupre in chapter 5, *Virtual Learning Environments: Second Life MUVEs to Leverage Student Ownership* present their research on using

Second Life in education and discuss the application of Adam's Knowledge Development Model for Virtual Learning Environments. The next chapter, *Exploring the Correlation between Online Teacher Dispositions and Practices in Virtual Classrooms and Student Participation and Satisfaction* by Carol Shepherd and Madelon Alpert, discusses the importance of teacher disposition in online educational environments and its relation to a greater student satisfaction and participation. Keysha Gamor concludes the first section with her chapter titled, *Signs and Guideposts: Expanding the Course Paradigm with Virtual Worlds*, exploring ways in which we can use the flexibility of virtual worlds to meet the needs of real-life traditional courses.

The next section of the book, **Section 2: Roadmaps from Theory to Practice**, highlights projects and research endeavors of educators and practitioners that are using virtual worlds in various contexts. The chapter, *Collaborative E-Learning Techniques: Learning Management Systems vs. Multi-User Virtual Environments* by Konstantinidis, Tsiatsos, Demetriadis and Pomportsis, discusses and compares the potential of Learning Management Systems and MUVEs to facilitate the implementation of traditional face-to-face collaborative learning techniques. Bucciero, Di Blas, Mainetti, Paolini, and Poggi in *How to Build Effective "Edutainment" Experiences in MUVEs* discuss building effective and engaging edutainment experiences in virtual worlds from their experiences. In chapter 10, the authors evaluate the outcome of a two year experimental project with Second Life as a teaching tool in *Learning by Building in SL: A Reflection on an Interdisciplinary and International Experience* by Denard, Salvatori and Simi. In *Trip to the Virtual Career World*, authors Wunderlich, Forbes, and Mills discuss their experiences at Old Dominion University Career Management Center with using Second Life as a medium for students to interact with employers. Following in chapter 12, *Web Based Authoring for Virtual Worlds Using PIVOTE*, David Burden and Andrew Jinman talk about the PIVOTE system and how it can be used to assist educators in virtual world educational exercise development. In *Immersive Education Spaces Using Open Wonderland: from Pedagogy through to Practice* by Gardner, Gánem-Gutiérrez, Scott, Horan, and Callaghan, the authors present a case study highlighting activities carried out as part of the SIMiLLE project to create a culturally sensitive virtual world to support language learning. Concluding Section 2 is a chapter by Feng and Song titled, *Teaching and Learning in Second Life: A Case Study*, where a case study is discussed on the diffusion of a virtual world on a university campus.

Section 3 is the next main section of the book titled **MUVEs in the Classroom: Experiences, Lessons and Applications** that focuses on applications of MUVEs in the classroom and the shared experiences and lessons provided by several authors. Chapter 15, by Elizabeth Wellman and Cathy Arreguin titled, *Science through Second Life: A Case Study of MUVEs in an Urban 9th Grade Classroom*, examines the opportunities and challenges educators face in creating a learning environment in Teen Second Life on the topic of environmental sustainability. Following, *Virtual Worlds – Enjoyment, Motivation and Anonymity: Environments to Reengage Disaffected Learners with Education* by Marc Thompson considers the effectiveness of virtual worlds on reengaging disaffected learners. Focusing on the crucial role of the teacher in learning through immersive technology, particularly with a videogame called Quest Atlantis, the authors Gresalfi, Barnes and Pettyjohn discuss their experiences in chapter 17, *Why Videogames are not Teacher-Proof: The Central Role of the Teacher when Using New Technologies in the Classroom*. Next in, *Constructing an Experience in a Virtual Green Home* by Mary Ann Mengel, the author presents how students in an environmental science course learned to make environmentally conscious decisions by visiting a virtual green home in Second Life. Marc Conrad's chapter, *Teaching Project Management with Second Life*, discusses the author's experiences on using Second Life in teaching Project Management in a unique way in the Department of Computer Science and Technology at the University of

Bedfordshire. Next in chapter 20, by Bjoern Jaeger and Berit Helgheim titled *Virtual Team Role Playing: Development of a Learning Environment*, the authors highlight their experiences in using and developing a virtual team role play learning environment in Second Life. In *Cross-University Collaborative Learning: Extending the Classroom via Virtual Worlds* by Massey, Montoya, and Bartelt, the authors, explore the use of various collaborative tools for a cross university course using virtual teams of students for a project. The chapter emphasizes how educators can use virtual worlds in the classroom for collaborative work. Next is a chapter by Jan Baum who discusses the pervasiveness of the Web in society and how tools like Second Life and other virtual worlds can be used for collaborations, learning, training and other positive interactions. Professor Baum highlights her work with Second Life and the experiences with her students in the Object Design program in *Object Design in Virtual Immersive Environments*. The authors Wu and Koszalka in their chapter, *Instructional Design of an Advanced Interactive Discovery Environment: Exploring Team Communication and Technology Use in Virtual Collaborative Engineering Problem Solving*, examine the instructional design of, and research on a MUVE that can be used for a distributed collaborative engineering course. The authors also discuss several frameworks on this topic related to social learning, media stickiness, and cognitive imprinting. Next in chapter 24, *Towards Usable Collaborative Virtual Reality Environments for Promoting Listening Comprehension*, by Garcia-Ruiz, Edwards, Aquino-Santos, Tashiro and Kapralos, the authors investigate if educational virtual environments can be developed to practice listening comprehension skills for second language learners. The next chapter focuses on a case study involving the understanding of communicative and pedagogical processes with Second Life in the context of second language learning by modeling lessons of Portuguese as a second language in an immersive fashion in, *Second Language Teaching in Virtual Worlds: The Case of European College Students under the ERASMUS Program* by Frias, Fernandes and Cruz. Concluding the book is a chapter by Regina Kaplan-Rakowski titled *Teaching Foreign Languages in a Virtual World: Lesson Plans*. In this chapter, the author uses her experiences with virtual worlds to create and explain several lesson plans and language based activities that can be used by educators wanting to explore the potential of virtual worlds or other immersive environments.

It is our sincere hope that the chapters in this book are helpful to those wanting to know more about virtual worlds in the context of education and how they can be used to help students learn in new and innovative ways. We foresee that as new generations of learners enter schools and universities, these new tools and simulations will one day be more commonplace. Works such as this volume will serve as a foundation to the next generation of teachers, who will easily interact with students through multiple methods, including virtual ones.

We again want to thank all of the contributing authors of this book for taking the time to share their research and experiences. It is through their hard work and experimentation that we can begin to see the great things that have been done already and to start thinking about the potential for education in the future.

Giovanni Vincenti
Towson University, USA

James Braman
Towson University, USA

Acknowledgment

Projects like these never happen in a complete vacuum. It takes the combination of great effort and dedication of many people to make it a success. Editing books can be a slow process, taking many twists and turns, but with a talented group of people working together, great things can happen. That being said, we would like to sincerely thank the contributing authors of this book, whose talent was the driving force that allowed this book to be possible in its current form. It has been an absolute pleasure working with such a gifted and dedicated group of individuals, driven by their passion for pushing educational boundaries through their research and experimentation in using various technologies and virtual worlds. Without your hard work and willingness to share your ideas, none of this would have been possible.

We would also like to express our deep appreciation to the members of the Editorial Advisory Board for their time helping to review the many chapters and documents. Thank you to all the additional reviewers who volunteered their time and energy towards making the book successful. And as always, we would like to thank the publishing team at IGI for their help, patience, and guidance throughout the process. We are very grateful to have been allowed the flexibility of including a diverse set of topics and ideas in our book.

Last but certainly not least, we would also like to also thank our families, friends, and colleagues for their support and patience throughout this project, as always. We are often considerably invested in our many projects, and can always count on your support as we continue to work towards many aspects at improving education, research, and the use of virtual worlds. Thank you to everyone who made this book possible!!

Giovanni Vincenti
Towson University, USA

James Braman
Towson University, USA

Section 1
Pedagogy and MUVEs:
A Necessary Intersection

Chapter 1
Linking MUVE Education and Best Educational Practices

Michael N. DeMers
New Mexico State University, USA

ABSTRACT

A major impediment to the adoption of multi-user virtual environments (MUVEs) is a misperception that their use is more a function of their exotic nature than their ability to deliver a quality learning experience. The linkage between best educational practices and the use of MUVEs as educational venues shows a mix of strong and weaker linkages parallels that of traditional education. MUVEs are extremely adept at providing active learning experiences, providing scenarios for students to examine their preconceptions, creating real-world settings for learning, and for developing collaborative environments and student-faculty interactions. There is evidence that, when well designed, educational environments support different learning styles, although this is poorly studied. The remaining best educational practices demonstrate either loose associations, or lack demonstrable examples for their support. These practices revolve around feedback both to students and to the instructor, and course assessment. Despite substantial research on these practices there seems ample opportunity for virtual worlds to provide not only comparable, but often-superior examples of best practices when applied properly. This inference should encourage others to experiment at both teaching in virtual worlds and researching the educational outcomes from them.

INTRODUCTION

Progress in the adoption of multi-user virtual environments (MUVEs) as potential venues for online education is not occurring with the speed

DOI: 10.4018/978-1-60960-545-2.ch001

that some who are already engaged in it might expect. Impediments to this ready adoption include fear of technology, steep learning curve, the need for high speed internet, lack of institutional support, and a reticence on the part of educators to use a game for a learning venue. While some of these have been examined in the literature, one major deterrent to this adoption has not been examined in detail. Some educators see that best practices for education are being sacrificed for the adoption of an exotic technology. Perhaps more importantly, administrators often share this view and are, therefore, not willing to invest the often-minimal financial resources necessary to allow their faculty the opportunity to experiment with it. This chapter examines, through examples of educational venues throughout the MUVE known as Second Life, each of the ten (10) recognized "best practices in education." Its intents are to:

1.   Dispel the myth that using MUVEs as a venue for education is just another fad based on charismatic forms of technology.
2.   Open a dialogue for investigating ways of achieving best practices in education through the use of the tools of Multi-user Virtual Environments (MUVEs) such as Second Life.
3.   Encourage others to develop effective learning environments inside virtual worlds that meet the criteria of best practices.

In preparation for this examination it is best to define the terms and conditions of the discourse. Best practices are generally understood to represent methods, processes, techniques, or activities that are more effective at producing a desired outcome than others delivered in the same circumstance. Some would call best practices the most efficient and effective methods of accomplishing a particular task. For this chapter I will assume that one is seeking to determine not whether or not approaches employed in MUVEs are the preeminent of these best practices, but rather that attempts at replicating known best practices for education are feasible. Evidence for this feasibility is provided based on observation and established research. Where best practices are not explicitly or obviously demonstrated this chapter suggests

possible ways in which they might be established and how their effectiveness might be examined.

There are many best practices for education depending on the application and setting. There are best practices for lecturing, best practices for evaluation, best practices for distance education, and best practices for online education. Assuming that education within a MUVE is not normally going to reflect the traditional Victorian model of education, it is safe to assume that best practices for delivering lectures are of little interest here, and evaluation is only one small portion of the overall teaching and learning best practices with which this chapter is concerned. One could easily assume that, because teaching in virtual worlds is a method of online education, that the ten best practices of online education would be those most appropriately evaluated. While this is something that needs to be examined, the approach here is to show that general best practices for education – those most commonly associated with face-to-face classes are reproducible not just in an online environment, but in a 3-D virtual environment. If best practices for traditional educational venues can be shown to be effective in virtual worlds then there is a likelihood that innovative educators, both face-to-face and online, will consider the use of virtual worlds for teaching.

The process of examining the relationship between best educational practices and the use of virtual worlds for delivery begins by listing the commonly acknowledged ten best practices of education along with a short description of each. While there is no one set of ten best practices, most lists include those examined here. Their enumeration and initial description provides a context for their implementation inside a virtual world. Each also provides face-to-face examples of how these practices are applied to provide comparisons for potential virtual world contexts. This initial discussion informs the examination of Second Life practices.

Brief Review of Ten Best Practices in Education

Most formal and informal discussions of educational best practices include the following ten. This section defines each and provides examples of their application in traditional educational venues.

1. Engage Students in Active Learning Experiences

Active learning is a general term for methods of education in which the responsibility for learning rests with the learner rather than the instructor (Bonwell & Eison, 1991). Active learning, sometimes called learning-by-doing requires the student to take part in the learning process through such activities as discussions and debate, role-play, case studies, or even teaching each other (Martin, 1985; Martin & Oebel, 2007). A common approach to active learning is experiential learning popularized by Kolb (Kolb & Fry, 1975) that is a process of making meaning from direct experience. Whatever the method active learning is a superior method to lecture if the primary goal is to develop thinking and/or writing skills (Bonwell & Elison, 1991).

2. Set High, Meaningful Expectations

As one might guess "high" expectations is a relative term yet and is fairly well understood by both educator and student alike. There is general consensus that higher expectations result in improved learning (Bamburg, 1994). Perhaps what is more important in this best practice is that the expectations be meaningful. Today's millennial student is more likely to see fantasy as a meaningful goal and see it as a component of serious or practical work (Cameron, 2005) compared to previous generations of learners. This suggestions that the meaning of course or assignment expectations can be related to fantasy scenarios either alone or in addition to practical applied work.

3. Provide, Receive, and Use Regular, Timely, and Specific Feedback

Feedback is often thought of as reporting of as reporting of grades and correcting student mistakes, but feedback in education is bi-directional and far broader in scope than that. This is especially true for online education where the students are expected to take ownership of their own learning. Moreover, the millennial student is less patient and more apt to require a shorter turn-around time for such feedback than his or her non-millennial counterpart. Research by Nicol and Macfarlane-Dick (2006) for example, was responsible for the development of seven characteristics of good feedback especially for self-regulated learning environments such as is common in the constructivist model of learning.

1. Helps clarify what good performance is (goals, criteria, and expected standards).
2. Facilitates the development of self-assessment (reflection) in learning.
3. Delivers high quality information to students about their learning;
4. Encourages teacher and peer dialogue around learning.
5. Encourages positive motivational beliefs and self-esteem.
6. Provides opportunities to close the gap between current and desired performance.
7. Provides information to teachers that can help in shaping the teaching.

4. Become Aware of Values, Beliefs, and Preconceptions: Unlearn if Necessary

Preconceptions, value systems, and beliefs; no matter how they are acquired, have an often profound impact on the learning process. Recent research in science education, for example, has shown that students think through a process of analogs but that they tend to use analogs in different ways (Zhou, Nocente, & Brouwer, 2008). This suggests that while the science teacher presents an analog expecting one result, they may get another. Much of this is a function of preconceptions about how things work. This requires that the instructor often shock the learner by dispelling such preconceptions through direct observation and analysis. In short, as the Zen story states, "How can I show you Zen unless you first empty your cup" (Senzaki, 2004)

5. Recognize and Stretch Student Styles and Developmental Levels

There are many kinds of learners and many classifications for those learners. One can base learning styles on the VARK (visual, auditory, reading, kinesthetic) model (Fleming & Mills, 1992), or one might want to refer to the more multi-dimensional Memletics Learning Styles inventory (Institute for Learning Styles Research, 2006), or one might be more inclined to use Kolb's (1984) convergers, divergers, assimilators, and accommodators model. These and others provide guidance but all indicate that different students learn differently. Many learners may demonstrate different learning styles under different circumstances. Beyond that, however, is the concept of Perry's (1970) development levels that indicates that students move from viewing truth in absolute (right and wrong) terms, often based on the word of some authority to one of acknowledging conflicting versions of the truth based on alternative scenarios and circumstances. In all of these cases it is crucial that students be allowed to experience learning in multiple ways and be encouraged to consider alternate possible realities.

6. Seek and Present Real-World Applications

It is commonly believed that practical, realistic work is both more useful to society and more engaging for the student. While the utility to society and to the overall educational mission is in ques-

tion, at least in universities, (Evans, 2010) there are many benefits to real-world applications and experiential learning opportunities. These benefits include increased intellectual achievement, an ability to deal with complex situations, and an easier transition to the workforce (Eyler, 2009). As demands to supply talented employees in an increasingly technical workplace then providing practical experiences seems a necessity.

7. Understand and Value Criteria and Methods for Student Assessment

Another basic tenet of teaching is that learner assessment is necessary (Benson, 2003), and that if done effectively, it can improve both teaching and learning. Student output for assessment can include anything from models and movies to papers and PowerPoint presentations; oral presentations, performances and e-portfolios; and the associated grading rubrics; as well as multiple types of exams. The assessments can be faculty led, peer-to-peer, or even performed by the learner. Importantly, as Benson (2003) pointed out neither the basic principles of assessment nor the fundamental need for assessment have changed regardless of the face-to-face or online mode of delivery.

8. Create Opportunities for Student-Faculty Interactions

Traditionally the faculty member has been viewed as a primary input to the development of the learner, whether performing as a source of information or as a guide to other resources. Logically, the continual and repeated exposure to the source of information or guidance should result in improved learning outcomes. Endo and Harpel (1982) as well as Pascarella and Terenzini (1980) indicate that increases in faculty-student interactions, whether formal or informal, result in improved student intellectual gains, and retention of university freshmen. Subsequent research seems to verify these earlier results (Kuh, 1995;

Kuh & Hu, 2001; Lamport, 1993). This suggests that opportunities for faculty and students to interact, whether these interactions are directly course-related or informal and indirect, improve the likelihood of student success.

9. Create Opportunities for Student-Student Interactions

An oft-ignored component of student learning is that of student-student interactions – not just collaborative activities for coursework, but as a support mechanism through the formation of a learning community (Johnson, 1981). Johnson (2000), for example, found that the sense of community is strongly associated with student academic success. Student-student interactions not only provide a support mechanism for the learner but they also provide opportunities for students to exercise their skills at collaboration necessary in many workforce settings.

10. Promote Student Involvement through Engaged Time and Quality Effort

Student involvement is at the heart of the constructivist model of learning where active participation is the rule rather than the exception. Yet even in traditional educational models, the degree to which the student becomes actively involved in their own learning is shown to result in higher rates of obtaining university degrees, shorter times to complete degrees, and higher overall grade point averages (Syanum & Bigatti, 2009). Because best practices eight and nine allude to social engagement and a general sense of belonging, it is safe to assume that best practice ten involves academic and intellectual engagement. Academic engagement is most often measured based on student attendance and/or tardiness while intellectual engagement focuses primarily on a student's motivation, interest, and enjoyment of a course or course activity (Willms, Friesen, & Milton,

2009). To be successful at this best practice it is necessary to create a learning environment where students are present, motivated, interested, and even enjoying the process.

MUVE and Best Educational Practices

It is unlikely that any educator is ever going to be 100% successful at all ten of the previously listed best educational practices, and certainly not simultaneously. Most often one can hope to achieve some of these during each class experience. One exercise might not be as enjoyable or as engaging as another but it may strongly encourage student-student interactions, another might accurately represent a real-world scenario but it's length and complexity might limit quick forms of feedback. A class discussion involves student-student and student-faculty interaction. It might also challenge student beliefs and force them to think of alternative possibilities, but the grading criteria might be less well articulated than a set of mathematics problems where there is a single correct answer for each problem.

If it is not likely that traditional courses can satisfy all ten of the best practices, it is equally unlikely that courses offered in virtual worlds will either. The purpose for both is to strive for attaining as many of these practices as often as possible over the span of an entire course. This portion of the chapter focuses then, not on the attainment of perfection through MUVE-based education, but on whether or not there are available circumstances, represented by documented examples, for educators to at least match the potential of traditional classroom circumstances. Where examples do not exist, the chapter provides suggestions from the author's own experiences as substitutes. Finally, where the attainment of the best practice is difficult or even impossible this chapter provides a detailed description of the limitation and a discussion of the alternative possibilities or suggestions as to its possible relevance within the context of virtual worlds.

1. Engage Students in Active Learning Experiences

Traditional lectures and other passive learning experiences are still common in virtual worlds such as Second Life. While virtual lectures provide a traditional delivery format for the online student, perhaps one of the strengths of virtual worlds is that they facilitate active learning opportunities easily, at minimal costs, and through both virtual and hybrid environments. Take, for example, Harvard's CyberOne: Law in the Court of Public Opinion course that was offered at three levels of participation: face-to-face, hybrid, and fully immersed in Second Life (Brown & Adler, 2008). In this case Second Life provided an opportunity for students to pursue legal discourse and discussion for extended periods of time in a synchronous environment.

The use of role-play is also a common active learning strategy that can be found in many scenarios in MUVEs. A recent effort by Loyalist College involved the creation of a Canadian border simulation (Hudson & Degast-Kennedy, 2009) (Figure 1). The project involved an experimental design that included three groups of participants: (a) active student learners who participated hands-on in the simulation, (b) passive student learners who observed the simulation and later actively participated in discussions, and (c) volunteer participants who would play the roles of travelers passing through the crossing. The simulation recreated the interview process, document examination, and determination of whether they would be allowed entry. Moreover, the volunteers were encouraged to express different emotional states to allow the student crossing guards to practice their skills at handling these situations.

Results of this classic role-play simulation indicated that the students gained real-world

Figure 1. The Border Crossing Simulation from Loyalist College. (The setting allows the students to role play as crossing guards and to experience the reactions of those passing through the crossing.)

experience where a real scenario would not be possible, and developed essential interview skills. Post-class interviews also showed that the students demonstrated high levels of engagement and satisfaction in the learning experience. More importantly, those who actively participated achieved substantially higher exam grades than those who did not. This example provides a template for other role-play scenarios that can be afforded by MUVEs.

There are many other ways in which active learning can take place in MUVEs. Perhaps one of the most impressive types of active learning scenarios in virtual worlds includes the development of virtual labs as exemplified by the biosciences lab at the University of East London (Cobb, Heaney, Corcoran, & Henderson-Begg, 2009). This experimental study recreated a virtual Polymerase Chain Reaction (PCR) experiment in Second Life designed to amplify DNA for use in molecular biology, biotechnology, and forensics. One group of students performed the experiments in Second Life while a control group performed it in real life. Results of this experiment showed that it was well received by the students, with 92%

of the students asking for more experiments to be conducted in Second Life. Although both groups of students improved their exam grades, those who did so in Second Life required less teaching assistant intervention. These examples show that virtual worlds are ready-made for successful active learning experiences if well designed.

2. Set High, Meaningful Expectations

There are few specific explicit examples of setting meaningful expectations, although they are often implicit in the content. The virtual laboratory developed for the University of East London (Cobb et al., 2009) and the exquisitely designed experiments of Genome Island (Clark 2009) are both examples of high end experimental models all requiring substantial application of the scientific method (Figure 2). Their advantage, beyond creating high expectations relative to the level of subject matter is that the experiments can be repeated continuously, thus allowing students an opportunity to repeat parts or all of the experiments for additional learning opportunities.

DeMers (2010) provided learning objectives and behavioral indicators for boxed laboratories in Second Life designed to augment their knowledge of geographic information systems. Each behavioral indicator had scores associated with task completion. This is simpler, but essentially the same approach Clark (2009) took in her genetics experiments where supplies and instructions were all provided and expected results were explicitly stated.

Among the most detailed examination of the use of educational standards in virtual world education is represented by the work of Schiller (2009). This virtual commerce experiment explicitly developed an assessment framework to evaluate results demonstrates the scientific method applied within virtual worlds.

The learning objectives included:

Figure 2. The calculation of hybrid cross results and statistical analysis of the Learning objectives and processes in the Second Life exercise.

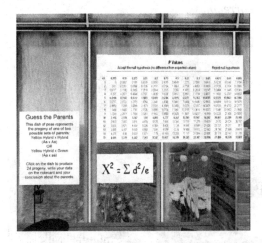

1. Understand the concept of a virtual business
2. Learn about some specific examples of virtual business and how such a business functions in virtual worlds.
3. Learn from each other and develop interpersonal skills in performing tasks.

The assessments were conducted by examining reflection essay questions, snapshots, chat logs, group presentations, peer-reviews, and a post project survey that each student was responsible for producing. Overall the students met the expectations the instructor set for the course and found the examination of the Second Life business model relevant to them as business students. This type of connection can easily be accomplished for many disciplines.

3. Provide, Receive, and Use Regular, Timely, and Specific Feedback

As with best practice two there seems to be no research specifically targeting the issue of feedback. There are certainly opportunities for informal feedback when the students and their instructors appear together as avatars in the same location in

Figure 3. A visual multiple choice examination tool in Second Life. The student touches the picture of their choice gets an immediate result of its correctness.

virtual space. Opportunities also exist to provide graded exercises and, although this is not explicitly stated, it is assumed that such is the case with the virtual laboratories of Cobb, Corcoran, and Henderson-Begg (2009) and Clark (2009). Certainly Schiller's (2009) extensive graded materials provide ample opportunity for feedback.

Providing education feedback in a virtual world is not a built-in feature of virtual worlds as they arc not themselves constructed for education. In fact, in face-to-face courses the primary mechanism for providing student feedback on progress is most often done through a form of learning management system (LMS). Fortunately Kemp and Livingstone (2006) produced a virtual learning management system called Sloodle, built on the Moodle engine. This tool provides the same opportunities for regular feedback as face-to-face learning management software. Other LMS-like tools are constantly being added to the Second Life toolkit and these will likely be ported over to other virtual worlds. Additionally, there are survey tools in Second Life that are relatively inexpensive and, while designed originally for

merchant surveys, can provide the educator with important information needed to modify a course to better meet student needs.

As more learners become gamers the speed at which they expect to receive feedback increases (O'Connell, Grantham, Workman, & Wong, 2009). This necessitates both rapid response on the part of the faculty member and the use of computer mediated responses. Some of the virtual world quizzing tools (Figure 3) and in-world learning management systems, such as the pathways learning management system (http://www.pathwayslms.com/pathwayslmsmanual.pdf) use in-world programming tools to provide instantaneous feedback. These types of tools are likely to be critical to the delivery of education within virtual worlds.

4. Become Aware of Values, Beliefs, and Preconceptions: Unlearn if Necessary

Second Life education has the capability to examine a vast array of social and cultural characteristics and settings. Because there are literally tens of thousands of simulations, many of which resemble widely varied locations around the world the opportunities are nearly endless. In the author's short four years in Second Life he has communicated with people from Europe, Asia, Oceania, and Latin America. In a flash one can visit nearly exact replicas of Russian's Red Square, a tent city in Darfur (Figure 4), or the Great Wall of China. Most importantly, however, virtual worlds allow opportunities to converse with people of different places to gain insights from those interactions, and perhaps more to the point, to dispel erroneous beliefs.

One example of this was provided at a meeting of the Association of American Geographers in which Merrill Johnson (2009) described the adventures of his students after visiting a Russian simulation built by Russians. When they discussed their experience, expounding on the accuracy of

Figure 4. The tent city of Darfur is one of a number of locations where students can examine their views, preconceptions and attitudes and perhaps even act on them.

the simulation they then expressed consternation because everyone around them was speaking Russian. Johnson quickly used this as a teaching moment rather than deriding the students on their recognition of the obvious. This exemplifies how virtual worlds can engender in even simple observations, a new relevance, a new realism, and a new recognition.

One of the more spectacular uses of virtual worlds for dispelling preconceptions is the simulation of the visual and auditory experiences of schizophrenics (Yellowlees & Cook, 2006). Yet another uses the differences between real and virtual realities to allow students to unlearn what they think they know about physics (dos Santos, 2009). Another powerful example is Virtual Ability Second Life Island in which many myths and misconceptions about people with physical handicaps can be examined, especially regarding their interest in becoming part of social groups. These are but a few of the many opportunities virtual worlds present for helping students become aware of their values, beliefs, and preconceptions by giving them opportunities to confront them. It is important to recognize that, as Diehl and Prins (2008) put it, "Although the cross-cultural exchanges in *SL* do not guarantee intercultural literacy, they provide

participants with opportunities to move in that direction." The same could be said of examining other values, beliefs, or misconceptions.

5. Recognize and Stretch Student Styles and Developmental Levels

Modern 3-D virtual worlds are currently capable of providing reading material, video, presentation hardware, voice, a wide array of multi-media, and even 3-D building and visualization opportunities. Lim (2009) suggests there are six basic learning environments within Second Life:

- **Learning by exploring:** visiting simulations and possibly including inferential analytical tasks
- **Learning by collaborating:** millennial learners excel at collaborative problem solving and discussion-based inquiry
- **Learning by being:** explorations of self and identity using things like role-play and performance
- **Learning by building:** building or scripting (programming) for tactile learners involved in math, physics, aesthetics, and others
- **Learning by championing:** initiatives involving students in real-life causes in a service-based approach to learning
- **Learning by expressing:** representing in-world activity to the outside world such as authoring blogs, podcasts, machinima (cinema in virtual worlds), and posters

All of these types of learning support, to varying degrees, one type of learner or another. DeMers (2010) used Kolb's learning styles inventory and, based on a determination that geographers were accommodators, to develop experiential learning modules that were appropriate for that type of learner. Although there is little written about the linkage between learning styles and virtual world education there is ample opportunity for both the exercise of different learning styles and the analysis of how this might best be done in Second Life.

6. Seek and Present Real-World Applications

The idea of realism in education developed in the 16th and 17th centuries during the period of scientific inquiry functions with an acknowledgement that things exist whether we are aware of them or not. This philosophy of education establishes that one of the purposes of education is to prepare people for the real world. Perhaps most importantly, realism-based education tends to build on a body of knowledge, and that realities can be observed, experienced, experimented with, and explored.

Virtual worlds are replete with real-world constructs and educators in MUVEs have taken advantage of this realism. You have already seen examples from genetics (Clark 2009, Cobb et al., 2009), psychology (Yellowlees & Cook, 2006), physics (dos Santos, 2009), border security (Hudson and Degast-Kennedy, 2009), and many more. The number of potential project-based applications is limited only by the imagination of the educator (Jarmon, Traphagan, & Mayrath, 2008).

Interestingly however, while one of the best educational practices recommends the use of real-world applications, recent research shows that the new generation of students, the millennial generation, are much more likely to accept fantasy and play as part of a more serious, real-world work activity (Cameron, 2005). This might suggest that the importance of presenting students with real-world applications is becoming less important as a best practice than in the past. It might even mean that the millennial student may not need real-world applications for learning at all. At a minimum this might suggest a re-evaluation of at least this individual best educational practice. A comparative analysis of real versus contrived exercises inside virtual worlds might prove a useful contribution to the educational literature.

7. Understand and Value Criteria and Methods for Student Assessment

You have seen several examples where faculty have developed grading criteria and have shown the general increase in grades (Clark, 2009; Cobb et al., 2009) through the use of virtual worlds for learning. Shiller's (2009) work was perhaps the most robust in that it indicated some specific tools that could be used for assessment and the general learning objectives that could be examined. DeMers (2010) outlined a bit more detail on learning objectives and behavioral indicators, but he also pointed out the limitation of his study in that, unlike the work of Hudson and Degast-Kennedy (2009) no systematic examination of the actual learning benefits of the virtual world environment was developed. DeMers suggested pre and post exams while Hudson and Degast-Kennedy used a control group against which the experimental group's outcomes could be compared.

There are many ways to assess students in virtual worlds including the use of in-world testing tools. Some of these tools provide real-time response to the student, a property that will prove beneficial to the millennial student. What remains is for those teaching in virtual worlds to begin the systematic examination of:

- What type of learner benefits most from an assessment standpoint
- What virtual world environments produce the best results
- What assessments work best in virtual environments

These are the fundamental questions that need to be answered and this chapter in part is meant to encourage others to pursue this type of research.

8. Create Opportunities for Student-Faculty Interactions

Some learning activities in Second Life are controlled through elegant programming that allows objects, intelligent agents if you will, to perform much of the instruction in Second Life. Take as a couple of examples The Ohio State University Medical School's eight and one half minute simulation of the human testes (Danforth, 2010) and simulation-based training in virtual worlds (Chodos, Naeimi, & Stroulia, 2009). While these are often quite well done, and even expedient, they are seldom a substitute for student-faculty interactions.

Many instructors are present with their students during exercises, building, presentations, performances, and discussions within virtual worlds. This author, for example meets with his students in Second Life for review sessions on Sunday evenings. In general the students seem to appreciate the willingness of faculty to spend time with them for such activities. Additionally, this author's students stated that their presence and that of the faculty member as avatars seemed to lessen the fear of embarrassment during question and answer sessions.

Among the better-received aspects of student-faculty interactions, however was acknowledged by Clark's (2009) students. Her survey results indicated that some of the students found that they had more access to the faculty member during off-class times than in their face-to-face classes. While this may be a function of perception, or of logistics (students not having to actually travel to the faculty office) it clearly illustrates that access to the faculty in virtual worlds is expedited and potentially to a higher degree than in face-to-face environments.

9. Create Opportunities for Student-Student Interactions

Student-student interactions in virtual world education can be, as with real world environments, both formal and informal. The author gets his students together for formal activities such as lectures, discussions, and group building projects but also includes social events, informal poster

sessions, and facilitates the class interactions of students. Each student is expected to become friends (a process of sharing contact information) in their virtual world with other students so that they are aware of the presence of others when they are in-world.

Among the most powerful student-student interactions is the collaborative assignment that has been suggested by Andreas, Tsiatsos, Terzidou and Pomportsis (2010) to improve and augment face-to-face student interactions. They also found that such collaborations were more effective than other approaches to distance collaboration and communication. Bourke (2008), for example, found that collaboration around the development and visualization of a 3-D molecular model enhanced student's understanding of these complex structures. And Burgess et al. (2010) showed that in-world collaborations enhanced cognitive presence, social presence, and teaching presence.

Virtual worlds are well designed for student-student interactions in virtually all types of disciplines. Students who work together on performances (e.g. reading Shakespeare, performing reenactments), role-play, building, discussions and many other forms of learning can meet with far fewer logistical limitations than in face to face environments. The only thing that needs to happen is for the educational designer to create an appropriate environment.

10. Promote Student Involvement through Engaged Time and Quality Effort

Student involvement in virtual worlds has been documented in several cases where students themselves indicate that the course content and projects were "fun." While many reactions by students to learning in virtual worlds include negative comments about technology and user interface most students seemed to adapt to this within a reasonable amount of time. Research by Cheal (2009) indicated that students preferred exploring, changing the avatar appearance, communicating with people from other countries and building communities. Lowe and Clark (2008) surveyed students and found that for their Mendelian genetics course there were mixed responses but that there were more positive reactions than negative. While some of their students indicated a great deal of enjoyment from the use of virtual worlds in the course, others expressed a keen dislike for technology in general.

This latter response indicates an important consideration for the use of virtual worlds to engage students and provide them with quality effort. Those who are averse to technology are not likely to be predisposed to its use or to enjoying learning in this manner. Suggestions that the millennial learner might be more well adapted to the technology, while seemingly obvious, are not supported by research data. Some millennial learners seem more focused on limited technologies such as iPods or texting and less well adapted to other forms of online interaction such as gaming worlds. This might suggest that gamers would be well adapted to this and Cheal's (2009) research seems to bare this out. Still there is a need for additional research in this area.

SUMMARY

This chapter examined the relationships between the generally recognized ten best educational practices and the use of multi-user virtual worlds (MUVE) for the development and delivery of course content. There are areas where the use of these environments seem to link especially well to some of the best practices. They seem, for example well adapted to the creation of active learning experiences (#1) although the level of engagement might be as much a function of the level of computer savvy of the student as of the exercise.

As a means of making students aware of their preconceptions, views, and beliefs, virtual worlds seem to provide an enormous capability to present learning opportunities. Virtual worlds can be in any culture, any situation or circumstance, involve any faith, include any country, involve many scenarios, and even create new and completely fictitious worlds for students to examine. Many of these scenarios and settings would be logistically difficult or even impossible to reproduce in real world classrooms.

Virtual worlds allow for many types of learners although some of these are poorly studied. Many real-world scenarios for students to examine can be more easily created in a virtual world than in a real one. Imagine, for example having a class create a small business in real life as opposed to creating one in a virtual world where the cost for the entire business might not exceed $100. Interactions, including student-student and student-faculty are easily developed inside virtual worlds.

There are loose associations between some of the remaining best practices, and some of these linkages have never really been tested through experiments and practical examples. Overall, virtual worlds seem to offer many possibilities both for education and for educational research. Each of the linkages presents a separate and perhaps critical avenue of research that, if pursued, will provide a clearer picture of the degree to which virtual worlds can recreate these practices. It might also be important to identify ways of effectively using virtual worlds through design models and the application and development of new and innovative educational best practices (Girvan & Savage, 2010; O'Conner, 2010; Wang & Hsu, 2009). What is known is that the numbers of educators experimenting with teaching in virtual worlds is increasing and the numbers of virtual worlds available for them are also increasing. The use of virtual worlds for teaching may, because of its newness and exotic nature seem to be a passing fad brought on by the charismatic nature of the gaming technology. Given the dedicated effort of a growing cadre of new educators, many of whom risk ridicule to experiment with these approaches, the likelihood of MUVE-driven education is almost a certainty.

REFERENCES

Andreas, K., Tsiatsos, T., Terzidou, T., & Pomportsis, A. (2010). Fostering collaborative learning in second life: Metaphors and affordances. *Computers & Education, 55*(2), 603–615. doi:10.1016/j.compedu.2010.02.021

Bamburg, J. (1994). *Raising expectations to improve student learning.* Oak Brook, IL: North Central Regional Educational Laboratory.

Benson, A. D. (2003). Assessing participant learning in online environments. *New Directions for Adult and Continuing Education, 100,* 69–78. doi:10.1002/ace.120

Bonwell, C., & Eison, J. (1991). *Active learning: Creating excitement in the classroom.* (AEHE-ERIC Higher Education Report No.1). Washington, DC: Jossey-Bass.

Bourke, P. (2008). Evaluating Second Life as a tool for collaborative scientific visualization. *Proceedings of the Computer Games and Allied Technology.*

Brown, J. S., & Adler, R. P. (2008). Minds on fire: Open education, the long tail and learning 2.0. *EDUCAUSE Review, 43*(1), 16–32.

Burgess, M. L., Slate, J. R., Rojas-LeBouef, A., & LaPrairie, K. (2010). Teaching and learning in Second Life: Using the community of inquiry (Coi) model to support online instruction with graduate students in instructional technology. *The Internet and Higher Education, 13*(1), 84–88. doi:10.1016/j.iheduc.2009.12.003

Cameron, D. (2005). The net generation goes to university? *Proceedings of the Journalism Education Association Conference.*

Cheal, C. (2009). Student perceptions of a course taught in Second Life. *Innovate: Journal of Online Education, 5*(5).

Chodos, D., Naeimi, P., & Stroulia, E. (2009). An integrated framework for simulation-based training on video and in a virtual world. *Journal of Virtual Worlds Research, 2*(1).

Clark, M. A. (2009). Genome Island: A virtual science environment in Second Life. *Innovate: Journal of Online Education, 5*(6).

Cobb, S., Heaney, R., Corcoran, O., & Henderson-Begg, S. (2009). The learning gains and student perceptions of a Second Life virtual lab. *Bioscience Education, 13.*

Danforth, D. R. (2010). Development of an interactive virtual 3-D model of the human testis using the Second Life platform. *International Journal of Virtual and Personal Learning Environments, 1*(2), 46–60. doi:10.4018/jvple.2010040104

DeMers, M. (2010). Second Life as a surrogate for experiential learning. *International Journal of Virtual and Personal Learning Environments, 1*(2), 17–31.

Diehl, W. C., & Prins, E. (2008). Unintended outcomes in "Second Life": Intercultural literacy and cultural identity in a virtual world. *Language and Intercultural Communication, 8*(2), 101–118. doi:10.1080/14708470802139619

dos Santos, R. P. (2009). Second Life physics: Virtual, real or surreal? *Journal of Virtual Worlds Research, 2*(1).

Endo, J., & Harpel, R. L. (1982). The effect of student faculty interactions on students' educational outcomes. *Research in Higher Education, 16*(2), 115–136. doi:10.1007/BF00973505

Evans, M. (2010). The universities and the challenge of realism. *Arts and Humanities in Higher Education: An International Journal of Theory. Research and Practice, 9*(1), 13–21.

Eyler, J. (2009). The power of experiential education. *Liberal Education, 95*(4), 24–31.

Fleming, N. D., & Mills, C. (1992). Not another inventory, rather a catalyst for reflection. *To Improve the Academy, 11*, 137-155.

Girvan, C., & Savage, T. (2010). Identifying an appropriate pedagogy for virtual worlds: A communal constructivism case study. *Computers & Education, 55*(1), 342–349. doi:10.1016/j.compedu.2010.01.020

Hudson, K., & Degast-Kennedy, K. (2009). Canadian border simulation at Lyalist College. *Journal of Virtual Worlds Research, 2*(1).

Institute for Learning Styles Research. (2003). *Institue for Learning Styles Research*. Retrieved from http://www.learningstyles.org/

Jarmon, L., Traphagan, T., & Mayrath, M. (2008). Understanding project-based learning in Second Life with a pedagogy, training, and assessment trio. *Educational Media International, 45*(3), 157–176. doi:10.1080/09523980802283889

Johnson, D. W. (1981). Student-student interaction: The neglected variable in education. *Educational Researcher, 10*(1), 5–10.

Johnson, J. L. (2000). Learning communities and special efforts in the retention of university students: What works, what doesn't, and is the return worth the investment? *Journal of College Student Retention: Research. Theory into Practice, 2*(3), 219–238.

Kemp, J., & Livingstone, D. (2006). Putting a Second Life "Metaverse" skin on learning management systems. *Proceedings First Second Life Education Workshop, Part of the 2006 Second Life Community Convention*, (pp. 13-18).

Kolb, A. Y. (1984). *Experiential learning: Experience as the source of learning and development*. Englewood Cliffs, NJ: Prentice-Hall.

Kolb, D. A., & Fry, R. (1975). Toward an applied theory of experiential learning. In Cooper, C. (Ed.), *Theories of group process*. London, UK: John Wiley.

Kuh, G. (1995). The other curriculum: Out-of-class experiences associated with student learning and personal development. *The Journal of Higher Education, 66*(2), 123–155. doi:10.2307/2943909

Kuh, G., & Hu, S. (2001). The effects of student-faculty interaction in the 1990s. *The Review of Higher Education, 24*(3), 309–332. doi:10.1353/rhe.2001.0005

Lamport, M. (1993). Student-faculty informal interaction and the effect on college student outcomes: A review of the literature. *Adolescence, 28*(122), 971–990.

Lim, K. Y. T. (2009). The six learnings of Second Life. *Journal of Virtual Worlds Research, 2*(1).

Lowe, C., & Clark, M. A. (2008). Student perceptions of learning science in a virtual world. *Proceedings 24th Annual Conference on Distance Teaching and Learning*.

Martin, J. P. (1985). *Zum Aufbau didaktischer Teilkompetenzen beim Schüler. Fremdsprachenunterricht auf der lerntheoretischen Basis des Informationsverarbeitungsansatzes*. (Dissertation). Tübingen: Narr.

Martin, J. P., & Oebel, G. (2007). Lernen durch Lehren: Paradigmenwechsel in der Didaktik? *Deutschunterricht in Japan, 12*, 4–21.

Merrill, J. (2009). *Identify formation and expression in Second Life: Implications for the use of virtual places in education*. Paper session: Virtual Learning Environments and Geographic Education. Association of American Geographers Annual Meeting.

Nicol, D. J., & Macfarlane-Dick, D. (2006). Formative assessment and self-regulated learning: A model and seven principles of good feedback practice. *Studies in Higher Education, 31*(2), 199–218. doi:10.1080/03075070600572090

O'Connell, T. A., Grantham, J., Workman, K., & Wong, W. (2009). Leveraging game-playing skills, expectations and behaviors of digital natives to improve visual analytical tools. *Journal of Virtual Worlds Research, 2*(1).

O'Conner, E. A. (2010). Instructional and design elements that support effective use of virtual worlds: What graduate student work reveals about Second Life. *Journal of Educational Technology Systems, 38*(2), 213–234. doi:10.2190/ET.38.2.j

Pascarella, E., & Terenzini, P. (1980). Student-faculty and student-peer relationships as mediators of the structural effects of undergraduate residence arrangement. *The Journal of Educational Research, 73*(6), 344–353.

Perry, W. G. (1970). *Forms of intellectual and ethical development in the college years: A scheme*. New York, NY: Holt, Rinehart, and Winston.

Schiller, S. Z. (2009). Practicing learner-centered teaching: Pedological design and assessment of a Second Life project. *Journal of Information Systems Education, 20*(3), 369–381.

Senzaki. (2004). *101 Zen stories*. Whitefish, MT: Kessinger Publishing, LLC.

Syanum, S., & Bigatti, S. M. (2009). Academic course engagement during one semester forecasts college success: Engaged students are more likely to ear a degree, do it faster, and do it better. *Journal of College Student Development, 50*(1), 120–132. doi:10.1353/csd.0.0055

Wang, S., & Hsu, H. (2009). Using the ADDIE model to design Second Life activities for online learners. *TechTrends: Linking Research and Practice to Improve Learning, 53*(6), 76–82.

Willms, J. D., Friesen, S., & Miltion, P. (2009). *What did you do in school today: Transforming classrooms through social, academic, and intellectual engagement*. Toronto, ON, Canada: National Report, Canadian Education Association.

Yellowlees, P. M., & Cook, J. N. (2006). Education about hallucinations using an Internet virtual reality system: A qualitative survey. *Academic Psychiatry, 30*(6), 534–539. doi:10.1176/appi.ap.30.6.534

Zhou, G., Nocente, N., & Brouwer, W. (2008). Understanding student cognition through an analysis of their preconceptions in physics. *The Alberta Journal of Educational Research, 54*(1), 14–29.

KEY TERMS AND DEFINITIONS

Active Learning: A general term referring to several modes of instruction that focus on the learner taking responsibility for his or her own learning.

Constructivist Theory: A theory of knowledge that argues that humans best generate knowledge and meaning from experience. It also argues that learning is best acquired through active participation rather than passive receipt of information.

Educational Best Practices: A collection of methods, approaches, and techniques that have proven successful in both engaging students and producing acceptable levels of student outcomes from the learning experience.

Experiential Learning: A specific type of active learning based on the idea that students learn best when they have the opportunity to create meaning from direct experience.

Millennial Learner: A cohort of learners generally born between 1982 and 2002 whose characteristics include a belief that their problems are the nation's problems, an expectation of safety, confidence, team orientation, conventional, pressured, and with a propensity to achieve.

Multi-User Virtual Environment (MUVE): A term to describe massively multiplayer online role-playing games (MMORPG) that allows multiple participants, represented as 3-D digital versions of themselves (avatars) to interact simultaneously inside a virtual 3-D world. Because these virtual worlds stay in place they are often referred to as persistent virtual environments.

Second Life: A commercial virtual world developed by Linden Research, Inc. and launched in June 23, 2003. Using a separate piece of client-side software called a viewer, Second Life allows residents to interact, move, communicate, program, animate, and build 3-D objects.

Chapter 2
Mapping Current Teaching and Learning Practices to Multi-User Virtual Environments

Niccolo Capanni
Robert Gordon University, UK

Daniel C. Doolan
Robert Gordon University, UK

ABSTRACT

During the course of this chapter, the authors will examine the current methods of pedagogical teaching in higher education and explore the possible mapping into a multi-user virtual environment. The authors consider the process of construction and delivery for a module of student education. They examine the transition of delivery methods from the established, slow changing traditional media, to the modern flexibly of community based, open source driven methods which are the foundation of virtual environments.

INTRODUCTION

Explanation of Terminology

In degree courses at the Higher Education (HE) level, students are typically taught several distinct subjects in parallel. We refer to each of these subjects as a "module". Although modules are sometimes spread across a number of academic terms, more often than not each module would run for a single term. We consider a "course" to be the body of academic work that leads to a degree exit award such as BA, BSc, BEng, MA or MSc.

Teaching in Practical Usage

For the purposes of this explanation we will use a generalized and typical module format. The format has been populated with material from a module concerned with Internet development technologies. This is only to assist understanding of the module descriptor. Such a module is loosely

DOI: 10.4018/978-1-60960-545-2.ch002

Figure 1. Generalized and typical module descriptor

Pre-requisites for Module Course entry requirements only. **Co-requisite Modules** None. **Precluded Modules** None.	**Indicative Student Workload** *Contact Hours* Full Time Lectures 24 Laboratories 24 Tutorials 12 Assessment 5 Directed Reading 30 Private Study 55
Aims of Module 1. To enable the students to explore the key concepts of web systems development. 2. To develop the students' skill in the practical design, development and management of web systems.	**Mode of Delivery** Key concepts are introduced and illustrated through the medium of lectures. Laboratory sessions provide a series of exercises designed to develop proficiency in techniques essential to the development of web systems. Tutorials will address specific technical points which will aid subject knowledge and practical skills.
Learning Outcomes for Module On completion of this module, students are expected to be able to: 1. Design and implement web pages appropriate to a given objective. 2. Demonstrate proficiency with the individual technologies required in the construction of web pages. 3. Develop web based server side applications.	**Assessment Plan** There will be one coursework-based assessment covering all the learning outcomes.
Indicative Module Content Concepts of internet and web development, historical and current . business applications and methods. Construction of web sites, at a site design and page design level. Technologies such as HTML, CSS, client side scripting and server side scripting.	**Keywords** Internet, Intranet, World Wide Web, HTML, CSS, client side scripting, Internet protocols, server side scripting

defined in the descriptor given in Figure 1. This module format has been adapted for delivery to students of varying backgrounds and expectations: undergraduates, direct entry degree year students and master's students. This variety has permitted the module leader/s to take advantage of different delivery and assessment methods based on the audience demographics.

The description in Figure 1 is sufficiently specific that the students know what to expect, without a rigidity which prevents module adaptation to new technologies or greater course requirements.

The module terms shown in Figure 1 are explained in areas of related purpose as follows:

- The first properties show whether a module has any pre- or co-requisites and whether it shares sufficient similar areas to preclude any other modules. However these properties are retrospective, looking to earlier modules, and later advanced modules may rely on the student first successfully completing this one.

- Module aims establish what skills the student should have mastered by completion. Learning outcomes explain how these aims will be summatively assessed, while the assessment plan describes the nature of the examination/s.

- Workload gives the specific contact time and type of contact as well as indicating the assessment burden and the expected non-contact time the student should spend in directed study or in improving their skills/knowledge in the subject area of the materials delivered.

- Keywords cover the subject areas that will be addressed. Indicative content gives the students a broader idea of how the module will be composed, but retains flexibility to allow the module lecturer to maintain relevance and introduce variation.

- Mode of delivery specifies how the knowledge and skills will be delivered during the indicated contact time. These modes cover lectures, laboratories and tutorials as described in the section "Deconstructing a Traditional Module".

This "mode of delivery" is of importance to this chapter. It supports the purpose of changing the educational environment as a method of delivering the same skills and knowledge in a more efficient, productive or practical manner. What is being discussed here is not the concept of teaching something new, but the concept of new teaching.

STUDENT BACKGROUNDS

Module descriptors such as Figure 1 are relevant at both the undergraduate and postgraduate level. At undergraduate level, students may arrive at a module from various backgrounds. First year students come from the shared background of no presumed experience of university education. Students in subsequent years come from two main sub-divisions; those who have progressed though the previous year/s and those who have received alternate entry to the current year, almost always after completing a pre-approved Higher National Certificate (HNC) or Higher National Diploma (HND) degree at a college of further education.

This differentiation of backgrounds immediately means that some students in a class may have experienced subject delivery through a standard lecture, laboratory and tutorial format and be familiar with the coursework, computer based assessed laboratories, and written exams of a particular university. The remainder of the class may be used to a more practical delivery and continuous assessment-feedback learning cycle.

Students may also come from a range of ages and have very different experience backgrounds. They range from recent school graduates in their late teens to adult learners returning to education or retraining who may be a similar age to or decades older than other students. Likewise

their previous knowledge of module content may differ greatly in both recreational and practical terms, while their experience and expectation of university educational delivery and assessment will also differ broadly.

The diversity of the student body means that modules must be delivered in a manner that suits the known demographics of the intended audience and does not significantly disadvantage any particular group of students.

Module on Course Dependency

The module creation process begins with considering how it fits the requirements of a course of study or how it covers a specific body of knowledge to an acceptable level. The aim/s of the module may be established at this point. Central to the aims are the key concepts and skills the students acquire from partaking in the module. Once these have been determined the leaning outcomes, which are examined through summative assessments, may be stated. If the module is to be a section of a larger course of study then the module leader considers three major factors: pre-requisite modules which establish the expected knowledge of the students, any modules for which this one under consideration is a pre-requisite and, most complex of all, any co-requisite modules which must be developed in parallel. (An example of co-requisites is a project management module delivered in conjunction with a technical module. The former is used to establish project management and collaboration skills, the latter as the medium or technology to base the project on).

In Figure 2, an example of the modules a student may take in a hypothetical four year honours degree course is shown. Repetition of a module name during a year indicates a double module with twice the credit and requirements of a single module. An example of pre-requisite modules can be shown by tracking the arrows from a module in one year to a module in a previous year, for example to take "Database Systems" in

Figure 2. Example course module map

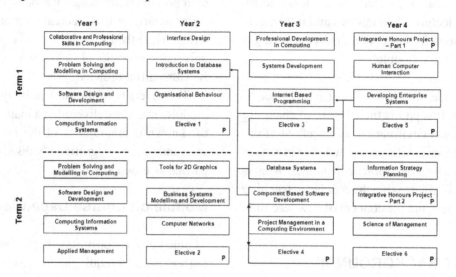

3rd year, a student must have passed "Introduction to Database Systems" in 2nd year. In some cases such as "Developing Enterprise Systems", there is a choice of pre-requisite modules which allows flexibility amongst course leaders as to what modules to include in earlier years. "Project Management in a Computing Environment" is a module that requires a co-requisite, either "Component Based Software Development" or a module chosen from the available electives. All electives may have precluded modules which cannot be counted towards the same course of study. A module descriptor as shown in Figure 1, provides clarification on these modules.

DECONSTRUCTING A TRADITIONAL MODULE

Module Structures

Modules are usually broken down into a hierarchy of smaller, more specific subjects which we will refer to as "topics". This module structure allows students to engage with material in more manageable amounts and assists with the development of a module's narrative through signposting. This narrative tells the story of the module, allowing students to visualize how all the parts link together and helps them see the bigger picture by understanding each component.

Topic Delivery

Topics make use of different delivery methods and media, which are described in familiar terms such as: lectures, laboratories, tutorials and so forth. These delivery methods may follow an individual narrative or may be paired / partnered so the different activities support each other. In this manner the narrative should follow a natural transition through the series of lectures. Likewise the other delivery methods, such as laboratory and tutorial sessions may follow a similar structure. Alternatively / additionally each lecture may deliver theoretical material which is practiced or re-enforced by specific partner laboratory or tutorial sessions.

Lectures usually take the format of a one-to-many computer-aided presentation in a lecture theater. The mass delivery approach is symptomatic of the restrictions imposed by large class sizes which prohibit unscripted one-to-one interaction. During these lectures, use will be made of presentation notes, such as PowerPoint, which can be electronically delivered to the students before the class. Due to the nature of the subject there may also be the interjection of other materials, such as video, live web site examination or predesigned examples.

The difficulty of maintaining audience attention during mass delivery lectures is notorious and has been the subject of a great deal of research. Garber (2001) coined the phrase "death by PowerPoint" to describe the effect of long lectures consisting of monologues backed only by PowerPoint presentations - this is exacerbated when the lecturer simply reads directly from the slides. A short respite or narrative change has long been known to boost information absorption; therefore the utilization of different media can have a good effect on audience learning (Johnstone & Percival, 1976). Student engagement is deeper with attention-holding lectures and so audience expectation increases, which in turn encourages attendance. The media used must be carefully chosen; as a student who had been searching for subject material online recently pointed out, "the only thing more boring than watching a lecture monologue is watching a video of a lecture monologue". Lectures are traditionally delivered in a lecture theater, with the audience focus on the performance of the lecturer. The lectures are best used to deliver subject knowledge and direct the students to further reading resources. The series of lectures provides the narrative for the module which is supported by the other activities.

Laboratory sessions provide hands-on exercises which follow the subject delivered in the lectures and convert knowledge into practical proficiency with relevant techniques. These take the form of computer-based exercises with the subject lecturer who engages on a one-to-one or small group basis. The students follow worked examples with supporting materials and advance to unsupported examples where they must apply their new skills to unknown problems. Often they will be directed to online resources for assistance.

Tutorials are used to address specific technical points which will aid the subject knowledge imparted in the lecture and the practical skills developed in the laboratories. They may be held in classrooms or computer laboratories depending on the specifics of the tutorial. The tutorials are structured to impart understanding of the knowledge or skills and not to deliver new knowledge or practice techniques that have expected outcomes.

The lecture, laboratory, tutorial format has been given here in context of a module similar to that presented in Figure 1. However the concepts are directly transferable to many other fields and adaptable to almost all HE courses, for example Life Sciences, Engineering, Arts.

Technology Transition

Methods of education have remained remarkably consistent during the decades, arguably the centuries, preceding the computer age. With globally recognized qualifications and a well established system of delivering lectures, it has been understandably difficult to institute changes in these methods. If the transitions in delivery methods are summarized and linked to the technologies, we can view them, with relevance to this chapter, in four stages.

Pre-Computing Technologies

Once the lecture advanced from purely oral delivery, chalk and blackboards became synonymous with the classroom and lecture theatre. Noticeable technology changes were the revolving blackboard and colored chalk. The benefits of the blackboard were restricted by the temporary nature of any lecture as the material had to be re-written for every class and the simplicity of the delivery was limited to hand written chalk in a few colors. Unfortunately with these hand writing technologies, the attention of the student was often given to scribing faster than the lecturer's notes could be wiped clean or revolved over the top.

The transition from blackboards and chalk to magnetic whiteboards and multi-color marker pens defined a significant first step. This gave the lecturer the choice to retain their previous method of delivery; walk in – write on board – walk out. Many chose to do just this, and consequentially for their classes very little changed. However some made use of the new media to introduce greater color and prepared magnetic material. For these education pioneers, this new technology allowed greater annotated explanations and by utilizing prepared material, freed up time from writing to discussion or deeper explanation. For the first time, the technology also permitted reuse and development of materials on a mass delivery level. This in turn reduced transcription errors.

Such is the persistence of these technologies that while students have, to a great extent, abandoned the skill of hand written note taking, the blackboard and whiteboard are still in use today. The freestyle enhancement they provide for the lecturer remains an important tool in education.

Transition to Computer Based Delivery

Over Head Projector (OHP) transparencies started to be introduced within the education sector in the 1950's and 1960's. Having lasted well up to the end of the 20th century such display technology can still be seen in lecture theatres even today, even if only as a dust-gathering homage to days gone by.. These were mostly phased out from the mid 1990's when the PC and overhead digital projection took center stage. Although not computer based, overhead projectors do represent a fundamental change in delivery methods, especially with regards to one great benefit and one significant disadvantage. Their benefit was that they allowed the serious reuse of printed materials and removed the necessity for the lecturer to write during the delivery. Their disadvantage was that they took the focus of the delivery away from the lecturer and moved it on to the presentation

material, effectively placing a barrier between the students and the lecturer. This allowed staff who were uncomfortable with student engagement and the performance of the lecture to disengage from it and hide behind their, or someone else's, material.

The PC could have allowed for a paradigm shift from the use of plain text and diagrams to the use of interactive multimedia elements that provided more entertaining means of lecture delivery. However the introduction of software such as PowerPoint has allowed for the extension of the weakness inherited from the preceding OHP system, and further removed the lecturer from the skills of delivery.

Just as some education enthusiasts championed the enhancements of whiteboard technologies, similar groups of progressive doers fully engaged with the computer technology as a method of enhancing, rather than replacing, delivery.

Virtual Environments

The central method employed by traditional teaching - that of a formal oral presentation/monologue given to an audience of learners - has changed little.. Advancements in the Internet and Virtual Environments now present a completely new form of media for interaction which is accessible to all irrespective of geographic location. This may also provide for a level of anonymity whereby students are no longer self-conscious about asking questions, and therefore will actively engage more to understand the material presented.

Virtual environments are a useful tool to empower student interaction and allow them to take ownership of their learning process in a communicative manner. The open source community has produced some very useful environments; these have broken the control of the fixed structures of "paid for" educational environments. The creativity and rapid development in response to "customer" feedback that the open source community is capable of has permitted rapid technology transition and enhanced the acceptance of such technology by including the users in the development community.

The key players in this new community are Drupal™ (http://drupal.org/) which is an open source content management platform and Moodle™ (http://moodle.org/) which is a Virtual Learning Environment. Drupal allows the development and implementation of websites from simplistic individual blogs to fully integrated group or community driven sites. It removed the need to develop page content using mark-up languages and provides structure, operation, information organization and behavior as key components. Moodle enables educators to create effective online learning sites that can be adapted to the needs of an institute and then down through schools to individual modules and even to the requirements of individual participants. Individual staff and students can create electronic avatars as representations of their needs, skills, resources and interactivity with the virtual community.

An alternative to open source platforms are the well established proprietary systems from Blackboard Inc. For the past several years, thousands of universities throughout the globe have been using the Blackboard Academic Suite as their e-Education delivery platform of choice. The Blackboard Learn product line consists of three elements: the Learning, Community, and the Content systems. The community system is essentially a portal whilst the other two deal with content management.

With the ever increasing popularity of mobile devices, we have seen the redevelopment of many of these services for the mobile platform. Moreover, given the mobility of these devices one has the opportunity to access content in a manner quite different from that possible via a desktop machine of fixed geographic location. Blackboard's Mobile™ Central for the iPhone is an example of such a service. Upon launch one is presented with the "Springboard" which provides an interface with all the services a university may wish to offer. One of the useful features of this product is "Maps". Maps allows the user to navigate through a campus map and search for particular buildings. In addition to this, thanks to GPS technology a user can pinpoint his location and thereby get a frame of geographic reference. Not only this, but one can also access public transport information or take a virtual tour of the campus. The virtual tour feature allows the participant to view images of the campus buildings, listen to audio descriptive content and even watch videos regarding the areas around campus. We are seeing that these services are being integrated with one another. As an example, one can carry out a search of a particular module to find all the details about timetables, information about the instructor and to see on the map where the lectures are being held. Students who have started using this Application have found it extremely useful, from first year students who are getting to know the campus, how things work and student life in general, to those in their final year of study. Students in their final year have been surprised by how many things are going on around campus that they were not aware of before the transition to the mobile platform. Clearly what started as just standard services to provide lecture content in terms of PowerPoint slides and lab notes has transitioned to an integrated facility that provides a wide range of services. These services are not only focused on lecture material, but constitute a more holistic set of services that allow the users to readily find and access any campus wide information they may need, as well as presenting information that they may have never known existed in the first place. We are now in the era of integrated rich media applications where the university learning experience is far more than just lecture material. It is the whole "university experience" where there is now a strong interplay between social and academic networking, communications and the means of material delivery.

Many universities have moved from the proprietary Blackboard to the open source Moodle for content delivery. Moodle is in use at well over 50,000 sites, including the Open University (Sclater, 2008) which has the largest number of registered users at over 650,000 (http://moodle. org/stats/). There have been a number of initiatives in developing mobile versions of Moodle in recent years. The first implementation for the iPhone called mTouch became available in April 2010 and provides access to all the standard services one can expect from Moodle itself (Sulcic, 2010). A research project called "Moodbile" made use of J2ME to develop a mobile client application for the Moodle system facilitating a number of activities such as forum, wiki, mail, glossary, calendar and access to the grades and qualification (Alier, Casany & Piduillem, 2009).

Moodle has also been used as the platform for an Alternate Reality Game (ARG) to promote language learning. One project "ARGuing for Multilingual Motivation in Web 2.0" developed a game called "Tower of Babel" (Connolly, 2009). The game took place over an eight day period in April 2009. It featured a developing and dynamic storyline and required students to develop collaborative guilds, carry out quests, develop profiles, participate in forums and deal with various multimedia content. It was played by over 300 students and 95 teachers from 28 schools in 17 countries. Clearly it can be very advantageous to use Moodle as a base platform for the development of multi-user gaming environments for education.

It is quite evident from this that there is a change happening as we speak. The move to get away from the tied down desktop system and to get mobile is one facet. The other is to use this technology to empower the development of interactive learning games. Augmented reality is also coming to the fore with several AR Web Browsers now available such as Layar (http://www.layar.com) and Wikitude (http://www.wikitude.org). With the advent of standards such as Augmented Reality Markup Language (ARML) the development of highly immersive multi-user virtual environments should be all the more accessible in the years to come (Lechner & Tripp, 2010).

With the advancement of technology we have seen the transition from traditional in-class oral presentations to a realm there the classroom is the world. Content delivery systems such as Drupal and Moodle have dramatically reduced the once ubiquitous skill of note taking. This can be both a blessing and a curse, but has freed up valuable contact time for more interactive discussions between students and educators. Alternate reality gaming is another avenue that learning environments have taken, that allows students to engage with course material through problem solving exercises in a virtual world. Such techniques of introducing material helps to re-enforce the learning material they may have engaged with through standard VLEs. Mobile technology has taken engagement one step further by allowing students and teachers alike to access materials no matter where they are, thereby freeing them from the bounds of desktop computing. This allows them to teach and learn in a manner that complements the myriad of learning styles that people have. The use of AR technologies can be used to place the material presented in context with the environment one sees. This provides the user with instant access to information about objects they see and places they visit in the real environment. The learning environment has clearly now evolved from the classical approach that has been to the fore for the past recent centuries to one in which the entire globe itself is the environment in which we can teach and learn.

Applicable Virtual Environments

One can typically expect to find a diverse set of skills and abilities amongst students studying computer science. Therefore, it can often be very difficult to find the correct level, balance and depth at which one should teach subjects such as computer programming. It is necessary to nudge a class along at a steady pace to ensure students do not get lost along the way. Many concepts in programming can be quite abstract, henceforth gaining an understanding of these fundamentals and techniques can be difficult for many, whilst being second nature to others. Attempting to ensure that all the students have a firm grasp of these essential skills can often come at a price to the students who have gone well beyond the mastery of such things. The students at the top of the class can often become bored; consequently this can result in their performance dropping due to lack of academic stimulation and interest. Online computer programming competitions can often be a useful outlet for these students to further enhance and hone their abilities.

The topcoder.com portal provides a multitude of environments for students to improve many of their skills. Probably the most interesting of these is the Algorithm Competitions area. Once a student signs up, they may take part in as many competitions as they like - typically a few competition sessions are run each week. Competitors get a number of problems ranging in complexity to solve, and gain points for the speed at which they can develop an effective solution that meets the specified criteria. The website provides a Java based environment within which students may develop their solutions using a variety of programming languages (Java, C#, C++ and VB.NET). All the tools for editing and testing the applications are firmly integrated into one single cohesive user interface.

Each competition is divided up into three distinct sections: coding, challenge and testing. The coding phase is a timed event where the user must attempt to complete three problem solving challenges within a 75 minute time limit. The next phase allows students to challenge other participants by attempting to break the solutions of their fellow competitors. Those whose algorithms are successfully compromised will lose points for that particular task. The challengers will, in-turn gain a 50 point reward. This phase of the competition lasts for 15 minutes and is followed by the system testing phase, in which an automated tester applies a set of inputs with the expectation

of certain outputs. Each competitor has a public profile page upon which some general information is displayed along with some statistics including a point based rating system. An additional incentive for competing is the possibility of receiving a monetary reward. The system also acts as a platform that may assist successful competitors in securing employment.

In summary, the topcoder.com portal can provide high achieving students who may already have a concrete grasp of programming fundamentals (amongst other skills) with an outlet that can put their problem solving skills to the test. Not only this, but for those who do well there may be both monetary and job prospect rewards at hand. Participants can interact through an online environment but the top competitors also have the opportunity of taking part in the real world. The 2010 finals were held at the Mirage Hotel, Las Vegas. This brings together people from all across the world and allows those participating to match up the real person with their online virtual representation.

The previous example made use of a web based virtual environment in which interaction was carried in a text based manner. The basic installation of the Moodle VLE allows for interaction through the use of forums, blogs, group areas, quizzes, databases and so forth. Many such facilities allow for large volumes of text based discussion to be generated. This can often be of benefit to students studying subjects that have a large emphasis on written skills. On the other hand the sheer quantity of text generated can be self defeating, as navigation and absorption becomes unmanageable. One might read a great deal about the underlying ideas and history surrounding a painting for example, but may gain a far greater appreciation of it by experiencing it within its proper environment. Therefore, photorealistic representations of distant museums and the like can give geographically disparate students a real sense of the true underlying principles that the curators believe the artist was trying to portray in the piece. The Virtual Tour of Hawaii website (http://www.vthawaii.com) provides viewers with thousands of high quality 360° virtual reality panoramas that provide a real sense of being physically present. You can essentially visit the Hawaiian Islands without ever leaving the comfort of your home.

Multi-User Virtual Environments can often be described as Massively Multiplayer Online Games (MMOGs) that may or may not focus around the concept of a "game". Probably the most widely known virtual environment is Second Life, which allows teens and adults to interact in a 3D virtual world. The relatively unconstrained virtual reality interactions enabled by Second Life have found their way into other virtual environments, including those for education. Chover, Belmonter and Remolar (2002) made use of the Crystal Space game engine (Tyberghein, 2002) to develop a virtual classroom which was designed to represent a lecture room as faithfully as possible. Some of the features included a blackboard, slide projector and laser printing facilities. One could interact through the use of avatars and chat sessions. Kao and Galas (2005) conducted a study on children's perceptions and their experiences of the RiverCity and Whyville virtual environments. They found that the customization of the avatars, which allowed the students to tailor the attributes of their virtual selves within the world, was an important facet within the environment. Chatting facilities were also found to be of use, both for educational and social interaction. Truly virtual characters within the world had a limited response to questions; hence the need for further research in to Artificial Intelligence technologies to ensure such characters can readily pass a basic Turing test. Recent advances in this area have come in the form of IBM's "Watson" machine which successfully competed against two of the most successful and celebrated contestants of the game show "Jeopardy" during the period of 14 - 16 February 2011. This clearly shows that machines now have the capability of 'understanding' and processing natural language with speed, accuracy and confidence.

With the advent of the world's first 3D Television by Samsung in 2010, it is expected that highly immersive environments will be the future for education and the entertainment industry. This will go hand in hand with an emphasis on visual realism. Such technology is beginning to appear in secondary school. For example, students can now explore the workings of a human heart in 3D when previous generations studied static pictures. The 3D environment allows the heart to be seen to beat; the chambers expand and contract, the operation of the valves and the flow of blood. Observing the dynamic process lead more rapidly and naturally to an understanding of how the system works than can be gain from text and pictures alone.

Advantages to Learning in Virtual Worlds

Even the simplest of virtual worlds, as were prevalent in the early 1990's, facilitated the development of tightly knit communities that were underpinned by the very same characteristics one may see in our everyday lives. Such worlds comprise of numerous social communities that entwine and interact with one another on multiple levels, even though such worlds may be purely text based (Rheingold, 1993). The virtual characters can be seen playing off against each other on many of the fundamental levels one sees in social groupings within the real world. The formation and destruction of bonds between two or more persons may create both friends and enemies in either world. The amalgamation of persons of similar disposition and interests allows for larger social group interactions and connections to be made.

Inherently humans have an underpinning desire to socialize For those who may be unable to partake in real world social interactions due to physical or mental constraints, online virtual worlds can provide an essential outlet for their social needs.

Many can also find it difficult to interact socially with new people, and the anonymity of interacting with others through the use of avatars provides a level of security that they would not encounter in the real world. Once these avatars existed in the imagination driven, text based, domains of Geeks. They have been made more socially acceptable through broad entertainment media of television and films. This popularisation can be readily seen in the virtual worlds of "Society" and "Slayers" as featured in the 2009 film Gamer directed by Neveldine and Taylor.

People interacting through the use of avatars have fewer inhibitions and are more willing to express themselves without worrying about what others may think. Getting students to interact in a lecture room environment can often be very difficult at best. Students rarely have the self confidence to stand out from the crowd and answer a question, and the main reasoning behind this is fear; the fear of being incorrect and the fear of what their peers may think. Even asking a question to a student body that simply requires a show of hands can often give a skewed representation of what they may really think. In such situations one can clearly see that some students will immediately raise their hands, followed by a number of others that will follow suit after a short initial delay while they deliberate if they should or not (where one leads many will follow).

Multi User Virtual Environments can also be especially useful as an assessment tool, in particular where group work is involved. In a typical group scenario the students must work as a team to analyze a problem, devise an appropriate solution and implement it. In reality one or two members of the group often carry out the majority of the work while the others may do little or nothing. This can sometimes lead to arguments amongst group members. Those who take a greater lead in the project often do too much work to counteract the limited effort applied by others. In terms of assessment if can often be difficult to determine who did what. To aid in the determination, each individual in the group may be required to write a short report outlining their participation throughout the project. One may also include some form marking grid for the purposes of peer assessment which imparts some degree of confidence for the level of participation of each group member.

Much of the stress that is created in such assessments can be alleviated by using virtual environments that can provide interactive feedback to the assessor on the progress of each individual student. As students work through a problem one can see time stamped logs of their progress. The lecturer can immediately get an appreciation of how students are progressing and can detect if certain students are off the mark. Additional tutoring may be provided as and when necessary to clarify any misunderstood concepts. Overall it can help to streamline the assessment process aiding both students and lecturers alike.

Virtual environments can provide the students with an interactive, fun and entertaining means of learning that fits with the ever increasing pace of technological advancement. This however must be met with a certain degree of caution and monitoring of student progress. Given that students may be less inhibited by what they may say in a virtual world they can easily say things to other students that may cause offence. Therefore, whilst a lecturer may get a far better insight into the progress of each student, they must also constantly monitor the conservations between group members to ensure that students are not being bullied or offended in any way by their peers. Such situations can be avoided by ensuring a code of conduct is established from the outset. Probably the best means for establishing such rules of interaction is for the students themselves to determine what they consider to be appropriate conduct and sign off on it in some manner. Hence the system should in essence be self policing, allowing for a less critical analysis of the interactions by the tutor.

The advantages of MUVEs clearly outweigh any elements that may detract from the use of the technology. They can enhance social interaction and collaboration across a disparate geographic region. Project based learning can be enhanced and a clear improvement can be seen in student progress. It has long been known that one of the best ways of learning is by doing; hence virtual environments that focus on problem-based scenarios and get the students to think for themselves are key to enhancing learning and retention.

Students are generally assessed by grading them in some way such as "A, B, C, D", but virtual worlds facilitate the possibility of an alternative, in the manner of increasing particpants' ranking or "in-game" points. This in turn can have a positive motivational impact. In an examination of game play interaction for the purposes of entertainment one can readily see the desire amongst gamers to see their name appearing on the "high scores" table. Hence the conception of such scenarios to motivate student learning.

CONCLUSION

Transition or Avoidance of New Technologies

We can associate available technology with opportunities but this does not necessitate lecturer participation. A lecturer may or may not chose to adopt these technologies and evolve their skill set in concert with them. Inevitably many people are resistant to change, especially when such change involves an increase in workload such as the updating or replacement of teaching materials. A lecturer may ask why should they engage with new technologies when their present mode of delivery appears to be more than adequate?

This resistance has been seen before when educators moved from the fixed technologies of the blackboard and whiteboard by the retention of the same methods and the adoption of bad habits in the subsequent technologies of the OHP and PC ages. If educators don't pursue these changes as opportunities to enhance learning at an early

stage, new technologies will become standard just in time to be replaced.

A dangerous precedent began with the PC age. As students began to grow up with household technology that was new to the previous generations who were teaching them, often the student was more skilled or knowledgeable about certain aspects of the technology. Resistance to change by staff only increased this knowledge gap.

The potential for a re-assertion of this precedent has occurred with the introduction of Virtual Environments. Different reasons may well apply with this as schools are often early adopters of new technology, and have been so with virtual environments. Virtual environments are now considered established technology, but they have not been fully adopted by HE institutes and many are still in a transitional period. Some staff actively avoid new technology or are willing to commit the technology "sin" in which they adapt their use of new technologies to allow them to deliver materials in the same manner as before and behave in the same way as they did with the previous technology. Their students may be far more familiar with such environments on entering the HE institute as they have already been exposed to them in school.

Applying MUVEs to Teaching & Learning

The use of MUVEs to enhance teaching and learning in HE has both advantages and disadvantages. Firstly such systems are often complex and require a systems administration team who are willing to provide the hardware, software and technical skills to set up and maintain the software system. Secondly, as with any VLE system content must be developed to populate the world, this is typically the remit of the lecturers. As such, some may be apprehensive at having to learn a new system. Others who may be more technologically confident may engage more readily, but still have to invest a great deal of time to map their present material to a new paradigm of interaction and delivery. Training in the use of these new systems is essential to ensure staff are fully versed in the capabilities of the system so they can move forward and use it to the height of its potential.

It is one thing to train the staff, but students also must be trained on how to use the system if they are expected to be fully engaged. One may say that VLEs like Moodle are intuitive and easy to understand but in many cases of observation, students' interaction with such systems and their fundamental understanding on how they work is severely lacking. This is especially prevalent in the case of non-computing students. Therefore for any virtual environment to be a success it is imperative that a well defined and clear cut training program is provided to both students and staff.

With the proper investment of resources, teaching materials and training, virtual environments can have a very positive effective on the learning process. Students can engage and learn at their own pace and in their own time. An analysis of Moodle logs typically shows that many students log on and download material in the early hours of the morning - this is often due to work commitments after a spending a day at university. A key benefit of such systems is the ability to provide students with an environment in which they can interact, carry out experiments, solve problems and learn using a problem solving based approach, thereby solidifying the general concepts and fundamentals they may learn in a standard lecture environment. With the rapid growth of mobile technology and unlimited Internet connectivity, the way in which the students of today and tomorrow learn has forever been changed. No longer are students confined to learning in the standard classical classroom setting typical of 200 years ago. Students now have the ability to learn and engage with material no matter where they are or what they are doing. The future lies in the amalgamation of MUVEs and mobile technology.

REFERENCES

Alier, M., Casany, M. J., & Piduillem, J. (2009). Towards mobile learning applications integration with learning management systems. In Goh, T. T. (Ed.), *Multiplatform e-learning systems and technologies: Mobile devices for ubiquitions ICT-based education* (pp. 182–194). Hershey, PA/ New York, NY: Information Science Reference.

Chover, M., Belmonter, O., & Remolar, I. (2002). *Web-based virtual environments for teaching.* Eurographics/ACM SIGGRAPH Workshop on Computer Graphics Education.

Connolly, T., Boyle, L., & Hainey, T. (2009). Arguing for multilingual motivation in Web 2.0: A games-based learning platform for language learning. *Proceedings from The 3rd European Conference on Games Based Learning.*

Garber, A. (2001). Death by Powerpoint. *Small Business Computing.com.* Retrieved from http://www.smallbusinesscomputing.com/biztools/article.php/684871

Johnstone, A. H., & Percival, F. (1976). Attention breaks in lectures. *Education in Chemistry, 13*(2), 49–50.

Kao, L., & Galas, C. (2005). *A totally different world: Playing and learning in multi-user virtual environments.* Digital Games Research Association, Seattle, WA. Retrieved from http://www.cathleengalas.com/papers/4TotallyDifferentWorldDIGRA05.pdf

Lechner, M., & Tripp, M. (2010). ARML – an augmented reality standard. *Proceedings from Mobile World Congress, Augmented Reality Summit.*

Rheingold, H. (1993). *The virtual community: Homesteading on the electronic frontier.* Reading, MA: Addison-Wesley.

Sclater, N. (2008). *Large-scale open source e-learning systems at Open University UK*. Educause Centre for Applied Research. Retrieved from http://net.educause.edu/ir/library/pdf/ERB0812.pdf

Sulcic, A. (2010). *Taking Moodle out of the class-room: Making learning mobile, context-aware and fun*. Moodle.si 4th International Conference.

Tyberghein, J. (2002). *Crystal Space game engine*. Retrieved from http://crystal.sourceforge.net

KEY TERMS AND DEFINITIONS

Algorithm: First created by the ancient astronomer and mathematician Al-Khwārizmī. It is essentially a concrete list of specific instructions that are required to fulfill a designated task.

Course: Under the UK education system a course is considered to be a body of academic work that leads to a degree exit award such as BSc or MSc.

Higher National Certificate (HNC): This is an award provided to students upon completion of a one year course at a college of further education. Such students may often find that they can apply for the first year of a university degree program for which they previous lacked school level qualifications, or they may have sufficient credit to transfer into the second year of such a degree program.

Higher National Diploma (HND): This is an award provided to students upon completion of a two year course at a college of further education. Such students may often find that they can transfer into to the second or third year of a university degree program.

Marking Grid: A marking grid is essentially a matrix of grades with a corresponding list of expected outcomes required to achieve an expected grade. Typically such grids work with the symbols "A, B, C, D, E, F & NS", NS being a non-submission.

Module: A module is a distinct unit of teaching. In degree courses at Higher Education (HE) level, students are typically taught several distinct subjects in parallel. Each of these subjects is referred to as a "module". A module typically runs for a single academic term (twelve weeks).

Moodle: Moodle is an online Virtual Learning Environment (VLE) that may be freely downloaded from http://moodle.org/. It is essentially a Content Management System (CMS) -for the delivery of educational material to students. The server side application is PHP based and installations of the system can be updated and tailored to meet specific needs by the installation of numerous additional plugins.

Turing Test: This is a test proposed by Alan Turing to determine a machine's ability to demonstrate intelligence. It requires a human to interact with one machine and one human using natural language conversation. If the first human is unable to tell the machine from the other human then the machine has passed the test.

Virtual Reality Panoramas: Usually generated by stitching a number of digital still images together to create a 360° view of a scene. Quick-Time VR is a popular technology to use for this. One may also find that some Flash and Java Applets can provide a similar level of functionality. Some VR scenes include the use of 'hotspots' allowing the user to jump from one scene to the next.

Chapter 3
Learning Places:
A Case Study of Collaborative Pedagogy Using Online Virtual Worlds

James Barrett
Umeå University, Sweden

Stefan Gelfgren
Umeå University, Sweden

ABSTRACT

The chapter, based on a set of developed teaching scenarios, discusses how virtual worlds, in particular Second Life, can be used in student centered pedagogy; intertwining theory and practice, emphasizing process-thinking, critical perspectives, and strengthen the confidence and independence of the student. Drawing upon experiences from traditional education, Web 2.0-tools, and problem based pedagogy grounded in project work, social media, engineering, and digital humanities, this chapter presents a pedagogy based upon the concepts of participatory culture, and co-creation on the part of students in the learning process. The authors have been involved in developing the core curriculum for a term-long (four month) course for Museum Studies. A problem based, student centered pedagogy is both integrated and contrasted with traditional classroom settings, that are also part of the planning, implementation, and assessment stages of the course. Based upon the practical experience of conducting this course, the article critically discusses ICT and problem oriented learning on a general level – including the benefits and disadvantages for the student and for the teachers. How this approach to learning, from the experiences in virtual worlds, can fit in to the established structure of learning goals, lectures, examination, and assessment is questioned in the chapter, based on the experiences gathered from teaching the course.

INTRODUCTION

This chapter emphasizes the potentials for using virtual worlds in student-based pedagogy. Virtual

worlds are three-dimensional, persistent environments that are distributed over the Internet, which function as spaces for communication, co-operation and sharing from one to many users. We give examples from a course developed and

DOI: 10.4018/978-1-60960-545-2.ch003

conducted within the framework of the Museum Studies Program at Umeå University, Sweden. Based on these examples we also draw some general conclusions – both positive and negative – regarding the practice of pedagogy using virtual worlds.

HUMlab (a digital humanities computing lab), in a partnership with the Department of Culture and Media, has hosted the digital components of term-long courses in Museum Studies and Culture Analysis. The project described below started when representatives from the Museum Studies Program approached staff in HUMlab to discuss possibilities for their second year undergraduate students learning what they referred to as "digital competence", without any further profound precision. The initial aim was to give the students basic knowledge in PowerPoint, and in audio and photo editing. Starting from that fairly vague concept, we came up with the idea to let students build multimedia exhibitions in the virtual world of Second Life (SL) during a full term-long course.

Teaching and learning with virtual worlds involves extensive planning, a coordination of the elements that are specific to the media, and an attention to the contexts provided by the subjects taught. The coordination and synthesis of the theoretical and administrative components between the digital realm of HUMlab and the classrooms of Culture and Media presented a series of challenges. Three dimensional multimedia virtual worlds can be a challenge to educators that are used to books and two-dimensional images. In our own experience, we have mostly avoided the recreation of classrooms and lecture halls in virtual worlds, such as ActiveWorlds and Second Life. Instead we have presented virtual worlds, mainly in the form of Second Life, to students as a tool for their own expression. The dynamics of successful group work, and an array of skills for digital literacy (visual, audio, design, composition and convergence) form the major learning goals of the courses.

The overall aim of the term for the students is to learn theoretical perspectives on interpreting our contemporary society. The SL-based element is intended to fit with more traditional style of learning of the course. On one hand Second Life became an environment to work with the different theoretical perspectives studied during the course. The students took lecture-style classes in gender, class, religion, sexuality, ethnicity, and globalization. On the other hand, SL became one tool among several in the pedagogical tool-set in combination with written examinations, seminars and discussions, each based around a core curriculum. There was an attempt to bridge the gaps between theory and practice through the use of Second Life. Involvement in technology became the means for both learning how to build an exhibition, and for reflection upon digital media as a way to present information. A secondary aim with the whole project was to give the students "digital competence" – in that we include for example an understanding of the affordances of various digital media, knowledge in handling different programs, a critical and reflective approach to digital media, and how to present information in different media.

All teaching in Second Life was conducted in HUMlab. HUMlab is a center for the humanities and information technology, often carried out through a multidisciplinary approach, but with a special focus toward the disciplines at the Humanities Faculty. Work along similar lines to the museum studies project involving virtual worlds has been done in HUMlab before. HUMlab ran the project "Virtual weddings and the real wedding of linguistics, literature and cultural studies" in 1998-2004 (Svensson, 2002). Instead of writing a traditional third year essay, students in language studies visualized and presented their ideas in the virtual world of ActiveWorlds. Each year the project centered around one complex concept – such as Weddings, Realities, City or Monstrosity. Students constructed and visualized their "essay" through building environments, linking objects, sound, picture and hypertexts. In another HUMlab project, "Immersion, experience and understanding: Virtual theatres in drama teaching", students in drama and film studies used virtual worlds to get a better understanding of the role of environment in relation to historical plays and theatres (Rosenqvist, 2004).

Digital tools and working methods were used to give the students possibilities to build their own theatres and thereby reflect upon the contextual factors affecting the plays. These two projects, as well as the SL-project of this article, use a simulation based learning approach, in order to activate and engage students in their own learning processes (the background to HUMlab's Second Life involvement is further described in Barrett and Gelfgren (2009). The experience, based upon these different projects, is that when you change forms for lecturing and make students more responsible for the learning process you let loose creativity and thereby help the students to find new ways for learning (Deutschmann & Panichi, 2009, pg 34).

An important starting point in order to understand how the museology project is developed is our own personal relation to both computer mediated pedagogy and teaching. Both authors have previous experience in a more student centered, and problem oriented learning on different courses when working as teachers at university. Barrett is currently a PhD student in English literature and is writing a thesis on digital literature and literacy. He also has a background in journalism and is active as a musician and performance artist. Gelfgren, working as associate professor at HUMlab, has a background in construction engineering, religious studies and the history of ideas. He wrote his dissertation on 19th century Swedish revivalism.

Pedagogical Frameworks

To understand the motivations behind the pedagogical framework used in HUMlab for teaching with virtual worlds, two broad categories are relevant. On one hand, approaching the media as a three-dimensional palette with which the students can create in networks of collaborative authorship is one focus for teaching with virtual worlds. Simultaneously, virtual worlds are also teaching platforms, with Virtual Online Traveler and Second Life being examples, which are used to deliver traditional teacher-centered lessons in real time over the Internet. Virtual worlds are synchronous media whereby participants can communicate with each other in real time, accompanying that communication with activities and actions. It is also possible to build three-dimensional structures in virtual worlds and populate them with objects and artifacts as well as actors. Some examples of the dominant pedagogical perspective for collaboration using virtual worlds include *Virtual Macbeth* led by Angela A. Thomas, Bernard Frischer's *Rome Reborn* (www.romereborn.virginia.edu), and the *Virtual Harlem* (www.evl.uic.edu/cavern/harlem) project led by Bryan Carter. In these projects the virtual world is created for the students to interact with. While in many cases the students can add content to the virtual world platform, the emphasis is on the delivery of learning materials to the student. The student projects from HUMlab differ from these excellent projects in that the students build the spaces during their learning. Creative expression along with learning and participation are what drives the HUMlab virtual worlds projects as students create in a critical sense while they are taking part in discussions and teaching.

The pedagogical framework for the courses conducted in HUMlab using virtual worlds calls on a number of pedagogical knowledge bases. These include Simulation Based Learning (SBL), virtual worlds as textual environments, virtual worlds as simulative environments, and mixed reality environments for learning.

Virtual Worlds as Toolkits for Learning

Learning with virtual worlds can be classified into two broad divisions. As a textual environment, a virtual world allows for creative expression and knowledge formulation. Students can create a three-dimensional representation of the themeselves, and discuss issues, questions or ideas under consideration in the studied course. Into these three-dimensional spaces can be placed links to web pages, written texts, audio and video. Within these spaces students can interact with each other, as well as specialists in the relevant fields of study, and people from the wider national and international community. The work of students can be published in a platform that allows for real time feedback and critique as well as synchronous collaborative learning. Materials can also be downloaded from within the virtual space. The textuality of virtual worlds allows for a unique synthesis of collaboration and representation. Students can make things in virtual worlds together. The latter of these two opens up virtual worlds to simulation-based learning.

Simulation Based Learning

The simulative properties of virtual worlds render them a powerful tool for creating learning situations that are otherwise impossible or very difficult to achieve with the text based materials of the more traditional pedagogy systems. Simulation Based Learning (SBL) as a model for training has been found to be superior to problem based learning in the education of medical students (Steadman et al., 2006). However, a delivery-based model of pedagogy remains the central tenant in many SBL theoretical accounts (de Jong et al., 1984; Rose, Eckard, & Rubloff, 1998; Bodemer, 2004), whereby the learner is introduced to, and must comply with, an already existing simulative learning platform. The work conducted in HUMlab with simulative learning environments differs from the usual delivery model of SBL, as it is profoundly constructivist on a level that is not even common in the use of virtual worlds in learning. The SBL work conducted in HUMlab emphasizes the active role of the students in learning models by creating virtual situations or scenarios in which they need to make decisions and consider information that can only be presented as abstract and conceptual in problem based learning situations. The simulative property of virtual world as a media form creates a situation where new perspectives are introduced to the students, through their own activities.

Mixed Reality Environments

Another challenge posed by the virtual spaces of such online worlds, as Second Life is their integration with the physical spaces which the students and teachers inhabit daily. In the case of the partnerships between the Department of Culture and Media, the classroom and digital humanities lab are joined by virtual spaces in learning. The open and non-centralized plan of HUMlab results in it being a major locus for meetings and collaboration between students and staff during the teaching term. Wireless broadband is open for all students and staff in all parts of the university, lending it to group and individual work being conducted in mixed, on and offline, situations. The virtual spaces of Second Life are also used for meetings, discussions and teaching. Augmenting the classroom, lab and virtual spaces, the student and staff blogs became tools for asynchronous communication with questions, comments, and recounting of course elements.

Problem Orientated Project Pedagogy (POPP)

POPP represents a crossover point between the situation based learning of the simulative elements used in teaching with virtual worlds and the problem based learning of the classroom. "The POPP-approach offers great potentials in designing and practicing virtual learning environments. It enables genuine collaboration among students; the possibility to work with real-life problems; the possibility to integrate work experience with theoretical methodological reflections" (Dirck-inck-Holmfeld, 2002, pg 31-32). The model for how we organized students into groups and the work that these groups conduct in relation to the spaces they occupy in the virtual worlds is based largely on the principles of POPP. According to the principles of POPP:

"Knowledge needs to be constructed through a collaborative process in which the students create and critically reflect upon a problem. Illeris (1974) relates the didactic principles of problem-oriented project pedagogy to Piaget's development theory: Problem orientation implies accommodative learning, i.e., learning which breaks down existing cognitive structures and builds up new ones. However, Illeris (1974) emphasizes that Piaget's theories can only be considered as point of departure for an alternative learning psychology" (Fjuk, 1998, 27-28).

Early in the courses students were asked in their groups to identify problems, issues or questions that they were interested in working with, in relation to the teaching they were receiving in lectures and seminars. The choice of a single theme based on a problem or issue taken from the areas of class, gender and sexuality become the theme they worked with in the virtual world space.

Design

The use of virtual worlds for simulation based learning in higher education requires careful attention to design. Design includes both the course and the possibilities for use that the virtual world embodies. Accordingly, planning course outcomes should be considered in relation to the affordances of the virtual world. Course planning by HUMlab includes a cohesive system for the parts of the

course that are conducted both in the classroom and in the digital environments. How the simulative virtual world media is to be integrated with the problem-based materials of the courses should be a defining criterion in the planning. In the relationship between the students, the materials and the goals of the courses, it is design that allows for collaboration and cohesion in the groups.

Design issues in teaching and learning with virtual worlds is an area unto itself and worthy of much more than can be provided in this discussion. In our own situation we chose to pursue a design that did not follow a delivery model. We did not build classrooms or embed media for students to consume and discuss in the virtual world. Rather, we treated the virtual space of Second Life as a blank three-dimensional canvas, upon which the students were to articulate their arguments, questions, hypotheses and observations.

Ethics

The general inability of legal prefaces, such as the End User License Agreement (EULA) and Terms of Service, to govern specific instances of individual behavior in a virtual world calls for a system of virtual ethics to be adopted by all users in educational contexts. Charles Ess (2009), Melissa Blades and Sarah Vermylen (2004), and Victoria MacArthur (2008) have conducted research on ethics in the contexts of virtual worlds. Virtual ethics address, among other things, the ethical considerations raised by the immersive, real time, interactivity of three dimensional virtual media spaces, and the actions and interactions this technology makes possible. Ethics in the use of virtual worlds in learning should be primarily concerned with privacy and attribution. The privacy of individuals must be protected in the collection of data in virtual worlds and this includes the identity of avatars. Permissions must be gained for the publication of field research from virtual environments, including statements from avatars and any material that is recorded that includes them, which could be later used to identify them (virtually or otherwise).

An Overview of the SL Project

At the time of writing, the museum studies course has been given twice in HUMlab. After the first time we took our own experiences and the evaluations from students and staff, which led to adjustments in the course planning. Problems were mainly related to the difficulty in integrating the Second Life-based project with the more traditional course content. The students (and also staff from the Museum Studies Program) had problems in relating the two tracks to each other. So, adjustments were made with the intention of the whole course being more coherent and integrated.

Each Second Life project runs for one full (four month) semester. The end product is to be a full exhibition of student work, both in the virtual world and in HUMlab, relating to the content of the course – even though the process reaching the goal is considered more important than the final construction. The students work in groups of three to four persons. Teachers from the student's home department allocate the groups.

The semester is divided into four different classes, each focusing on a specific theme, such as gender, class, ethnicity/religion, locality. At the same time the classes are comprised of four different modules, the Second Life-project is intertwined into all four, running like a "red thread" through the whole semester. Therefore progression in Second Life has to be integrated into the different single standing classes.

During the first module the students are given an introduction to Second Life. A short introductory lecture on SL, and thereafter the students created their accounts and started creating their avatars supported by supervision if needed. During the first module they are encouraged to spend as much time as possible "living in" and exploring the virtual world. The students were also assigned to some tasks in order to push them to live and hang out in the world to discover and learn about places and persons. The aim is to teach them how to navigate the world, identify with their avatar, and to give them an understanding of the world as a medium – to understand the affordances of the world. This aspect cannot be overemphasized. Many students focus on the final exam and want to start building as soon as possible, but we want the students to learn and experience the virtual world first. In the end of the first module they are given a short introduction to building, but it is not until the second module that the students are given more profound knowledge in building and sculpting in SL through lectures, workshops and supervision. During the third module the building skills are deepened, aiming toward the final result. The last module is to a large extent devoted to the student's own work.

Teachers are available throughout the whole semester, often working in the same studio environment (HUMlab) as the students. Each module includes a few hours of scheduled but voluntary, from the student perspective, drop-in supervision. Because of the online nature of virtual worlds such as Second Life, teaching is often outside regular office hours. Second Life is a global community and therefore works on global time. Combined with the comments sections on the student blogs, it was not unusual to be interacting with students working on the projects in the evenings or on weekends, answering questions and responding to problems.

Tasks were assigned within the groups as a result of the design of the virtual world platform. These roles include the creation of content inside the virtual world using Linden Scripting Language (LSL) code scripting, objects, landscaping, multimedia content (audio, images, text) and virtual cinematography (machinima). The affordances of Second Life result in the groups organizing themselves around the technology and enacting roles that suited the subject areas in relation to curatorial and museum work. Often a coder would emerge from the group, with another student working with images, another with audio, someone looking into copyright and another would collect materials for the displays. These specializations were collaborative and arbitrary, with skills and competencies determined within the groups regarding who did what. Early in the second running of the museum studies course two students declined to do the course based largely on its focus on technology. These students concluded that they we interested in physical spaces and materials and they did not see the benefits that could be had from simulations. It is likely the students who declined the course experienced other forms of trepidation, as they did not discuss their concerns with the HUMlab staff involved in the project. In regards to use of virtual world platforms and higher education, student preconceptions and fears are a very large barrier to communication and learning. Much energy needs to be devoted to introducing even so-called digital natives to the media and encouraging them to use it in a collaborative and learner-directed manner.

An example from the use of Second Life in relation to both use and design, and how the two meet, involves a group dynamic for working together based on the allocation of land and how land can be owned. The teachers leading the course from the Culture and Media Department broke the students into groups of three to four members. These groups were allocated land, which had to be sold to the leader of each group according to the design of Second Life. Once the student owner of each parcel of land accepts the purchase, for zero dollars, they can create a group and invite the members of their allocated group to join and share in most of the privileges of land ownership. They can deed the land to the group and assign roles to each member. Roles allow members to build and edit objects (prims) on the group-owned land parcel. Only the original owner of the land can perform editing of land, so-called terraforming. Once the students are group owners of the land and each possess equal abilities to effect agency in Second Life, a certain degree of collective pressure is asserted regarding the performance of

tasks. From the examples related to land ownership in Second Life it is possible to imagine how the design of the software affects the structure of the group dynamic in learning. A leader emerges in each group, with tasks allocated according to the structures of the land ownership.

A further example of how these scenarios open students to new and very practical inputs is from the realms of copyright law. One group of students had made a digital copy of an extract from a commercially released documentary film for inclusion in their virtual world installation on social class and education. During a round-table discussion with teaching staff and other students it was revealed that permission had not been obtained for using the film material. With only a week before assessment the students were thrown into a panic with the realization that without permission they could not use the film. Obtaining permission from an author or publisher was not something they had considered. A period of reflection following the situation with the film, allowing students to reconsider their perspectives on copyright law and discuss its implications in relation to museums with teachers.

In the HUMlab-led sections of the courses students create the learning objects as they progress. These objects can take a number of forms. Early in the course drawing, sketching and the composition of models are used to give form to ideas and concepts. Once the students move into the virtual spaces of the online worlds they use the editing tools of the virtual world programs to make objects and artifacts. When the three dimensional frame of the virtual space is ready, students then move into video, audio and text production for media to be included in the world. Once the in-world projects are complete the students then document them with videos and still images, which includes post-production techniques. Throughout the course students are encouraged to maintain blogs for documentation and reflection regarding their progress in the project.

Figure 1. Genesis: Students arrive for the first time on the HUMlab Island

Figure 2. Mixed Stream: Video stream and class conducted both in Second Life and in HUMlab

The students are introduced to different software useful for their final exhibition. They were introduced to film, sound and image editing, and how to integrate various forms of media into their buildings. Basic three-dimensional modeling skills are included in the course. For the whole semester students were also given tips through the teacher blog where they could look for help on the Internet, for example tutorials on YouTube, inspirational sites in Second Life, web pages, and other related blogs.

Each course section ended with an evaluation done by teacher, both from HUMlab and from the Museum Studies Program. The evaluations pinpointed reactions to the content of the course and how the student's work was progressing. Each theme also had a lecture with focus on the specific issues dealt with in relation to Second Life and/or virtual worlds in general, for example "Gender and sexuality in virtual worlds", "Space and place in virtual worlds" and "Religion in virtual worlds".

Student Impressions

When the students were given their Second life accounts and avatars they arrived at the HUMlab Island for the first time. They were met by a flat empty surface on a large deserted island; it was to be their in-world home for the next four months. After the initial trial and error experiences they were sent to a few places to visit from a museological point of interest. Thereafter they are let loose, encouraged to live and learn Second Life, supported by the teachers whenever they want supervision. However, even if we emphasized the need to explore and learn the world, many students quite immediately (as mentioned) focus on the final exam – the exhibition. They were given an introduction in building at the end of the first class, and they are generally both anxious and eager about starting building, not from the perspective of the process but for the goal they believe is the aim of the course.

At the same time, different students approached the problem from different angles. Some students started constructing just for the sake of it, without any long term planning, no matter what they built. Their aim was just to start building in order to learn the means. Other groups started thinking about the form and the content and were astounded (almost paralyzed) by the complexity of the assignment. So, early on it was possible to see a variation in attitudes toward the assigned task and to Second Life, even though no one had any experiences from SL at forehand.

From the second module, the SL-project is more clearly directed toward constructing an exhibition. HUMlab had the possibility to invite a professional and skilled SL-builder for a workshop together with the students. They are also introduced

Figure 3. Early Build: Experimental building by Museum Studies Students

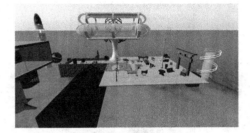

Figure 4. Dogville: Project based on the Lars von Trier film and gendered space

to and have workshops on Photoshop (for photo editing), and Camtasia (for on-screen filming). At the end of the third module there is a workshop specifically aiming at integrating various forms of media format into the exhibition. During the last quarter of the term the students have the possibility to suggest themes for scheduled supervision and workshops based upon their specific needs at the time.

The exhibitions are assessed through group presentations in front of teachers and fellow students. The technical quality is examined, but the most important part of the exhibition is the process leading to the final result. The students have to be able to reflect upon and discuss their choices and the ways leading up to their concluding results.

A week after the final examination a public vernissage is held, showing the exhibition for anyone interested – both in the physical world and in Second Life. The event was announced at the university through posters and email, the local press and through mailing lists, appropriate Facebook groups and personal contacts. The first year there were approximately 40 visitors at the vernissage and the second year about 70 people attended. The students know about the vernissage from the very beginning of the project, which adds a feeling of seriousness to the whole project.

Feedback from students was gathered using a standard form with eight questions distributed at the completion of the course. The questions were designed to elicit the expectations and critical reflection from the students. The initial

reactions from students included that the course was going to be difficult and they did not know what Second Life was. In the post-course feedback students expressed doubts about the level of competency they had gained from the course in terms of digital media, one student states "I am doubtful that the knowledge I have today would be seen as a cutting edge but it clearly is a start and it is certainly a great deal more than those that already work in museums have". Along with a general competence, students expressed a sense of inspiration from the learning experience, one stating an intention to continue working with the virtual world and simulation format with "several ideas of my own". This expansion of interest and perceived competencies included for some students other digital media formats dealt with in the course, such as video, blogs, and wikis. The overall feedback from the students using the questionnaire was positive, with reservations about

Figure 5. Class Room: Origins of class in education

the level of effort demanded from the course and regarding how much they believed they had gained from it in terms of their own abilities.

Collaborative Learning in Virtual Worlds

During the Second Life project we assume the students can and want to solve the loosely defined tasks. They are supported by introductory lectures and workshops, teaching them the necessary software and skills. A problem-orientated pedagogy empowers the students and their learning, but it also necessitates a transformation of power structures in the learning environment. The students have to be more active than in traditional situations, and the teacher no longer has the authoritative role that (s)he usually has. The teachers from Mueum Studies often expressed that they did not have the time to learn SL, and the problem-oriented pedagogy forced them to realize they had another role than the usual lecturer. They rather became the supervisor or the facilitator, which is vitally important to understand in this kind of pedagogy (Bauersfeld, 1995). There were different ways to handle this new situation – both from the student's and the teacher's perspectives. The teachers from the Museum Studies Program had to deal with both the new role as teachers and the fact they did not know much about the technology involved, even if most of them were happy about the collaborations within the project.

The students were sufficiently competent with the most basic use of computers – emailing, browsing the net, some gaming, reading blogs, some social media services – but none were familiar with virtual worlds, and in the beginning they were hesitant and reluctant toward SL. The overwhelming experience of digital culture for the students was more on the consumer side, rater then as active and reflective producers of content. One student rejected Second Life as "soo 2003", implying that the market-driven, commodity-based hype is over, and therefore it is no longer a

Figure 6. Power Map: Expressions of Power in 3D space

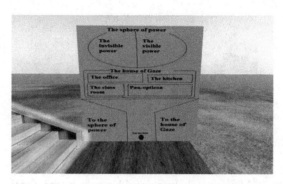

relevant medium. The teachers from the Museum Studies Program had little or no experience in virtual worlds, but they were given an introduction in the beginning of the term so all of them had at least their own avatar.

Among the students there were at least two different strategies. One group dived into Second Life with a trial and error-attitude, as mentioned above. This group of students looked at different sites, met other people, had some experiences, and started building randomly, no matter the final use of whatever they build or learned. The other group had a higher threshold to climb. Instead of starting by discovering the possibilities (and constraints) of SL, they began by discussing and planning the final exhibition, and hence postponing the basic work that actually had to be done. It is the first, trial and error-approach that is preferential for the outcome of the project. The practical learning process has to be achieved through integrating the traditional theoretical ways of learning with more practice/simulation based learning, alongside the aims, means and goals of communication that are at hand.

The Student's Learning Process

Through a problem oriented project pedagogy approach, the intention was to empower the students and let loose their creativity. All groups initially had a preliminary idea about what they

Figure 7. Silent Spring 1: Environment and Class Project

Figure 8. Silent Spring 2: Environment and Class Project

wanted to do. Lectures and seminars on theoretical perspectives gave the students angles on previously mentioned issues such as ethnicity, class and gender in virtual worlds. In order to visualize and turn theory into objects and spaces they had to thoroughly discuss the content of the curriculum, which improved the understanding of the subjects studied.

Apart from just using Second Life as a platform for building and visualizing concepts, SL was also used as a field for empirical studies. The mere creation of the personal avatars made the student aware of various perspectives. What happens if the avatar is made the opposite sex of person operating it? What kind of reactions do they face in meeting other people? What kind of signals do clothing and body shape of the avatar send to others? What does the possibility to fly and teleport all over the world imply for a sense of place and gaze? What does the entire gender coded environment, with sex shops and clubs, imply? How are religious faith and practice conducted in different settings? And so on. Second Life can, simply speaking, be seen as a digital representation of our physical world, giving the students the possibility to study all sorts of environments, reaching them with just a mouse click.

While the students work on their exhibitions they struggle a lot with Second Life as a social arena, and with technology and the difficulties with construction the things they imagine they

wanted to do. They have to put a lot of effort in making whatever they want to do, and there were a lot of complaints during almost the whole term. However, this turned out to be one part of the success of the project in the end. To call upon a well known C. S. Lewis quotation: "The happiness I feel now is the pain I had before". The investment in the course was well rewarded at its end with many of the students aware that they had participated in something so different from the dominant formula for learning.

It is difficult to conceptualize the actual process of how and what the students learned. But through intertwining theoretical perspective on cultural phenomenon, introductions and workshops on digital perspectives and tools, continuous supervision, with student based group-wise work, aiming toward one openly defined exhibition, we could support the student's learning process. At least that is what we were told by the students and what many of them wrote in the final assessment of the course. A few students wrote that they were skeptical in the beginning, but the process as a whole had been interesting. Other students claim the end result was good, despite all the anxiety during the term. Overall student feedback was positive to the courses but somewhat negative to the degree of reliance upon student-led learning, due largely to the demands it places on them. There were also negative comments about the integration of the SL project into the more traditional track of the course. Generally students expected to be shown how to use the virtual world platform, instead of finding out through trial and error.

Realities of Virtual Worlds in Learning

It is very clear that problem based pedagogy has great potential in relation to the use of virtual worlds in learning, through letting the students be responsible for their own process of learning. The original aim of the SL-project was to give the students "digital competence", at least on a basic level. They were supposed to learn some digital tools and software, but also learn how to present information and interact with potential museum visitors in a digital milieu. The added value of working in a virtual and spatial environment, which allows students to simulate the process of planning and building an exhibition, is a part of this competency. Apart from the initial explicit requirements there were other advantages with working in Second Life. The fact that the students work together as a team gives them skills and insights into processes they normally would not have encountered in lecture-style learning environments, similar positive experiences are also described by Lona Dircknick-Holmfeld (2002).

Building an exhibition in a virtual world has the great advantage that it is possible to build full-scale models for a relatively small amount of money. The students have in virtual worlds all the means at hand for simulating and practicing the planning and building of a full exhibition space, which is very difficult to manage in other ways. They have to take into account the importance of space, scale and composition, which is something every curator has to do. It is also possible for the students to experience the exhibition on site, and make adjustments throughout the process of creation.

A main focus for whole term is to give students analytical tools to interpret our contemporary society. Through constructing exhibitions they

Figure 9. The Class Game: Designation of class based on an in-world game

had to visualize what they have learned, which undisputedly adds something vital to the learning process. In the usual case the students would discuss related issues in seminars and in different forms of written assignments. Now instead the students sat by their computers making sketches on paper, trying to combine visualization with theoretical perspectives. We firmly believe that in working across media and in virtual spaces, which differed dramatically from usual academic work, activated other forms of creativity.

Learning "digital competence" was at the core of the Second Life project, but the students learned so much more through this loosely defined problem oriented project approach. Apart from building in SL they have to think about how to write text suitable for the format – whether it was for SL, blogs or other web pages. They learn to record and edit pictures, films and sound, and how to integrate the different forms of media into a virtual exhibition. The students learn how to link content to other digital channels, video, photos and audio. In other words, the students learned "digital literacy" – to read and interpret digital content in relation to its form, knowing both limitations and the potential of digital content making. Paul Gilster claims "Digital literacy is the ability to understand and use information in multiple formats from a wide range of sources when it is presented via computers. [Literacy] has always meant the ability to read with meaning, and to understand" (1997, 1-2). Camilla Scavenius Lopez (2002) has a similar understanding of literacy, and stresses that learning in a digital age must include a "Fourth Cultural Technique" – understanding information technology – apart from traditional reading, writing and mathematics. This so-called fourth competence can be divided into three steps, firstly, to understand and use computers and software, secondly, to communicate and navigate in a digital environment, and to relate to available information, and finally, to understand the digital content, and to relate it to social contexts. The way to teach this multifaceted competence is to integrate perspectives on ICT into classes, which also is the ambition of the SL project.

The project runs for a whole semester and involves a rather complex process. The students have to plan the exhibition in order to finish it in time, and it also required economic planning since some parts of the construction work cost money. The students are given a budget at the start of the course, with real money used to buy the currency of Second Life. Consequently the students are forces to plan and run a long-term project, closely connected to real life scenarios. They also had to deal with group dynamics, balancing visions with competences and technical constrains, division of work and matters concerning conflicts and leadership. One interesting aspect is how the students deal with language. Every group voluntarily made their exhibitions in English, despite the first language generally being Swedish, and the results aimed at a potentially broad audience in Second Life. Finally issues regarding copyright and ownership are raised when students want to import digitally available content as films and pictures – therefore they have to investigate the whole legal aspect of publishing on the Internet.

A reevaluation of ethics in teaching is provoked by the use of the simulative attributes provided by virtual world platforms. The barriers that both insulate and protect with traditional classroom teaching are not part of the use of virtual worlds in learning. Along with this increased freedom comes an increased responsibility in regards to how students can use the media and what they are exposed to in learning. Decisions concerning ethics in teaching and learning regarding virtual worlds should be made at the design stage of course planning. Ethics should be included in course descriptions and can even be discussed in course objectives, as is illustrated by the above example regarding copyrighted material and student use.

The exhibitions are examined and assessed at the end of the term (more about the assessment below). The whole course ends with a public vernissage, using HUMlab's extensive screenscape and in Second Life, to which anyone interested is welcome. Parents, fellow students, teachers, university staff, and so on, attend the exhibition. The vernissage makes the whole project more "real" and serious in a sense. The students have to stand up in front of their work, show its results and give guided tours in their exhibitions. Despite all the hardship during the course, or maybe because of all their work and worries, they are very serious about this part of the project showing great pride in their work.

Archive

The archiving of materials created in virtual online worlds is a deeply problematic area. In a proprietary model such as that adopted by Linden Labs, the owner and publisher of Second Life, while the content is user owned in the world, it falls closer to a leasehold arrangement than outright ownership. The contents of Second Life cannot be hosted anywhere else other than in Second Life. Other virtual world platforms, as for example Active-Worlds, have different proprietary arrangements when it comes to the control and ownership of the in-world content. The intellectual property rights of the virtual world should be closely considered when designing the course. In relation to archiving, the rights to content are what determine the form of the archive for student work. In the courses conducted by HUMlab, we have maintained the work of students in the world. The islands where the work is situated on are kept in the state the students left them when they finished their courses. This is of course a short-term solution. Video and still images of the student projects have been collected and archived at every stage of the course. Another solution that is being considered is the miniaturization and storage of student work in the world.

Assessment

One challenge is how to assess the final examinations. As mentioned briefly above, examinations do not explicitly evaluate the technical solutions or the technical complexity of the exhibition. This has really not been a problem since all the groups have done their very best and achieved well over all expectations. Complexity is just not always a sign of good quality. It is rather the process leading up to the final construction that is assessed. Still, it is necessary to develop good procedures in order to assess this kind of simulation-based work in a satisfactory way, both from teachers', and students' point of view. We are currently at a point where we need to develop the way we grade the exhibitions, so here are some thoughts on assessments, which need to be developed further.

First of all the goals with the exhibitions have to be shared and agreed upon within the group of teachers involved in the course, and the goals have to articulated and also communicated to the students. It could be something like "the exhibitions has to relate to at least two themes dealt with during the semester", and "the grade of analysis must exceed a descriptive level using a clear theoretical perspective", and in that way measure quality in a quantifiable manner. The problem with such an approach could be that it narrows down the imaginative scope of the students, and makes them focus on the end product too much. We want the students to embark on their project with open and creative eyes, and not just working to meet imposed assessment requirements.

What we have assessed is to what extent the students reflect upon the process they have gone through. What has been of interest is the questions; "Can they describe and reflect upon the process leading to the final exhibition?" and "Can they motivate choices they have made?" During the semester the students are encouraged to blog about their work, using the blog as a log book it is possible for the teachers to see what the students are doing and to have the possibility to comment and support the students in their work. The blogs have the added advantage that in the end of the semester it is possible for the students to go back to their log and see what they have been thinking and working on, by using the blogs to recapture their ideas and provide a record of the processes involved. These reflections and observations become cumulative, with the following term's students taking over the same blogs and benefiting from the knowledge base that has been created.

CONCLUSION

The use of online virtual worlds in collaborative, problem orientated, and project based simulative pedagogy represents a possible shift in learning and teaching that is part of a much larger set of relationships active globally today. From urban India to the Australian outback, from the Sámi schools of Lapland to the favelas of Rio, digital media in a variety of forms, from mobile phones to Open Source software, can make an impact on how learning is achieved. What we have described here is one small part in this great adventure with meaning. Perhaps what is most striking in our experience has been how the traditional power relationships and the assumptions they are based upon within transference-centered learning seem to be no longer relevant.

In many of the situations described above the students are not sure of how to be students and teachers are equally uncertain about how to be teachers, when the classroom includes a room with no walls where people make things together. The teacher is no longer the only source for information, but is now the navigator, or the *kybernētēs*, a guide for the group of learners dealing with potentially hundreds of choices and pieces of information in a single day. This is a complex process questioning many concepts of traditional teaching. The tricky question is how to make use of the positive aspects of collaborative, problem oriented learning, and without throwing away the positive aspects of traditional pedagogy and scholarship.

Ethics, interactive and experience design, group dynamics and human resource management, language and media literacy, computer sciences, engineering, law and the visual arts are just some of the areas called upon in leading the navigation through the courses described above. No one person can do this alone, and team teaching is a necessity that has proven effective in HUMlab. The technical support from the systems administrators, programmers, and digital production crew in HUMlab has been invaluable. The research and administrative staff of HUMlab have actively supported the teaching and learning in virtual worlds by becoming involved. Such a networked model for learning that emerges is made possible by the use of virtual worlds but it is much more than that. The technology that mediates the teaching and learning is not creating it. People do that; they always have and always will.

REFERENCES

Barrett, J., & Gelfgren, S. (2009). Spacing creation: The HUMlab Second Life project. In Molka-Danielsen, J., & Deutschmann, M. (Eds.), *Learning and teaching in the virtual world of Second Life* (pp. 167–183). Trondheim, Norway: Tapir Academic Press.

Blades, M., & Vermylen, S. (2004). Virtual ethics for a new age: The Internet and the ethical lawyer. *Georgetown Journal of Legal Ethics*.

Bodemer, D., & Plötzner, R. (2004). Encouraging the active processing of information during learning with multiple and interactive representations. *Proceedings of the 5th International Workshop of SIG 6 Instructional Design of the European Association for Research on Learning and Instruction (EARLI)*, (pp. 127-138).

Carter, B. (n.d.). *Virtual Harlem.* Retrieved on June 14, 2010 from http://www.evl.uic.edu/cavern/harlem

de Jong, T., van Joolingen, W., Scott, D., de Hoog, R., Lapied, L., & Valent, R. (1994). SMISLE: System for Multimedia Integrated Simulation Learning Environments. In de Jong, T., & Sarti, L. (Eds.), *Design and production of multimedia and simulation based learning material* (pp. 133–167). Dordrecht, Netherlands: Kluwer Academic Publishers.

Deutschmann, M., & Panichi, L. (2009). Instructional design, teacher practice and learner autonomy. In Molka-Danielsen, J., & Deutschmann, M. (Eds.), *Learning and teaching in the virtual world of Second Life* (pp. 27–44). Trondheim, Norway: Tapir Academic Press.

Dircknick-Holmfeld, L. (2002). Designing virtual learning environments based on problem oriented project pedagogy. In Dirckinck-Holmfeld, L., & Fibiger, B. (Eds.), *Learing in virtual environments* (pp. 31–54). Frederiksberg, Denmark: Samfundslitteratur.

Egidius, H. (1999). *PBL och Casemetodik: Hur man gör och varför*. Lund, Sweden: Studentlitteratur.

Ess, C. (2009). *Digital media ethics*. Cambridge, UK: Polity Press.

Fjuk, A. (1998). *Computer support for distributed collaborative learning. Exploring a complex problem area.* Unpublished doctoral dissertation, University of Oslo, Norway.

Frischer, B. (n.d.). *Rome reborn.* Retrieved June 16, 2010, from http://www.romereborn.virginia.edu

Gilster, P. (2007). *Digital literacy.* New York, NY: Wiley Computer.

Heinrich, B. (1995). Language games in the mathematics classroom: Their function and their effects. In Cobbs, P., & Bauersfeld, H. (Eds.), *The emergence of mathematical meaning: Interaction in classroom cultures.* Abindgon, UK: Routledge.

Illeris, K. (1981). *The pedagogy of counter-qualification.* Copenhagen, Denmark: Unge Pædagoger.

MacArthur, V. (2008). Real ethics in virtual worlds. *Proceedings of the Conference on Human Factors in Computing Systems.*

Rose, A. Eckard, D., & Rubloff, G. (1998). *An application framework for creating simulation-based learning environments.* Human-Computer Interaction Laboratory, Institute for Systems Research. University of Maryland, North Carolina State University, (HCIL Technical Report No. 98-07).

Rosenqvist, C. (2004). *Immersion, experience and understanding: Virtual theatres in drama teaching.* Retrieved from http://gupea.ub.gu.se/dspace/bitstream/2077/18100/1/gupea_2077_18100_1.pdf

Scavenius Lopez, C. (2002). Le@rning in a digitised society. In Danielsen, O., Nielsen, J., & Sørensen, B. H. (Eds.), *Learning and narrativity in digital media.* Frederiksberg, Denmark: Samfundlitteratur.

Steadman, R., Coates, W., Huang, Y., Matevosian, R., Larmon, B., McCullough, L., & Ariel, D. (2006). Simulation-based training is superior to problem-based learning for the acquisition of critical assessment and management skills. *Journal for the Society of Critical Care Medicine, 34*(1).

Svensson, P. (2002). Virtual weddings and a real wedding of linguistics, literature and cultural studies. Retrieved on June 16, 2010, from http://www.rhu.se/activities/projects/financed_projects/q-s/svensson_patrik_98_slut.pdf

Thomas, A. (n.d.) *Virtual Macbeth.* Retrieved on June 19, 2010, from http://www.virtualmacbeth.wikispaces.com.

Chapter 4
Using the Interaction–Combinations Integration Model to Explore Real–Life Learning in User–Created Virtual Worlds

David M. Antonacci
University of Kansas Medical Center, USA

Nellie Modaress
University of Kansas Medical Center, USA

Edward Lee Lamoureux
Bradley University, USA

David Thomas
University of Colorado Denver, USA

Timothy Allen
Wharton Research Data Services, USA

ABSTRACT

User-created virtual worlds are emerging technologies with rapidly growing acceptance in education. Of the various reported educational uses of these virtual worlds, the focus of this chapter is on virtual worlds for constructivist learning activities, because this use has application to many real-life courses and has the potential to transform teaching and learning. To assist educators with recognizing and understanding virtual world learning activities, Antonacci & Modaress (2005, 2008) developed the Interaction-Combinations Integration model. However, this model has not been studied in actual virtual-world learning practice. Using a case study method, this chapter examines the usefulness of this model to organize and describe actual virtual world learning activities, provides additional learning activity examples, and describes what was needed to implement and conduct these learning activities.

DOI: 10.4018/978-1-60960-545-2.ch004

INTRODUCTION

User-created virtual worlds, such as Second Life (Linden Lab, 2010a), ActiveWorlds (Activeworlds Inc, 2010), and There (Makena Technologies, 2010), are emerging technologies with rapidly growing acceptance in higher education (New Media Consortium, 2007). These virtual worlds are 3D simulated environments created by their users, and simultaneously played by thousands of people around the world.

Unlike traditional computer games and simulations, where people interact with a preprogrammed environment, user-created worlds allow their users to create their own world and interact with it and other users in it. This ability to create and interact with your own simulated world offers some exciting possibilities for teaching and learning.

BACKGROUND

Educators on the Second Life Educators List (Linden Lab, 2010b) have reported using Second Life in three primary ways. Some faculty are having students study the virtual world itself as part of a course on gaming, online culture, or virtual world technology. Though appropriate for these courses, this use has limited application to the majority of real-life courses.

Other faculty are using virtual worlds as a communication medium. This includes in-world lectures and presentations, online discussions or chats, student-built displays instead of traditional reports, and machinima which is real-world film-making from the virtual world engine. While this use of virtual worlds is still being developed and explored, other communication media exist which may be more effective and efficient, and this use is more of a translation of existing teaching practices to a virtual world environment, instead of a transformational use that changes teaching and learning practices to leverage the unique affordances of virtual world technology.

Finally, faculty are using virtual worlds for constructivist learning activities. By constructivist learning, we mean a theoretical view of learning where knowledge is constructed by the learners as they actively problem solve in an authentic context, as opposed to more traditional instruction where knowledge is seen as an object transmitted from teacher to learner (Jonassen, Peck, & Wilson, 1999).

Of those three reported uses, the focus of this chapter is using virtual worlds for constructivist learning activities. This use has application to many real-life courses instead of a limited number and has the potential to transform teaching and learning rather than simply translate existing classroom practices, such as lectures, to the virtual world.

However, considering the new and emerging nature of virtual world technology, it can be challenging to recognize these educational possibilities and enable educators to integrate virtual world learning activities into their real-world courses. To confront this challenge, Conklin (2007) identified and described more than 100 possible educational uses of Second Life. Her list included numerous ideas for Art, Business, Computer Science, Education, Law, Mathematics, Psychology, Religion, Science, and Sociology.

As an alternative to describing specific educational activities, Antonacci and Modaress (2005, 2008) developed the Interaction-Combinations Integration model to help educators connect real-life course topics to potential virtual world learning activities. In their model, virtual worlds, like the real world, consist of people and objects. Those two things can interact in three possible combinations: people-people, people-object, and object-object. Much of what is taught can be categorized into those three interaction combinations. Once an educator has identified what interaction type corresponds to a course topic, the model then suggests several virtual world activities for that interaction type.

For example, some courses teach interviewing or selling skills, which would be person-person interaction types. Virtual world role playing is one possible learning activity for this interaction type. Other courses teach people how to interact with objects (person-object interaction), such as operating equipment or building structures. One possible learning activity is having students actually build a structure and interact with it in-world. Many courses teach people about physical and procedural processes (object-object interaction), such as soil erosion or assembly line production. A possible learning activity for object-object interaction is having students interact with an instructor-developed in-world simulation, or a better activity might be having students create their own in-world simulations.

MAIN FOCUS OF THE CHAPTER

Though the Interaction-Combinations Integration model (Antonacci & Modaress, 2005, 2008) provides a theoretical framework for organizing and understanding virtual world learning activities, it has not been studied in actual virtual world learning practice. This model also provides only a few learning activity examples for each interaction type, and these examples are proposed examples, not grounded in actual practice. Finally, this model does not describe what is needed to design and develop such learning activities nor how to conduct such activities in-world.

The purpose of this chapter is to further examine this model with actual virtual world teaching and learning experiences. Specifically, this chapter:

- Examines the usefulness of this model to organize and describe actual virtual world learning activities.
- Provides additional learning activity examples from actual virtual world learning activities.

- Describes what was needed for these learning activities and how they were conducted.

Method

A case study method was used for this chapter. Three co-authors (Lamoureux, Thomas, and Allen) were purposefully selected (Lincoln & Guba, 1985) because they had used Second Life for real-life learning, and each had included a learning activity corresponding to one of the three interaction types of the Interaction-Combinations Integration model (Antonacci & Modaress, 2005, 2008).

Co-authors were asked to describe their in-world teaching experience. A case outline (Appendix A) was developed and provided to all co-authors to assist each in fully examining their in-world experience and to provide some consistency among the case descriptions (Bogden & Biklin, 1998). However, this outline was presented as a guide. Co-authors were encouraged to include missing outline topics they considered important to their case and to ignore outline topics which did not apply.

Member checks were conducted throughout chapter development (Lincoln & Guba, 1985). Each case was reviewed by all authors and edited based on suggested improvements. This was an iterative process, with repeated revisions until all authors agreed their cases were adequately described. Similarly, the entire article was reviewed and revised by all authors until consensus was reached.

PERSON-PERSON INTERACTION CASE: FIELD RESEARCH IN SECOND LIFE (LAMOUREUX)

Bradley University, in Peoria, Illinois, serves approximately 5,000 undergraduates, 65 of whom major in the Department of Interactive Media, housed within the larger Slane College of Communication and Fine Arts (CFA). In January 2007, five students enrolled in and completed a trial offering of Multimedia 491: Field Research in Second Life, taught by Ed Lamoureux, Ph. D. Experience from this trial course indicated the need for multiple courses. Multimedia 333: Introduction to Field Research in Virtual Environments and Multimedia 444: Field Research in Virtual Environments were approved as regular course offerings in the spring 2007. Additional changes to the courses were approved for implementation beginning fall, 2010.

Lamoureux had originally opposed curricular participation in game development due to its regular association with violence and quest-based fantasy. However, as the program developed (now including a concentration in game design) and faculty agreed to keep programmatic interest in game development focused (primarily) on learning and simulations rather than commercial and entertainment game design, Lamoureux recognized the need to begin developing expertise in at least some aspects of game-related activities.

Motivation for developing the course was initially provided by the foray into Second Life by the New Media Consortium (NMC) of which Bradley University, especially the Department of Interactive Media, is a member. NMC selected Second Life as the virtual world of their choice for understanding teaching and learning in online game environments. While not immediately drawn to Second Life, Lamoureux eventually contacted NMC assessing their interest in the development of a Field Research Methods course to be taught entirely within Second Life. NMC leadership expressed interest and planning began in late spring, 2006. Lamoureux became Professor Beliveau in Second Life.

The initiative appeared to fulfill a number of important curricular needs for the Department of Interactive Media and the author. Activities in Second Life provide an excellent opportunity to teach students about virtual worlds/immersive environments in a game that is neither based on

violence nor quest. Most of the Interactive Media students at Bradley want to learn to author 3D, immersive media. Doing meaningful things in Second Life (like holding class, making presentations, observing others, etc.) helps students further understand the products they want to someday make while at the same time, showing them that games are far more than just playing, especially shooting. The course teaches students to better understand how new media impacts society by learning a valuable and oft-used strategy/method for doing research, ethnographic field methods, that they may later use in their professional lives to study how new media is used.

The course also presented advantages to the author. Teaching online, in a virtual world helps keep one engaged and relevant to students. This course provides the opportunity to teach ethnographic methods to neophyte researchers in an environment that is safer for both students and subjects than is real life.

And not to be ignored, Second Life offers a distance education platform currently unmatched by other modalities, thereby giving the Interactive Media Department a chance to offer classes over an otherwise "dark" period at Bradley. Though we can offer courses in the January and May interims, few students want to stay in Peoria over semester breaks in order to take courses.

The author spent a couple of months getting oriented to Second Life, initially as a free account and later as a premium subscriber. Without 3D building or script coding skills, the author's experience of Second Life was probably similar to that of many "newbies": The Second Life learning curve was steep and many hours were spent learning to navigate and participate. NMC's support was important along the way as the NMC Second Life campus provided a friendly place to hang out until land was acquired. Many NMC activities brought contact with and information from others interested in teaching and learning in Second Life, and using the NMC campus for class saved one the effort required for building learning environments and developing supporting materials. Later, the author purchased a small plot of land where class meets. Bradley University also supports an island; students use its sandbox and can interact, socially, with other Bradley students on the island.

Class syllabi and materials were developed over the course of approximately 3 months. Strict application procedures were used to limit enrollment in the trial offering to students: (1) with computers, peripherals, and network connections that met Second Life's technical specifications and (2) demonstrated interest and experience in Second Life. Subsequent offerings of the classes do not require Second Life experience as the first course in the two-class sequence is designed, in part, to provide that grounding.

One of the principle issues in the development of the course concerned the nature of the class as a research methods experience in which students would collect social scientific data. In addition to the actual concerns for the protection of human subjects, preparations to do research within Second Life initially needed to meet two other constraints. First, Linden Lab had a set of research policies, an application process, and an approval process. During the preparation for the class, these procedures were completed and submitted to Linden Lab. Not long thereafter, however, Linden Lab removed themselves from the project approval process, relying instead on the human subjects protection procedures of researchers' universities and the Second Life Terms of Service (TOS) that set out privacy protections for residents.

Second, the Bradley University Committee on the Use of Human Subjects in Research has a procedure in place for approving research projects. Normally, field research would be exempt from full committee approval. If the research were done in the real world one would only file an application for the exemption. However, after showing Second Life to the committee and discussing the nature of the class, they decided that since subjects' names are always displayed, each

individual student would have to go through the full application and approval process for their research project. Given this was an introduction to field research, that students were new researchers, and that the class took place over the course of only three weeks, the author was very concerned about the constraints the process might place on students. However, while preparing the class materials, the author became convinced that the class activities fall within the exemption category and therefore made an appeal to the committee chair, who agreed to reduce the obligations. As a result, the faculty member filed a single application to the committee as the primary investigator with students as co-investigators. The application listed the general thrust of the research students would study and do (observing naturally occurring groups in everyday life—in this case, in a virtual world—in order to better understand and explain how communication and social interaction works to establish order in communities of practice) and listed planned protections.

Despite establishing a larger than usual number of subject protections, interactions with the human subjects protection committee has continued to be problematic over the years and across a number of offerings. Currently, the committee (once again) requires separate research proposals from each undergraduate student. As a result, data collection has been removed from the first course in the sequence. Instead, in that course, students complete all the protection procedures (to learn them) but only practice data collection (no data is collected for analysis). In between the two classes, students apply for permission for the research projects in the second course. Some projects have been turned back, mostly due to the application of inappropriate standards by the committee because of their misunderstandings about virtual worlds and the research therein. For example, one project was denied expedited review (necessary so students can start their projects at the start of the term) because the student was working within a Sim for gay and lesbian avatars; the committee thereby assumed that the users behind the avatars are members of a protected class and that the project required full review.

The class utilized a broad series of human subjects protection techniques including:

- Following the Linden Lab TOS.
- Creating a Researcher group identification for all student avatars. Once data collection and class began, the designation was displayed prominently on all student researchers/avatars at all times.
- The Chairman of the Bradley University Committee on the Use of Human Subjects in Research reviewed and approved the application for exemption from full review for field research.
- Each student created a human subject protection (HSP) handout, as a note card, offered to any avatar who inquired as to the research work or the researcher's presence.
- Full maintenance of subject confidentiality in data management (coded names, etc).
- Forbidding students from copying and saving transcripts of talk from subjects from whom they had not gotten permission and who had not been given an HSP handout.
- Forbidding students from using camera controls to see through objects and into spaces where they are not co-present with the subjects.
- Publishing the URL for the student course blogs on the course site as a way to give back information to the communities of practice via the potential for increased awareness and understanding both on the part of the community and of outsiders.
- Regular faculty review of the student blogs to catch any beginner mistakes that might compromise subject protections.
- Blocking out avatar names and faces in cases of publishing photos of subjects without their permission.

- Copies of final papers posted to the student blog for the benefit of the subject communities and others. (This feature can compromise the "exempt from review" status of the research as such posting constitutes publication.)

The course was conducted in three-hour time blocks, Monday through Friday evenings. The first hour of the class was dedicated to lecture and discussion over reading material and conceptual content. This activity was supported by the provision of a lecture note sketch, by way of an in-world note card, prior to each lecture. Each lecture and discussion session was preceded by a brief quiz over the previous night's material. The quiz was conducted in text chat to keep a record of student responses.

After the quiz, lecture/discussion, and a short break, students each made presentations concerning their research activities over the past 24 hours. Some of the presentations focused specifically on their progress completing course assignments of which there was a step-wise series to develop research process. At other times, their reports simply featured descriptions of what they had accomplished the previous day.

After another short break, the final hour was dedicated to time for students to accomplish field research. Each avatar was monitored so that they would work in the field at least that hour, daily. Students were encouraged to do additional research at other times as well. Further, the instructor made three visits to the field with each student to observe their technique and to monitor their progress. This is one of the advantages of teaching field research in Second Life over real world: One can easily transport/teleport from location to location to accomplish multiple field supervisions in a short period of time.

During the class, students learned the fundamentals of qualitative field research methods in the ethnographic tradition, adjusted to the characteristics of online virtual worlds, including (but not limited to) subject protection, observation, mapping, interviewing, note taking, note rendering, and document analysis. Students completed the beginnings of a research project at a level approximate to a research prospectus for an undergraduate senior thesis. Four students completed research projects; one was tasked with making a machinima movie about the course instead of a research project [http://interactivemedia.bradley.edu/ell/490/final_piece_web.mov?q=com/faculty/lamoureux/website2/490/final_piece_web.mov].

Each student was able to complete the work as assigned; however, one of the four students doing a research project was unable to get a sound footing in the community of practice in which he was interested, so his resultant project was less than satisfactory. Students showed facility in Second Life as was predicted by the application/selection procedures used to pre-certify those abilities. Little technical trouble in Second Life was encountered, beyond the usual downtimes associated with grid maintenance and/or crashes. Class intrusions were minimized by using a skybox for classroom. The few intrusions that did occur were brief and polite. A number of individuals (teachers, reporters, graduate students) were allowed to visit the class as observers.

The course engendered much positive press coverage, providing the Department, College, and University with significant public relations advantages. By all accounts, the class was a success. However, the class, and the subsequent multiple offerings, has (to this writing) failed to capture the interest of students at Bradley. From the author's perspective, Second Life seems to appeal more to teens (on the Second Life Teen Grid) and faculty (on the main grid) than to college-age students. The lack of quest, reward, and action appears to depress interest, even in students for whom the development of virtual worlds may be central to their career tracks. An additional factor may be at work here: The content of the course (research) may be of less interest to students than would be

a course that is focused on digital work such as 3D building, animation, or coding.

Additional information about Lamoureux's work in Second Life can be found at http://interactivemedia.bradley.edu/ell/slstuff.html, and more information about his course, MM 490: Field Research in Second Life, is available at http://interactivemedia.bradley.edu/ell/490/mm490.html. Materials from the two-course sequence may be found at http://interactivemedia.bradley.edu/ell/333/mm333ja09.html and http://interactivemedia.bradley.edu/ell/444/mm444_09.html.

Beginning in fall, 2010, the first course in the sequence will be (re)titled IM 344: Virtual World Building and Research. The course will shift the focus from ethnographic research to building an entrepreneurial presence in Second Life. Research techniques will be introduced as part of the business development cycle. This course should appeal to Interactive Media students who are interested in building and scripting as they learn to apply skills to develop a working enterprise within virtual space. The second course in the sequence, IM 444, remains a field research methods course that will enable students to study the ways that Second Life residents interact with the business established in the initial course.

PERSON-OBJECT INTERACTION CASE: URBAN PLANNING IN THE GAMING WORLD (THOMAS)

The University of Colorado at Boulder is the flagship institution in the University of Colorado system and the state's largest campus with more than 24,000 undergraduates and 4,000 graduate students. Within the University, the College of Architecture and Planning provides undergraduate and graduate education in architecture and urban planning and design. The college has approximately 400 graduate students and 600 undergraduates.

Planning in the Gaming World was proposed as a course to increase the awareness of and interest in urban planning and design inside the college. Typically, students entering the college come to pursue architecture-oriented studies through the Bachelors of Environmental Design or the more general Design Studies degree.

The initial idea was to use games such as SimCity (Electronic Arts Inc., 2010) to introduce basic planning concepts to undergraduates in an effort to broaden their understanding of the built environment and encourage them to consider further studies in planning. As the course has evolved over four semesters, it has grown to include a media studies element where the students are challenged to consider how the digital medium affects environmental design in its various forms—architecture, landscape architecture, and urban planning.

Because the course is offered as an upper division elective and is listed in the course catalog as only open to college majors, the enrollment typically consists of roughly 75% students in architecture-oriented majors and 25% in those from planning. Class standing skews toward juniors and seniors.

Perhaps ironically, given the subject matter, the course runs as a traditional in-class experience. Students attend class face-to-face and spend the majority of class time in a computer lab. As such, all game or virtual activities take place in the classroom, with each student using a lab computer—including the various exercises and experiences that take place inside Second Life.

Thanks to SimCity, videogames have an obvious standing in the domain of urban planning. A course posited to teach planning using games finds itself in the domain of videogames, even in spite of the longer legacy of more traditional design games.

Problematically, videogames as a field do not offer many other obvious examples that work as parts in a planning education. City Life (Cities XL, 2010) has emerged as a more European-style Sim-City clone and a variety of historical simulations and real-time strategy games provide potential, but not direct, extensions to the curriculum.

Second Life provides a more open-ended opportunity to extend the exploration of planning topics. To date, we have used variants of three different course activities based in Second Life.

The first activity, "Interesting (Virtual) Place", charges students to explore Second Life on their own and to return with a report, reflecting on the nature of place and speculating on what constitutes an interesting place. This conversation and report mirrors an earlier in-class discussion challenging students to consider the most interesting urban environments they have experienced and to consider what makes those places work.

The "Thing I Built" activity allows students to creatively express themselves while demonstrating mastery of basic in-world building. This activity develops building skills needed for the course capstone project.

Additionally, both the "Interesting (Virtual) Place" and "Thing I Built" assignments prepare students for a more in-depth building project in the world, and the results reflect a basic sensitivity to the underlying culture and norms of life in Second Life.

The capstone project, "Use in Conflict", provides the students with a project comprised of twin challenges. First, contrary to much of the design education, students are placed into groups and asked to produce a collaborative project. Second, each group undertakes a project with obvious and potential conflicts. Each of the three groups work in shared in-world land and pursue to complete one of the following objectives and themes:

- **Build a place to learn:** A driving school complete with classroom and outdoor track
- **Build a place to relax:** A Japanese meditation garden
- **Build place to have fun:** A nightclub with various themed rooms

This project provides students with the chance to integrate many of the planning and design concepts covered in the course, experience more real-world collaborative design work, and touch on the nature and difficulty in urban planning of dealing with conflicting use in the built environment.

By artificially constructing a situation in conflict, the students are forced to reconcile their individual design ideas first with their own group, and then with the rest of the class. Limited land and an associated object/prim building allowance further challenges the students and groups to work through a community process to reach mutually beneficial ends.

By building in the virtual world, this exercise avoids the usual cognitive dissonance of role-playing and further focuses the students on tasks that fit with their undergraduate training as environmental designers. While Second Life lacks fidelity in terms of the complexities of real-world urban planning, it provides an interesting learning space. Second Life's abstractions of form and simplified design negotiation allow students to develop an understanding of the role of conflict and compromise in the shaping of cities, a critical element SimCity lacks.

In terms of the interactions model proposed in this paper, this particular class project focuses heavily on people-object interaction, but places the objects as a visible manifestation of the more important people-people interactions taking place in the classroom and during on-campus work sessions.

While this might seem to strain the model as proposed, in fact, it suits a core concept of understanding the built environment as a product of social interaction—that is to say, our physical environment (people-objects interaction) exists in organized space almost purely as a result of social (people-people) interaction.

As this course has been developed over time, issues and challenges have been encountered. Funding for this project, a potential challenge for any project, relies on free basic Second Life accounts. There has been no outside funding or student costs incurred by using Second Life in this course.

The students in this class were generally upper classmen, with moderate to extensive experience with 3D design tools. As a result, students found building in the world exceptionally frustrating. They were familiar with how advanced 3D modeling tools work, and they had a reasonable expectation of high-performance object manipulation simply not available in Second Life's dynamic world.

After the first two semesters, the course de-emphasized building in the world, especially with regard to any assessment, to help mitigate this frustration. Assignments that require building, but do not attempt to assess the quality of the build, replaced more outcome-based design evaluations.

Further, as student experience of virtual space continues to expand through exposure to video-games and game environments, such as World of Warcraft (Blizzard Entertainment, 2010), issues surrounding graphic fidelity and system performance inside Second Life grow in concern. Students expect any game or game-like system to run at higher frame rates, use higher-quality textures and larger object models, run with less lag, and have more overall professional design quality than Second Life can currently support. As a result, the course instructor must continually re-emphasize the reasoning behind using virtual worlds over other alternatives.

The term "virtual world" creates a theoretical difference that can mislead anyone intent on using synthetic spaces in the classroom. Because, if one world is real and the other is virtual, then the properties of the virtual world can easily be taken as either a non-material presentation of the real world or an indigenous other place with no tie to nominal reality. Either of these conclusions will lead to conceptual problems, because a place like Second Life bridges both concepts.

Bringing students into Second Life entails not so much the issue of orienting them to the symbolic or semiotic match-ups between the real and the virtual (a portal is a door in Second Life and an avatar is really a person at a keyboard), nor of simply teaching them the conventions of virtual world social practices (AFK means someone is away from their keyboard). Because, while these two perspectives provide a base for experiencing a virtual world, more problematic issues arise in understanding the interactions between the symbolic space and social interactions. How, for instance, do students deal with the complex potentials in dealing with people pretending to be vampires in a vampire world? Or, how to decode play from serious social content or symbol from fantasy?

Pedagogically, Second Life suggests a better approach. Frankly treating these disjunctions and allowing students full volition in the world. Permitting students the maximum amount of latitude in avatar customization, for example, provides a basis for exploring these lines and overlaps. Giving permission to access all places on the grid, regardless of content or rating is another strategy. In contrast, attempting to recreate classroom spaces, norms, and conduct tends to strengthen student's perception of the virtual world as an inferior shadow of or arbitrary location for education.

As an extension, minimizing the use of Second Life as a simulator provides another interesting, if contrary, approach to using virtual worlds. Instead of asking students to pretend that the virtual world largely or meaningfully reflects the real world, allowing them to experience the virtual world as a synthetic place, provides a potentially innovative landscape for education.

Future iterations of this course will use more paper-based games and integrate basic game design assignments to help diversify the experiences and to push students to explore planning concepts in greater detail. The rationale behind these moves stems from a desire to have students experience urban environments rather than simply deal with their representations, and an effort to get students to experience the more difficult concepts of urban planning and design as social interactions and

process through game play rather than simply as acquirable facts and knowledge.

Future improvements to the Second Life technical architecture, such as the ability to import 3D geometry from tools like 3D Studio Max (Autodesk Media and Entertainment, 2010) or Google Sketch Up (Google Inc., 2010), will also open up project possibilities and dramatically improve the usefulness of Second Life to a design and planning education.

OBJECT-OBJECT INTERACTION CASE: GAS TANK SIMULATION (ALLEN)

As of 2009, Crompco was a 160-person limited liability company (LLC) in Plymouth Meeting, PA, located just outside of Philadelphia. Crompco was founded in the early 1980s, and shortly after, bought by Rusty Carfagno, the current CEO. Since being founded, Crompco has grown to become the largest independent tank testing company in the world, with a service footprint extending from Maine to Florida, and as far west as Ohio and Texas. As of 2009, the company consisted of approximately 30 office employees, and 130 field technicians who typically work in two-person crews. Crompco's clients are the biggest companies in the world, including ExxonMobil, Hess, Sunoco, Shell (Motiva), Lukoil, and many more. Crompco tested approximately 20,000 stations per year in various capacities, from full regulatory compliance testing to company-specific inspection and replacement programs. The fleet of 70 trucks was top-notch, allowing for many parts to be taken on-site for minor repairs, which often avoided the need for an expensive return trip and re-test on faulty equipment. Crompco has been recognized as the tech leader within the sector, leading the way with fully automated field data capture first through iPaq hand-held devices, and now Tablet PCs, as well as innovative work in Second Life. Crompco was the first company to use Second Life for corporate training purposes, in January of 2004.

Ed Kubinsky was Crompco's Director of Special Projects and led a team consisting of Timothy Allen, Head of Technology; Tracy Richmond, Safety Coordinator; and Chuck Pedano, Vice President. Kubinsky and Richmond trained the new hires in their respective fields of expertise: Richmond on safety and OSHA regulations and Kubinsky on the testing services performed in general. Allen coordinated upgrades for the virtual training system through requests from Kubinsky and Richmond, and he trained them on any new features added to the system.

Rather than training each new recruit on Second Life, which has a fairly high learning curve, the virtual world was projected onto a large screen for viewing, and the Crompco avatar was driven by an expert user, typically Kubinsky or Allen. This training was used for all new field technicians, as it introduced all the basics of gas station layout and Crompco safety requirements. The piping, pump, and pressure systems that lie underneath the asphalt of a tank field are fairly complex, and there are many different configurations to which a gas station can be built (about 15 standard configurations, excluding rare exceptions). Having new field technicians understand the complex systems, potential dangers, and a general knowledge of the mechanical and electronic systems before working in an environment with tens of thousands of gallons of gasoline is absolutely essential. Fortunately, within Second Life, nothing is flammable!

The virtual gas station was the brainchild of Allen, a long-time Second Life resident. In early 2004, Allen started to ask himself how Second Life could be used for purposes other than entertainment and showed the virtual world to Crompco's Vice President, Chuck Pedano, a tech enthusiast and supporter. Together, they agreed that making a virtual gas station would be useful for quite a few purposes. First and foremost would be training new hires, but as the Second Life adoption

rate continues to increase and computer speed improves, plans are to also train station managers and show companies where problems exist on their current stations. In the future, Second Life could provide a central location for nationwide training as well.

The initial project objectives were to show several key systems: the tanks, the lines that take the product from the tanks to the dispensers where gas is pumped, the submersible turbine pumps (STPs), siphon bars, and the full Stage II vapor recovery system. While that may be Greek to anyone outside of the industry, these components are the basic essentials to understanding how to test a station's components to ensure the station is in environmental compliance.

Prior to training new recruits on Second Life, a white board with dry-erase markers was used. The trainers would draw a bunch of underground tanks, pumps, dispensers, and piping. After about five minutes, the new recruit's attention and interest was waning. Also, this approach did not really get the point of how gas stations worked across to the new hires. Understanding gas station operation would not "click" in their minds until they saw a station under construction and could see the system under the asphalt.

To enable the new recruits to see the underground system, a Second Life gas station was built in January 2004, rolled out in several weeks. With the click of a mouse, they can see under the asphalt and inside the dispensers. Additionally, color-coding was used to make identification of sub-systems easier. It immediately received quite a bit of attention as one of the first projects using Second Life for a real-life purpose. More importantly, this new, vibrant, engaging form of training has had a measurable impact. In the past, it could be six months before a new recruit got a chance to see a station under construction, and observe the piping, pumps, and tanks that are typically hidden by asphalt. With the new training, they got that chance in their first week. As a result, testers received a much clearer picture of how these entire systems work before going out into the field, and this also helped reduce the overall training period before they were ready to move from apprentice to foreman status.

After the initial development period, educational slide shows were added to the gas station, showing real-life pictures of testing equipment, how tests are performed, and safety regulations. These slide shows allow a true multimedia review of the materials being learned. Second Life has been a great platform for their corporate training needs. They considered this project to be a success, and they counted all the media attention they have received as a nice bonus. Additionally, the lessons learned developing and using the gas tank simulation can be applied to many fields: architecture, HVAC, planning of public spaces, and many more.

DISCUSSION

This chapter examined the usefulness of the Interaction-Combinations Integration model (Antonacci & Modaress, 2005; 2008) to organize and describe actual virtual world learning activities. Examples were found corresponding to the three interaction types proposed by this model: person-person, person-object, and object-object. Additionally, the described learning activities as well as the problems, issues, and concerns mentioned for each case provide some support that these learning activities, based on interaction types, are unique and different from each other. For instance, numerous issues with in-world building were mentioned in the urban planning case, but building was not mentioned at all in the field research case.

At the same time, this chapter reveals some learning activities may include more than one interaction type. In the urban planning course, for example, the capstone project included several objectives. The primary objective was to apply course concepts to the design and development of built space, person-object interaction. However, because this activity was done as group projects, students learned about collaborative design work as well, which would be person-person interaction. Furthermore, including constructivist learning activities does not preclude using the virtual world in other ways. Not only did the field research course include virtual world learning activities, but it also used Second Life as a communication medium for instructor and student presentations and for quizzing.

While this model provides a useful framework for identifying and categorizing real-life course topics by interaction type, without good suggestions for learning activities, educators may not be able to locate suitable in-world learning activities. This chapter makes an important contribution by providing three additional learning activity examples from actual virtual world learning activities, one for each interaction type. The field research activity described in this study is significantly different from the role-playing activities described in previous Antonacci & Modaress (2005, 2008) work. Although the urban planning capstone project is similar to previously described work, the "Interesting (Virtual) Places" activity within that course adds an example of a virtual world learning activity for learning person-object interaction, without having students building or scripting. Similarly, the gas tank simulation supplies another example of a learning activity for learning object-object interactions, and by using a demonstration format, it puts forward an approach which avoids having students learn to use the Second Life program all together.

To help educators implement these virtual world learning activities, this chapter also offers rich descriptions of what was needed for these learning activities to succeed and how they were conducted. Although each activity and context has its unique considerations, several common themes emerged. First and foremost, each activity focused on specific educational needs—learning drove these educational innovations, not the technology. Second, virtual worlds were used for learning activities that would be difficult, costly, dangerous, or impossible to do in real life—that is, the virtual world afforded some important advantages over real life or other technologies.

Another common theme among these cases is the learning curve for using a virtual world. Lamoureux and Thomas both mentioned the time and frustration of learning Second Life for instructors and students, and Allen specifically implemented a demonstration format to avoid some of these complications. As virtual worlds become more commonplace, instructors and students will already be familiar with this technology, and this barrier may be reduced, much like word processing and Internet skills, once requiring class time to learn, are now assumed today.

Each case also described an approval process before implementing their virtual world learning activities. Lamoureux reported the most resistance to this innovation. But, Thomas obtained formal course approval, and Allen sought approval of his corporate vice president. Again, as virtual world technology diffuses, such approval may not be needed.

Finally, the learning activities described in these cases developed over time. No activity was perfect from the start, and each was modified, refined, and improved as the instructors gained experience teaching it. Unlike classroom instruction in which instructors have ample experiences to guide their actions, teaching and learning in virtual worlds is so new that very few instructors have any experience in this area at all. It will take time for each instructor to understand and adapt to this learning environment, and it will take time before research and best-practices can inform our practice.

CONCLUSION

In closing, the authors would like to encourage interested educators to begin exploring virtual worlds as a tool for teaching and learning. As this technology develops and becomes more widespread, you will be ready to successfully integrate virtual world learning activities in your class. As shown in this chapter, this process takes time, and it involves identifying, developing, and refining virtual world learning activities, learning to use the technology itself, obtaining approval to use the technology, and gaining experience teaching with it.

REFERENCES

Activeworlds Inc. (2010). *Active Worlds*. Newburyport, MA: Activeworlds Inc. Retrieved May 26, 2010, from http://www.activeworlds.com

Antonacci, D. M., & Modaress, N. (2005). *Second Life: The educational possibilities of a Massively Multiplayer Virtual World* (MMVW). EDUCAUSE Southwest Regional Conference.

Antonacci, D. M., & Modaress, N. (2008). Envisioning the educational possibilities of user-created virtual worlds. *AACE Journal, 16*(2), 115–126.

Autodesk Media and Entertainment. (2010). *3D Studio Max*. Montreal, Canada: Autodesk Media and Entertainment. Retrieved May 26, 2010, from http://www.autodesk.com/3dsmax

Blizzard Entertainment. (2010). *World of Warcraft*. Irvine, CA: Blizzard Entertainment. Retrieved May 26, 2010, from http://www.worldofwarcraft.com

Bogden, R. C., & Biklin, S. K. (1998). *Qualitative research in education: An introduction to theory and practice*. Boston, MA: Allyn & Bacon.

Cities, X. L. (2010). *City Life*. Paris, France: Cities XL. Retrieved May 26, 2010, from http://www2.citiesxl.com

Conklin, M. S. (2007). *101 Uses for Second Life in the college classroom*. Elon, NC: Elon University, Department of Computing Sciences. Retrieved May 26, 2010, from http://citeseerx.ist.psu.edu/viewdoc/download?doi=10.1.1.133.9588&rep=rep1&type=pdf

Electronic Arts Inc. (2010). *SimCity*. Redwood City, CA: Electronic Arts Inc. Retrieved May 26, 2010, from http://www.ea.com

Google Inc. (2010). *Google SketchUp*. Mountain View, CA: Google Inc. Retrieved May 26, 2010, from http://sketchup.google.com

Jonassen, D. H., Peck, K. L., & Wilson, B. G. (1999). *Learning with technology: A constructivist perspective*. Upper Saddle River, NJ: Merrill-Prentice Hall.

Lincoln, Y. S., & Guba, E. G. (1985). *Naturalistic inquiry*. Newbury Park, CA: Sage Publications.

Linden Lab. (2010a). *Second Life*. San Francisco, CA: Linden Lab. Retrieved May 26, 2010, from http://www.secondlife.com

Linden Lab. (2010b). *Second Life educators list*. San Francisco, CA: Linden Lab. Retrieved May 26, 2010, from https://lists.secondlife.com/cgi-bin/mailman/listinfo/educators

Makena Technologies, Inc. (2010). *There*. Silicon Valley, CA: Makena Technologies, Inc. Retrieved May 26, 2010, from http://www.there.com

New Media Consortium. (2007). *The horizon report: 2007 edition*. Austin, TX: New Media Consortium. Retrieved May 26, 2010, from http://www.nmc.org/pdf/2007_Horizon_Report.pdf

KEY TERMS AND DEFINITIONS

Constructivist Learning: A theoretical view of learning where knowledge is constructed by the learners as they actively problem solve in an authentic context.

Human Subject Protection: A procedure to protect human subjects (e.g., distress, physical harm, confidentiality) in research studies.

Interaction-Combinations Integration Model: A technology integration model to help educators connect real-life course topics to potential virtual world learning activities, using three interaction combinations: people-people, people-object, and object-object.

Second Life: A user-created virtual world developed by Linden Lab based San Francisco, CA.

Technology Integration: The process of incorporating communication and information technologies into teaching and learning.

User-Created Virtual Worlds: 3D simulated environments created by their users, and simultaneously played by thousands of people around the world.

APPENDIX A: CASE OUTLINE

1.   Larger organizational context of project
     a.   Name
     b.   Type (non-profit, corporate, higher education, etc.)
     c.   Size
     d.   Location
     e.   Mission/purpose/goals/objectives
2.   Division/Department context
     a.   Name
     b.   Type (training department, school of education, etc.)
     c.   Size
     d.   Mission/purpose/goals/objectives
3.   Course context
     a.   Name
     b.   Description
     c.   Type (required, elective, etc)
     d.   Target audience (adults, masters level, new hires, etc)
4.   Project
     a.   Knowledge or skills gap/need which led to the project
     b.   Objectives
     c.   Learning activity description (What do the participants/teachers/ learners/clients do?)
     d.   Why Second Life? (advantages over face-to-face or other technologies)
     e.   Evaluation methods
     f.   Student outcomes
     g.   Funding (amount, source)
     h.   Technical requirements (hardware, support, training)
     i.   Development and maintenance needs (personnel, time, financials, incentives, rewards)
     j.   Student learning curve for learning/using Second Life
5.   Lessons learned (problems, concerns, issues, challenges, and solutions)
6.   Recommendations
7.   Future plans

Chapter 5

Virtual Learning Environments:
Second Life MUVEs to Leverage Student Ownership

Mitzi P. Trahan
University of Louisiana at Lafayette, USA

Nan B. Adams
Southeastern Louisiana University, USA

Susan Dupre
University of Louisiana at Lafayette, USA

ABSTRACT

The purpose of this chapter is two-fold: first, to present an overview of research related to Second Life, one of several Internet-based multi-user virtual environments (MUVEs); and second, to demonstrate that practical applications of MUVEs in education and professional development can be merged with an existing model for learning in virtual learning environments. While the three-dimensional environment of online worlds like Second Life exhibit game-like ambiance, there is serious business going on "in-world" as educators experiment with this technology in increasing numbers. In particular, Second Life is being used as a vehicle for university course delivery, conference sessions, informal meetings, collaborative projects, and creative products. As a result, Second Life (SL) and similar platforms have become the subject of recent research attention from those who seek to understand the current and potential educational value of this online phenomenon.

The growing experimentation with multi-user virtual environments for educational purposes demands rigorous examination of all aspects of these digital worlds. While their use appears to enhance and expand traditional distance learning, educators acknowledge that barriers to access remain, including a steep learning curve for orienting users to MUVE navigation and functionality. The application of Adams's Knowledge Development Model for Virtual Learning Environments provides a framework for the design of in-world learning opportunities and activities, many of which tend to mirror pedagogical best-practices in Real Life (RL).

DOI: 10.4018/978-1-60960-545-2.ch005

INTRODUCTION

As educators seek to expand options for teaching and learning in the digital age, a growing number are testing the educational potential of emerging technology in the form of 3-D virtual environments. Second Life®, an Internet-based multi-user virtual environment (MUVE), has great potential applications in education and professional development. In this chapter, Second Life will be used to ground the dialogue of MUVE's and to demonstrate how educational activities can be accomplished in-world; more importantly, we will explore the idea that education can be enhanced with these cutting edge technologies. As we approached the topic, three questions emerged:

1. What constitutes effective virtual educational delivery options aimed at creating full learning experiences, and are these options available within Second Life?
2. What is required to prepare teachers and students for virtual world classrooms?
3. What learning objectives and outcomes can Second Life help students to achieve?

Literature Review

As in the case of any new technology, researchers often begin by exploring efficacy and application of the innovation; this phenomenon is no different for Second Life (SL) research. Overall, digital technology is impacting how individuals manage and process vast amounts of available information as well as significantly changing traditional ways of communication knowledge. Boland (2009a) suggests that evidence is building in favor of using Second Life as a viable learning environment. Yet, more research and empirical evidence is needed to demonstrate what genuine learning outcomes are possible. Educators must be responsive to the increased demand for informational technology, while simultaneously exploring its implications for teaching and learning. Ultimately, SL research

should help to inform instructional design and connect the findings in a way that will help teachers and learners appreciate the potential of SL as an alternative learning environment.

In recent years, information technology scholars have examined the impact of self-efficacy and cognitive beliefs regarding the effectiveness of technology as learning tool (Venkatesh & Davis, 2000). Additionally, the efficiencies of virtual learning environments (VLEs) have been the focus of much of the technology research. Another path to determining the usefulness of technology has been to examine technology performance predictors (Moore & Benbasat, 1991). The purpose of this inquiry was also one of discovery.

Recognizing that research on multi-user virtual environments is in its infancy, the authors reviewed the current literature in order to identify study variables and categorize recurring educational research themes. Many traditional educational outcomes and variables have surfaced as the focus of early SL research. However, the research framework seems to be moving beyond concrete outcomes such as, impact on student test scores, to process outcomes that recognize a paradigm shift in teaching and learning with technology. For instance, there seems to be a trend towards examining the benefits of SL through the lenses of personal and social engagement. Brown (2009) advanced theories of presence, positioning, and community that inform individual perceptions of social connectedness, the role of the facilitator, and emotional aspects of cognitive activity. In her study, she hypothesizes that cognition and emotion are inseparable and that virtual experiences amplify memory and learning. Brown concludes that Second Life provided a "strong sense of presence.... Communicating synchronously with students and seeing their avatars promotes a sense of being with people in a fixed place and time" (p. 11).

Therefore, a need exists to combine instructional design, which can capitalize on the unique qualities of virtual environments like Second Life, with learning theory that predicts the impact of learning in such environments. Constructivism provides the connection. While not a new perspective, constructivism can be used to address what Duffy and Jonassen (1992) defined as two primary changes in our society: first, the sheer volume of information we must manage, and second, the new opportunities provided through technology. In a constructivist approach, it is the interaction between the learner and the environment that creates knowledge, and Antonacci and Modaress (2008) remind us that many activities taking place in a virtual world like Second Life require active participation and engagement. The following literature review is organized around two major conceptual frameworks: (1) Individual or Cognitive Constructivism and (2) Social Constructivism. The primary difference between the two is that individual constructivism refers to working in isolation, whereas group work is the defining characteristic underlying of social constructivism. Constructivism, as presented in this paper, is grounded in its function as a learning theory.

Individual Constructivism

Individual constructivism is a learning theory that states that students learn by doing and emphasizes the active role of the learner in knowledge construction (Woolfolk, 2007). The American Council of Education (Oblinger, 2001), for example, report that "the curriculum of the virtual college is composed of specific courses which involve the interaction between the learner and the instructor, among learners and/or between learners and learning resources conducted through one or more media... (p. 15). Girvan and Savage (2010) suggest that the obvious pedagogy for use in virtual settings will be those with tools that provide the flexibility to build learning objects and activities in a persistent environment. Rather than the rote memorization typical of knowledge- and skills-based learning, students should be provided the opportunity to experience their own personal

cognitive processes to integrate and construct knowledge in their own way.

Student-Centered Learning

A predictor of success in online environments is that students are challenged to take a greater role in reflective and active learning as they are being guided instead of being told. For example, Harvard University's River City, a MUVE designed for middle school students, asks participants to apply modern technology and knowledge to problems faced by previous generations—specifically, to determine why people in a town are becoming ill (http://muve.gse.harvard.edu/rivercityproject/9). In this application, participants use simulations that allow them to formulate and test hypotheses based on data collected in-world.

One of the hallmark characteristics of transformative learning is the ability to control one's learning. Todd (1999) talks about reengineering schooling and, thus, reforming education via information technology. He argues that students need to be empowered and supported to adopt learning with technology. This is definitely true with SL in particular as students (and teachers) work to overcome the technological challenges of creating and navigating their *student avatars*. A fundamental challenge to embracing educational technology lies in students' ability to incorporate three dimensions of information literacy: thinking, reasoning, and reflecting processes – cognitive doings – as well as behavioral doings" (Todd, 1999, p. 9).

Learner Autonomy

Little (1996, as cited in Schwienhorst, 2002), defines autonomy as a "capacity for detachment, critical reflection, decision-making, and independent action." According to Eck, Legenhausen, and Wolff (1994), the autonomous learner becomes an effective communicator and intentional metacognitive learner. Similarly, Albert Bandura

(1985) believed that the phenomenon of changing one's thinking can only occur through the ability toward self-reflection. It can be argued that these defining characteristics are predictive of success in many typical online environments that require the learner to work in isolation.

Self-Efficacy

Self-efficacy is a precursor to motivation and specific behaviors towards completing an activity. For that reason, a cycle of self-examination and interpretation of one's ability will subsequently alter future performance. Accordingly, self-efficacy can be conceptualized as a future oriented belief of performance in a context-specific assessment of success. Further, computer self-efficacy has been shown to be a strong indicator of computer use behavior in the context of both hardware and software applications (Argarwal, Sambamurthy, & Stair, 2000).

Zhang and Espinoza (1998) have indicated that low computer self-efficacy negatively impacts an individual's ability to perform at his or her fullest potential. At times, new users of technology experience fear and uncertainty that can produce negative and even demoralizing feelings towards a technology tool. This is particularly relevant as learners transition to MUVE and the steep learning curve associated with Second Life. For example, Hollander and Thomas (2009) found that, understandably, student with minimal experience in 3-D modeling had the greatest difficulty, but even students with experience felt that SL was limited and became frustrated. By the end of the class, however, students' teamwork skills, problem-solving abilities, and the ability to integrate knowledge and skill using authentic experiences were greatly enhanced through SL. A fundamental concept to self-efficacy is that, as mastery experience increases, so does self-efficacy (Woolfolk, 2007).

Social Constructivism

A basic premise of constructivist learning environment is that the environment promotes engagement and reflection that, in turn, provides for collaboration (Driscoll, 1994). Closely tied to this thought is the value of a sense of community. Social interaction can easily be encouraged in SL by embedding group learning activities that promote both individual development and collaborative learning. Bandura (1977, 1985) also speaks to social constructivism and encourages social interaction by learners as a way to improving learning. Interestingly, Senges and Alier (2009) note that online communities evolving through virtual environments like Second Life tend to become learning communities. In addition to acquiring specific knowledge related to the group's interests, participants also learn and practice advanced communication, organization, and technology skills as they adapt to their part in a collaborative—and often global--network. This social networking trend (evidenced by the popularity of applications such as Facebook and Twitter) is the result of the dissolution of distance produced by enhanced online communication; this trend is changing the landscape of learning by enhancing our ability to collaboration and is fully embraced in Second Life.

Hollander and Thomas (2009) propose that, "Second Life provides a heretofore unprecedented tool for teaching planning" (p.108). In their study exploring collaborative experiences in SL, they posed the research question, "What are some of the implications of moving education off the drafting table and pin-up wall and into an active, simulated computer–based world?" Qualitative findings indicated that students not only enjoyed late night interactions but actively supported each other in the SL classroom space. Recent studies at Australia's Griffin University explored the potential of using virtual environments to support small group discussions by comparing student responses in the SL virtual learning environment

(VLE) with those that took place in the more traditional Blackboard learning management system (LMS). Findings reveal an increase in depth of discussions, as well as greater prompted and unprompted contributions, attributed by the author to the sense of physical presence available in Second Life (Zagami, 2010).

The availability to interact 24/7 has already been recognized as an advantage in many online course delivery systems (Trahan, 2004). Unlike many asynchronous platforms, SL offers the ability to envision and create a new educational in-world culture:

- A *classroom* with limitless virtual world synchronicity
- A *classroom* that has the potential to reverse social isolation
- A *classroom* that spans global distance and culture

An Introduction to Second Life

Second Life (SL) is a virtual world created and shaped by its inhabitants. While the three-dimensional online simulated environment of Second Life exhibits a game-like ambiance, there is serious business going on *in-world*, including the business of education. Organizations such as the International Society for Technology in Education (ISTE) and educational institutions including Harvard University have purchased real estate inside Second Life for use as platforms for learning (International Society for Technology Education, 2009; Linden Research, Inc., 2009a). Research conducted in and delivered through Second Life educational portals reveal the recreation in Second Life of educational opportunities and activities that mirror pedagogical best-practices in the real world (RL); however, barriers to access remain, including a steep learning curve associated with orienting users to the MUVE.

Linden Research Inc., the San Francisco-based company that owns Second Life, considers education to be a core function of its virtual world (Linden Research, Inc., 2009b). Beginning with a one-square kilometer of real estate, Second Life has grown to encompass 600 square kilometers with registered users numbering in the millions (Waters, 2009). Today, Second Life is accepted as the most robust of all virtual environments; its well-established landscape began as an experiment in exploration (Rymaszewski et al., 2007). Users of this digital simulation, called *residents,* are represented by *avatars*, virtual personas that many users view as an expression of their own creativity (Jamison, 2008). Residents are guided through avatar creation on their first visit, and each avatar is given a program-generated last name to provide a degree of anonymity if desired.

After entering the virtual landscape, residents move through the many communities of Second Life by walking, running, flying, and even teleporting. Just as in *first life*, there are shopping areas, clubs, schools, and places that should be avoided. For this reason, Linden Labs has bifurcated its virtual reality by establishing a Teen Grid for students ages 13 through 17 (Waters, 2009). SL residents can play games, construct buildings, buy and design clothing, and operate businesses with Linden dollars, which are trading at approximately 250 Linden Dollars (L$) to the US Dollar (Linden Research, Inc., 2009b). However, the space itself is secondary; what draws participants to Second Life is the enjoyable experience of connection that results when avatars gather in the same space at the same time (Johnson, Levine, & Smith, 2008).

Course Delivery Options in Second Life

First-time users of Second Life will recognize similarities to popular online games like *World of Warcraft* (WOW); the emerging gaming culture has created a thirty-billion dollar industry and redefined gaming activities to include communication, entertainment, training, and education (Natkin, 2006). These well-established gaming activities are also present in Second Life, allowing SL to provide an economical way to distribute educational content over the Internet (Yellowless & Cook, 2006). However, virtual words are not games; rather, they are online social environments to which a physical presence has been added (Johnson, Levine, & Smith, 2008). While a traditional learning environment can be created in Second Life, it is also feasible to utilize unusual and perhaps more engaging non-traditional situations and locations that are only available through a virtual world. Museums, laboratories, and classroom simulations all become possible tools in an educator's efforts to encourage collaboration, social engagement.

Just as in online games, Second Life avatars can see each other; they can communicate with each other through voice chat, text chat, and instant messaging. Nametags levitate above the head of every avatar, and a built-in translator expands communicative and collaborative possibilities. In Second Life, all interaction is synchronous and is similar to real-life video conferencing, and interactions can be video-taped for later viewing. These options provide all users with increased opportunities for global understanding, dialogue, and self-reflection. Real world programs such as Global Kids have capitalized on these expanded communication options by using SL's Teen Grid (TSL) to host workshops to connect New York City teens for discussions on genocide, racism, child trafficking, and the digital divide in an effort to build leadership and critical thinking skills (http://www.globalkids.org).

Jon Wardle notes that higher education has begun to recognize the need to extend learning opportunities for all learners: "Lecturers and students are both starting to understand that online learning doesn't have to be a poor alternative to traditional campus-based courses. The days of the very bad, old-school correspondence courses are over. Now the future is about trying to discover new pedagogies which might not work face-to-face, but work wonderfully online" (Tobin, 2009).

Educators experimenting with course delivery in Second Life will find that most, if not all, of the traditional options are also available in-world, as well as many options that are only available in a virtual environment. The International Society for Technology in Education (ISTE) has created a vibrant educational community on its own real estate called ISTE Island for the purpose of encouraging and supporting professional development among its members. It offers a "New Educator Pilot Program" with live volunteers called *docents* available to assist during scheduled hours. ISTE takes the position that the wide array of built in learning activities such as communication and collaborative projects opens the door to creative pedagogical potential (International Society for Technology Education, 2009).

Another such island community is Lighthouse Learning, established by Kathy Schrock, the administrator for technology for Nauset Public Schools. Designed as venue for traditional professional development and collaboration, the island is host to meetings, presentation, and training materials needed to provide K-12 teachers with the skills needed to move to content-specific Teen Grid islands (Schrock, n.d). Its virtual meeting rooms and auditoriums provide gathering places for teachers in an environment similar to those they might find in a real-world setting; the difference, of course, is that all social networking is done through avatars (Waters, 2009).

Regardless of the location, students and teachers or facilitators in Second Life encounter a plethora of options for collaboration, communication, and exploration. Residents can meet in traditional setting such as classrooms and lecture halls, or in non-traditional settings like beaches or parks. They can share information through slides, audio, video, discussions, presentations, group projects, simulations, and explorations (Kay & Fitzgerald, 2007). They can jump into a hurricane, be battered by a tsunami, or travel to distant planets. Because it is a user-created environment, Second Life offers a remarkable learning platform for flexible delivery of instructional content.

Preparing for a Virtual World

Before educators embrace Second Life as a learning platform, however, a level-headed evaluation of the challenges facing users must be considered. Often cited is the steep learning curve associated with Second Life utilization, which can be partially blamed on the user interface (Boland, 2009b; Tobin, 2009; Trotter, 2008). This challenge could be overcome with scaffolded mentoring of new users, but planning for an orientation to Second Life should be part of any educator's game plan.

Adoption issues also include the technology requirements for running the application, including fast computer processors, quality graphics cards, and broadband Internet access (Kay & Fitzgerald, 2007). Additionally, while a basic subscription is free of charge and sufficient for basic participation, a myriad of desirable options and accessories are available from in-world vendors and from Linden Labs itself; these often hasten an inhabitant's desire to spend real world cash (Trotter, 2008).

The Second Life application itself requires the downloading of a connection interface, which can be painstakingly slow. This application does not run on open standards; as a result, it is not possible for schools and universities to host their virtual worlds on local servers. Because all activity occurs on Linden Lab servers, there are a limited number of *prims*, the basic building block of Second Life, and there are limitations on the number of avatars (between 50 and 70) who can meet in a single area (Kay & Fitzgerald, 2007).

Assets purchased in Second Life are not portable, and inhabitants are dependent upon Linden Labs for maintenance and upkeep of the Second Life grid (Trotter, 2008). Performance issues often occur during times of regular server maintenance, and the client-end software must be updated about once a month. Inhabitants have reported recent sluggish performance, partially the result of a rapidly expanding population.

Since Second Life mirrors first life, legal and social issues can be expected. Residents must follow terms of service and community standards set by Linden Labs, who reserves the right to cancel accounts without legal recourse (Linden Research, Inc., 2009b). This is often the fate of *griefers*, those who purposefully disrupt the in-world experiences of other inhabitants. Ethical issues related to educational research have also recently been addressed (Ess, C. & the Association of Internet Researchers, 2002).

In addition to these challenges that would affect any users, particular issues exist when Second Life is considered for educational use. Because of its similarity to games, outsiders may view the platform as inappropriate, and network administrators may block access under the heading of gaming. The problem of anonymity in Second Life could also be a concern, but this issue is common in any form of online teaching (Kay & Fitzgerald, 2007). Finally, legal issues for institutions related to intellectual property rights and indemnity have yet to be tried in real-world courts, but this, too, is probably only a matter of time.

In light of the increasingly widespread interest in the use of 3-D MUVEs and profound implications for teaching and learning, cutting edge research and the advancement of conceptual models to ground future investigations are currently needed to explore the potential of virtual world for educational course delivery.

A KNOWLEDGE DEVELOPMENT MODEL FOR VIRTUAL ENVIRONMENTS

When designing educational strategies for virtual learning environments, the links between effective real world learning strategies and virtual world learning strategies have been suggested. Adams (2007) developed a Knowledge Development

Figure 1. Recursive model for knowledge development in virtual environments

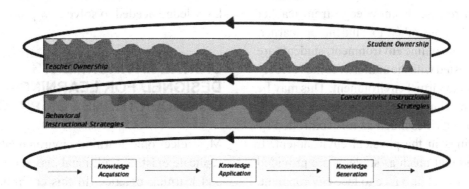

Model for Virtual Learning Environments based on effective real world learning theory and both behavioral and constructivist teaching and learning strategies. This model identifies three interrelated dimensions: (1) the learner's developing knowledge approach, (2) the teacher-student relationship with regards to knowledge authority, and (3) suggested teaching approaches. The dimensions of this model were validated as representing dimensions that were conducive to the development of knowledge in virtual environments (Adams, DeVaney, & Sawyer, 2009). Much as Vygostky (1978) describes learning as a recursive process, it is assumed that each of these dimensions is cyclical and recursive and that this process may have several different instances occurring simultaneously, as shown in the Figure 1.

The model above combines the dimensions of knowledge approach, the teacher-student relationship with regards to knowledge authority and teaching approach to demonstrate the recursive and scaffolded design for creation of virtual learning environments. At this time, the author would like to offer a practical observation. In the context of course progression found in most learning institutions, these progressive knowledge approaches may occur repeatedly during one course or learning unit, or may stretch across two or more learning units or courses. The focus is to insure that all levels of knowledge engagement should

be considered when creating complete knowledge transfer and foster ownership.

Dimension 1: Knowledge Approach

The first dimension of the model represents a continuum of recursive learning outcomes that are best described through the developmental processes of: (1) Knowledge Acquisition; (2) Knowledge Application, and (3) Knowledge Generation.

Knowledge Acquisition refers to the users initial student contact with the knowledge base. This often involves an interaction between the learner's pre-existing framework of understanding and exposition to new knowledge structures.

Knowledge Application refers to the process of building and combining concepts through their use in the performance of meaningful tasks.

Knowledge Generation refers to the testing and tuning of conceptualizations through use in applied contexts.

Through these applied contexts, new constructions may emerge or 'holes' in knowledge may emerge. The knowledge generation phase gives rise for a recursion of the process by exposing new areas of need for knowledge acquisition.

Dimension 2: Knowledge Authority

The Dimension of Knowledge Authority describes the Teacher-Student Relationship within the learning environment. Vygotsky (1978) discusses the gradual release of knowledge from teacher or knowledgeable other to student or learner. Uniquely in the online environment, students are initially invested with the authority to move freely throughout the virtual environment. This may be controlled by timed offering of certain material and certain activities much as it is controlled by class meetings in the physical environment. It is suggested that much as students are provided the entire textbook in a face to face environment, virtual environments should be presented in their entirety (as a whole learning experience rather than disjointed parts) with the gradual release of knowledge authority from teacher to student demonstrated by the course organization. This provides a whole rather than partial view of the virtual reality construction of the knowledge to be explored. This also allows students to continually view the entire construction of the knowledge as they set about exploring the dimensions that make up this full construction.

Dimension 3: Teaching Approaches

Teaching approaches range from the most behavioral strategy of drill and practice, through programmed instruction to constructivist strategies that include discovery learning and scaffolded learning activities. This model suggests that all of these techniques are useful in the virtual learning environment. A natural use of these strategies might begin with more behavioral strategies to convey basic terminology and other supporting skills and progress to constructivist teaching approaches to foster the Knowledge Application and Knowledge Generation goals of this model. Scaffolding of learning activities to continually expand the student Zone of Proximal Development (Wertsch, 1984) should be a central focus for continued knowledge transfer and generation. For when new knowledge is being generated, student ownership of both existing and newly generated

knowledge is central to the new constructions of knowledge needed to solve new problems.

DIGITAL ENVIRONMENTS DESIGNED FOR LEARNING – CONSIDERATIONS FOR PRACTICE

Most electronic learning environments seek to replicate existing traditional classroom teaching and learning practice. In this environment you often find word intensive pages that are intended for students to read and be expected to 'know' for a later demonstration. While these learning sites may be easy to construct, they are hardly virtual environments that create a variety of learning opportunities to foster knowledge development. Their focus is Knowledge Acquisition and they imply that knowledge authority is possessed by the teacher or site creator and are not particularly open to student manipulation

As a virtual learning environment is developed the teacher or developer of the environment must consider the overall goals for student learning and within each of these goals determine the knowledge acquisition concerns, the knowledge application activities and determine how to foster knowledge generation through the discovery process. Using the Knowledge Development Model for Virtual Learning Environments, the following strategies are suggested for each of the proposed knowledge approaches:

Knowledge Acquisition

If the goal for a certain learning activity is to foster knowledge acquisition, access to programmed instruction segments that provide supporting terminology and initial concepts to be used as building blocks for more sophisticated learning activities should be considered. Discovery learning may also be employed as the context and various Programmed Instruction modules or activities that require the student to access and obtain information that defines the knowledge structures for a given area for learning may be supplied to inform this discovery process. Tutorials, informational web pages and databases to support student knowledge acquisition are useful tools for this phase of student learning.

Knowledge Application

Traditionally, knowledge application tasks include laboratory work, writing, preparing presentations and other activities that require the student to construct acquired knowledge to solve existing problems that have somewhat predictable outcomes. Collaboration among students often reinforces this process. Discovery learning also easily fits the context for knowledge application. The design of presentations or web pages that demonstrate a construction and application of the knowledge under investigation are appropriate virtual learning tools. These student products may be included for review as part of the virtual environment and serve to develop student ownership of course content, which is critical to fostering knowledge generation among students. The posted or delivered presentations demonstrate student knowledge and investment in the learning activities and ultimately student ownership of the knowledge. These constructions also allow the instructor to uncover common misconceptions about the knowledge base and facilitate discussion about these misconceptions to increase knowledge. Collaborative environments such as Second Life, with strategies such as chat, threaded discussion boards, instant messaging and other collaborative tools are useful to facilitate knowledge application strategies.

Knowledge Generation

A different level of discovery learning may be employed for fostering knowledge generation. Student ownership of this process is critical. Student brainstorming of problems to be solved creates the context for this ownership. Collaboration among students and between students and faculty becomes a vital aspect of generation of new knowledge, and Second Life may provide the virtual environment to foster high quality collaboration and discussion. Additionally, private discussion forums or the private chat feature of SL that allows for risk taking may aid this process. As with knowledge application, collaborative environments such as chat, threaded discussion boards, instant messaging and other collaborative tools are useful. The design of presentations or web pages that demonstrate new construction and application of the knowledge under investigation are appropriate virtual learning tools. These student products should be provided space for private development either by singular students in collaboration with faculty or within student groups with faculty collaboration. The final projects should be included as part of the virtual environment and may be the capstone discussion activity of the learning cycle. The fact that this discussion may take on a real time interaction with lifelike avatars may add to the quality of the feedback and response. These projects may easily reveal new areas of knowledge for exploration and may serve as the catalyst for another recursive learning cycle.

CONCLUSION

According to both individual cognitive and social constructivism theories, Second Life has the potential to provide a rich, interactive classroom learning environment. Learners can walk or fly to and through virtual lands solving problems on their own or as a team communicating with other classmates. Course content can now be discovered visually *in-world*, promoting engaging and challenging authentic activities which have the potential to transform knowledge beyond pure student learning outcomes to richer, deeper, personalized transformative life-long cognitive learning processes. Learner-centered opportunities are ideally adaptable to Second Life—teachers and students initially share power in transformative learning environments. Teachers increasingly relinquish responsibility for learning to students allowing them to creatively take charge of constructing knowledge. While researchers caution that this technology is in its formative years with relatively minimal existing use and experimentation, Second Life seems to have considerable pedagogical potential for education. Virtual worlds such as Second Life offer great promise for true transformative learning.

Adams's Model for Knowledge Development for Virtual Learning Environments (2007) provides a framework for the development of learning and teaching strategies based on individual and social constructivist learning theory. The three dimensions of this model provide perspective for the role of the teacher, context for the role of the student and guidance for the development of educational strategies within virtual learning environments.

In an age in which text-based online instruction was considered progressive, Duffy and Jonassen (1992) believed that visual experiences would become the futuristic pedagogy for individual and group learning. Certainly, the 21st century with its expanded digital applications has forced a reevaluation of instructional approaches and of learning processes in order to capitalize on this emerging technology. Visual experiences delivered through virtual learning environments like Second Life offer the chance for educators to make digital classrooms a reality—a virtual reality.

REFERENCES

Adams, N. B. (2007). Toward a model for knowledge development in a virtual environment: Strategies for student ownership. *International Journal for Social Sciences, 2*(2), 71–77.

Adams, N. B., DeVaney, T. A., & Sawyer, S. G. (2009). Measuring conditions conducive to knowledge development. *The Journal of Technology, Learning and Assessment, 8*(1).

Antonacci, D. M., & Modress, N. (2008). Envisioning the educational possibilities of user-created virtual worlds. *AACE Journal, 16*(2), 115–126.

Argawal, R., Sambamurthy, V., & Stair, R. (2000). The evolving relationships between general and specific computer self-efficacy: An empirical assessment. *Information Systems Research, 11*(4), 418–430. doi:10.1287/isre.11.4.418.11876

Bandura, A. (1977). *Social learning theory*. Englewood Cliffs, NJ: Prentice Hall.

Bandura, A. (1985). *Social foundations of thought and action: A social-cognitive theory*. New York, NY: Prentice Hall.

Boland, I. H. (2009a). *Efficacy of the 3D multiuser virtual environment (MUVE) Second Life of learning in cognitive constructivist and social constructivist practices*. (Unpublished dissertation), Capella University.

Boland, I. H. (2009b). Learners' love/hate relationship with 3D worlds. *Learning Solutions*, 10-13.

Brown, A. (2009). *A second look at Second Life: Virtual worlds and education*. Paper presented and the annual NECC conference, Washington, D.C.

Driscoll, M. (1994). *Psychology of learning for instruction*. Boston, MA: Allyn & Bacon.

Duffy, T., & Jonassen, D. (1992). *Constructivism and the technology of instruction: A conversation*. Hillsdale, NJ: Lawrence Erlbaum Associates.

Eck, A., Legenhausen, L., & Wolff, D. (1994). The use of telecommunications in a learner-oriented second-language classroom. In Gienow, W., & Hellwig, K. (Eds.), *Interkulturelle Kommunikation und prozeßorienterte Medienpraxis im Fremdsprachenunterricht: Grundlagen, Realisierung, Wirksamkeit* (pp. 43–57). Seelze, Germany: Friedrich Verlag.

Ess, C. & Association of Internet Researchers (2002). *Ethical decision-making and Internet research: Recommendations from the AOIR Ethics Working Committee.* Retrieved October 22, 2009, from Association of Internet Researchers: www.aoir.org/reports/ethics.pdf

Grivan, C., & Savage, T. (2010). Identifying an appropriate pedagogy for virtual worlds: A communal constructivism case study. *Computers & Education, 55,* 342–349. doi:10.1016/j.compedu.2010.01.020

Hollander, J. B., & Thomas, D. (2009). Commentary: Virtual planning: Second Life and the online studio. *Journal of Planning Education and Research, 29,* 108. doi:10.1177/0739456X09334142

International Society for Technology Education. (2009). *Member networking: ISTE in Second Life.* Retrieved October 21, 2009, from http://www.iste.org/Content/NavigationMenu/Membership/Member_Networking/ISTE_Second_Life.htm

Jamison, J. (2008). *Educators in a strange land: The experience of traditional educators when immersed in the virtual environment of Second Life.* (Doctoral dissertation). Capella University, Minneapolis, MN.

Johnson, L., Levine, A., & Smith, R. (2008). *One year or less: Virtual worlds.* The 2008 Horizon Report: Australia–New Zealand Edition.

Kay, J., & Fitzgerald, S. (2007). *Exploring the educational uses of Second Life.* Retrieved October 23, 2009, from http://sleducation.wikispaces.com/educationaluses_page1#distance

Linden Research, Inc. (2009a). *Virtual environments enable new models of learning.* Retrieved October 1, 2009, from http://www.guardian.co.uk/education/2009/apr/21/elearning-university-of-london/print

Linden Research, Inc. (2009b). *What is Second Life?* Retrieved September 22, 2009, from http://secondlife.com/whatis

Little, D. (1996). Freedom to learn and compulsion to interact: Promoting learner autonomy through the use of Information Systems and Information Technologies. In R. Pemberton, E. Li, W. Or, & H. Pierson (Eds.), *Taking control: Autonomy in language learning.* Hong Kong, HK: Hong Kong University Press.

Moore, G. C., & Benbasat, I. (1991). Development of an instrument to measure the perceptions of adopting an Information Technology innovation. *Information Systems Research, 2*(3). doi:10.1287/isre.2.3.192

Natkin, S. (2006). *Video games and interactive media.* Wellesley, MA: A. K. Peters.

Oblinger, D. G., Barone, C. A., & Hawkins, B. L. (2001). *Distributed education and its challenges: An overview. American Council on Education.* ACE.

Rymaszewski, M., Au, W. J., Winters, C., Ondrejka, C., & Batstone-Cunningham, B. (2007). *Second Life: The official guide.* Indianapolis, IN: Wiley.

Schrock, K. (n.d.). *Second Life: Interactive professional development.* Retrieved October 31, 2009, from http://www.hotchalk.com/mydesk/index.php/editorial/44-online-professional-development/86-second-life-interactive-professional-development-pt-1

Schwienhorst, K. (2002). Why virtual, why environments? Implementing virtual reality concepts in computer-assisted language learning. *Simulation & Gaming, 33,* 196.

Senges, M., & Alier, M. (2009). Virtual worlds as environment for learning communities. In Lytras, D., Tennyson, R., & Pablos, P. (Eds.), *Knowledge networks: The social software perspective.* Hershey, PA: IGI Global.

Tobin, L. (2009, April 21). From video marking to Second Life, technology is transforming the options for online students. *The Guardian*. Retrieved October 22, 2009, from http://www.guardian.co.uk/education/2009/apr/21/elearning-university-of-london/print

Todd, R. J. (1999). Transformational leadership and transformational learning: Information literacy and the World Wide Web. *NASSP Bulletin*, (March): 1999.

Trahan, M. (2004). *Online college students*. Unpublished research study.

Trotter, A. (2008). Educators get a Second Life. *Education Week*, *27*(42), 1.

Venkatesh, V., & Davis, F. D. (2000). A theoretical extension of the technology acceptance model: Four longitudinal field studies. *Management Science*, *46*(2), 186–205. doi:10.1287/mnsc.46.2.186.11926

Vygotsky, L. S. (1978). *Mind and society: The development of higher mental processes*. Cambridge, MA: Harvard University Press.

Waters, J. (2009, January). A Second Life for educators. [from http://www.technteach.info/asecondlifeforeducators.pdf]. *T.H.E. Journal*, 1–6. Retrieved October 22, 2009.

Wertsch, J. V. (1984). The zone of proximal development: Some conceptual issues. *New Directions for Child and Adolescent Development*, *1984*, 7–18..doi:10.1002/cd.23219842303

Woolfolk, A. (2007). *Educational psychology* (10th ed.). Boston, MA: Allyn and Bacon.

Yellowless, P., & Cook, J. (2006). Education about hallucinations using an Internet virtual reality system: A qualitative study. *American Psychiatry*, *30*, 534–539.

Zagami, J. (2010). *Second Life as an environment for education*. Paper presented at ISTE 2010 (International Society of Technology in Education (ISTE), Denver, CO.

Zhang, Y., & Espinoza, S. (1998). Relationships among computer self-efficacy, attitudes towards computers, and desirability of learning computer skills. *Journal of Research on Computing in Education*, *30*(4), 420–431.

KEY TERMS AND DEFINITIONS

3-D Virtual Environments: Often referred to as in-world or virtual world delivery platforms.

Digital Communities: Mutual interest groups organized formally or informally for social networking who interact through Internet-based technology.

Multi-User Virtual Environment (MUVE): A computer-based virtual world designed to support interaction between many users.

Online Teaching and Learning: The process of utilizing Internet-based technology to facilitate interactions between teacher and students.

Second Life®: An Internet-based three-dimensional multi-user virtual environment (MUVE) trademarked by Linden Labs, Inc. in which digital technology simulates a real-world environment and users interact through virtual representatives called avatars.

Virtual Education: Synchronous or asynchronous learning that relies on digital technology the delivery of instructional content.

Virtual Learning Environment (VLE): A system designed to support computer-based teaching and learning, or e-learning, through which learners can access information, download content, or interact synchronously or asynchronously with teachers and peers.

Virtual Learning Experiences: A variety of educational activities conducted using digital technology.

Chapter 6

Exploring the Correlation between Online Teacher Dispositions and Practices in Virtual Classrooms and Student Participation and Satisfaction

Carol M. Shepherd
National University, USA

Madelon Alpert
National University, USA

ABSTRACT

Greater teacher efficacy in online teaching and teaching in a virtual world appears to be positively correlated with certain exhibited dispositions and practices. Inferential measures of dispositions such as friendliness, enthusiasm, active involvement, patience, and tolerance, among others, exhibited by professors in online instruction lead to greater student participation and satisfaction. By analyzing four professors teaching in the virtual world environment, two with positive student reviews and two with negative or mediocre student reviews, certain teacher dispositions and practices emerged. Three areas were studied: instructor participation with students, the tone of communication with students, and the creation of a community of learners in a virtual world. Instructor participation with students was measured by the interaction and guidance in discussion board questions, comments on graded student work, the amount of measured user time of the instructor while teaching online, and student evaluations. The tone of communication with students was measured by professor communications with students in the discussion boards, virtual office responses to student questions, and whole class as well as individual emails. The creation of a community of learners in a virtual environment helps to foster a sense of belonging, and was measured by activities such as informal course announcements, media, emails, and student and professor biographies, indicating that the instructor is interested in each student. There

DOI: 10.4018/978-1-60960-545-2.ch006

are two perspectives to online instruction: that of the student as well as that of the instructor. In order to provide a valid base for analysis, it is important to consider both. A search of the literature revealed almost no information in the areas of focus of this study. Further research is needed to identify positive behaviors by instructors leading to greater online instructor efficacy when teaching in virtual worlds.

INTRODUCTION

Access to higher education is now possible through the use of technology. Distance education is widely accepted as high quality education. Technology and the creation of virtual environments allow the learning to be personalized according to the individualized needs of each student. Although mentally and visually stimulating, involvement in the virtual world can be isolating for the individual. Therefore, it is important for the instructor to be supportive and to create a sense of community that bonds the class and enables the students to function as a cohesive unit.

In a study of student interaction in virtual classrooms, the authors found that online courses were superior to real world courses in regard to the effectiveness of student interaction with each other and with the instructor resulting in courses that were also more effective. Whether it is in traditional classrooms or in a virtual environment, student interactions with each other and with the instructor are vital to learning and teaching effectiveness. Students expect this human interaction, and instructors must provide it in order to be effective. In a virtual world, virtual interactions and virtual discussions must be cultivated (Hay, Hodgkinson, Peltier, & Drago, 2004).

As an increasing number of students elect to pursue their degrees online, it becomes critical to identify and implement teaching behaviors that support student learning. Greater teacher efficacy in online teaching appears to be positively correlated with certain exhibited dispositions and practices. Inferential measures of dispositions such as friendliness, enthusiasm, active involvement, patience, and tolerance, among others,

exhibited by professors in online instruction in virtual worlds lead to greater student participation and satisfaction.

Teacher reform agencies in the United States, such as the National Council for Accreditation of Teacher Education (NCATE), the largest accrediting agency, emphasize the importance of certain dispositions in teacher candidates and require that student dispositions are assessed and supported in teacher education programs. Additionally, the Interstate New Teacher Assessment and Support Consortium (INTASC) now measures whether a teacher's internal existence aligns with appropriate professional dispositions. There is an effort by various agencies to professionalize the field of teaching, which has a long history tracing back to the days of early colonization. These agencies are following a pattern formed by successful elite professions, such as medicine and law, which have been able to convince society that their members possess certain specialized skills and knowledge that should be respected and valued. Members of these professions internalize the dispositions, or legitimate ways of knowing and behaving, that are valued by each profession and which are known as virtue ethics (McKnight, 2004).

DISPOSITIONS

According to Aristotle, a disposition is related to a specific desire toward a virtuous or vicious end. This is very similar to the concept of the virtue ethic. Dispositions become part of people's ingrained behavior, and are developed after they have experienced a significant portion of their lives. Reason and emotion become harmonious, and virtue is enacted out of understanding and love. Those who have certain dispositional behaviors and desires and are receptive to reason and deliberation are able to effect positive change over time (McKnight, 2004). Although they become a developed and ingrained behavior, dispositions are not to be confused with habits. Habits can be changed, whereas dispositions become an integral part of a person's life and ethical behavior.

Reformers seeking professionalization in the field of teaching argue that student learning is dependent upon the behavior of the teacher. Ultimately, teaching behavior is based on the educator's internal dispositions. Therefore, teaching dispositions must somehow be observed, analyzed, and explained to determine those most desirable in online instructors. Dispositions such as friendliness, enthusiasm, active involvement, patience, and tolerance, among others, exhibited by professors in online courses have been shown to result in greater student participation and satisfaction.

These qualities are as important as knowledge and performance (Helm, 2004). Observation of such dispositions is challenging. They are internal in nature, and difficult to define. It is easier for individuals to recognize them when exhibited in others' behavior. In order for these dispositions to be identified and assessed, colleges and universities include the identifying of certain teacher dispositions as a part of their training programs for teachers. One such measure of assessment is the California Critical Thinking Teacher Disposition Inventory (CCTTDI), which uses a seventy-five question format that deals with critical thinking. Another is the Gibbs and Gambrill survey, a thirty-five question inventory also dealing with critical thinking. The University of the Cumberland's teacher education program utilizes scoring rubrics, indicating whether the student is showing evidence of certain dispositions. The College of Saint Benedict, in conjunction with Saint John's University, uses entry interviews to assess teacher candidate dispositions. Questions are designed

to elicit responses showing such dispositions as communicating effectively, encouraging and facilitating positive growth in others, and reflection (Helm, 2006).

Giovanelli (2003) found there is a positive correlation between having a reflective disposition toward teaching and effective teaching. Reflective teachers make better educators. Bandura's (1979) social learning theory stresses the importance of reflection in regard to human functioning. Reflective self-awareness deals with individuals' thoughts about self and how they gain knowledge of their social and physical environment. This perception of self-efficacy relates to how people learn to understand themselves and how this understanding affects their behavior. In a virtual world, where standards for behavior are sometimes lax, understanding how people learn and coordinating that information with the learning contexts is an important task for instructors (Smith & Berge, 2009).

Understanding and measuring disposition-related practices in online teaching in virtual worlds is a challenge facing educators and the administrations assessing their competence. However, this assessment of teaching competence in the online environment is vital for continuous professional growth and improvement (Reynolds, 2007).

METHODOLOGY

Dispositions must be observed in order to be analyzed. In this study, our data was obtained from the study of instructors as well as students. Written communications from students were used, as well as feedback from the researcher actively enrolled as a student in the courses. Dispositions exhibited online by instructors are sometimes different from those exhibited in the actual classroom. Teaching in a virtual world creates a unique learning environment and necessitates a different delivery system. Therefore, it is critical that online instructors focus on demonstrating dispositions such as friendliness, enthusiasm, active involvement, patience, and tolerance, among others.

There are two perspectives presented in online instruction: that of the student as well as that of the instructor. In order to provide a valid base for analysis, it is important to consider both. To obtain this data, one researcher anonymously enrolled in four online classes having a one-month format and using the Blackboard platform, and participated in each class as a student. She was treated as a student, and held to the same standards. Two of the instructors who had been selected for this study generally received high evaluations from students, and two generally received low or mediocre evaluations. By analyzing the activities and techniques of the four professors teaching in the online environment, two with positive student reviews and two with negative or mediocre student reviews, certain teacher dispositions and practices emerged. Both the instructor view and the student view were considered. Three areas were studied: instructor participation with students; the tone of instructor communication with students; and the instructor's creation of a community of learners online. Instructor participation with students was measured by the interaction and guidance in discussion board questions, comments on graded student work, the amount of measured user time of the instructor while teaching online, and student evaluations. The tone of communication with students was measured by professor communications with students in the discussion boards, virtual office responses to student questions, and whole class as well as individual emails. The creation of a community of learners online helps to foster a sense of belonging, and was measured by activities such as informal course announcements, media, emails, and student and professor biographies, indicating that the instructor is interested in each student.

INSTRUCTOR PARTICIPATION WITH STUDENTS

Instructor participation with students was measured by the interaction and guidance in discussion board questions, comments on graded student work, the amount of measured user time of the instructor while teaching online, and student evaluations. Studies have shown that students in those virtual classrooms who received the greatest influence by the professor exhibited the most sophisticated thinking and learning. It is critical that the instructor be available to facilitate and guide the threaded discussions and the virtual world activities in order to keep the students focused on the topic and to elicit cognitive involvement from them. The teacher must be both prepared and willing to guide the learners through this process of cognitive presence (Jonaitis, 2007). In the virtual world of online learning, instructors must maximize the importance of the reflective process, to encourage students to ponder and then effectively express their ideas and beliefs. In addition, INTASC and NCATE expect teachers to demonstrate the dispositions to provide learning opportunities that are specifically adapted to the needs of diverse learners (National Council, 2008).

Effective online and virtual world instructors demonstrate their presence by active involvement; this is based upon their availability to communicate with students on a regular basis. Their accessibility encourages students to communicate with them and be part of the cognitive process. Maintaining a dialogue or interaction online with students decreases the isolation that many students feel. Based upon two online classes using the one-month delivery format, with an average enrollment of 19 students per course, the effective professors sent 111 emails per class. The communications were primarily between the instructor and individual students. In addition, the instructors sent two to four whole-class emails per week.

Conversely, the ineffective instructors seldom demonstrated their presence by any involvement.

For example, one professor who did not participate in the class, with no email responses for the entire third week, emailed the class at the end of the week and stated, "I will attempt to make a contribution to your Unit IV discussion." At the end of the fourth week, at the close of the course, with no responses to students' discussions or emails during the week, he emailed the entire class again, stating, "I was unable to be more active in Unit IV as I have been spending time reading your work." The second instructor also commented to students that she was unable to respond to them in their discussions because she needed to spend her time grading their papers.

Many online classes use a virtual office which encourages students to post queries that the whole class has access to and which typically would be of interest to everyone, i.e. "Where can I find the verification form used during the classroom observations in a school?" or "Where can I find the rubrics used to grade the assignments?" Most questions were posted during the first week of class while students were familiarizing themselves with the online format. Many of the questions tended to be navigational concerns about where students could locate materials within the online course. Some resources were under the "Doc Sharing" tab while others were located under "Course Materials." All four classes had a virtual office and averaged 22 student questions per class. Students expect and want a speedy response; a student comment on the final course evaluation of one of the effective instructors captures the positive atmosphere that educators aspire to: "….. was always available to answer questions," which supports the need for online instructors to be available on a daily basis, ideally 24 hours a day, 7 days a week. Conversely, the virtual office of the less effective instructors was populated primarily by students responding to the concerns of other students, rather than the professors making responses to the class. When the professors did respond, it was with comments such as, "Check the syllabus."

Examination of user time was determined by the online course data collection program built into the course shell. This data is evidence of the active involvement and presence of the professor throughout the course. Time is typically devoted to engaging with students in activities such as: maintaining a strong presence on discussion boards by responding to student postings in a timely way, partaking in scheduled chats, and grading student assignments within five days or less of submission. The more effective professors for the two classes studied averaged 114 hours per class each month, whereas the less effective professors averaged 72 hours.

There are numerous means of communication that afford instructors the opportunity to reach out to students, including: introductory emails a week prior to the start of the online class to insure that students have their texts from the first day of class; online announcements that are visible and accessible throughout the course; discussion boards where personal stories and experiences can be cited within the context of the assignment; and virtual offices that answer student concerns with a timely reply from the instructor which decreases the anxiety levels of students. It is vital that instructors maintain a physical presence in the activities of a virtual environment. During these various online communications professors reveal their patience, tolerance, friendliness and enthusiasm. Effective educators utilize these means of communication with some degree of frequency, whereas ineffective ones generally do not.

The amount of measured user time of the instructor while teaching online in a virtual world is vastly greater than when teaching in a traditional classroom. Rather than waiting for the standard twice-weekly meetings, students in online classes want almost immediate responses to their concerns. The instructor is expected to respond to student queries at least within a twenty-four hour period. Even though the requested information may often be found in the syllabus or in other information already provided in the online course, students do not want to be told to look for it there. They want the professor to access that information for them and carefully explain it to them. Teaching in a virtual world involves waiting. Sometimes, it is necessary to give students time to reflect on knowing, or to make connections between academic learning and life experiences (Hendricken, 2004). This is important in helping students establish patterns of lifelong learners, and to help them differentiate between learning and experience.

Bandura's social learning theory is based on the concept that people are unable to learn for themselves, and require a model to help them establish their behavior. In a virtual world, students construct or learn their behavior by observing others, or "lurking" before acting. After observing the behavior of the instructor and classmates, students then have the opportunity to imitate behaviors that elicit positive reactions from others. Instructor participation during this modeling stage is vital, to establish acceptable criteria for class behavior (Smith & Berge, 2009).

TONE OF COMMUNICATION WITH STUDENTS

The tone of communication with students was measured by professor communications with students in the discussion boards, virtual office responses to student questions, and whole class as well as individual emails. This refers to both formal and non-formal communication opportunities. Participation in non-formal communications, such as virtual office questions and other student email questions, was generally the result of the learners' personal preferences. It can be very difficult to establish a personal connection without at least one face-to-face interaction. This is where the cyborg, avatar, puppet, or the surrogate which the student chooses can be effective. However it is achieved, the personal relationship that is developed between the professor and the student

is important in encouraging learner persistence (Jonaitis, 2007).

The tone of communication is critical; words and actions need to convey friendliness as well as enthusiasm. The online environment denies the reader the ability to interpret body language or to hear the tone of voice being used. The adage, "It's not what you say, it's how you say it," captures the essence of communication in cyberspace. A major drawback to comparing life in a virtual world to life in the real world, referring to Bandura's social learning theory, is that students are unable to imitate attitudes or emotional reactions exhibited by the participants (Smith & Berge, 2009).

The communications of many professors, particularly those who are considered effective, is enhanced with the inclusion of graphics, pictures, or actions which can convey an emphasis or a sense of humor along with a strong visual impact. When writing comments to students or grading their work, instructors should be encouraged to use the student's first name to make the constructive criticism less formal and austere. As a student stated in the course assessment, "I felt like there was a real person on the other side of the computer." Conversely, when a professor does not have a presence in the course, a student asked, "Why do we need a professor for this course? We could just get the book and learn by ourselves!"

Class Biographies during the first week of meetings are an opportunity for the professor and students to introduce themselves to each other and share a snapshot of their lives. One of the effective educator's biographies is called "Apples to Oranges" and sketches her lifetime journey from growing up in New York City to currently living in California. Another instructor uses a PowerPoint presentation with pictures of herself, her family, and her interests, accompanied by various audio effects. Many students scan photographs of their family which further personalizes their life stories. In a virtual world, teachers and students can use numerous ways to share a part of their lives, or the lives they wish to portray to the class. All participants gain personal insights and a sense of knowing the others. Conversely, the two less effective educators simply included their professional resumes, and did not respond at all to the student biographies.

For the past two years the two effective online instructors referred to in this chapter have been using telephonic communication as a means to personally interact with their students. Individual calls are made during the second week of class; typically, students are shocked and amazed when they discover who they are talking to. The telephone chats tend to be upbeat and encouraging. This friendly telephone call provides an opportunity to answer questions for the student as well as the instructor. Sometimes it affects retention, as students might be considering dropping the class, but are encouraged to remain enrolled. The students appreciate the personalized attention and time. This presents the professor with an opportunity to use the time for individual mentoring and coaching. On a course evaluation a student shares: "I applaud instructor....on making individual phone calls to all the students. This was a very effective way of creating rapport and getting to know one another. In fact it was a perfect example of a teacher role modeling how to motivate students; after I felt she knew me, I was eager to perform at my best to fulfill her high expectations of me!"

When commenting on student work, it is important for instructors to be aware of the tone of their writing. Professors need to recognize and acknowledge the level of cognitive development of the learners, as well as the learning capacity of each student. Not all students are in identical zones of proximal cognitive development (ZPD). The instructors must provide a safe learning environment that meets the developmental needs of the learners and nurtures and supports them in developing the appropriate strategies for success (Jonaitis, 2007; National Council, 2008).

Virtual worlds provide a means for making subject matter content accessible to all students, without prejudice toward their physical constraints or life styles. They are extensions of the communication exchanges of the material world. Approximately 50 to 200 million people use Second Life, multi-user virtual environments (MUVEs), and other virtual worlds (Anonymous, 2008; Springer, 2009). Physically coded social identity markers such as gender, age, race, and physical condition are eliminated in the world of cyberspace, freeing the individuals of such potentially limiting identifiers and enabling them to be imaginative and don their identities of choice in the less judgmental virtual world. Students can adopt their gender of choice; their desired age; and their form, whether it is animal, vegetable, or something out of science fiction. This selected protean self, cyborg, avatar, puppet, or surrogate is then projected into the virtual world of cyberspace (Pomeroy, 1996).

Participating in these virtual worlds has been shown to enhance the lives of people with physical disabilities, improving their fine motor skills, eye/hand coordination, and spatial awareness. People with physical disabilities may often be isolated, but in a virtual world they are able to communicate with others, and may or may not elect to reveal their personal limitations. Second Life enables speech recognition, and also provides individuals with the opportunity to change their physical status and appearance. Assistive technology users may participate in virtual classrooms without having classmates or the instructor aware of their physical constraints.

In the freedom that this virtual world provides, individuals are more likely to utilize their ambiguity and express themselves more freely than they might in the confines of the everyday world. It is important for instructors in online courses and virtual worlds to encourage this freedom of expression in ways that will enhance the communications within the class. Encouraging varying viewpoints and creating openness to new ideas is most evident to students based upon the tone of the instructor's writings and actions. This tone is very important. As an example, in commenting on student work, one of the less effective instructors accused this researcher/student of using sarcasm, and gave her a strongly worded lecture on appropriate behavior in a graduate class and warned her to behave properly if she ever wished to achieve on the graduate level. This was quite a surprise to the student, who was herself a university professor. No sarcasm on her part had been intended. Whereas face-to-face communications are accompanied by gestures and tone of voice, it is easy to misinterpret the written word or the actions of an avatar manipulated by a beginning student in virtual reality. Instructors should not make assumptions as to a student's intent, particularly if it is a negative assumption. This type of judgmental interpretation can seriously affect the tone of communication with students.

CREATION OF A COMMUNITY OF LEARNERS

For some individuals, because of their sexual proclivities or physical disabilities, conducting authentic lives in the real world can be difficult. However, in cyberspace, these sometimes limiting factors do not necessarily constrain them. Through virtual worlds, many people have found an increased sense of connectedness and belongingness, as well as higher self-esteem, optimism, and improved physical well-being. Some even lead more productive real world lives as a result of their experiences in the virtual world (Cabiria, 2008).

The creation of a community of learners online was measured by activities such as informal course announcements, media, emails, and student and professor biographies, indicating that the instructor is interested in each student. A critical component of learning is the social integration and interaction between students as well as between the professor and the students. However, there are several perspectives as to the definition of social integration and how it impacts the cognitive development of students in virtual

worlds and in online classes. Learning styles may have an effect on students' enjoyment of a class, but not on their participation. Online instruction and participation in a virtual world is not face-to-face instruction. Pedagogy that is effective in the traditional classroom does not always prove effective in the virtual environment. Instructors must utilize new and innovative strategies for online community development (Jonaitis, 2007).

In a study of undergraduate online learning, Jonaitis (2007) discovered the significance of participation by the instructor in the class as a vital aspect in encouraging a community of learners. Of utmost importance was the quality of the interaction. Students needed to know the instructor recognized them as individuals, and had an investment in their success and learning experience. The quality of the online experience is positively correlated with the human interactions present in the experience. Without this personal interaction and specialized attention, both professor and student can feel disconnected and isolated in cyberspace.

The creation of a community of learners in the online environment is dependent on all of the various means of communication studied during this research. However, it is the tone of the interactions that enhances the sense of community. The researchers strongly feel that the use of class biographies and telephone contact with students is the cornerstone to creating a community of learners online. The supportive instructor ensures that students have resources and materials readily available to them. These include: media, webliographies, models of assignments, grading rubrics and all necessary documents needed for students to successfully engage in the virtual world learning assignments and activities. These constantly need to be updated and monitored to present the most recent and relevant information to students.

Additionally, many instructors include synchronous activities, those that require all participants to be online at the same time. These two way audio experiences can take the form of chats or webconferencing; both encourage an open dialogue and personalize the sterile atmosphere of an online class. One of the effective online instructors conducted weekly synchronous chats, in which she responded to student concerns, discussed the class work, and personalized the online experience. However, depending on where the students are located this can be a scheduling challenge when dealing with international students who reside in different time zones. However, it certainly adds another dimension to communicating with students. The same is true of activities in a virtual world, where members interact with each other, and where actions are sometimes dependent on the reactions of others.

Asynchronous techniques allow students to log on at their convenience and include activities such as: threaded discussions, blogs, and wikis. Podcasts are an exciting way to have audio and visual components and can be an effective medium for lectures, so that students can actually hear their professor's voice. One of the effective instructors prepared PowerPoint presentations for the students, using her picture with animated eyes and lips, and her recorded voice talking to the students. Another way of sharing this personalization with students is through the use of various software programs, such as Crazy Talk, that combine animation with sound.

Educators recognize that the creation of a caring learning community positively affects student participation and enhances student success. When teaching in a traditional classroom many instructors employ teaching techniques and demonstrate personal attributes that engage students, which help to build a rapport between the professor and the students. Because it can be challenging to create this rapport in a virtual environment, an effective instructor must find alternative ways to engage the class. A student's comments on the course assessment provide a student perspective, "...the instructor made it a point to contact me and the rest of the class by phone to introduce herself and to meet me; in our exchange she gave

Table 1. Evaluation averages of effective and ineffective instructors

(Scale: 0-5) 0-Low, 5-High	EFFECTIVE EDUCATOR	INEFFECTIVE EDUCATOR
Grade Point Average of Students:	3.39	3.82
Student Self Assessment of Learning:	4.02	3.64
Student Assessment of Teaching:	4.46	2.81
Student Assessment of Course Content:	4.14	4.36

me some sage advice. She replied to everyone in the discussion boards every week, another first!"

Professor evaluations and feedback are an essential part of the reappointment and promotion cycle for faculty at institutions of higher learning. The following data were collected and compiled from a university course assessment that students are asked to complete the last week of class; however, participation is voluntary and anonymous. The data presented are based upon a five point scale, taken from the four focus online classes during the past eighteen months of this research. Two of the classes were taught by the effective instructors, and two by the less effective instructors. Resulting data from each of the two groups were averaged.

CONCLUSION

This chapter and research have examined exhibited dispositions and practices of effective online educators, active involvement by the instructor, the tone of communications with students, and the creation of a community of learners. The premise is that when these dispositions and practices are present and are evident to students, there will be greater student participation and satisfaction in online learning and virtual world environments. University assessment of effective online teaching in a virtual world is of utmost importance for professional improvement and effective program administration.

Teaching through the use of virtual worlds is going to become the new traditional format for online instructors and students enrolled in online classes. Second Life is only the forerunner in the development of MUVEs that will be used in distance education. Technology will ultimately afford users the opportunity to see, smell, hear, and feel things never before experienced by them in the real world. This is reminiscent of Aldous Huxley's (1932)*Brave New World*, where people were able to attend the movies, referred to as the feelies. By putting their hands on a bar across the front of their seats, audiences could see, smell, hear, and feel the same sensations experienced by the actors.

Harvard and Stanford Universities, among others, have virtual campus extensions in Second Life that are fully funded. The University of Baltimore has maintained hybrid classes, using both the traditional classroom and Second Life as an additional platform. With so many of today's students being proficient gamers, this Second Life platform is an excellent means of extending the learning environment beyond the traditional classroom. It affords both students and instructors the excitement and challenge of a game, combined with the opportunity to participate in class any time, from any place (Smith & Berge, 2009). The challenge for educators will be to find ways to present problem-solving scenarios that have realistic solutions and viable consequences while students are operating in an imaginary world.

The authors would like to offer some suggestions for those educators who are teaching online and using virtual environments. Before the class begins, email the students, welcoming them to the class and providing them with a course syllabus with the required texts, activities, and other necessary information. When the course begins, provide a rubric or rubrics for assessing assignments, and models of the student coursework. Provide guidelines for acceptable avatar behavior in a virtual world. Offer a personalized instructor biography, not merely an impersonal resume. Most importantly, have a positive presence in the class. Give yourself permission to enjoy the thrill of the game and the challenge of the new and exciting experience.

REFERENCES

Anonymous. (2008). Living a second life online. *Newsweek, 152*(4).

Bandura, A. (1979). Self-referent mechanisms in social learning theory. *The American Psychologist, 34*(5), 439–441. doi:10.1037/0003-066X.34.5.439.b

Cabiria, J. (2008). *A Second Life: Online virtual worlds as therapeutic tools for gay and lesbian people.* (Doctoral dissertation). Fielding Graduate University, Santa Barbara, CA.

Giovanelli, M. (2003). Relationship between reflective dispositions toward teaching and effective teaching. *The Journal of Educational Research, 96*(5), 293–309. doi:10.1080/00220670309597642

Hay, A., Hodgkinson, M., Peltier, J., & Drago, W. (2004). Interaction and virtual learning. *Strategic Change, 13*(4), 193–204. doi:10.1002/jsc.679

Helm, C. (2006). The assessment of teacher dispositions. *Clearing House (Menasha, Wis.), 79*(6), 237–240. doi:10.3200/TCHS.79.6.237-239

Hendricken, V. (2004). From teaching to mentoring: Principle and practice, dialogue and life in adult education. *Journal of Distance Education, 19*(2), 93–98.

Huxley, A. (1932). *Brave new world.* London, UK: Chatto and Windus.

Jonaitis, S. (2007). Learner control in undergraduate online learning: Instructor perspectives. (Doctoral dissertation). Michigan State University, East Lansing, MI.

McKnight, D. (2004). An inquiry of NCATE's move into virtue ethics by way of dispositions (Is this what Aristotle meant?). *Educational Studies, 35*(3), 212–230.

National Council for Accreditation of Teacher Education. (2008). *Professional standards for the accreditation of teacher preparation institutions*.

Pomeroy, S. (1996). Gendered places, virtual spaces: A feminist geography of cyberspace. (Doctoral dissertation). University of California, Berkeley, CA.

Reynolds, T. (2007). *Identifying and measuring educator effectiveness dispositions in online teaching.* Paper presented at the meeting of the International Council for Education on Teaching, San Diego, CA.

Smith, M., & Berge, Z. (2009). Social learning theory in Second Life. *Merlot Journal of Online Learning and Teaching, 5*(2).

Springer, R. (2009). Speech in a virtual world. *Speech Technology, 14*(5), 42–43.

KEY TERMS AND DEFINITIONS

Asynchronous: Digital communication not happening at the same time.

Dispositions: A habit, or tendency to act in a specific way.

Lurking Presence: The state of watching the activity in a virtual world, before taking action. Frequently practiced by beginning users in virtual worlds.

MUVEs: Multi-user virtual environments or worlds.

Second Life: A three-dimensional virtual world, where users can create and manipulate an avatar and a fantasy world.

Synchronous: Digital communication happening at the same time.

Virtual Ethics: Incorporates dispositions as a tendency to act in an ethical manner.

Virtual Office: A feature in the Blackboard platform that enables students to ask questions of the professor about class requirements, procedures, etc. The questions and responses, from the professor as well as from other students, can be viewed by the entire class.

Chapter 7
Signs and Guideposts:
Expanding the Course Paradigm with Virtual Worlds

Keysha I. Gamor
ICF International, USA

ABSTRACT

Experiential learning has long been touted as critical to deep understanding, learning, and ownership of knowledge. Technology has ushered in many new ways for people to interact; a virtual world is one such category of technological tools that enhance engagement in a learning experience. Using a virtual world for instruction does not and should not be an 'all or nothing' proposition. Virtual worlds are flexible, rich, collaborative environments which can be used in a variety of ways to augment a traditional, instructor-led course, Web-based courses, and other types of courseware, in addition to serving as a 'stand-alone' solution. Grounded in experiential learning and constructivist theory, this chapter explores ways in which one may exploit the flexibility of a virtual world to meet the real-life demands of traditional courses.

Mankind likes to think in terms of extreme opposites. It is given to formulating its beliefs in terms of Either-OR's, between which it recognizes no intermediate possibilities. When forced to recognize that the extremes cannot be acted upon, it is still inclined to hold that they are all right in theory but that when it comes to practical matters circumstances compel us to compromise.

Educational philosophy is no exception. –Dewey ~ Experience and Education, 1938

Tell me, and I will forget. Show me, and I may remember. Involve me, and I will understand. –Confucius ~ 450 BC

DOI: 10.4018/978-1-60960-545-2.ch007

INTRODUCTION

Experiential learning has long been touted as critical to deep understanding, learning, and ownership of knowledge (Dewey, 1938; Dede, 2007; Kolb, 1984a). Technology has ushered in many new ways for people to interact; a virtual world is one such category of technological tools that enhance the way in which we may engage in a learning experience. Some believe that in order to use a virtual world in a 'mature manner', one must evolve to using the virtual world to do 'work'. While our definitions on 'work' may differ, it is essential to simply use the virtual world to solve whatever challenge it is suited to address. Using a virtual world for instruction does not and should not be an 'all or nothing' proposition. Virtual worlds are flexible, rich, collaborative environments which can be used in a variety of ways to augment a traditional, instructor-led course in addition to serving as a 'stand-alone' solution. Virtual worlds provide a unique environment for problem finding because they provide a multisensory, immersive, graphically rich way to represent an authentic environment, communicate, collaborate, coexist, and co-create with other participants (Gamor, in press; Holden, Westfall & Gamor, 2010). This chapter explores ways in which one may exploit the flexibility of a virtual world to meet the real-life demands of traditional learning situations.

BACKGROUND

Rather than starting from a blank screen, the author applies theories, methodologies, models and other constructs that have (in some cases) been used for decades in developing traditional instructor-led courses, courseware, and web-based courses. In some cases, the theories, methodologies, models, and other constructs have been modified in order to expand them to the new modality under discussion: virtual worlds.

As with any technology, it is important to apply lessons learned in order to optimize the use of the new tool under consideration. In this case, appropriate lessons learned are drawn from learning theorists (such as John Dewey, Benjamin Bloom, and David Kolb), instructional methodologies or models (such as TRADOC Levels of Interactivity and the 3D Learning Maturity Model), and other constructs (such as the Push-Pull Paradigm). While it is out of the scope of this chapter to address every relevant theory, methodology, model, or other construct, salient points from each of the issues foundational to this chapter are discussed from the perspective of a select, representative few. Specifically, experiential learning theory is pivotal to understanding the *power* of a 3D world and the instructional design *responsibility* necessary to achieve optimal immersive learning experiences. Awareness of instructional methodologies and instructional design considerations is critical for conceptualizing virtual worlds as an instructional tool. Knowledge of relevant learning models help to contextualize the affordances of virtual worlds into a familiar framework, and new constructs designed around the newer media used in the classrooms today can help to light a path for educators trying to figure out how to use the technology rather than have the technology become yet another box to check.

From John Dewey (1938) to David Kolb (1984a; 1984b), theorists have described experiential learning as educational events in which the participant's subjective experience is fundamental to the learning process. In this sense, it is not just about 'what is presented', but about 'how a learner interacts with the what'. Equally important, it is also about how the learner applies the newly acquired knowledge to other experiences. Experiential learning models are not in scarcity and are the subject of renewed discourse given recent developments and advancements in social media and immersive learning technologies.

In one case in particular, researchers have borrowed from the concept of a process improvement

Figure 1. Comparison of the TRADOC Levels of Interactivity and the 3D Learning Maturity Model

LEVELS OF INTERACTIVITY	3D LEARNING MATURITY LEVEL	COMPARATIVE DESCRIPTION
Level 1 - Passive.	Maturity Level 1- Mimicking Existing Classroom Structures	• The student acts solely as a receiver of information. Students read or listen to information. • Avatars sit in classroom/auditorium seats, raise their hands and wait to be called. They receive information from the lecturer. Learning focuses on facts, terminology, and other types of declarative knowledge.
Level 2 - Limited participation	Maturity Level 2- Expansion of Existing Learning Structures	• The student makes simple responses to instructional cues. • Avatar participation would be in the form of guided tours, scavenger hunts, or some type of group work. Used for providing declarative knowledge as well as providing examples.
Level 3 - Complex participation.	Maturity Level 3- Practicing the Authentic Task	• The student makes a variety of responses using varied techniques in response to instructional cues. • Avatars engage in role play, process practices, or some other decision-making exercises/simulations. Useful for soft skills, procedural, or psychomotor skills practice.
Level 4 - Real-time participation.	Maturity Level 4- Working	• The student is directly involved in a life-like set of complex cues and responses. • Avatars work together within the 3D space to create a product. They are involved in problem solving and social networking.

model (the CMMI capability maturity model) to structure a concept of learning into a progressively interactive learning framework titled the "3D Learning Maturity Model" (Kapp & O'Driscoll, 2010). This is a useful construct to the extent that the level of interactivity that is designed into the design of a virtual world requires a mature understanding of the power and affordances of the tool. Once this basic understanding is attained, then designers can create worlds that scaffold learning using levels of interactivity as a conduit.

While the Kapp and O'Driscoll model was designed for a 3D immersive learning environment as the medium, it is remarkably similar to the TRADOC Levels of Interactivity model which was designed to structure an understanding of interactivity in courseware development (Department of Defense [DoD], 2001). Thus, it would probably be useful to compare the Kapp and O'Driscoll model to the TRADOC model since the latter offers a bridge to the familiar. The U. S. Army Training and Development Command

developed the TRADOC Levels of Interactivity to define standard expectations regarding interactivity for courseware development. This framework has been adapted many times over, but the basic tenets are essentially the same. (The author of this chapter limits this comparison to interactivity and excludes navigation considerations due to space limitations. See Figure 1, Comparison of the TRADOC Levels of Interactivity and the 3D Learning Maturity Model.)

A closer examination of the two models provides some degree of relief as it is evident that Kapp and O'Driscoll apparently considered lessons learned from the training and development industry in the design of their new model. The Kapp and O'Driscoll 3D Learning Maturity Model addresses the general attributes of the environment itself and maps the attribute to the level of interactivity it enables. For instance, in keeping with TRADOC's Level 1 as passive, the 3D Learning Maturity Level 1 is described as one that often immerses avatars a facsimile of a real-life classroom or lecture hall environment. Given this physical attributes of the 'passive' virtual environment, it also takes on the traditional expectations and norms of a real-life classroom environment, thus shunning, to some extent, the affordances which make virtual worlds unique and worthwhile in the first place. TRADOC's Level 2 calls for limited participation in the form of information recall and limited response to instructional cues. Similarly, 3D Learning Maturity Level 2 outlines a little more interactivity in the form of scavenger hunts and guided tours, for example. Again, the affordances of a virtual learning environment have not been realized fully at this level although this level would probably yield a more memorable experience than that which is attainable from Level 1. Level 3 of TRADOC's Level of Interactivity model stipulates complex participation, which is discussed in terms of as role playing and communication. The 3D Learning Maturity Level 3 specifies that maturity at this level involves practicing the authentic task. Both models identify participation at this level as engaging in role play, practicing a process or some other simulated real-life experience which may be encountered in the real world. Finally, at TRADOC's Level 4, the Army identifies this as real-time participation. Generally, this was possible via a blended learning approach, which may include a simulation-based asynchronous and/or live synchronous instruction (DoD, 2010). 3D Learning Maturity Level 4 is simply defined as 'Work'. While 'work' could be defined in many ways, Kapp and O'Driscoll labeled it as a discrete event or series of events leading to a final product or deliverable.

It appears as though there is yet another maturity level that could be used to expand the 3D Learning Maturity Model. Perhaps the highest level of maturity in a 3D synchronous learning environment is not an event at all, but rather the institutionalization of the environment itself into the toolset of the organization. In other words, the highest maturity level currently achievable in a 3D virtual immersive environment is when the environment itself becomes part of how the organization does business or how student cohorts work together to provide multiple types of peer support beyond their initial, common educational experience. In this sense, the interaction is not a single event nor is the intent to reach some specific end in and of itself. The purpose of the environment is to facilitate a type and level of interaction on an ongoing basis that is necessary for carrying out business at the targeted level and in the desired manner.

For example, a tool such as Green Phosphor's Glasshouse has as its primary objective to be a 3D data analytical workspace—to be a 21st century business tool which enables users to view and manipulate data in ways never before possible. Since the software acts as a sort of middleware, it is platform agnostic. The CICP code was developed to ensure the tool's compatibility with any virtual world. Using this tool as an example, Glasshouse is a space wherein data analysts could meet together to view data and drill down into it. They could make predictions and find relationships that would normally remain hidden in 2D data. Such a tool has the power to revolutionize how data analysis occurs today. It could also help to address the huge gap in available, qualified data analysts since lesser experienced analysts could find patterns or make discoveries and share them with more experienced or expert analysts for input and analysis. In this case, the Glasshouse appliance is used as a learning environment, a training environment, and a business tool.

In a higher education context, a 3D space at the proposed maximum level of maturity could be a 3D social network which may have started out by an instructor whose intent was to have students incrementally build a world relevant to their specific domain. Through the act of co-creation, instructor facilitation, peer-to-peer support, and community building evolve as well. Perhaps this activity was conceived as a discrete task for a specific course but expanded when the stakeholders discovered the power and value that could lie within should they envision the world's mature state as a dynamic place for people committed to a particular course of study or major to experience the program, helping one another along the way and experiencing a wide range of course activities, events, and communities within the world. One such example is Appalachian State University's AppEdTech Virtual Community based upon a proprietary version of ActiveWorlds virtual world platform. AET Zone is described as a learning community that supports faculty, students, and alumni affiliated with the graduate Instructional Technology, Library Science, Curriculum and Instruction, and Educational Administration programs. (Bronack et al., 2008a). AET Zone researchers report that:

...sections of the same class as well as sections of different classes are working together to discuss issues in each other's schools and districts.... [S]tudents are much more engaged in authentic conversations, projects and tasks than we had experienced before. We attribute this to the development of wider communities of practitioners working together in the 3D world. (Gilman, Tashner, Bronack, Riedl, & Cheney, 2007)

Among the important lessons learned, ΛET Zone researchers recommend the following guiding principles:

- **Consider the principle of least effort***(Don't use virtual worlds when a simpler method would suffice.)*
- **Design spaces thematically***(Take advantage of the opportunity to contextualize learning in a graphically rich space, immersing participants in an experience.)*
- **Promote presence***(Create opportunities for participants to interact with one another and the environment.)*
- **Understand human behavior***(Apply lessons learned from online learning and*

adult learning theories at a minimum.) (Bronack, Cheney, Riedl, & Tashner, 2008b).

(Note: The author of this chapter added parenthetical comments.)

Analyzing the experience of learning in 3D through a comparison of the TRADOC Levels of Interactivity and the 3D Learning Maturity models is useful, but there are additional frameworks that may also provide lessons learned to help use a virtual world more effectively. Bloom's Taxonomy is a tried and true classification framework defining how people think and learn according to three domains: cognitive, affective, and psychomotor. With more emphasis on the six cognitive levels of complexity, it identifies the most complex levels as analysis, synthesis, and evaluation. This classification helped to identify what we now know as higher order thinking skills (HOTS) and how they map to learning objectives (Bloom, 1956). Using Bloom's Taxonomy can be a valuable lens through which to view learning in 3D immersive environments, such as virtual worlds. Anderson and Krathwohl's (2001) and Forehand's (2005) revisions of Bloom's Taxonomy centered on terminology, structure and emphasis, and the efforts helped to frame the cognitive, affective, and psychomotor domains within the context of action verbs. While none of these components fit neatly into a little box, Figure 2 illustrates the similarities and synergies among a selection of relevant frameworks within the context of an experiential learning model.

Kolb's Experiential Learning Theory is designed as an iterative model. While a learning experience could be designed to follow each 'step' in a linear manner, any one of the steps could be a starting point for a 3D learning experience. Likewise, a 'concrete experience', for instance, does not have to be 'passive' or 'mimic a classroom'. Figure 2 shows one way to view the frameworks when juxtaposed against one another. They are interconnected and useful in

Figure 2. Comparison of frameworks relevant to learning in virtual worlds

Experiential Learning	Concrete Experience	Reflective Observation	Abstract Conceptualization	Active Experimentation	
Levels of Interactivity	Passive	Limited Participation	Complex participation	Real-time participation	
3D Learning Maturity Model (*Expanded*)	Mimic classroom	Expand existing Structure	Practice task	Work	Operational Institutionalization
Bloom's Taxonomy	Remember	Understand	Apply Analyze Evaluate	Apply Analyze Evaluate Create	Apply Analyze Evaluate Create

Ideal VW Learning Experience

conceptualizing the design of a 3D learning experience. There is also the glaring observation that, like web-based training, 3D immersive learning environments, such as virtual worlds, also offer a range of interactivity which should be considered within the context of the learning objectives and affordances of the environment.

VIRTUAL WORLDS AS PART OF AN INSTRUCTIONAL TOOLKIT

Understanding the lessons learned from early theorists and scholars help to illuminate the way ahead for newer technologies. While there is a requirement to expand some of the early theories, models, and other constructs, there is no need to start from nothing. In the same vein, it is also unnecessary to discard existing learning assets. Just as there is no 'one size fits all virtual world', there is also no one size fits all tool or application for teaching and learning. Indeed virtual worlds are just an addition to our toolkit. It is, therefore, critical to determine how to incorporate it into an already functioning instructional approach. An examination of existing tools and goals will help to determine how a virtual world could be incorporated into an existing course or learning experience.

Figure 3. Educational Uses of Social Media & Virtual Worlds. Educational Uses of Selected Social Media Tools illustrates direction and temporal attributes of social media and immersive environments

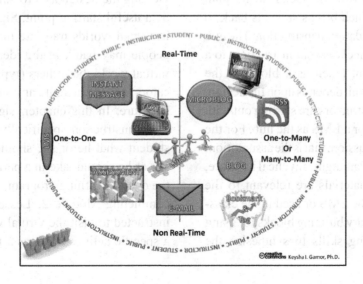

Figure 4. The Push-Pull Paradigm is based on the Concept of Purposeful Resource Integration

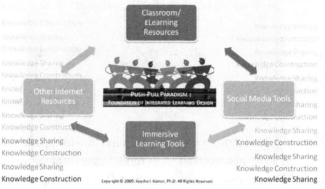

The concept for integrating virtual worlds into an existing course, online curricula and/or social media plan is based on a construct the author calls the Push-Pull Paradigm (Figure 4).

This construct assumes an integrated approach to applying curriculum materials for a course, wherein learning resources, social media, and internet resources are well conceived in order to push students outside the learning management system (LMS) or classroom toward other resources in a just-in-time/learner-centered manner as well as to nudge them toward their peers and external experts as resources. The relevancy of resources and design of the social media plan creates the 'pull' which brings students back to the 'hub' for the foundational instruction. The hub can be anything from classroom instruction, to a social media element (such as a blog), to the virtual world itself. It all depends upon the design. In most all cases, instructors are starting out with a traditional course or a LMS as the hub. For the purposes of this discussion, that is the assumption. Since the Push-Pull Paradigm is cyclical in nature, all resources and materials are relevant to the materials stored in the LMS or used in the classroom and are necessary building blocks for using higher order thinking skills to synthesize the

material learned on one's own with a broader, contextualized understanding of the learning objectives of the course. See Figure 5.

A key point to remember: Social media or technology without an objective is just something else to do. Relevance is critical to acceptance, compliance, interest, motivation, and engagement.

Signs and Guideposts in Virtual Worlds

In order to achieve any one of the implementation solutions to be described later in this section, viewing the design as a roadmap metaphor may be a useful starting point. Signs and guideposts in virtual worlds translate into structure. Many people may baulk at the idea of structure in a virtual world, but others (typically trained educators) cannot imagine any world without some structure. In this chapter, signs are defined as direct instruction specifically explaining to the student what he or she should do or what path she or he should take in a particular sequence in the overall learning program. For example, after completing Module 2, Lesson 3, students are instructed to visit the virtual world to engage in a specific activity, such as a tour or a role-play

Figure 5. The Push-Pull Paradigm encourages the use of multiple resources to foster the development of a balanced, well-rounded understanding of a concept, topic, and theme. This construct is applicable to social media and immersive learning tools

Creating lasting effects of learning require the use of many different devices from the instructional designer's toolkit. Social networking tools have become critical instruments in helping learners construct and share knowledge.

Uses of social networking tools in the traditional or virtual classroom have to be designed around an understanding of the power of social networking software to help build the community that will share them. To do this, an instructional designer must be aware of web cultures, values, and practices that constitute the reality of how communities commonly use such applications.

If implemented properly, social networking tools have the power to become an extension of the learners' reality construct, thereby making the educational uses of these tools plug in more naturally into their ways of viewing the tools' value, not only as a social tool, but also as an educational resource. This results in an extension of the traditional or virtual classroom, enabling learning and knowledge construction to occur in myriad ways inside and outside the formal course construct.

Realistic applications of social networking tools to conduct authentic transactions and to do actual work is paramount to their successful implementations in a course. Otherwise, they become little more than just another task that has to be done.

Indeed, carefully crafted, social networks developed with a specific course in mind can extend into an ongoing system of peer-to-peer support that will persist long after the formal course event has ended. Most educators yearn for their students not only to construct knowledge, but also to evolve into lifelong learners who are building necessary skills they can use in other courses, on their jobs, and in their personal lives.

© 2009 Keysha I. Gamor, Ph.D. May be used with attribution to author

exercise. Guideposts, on the other hand, are like guardrails that keep the student from falling off course too far. An example of a guidepost might be note cards, objects, bots or other element that is strategically programmed and placed into the virtual world for the specific purpose of providing support, facilitating a particular train of thought. While this strategy is not prescriptive, as with the signs previously described, it is facilitative and somewhat structured. Although the intent of a virtual world is to help the students explore, adult learning theory tells us that learners have limited time and need to have some understanding of what is expected of them. Learning experiences can be designed to provide both freedom and seemingly endless learning opportunities without overwhelming lack of structure and clarity. Indeed, in the 'real-world' we enjoy the comforts of signs and guideposts all the time without losing the depth of experience that life has to offer. We have the option of heeding them and depending upon them as little or much as we deem necessary. The same is true of virtual worlds.

A learning experience in a virtual world can be designed to (1) Augment existing training material managed through a Learning Management System (LMS), taking on similar, high level structure (activity, lesson, module, course) for content management purposes. This design can include simple simulations or embody an entire learning experience through an extended combination of learning opportunities, utilizing a wide variety of instructional strategies designed to optimize goal achievement (such as, a course equivalent); or (2) Serve as a discrete, stand-alone instructional or collaborative event, (such as, a meeting, workshop, seminar, or conference).

The rest of this section details the ways in which virtual worlds can be incorporated into an existing learning program, with a traditional classroom or LMS as the hub. The section begins with the simplest approach and progresses to the most complex implementation.

Augment Existing Training

Learning doesn't have to mimic chapters or sections of a book. While applying a modularized approach to designing virtual learning experiences is not ill-advised, it will somewhat limit the

Figure 6. 3D Immersive Environment Implementation Continuum Illustrates the Range of Uses of Virtual Worlds in a Learning Program

possibilities of what you can do in so far as your treatments become more of discrete events, posing a bit like learning simulations. There's nothing *wrong* with this approach, but virtual worlds can offer so much more with a little more analysis and planning. That being said, this 'modularized' approach may be a good one for helping to build a bridge to the familiar for your learners and to help you adjust to designing learning opportunities for virtual worlds. It is also a good way to phase in virtual worlds into an existing learning program, priming both your culture and your design staff for immersive learning, as well as mining your content for suitable objectives and applications. More than likely, you already have a LMS with content that your organization has invested in significantly. In this case, in your proof of concept phase, you should design your program such that virtual worlds are used to enhance the existing learning experience with opportunities to collaborate with peers, foster higher order thinking skills in your target population, and help to build a community amongst your intended audience.

Starting with what we already know about course development and sequencing content may help instructors and instructional designers use virtual worlds to augment existing curricula and discover unique, meaningful uses of virtual worlds. The 3D Immersive Environment Implementation Continuum shown in Figure 6 illustrates how virtual worlds can be used to support various components of a learning curriculum.

The Virtual World Implementation Continuum illustrates that there are multiple possibilities for how virtual worlds may be used in a learning environment. Whether applied in traditional, face-to-face classroom or e-learning settings, the unique

affordances of virtual worlds can enrich most any learning experience. Using virtual worlds in a learning context does not have to be an "all or nothing" proposition. Indeed, there is a risk of losing some of the inherent benefits of virtual worlds (persistence and community-building through co-existence and collaboration) when applied in an ad hoc manner; however, when the decision to use this implementation approach is confirmed, it should have little impact on the overall experience since the requirement may not have underscored these specific affordances (persistence and long-term community-building) as critical for goals set forth in the needs analysis. A closer examination and understanding of each implementation option will help to refine the requirements even further.

Activity

Through the use of Immersive Activity Objects (also thought of as Discrete Learning Events), virtual worlds provide a platform for experiential activities that illustrate, for example, a concept that can be applied in a real-world scenario in-world or in context. This use of virtual worlds is supplemental and would be suitable for augmenting instructor-led or e-learning courses. Using virtual worlds in this manner adds another dimension to a blended-learning solution that gives learners the opportunity to conduct several higher-order thinking skills at once by using practice, replay, multiple perspectives, role playing, metacognitive analysis, review/dialog, and feedback. This use of virtual worlds could be compared to a simulation with the added dimensions of coexistence and persistence. A virtual world environment enables many participants serving in different roles as many times as they would like. The world remains as the group leaves it, facilitating review, analysis, and reflection. Imagine recording sessions and using them with different classes, offering participants the opportunity to consider multiple perspectives other than those presented in their immediate learning event. Imagine the benefit of having the opportunity to discover and/or solve another problem that resulted from the decisions made in the previously experienced event. In this sense, learning is not disjointed, but fluid—just like real life, with real consequences but with low risk. Using your entire integrated learning foundation, you might find your students microblogging (tweeting) about events in the virtual world, quoting or paraphrasing material from a LMS resource, building creative responses to assignments, collaborating across course sections and more. This is a snapshot of a fully functional, well-integrated learning framework design.

Lesson

You may find that your instructional requirements analysis indicates that your target audience is having challenges in a particular area. Let us assume that the problem is with a complex, abstract concept and that the content in your LMS does not appear to be helping your learners reach the level of competence that your goals define. This is a great opportunity to examine whether or not virtual worlds may help. You could start out with one discrete activity as a 'pilot' and phase in transitioning the entire learning event to virtual worlds if the outcomes from your analysis and your 'pilot' support such action. This is not an activity or knowledge check equivalent. Facilitating an entire lesson in a virtual world could be valuable if, for example, the main goal of the lesson is based on situated cognition. For instance, in a course on harassment (while students could read about the harassment laws, scenarios, and anecdotes) constructing a personal understanding would best come from experience.

Build consequences into the scenario and the student motivation will likely peak as focus grows more intent. Sound like a game? This is no game, for in real-life, consequences result from our actions. It is better to learn how to analyze a scenario, identify a problem, and solve the problem in an environment where the cost of failure is lower than to experience them in real life where the cost is generally exponentially higher and more difficult to correct. In the case of experiencing the world of harassment within a virtual environment, on the other hand, failure (according to experiential learning theory) simply provides more learning opportunities and increased knowledge transfer to the real world (Kolb, 1984a, 1984b).

Module

Some content may benefit from having an entire immersive module. In these cases, the content is such that reading about it and discussing it alone does not provide a meaningful, memorable, personal understanding of it. For instance, experiencing a module on Interacting with the Press would have much more meaning than just reading one. What does it mean to: "Be careful about your choice of words when speaking to members of the press?" or "Can seemingly innocent comments put people or a country at risk?" These concepts are not easy to express in words only. Crafting a realistic scenario wherein students can participate in and examine an interview from multiple perspectives would enable them to understand the complexities of both monitoring one's own words and behavior, and also being aware of the words and behavior of those surrounding them. Such a design requirement would also necessitate an opportunity for practice. Role playing, in addition to observation, would be a useful exercise. Participants could be divided into teams to design a scenario. Afterwards, they could present their scenario, asking the observers to predict behaviors and outcomes as they go along.

Learning facilitators could contribute by sharing real interviews from the Internet and discussing the salient issues. There are many options when there is an instructional need to provide first-hand experience in order to understand and construct personal knowledge about a given topic. Learning facilitators could bring in expert interviewers as part of the immersive experience. Last, but not least, a feedback session provides opportunities for reflection. To conceive of an entire module in a virtual world need only start with a story. What is the narrative or theme of the module? What components must be designed and developed to make the environment realistic and authentic? What characters are involved? What emotion, logic, or ethical issues are pertinent to the module? How will ethos, logos and pathos be represented thematically? Can you have your students help to build the module as part of their learning experience? In other words, is it possible for you to modularize the construction of your module? If so, what should students build in order to accomplish the objectives of the module? Careful planning will ensure the commitment of your students and success of the experience.

Course

The author defines a course or an extended learning experience as a set of immersive events centered on an overall course goal and a specific set of learning objectives. Under what circumstances would it be useful to facilitate an entire course or extended learning experience in a virtual world? Virtual worlds would significantly benefit a course or learning experience whose objectives are bound to higher order thinking skills that require analysis, synthesis, and evaluation opportunities. A good example is viewing a "course" as an evolving group of learning experiences designed to help learners gain first-hand experience in analyzing defect detection; predicting outcomes of accurate and inaccurate detection skills; and testing alternate actions. Further, incorporating a knowledge support network in an extended learning experience by inviting subject matter experts, former learners, or participants representing multiple perspectives may build a community that could continue well after the formal "course" construct has come to an end rather than simply as a discrete set of learning experiences. The group dynamic should not be underestimated (Johnson & Johnson, 1996), especially in virtual worlds, for it is a prime environment for many learners to come together simultaneously in a graphically rich, interactive context. In this case, learners continue to have access to an environment that could serve as an environment wherein they can refresh skills, volunteer as a mentor, and share real-life experiences. In addition, such a learning experience can provide instructors and learners more context and performance-specific feedback during the experience, rather than simply the didactic responses typically seen at the end of online instruction events. Since the feedback occurs during the learning process, rather than after, learners can analyze the feedback and make necessary modifications as they go through the experience. These are powerful benefits of immersive learning in virtual worlds, but how much more effective would it be if the world encompassed the very tools used to conduct the work in the 'real world'. In this case, the instructional and learning tool is also the business tool. This would enhance transfer of knowledge to the real work setting since there is no learning curve to master pertaining to the job tasks.

Offering a course entirely in a virtual world brings with it many opportunities to challenge the way we teach and learn in order to work smarter. Given the technologies designed to improve productivity, access, and communication, it is time that the affordances of these technologies used drive the way they are applied. In the world of 'contact hours for course credit' having some construct for calculating the level of effort required for successful course completion is important. While the previous construct may be helpful in assisting course developers calculate level of effort necessary, contact hours required, and equivalent credit hours, it does not (and should not) have to dictate the design of the course or extended learning experience itself.

Program

An entire learning program is normally comprised of a variety of media and resources applied within a set of learning experiences designed to address multiple, related subjects. The main thrust of a program can benefit from having a virtual world as its central platform if higher order thinking skills, context, and/or access to experts are critical. Consider a "town hall, student union, cohort, or conference hall" metaphor. The virtual world could serve as a meeting place, learning platform, or a place organized around themes, which facilitators and participants generate, develop, and maintain. David Jonassen and colleagues (1995), leaders in constructivist learning theory and methods maintain that "constructivist environments engage learners in knowledge construction through collaborative activities that embed learning in meaningful context and through reflection on what has been learned through conversation with other learners" (p. 13). With this model, the interactions may be directly and indirectly evaluated within the community to understand a learner's individual performance. Instead, perhaps these interactions will be evident from the performance observed during the specific learning events or experiences comprising the overall course or program. Using this construct, the virtual world becomes the 'learning or communications portal', the central place for all activities associated with a comprehensive learning experience. As discussed earlier in this chapter, some institutions are already experienc-

ing unparalleled success with this implementation option.

Design Discrete Collaborative Events

As an instructional designer, learning manager, project manager or instructor, you may find that your requirements only indicate that replacing your webinars, meetings, and conferences with their virtual equivalents is ideal. Cost savings due to reduced travel, decreased employee time spent away from the office, and interest in broadening your audience base may be indicators that make virtual worlds an appealing option. Perhaps you do not wish to have an extended experience beyond the discrete event (i.e., you're not interested in building a community), and you are unsure whether or not you want to archive such events for later reference. With virtual worlds, you have the option of doing either or both.

Virtual worlds are also attractive as analytical workspaces because you can summarize, analyze, and calculate data faster and in a graphically rich, 3D space, enabling one to examine the data from multiple perspectives with multiple participants. The shape, structure, and flow of your 'course equivalent' or collaborative event entirely depend upon your goals and objectives. You can develop experiences to augment existing training, create collaborative events to a broader audience, or provide unique opportunities for staff to analyze data in 3D.

In any case, it is critical to conduct a thorough requirements analysis first. A Gartner press release (2008) indicated that 9 out of 10 virtual worlds programs fail within 18 months of launch due to lack of planning and identification of concrete requirements. Whatever implementation option your analysis supports, remember to take advantage of the inherent attributes of your 3D immersive learning space to create a meaningful, memorable learning experience.

FUTURE RESEARCH DIRECTIONS

Future research in virtual worlds could take on myriad directions. Indeed, there are a great deal of questions to be answered and discoveries to be made. However, there are some basic concerns which should be considered in the near term in order to help facilitate the continued growth and adoption of this technology.

Currently, many virtual world projects are still in a pilot or proof of concept phase. It is necessary that, as an industry, lessons learned are shared across sectors. DoD and higher education institutions are leading the way ahead in the use of virtual worlds. To avoid inadvertently duplicating effort or, worse yet, repeating the same mistakes, perhaps a national initiative could help to foster collaboration.

Costing models also present significant barriers to entry. In order to avoid similar business challenges that LMS vendors faced, it is also critical that the virtual world clients help shape new pricing structures so that access is aligned with a variety of use models, thus making the tool more accessible to small and large organizations or individuals.

Finally, as end users, we must help identify ways this medium can become part of the institution—not as tool, but as part of the culture and nature of the work we do. It may be a lofty goal, but imagine a tool that accomplishes what e-mail, the Internet, and the SmartPhone still attempt: to work smarter, not necessarily harder. Why not train on the very tools we will use for real work?

CONCLUSION

Virtual worlds can be used in a traditional classroom setting as effectively as they can be used as a total learning design approach. Frameworks exist which can help us to make 'sticky' virtual worlds in much the same way as we learned to create and why we should create sticky web sites. Theories and models on learning and communication which have stood the test of time can be brought to bear in identifying methodologies for developing meaningful, memorable learning experiences in virtual worlds. The best way to learn about virtual worlds is through experience. Get an account and an avatar and start dreaming of ways to transform the experiences associated with your courses. Analyze thoroughly, plan well, start small, but aim big. The 3D immersive learning environment is a critical 21st century learning medium, and today, we help to shape the future of learning.

REFERENCES

Anderson, L. W., & Krathwohl, D. R. (Eds.). (2001). *A taxonomy for learning, teaching, and assessing: A revision of Bloom's taxonomy of educational objectives.* New York, NY: Longman.

Bloom, B., & Englehart, M. Furst, E., Hill, W., & Krathwohl, D. (1956). *Taxonomy of educational objectives: The classification of educational goals. Handbook I: Cognitive domain.* New York, NY, Toronto, Canada: Longmans, Green.

Bronack, S., Cheney, A., Riedl, R., & Tashner, J. (2008b). Designing virtual worlds to facilitate communication: Issues, considerations, and lessons learned. *Technical Communication, 55*(3), 261–269.

Bronack, S., Sanders, R., Cheney, A., Riedl, R., Tashner, J., & Matzen, N. (2008a). Presence pedagogy: Teaching in a 3D virtual immersive world. *International Journal of Teaching and Learning in Higher Education, 20*(1), 59–69.

Dede, C. (2007). Reinventing the role of information and communications technologies in education. *Yearbook of the National Society for the Study of Education, 106*, 11–38. doi:10.1111/j.1744-7984.2007.00113.x

Department of Defense. (2001). *Department of Defense handbook: Development of interactive multimedia instruction (IMI), part 3 of 5 parts.* (MIL-HDBK-29612-3A).

Department of Defense. (2010). *TRADOC revised levels of interactivity.* Retrieved July 1, 2010, from http://www.atsc.army.mil/tadlp/

Dewey, J. (1938). *Experience and education.* New York, NY: McMillian.

Forehand, M. (2005). Bloom's taxonomy: Original and revised. In M. Orey (Ed.), *Emerging perspectives on learning, teaching, and technology.* Retrieved June 2, 2010, from from http://projects.coe.uga.edu/epltt/

Gamor, K. (In press). What's in an avatar? Identity, behavior, and integrity in virtual worlds for educational and business communication. In Proctor, R., & Vu, K. (Eds.), *Handbook of human factors in Web design* (2nd ed.). New York, NY: CRC Press.

Gilman, R., Tashner, J., Bronack, S., Riedl, R., & Cheney, A. (2007). Crossing continents: Bringing teachers and learners together through a 3D immersive world. *Educators' eZine*, April 2007. Retrieved June 15, 2010, from http://www.techlearning.com/ story/showArticle.php? articleID=196604336

Holden, J., Westfall, P., & Gamor, K. (2010). *An instructional media selection guide for distance learning: Implications for blended learning and virtual worlds* (6th ed.). Boston, MA: USDLA.

Johnson, D. W., & Johnson, F. P. (1996). *Joining together: Group theory and group skills* (6th ed.). Boston, MA: Allyn and Bacon.

Jonassen, D., Davidson, M., Collins, M., Campbell, J., & Haag, B. B. (1995). Constructivism and computer-mediated communication in distance education. *American Journal of Distance Education, 9,* 7–26. doi:10.1080/08923649509526885

Kapp, K., & O'Driscoll, T. (2010). *Learning in 3D: Adding a new dimension to enterprise learning and collaboration.* San Fransisco, CA: Pfeiffer.

Kolb, D. A. (1984a). *Experiential learning: Experience as the source of learning and development.* Englewood Cliffs, NJ: Prentice Hall. Retrieved April 29, 2009, from http://www.learningfromexperience.com/images/ uploads/process-of-experiential- learning.pdf

Kolb, D. A. (1984b). *Experiential learning.* Englewood Cliffs, NJ: Prentice Hall.

Section 2
Roadmaps from Theory to Practice

Chapter 8
Collaborative E-Learning Techniques:
Learning Management Systems vs. Multi-User Virtual Environments

Andreas Konstantinidis
Aristotle University of Thessaloniki, Greece

Thrasyvoulos Tsiatsos
Aristotle University of Thessaloniki, Greece

Stavros Demetriadis
Aristotle University of Thessaloniki, Greece

Andreas Pomportsis
Aristotle University of Thessaloniki, Greece

ABSTRACT

This chapter compares the potential of Learning Management Systems (LMSs) and Multi-User Virtual Environments (MUVEs) to facilitate the implementation of traditional face to face collaborative learning techniques in an online environment and discusses the benefits and challenges of an integrated approach. Initially, the chapter focuses on the application of collaborative learning techniques in traditional and computer supported didactical settings. Following this, the practice of utilizing LMSs in the contemporary educational process is analyzed, and the use of MUVEs in order to facilitate collaborative learning at a distance is subsequently presented. Ultimately, the chapter aims to clarify how the fruitful combination of these two technological approaches to the collaborative learning pedagogy can both diminish their weaknesses and amplify their strengths. For this reason, the final section of the chapter focuses on presenting an integrated approach, which merges two open source solutions: the popular LMS Moodle with the promising MUVE OpenSim.

DOI: 10.4018/978-1-60960-545-2.ch008

INTRODUCTION

Collaborative learning can generally be defined as learning activities expressly designed for, and carried out by pairs or small interactive groups (Barkley, Cross, & Howell, 2004). Research has demonstrated that learning is most effective when students work in groups, verbalise their thoughts, challenge the ideas of others, and collaborate to achieve group solutions to problems (Lehtinen & Hakkarainen, 2001; Johnson et al., 2002; Shih & Yang, 2008). Moreover, students who work in small groups tend to achieve relatively higher levels of academic outcomes and are more likely to develop the skills needed for a successful career (Joseph & Payne, 2003). Cooperative learning differs from collaborative learning in that, in cooperative learning, the use of groups supports an instructional system that maintains the traditional lines of classroom knowledge and authority (Flannery, 1994).

Taking into consideration the complete spectrum of available learning paradigms (Strijbos, Kirchner, & Martens, 2004) suggested by esteemed pedagogical theorists such as: Watson and Skinner (behaviourism), Bruner (discovery learning), Ausubel (meaningful learning), Piaget (constructivism), Rumelhart (schemata), Schank and Abelson (scripts), Spiro (cognitive flexibility), Bransford (problem-based learning) Brown (situated cognition), Salomon (distributed cognition) and Engestrom (activity theory), one can safely deduce that the practice of collaborative learning is mostly related to the principles of Vygotsky's dialectical/social constructivism.

Social constructivism focuses on an individual's learning that takes place because of their interactions in a group. This is not to be confused with social constructionism, which focuses on the artifacts that are created through the social interactions of a group.

Therefore, social constructivism is a sociological theory of knowledge that applies the general philosophical constructionism into social settings, wherein groups construct knowledge for one another, collaboratively creating a small culture of shared artifacts with shared meanings. The major theme of Vygotsky's theoretical framework is that social interaction plays a fundamental role in the development of cognition (Wertsch, 1985). Every function in the child's cultural development appears twice: first, on the social level, and later, on the individual level; first, between people (inter-psychological) and then inside the child (intra-psychological).

The potential for cognitive development depends upon the "zone of proximal development" (ZPD): a level of development attained when children engage in social behavior (Vygotsky, 1962). In other words, the range of skill that can be developed with adult guidance or peer collaboration exceeds what can be attained alone. The idea of ZPD has been useful for understanding mechanisms in collaborative learning. More advanced peers are likely to be operating within one another's proximal zones of development, modelling in the collaborative group, behaviors more advanced than those they could perform as individuals.

With this fundamental theoretical infrastructure in place, the major goal of collaborative learning becomes to support social interaction and encourage the learner's cognitive processes (Ertl, Kopp, & Mandl, 2007). Collaborative arrangements have been found to be superior to both competitive and individualistic structures on a variety of outcome measures, generally showing higher achievement, higher-level reasoning, more frequent generation of new ideas and solutions, and greater transfer of what is learned in one situation to another (Barkley et al., 2004).

From a motivationalist perspective, collaborative incentive structures create a situation in which the only way group members can attain their own personal goals is if all the members of the group are successful. In these conditions, group members must both help their group mates to do whatever helps the group to succeed, and to encourage their group mates to exert maximum effort (Slavin, 1997). On the other hand, social cohesion theorists emphasize the idea that students help their group mates learn because they care about the group. The social cohesion perspective focuses on teambuilding activities in preparation for collaborative learning, as well as group self-evaluation, instead of external incentives and individual accountability.

From a constructivist perspective, collaborative learning can be viewed as one of the pedagogical methods that can stimulate students to negotiate information such as: abstract, ill-defined and not easily accessible knowledge and open-ended problems, and to discuss complex problems from different perspectives (Veerman & Veldhuis-Diermanse, 2001). This can support learners to elaborate, explain and evaluate information in order to re- and co-construct (new) knowledge or to solve problems.

In the following sections, this chapter examines traditional approaches to collaborative learning and presents the Jigsaw technique as an example. Next, computer supported collaborative learning is analyzed through a comparison of Learning Management Systems (LMS) and Multi-User Virtual Environments (MUVE). Subsequently, an integrated approach of the LMS Moodle and the MUVE OpenSim is presented, and the associated challenges are evaluated. After this, a conceptualized platform and an example of its application are discussed. Finally, the sections on future work and conclusions bring the chapter to a close.

TRADITIONAL COLLABORATIVE LEARNING

Collaboration with other students provokes activity, makes learning more realistic and stimulates motivation (Petraglia, 1997). Students can ask each other questions and discuss problems from different perspectives. They can propose various answers and solutions and evaluate them on different criteria. Research (Lehtinen & Hakkarainen, 2001) has shown that groups which consist of members with different but partially overlapping expertise are more effective and innovative than groups with homogeneous expertise.

In general, traditional collaborative learning techniques can be organized into five types (Barkley et al., 2004): (a) discussion: where student interaction and exchange is achieved primarily through spoken words, (b) reciprocal teaching: where students purposefully help each other master subject matter content and develop discipline-based skills, encouraging interdependence, (c) problem solving: where students focus on practicing problem-solving strategies, (d) graphic information organizing: where groups use visual tools to organize and display information, and (e) collaborative writing, where students write in order to learn important course content and skills.

As an example, we will examine a reciprocal teaching collaborative learning method: the Jigsaw technique (Figure 1). This technique has a three-decade track record (Aronson & Bridgeman, 1979) of successfully reducing racial conflict and increasing positive educational outcomes. Here, students develop knowledge about a given topic (creating expert groups) and then teach this knowledge to others (i.e., the initial Jigsaw groups). Just as in a Jigsaw puzzle, the participation of each student is essential for the completion and full understanding of the final product. In other words, if each student's part is essential, then each student is essential; and that is what makes this strategy effective.

Several pedagogical advantages have been attributed to the Jigsaw collaborative technique (Aronson & Patnoe, 1997). These educational benefits include listening encouragement, engagement, and empathy by giving each member of the group an essential part to play in the academic activity. Group members must work together as a team to accomplish a common goal and each student depends on everyone else. No student can succeed completely unless everyone works to-

Figure 1. The Jigsaw Collaborative Learning Technique

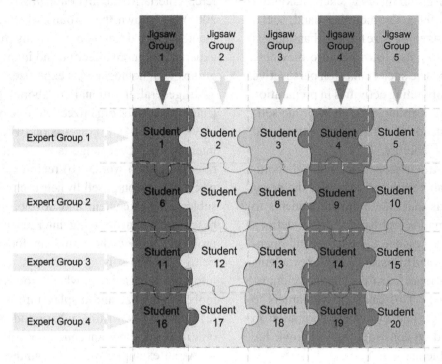

gether. This "collaboration by design" facilitates interaction among all students in the class, leading them to value each other as contributors to their common task.

COMPUTER SUPPORTED COLLABORATIVE LEARNING

Students' lives outside of school and college are increasingly media-rich and stimulating – which reflects the wider technological revolution taking place in society. As a result, education is becoming disconnected. The classroom is a sort of 'virtual reality'; a drab, technology-free zone that bears little relation to the increasingly technological reality of the students' lives outside of the classroom.

According to Resta and Laferrière (2007) there exist four instructional motives for the use of technology in support of collaborative learning: (a) to prepare students for the knowledge society

(collaboration skills and knowledge creation), (b) to enhance student cognitive performance or foster deep understanding, (c) to add flexibility of time and space for cooperative/collaborative learning, and (d) to foster student engagement and keep track of student cooperative/collaborative work (online written discourse).

However, according to the theory of connectivism (Siemens & Downes, 2005), learning (defined as actionable knowledge) can reside outside of ourselves (e.g., within an organization or a database), is focused on connecting specialized information sets, and the connections that enable us to learn are more important than our current state of knowing. Connectivism is considered as a more appropriate learning theory for online learning than older theories such as behaviorism, cognitivism, and constructivism (Ally, 2004). This position rests on the idea that the world has changed and become more networked, so learning theories developed prior to these global changes are less relevant. Research by Lin (2001) reveals that creating learning communities and providing supports are the two most essential pedagogical issues for the success of a networked learning environment.

Educational institutions, however, tend to take traditional classroom ideas and pedagogy and substitute them into non-contiguous collaborative learning environments paradigms (Strijbos et al., 2004). The assumption is that, since these environments have features that allow the interaction that we see in the classroom (e.g., messaging, real-time meetings, and shared applications), traditional pedagogy can be used. The proximate result is often disgruntled or disappointed students and instructors, motivation that is quickly extinguished, poorly used environments, wasted time and money, and showcase environments that are often not much more than computer assisted page-turning.

Learning Management Systems

A Learning Management System (LMS) is usually a Web-based system facilitating the organization and coordination of the learning material of an educational institution. LMSs also facilitate communication and collaboration of the students through the support of communication, collaboration and Web2.0 tools such as forums, blogs, wikis, chat rooms etc.

Learning Management Systems are widely used to support blended learning. The main goal of blended learning is to combine the best features of traditional education with the most prominent characteristics of online teaching, so as to encourage independent learning and decrease the required classroom time. In order for the above goal to be accomplished, it is of vital importance to guarantee the correct ratio in the use of the different educational means.

According to Trasler (2002) the advantages of blended learning include: (a) an ease in functionality and student time organization; (b) increase

in interaction between students, or students and instructors; (c) spatial and temporal flexibility; (d) increased learning; (e) decrease in student drop outs; and (f) adjustability to each student's preferences (e.g., personalized learning).

The most important features of Learning Management Systems (LMSs) are adaptability, personalization, extensibility and adaptation (Graf & Beate, 2005). Adaptability includes all the facilities that allow the customization of the platform for the educational institution's needs (e.g., the language or the design) while personalization aspects indicate the facilities of each individual user to customize his/her own view of the platform. With regard to the degree of extensibility, this can vary in open source products based on the availability of a good programming style or a documented application programming interface (API). Finally, adaptivity indicates all kinds of automatic adaptation to the individual user's needs (e.g., personal annotations of learning objects or automatically adapted content).

Open source systems such as Sakai and Moodle offer unique advantages over proprietary systems such as WebCT and Blackboard (Idaho State University, 2007): (a) the source program code is available, so open source applications are much more customizable than proprietary systems, (b) there is a community of developers at universities and corporations that add functionality to the systems and contribute those new modules back to the entire community for inclusion in the product, (c) open source solutions do not require license fees, (d) active open source communities have been providing support for their products successfully for quite some time, and (e) for very active open source communities, this results in a quickly evolving product.

Moodle is one of the most popular contemporary open source Web-based LMSs. Its strengths are the realization of communication tools, and the creation and administration of learning objects. Additional strengths include its usability, the comprehensive didactical concepts supported and the tracking of data (Graf & Beate, 2005). According to research results (Konstantinidis, Papadopoulos, Tsiatsos, & Demetriadis, 2010a), Moodle is highly accepted by instructors as a helpful and useful system which caters for their educational needs. Specifically, all instructors declared that Moodle helped them in their teaching duties, enhanced their communication with students, and made course material distribution a lot easier.

Multi-User Virtual Environments

Continuous enhancements in computer technology and the current widespread computer literacy among the public have resulted in a new generation of students that expect increasingly more from their e-Learning experiences (Monahan, McArdle, & Bertolotto, 2007). To keep up with such expectations, e-Learning systems must go through a radical change from the initial text-based environments to more stimulating multimedia systems.

Growing research shows the educational effectiveness of constructivist and collaborative learning in 3D MUVEs (Shih & Yang, 2008). Several MUVE features are considered supportive of knowledge construction, self direction, immersion, interactivity, and education. Such rich multimedia spaces are fundamentally changing the way we consider learning, social interaction, and self-expression (Johnson, 2007).

MUVEs are becoming another empowering, world-flattening educational technology, very much like the Web before them. Beyond the direct mappings of traditional lecture formats, MUVEs can enable novel collaborative learning and educational interactions (Djorgovski et al., 2009). Furthermore, MUVEs provide opportunities to use simulation in a safe environment to enhance experiential learning, allowing individuals to practice skills, try new ideas, and learn from their mistakes (Beard, Wilson, Morra, & Keelan, 2009).

Students were asked to comment on the general advantages and disadvantages of using 3D CVLEs for collaboration. The most important advantages of this pedagogical approach were considered to be spatial and temporal flexibility, innovation and originality of method (e.g., 83% of students entered the environment outside of the educational process simply to explore the new environment) and enhanced communication and collaboration tools. On the other hand, disadvantages included lack of face to face interaction, increased technological dependency and learning overhead imposed by the new tools.

Second Life (SL) is the most popular 3D MUVE. It is mainly a consumer application but has been used extensively by universities (e.g., MIT, Harvard, Edinburgh University etc.). It offers distant learning capabilities that allow teachers to design, implement and support online courses easily (Konstantinou, Varlamis, & Giannakoulopoulos, 2009). Research (Konstantinidis, Tsiatsos, Terzidou, & Pomportsis, 2010b) shows that students have mixed opinions regarding the capabilities of SL to support collaborative learning techniques, as opposed to the traditional face to face method. For example, more than 40% of the students agree that it was harder to collaborate through SL in comparison to the traditional method, while 50% of the students believe that the effectiveness of collaboration was reduced. In general, students find the traditional method easier (87%), more direct (93%), and more useful (62%). On the other hand, they find the SL approach to collaboration much more interesting (87%).

On the other hand, OpenSim is an open source 3D MUVE solution, which offers high compatibility with Second Life and communication protocols for other platforms. Although, it is still in the alpha phase of development, it has been used extensively by universities and companies (e.g., IBM, Microsoft). According to Radoiu (2008), OpenSim operates in one of two modes: (a) standalone mode: a single process handles the entire simulation, and (b) grid mode: various aspects of the simulation are separated among multiple processes, which can exist on different machines. Responsibilities are divided among five servers: user server, grid server, asset server, inventory server and simulation server.

OpenSim is especially suitable for research purposes because it is open source and allows free land. Moreover, since it is a private server, researchers can have any experiences without bad influence to others. Being an open source application can grant designers the freedom of creating a multitude of user interfaces, simulations and environments and enhancing OpenSim with needed collaborative learning functionality. In contrast to conventional virtual learning platforms including LMSs and Content Management Systems (CMS), OpenSim provides two important and relevant resources: immersive interaction and synchronous dialogue through multiple concurrent channels (e.g., voice and text chat).

A Comparison of LMSs and MUVEs

Like Moodle, most LMSs offer affordances beyond simple document repositories, by featuring discussion forums, online chat rooms, grade books and the ability to give automatically marked tests such as multiple choice questionnaires (Kemp, 2006). There is, however, relatively little use of multimedia, authentic learning and established collaborative learning techniques.

Therefore, in terms of enhancing the experience of learning, it seems clear that MUVEs should have some distinct advantages over traditional LMSs. For example, the 3D immersive format has significant potential for facilitating collaborations, community and experiential learning. Moreover, compared to other electronic tools for distance communication, there is an improved sense of presence and the ability to build rich 3D demonstration models, leveraging the power of modern computers to allow students to experience phenomena of interest, which would have otherwise been impossible due to issues of cost, safety, time, or scale.

On the other hand, MUVEs are very poor document repositories and have considerable hardware demands. Furthermore, the limited ability to contain disruptive students or avoid environment distractions is another problem.

In MUVEs, teachers have the freedom to weave their own metaphors and build domain-specific settings in 3D environments. However, according to Liu (2006), the creation of engaging teaching and learning aids or effective research tools requires not only strong scripting skills, visual design skills, and 3D modeling skills, but also expertise in subject contents. As a result, a multi-discipline team with a diverse skill set is likely to be more productive in a MUVE than individual instructors or researchers with expertise in only one discipline. For this reason we propose an integrated approach presented in the following sections.

MOODLE AND OPENSIM: AN INTEGRATED APPROACH

No pedagogical approach or technological solution is flawless and there is no single ideal educational environment. However, a successful combination of specific approaches and systems can surpass most shortcomings. In other words, the advantages of one approach can be utilized to overcome the disadvantages of another. Based on this fact and depending on the set objective, collaborative learning techniques can be used independently of, or in combination with each other (Dillenbourg, 2008). Recent computer supported collaborative learning techniques are not restricted anymore to collaborative learning but can include individual learning activities (i.e., reading papers, writing a summary, etc.) as well as class-wide activities with the teacher (i.e., introductory lectures, debriefing sessions, etc.).

The metaphors for MUVE teaching and learning do not reference a fully rounded learning experience (Bennett & Peachey, 2007) – rather they offer a mature option against face to face tuition, with opportunities for collaborative and community-based interaction and learning in a situated constructivist environment. On the other hand, a VLE can offer documented learning paths, social book marking and networking options, act as an information repository, enable class planning (e.g., calendar, assignment deadlines etc.) and offer assessment facilities, online learning activities and SCORM compliant assessment data.

SLoodle (Simulation Linked Object Oriented Dynamic Learning Environment) is a suite of tools which enhances e-Learning support for teaching and learning in Second Life (SL). SLoodle is provided as a free plug-in for Moodle, and allows the integration of Moodle and SL (SLoodle 0.4 Brochure, 2009). The purpose of the SLoodle mashup is to create a blended online learning experience that locates SL within the MUVE environment so it is a synchronous, active tool supported by the asynchronous LMS context, repository, forums and course material.

The major features of this integration include: (a) a Web-intercom (a chat-room that brings Moodle and SL chats together), (b) a registration booth (providing identity management for both platforms, linking students' avatars to their Moodle user accounts) and (c) the presenter (through which users can author SL presentations mixing slides, Webpages and video through Moodle).

In similar fashion, the envisaged Moodle and OpenSim integration would aim to successfully facilitate collaboration, by supporting standardized collaborative learning scenarios and techniques. The inherent design philosophies of the two platforms, however, do not incorporate many of the fundamental principles of collaborative learning. Therefore, the integration of two such versatile, yet different, educational and technological approaches yields multiple scientific, pedagogical and technical challenges which must be addressed in order to facilitate their successful and efficient integration.

Integration Challenges

The scientific challenges mostly concern the ability of assessing or validating learning in formal contexts. This is particular with e-Learning, immersive learning environments and simulations, where learning is often an open-ended, exploratory and experiential learning process.

An update to traditional assessment, Assessment 2.0, is proposed by Elliott (2008). The updated system will embrace the Internet and, more specifically, Web 2.0. The type of assessment activity best suited to the contemporary learner would exhibit some or all of the following characteristics:

- **Authentic:** involving real-world knowledge and skills.
- **Personalised:** tailored to the knowledge, skills and interests of each student.
- **Negotiated:** agreed between the learner and the teacher.
- **Engaging:** involving the personal interests of the student.
- **Recognise existing skills:** willing to accredit the student's existing work.
- **Deep:** assessing deep knowledge – not memorisation.
- **Problem oriented:** original tasks requiring genuine problem solving skills.
- **Collaboratively produced:** produced in partnership with fellow students.
- **Peer and self assessed:** involving self reflection and peer review.
- **Tool supported:** encouraging the use of ICT.

Moreover, pedagogical interoperability challenges hinder the integration process. In contemporary education, collaborative learning techniques are seldom used separately. Identifying and combining complementary and compatible pedagogies remains an open issue, worthy of further research initiatives. Pedagogical mashups such as SLoodle offer the ability to make best use of both sets of metaphor to establish a fully blended online learning experience, offering the immediacy, dynamic interaction and high production values required for activity sessions in combination with the repository, time management and assessment opportunities offered by a VLE environment.

The majority of the students feel more comfortable when a combination of both traditional and neoteric methods of teaching is used (Michailidou & Economides, 2003). In particular, they propose that an innovative educational environment should only be used when it truly improves learning and when practical difficulties arise, like in the case of distance learning. Therefore, designers should not seek the goal of recreating all the curricula offered by particular courses in a 3D MUVE (Prasolova-Førland, 2008). Designers should choose educational topics and concepts where the 3D visualization and simulation will have clear advantages compared to the more traditional presentation modes such as slides, articles and diagrams.

Finally, from a technical point of view, the seamless integration of 2D and 3D educational tools, resulting in an efficient, accessible and accomplished system remains a challenging task. For instance, 2D applications provide mostly a private experience, while 3D environments are inherently a community, providing a different social dynamic. Therefore, technical challenges include bridging the different systems, defining standards, and envisaging innovative interfaces.

Conceptualized Framework

In this section we present a conceptualized framework (Figure 2), which we will attempt to develop and assess in forthcoming research, in order to circumvent the challenges stated above and evaluate possible solutions. In a nutshell, the framework proposes that the collaborative learning techniques are implemented as a module for the Moodle platform, in analogous fashion to the

SLoodle set presented previously, but executed in the OpenSim environment.

Combining these two types of educational approaches may allow instructional developers and teachers to explore exciting new opportunities for collaborative learning on the Web and within 3D Multi-User Virtual Environments. However, according to Fortney (2007), it is necessary to avoid the pitfall of disguising old ideas with new technology, and surpass the challenge of identifying scenarios where 3D MUVEs achieve greater benefits than more traditional, familiar solutions.

The difference with SLoodle is that here, the tutor will be able to select an educational scenario and based on its requirements several actions are carried out automatically: tools (e.g., forums, chat rooms etc.) are added, users are organized into groups and the 3D MUVE is adapted accordingly (e.g., seat positions, presentation boards, group and public rooms etc.). The scenario is then executed and at the end the tutor can begin a new one if necessary.

For example, if the educator chooses to utilize the Jigsaw collaborative learning technique, the appropriate form is presented and s/he is asked to fill it in, in order to define the parameters of the educational scenario (part 1 of Figure 2). Example form fields could include: number of students, number of jigsaw/expert groups, topics of study per jigsaw/expert groups, available tools etc. After defining the Jigsaw scenario, the system automatically calibrates the course organizational structure with relevant areas, tools and activities (part 2 of Figure 2) based on the parameters provided by the educator. For example, tools can include unique forums for each individual jigsaw/expert group, or wikis per examined theme.

Next, based on the requirements of the scenario, an architectural design is created for the 3D environment within OpenSim (part 3 of Figure 2). For example, based on the defined number of jigsaw/expert groups, the necessary number of group rooms, tools and apparel is created. In addition, default rooms such as the central presentation area,

Figure 2. The conceptualized framework combining the Moodle and OpenSim platforms

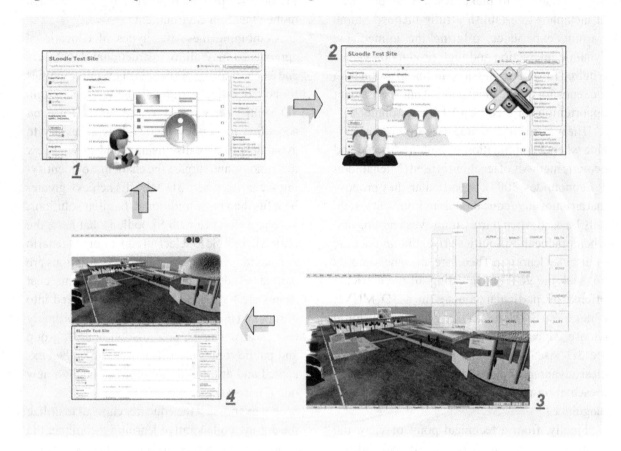

the library (containing links to relevant literature) and the lockers room (containing team clothing and avatar gestures) are also built.

Finally, the collaborative learning scenario is executed, combining the different types of affordances facilitated by either the VLE or MUVE (part 4 of Figure 2).

FUTURE RESEARCH DIRECTIONS

Although researchers are encouraged to apply what they know about face-to-face collaborative learning in their analysis of online interaction in CSCL environments (Resta & Laferrière, 2007), future CSCL studies should focus less attention on the question of whether CSCL is better than face-to-face collaborative learning, but rather focus on

what is uniquely feasible with new technology. More specifically, additional research is needed in the topics of student characteristics (particularly of the neo-millennial students), design elements of CSCL and organizational issues related to implementing CSCL in higher education to determine the essential conditions that must be in place for effective use by faculty.

Moreover, Assessment 2.0 (Elliott, 2008) poses challenges for teachers – who are often the epitome of the digital immigrant. Not only might they lack the IT skills needed to understand Web 2.0 services but they may lack the knowledge and experience required to appraise students' work produced using these tools. Furthermore, teachers also lack the rubrics required to assess Web 2.0 skills. Therefore, research must yield specific rubrics which are required in order to address self- and peer-assessment, and collaboration.

The implementation of the suggested approach, described in the previous section, constitutes future work for our research team. Our ultimate aim is to assess the applicability of the OpenSim and Moodle combination for collaborative learning by developing virtual tools and metaphors and exploiting the representational richness each medium provides. The results of our study will be discussed and analyzed, with a focus on student collaboration; avatar representation and learning space awareness in future work.

CONCLUSION

Students who are "digital natives" (Bennett & Peachey, 2007) have limited patience with the current formal, structured educational system. They think, play and learn in environments that are fast-paced, multimedia, multimodal, interactive and, of course, digital with expectations of engagement and high production values at all times. These volatile, interconnected, and complex social milieus call for learning options that are critical, collaborative, creative, and futures-oriented.

In facing the challenges of restructuring educational environments to accommodate rapid change, educators need to restructure the way they view learning and learner engagement, and adapt learning environments to take best advantage of educational opportunities made possible by new technologies.

The new era of ubiquitous technology-enhanced and socially-mediated life-long-learning beckons. Research has shown that new-tech disguising old ideas is almost certainly doomed to failure. Educators, instructional designers, and researchers are already forming new pedagogies and discovering patterns of learning and learning tools that have not even been tapped in real life distance education environments. The possibilities for exploration and development of new practices in distance education using a combination of MUVEs and LMSs are worth exploring.

REFERENCES

Ally, M. (2004). Foundations of educational theory for online learning. In Anderson, T., & Elloumi, F. (Eds.), *The theory and practice of online learning*. Athabasca, Canada: Athabasca University.

Aronson, E., & Bridgeman, D. (1979). Jigsaw groups and the desegregated classroom: In pursuit of common goals. *Personality and Social Psychology Bulletin*, *5*, 438–446. doi:10.1177/014616727900500405

Aronson, E., & Patnoe, S. (1997). *The jigsaw classroom: Building cooperation in the classroom*. New York, NY: Longman.

Barkley, E., Cross, P., & Howell, C. (2004). *Collaborative learning techniques: A handbook for college faculty*. San Francisco, CA: Jossey-Bass.

Beard, L., Wilson, K., Morra, D., & Keelan, J. (2009). A survey of health-related activities on Second Life. *Journal of Medical Internet Research*, *11*(2), e17. doi:10.2196/jmir.1192

Bennett, J., & Peachey, A. (2007). Mashing the MUVE: A mashup model for collaborative learning in Multi-User Virtual Environments. *Proceedings of the Interactive Computer Aided Learning Conference* (ICL2007).

Dillenbourg, P. (2008). Integrating technologies into educational ecosystems. *Distance Education*, *29*(2), 127–140. doi:10.1080/01587910802154939

Djorgovski, S. G., Hut, P., McMillan, S., Vesperini, E., Knop, R., Farr, W., & Graham, M. J. (2009). Exploring the use of virtual worlds as a scientific research platform: The Meta-Institute for Computational Astrophysics (MICA). *Proceedings of Facets of Virtual Environments (FaVE 2009)*.

Elliott, B. *(2008). Assessment 2.0.* Proceedings of the Open Workshop of TenCompetence, Empowering Learners for Lifelong Competence Development: Pedagogical, Organisational and Technological Issues.

Ertl, B., Kopp, B., & Mandl, H. (2007). Supporting collaborative learning in videoconferencing using collaboration scripts and content schemes. In F. Fischer, I. Kollar, H. Mandl, & J. M. Haake (Eds.), *Scripting computer-supported collaborative learning* (pp. 213-236). New York, NY: Springer Science and Business Media, LLC.

Flannery, J. L. (1994). Teacher as a co-conspirator: Knowledge and authority in collaborative learning. In Bosworth, K., & Hamilton, S. J. (Eds.), *Collaborative learning: Underlying processes and effective techniques* (pp. 15–23). San Francisco, CA: Jossey-Bass.

Fortney, K. (2007). *Using Second Life to provide corporate blended learning solutions*. Second Life Education Workshop.

Graf, S., & Beate, L. (2005). An evaluation of open source e-learning platforms stressing adaptation issues. *Proceedings of IEEE International Conference on Advanced Learning Technologies (ICALT2005)*.

Idaho State University. (2007). *Instructional Technology Resource Centre*. Retrieved March 2010 from http://www.isu.edu/itrc/resources/LMS_FINAL_REPORT_MOODLE.pdf

Johnson, L. (2007). *Why creativity matters*. Second Life Education Workshop.

Johnson, S. D., Suriya, C., Won Yoon, S., Berrett, J. V., & La Fleur, J. (2002). Team development and group processes of virtual learning teams. *Computers & Education, 39*, 379–393. doi:10.1016/S0360-1315(02)00074-X

Joseph, A., & Payne, M. (2003). Group dynamics and collaborative group performance. *ACM SIGCSE Bulletin Archive, 35*(1), 368–371. doi:10.1145/792548.612008

Kemp, J. (2006). Putting a Second Life "Metaverse" skin on Learning Management Systems. *Proceedings of the Second Life Education Workshop at the Second Life Community Convention*.

Konstantinidis, A., Papadopoulos, P., Tsiatsos, T., & Demetriadis, S. (2010a). (Manuscript submitted for publication). Selecting and Evaluating a Learning Management System: A Moodle evaluation based on instructors and students. *International Journal of Distance Education Technologies*.

Konstantinidis, A., Tsiatsos, T., Terzidou, T., & Pomportsis, A. (2010b). Fostering collaboration in Second Life: Metaphors and affordances. *Journal of Computers and Education, 55*(2), 603–615. doi:10.1016/j.compedu.2010.02.021

Konstantinou, N., Varlamis, I., & Giannakoulopoulos, A. (2009). *Using 3D worlds in an educational network*. 13th Pan-Hellenic Conference on Informatics.

Lehtinen, E., & Hakkarainen, K. (2001). *Computer supported collaborative learning: A review*. Retrieved April 2010 from http://www.comlab.hut.fi/opetus/205/etatehtava1.pdf

Lin, C. S. (2001). The experiences in running a cyber school in improving study. *Selected Papers of International Conference on Information Technology in Education of Schools*, (pp. 101-113).

Liu, C. (2006). Second Life learning community: A peer-based approach to involving more faculty members in Second Life. *Proceedings of the Second Life Education Workshop at the Second Life Community Convention*.

Michailidou, A., & Economides, A. A. (2003). E-learn: Towards a collaborative educational virtual environment. *Journal of Information Technology Education, 2*, 131–152.

Monahan, T., McArdle, G., & Bertolotto, M. (2007). mCLEV-R: Design and evaluation of an interactive and collaborative m-learning application. *International Journal of Emerging Technologies in Learning, 2*(2), 47–53.

Petraglia, J. (1997). *The rhetoric and technology of authenticity in education.* Mahwah, NJ: Lawrence Erlbaum.

Prasolova-Førland, E. (2008). Analyzing place metaphors in 3D educational collaborative virtual environments. *Computers in Human Behavior, 24*(2), 185–204. doi:10.1016/j.chb.2007.01.009

Radoiu, D. (2008). Virtual organizations in emerging virtual 3D worlds. *Studia Univ. Babes-Bolyai, Informatica, 53*(2).

Resta, P., & Laferrière, T. (2007). Technology in support of collaborative learning. *Educational Psychology Review, 19*, 65–83. doi:10.1007/s10648-007-9042-7

Shih, Y.-C., & Yang, M.-T. (2008). A collaborative virtual environment for situated language learning using VEC3D. *Journal of Educational Technology & Society, 11*(1), 56–68.

Siemens, G., & Downes, S. (2005). Connectivism: A learning theory for the digital age. *International Journal of Instructional Technology and Distance Learning, 2*(1).

Slavin, R. E. (1997). *Research on cooperative learning and achievement: A quarter century of research.* Annual Meeting of Pedagogical Psychology.

SLoodle 0.4 brochure. (2009). Retrieved December 2009 from http://www.scribd.com/doc/14996661/SLOODLE-Brochure

Strijbos, J. W., Kirschner, P. A., & Martens, R. L. (2004). *What we know about CSCL: And implementing it in higher education.* New York, NY: Kluwer Academic Publishers. doi:10.1007/1-4020-7921-4

Trasler, J. (2002). Effective learning depends on blend. *Industrial and Commercial Training, 34*(5), 191–193. doi:10.1108/00197850210437111

Veerman, A., & Veldhuis-Diermanse, E. (2001). Collaborative learning through computer-mediated communication in academic education. *Proceedings of Euro-CSCL 2001.*

Vygotsky, L. S. (1962). *Thought and language.* Cambridge, MA: MIT Press. doi:10.1037/11193-000

Wertsch, J. V. (1985). *Cultural, communication, and cognition: Vygotskian perspectives.* Cambridge, UK: Cambridge University Press.

KEY TERMS AND DEFINITIONS

Collaborative Learning (CL): CL is a general term used for the description of educational practices based on the simultaneous cognitive and mental effort of multiple students or/and educators.

Computer Supported Collaborative Learning (CSCL): CSCL is a method of supporting collaborative learning using computers and the Internet.

Learning Management System (LMS): An LMS is a software application for the administration, documentation, tracking, and reporting of training programs, classroom and online events, e-Learning programs, and training content.

Moodle: Moodle is an open source Learning Management System (LMS). It has become very popular among educators around the world as a tool for creating online dynamic Web sites for their students.

Multi-User Virtual Environment (MUVE): MUVEs enable multiple simultaneous participants to: access virtual contexts, interact with digital artifacts, represent themselves through "avatars" (in some cases graphical and in others, text-based), communicate with other participants (in some cases also with computer-based agents), take part in experiences incorporating modeling and mentoring about problems similar to those in real world contexts.

OpenSim: OpenSim is an open source solution, which offers high compatibility with SL and communication protocols for other platforms. Although, it is yet in the alpha phase of development, it is used extensively by universities and big companies (such as IBM, Microsoft, etc.).

Second Life (SL): SL is the most popular 3D MUVE. It is mainly a consumer application but has been used extensively by universities (e.g., MIT, Harvard, Edinburgh University etc.). It offers distant learning capabilities that allow teachers to design, implement and support online courses easily.

Virtual Learning Environment (VLE): Virtual Learning Environments (VLEs) are learning management software systems that synthesize the functionality of computer-mediated communication software and on-line methods of delivering course material.

Chapter 9
How to Build Effective "Edutainment" Experiences in MUVEs

Alberto Bucciero
University of Salento, Italy

Nicoletta Di Blas
Polytechnics of Milan, Italy

Luca Mainetti
University of Salento, Italy

Paolo Paolini
Polytechnics of Milan, Italy

Caterina Poggi
Polytechnics of Milan, Italy

ABSTRACT

This chapter is about how to make an effective use of MUVEs (Multi-Users Virtual Environments) in formal education. It draws on the authors' experience with four different programs deployed since 2002 involving, so far, more than 9,000 students from 18 European countries including Israel and the USA. The chapter is intended as a set of "lessons learned" on all of the relevant aspects of this kind of enterprise, from design to implementation and actual deployment. It is therefore meant as a short "users" guide for building effective and engaging edutainment experiences in virtual worlds.

INTRODUCTION

Multi-user 3D environments have become popular, due to the success of Second Life, in a number of fields, especially eEntertainment and eMarketing.

They can be used for cultural heritage, for example, in Kenderdine's "Ancient Olympia, Home of the Gods" (Kenderdine, 2001), Johnson's "Monticello, the home of Thomas Jefferson" (Johnson, 2005) or the "Theban Mapping Project" (Johnson, 2003). They can also be used for naturalistic heri-

DOI: 10.4018/978-1-60960-545-2.ch009

tage as in "Wolf Quest" (Schaller et al., 2009). It is less well-known, outside a small circle of researchers and professionals, that they can also be used for education.

Among the most well-known examples of virtual worlds for education are: Barab's Quest Atlantis, a persistent virtual world where children as young as nine engage in curriculum-related quests to save an imaginary land from environmental disaster (Barab, Thomas, Dodge, Carteaux, & Tuzun, 2005; Barab, Gresalfi, & Arici, 2009); Dede's River City, where teams of high school students investigate the social, health and environmental causes of an epidemic in a 19th century virtual town (Dede, Clarke, Ketelhut, Nelson, & Boeman, 2005); and Bers's Zora, a virtual environment used by children with psychological, mental or physical problems, who can find a way to express themselves and tell their stories by manipulating virtual objects and characters (Bers, 2001).

While most of the cultural heritage 3D virtual worlds can also be categorized as "informal education", i.e. a situation where the visitor does not necessarily have a precise learning goal, although he/she may be expected to learn something during the experience, only a few attempts are related to "formal education", i.e. a situation where a group of pupils, possibly under the guidance of a teacher, have precise learning goals, to be achieved with a well-defined effort. Formal education has to meet stringent requirements, such as organized groups of pupils, organized scheduling, time constraints, possible conflict with standard curricular activities, etc. These constraints make it difficult to introduce collaborative technologies in formal education, since collaboration implies that different (groups of) pupils need to harmonize their constraints and their learning goals with the constraints and goals of other (groups of) pupils. The "added value" of the experience in terms of benefits must therefore be guaranteed for teachers to enroll in the activity.

In this chapter, we would like to introduce our experience with the design, implementation

and deployment of educational experiences using MUVEs in formal educational settings. It is based on our long-term experience with more than 9,000 pupils, aged 12 to 19, from 18 European countries plus Israel and the USA. The chapter therefore aims to provide a set of organized 'lessons learnt' directly from the field. It will deal with general issues to be raised while building an effective 'edutainment' experience using collaborative technologies and 3D environments.

The Case Study: L@E

Learning@Europe (L@E) is an edutainment experience for European high school students based on a multi-user online virtual world, involving also a set of forums for asynchronous communication, and a body of educational material (in the format of interviews with leading international experts) which participants download from the website.

The subject matter of L@E is European modern history, and participants (groups of schools from at least three different countries) are asked, after having studied the content, to contribute knowledge, material evidence, and culture-specific perspectives from their country and national history, thus helping to build a broader picture of a historical phenomenon which affected Europe both at local and international level. The activities in an L@E experience include synchronous discussion (via chat) and team games in the 3D world, discussion on asynchronous online forums, and collaboration, both face-to-face among classmates and on the forums between remote partner classes, to produce the assignments: digital representations of knowledge synthesizing the results of students' research and discussion.

L@E was built upon previous experiences with MUVEs for education: Virtual Leonardo (Barbieri & Paolini, 2001), a digital 3D reconstruction of the Museum of Science and Technology in Milan, SEE (Shrine Educational Experience), where students from Europe and Israel would meet in a 3D environment evocative of the Shrine of the

Book section of the Israel Museum in Jerusalem to discuss religious, historical and sociological issues related to the Dead Sea Scrolls, and Stori@Lombardia, again a 3D world (a fantasy castle), where the subject matter was medieval Lombardy in Italy. In its turn, L@E has created a new program: Learning@SocialSport (www.learningatsocialsport.it) on the social, ethical, psychological and medical issues of sport, aimed at young Italian athletes. L@E is the most prominent of all the above projects (in terms of participants, complexity, evaluation, etc.) and therefore we have selected it as a case study for this paper.

GOALS AND REQUIREMENTS

MUVEs-based educational experiences may be considered a form of 'edutainment', that is, a blend of entertainment and education (where entertainment acts as a driver for education). Therefore we may state that the two high-level goals of any edutainment experience are to entertain and to be educational. Taking into consideration the main categories of stakeholders helps further goals emerge, as the reader can see in Figure 1.

The requirements are related to the main goals of an edutainment experience: to entertain and to be educational. Further requirements are related to the collaborative nature of MUVEs and some constraints.

The entertainment requirements of MUVEs can be refined, making reference to those dimensions that are commonly acknowledged as fundamental in the various taxonomies of fun (Di Blas & Poggi, 2008): challenge, fellowship and mimesis (Caillois, 1961; Hunicke, LeBlanc, & Zubek, 2004; Johnson, 2005). Challenge means overcoming obstacles; it may involve conflicts, competition and time-pressure. Players are 'pushed to their limits'. Fellowship is the social element of games, rewarding for the emotive component and the possibility of improving one's social status. Fellowship naturally goes with collaboration: in MUVEs, players typically organize themselves into guilds to overcome obstacles, beat a monster, etc. Eventually mimesis concerns the possibility for users to 'escape into another world', experimenting with different personalities and expressing their own creativity.

Education is the other primary goal of edutainment applications. In a broad sense, learning can

Figure 1. Stakeholders of an edutainment experience

STAKEHOLDERS	
Students	They are the intended users of the system, surely interested in one of the two main goals (to be "entertained") but also to the second ("to learn"). They are likely to welcome a collaborative experience based on ICT, which they generally appreciate and use.
Teachers	They play the most active role into deciding whether to enroll in the activity or not. They are interested in the educational goal (including the possibility of putting into practice pedagogical approaches – see table 3). They welcome the entertainment component of the activity as a way to motivate the students.
School's principal	She must support the teacher's decision. She may be interested into including 21st millennium skills (so much sought-after by all school systems world-wide) in the curriculum and exploiting the technical equipments of the school. Elements of prestige (like in our case-study, international cooperation and visibility) may also be relevant.
Educational authorities	They share with the principal the goal of exploiting the technical equipments of the schools and promoting the acquisition of the 21st century skills. Further goals may depend on the concrete subject matter of the experience: in our case-study, they were also keen to support the development in young generations of a sense of European-ness.
Families	They act as supporters. They welcome both the educational outcomes as well as the engagement, if they see disaffection for school activities turn into affection.
Staff and developers	In our case-study (but these goals may be common to many): they want the program to be used, by as many schools as possible and to minimize the cost to make the service self-sustainable

Figure 2. A list of possible entertainment requirements

CHALLENGE
Include intellectual challenges (quizzes, mysteries, strategy problems)
Include physical challenges (e.g. requiring manual ability)
Include competition (with the game or with other users)
Include conflict situations
Make challenges hard, but always doable
Provide rewards for players at every skill level
State rules clearly
Give clear feedback on challenge results
Include race with time
Failure must have a cost
Advanced players must not get rewards for easy challenges
Allow multiple routes to make progress
Provide a compelling context for tasks requiring repeated practice
FELLOWSHIP
Support social interaction
Include collaborative tasks (achievable only through collaboration)
Provide occasions to increase social status
Provide features to express emotional states (e.g. emoticons)
MIMESIS
Provide compelling story or underlying metaphor
Provide dramatic and climatic elements
Provide customizable personal features
Support user authoring of content
Provide aesthetically compelling content

be meant as the acquisition of knowledge, skills and attitudes. Other requirements for an educational experience may be related to the possibility of implementing a specific pedagogical approach. Eventually, since we are in the field of formal education, there are also requirements for activities taking place during school hours and involving the class as a whole. Figure 3 incorporates these aspects.

MUVEs are intrinsically collaborative; otherwise, it would not make sense to be 'many in one place'. Therefore, a MUVEs-based educational experience must promote collaboration in all possible ways. This requirement impacts on many dimensions: entertainment (where team games must be devised rather than individual chal-

lenges), education (where collaborative learning, collaborative tasks and assignments, discussions and comparison must be foreseen) and also software, since the simultaneous presence of multiple users in a 3D world has a number of implications, e.g. in terms of coherence of the shared state, controlling access to active objects, and requirements of connection bandwidth.

Eventually, in addition to specific functional requirements, classic software requirements, and soft goals (such as usability and performance) common to any application, the design of computer-supported educational experiences must take into account a complex set of constraints, characteristic of the educational application domain. Taking into account the technological

Figure 3. Educational Requirements

KNOWLEDGE	
Knowledge	Make learners recall data or information.
Comprehension-1	Help learners understand meaning and interpretation of contents
Comprehension-2	Make learners state a problem in their own words
Application	Encourage learners to apply a concept in a new situation
Analysis-1	Help separate concepts into parts, so that the organizational structure may be understood
Analysis-2	Help learners distinguish between facts and inferences
Synthesis	Support learners in building a structure from diverse elements, creating a new meaning
Evaluation	Ask learners to make judgments about the value of ideas or materials.
SKILLS	
Group work	Support collaborative learning
Foreign language	Provide authentic opportunities to practice and improve functional skills in a foreign language
Technologies	Include opportunities to improve students' technical skills
Learning methods	Provide opportunities to explore new learning methods and tools
ATTITUDES	
Motivation	Increase motivation and engagement in school activities
Curiosity	Increase curiosity and interest in a subject
Relationships	Improve attitude of learners toward other learners, teachers, or other categories people
PEDAGOGICAL APPROACHES	
Multiple intelligences	Require the use of multiple intelligences, learning styles, and skills
Active learning	Learners must be protagonists of their learning, teachers play a facilitator role
Collaborative learning	Include collaborative tasks, where students must produce together a common output
Critical thinking	Incite learners to critically reflect on contents, highlight multiple perspectives, identify conflicts
Problem solving	Stimulate learners to solve problems
Peer scaffolding	Encourage and support learners helping their peers
Social constructivism	Provide occasions for discussion, sharing of multiple perspectives, and negotiation of new, more refined meanings
Drill and practice	Provide engaging and meaningful contexts for learners to practice
REQUIREMENTS FOR ACTIVITIES TAKING PLACE DURING SCHOOL HOURS	
Curriculum integration	The edutainment experience must fit in school curricula
Class involvement	The activity should involve all the students of a class, not only part of them.
Pre-requisite knowledge	Activities must be adequate to the participants' level of knowledge, or resources should be provided to fill in the gaps

equipment available in schools is obviously essential. Applications must run on school machines and school networks, access the Internet from the school's connection, comply with the protection features and policies regulating online access, and software and hardware resources. They must be tailored to the technological equipment currently available in European schools, which is not necessarily state-of-the-art. Analogous considerations apply if an edutainment application is designed for use in the learners' homes: the kind of equipment generally available to intended users, their level of computer literacy, and the scenarios and daily practices into which the application will be integrated, need to be assessed.

DESIGN OF MUVES-BASED EDUCATIONAL EXPERIENCES

In order to show how the above goals and requirements can be met in a concrete design solution, we now illustrate in detail our case study: Learning@ Europe. L@E is a highly complex experience blending ICT-based activities and 'traditional' learning.

L@E is structured upon a 6-7 week experience: four classes of high school students from different European countries take part in a cultural competition (two classes against two). Students meet together four times on a shared online 3D environment accessible over the Internet: four cooperative sessions distributed across two months, each session lasting about one hour. Two

Figure 4. Constraints Related to Technical Requirements

CONSTRAINTS	
Connection	Bandwidth
	Internet access
	Geographical location
Hardware	Video and audio card
	HDM, mouse, joystick, speakers...
	Processor
	Equipment available to users
Software	Operating system
	Additional software and plug-ins
	Installation and setting up
Support and Troubleshooting	School network's protections
	Field-testing
	Prevention strategies
	Emergency plans
	Short-term alternative solutions
	Maintenance
Time and scheduling	Integration in school time-tables
	Booking computer lab
	Integration in school calendar
Organization, Social, Political Issues	Lab-related school policies
	Teacher's computer literacy
	Availability of school technician
	Redundant messages and communication channels
	Short, clear, timely instructions
	Teacher support

students per class are represented in the 3D world by avatars. Meetings are devoted to cooperative activities, such as discussions (Figure 6, bottom right) and games (Figure 6, top right). Students meet their peers from different geographical areas, discuss relevant cultural matters with them, and play with them in the virtual world, divided in two teams. All games are based on cultural

Figure 5. Learning@Europe: 'storyboard' of the experience

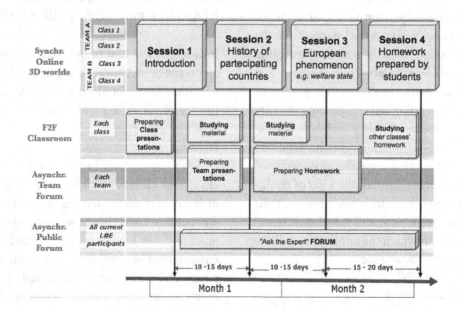

Figure 6. Screenshot of the 3D environment. Left: students share online pictures of their home countries. Top right: an avatar performs an ability game; bottom right: avatars gather around boards, the content of which will trigger cultural discussion

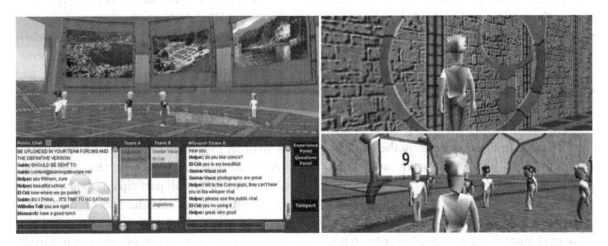

riddles requiring an accurate knowledge of the subject matter; competition is a powerful motivator, adding excitement to the experience. In addition, students are encouraged to work together with their remote team-members, strengthening ties with them. They interact via chat in the 3D world and asynchronously through online forums during the intervals between sessions.

The language of all interactions, interfaces and study materials is English. To achieve in-depth comprehension of the cultural themes proposed, further educational activities are performed in the intervals between sessions in the virtual world: students are asked to study a set of contents in the format of interviews with international experts, and to prepare a piece of homework in collaboration with their team members by doing some research: for example, they may have to relate a significant historical issue to its present consequences and analyze the traces left in their local context (e.g. the influence of languages or religion in the formation of national states).

Every synchronous online cooperative session lasts approximately one hour. Ten avatars move around in the virtual world: eight students (two per school), a guide and a helper, human tutors

'physically' present in the virtual world. While two students in each class control an avatar in the 3D world, others interact with remote peers via chat (a 2D chat separated from the 3D graphics) from a third and (since L@E 2005-06) a fourth computer; the rest of the class groups around them or follows from a projection screen, takes turns, and helps them answer questions. The guide and the helper play a critical role in keeping the session fast-paced, coordinating the students, making sure that no one gets lost or left behind, directing the activities, helping with technical problems, assigning scores and also penalties for rude behavior. From an educational point of view, their role is to provoke discussion among students by asking test questions and introducing new topics.

In order to avoid confusion, ineffective interactions and wasting time during the session, every single time slot is dedicated to a precise educational activity, and the guide makes sure that everyone keeps to it. The 'in-the-small' sequence of activities for each session includes:

- a few minutes' welcome: students chat and move around while the guide waits for everyone to log in

- a self-presentation from the four participating countries (in Session 1 see Figure 6, left), from the two teams (in Session 2), or of the final homework (in Session 4)
- a discussion based on the interviews (Sessions 2 and 3) or the final homework (Session 4)
- a team game based on the contents of the interviews (in Sessions 2 and 3 see 2 top right)
- a wrapping-up section where the guide assigns tasks for the following session, and all say goodbye.

As regards the 'in-the-large' sequence, the four sessions (Figure 5) are structured in order to lead from a general knowledge of the formation of national identities in Europe, to a progressively more focused view of a specific cross-national aspect which, eventually, students connect to their own local context and present culture.

- Session 1 introduces students to each other and to the cultural topic of the experience. They meet remote peers, show in turn pictures of their class and country (sent in advance for upload in the 3D), discuss the preliminary material (read before the session), and play the first game.
- In Session 2, students present their team's work and discuss the history of the countries involved; they also play a game based on the contents (a treasure hunt). At the end they are assigned materials on a specific European issue for Session 3, and the title of the research homework to be prepared for Session 4.
- In Session 3, a specific European issue is dealt with in depth, e.g. the role of languages in the formation of nation-states. Again, discussion and games take place. Afterwards students have another couple of weeks to complete the assignment (i.e. connecting a relevant European subject to

their local context). One week before the last session students submit their homework and read the works of the other schools.
- Finally, in Session 4 students present their homework, discussing with their peers. The final scores are also announced, and the 'crowning' of the winning team concludes the experience.

In order to guarantee the achievement of substantial educational benefits in terms of knowledge, and to allow all participants to start on the same footing, a set of materials is provided beforehand to schools, in the form of interviews with leading European scholars and auxiliary materials. An international scientific committee supervised the selection of approximately 20 interviewees (at least one from each of the countries covered). Experts are interviewed (in English) about the main events in the history of their country, and their perspective on some trans-national issues (such as the spreading of nationalistic ideals, the language differentiation, etc.). The staff edit and reorganize the interview transcripts into a set of thematic units. They also formulate a set of questions that guides and helpers will use to test the students' preparation, and collect related material to support comprehension, such as maps, chronologies and descriptions of important events or characters. These auxiliary materials help to fill in the gaps, as students from different countries, ages and school orientations will certainly have different background knowledge.

Students are asked to perform a number of assignments; assignments play an important role in getting students to actively reflect on the contents, work in groups with classmates and team-mates, and use electronic tools (from word processors and Internet search engines, to HTML and photo editors). For example, before Session 1, students are requested to send a class presentation (an HTML page with pictures of the students and a short text) and nine pictures representative of their town and country. During the first session students introduce themselves and meet their team partners; by the next session teams will have to collaborate on the forums to describe and compare their everyday life, and to research, explain and compare material evidence related to their national identity. They also have to create an HTML presentation to show their findings in the 3D world. Finally, for the last session they have to: (a) interview ten 'people in the street' about the way they perceive their national identity; (b) critically reflect on the role of a given historical issue in their country's history; (c) compare their findings with team partners, and synthesize their discussion in two short HTML presentations. During Session 4 they discuss their findings with the other team.

When online in the 3D environment, students interact via chat. The chat is a very fast-paced means of communication: while it effectively supports a fast exchange of short questions and answers, it is less suitable for discussions involving long and complex contributions, especially if chatting is not the only activity. In the 3D world users can also move around and explore the environment. Therefore, quick questions are asked in the chat in the 3D world, while more complex questions, requiring more thoughtful answers, are posed in a parallel 2D chat.

In the 3D world, a number of games are there to stimulate competition and, at the same time, to force team collaboration, provide excitement, and encourage exploration of the 3D world and its features. There is always interplay between the aspects of playing and the educational benefits which are sought; students are motivated to study the contents necessary to solve the cultural riddles embedded in the games. For example, in Session 1 the quiz requires players in the 3D world to perform ability games (e.g. flying through a series of circles: see Figure 6) as many times as possible, while team partners in the 2D chat can win facilitators for them by answering the guide's conceptual questions correctly. All games are cooperative: for example, in Session 3 the game

'find your way' requires one class per team to go as many times as possible through a path full of obstacles, where only the partner class can see the obstacles, and must give instructions via chat to the 'blind' team partners. Obstacles suddenly appear (facilitating the run) if the team-mates in the 2D chat give correct answers to the cultural quizzes.

Eventually, every class can stay in touch with remote participants between sessions and collaborate with them thanks to the online forums. The common forum is reserved for the four classes involved in an experience, the team forum is accessible only to the two classes composing a team, and the public forums are visible to everyone. Students and teachers can contact participants in other experiences and send questions to the experts of the scientific committee in the *meet the experts* forum. Students moderate team forums; the others are moderated by the guides. All communications between the schools (i.e. teachers) and L@E staff take place via email.

IMPLEMENTATION

Edutainment experiences are complex artifacts, involving many different stakeholders with various goals and requirements, as discussed above. In our experience with different tools based on shared 3D worlds, we have identified two main recurring problems:

- *Great variability of requirements*: in the phases that lead from the educational concept to the first application prototype, there is often the need to test several configurations that differ for environment/objects/ interactions/contents. This is aimed at understanding the best and most effective educational strategy to get the desired results. Obviously, this need of 'customizability' deeply is reflected in software implementation.

- *The need to generate several variants of the same collaborative experience prototype, fitting the virtual world to the particular user requirements*: the same virtual world must be 'dressed' according to the educational target and to the players involved (i.e. avatar skin, players' names, etc.)

For the above reasons, and for the need to generate a variety of applications, we came to the conclusion that we needed to build our own framework, based on industry standard, flexible and configurable, in order to support advanced collaborative features. Therefore, from the very first experience back in 2001, we developed our own framework (rather than a specific application) named WebTalk04 (WT04) (Bucciero, Mainetti & Paolini, 2005). WT04 supports complex cooperation features which have been tested with hundreds of 'direct users' and thousands of 'indirect users'. As a distinctive feature, WT04 is based on an XML configuration strategy, which allows an easy control of most of the advanced features, including collaborative functions such as public and whisper chat, cooperative object seeking, another eye's avatar view, etc. WebTalk04 proposes an XML declarative format to reduce programming need for non-expert designers of the collaborative experience (Barchetti, Bucciero, Mainetti, & Santo

Sabato, 2005). For this reason we examined the major issues concerned in the formal description of a collaborative virtual environment both from a static point of view, regarding how the virtual word is when it is generated, and from a dynamic point of view, regarding how it can evolve during the collaborative session, through a declarative description of the Event Conditioned Actions (ECA) which can be performed in the virtual environment.

The XML description of the scene graph and of the user-to-user or user-to-object interactions is the interface between the following subsystems (Figure 7):

- *WT04 runtime environment*, in which this XML file works as a declarative description of how the virtual world has to be rendered, as well as the way in which the action can take place and evolve.
- *WT04 authoring environment*, where the designer defines and fine-tunes the world structure and the specific behaviors attached to each user or interactive object.

As shown in Figure 8, we devised our logical architecture as a 3-tier system, detailed as follows:

Figure 7. WebTalk04 technical architecture

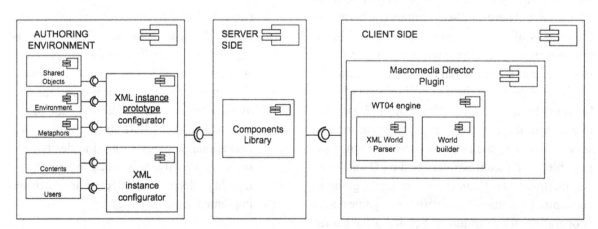

1. *Scene graph and behavior schema*: coded through XML schema, it represents the structure of a valid WT04 XML instance, where the elements composing XML instances are defined, together with the rules between elements and the supported data types.
2. *Scene graph and behavior instance prototype*: an XML document representing the skeleton of a collaborative session, where the designer had already defined geometries forming the virtual environment as well as the users' interaction rules.
3. *Scene graph and behavior instance*: the final and XML instance completed with all information and contents depending on the specific context (specific users involved, specific target of the experience, given topics, etc.).

In this way every actor involved in the authoring process has to manage a different and separate concern of the whole system:

1. Software architects develop *scene graph and behavior schema*, in other words the vocabulary of elements to be used to compose every XML instance describing a collaborative experience.
2. Session configurators build the *scene graph and behavior instance prototypes*.
3. Teachers (without particular technical skills) create a *scene graph and behavior instance* on the basis of a pre-built XML instance prototype.

When an XML instance is generated, the system is ready to start a collaborative session. The XML instance serialized file is sent to the clients' runtime environment (coded in Macromedia Director and Flash technology) which interprets the declarations and provides the instance with the right components taken from a library (on one hand it instances the right 3D models in the world, on the other it sets up the collaboration's rule that will govern the shared experience).

Collaborative Metaphors

One of the main features of the WT04 framework is the extensive support for collaborative metaphors. Collaborative metaphors (Barbieri & Paolini, 2001) are set of rules to support interaction and collaboration between users who want to explore complex content and information together. The rules determine how a community of users can be created and managed, how every member of the community can operate on his own or can cooperate with other members. Different types

Figure 8. WebTalk04 declarative system levels

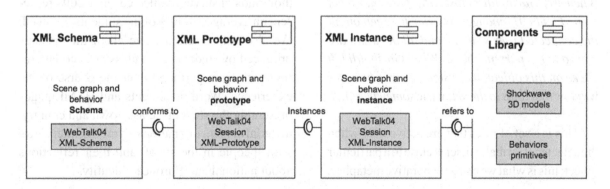

of situation, tasks, and users' roles determine different behaviors and therefore need different metaphors. WT04 offers a huge support to collaborative metaphors. We can set up in the XML configuration file a set of specific behaviors that can be applied to a specific metaphor. Therefore we can select what behavior is applied to a specific shared object at a particular moment. When a collaborative metaphor is activated, the corresponding set of interaction rules takes effect, and every object follows the right behavior to interact with the shared world. There are two different way to activate a metaphor:

1. *Explicit way*: it can be started manually (and asynchronously) by a power user.
2. *Implicit way*: an event in the virtual shared world generates a 'change metaphor sync message', which tells all clients to apply the new metaphor.

Thanks to the collaborative metaphor paradigm, we are able to manage complex interactions between entities in a virtual shared environment, specifying the current set of the collaboration's rules governing every aspect of the virtual world.

Let us now examine how we can translate an interaction rule into an XML based description used by a WT04 engine to control the mutual interactions generated inside the shared world.

Let us suppose that we want to map this interaction rule:

When user Garibaldi is close to the gate, the object named 'cube01' changes its color to green on all the connected user's clients and all the users are moved to the part number 2. When Garibaldi left clicks on this object, the system opens a browser window that links to the url: www.somewhere.net.

This is a set of rules that are active only when the selected (Garibaldi) user is close to a particular object: this is what we call collaborative metaphor.

Algorithm 1 is a fragment of the metaphor as serialized in XML format.

Obviously, by defining a huge number of metaphors and merging them together, we can govern the collaborative environment, recreating the exact collaborative situation we want.

EVALUATION

Sources and Monitoring Tools

In order to obtain a picture as complete as possible of the students' experience with Learning@ Europe, we collect data, both quantitative and qualitative, from many different sources.

We ask all participating teachers to complete five online surveys: one about their expectations before the beginning of the project, and one after each of the four cooperative sessions. After the final session we also ask teachers for a global evaluation of the project's educational impact. In addition, after the conclusion of the project, in-depth interviews or a focus group with a limited number of teachers provide assessment and insights about the surveys' results. Since 2004 we have collected hundreds of surveys, representing 70-90% of teachers.

We ask all participating students to complete two online surveys: one about their expectations before the beginning of the project, and one after the final cooperative session, asking for a global evaluation of their experience with L@E. The thousands of surveys collected since 2004 represent on average 30-40% of the students involved. We also collect and archive all of the artifacts produced by students (as a class or in collaboration with team partners) over the course of the experience: Word documents and HTML pages presenting the students' class, town and country, material evidence of national symbols, interviews with 'people in the street' and their reflections about national and European identity.

Algorithm 1. Fragment of the WT04 XML instance of a collaborative metaphor

```
<Object Name="Cube01" Physics="Yes">
    <Geometry>
          .................
      </Geometry>
      <Behavior>
              <Metaphors>
                      <Metaphor num="1">
                              <User name="Garibaldi">
                                      <OnLeftClick Far="400">
<Action Type="GoToUrl" where="www.somewhere.net"/>
                                      </OnLeftClick>
                                      <OnProximity Distance="3000" Persis-
tence="0">
                                              <Action Type="StarTrek"
Property="UsST2"/>
<Action Type="ChangeColor" Target="Cube01" Property="#green"/>
                                      </ OnProximity >
                              </User>
                      </Metaphor>
              </Metaphors>
      </Behavior>
</Object>
```

All online tutors (guide and helper) complete a short debriefing and an online report at the end of each cooperative session, describing the events and evaluating the session in terms of participation, pedagogical value, technical and organizational issues. In addition, every week tutors must complete a survey about the current status of the forums they are moderating, and at the end of the experience they must complete a global forum report.

The system automatically logs and archives the transcripts of all chat discussions which take place in the 3D worlds, as well as all of the messages posted on the forums, including information such as date and time of posting, author's nickname and IP address, users' log-in and log-out times in the 3D world. Quantitative analysis on this data provides information such as peak hours of forum use and average connection time of users. Interesting posts pointed out by moderators provide anecdotal evidence of the experience's impact in terms of engagement, cross-cultural exchange, formation of online communities of European students, English practice and historical reflection. In addition, a certain number of sessions are registered from the guide's monitor through Camtasia, a screen-capture tool, and/or videotaped by observers on-site in the schools.

The Impact

The impact of L@E, as well as of its 'kin' programs, has always been quite positive. We present here some selected results of the year 2006-07, the year in which we had the highest number of participants (for a thorough presentation of the results see Poggi, 2006).

Asked in a survey to evaluate the overall educational impact of L@E, 60.7% of the 61 teacher-respondents rated it either as very good or excellent, and 37.7% as good. Only one teacher found it less than good. Teachers' comments in the surveys show that they appreciated the new and stimulating educational format, the collaboration with European partners, and the positive impact on the students' motivation, learning, and engagement.

According to the teachers' survey responses and the reports of online tutors, the majority of students in each class achieved significant pedagogical goals, not only in learning historical facts, but also in terms of critical thinking, understanding of complex historical concepts, and acquisition of a broader view of European history: a view that overcomes national borders and looks at historical phenomena from multiple perspectives, taking advantage of the 'first-hand' information and fresh insights provided through discussion among students from different countries.

As regards improvements in attitudes, more than 51% of teachers rated as very good or excellent the improvements in the students' attitudes towards other cultures, and 36% reported a very good or excellent increase in students' motivation at school in general. In addition, almost 70% of teachers reported a general increase in the proficiency of their students.

Students confirm this data in the surveys: asked whether the L@E experience had made them change their mind about (1) the use of computers at school, (2) the use of English, (3) their nation, (4) other nations, (5) history and (6) Europe, 34% (498 respondents) wrote they had changed their minds about Europe and 42% about history. Many commented that they had realized that history can be interesting, especially when studied in this particular way, and that Europe has much more to do with their own identity than they thought. While 20% of students said that they had

acquired different views about their nation, 47% changed their opinions about foreign countries. Presenting one's nation to foreign peers, and seeing them presenting their own, is a powerful way to understand national identities in a European perspective. Many students also changed their minds about the usefulness of English and about computers as learning tools.

Eventually, there are improvements in skills. Students' improvements in the functional use of English as a second language are remarkable: all teachers except one reported at least good improvements, with 55.7% rating them as major or excellent. As regards what we may call the '21st century skills', positive improvements for new learning methods, group work, and the use of computers for studying are reported by over 90% of teachers.

Some Anecdotal Evidence

We present here some qualitative data extracted from teachers' and students' answers to open-ended survey questions.

The **overall impact** was generally deemed very high:

It has been a rewarding experience for students and teachers too. Here are benefits in the process of project: enhanced communication between teacher and student; collaboration; no restrictions to text only: interactivity, color, sound; the use of technologies; multicultural trans-national approach; students have shown remarkable improvements in a number of learning fields, have even shown a greater motivation. (A teacher, L@E 2005-06.)

Probably the most stunning benefits were related to changes of attitude, in terms of "Europeanness" and acceptance towards other nations/cultures. Students' comments suggest that the L@E experience, particularly the study of European history and the interaction with other European students, greatly enriched their perception of being Europeans, and improved their understanding of European identities.

I understand that Europe is ME. (A student, L@E 2006-07.)

I think that Europe is a one big family. (A student, L@E 2006-07.)

Now I think that Europe is not only an idea, but something concrete. (a student, L@E 2005-06.)

It helped me to get more involved at school, above all, as regards English and the history of the other nations. (a student, L@E 2005-06.)

Students' comments in the surveys suggest that L@E was a powerful **motivator**:

I think that history was boring to study but now I don't think so! Studying with the computer is really great! (A student, L@E 2006-07.)

The motivation was great, especially the curiosity for other cultures. All students, even the weak ones, were involved in the event [...]. They discovered they were useful for the session and later on they felt more motivated and integrated in the class. (A teacher, L@E 2005-06.)

Teachers also noticed increased knowledge and interest in history and in a wider, more 'European', approach:

My impression is that students have acquired a new and deeper interest in history. They have seen from different perspectives some events of European history they had studied so far in a more 'detached' and 'mechanic' way. It was very interesting to talk about national identities taking into account specific interviews and other students' homework. (a teacher, L@E 2005-06.)

As regards lateral skills acquired during the experience, 51% of students in L@E 2006-07 declared they had changed their minds about English. They realized that: "with English we can speak with people of other countries"; teachers noticed this increased interest too:

My students haven't become 'Shakespeares', but they really communicate in English more confidently. (L@E 2005-06.)

For the first time I saw my students reading and, above all, writing English on their own initiative! (L@E 2004-05.)

Students also changed their minds about using computers as learning tools and working in groups:

I saw a different way to use computers"; "now I know that it's not only for playing games; I would like to use computers at school for every subject! (L@E 2006-07.)

On the whole, excitement and involvement were high: "they were so enthusiastic and excited that it was difficult for us to calm down everybody; it is so different from a usual lesson that I'm not sure they have realized they have communicate in English; you know French students are so reticent to speak English, and in this situation you could feel that everything was going on well." (L@E 2006-07.)

CONCLUSION

The final discussion examines the most relevant issues not only on the ground of the Learning@ Europe experience (described in previous sections) but also taking into account other ICT-based educational experiences run by our laboratory. The most relevant one is PoliCultura (Di Blas & Boretti, 2009; Di Blas, Garzotto, Paolini, & Sabiescu, 2009; Di Blas, Paolini, & Sabiescu,

2010a; DiBlas, Paolini, & Torrebruno, 2010b; Di Blas & Poggi, 2008; Paolini, DiBlas, & Torrebuono, 2009), an experience calling thousands of students in Italy every year, organized into regular classes, to develop digital storytelling projects (i.e. multimedia presentations composed by audio, images' slideshows and text).

For the sake of readability, these conclusions are organized into four "lessons learned". We warn the reader that this is a simplification: all issues are interrelated and sometimes strongly interwoven in terms of their cause and effect for each other.

Lesson Number 1

Technology does not provide educational benefits directly, but as a component of an overall educational experience.

After a number of years of projects, and after thousands of users (from pre-school to higher education students), we reached a belief that would have shocked us when we started: generally speaking, technology does not provide any educational benefit "directly". This is not to say that learning experiences cannot be greatly enhanced by technology (see lesson number 2), but that there is no direct correlation between the use of technology and the achievement of educational benefits. In Learning@Europe, the actual learning follows activities like studying interviews with experts (as downloadable pdfs), discussing them in class, doing independent research, performing assignments, etc.

MUVE was used for gaming, quizzes, questions and answers, chatting and discussions: these activities are important (see lessons 3) but are not directly related to learning.

For some students (a small fraction), discussions over the forum was also important, but this of course is a much simpler collaborative technology, and in any case forums were never crucial: in some cases, forums were not used at all.

All the impact studies that we have carried out seem to indicate that there is no direct correlation between any specific learning and the technology. Still, technology plays a crucial role, as discussed in lesson number 2.

Lesson Number 2

The role of technology, in making the educational experience effective, is crucial but sometimes hard to understand, and more complex than it may look at first sight.

Despite our claim that technology does not directly provide educational benefits, almost all the teachers and pupils indicate that the learning experience would not have been so effective (and in some cases, even not feasible) without the technology. So what is the role of a MUVE and, more in general, of ICT in enhancing a learning experience? Let us try a few possible answers:

- **Feasibility (in a functional sense):** it is clear that without a collaborative technology it would be impossible to carry on a learning experience involving students from four different European cities. However, do we really need something as sophisticated as MUVEs but not simply e-mail and forums (that could be enough, from a purely functional point of view)?

- **Sense of glamour/modernity:** 3D environments, avatars, 3D gaming, action, real-time chatting, etc. all these activities generated in the participating students a feeling of being "introduced in the third millennium"; this feeling was particularly remarkable since it all happened at school and during school hours, generating a clash between third millennium technology and 18th century "technology" (blackboard, chalk, paper...). Overall, activities in the 3D environment lasted 4 hours per experience only, approximately 10-20% of the whole workload. Nevertheless, they were perceived as the distinctive and glamorous point of the experience as a whole.

- **Fun/entertainment/excitement:** some activities, and especially those in the 3D environment, were designed to provide fun. They could not be compared to videogames, but still the feeling was one of "gaming", with consequent engagement. In addition, the engagement was collective (a full class felt "united as a team", as some of them said) but not just individual. Videos show that while a couple of students were directly using the workstation, a number of others (up to five or six) were gathered around them, suggesting messages and answers, cheering and shouting. Participation rate and "virtual presence" were very high.

- **High visibility/challenge:** each class felt "important", since only a few classes in each country were participating, and in general, school authorities (at national or regional level) were directly involved. In addition, there was a competition, and each class wanted to win to honor their country, region, and/or school. Each class, each teacher and each pupil were highly competitive, both for individual pride and collective pride, given the international setting. It provided great challenges: the technology was new, the social setting was new, the educational frame was also new. No one had sufficient previous knowledge to rely on, and everyone felt as a pioneer and an innovator.

- **Team-building:** the difficulty of the challenge, the uncertainty about what to do, and the willingness to win the competition (or at least to show off) reinforced within each class the sense of "we are a team and we are going to make it".

- **Motivation:** all the above answers, in the end, sum up to a strong motivation for learning. Pupils dig into the material, read papers, train to answer quizzes, do additional research, in order to take part in the game and show off their knowledge to their teammates and opponents, have fun, and contribute to the performance and fate of their team.

So, in the end, motivation for learning is the crucial factor favored by the technology: this is neither an obvious nor a negligible factor. On one hand, it seems to contradict technology detractor positions: advanced technology at school seems to be an important ingredient for increasing pupils' motivation. On the other hand, it seems to contradict the extreme positions of technology fans, claiming that direct functional benefits are generated by technology.

It should also be noted that in several cases (roughly 25%, 30% of classes), teachers indicated that the motivation crossed borders of the specific experience (Learning@Europe, the storytelling activity, etc.): pupils were more involved in school activities in general, for a long span of time. So, bringing technology at school seems to be capable, at times, of providing pervasive and long-lasting effects.

Lesson Number 3

The design of a complex, technology-enhanced educational experience is a complex activity following unusual rules.

The architecture of the learning experience provided by Learning@Europe was not developed in a canonical manner, i.e. from requirements to design and then to implementation. Even the objectives to be reached were not clear in the beginning.

The starting point was the intuition that a 3D multi-user environment, used to connect different classes, could generate an engaging and socializing experience. Around this intuition, in order to shape the full experience, different elements were added: the architecture and geometries of the environment, the collaborative features, the activities, the games, the traditional learning activities, etc.

Such a design is supported by intuition, induction (by analogy), trial and error, and expert evaluation. Accurate monitoring of real-life experiences was also a source of inspiration to revise previous design decisions.

We call this style of design "organic design" (Bolchini, DiBlas, Paolini, & Poggi, 2010), since it corresponds to how organic life develops, rather than to how human beings create artifacts. The resulting design of the overall experience is perfectly rational (everything has a clear motivation and explanation), but it does follow a small set of requirements, though not in a strict sense.

Lesson Number 4 (Consequence of Lesson 3)

The design of a MUVE to support an educational experience is a complex activity following unusual rules.

Not only the learning experience, but also the technology seems to be based on organic design rather than on traditional design. Again, we could not even define the requirements, but only in a generic sense. We cannot demonstrate that all the technology features are the best possible answers to each specific requirement: we can argue that those technological features play a role and that in the end they work, in the sense that they get the job done. The analogy is with the "design of life": can we argue that "2 legs" are better than "8 legs" or than wings or than crawling like a snake? They are all plausible answers to contextual stimuli: the same reasoning applies to our technology solutions.

Overall we can conclude that MUVEs have great potential for fostering change and innovation at school, providing substantial educational benefits: Learning@Europe is a clear demonstration of this.

REFERENCES

Barab, S., Gresalfi, M., & Arici, A. (2009). Why educators should care about games. *Educational Leadership*, 76–80.

Barab, S., Thomas, M., Dodge, T., Carteaux, R., & Tuzun, H. (2005). Making learning fun: Quest Atlantis, a game without guns. *Educational Technology Research and Development*, *53*(1), 86–107. doi:10.1007/BF02504859

Barbieri, T., & Paolini, P. (2001). Broadcast and online cultural heritage: Reconstructing Leonardo's ideal city – from handwritten codexes to webtalk-II: A 3D collaborative virtual environment system. *Proceedings of the Conference on Virtual Reality, Archeology, and Cultural Heritage*, (pp. 61-66).

Barbieri, T., & Paolini, P. (2001). Cooperation metaphors for virtual museums. In Bearman, D., & Trant, J. (Eds.), *Proceedings Museums & Web*.

Barchetti, U., Bucciero, A., Mainetti, L., & Santo Sabato, S. (2005). *WebTalk04: A declarative approach to generate 3D collaborative environments*. VAST 2005 6th International Symposium on Virtual Reality, Archaeology and Cultural Heritage, 3rd Eurographics Workshop on Graphics and Cultural Heritage, (pp. 55-60).

Bers, M. U. (2001). Identity construction environments: Developing personal and moral values through the design of a virtual city. *Journal of the Learning Sciences*, *10*(4). doi:10.1207/S15327809JLS1004new_1

Bolchini, D., Di Blas, N., Paolini, P., & Poggi, C. (2010). Biological life cycle: A new interpretation for the evolution of ICT applications. *Proceedings of the Educational Design Research Conference: Local Change and Global Impact*.

Bucciero, A., Mainetti, L., & Paolini, P. (2005). Flexible 3D collaborative virtual environment: WebTalk04. *Proceedings of the 11th International Conference on Virtual Systems and Multimedia,* (pp. 669-680).

Caillois, R. (1961). *Man, play and games.* New York, NY: Free Press.

Dede, C., Clarke, J., Ketelhut, D., Nelson, B., & Bowman, C. (2005). *Students' motivation and learning of science in a multi-user virtual environment. American Educational Research Association.* AERA.

Di Blas, N., & Boretti, B. (2009). Interactive storytelling in pre-school: A case-study. *Proceedings of IDC 2009 (Interaction Design and Children),* (pp. 44-51).

Di Blas, N., Garzotto, F., Paolini, P., & Sabiescu, A. (2009). Digital storytelling as a whole-class learning activity: Lessons from a three-years project. *Proceedings of ICIDS 2009.* (LNCS 5915), (pp. 14-25).

Di Blas, N., Paolini, P., & Sabiescu, A. (2010a). Collective digital storytelling at school as a whole-class interaction. *Proceedings of IDC 2010.* (in print)

Di Blas, N., Paolini, P., & Torrebruno, A. (2010b). Digital storytelling at school: Does the TPCK model explain what's going on? *Proceedings of E-Learn 2010 Conference.*

Di Blas, N., & Poggi, C. (2008). Can ICT support inclusion? Evidence from multi-user edutainment experiences based on 3D worlds. *Proceedings of the Workshop Marginalized Young People: Inclusion Through ICT, IDC 2008.*

Di Blas, N., & Poggi, C. (2008). The PoliCultura competition. Introducing media literacy in Italian schools. In Leaning, M. (Ed.), *Issues in information and media literacy* (pp. 93–121). Santa Rosa, CA: Informing Science Press.

Hunicke, R., LeBlanc, M., & Zubek, R. (2004). MDA: A formal approach to game design and game research. *Proceedings of the Challenges in Game AI Workshop, Nineteenth National Conference on Artificial Intelligence.*

Johnson, B. (2003). *Disintermediation and the museum Web experience: Database or documentary-which way should we go?* Museums and the Web.

Johnson, B. (2005). Place-based storytelling tools: A new look at Monticello. *Museums and the Web,* 173-182.

Kenderdine, S. (2001). 1000 years of the Olympic games: Treasures of ancient Greece. Digital reconstruction at the home of the gods. *Museums and the Web,* 173-182.

Paolini, P. Di Blas., N., & Torrebruno, A. (2009). Media & communication literacy in higher education: Learning a foreign language. *Proceedings of World Conference on Educational Multimedia, Hypermedia and Telecommunications 2009,* (pp. 3210-3220).

Poggi, C. (2006). *Bridging the gap between goals and design.* (Doctoral Dissertation). Politecnico di Milano, Milano, Italy.

Schaller, D., Goldman, K. H., Spickelmier, G., Allison-Bunnell, S., & Koepfler, J. (2009). *Learning in the wild: What Wolfquest taught developers and game players.* Museums and the Web.

Chapter 10
Learning by Building in SL:
A Reflection on an Interdisciplinary and International Experience

Hugh Denard
King's College, UK

Enrica Salvatori
Università di Pisa, Italy

Maria Simi
Università di Pisa, Italy

ABSTRACT

This chapter will report on, and critically assess the outcome of a two year-long experimental educational project using Second Life (SL) as a teaching and learning platform. The project's main goal was to investigate the added value of a multi-user environment in a multi-disciplinary and international context for learning about history, archaeology, acquiring a scientific approach and methodology to historical reconstruction and 3D visualization, as well as the skills to use different media technologies for communication and collaboration. This chapter will describe educational facilities and resources as well as heritage visualization projects built in the Digital Humanities Island in SL, where the collaboration between King's College London and the University of Pisa took place.

INTRODUCTION

In July 2007, following a highly successful one-year Erasmus studentship of Marco Bani[1] (a student from the Digital Humanities degree at the University of Pisa) to the Centre for Computing in the Humanities (CCH) at King's College, Hugh

Denard, one of Bani's tutors at King's, submitted a proposal to the Director of CCH to start a collaboration with the Digital Humanities program of the University of Pisa (DH-Pisa).

The proposal was to jointly develop a "Digital Humanities" Island in Second Life (SL), to create a focus for a strategic relationship between CCH and DH-Pisa involving teaching, research and conferences to generate economies, synergies

DOI: 10.4018/978-1-60960-545-2.ch010

and opportunities by sharing costs, expertise, resources and contacts.

"Digital Humanities" Island, jointly hosted and developed by CCH and DH-Pisa, had the potential to be the basis for a wider international collaboration around shared sets of resources.

Given that both institutions offer modules in visualization for the humanities, this was also seen as an opportunity to develop a shared syllabus and associated teaching and learning resources, with a view to develop possible future collaborative initiatives in this area including internships.

A further aim was to develop joint cultural heritage projects, with DH-Pisa providing access to contacts, resources and authorizations necessary to undertake cultural heritage sites in Italy, and CCH securing additional cultural heritage visualization skills, equipment and methodologies. Projects envisaged included the complex in which "The Leaning Tower of Pisa" is situated, the Roman theatre at Lucca, and the historic, medieval walls of Pisa.

CCH and DH-Pisa also wished to study, collaboratively, the methodological implications of the Second Life platform in relation to current developments and debates, especially *The London Charter for the Computer-based Visualization of Cultural Heritage* (The London Charter, 2006). In particular, it was interesting to identify specific issues and opportunities that the SL platform raises regarding London Charter implementation, and to explore questions such as, for instance, whether a more or less fixed set of visualization and documentation conventions for humanities and cultural heritage uses of SL would be desirable, or whether a variety of approaches should be allowed to emerge in tandem with the technology as it evolves. A collaboration would allow researchers in both institutions to draw on their teaching and learning activities, developing and observing a wider range of case studies with student groups, and to provide a well-defined research agenda and set of approaches according to which participation by other humanities and

cultural heritage researchers in SL, including the EPOCH network of excellence (http://www. epoch-net.org/), could be encouraged.

Between 2007 and 2010, King's and Pisa made notable advances in realizing each of these objectives. Together, they established "Digital Humanities Island" (DHI), complete with welcome center, teaching, learning and display spaces and interactive guide, and successfully hosted a number of virtual exhibitions and "mixed-reality" live events there; in 2007-2008, they created several proof-of-concept cultural heritage visualizations in SL including of Galileo Galilei's Laboratory and the Leaning Tower of Pisa; in 2008-2009, they carried out a successful teaching and learning collaboration on ancient maritime archaeology; and in 2009, they secured funding for, and completed, a project on applying the London Charter (discussed below) within SL.

At the time of writing, we at Pisa and King's find ourselves, on the one hand pressed for the resources that would enable us further to evolve our shared teaching and learning activities, but also, on the other hand, poised to leverage our work in SL into real-life installations and planning consultations in both Pisa and London. The story of our collaboration thus far is one that encompasses ideals and errors, hopes and frustrations, achievements and, today, a renewed and revised sense of possibilities. This chapter will give an account of these pedagogical experiments and reflect upon what they have taught us about the use of virtual worlds in humanities teaching and learning.

HUMANITIES VISUALIZATION AND VIRTUAL WORLDS

The University of Pisa offers a degree in Digital Humanities, an interdisciplinary study program in which students receive a solid education in humanities together with the technological skills and methodologies to master the tools for processing cultural contents in different digital forms. Most of the students involved in the project specialize in a graduate-level program within a master degree in Digital Humanities, called "Graphics, interactivity, virtual environments". This study program aims to produce professionals for the cultural, entertainment and educational industry, by forming competences and skills for jobs which rely on creative expression by means of new technologies such as: virtual environments and augmented reality, graphics, 3D modeling, animations, multimedia production, digital audio, computer games, computer art, interactive performances and exhibitions. Given their specific background, students have the necessary competences to play an active role in the construction of artifacts in SL.

The Centre for Computing in the Humanities at King's College London offers a taught Masters in Digital Culture and Technology, which attracts students from the full range of traditional humanities disciplines as well from film and media studies, computer science and the social sciences. In an elective module called Applied Visualization in the Arts, Humanities and Cultural Heritage, students study significant examples of computer-aided, applied visualization – past, current and emergent – in teaching and research contexts, encompassing a wide range of purposes, technologies, approaches and methods and, working under the guidance of members of King's Visualization Lab (KVL), plan and carry out a visualization project. KVL has nearly fifteen years of expertise in the reconstruction and visualization of cultural heritage.

KVL now also has a significant profile in SL. In June 2007, generously supported by the Eduserv Foundation, KVL commenced work on its first major, teaching and learning project in SL, Theatron3 (Childs, 2009, http://www.theatron3.cch.kcl. ac.uk/). Theatron3 transformed the team's earlier, award-winning Theatron project (http://www. kvl.cch.kcl.ac.uk/theatron.html) into a range of content-rich, research-based virtual environments in SL comprising digital 19 milestones in European theatre design from the Theatre of Dionysus at Athens to the Teatro Olimpico at Vicenza, and from Shakespeare's Globe Theatre to the Schaubühne am Lehniner Platz in Berlin (Denard, 2005). Each virtual theatre has extensive associated historical and interpretative materials delivered through location-sensitive, media-rich Heads-Up Displays (HUDs) containing in-depth contextual and interpretative educational resources, as well as a framework enabling teachers and students to create their own versions of the HUD responsive to their own teaching learning objectives. In collaboration with the Higher Education Academy Subject Centers for English and for Dance, Drama and Music, Theatron3 also disbursed five small grants to university tutors to conduct pedagogical projects exploring its potential as a rich environment for practice-based learning, from creative writing to scene design, and from Shakespearean dramaturgy to mixed-reality performance. A report by the project's educational technologist, Mark Childs, can be found through the Theatron3 Website, above (Childs, 2009).

KVL is also notable for having instigated, and for continuing to lead the development of The London Charter for the Computer-based Visualization of Cultural Heritage (London Charter) – a set of internationally-recognized principles that provides a framework ensuring that digital visualization methods are, and are seen to be intellectually rigorous and robust. The London Charter insists upon intellectual accountability, or "transparency" that enables subject communities "to evaluate the choice of a given visualization method, and how it has been applied in a particular case without having to rely exclusively on the *authority claims* of the author" (Beacham, Denard, & Niccolucci, 2006). The current version of the London Charter (2.1, February 2009) sets out six main principles (each being elaborated through several sub-sections):

- **Principle 1 – Implementation:** The principles of the London Charter are valid wherever computer-based visualization is applied to the research or dissemination of cultural heritage.

- **Principle 2 – Aims and Methods:** A computer-based visualization method should normally be used only when it is the most appropriate available method for that purpose.

- **Principle 3 – Research Sources:** In order to ensure the intellectual integrity of computer-based visualization methods and outcomes, relevant research sources should be identified and evaluated in a structured and documented way.

- **Principle 4 – Documentation:** Sufficient information should be documented and disseminated to allow computer-based visualization methods and outcomes to be understood and evaluated in relation to the contexts and purposes for which they are deployed.

- **Principle 5 – Sustainability:** Strategies should be planned and implemented to ensure the long-term sustainability of cultural heritage-related computer-based visualization outcomes and documentation, in order to avoid loss of this growing part of human intellectual, social, economic and cultural heritage.

- **Principle 6 – Access:** The creation and dissemination of computer-based visualization should be planned in such a way as to ensure that maximum possible benefits are achieved for the study, understanding, interpretation, preservation and management of cultural heritage.

The deep and widespread impact of the London Charter, the current draft of which (2.1, February 2009) is available in English, Italian, Spanish, German and Japanese, is apparent not only in such occurrences as the Italian Ministry of Cultural Heritage and Activities funding of implementation case studies, but also in developments such as the newly-drafted Seville International of Virtual Ar-

chaeology (June 2010) which explicitly describes itself as an implementation of Principle 1.1 of the London Charter, which states that: "Each community of practice, whether academic, educational, curatorial or commercial, should develop London Charter Implementation Guidelines that cohere with its own aims, objectives and methods."

Interdisciplinary Education

In a series of separate and joint projects between October 2007 and June 2009, DH-Pisa and King's College built, on Digital Humanities Island, Galileo Galilei's Laboratory, the Leaning Tower of Pisa, the Tower of London, a Roman ship (Alkedo) and an orientation center, "Arketipo", equipped with a conference room, offices, tools for organizing meetings, information panels and an interactive guide called "IUMI". All the "builders" were students, under supervision and guidance of the teaching staff, and they did everything – the modeling and the development of tools – in the few months available within the curriculum.

The partners used SL not only as a building yard, but as a real area of collaborative work, given that the organizational and planning meetings were held in the virtual world as part of the practical lessons; the usefulness of SL as a platform for meetings and workshops indicates its significant value within the educational domain (a former example was the Kamimo Island, 2007).

The main barriers were thus not so much cultural or linguistic in nature (these exist, but can be largely addressed through the use of SL as a social networking tool) but rather reside in the concrete bureaucratic and administrative problems that affect the organization of joint courses in two (or more) universities: the differences and rigidity in timelines and schedules, unclear relationships between face-to-face lessons and independent study, the difficulty in accrediting the time students and staff spend working in the virtual environment, and the challenge of getting university authorities to understand the nature and benefits of these modes of teaching and learning as well as the shifts in working practice and assessment models they imply. If these barriers were reduced or eliminated altogether, SL could actually constitute a practical and economical platform for internationally-taught modules which would become "naturally" interdisciplinary because they would require students to learn and use a shared language: we do not refer here only to the spoken language, but to the specialized language of each subject material treated (in our case History, 3D Modeling, Art, Architecture, Computer Science), that differs from country to country.

The great interdisciplinary value, as well as potential limitations, of a Multi-User Virtual Environment (MUVE) such as SL lies in the fact that, within it, students can learn by doing, complementing the (often inadequate and un-motivating) combination of reading/writing or reading/explaining that characterizes the vast majority of university courses in the humanities (Kemp & Livingstone, 2006; Joseph, 2007; Ondrejka, 2008; Wankel, & Kingsley, 2009; Molka-Danielsen, & Deutschmann, 2009; Gütl, Chang, Kopeinik, & Williams, 2009).

The construction of the Arketipo learning and information center; the IUMI interface; Galileo's Laboratory; the Leaning Tower of Pisa; the Roman ship, Alkedo; and the East Wing of Somerset House, London enabled students to acquire, share and improve knowledge and skills not only in history and archaeology, but also in 3D digital modeling; digital video and audio; writing; reading aloud; human computer interaction and Web design; as well as advanced skills in independent learning; multi-partner collaboration; project planning and management; collective problem solving; implementation of relevant methodological standards; communication across disciplinary, cultural and technical divides, as well as how to assess the utility and potential of a technical platform for cultural content creation, technical development and exploitation.

In the volume edited by Molka-Danielsen & Deutschmann (2009), we discussed in some detail the pedagogical significance of the Arketipo, IUMI Interface, Galileo's Laboratory, and Leaning Tower of Pisa projects, all carried out during the 2007-2008 academic year. We briefly review these projects now, both because they provide essential context for the teaching and learning strategies underpinning the "Alkedo" and recently-completed Somerset House projects of 2008-2010, and because our experience of these later projects has given us further perspectives on the work of the 2007-2008 session.

CREATING AND DEPLOYING VIRTUAL LEARNING SPACES

We now turn our attention to the learning experience of creating and using the "virtual classroom" and "virtual learning infrastructure".

Arketipo

Arketipo is the conference center and meeting place of the DHI community. It was especially designed for teachers and students of Humanities computing; however the solutions adopted, some of them innovative, as well as the problems encountered, apply to any virtual environment which aims to reproduce traditional educational facilities.

We envisioned the center to become an effective *bonding place* where the reference community could meet and engage in a number of activities introducing them to the humanities computing culture. The conception of the building itself was ambitious and highly symbolic. All the constructions in Sl, including this building, are the result of student projects; this provides major skill acquisition opportunities including the ability to create from scratch a new "learning space" from minimal input from the supervisors. The chief builder, Francesco Genovesi, one of our most

Figure 1. Arketipo

skilled students, put a lot of imagination, care and effort in designing and building Arketipo; the result was a grandiose building, high quality when compared to the standards of SL (Figure 1).

The building hosts a garden dominated by the *tree of knowledge* rising among ancient ruins. The branches of the tree form the shape of a hand stretching towards the sky (Figure 2). You can sit on the tree to chat with fellow avatars (Arketipo blog, 2009).

Arketipo, however unique, is not much different from other virtual educational environments;

Figure 2. Knowledge Tree

it offers the virtual counterpart of traditional teaching places and tools: an auditorium, meeting places such as the garden, an exposition space, offices, slides projectors, blackboards …). Multifaceted information services integrate in SL information sources already available in the university setting: Web site, blog, forum, mailing list, RSS feeds.

Information is made available both in *asynchronous* mode, by way of special panels, interfaces, notecards, HUD displays and in *synchronous* mode, by means of lectures in the auditorium, meetings and contact hours with professors.

HCI (*Human Computer Interaction*) is the discipline concerned with the design, evaluation, and implementation of interactive computer systems for human users. The design of interactive, human-machine interfaces is no easy matter, and designing *avatar*-machine interfaces for *virtual worlds* can be even more difficult. In accessing a virtual world, the user must first learn the *client* interface before identifying the interface that has been created on purpose for the space where he/she is interacting through the avatar interface, which changes continuously depending on the places being visited. This lack of standardization often generates confusion.

Special care was dedicated to designing effective interactive devices and natural solutions for the "affordance"[2] of objects (Norman, 2002). New entry students and occasional visitors land exactly in the middle of the arrival platform, in front of the entrance hall of the center. They find before them a set of four pillar-like interactive panels: Rules, Teleport, Information, Iumi (Figure 1).

When approaching any of these panels, within a range of 5 meters, a round-rotating script associated to the buttons is enabled and a rotating text appears around the buttons, explaining their function. This is the only *non-static* element and is especially designed to immediately catch user's attention on the action to be performed. This rotating effect only appears within a certain distance from the avatar, thus preventing any visual interference

problem. Depending on the type of information, standard *notecards* are offered or SL's integration features are used to directly access Web pages with relevant content.

The *Teleport* allows a person to be immediately transferred to the desired location. In order to differentiate between levels in the building, a legend has been implemented in the *associating perception* style: the user easily associates the two upper buttons to level I and the lower two to level -I by exploiting form and color as clues. In practice, the black buttons refer to the upper level, the white buttons to the underground level. This idea was tested on different subjects and proved easily understandable and intuitive.

The first floor hosts a big semi-circular auditorium for conferences, fully equipped with a screen for slide and movie projection, blackboards, a teaching desk and a number of chairs for the audience (Figure 3).

In the underground floor there are a number of offices, fully equipped with uniquely designed desks and chairs, where professors can meet with students. Contact hours are advertised on message boards in the atrium in front of the offices. The underground floor also hosts a special secret room where the students can find other student's notes and suggestions on how to pass the exams.

Arketipo's exhibition hall is a place for showing the best projects completed by the students. They appear as pictures hanging on the wall, leading to Web sites when clicked. More complex is the solution adopted for showing 3D models of buildings. Since the number of prims is limited, we cannot afford to display all the constructions permanently on the island. The solution was to acquire and deploy a mechanism for displaying them on demand, a so-called *rezzing panel*. This device is able to store 3D objects composed of large number of prims, provided they are built in the appropriate way, and to reconstruct them when needed in the space outside Arketipo.

Figure 3. The Auditorium of Arketipo

The Value of Arketipo as a Learning Environment

Overall the solutions adopted to recreate a learning environment in SL were state-of-the-art and we consider this in all respects a valuable learning experience for our students and a great achievement for our team. The motivation and engagement of the best students was a driving force for other students to work jointly towards common goals and to contribute in a shared effort as part of a community. The educational value of this experience cannot be underestimated. Arketipo received a lot of attention in the metaverse the day of its inauguration, with enthusiastic comments from other educators and SL builders.

However, without a designated curator or manager, the actual use of the center was quite limited and the excitement of visiting the place accordingly quickly faded away; virtual venues evidently require proactive programming just as much as a physical venues.

We managed to use the auditorium for a few conferences and seminars with remote distance participants. Organizing slide and movie projections in the conference hall is not an easy task with current technology: It is to be planned and prepared in advance by people with the right technical skills and the right permissions to manage the virtual land. Depending on the client hardware the quality may be not satisfactory. For events with a large number of in-world participants, we experienced problems with the audio setting and with sometimes unbearable delays in rendering time. However, with the right technical know-how and facilities, live and mixed-reality events can enable an audience, which could otherwise not be present, to participate, either as avatars in SL or simply through accessing Web streaming video of the live event. In October 2009, for example, the Royal Irish Academy's Digital Humanities Observatory, with sponsorship from *Architecture Ireland*, arranged a public lecture by Denard on "Recreating Research, Art and Education in Shared Virtual Worlds", which took place in both Dublin City Council's Wood Quay Auditorium and the Arketipo conference room on Digital Humanities Island (Figure 4).

Just as many people attended the lecture virtually in Second Life as did physically in Dublin, and a moderator relayed questions from the virtual audience to the live event. While the sound signal lagged several seconds behind the physical event, virtual attendees nevertheless mostly re-

Figure 4. Audio-video stream from the Wood Quay Auditorium, Dublin, October 2009

mained present for the duration of the session. The technical and logistical effort of deploying this mixed reality mode could be justified by the presentation's reliance on visual, and especially virtual world, content.

While the physical audience enjoyed the heightened immediacy of physical co-presence in the Dublin auditorium, the virtual audience, as their avatars followed that of the presenter from site to site in Second Life, had higher status within the experiential hierarchy of the virtual world. Escaping the single, projected viewpoint to which the live audience in Dublin was constrained, each avatar's navigational choices created its own parallel "narrative" as a counterpoint to that of the presenter. The parity of their virtual presences invited a quite different quality of engagement from that offered to passive receivers of audio-video signals. At the same time, the physical audience's view of the virtual audience's avatars, as seen through the data-projected visual field of the presenter's avatar, accentuated their awareness of the ephemeral nature of the virtual event, as well as its randomness: the physical and the virtual, umbilically connected by the internet, seem to have exposed two different sets of "rules", as well as modes, of experience. In Second Life, what begins as an experiment in teleconferencing

quickly becomes an exploration of presence and performativity – the kind of creative collision that is common on this frontier. As of the time of writing, Arketipo remains live in SL as a virtual venue available for digital humanities-related activities.

As for the other educational facilities we have built, a few adventurous professors made some attempt to set up times for contact hours in their virtual offices. They managed to meet some enthusiastic first year students and a few of the students attending their courses. After a few weeks however nobody showed up any more and the experiment was discontinued.

The project team had a number of discussions about design decisions made in building Arketipo: we aimed for high quality and the result is impressive, but this was not without a cost. The number of primitive objects needed to achieve the desired degree of accuracy and detail was excessive: of the 15000 prims allowed in a sim, as much as 8000 were used by Arketipo alone; all the other educational activities and buildings had only 7000 prims left to share and this created some issue on how to ensure a fair allocation of prims to projects. A secondary effect of using such a huge count of prims, was the lagging experienced in rendering, which made Arketipo difficult to use with cheap hardware. Since the building was complete and quite spectacular, it was painful to have to destroy it and labor intensive to simplify it. Finally the decision was made to give up the underground floor and leave the rest.

Arketipo's quality did not go unnoticed: a copy of the building was sold to an educational institution of one of the big regions in Italy. Their main motivation in using SL was to reach a large number of students in high school, without moving educators to different locations. Their reasoning was along these lines: an avatar (student) per class, 30 students per class participating, 30 avatars in the auditorium, make nearly 900 students from different schools that can be reached simultaneously. At this time we cannot tell whether their expectations were met.

Overall our impression is that, given the current state of technology, for normal purposes, the use of SL as a virtual classroom, or more in general as a place for classes, seminars and conferences, does not offer clear advantages in comparison to other communication media such as Skype, teleconferencing or instant messaging. Specific tools for teaching (blackboards, slide and movie projectors) exist but are difficult to use, require some planning and have a clear additional cost. However, our challenge is to identify – or perhaps all we can do sometimes is guess, or intuit – those contexts and activities that might take on new dimensions if filtered through Second Life's evocation of virtual space and presence; this is the brave new world that we are, even now, only beginning to be able to perceive, much less chart.

IUMI: An Intelligent, In-World Interface

One fascinating student project, started in 2007-2008 and further refined and developed 2008-2010, has the ambition to develop an "intelligent" and cooperative in-world user interface for delivering location-aware and user-sensitive information.

Iumi is a *pseudo-animated* pet that can be worn on the avatar's shoulder and acts as a chatting companion during the visit to the DH island. The idea of the character was inspired by the logo of Informatica Umanistica (DH in Pisa), a bizarre combination of a book and computer screen (http://infouma.di.unipi.it/).

Iumi was created by Francesco Genovesi as an experiment in providing contextual and customized information about the virtual world objects in a natural conversational style form. This first instance of Iumi can be described as a context-aware user-adaptive guide, but the communication goes only in one direction: Iumi delivers information to the avatar (Figure 5).

The idea was further developed by Alan Zucconi, a computer science student, with a passion for Artificial Intelligence, by adding to the pet the functionalities of a *chat-bot*, i.e. a computer program able to carry out a possibly quite large set of language interactions according to a set of predefined rules and thus making it able to simulate a believable and sensible conversation with the user. Alan had already created a Web chat-bot, called Doriana, very successful with teenagers all over Italy, and was challenged to extend and adapt its technology to work within SL.

Figure 5. Iumi, Virtual Guide and Chat-bot

Iumi has been programmed in such a manner, that it can communicate with the avatar who wears it (i.e. the object owner) over a private channel; as an alternative, IUMI answers questions expressed in the public channel, when its name is explicitly mentioned. The request from the avatar goes to the chat-bot engine, residing on a server, where the answer is generated and sent back to the appropriate SL communication channel.

The chat-bot exploits location awareness in two different ways: (a) by volunteering appropriate information when the avatar enters a place or the range of an object for the first time *(location specific suggestions)*, and (b) by answering a set of pre-defined questions related to the location *(location specific answers)*. Communication is triggered upon entering the *range* of an object, by exploiting one of the positioning methods available. In practice, the avatar is free to go wherever it wants, and only when it happens to be in a specific context it gets from Iumi the information relevant to the context.

Iumi is also able to *adapt* to the avatar profile by offering different contents for different profiles. Living in an intercultural environment, Iumi is characterized by identity crisis: it does not know whether it is a book or a computer screen. Even if one of our missions as educators is to make both cultures coexist in our students, it is funny and engaging to imagine a tension between cultures that are so different. Thus, Iumi implements two profiles: *the computer science* and *humanistic* profiles according to the fact that our visitors may be more inclined towards technology or rather towards humanities: in the first case it delivers information more focused on the technological aspects, such as implementation methods and building techniques; in the second case, it will talk about the history of the buildings, important events, artistic aspects and so on. Other, maybe more significant, forms of adaptation to the user profile, are possible by writing specific rules and greatly enhance communication.

If everything else fails, Iumi has a large repertoire of sentences to express its inability to understand, a form of graceful decay mechanism to hide the shallowness of the interaction.

Finally, with the purpose of making the character more believable and human, Iumi's schizophrenia manifests itself in randomly generated sentences, which can be uttered once in a while. The sentences were collected within a forum, where contributors were DH students were challenged to invent ways to personalize Iumi's behavior.

This project was very significant since the result of the experiment is a proof of concept for how scholars, tutors and students may deliver location and user-sensitive information in world by using a natural paradigm of interaction. Other means of delivering information exist in SL, such a notecards or HUD's, but they are more artificial and more difficult to grasp than having a friendly conversation, even with the obvious limitations of today's natural language technologies. The possible extensions to the chat-bot are endless, as unlimited are the sources of information that the chat-bot engine can access; we tried for example to use a question answering system on contents from the Wikipedia, build as part of another project.

Equally important, and quite rewarding for us and for the students, was the possibility of working together at a truly challenging and interdisciplinary project, where different competences were required (programming, contents creation, graphics) and where the virtual world provides an ideal terrain for experimenting with real world issues such as location-aware behavior and real time human interaction, and the gratification of instant visibility of the project.

CREATING CULTURAL CONTENT IN SECOND LIFE

We now move from the learning experience of students creating and using the "virtual classroom" and virtual learning infrastructure, to that of creating and using virtual heritage content in Second Life.

Rebuilding the Tower of Pisa

Elisa Ciregia, then a graduate student of Digital Humanities at the University of Pisa (Ciregia, 2009) undertook to build a *London Charter*-compliant visualization of the famed, "Leaning" Tower of Pisa – the universally-recognized icon of the city and, indeed, of the nation as a whole. The effort was authorized the *Opera del Duomo* which carries the responsibility for the entire *Piazza dei Miracoli* area containing the *Duomo* (Cathedral), Leaning Tower, Baptistry, *Camposanto* and Museum. The central aims of Ciregia's project were twofold: (a) to test the capabilities of Second Life as an environment for both faithfully representing and providing, virtually, widespread public and information-rich access to precious monuments; (b) to strengthen the existing positive relationship between the *Opera del Duomo* and the Faculty of Humanities at the University of Pisa as a focus for exploring opportunities for further, shared activities relating to interpretation and dissemination.

Ciregia's model was rooted in her study of plans and technical documents relating to the Tower held by the Department of Civil Engineering at the University of Pisa. However, despite the effort to ensure the fidelity of the model to the original, the work presented many problems. The first challenge was the policy, then in force on Digital Humanities Island, that heritage visualizations, in the interests of consistency of user experience, should be built at 1:1 scale (using the in-world unit of measurement). This stipulation, together with the extraordinary complexity of the Tower, would have required a number of prims ("primitives" - the basic building blocks used to create three-dimensional content in Second Life) many times in excess of that available within Second Life in general and in the shared space of Digital Humanities Island in particular. Consequently,

Ciregia had to devise ways of greatly simplifying the model both decoratively and structurally. Rather than detailing each of the unique column capital designs on the actual Tower, for example, Ciregia was forced to use a single, standardized capital. Similarly, entering the "virtual" Leaning Tower, one finds it completely hollow; where the 296 stairs should be is, instead, an interactive teleport tool inviting avatars to beam themselves up to the top floor. Ciregia's deployment of subtly overlapping prims, as a necessary concession to the limited maximum size of Second Life prims (10m x 10m x 10m), gives the viewer a sense of, but does not accurately reproduce the Tower's cylindrical circumference (Figure 6).

Figure 6. The Tower of Pisa

The *London Charter* provided a highly accessible framework, for staff and students alike, to discuss the complex issues of intellectual integrity to which the Tower project gave rise, and assisted in maintaining an emphasis on the importance of following a rigorous scientific method even in a visualization designed to further popularize a monument. While Second Life imposes particularly stringent constraints on the modeling process, every type of modeling software, in fact, even the most accurate, involves operational decisions that affect the quantity and quality of information vehicles: there is no perfect model. To the question: "Can Second Life successfully accommodate and communicate to mass audiences high-quality, faithful, representations of complex, large-scale monuments?" the project established some not insignificant limitations, and in the process became a wonderful occasion to add to the bouquet of interdisciplinary learning other flowers, most notably restoration theory and practice, and the methods and problems of popularizing cultural heritage. These extended observations and understandings now become the starting point for future conversations about virtual heritage representation between the *Opera*

del Duomo and the University, as well as for curriculum development within the University.

Galileo Galilei's Laboratory

The next project followed, in some ways, a similar path to the Tower of Pisa project, since this virtual building too was "enriched" by notecards and audio files; but it also presented different challenges and problems. *Galileo Galilei's Laboratory* is a virtual representation of an actual building in the old slaughterhouse area of Pisa dating to the early 900s that today hosts the Museum for Computation Instruments (*Museo degli Strumenti di Calcolo*) in which the Galileo Galilei Foundation stores and displays to the public several Galilean experiments. The building and the virtual experiments were modeled as part of a taught module in *3D Graphics*, while students studying *Introduction to Historical Studies* produced audio and text files relating to the life of Galileo, his experiments and the history of science (Figure 7). The project explored not only the potential benefits that a virtual world might bring to two separate modules – one primarily historical and one primarily technical in nature – but also how

Figure 7. Galileo Galilei's Laboratory

inter-module collaboration might prompt us to rethink our learning objectives and outcomes in both of these, quite distinct, subject areas.

In the *3D Graphics* module, students first took photographs of the real Laboratory and of the Museum's physical reconstructions, designed by Professor Vergara Caffarelli, of experiments described by Galileo Galilei. Using these photographs both as primary reference materials for modeling and as sources for textures, they then undertook to build their own virtual reconstructions, in Second Life, of the "inclined plane", "pendulum", "inclined plane with pulley", "double pendulum" and "hydrostatic balance" experiments. Meanwhile, the students taking the *Introduction to Historical Studies* module undertook extensive readings on the life of Galileo and on the importance of his works in history of science. They then wrote, and recorded as audio files, informative texts suitable for the general public which the *3D Graphics* students, as well as publishing them through Web-pages, also embedded in the virtual library so that Second Life users could read or hear them by clicking on the experiments and pictures hanging on the walls.

What, then, was the significance of this pedagogical experiment? Overall, the opportunity to work in groups on shared objects in a common environment, the awareness that the project would produce something to be enjoyed by all people, and the continuous online interaction with teachers beyond the class schedule, all acted together to provide a powerful impetus towards learning and participation, which contributed notably to efficacy of the teaching process.

For the students of *Historical Studies*, the collaborative, virtual world-orientated process drew upon the traditional skills of reading books and articles, but also shifted the emphasis of these activities by conjoining them with the additional tasks of: (a) selecting from rich, complex and deep historical materials subsets to be deployed in the context of a particular exhibition/installation; (b) summarizing, explaining and correcting sources

to create new texts appropriate for a specific audience; (c) adapting content for use as hyperlinked segments, rather than as linear narratives; (d) authoring and publishing historical content for the non-print technologies of the digital, mass media age. In this way, the engagement with the virtual world platform, in addition to developing their knowledge and understanding of historical materials, also drew attention to, and developed their skills in confronting, the numerous, nuanced choices we make when we attempt to interpret and communicate the past in different contexts.

The virtual world environment also changes, and augments, the learning experience of students of *3D Graphics*. Firstly, and most importantly, their standard workflow, and conventional aims of modeling, have to be redesigned to make allowance for, as well as take advantage of, a collaborative, real-time, avatar-based, content-creation environment. A particular challenge in this respect is that of understanding the implications of working in an environment that, unlike most 3D modeling tools, is not designed to provide industry-level, or near-industry-level, graphical quality and performance, or to facilitate complex modeling operations, but rather aims to enable user-generated content and social interaction via a form of virtual embodiment. In this context, even the very aims of graphical representation need to be reconsidered: it may, for example, be more appropriate to think of the outcome itself as a kind of "laboratory" designed to invite and facilitate meaningful, creative interactions by users, rather than – as may be more commonly the case in 3D Graphics modules – as a polished, finished product to be "visited" or "used".

Other major challenges, or learning opportunities, are those of devising approaches to digitally representing three-dimensional cultural heritage that anticipate the requirements of both the user and the avatar. In the games industry, for example, the layout of the virtual terrain and the environment are laid out by the virtual world designer so as to optimize ease of navigation and viewing.

By contrast, real-world monuments, with their frequently complex, confined and irregular interior spaces, are rarely so obliging to the avatar: the camera (the "eyes" of the user, which typically floats behind and slightly above the avatar's body so that users can see their virtual selves in relation to their environments) finds itself stranded on a different level or different room to the avatar to which it supposedly belongs; avatars, trying to cross a room to view an object or climb virtual stairs, find the default avatar speed that the system bestows has them bumping into walls, overshooting doorways, or falling through gaps.

Computer games also typically do not aspire to hold themselves accountable to high standards of historical integrity, or to deliver extensive, detailed historical information. Historical visualization, however, operates in a domain in which the conventional means of communication is lengthy, linear text; the heritage visualization strategy must therefore also include plans for communicating the relationship of visualization to the historical sources from which it derives, for adapting historical materials into genres and formats that are appropriate to the virtual world, as well as for providing access to them through non-intrusive, intuitive interfaces.

Thus, 3D Graphics students confronted by *both* an avatar-based, user-generated, virtual world *and* complex cultural heritage content, must attempt to develop sophisticated responses to these several difficult challenges that a static, commercially-orientated 3D Graphics module would not normally encounter. The learning context that virtual worlds such as Second Life present to 3D graphics students in the humanities is therefore particularly demanding, both conceptually and technically.

Old-Style Modeling in a New Technology: Early Experiments at King's

While the students from Pisa were building Arketipo, the Leaning Tower of Pisa and Galileo Galilei's Laboratory, in the 2007-2008 sessions, students at King's College London were taking a different approach: each of them was asked to define, and then to realize, an individual visualization project within Second Life. Their proposals ranged from an interactive model of the Tower of London, to a media-rich, black-and-white simulation of part of the films set for Kevin Smith's 1994 film, *Clerks*.

At the end of the module, we found that students had either done unusually well, or unusually badly: if a student managed to surmount the technical challenges of content creation, they were inclined to lavish upon their work significant amounts of time and creativity, producing results with impressive attention to detail and imaginative use of textures and scripts providing exciting user experiences. By contrast, if individual students discovered themselves to have limited aptitude for 3D modeling – which is only one aspect of humanities visualization as a taught subject – they had no means of demonstrating their competence in other areas such as research, data capture and processing, project design, planning and documentation. On reflection, we noted that this isolated approach, while it provided excellent opportunities for able students, also unfortunately tended to imitate the product-orientated approach of conventional, off-line 3D modeling, and so failed to exploit the collaborative, real-time properties and potential of the Second Life environment.

In this 2007- 2008 session, we had indeed attempted to offer students an introduction to 3D modeling in Blender – an open-source version of an industry-type 3D modeling platform – before introducing them to Second Life's much less technically demanding 3D modeling system. As the semester progressed, however, we realized that, even if we had dedicated all of six of the available practical tutorials within the teaching schedule wholly to Blender, it would not have afforded sufficient training time to enable students to carry out a substantial, collaborative heritage visualization project, either individually or collectively. Given the diverse, and typically non-technical backgrounds of our MADCT students, we determined that Second Life, despite its severe limitations as a modeling platform, did at least provide an accessible introduction to some of the core principles of 3D content creation that students could draw upon if choosing further to pursue 3D modeling. More importantly, however, we were – and remain – convinced that the real-time and collaborative nature of Second Life, as well as accessibility to a mass audience, constituted challenges and opportunities significantly different in nature to static modeling that it is important for students of the Web 2.0 age to come to terms with. With that experience under our belts, we decided, in the following academic year, to concentrate the practical tuition exclusively on Second Life.

The Alkedo

The very significant success of the Galileo's Laboratory project at Pisa, with its combination of the two very different "cultures" of modules on *Historical Studies* and *3D Graphics*, both prompted us, at King's, to emulate its collaborative approach in the next academic session (2008- 2009), and also gave us the confidence that the virtual world could enable us to do what we would never previously have attempted, namely: to link modules in two different institutions in two different countries. We therefore prepared ourselves to undertake a much more ambitious, collaborative project.

In 1998, lying in the soft silt of an ancient river bed on the outskirts of Pisa, was found the remains of several boats spanning 1,000 years of maritime history from the Augustan age to medieval times, all wrecked, at one time or another, by violent tidal floods. One of these, Ship C, is the only Roman vessel ever to have been found with a name carved into her timbers: her deeply incised Greek letters clearly spell out the word "Alkedo" – Seagull. The Alkedo is a 13m-long vessel in the shape of a small, sail and oar powered Roman warship, which may have acted as a coast-hugging patrol boat, or a shuttle designed to carry personnel and supplies from port to larger, sea-going vessels in the fleet, or – perhaps retired from active service – the pleasure boat of a wealthy local. The hull and its contents have been lovingly and painstakingly preserved by the Centre for Restoration of Waterlogged Wood (*Centro di Restauro del Legno Bagnato*) at the Shipyard of Ancient Pisan Ships (*Cantiere delle Navi Antiche di Pisa,* http://www.cantierenavipisa.it/) and the ship will soon be the subject of a display in the new Museum of Ancient Pisan Ships (*Museo delle navi Antiche* di *Pisa)*, soon to open on the banks of the Arno in Pisa.

The archaeological riddle of this unique ship, the intrigue – even romance – of its lost histories, the complexity of its tidal environment and the energy surrounding its imminent transition from an archival object to a museologic exhibit made it a compellingly attractive subject. Equally promising was the existence of a substantial body of scientific documentation of the site, the ship and its contents, and a number of scholarly publications providing interpretation of the remains from a variety of perspectives.

Finally, the Centre for Restoration of Waterlogged Wood had also created a large-scale, physical reconstruction of the Alkedo, which would provide both a reference point and a rival hypothetical interpretation in relation to which we could situate our own virtual, reconstructive efforts.

Initially, we sought for a way for the students from Pisa and from King's to work together, but it quickly became clear that departmental and institutional constraints on the schedule and requirements of our curricula would preclude direct collaboration. We therefore, instead, devised a project with two associated, but autonomous, phases: in the first semester of 2008-2009, students at Pisa would model, in Second Life, the archaeological remains of the Alkedo; then, in the second semester, the students at King's would create, also in Second Life, a virtual reconstruction of the Alkedo as it may originally have been in its prime. The two projects, together, would provide different perspectives of the one, shared object, and would encourage each group of students to consider their own project in the context of a wider program of work.

This affiliation of the two "Alkedo" projects became significantly more substantive with the inception of an additional new joint King's-Pisa initiative: the *London Charter in Second Life* project (The London Charter in Second Life, 2009). Martin Blazeby (King's) and Beatrice Rapisarda (Pisa) applied for, and received, funding under the British-Italian Partnership Program for Young Researchers, 2008-9, a joint initiative of the Italian Ministry of University Education and Research (*Ministero dell'Istruzione dell'Università e della Ricerca*) in collaboration with the Conference of Rectors of Italian Universities (*Conferenza dei Rettori delle Università Italiane*) and the British Council. The funding enabled Blazeby and Rapisarda to convene a series of workshops in Pisa and London designed to develop tools, guides, a heritage visualization ontology and visual conventions to aid the implementation of *The London Charter* in Second Life. This joint venture resulted in both the Italian and UK student projects on Alkedo becoming constituent elements of a shared best practice investigation, and that students and staff in both institutions would be exchanging ideas and approaches on burning methodological issues of common concern during the course of the year.

At King's College London, the hypothetical reconstruction, in Second Life, of the original state of the Alkedo formed the focal point of both tuition and assessment for the whole, one-semester *Applied Visualization* module (Figure 8). By the time the King's students were about to embark on their phase of the project, the students from Pisa had largely completed their model of the archaeological remains of Boat C, and their tutors were ready to visit London for a three-day workshop with KVL as part of the *London Charter in Second Life* project. During their visit, they gave a presentation on the Alkedo, and expressed

Figure 8. Alkedo

the intention to leverage the visualization project into a real collaboration with the new Museum of Ancient Ships (*Museo delle Antiche Navi*) shortly to open in Pisa. This gave the students of *Applied Visualization* at King's a strong sense of being involved in a significant, international collaboration with a real-world dimension; one that invited, and would reward, their best efforts.

In 2008-2009, through the Alkedo project, we trialed, and subsequently in 2009-10 consolidated, the following combination of theoretical and practical tutorials. Throughout the semester, students attend a weekly, two-hour, traditional seminar which, in addition to discussing the history and theory of humanities visualization, provides tuition in the principles and practice of project management, and offers hands-on project review sessions, in which the tutor, Denard, helps the students to develop and monitor their project plan as the work unfolds, and to keep their activities in dialogue with both the *London Charter* and the specific assessment criteria of the module.

In addition, in the first six weeks of the semester, KVL Senior Research Fellow, Drew Baker, gives tutorials on conducting *London Charter*-compliant visualization projects in Second Life. In the first week of the practical workshop, tutors and students meet physically in a seminar room in

London. Thereafter, Baker and usually one or two students join the session virtually, while Denard and most of the students continue to meet physically. One of the laptops in the seminar room is connected to standard plug-in speakers, a Sony ECM F8 desktop conference microphone and Skype (rather than the unreliable Second Life voice client) to establish an audio link between the room and the remotely-located participants: this is an inexpensive and highly effective means of running a hybrid, virtual-physical session.

Baker and Denard ask students to complete, in their own time, a number of freely-available, in-world tutorials created by SL residents – in particular, the well-known "Ivory Tower Library of Primitives" – to ensure that they acquire rudimentary skills in modeling and texturing. This allows the workshops to concentrate on the more methodologically-rigorous standards and techniques of content creation that a collaborative, humanities context imposes, lending particular emphasis to: prim-efficient building; accurately introducing measurements and images of real-world assets into the virtual environment; permissions management; creating regular multi-inventory back-ups of project content; and iterative documentation of the visualization process.

Baker also provides, and teaches students to use, a number of Linden Scripting Language (LSL) scripts, that enable them to work with Universally Unique Identifiers (UUIDs) to achieve automated manipulation of in-world objects and absolute positioning and rotation of 3D assets. Mirror scripts accelerate modeling of symmetrical objects, while other scripts allow students to apply floating text to objects; develop heads-up displays (HUDs) that provide in world information to users; create links to external resources; embed rich media; and implement location-sensitive technologies such as chat engines, hot spots and sonar.

Examples of recommended good practice that Baker teaches include:

1. recording editing operations and queries on notecards stored within each object, or in the root object of each linked set of objects
2. when building, each student using, instead of the generic SL prims, their own set of primitives, stored in their inventory, each primitive pre-set with the correct permissions (i.e. allowing full permissions to group members) and containing a blank notecard ready for use in documenting parts of the visualization process
3. removing, after each work session, all "prim litter", so as to avoid wasteful expenditure of prims

At the end of the project, students submit their in-world content by "selling" the project to the tutor's avatar for L$0, with each individual object, texture and script set to give the "next owner" full permissions: this ensures that tutors are able to pack the project into a rezzer so that the model can be preserved without being permanently present – taking up prims and space – on the island.

The module's combination of theoretical and practical tuition, while details can always be further refined and improved, appears successful:

The mixture of a theoretical class and a practical class [provided] a very good framework for the course. The theoretical class allowed students to get an understanding about the arts and a perspective about visual regeneration of historic venues. It allowed me to gain a perspective on how scholars and practitioners used modern technology to try and unravel the secrets of the past. If not for this class, I would never have imagined the meticulous process one has to undergo whilst trying to regenerate an image of something that stayed in the past. (Student feedback from 2010)

The lecture in world format I really liked. The tutorials from Drew were good and enabled us to getting up and running pretty quickly. (Student feedback from 2010)

When the students began to work on the Alkedo itself, it became clear that the principles of interdisciplinary learning observed in the case of the previous year's recreation of Galileo Galilei's Laboratory remained valid: students engaged in the modeling work had to learn aspects of Roman-era shipbuilding, the morphology of the Pisan coast over time, and of marine archaeology excavation and preservation techniques, as well as how to make these concepts and materials accessible to a wider audience through the creation of a Website and documentary.

The student project team at King's, comprising eight students, assigned roles so that each student was responsible for some combination of defined tasks including: project management; historical research; translation into English of Italian sources; archaeological data acquisition and analysis; liaison with subject experts; in-world modeling (of interiors and exteriors); 3D Studio Max modeling (of artifacts) and creation of sculptured prims ("sculpties") in SL; texturing; scripting behavior of in-world objects; in-world visitor interface design; 3D animations; video documentary creation; wiki creation; Website design; Facebook page creation; publicity materials creation; glossary compilation; copyright management (Alkedo project, 2009).

We recognized, from the outset, that it would be necessary to devise a means of assessing this project that would give the students a clear framework of activity spanning project planning, content creation, documentation and dissemination, as well as requiring them thoughtfully to reflect upon the process in a structured way. The assessment model would also need both to reward individual effort and achievement, and to place a fair emphasis on collective responsibility for the project – a core principle of collaborative work. While the project would require teamwork, in which each student would attend to a particular set of tasks while at the same time remaining aware of, and coordinating with the work of others, the assessment model would have to cope with inevitable disparities. Indeed, commenting on the project after the fact, one student noted:

Group dynamics were hard to manage, with some people working a lot more than others, or working at different standards (Student feedback from 2009)

Student responses to this assessment model have been universally favorable:

"It's a good thing to get away from 3-5,000 word essay format which seems a terribly old-fashioned way of assessing such a forward looking subject." (Student feedback from 2009)

The model of the Alkedo that the students produced in Second Life was an impressive achievement: despite the limitations, as a modeling platform, of Second Life, through a combination of ingenuity and perseverance, the students meticulously captured the irregular contours of the boat, each rib and plank of the hull being composed of several, painstakingly measured and placed prims. Relevant literature was combed to allow the team plausibly to restore, from valid studies or *comparanda*, lost elements such as the anchor and steering oar. Each artifact found in the hull was modeled in 3D Studio Max, and converted into a sculpted primitive (Second Life's way of introducing complex organic shapes that its primitive-based modeling system cannot reproduce), and scripts attached to oars and sail to evoke the vessel's means of movement.

The project team conducted numerous experiments to determine successful ways of publishing documentation of the visualization process that would render the visualization "intellectually accountable", or "transparent", as stipulated by the *London Charter*. The challenge was to find an approach that would not be unduly intrusive for the casual visitor, but which would allow interested users to drill down to highly detailed documentation providing full "transparency".

The solution was combined in-world "hotspots" – detectable only by a change in cursor icon – which, when clicked, offer both notecards with information about the individual component in question and offering a live link to a Webpage where was presented full, illustrated documentation of both the evidence on which the component was based, and of the process of interpretation and visualization. The whole process of planning, research and modeling was captured via a wiki (Alkedo Project wiki, 2009) while a multilingual, interactive panel situated beside the SL model directed visitors to a separate Website designed to present the project and its methodology to the public (Alkedo Project, 2009).

The integration of product and documentation of process continued through to the brief audio-visual documentary created by the team (Alkedo Project video-documentary, 2009), which included footage of work in progress, animations illustrating topographical changes in the Pisan coastline over time, and a commentary on the theory and practice of implementing the *London Charter*. Finally a formal, 33-page report (available through the wiki) recorded and reflected upon the project's aims, process and outcomes, relating it to wider issues in heritage visualization, and a signed, collective statement – together with wiki entries and SL's record of which avatar created each object – allowed tutors reliably to track, verify and assess the quantity and quality of each participant's contribution. The deployment, by students and staff alike, of a formal methodological framework, such as the *London Charter*, encourages a mutually-reinforcing coalition of product- and process-orientated learning: documenting and reflecting on process contributes greatly to the conceptual, contextual and technical coherence of the activity and, consequently, of its outputs.

While the audio-visual documentary provides an elegant record of the project suitable for online or event-specific display, a A1 project poster affords the project a physical presence suitable for exhibitions. This focus on dissemination within the learning process is consistent with best practice within the field of historical visualization, which asks those engaged in creating digital representations of cultural heritage to attend to the value that their efforts have, beyond their own immediate contexts, for wider society:

The creation and dissemination of computer-based visualization should be planned in such a way as to ensure that maximum possible benefits are achieved for the study, understanding, interpretation, preservation and management of cultural heritage. (The London Charter 2.1 (February 2009) Principle 6: Access)

Student assessments of the experience were overwhelmingly and strongly positive, but not without qualifications. The following comment, in particular, reflects the difficulty of identifying a subject that strikes the right balance between being challenging and achievable, between being sufficiently clearly defined to provide focus, and open-ended enough to allow students scope for creative input:

I think choosing the right subject matter is important and it should be chosen specifically with Second Life in mind in order capture peoples' imagination. In this respect I thought the Roman ships were an average subject matter as I think there is more room improvisation on behalf of the student. I think the ship was basically a little bit too much like a building project - we get given a set of plans and then reconstruct it in 3D. Whilst this is clearly an excellent way to introduce people to Second Life I think we could have been stretched a bit more with the subject matter. (Student feedback from 2009)

Another reservation was the consequences of working in, and having content locked into, the proprietary Second Life system:

the fact that everything has to be done online and through [Linden Labs'] server meant a lot of restrictions on where and when one could model. At the end we could not save and export the model outside SL and this is a huge drawback I think, as we would have liked to be able to have each a copy of our hard work. (Student feedback from 2009)

The cost of the necessary decision to concentrate on Second Life to the exclusion of more standard 3D modeling tools is also noticed:

Whilst I liked working in Second Life and found it both useful and fun I'm not sure it laid the best foundation for getting deeper into the world of visualization... I'm now looking to use more advanced 3D software for visualizations and feel I would have been better placed if we had learnt to model in a more standard 3D environment. (Student feedback from 2009)

There is no question but that these are valid concerns, and indeed ones that tutors share; there are ways of both importing and exporting SL content, but none of them, yet, is easy, reliable or quick; and, short of extending the module into a second semester, the benefits of real-time collaborative content creation, as well as the excellent results achieved in Second Life, including elements of social engagement, validate our decision to concentrate on the SL platform, as further student comments attest:

[modeling in SL is] easy to pick up and quite quickly it becomes obvious that as a tool it has great potential. (Student feedback from 2009)

In addition, the cognitive effort required in modeling, the powerful stimulus given by the aim of producing a polished functional model for public consumption, and the added efficacy and motivational impetus of working in a group, clearly did also combine to make for a highly effective module on the digital reconstruction of the past:

we all had a sense of real achievement having collectively produced work on a larger scale than any of us could have hoped to individually (Student feedback from 2009)

This sense of achievement is not without foundation; later this month, tutors from both Pisa and King's will meet with the Director of the Museum to take forward, we hope, plans to create a permanent, public visual installation on the Alkedo based on our students' work in Second Life.

LEARNING BY VISITING AND PLAYING

If it proves difficult or impossible to enable students to undertake content creation in a MUVE, a good option is to use Second Life as a learning environment for "searching", "visiting" or "playing". The Leaning Tower of Pisa, Galileo's Laboratory, the Roman ship Alkedo and the Somerset House projects can now be viewed on Digital Humanities Island, and elsewhere in Second Life many other historical "reconstructions", such as the Basilica of Assisi, the Sistine Chapel, Stonehenge, the ancient city of Uruk, the Great Wall of China, the castle of Matsumoto, not to mention KVL's Theatron3 project, mentioned above.

Unfortunately there isn't yet a serious catalogue of the cultural heritage in Second Life, where it could be possible to understand - in accordance with the *London Charter* - if modeling followed a method, which are the limits, who the authors and with which purposes. In most cases, we must admit, we face poor quality models, created mostly by people with no educational purpose or scientific concerns. When, however, reconstructions are scientifically valid or at least acceptable, when digital models show rich data as result of interdisciplinary projects - as those described above - the teacher would face a "homogeneous context" (historical, artistic, cultural context) where actually "immerse" students making them interact, communicate, search, evaluate or answer to questions.

Several tools make these functions easy: from simple ones (notecard, chat, and inventory of objects) to more complex software. Second Life, for example, can be integrated with a popular and open source e-learning platform Moodle that can be used "in world" with its rich set of functions to distribute texts or images, create quizzes, manage classroom management and create glossaries. Obviously it depends on the purpose of the course and on the ability of teachers how using of Second Life, starting from a simple visit up to the construction of scenarios for a role play, with students and teachers for players.

We tried this option too in Galileo's laboratory: we thought to create three avatars from the characters of *Dialogue Concerning the Two Chief World Systems* (Sagredo, Simplicio and Salviati) making them interact with each other and any visitors. That project stalled for lack of financial support and some technical difficulties (partially solved improving IUMI guide, see below), but it can only be achieved spending time and money. The road, however, looks promising, especially if we carry on experiments in open source MUVEs, which allow a greater freedom in computer programming.

The Theatron3 project, in addition to the content-rich Heads-up Display, included the development of a "Director Tool" which allows users to compile sequences of actions and events, that are, during "performance", sent as in-world text prompts to each participating "actor". In one notable experiment, KVL Senior Research Fellow, Drew Baker, used this tool to facilitate the recreation of a medieval drama in the Cornish language, comprising sound clips, sub-titles and moving scenery. He even developed an "Audience HUD" that enabled spectators to cheer, boo or whistle, or even throw (virtual) rotten fruit, ensuring that the performance was a fully participative event. Theatron3 also actively encourages its users to bring and develop their own costumes,

props, scenery and scenarios and mixed-reality modes of engagement so that it becomes not just a place to visit, but a laboratory in which users can conduct their own, complex, experiments that exploit virtual embodiment within a spatial metaphor of Second Life.

Again, however, we recognize the need to create, in education just as in research, close collaboration between scholars of Humanities and Information and Communication Technology (ICT) experts, to go beyond a merely instrumental use of technology, and study, together, both how technology can influence the dissemination of humanistic knowledge and, conversely, how new technologies will evolve and change in response to the demands of the Humanities. Such endeavors become increasingly attainable as the discipline of Digital Humanities acquires more recognition within the scientific community (Dacos, 2010).

SOME CONCLUSIONS

Obviously the kind of work described above best suits "digital" students, who are not only able to live in Second Life and hopefully to create objects there, but who could also benefit from linking together different courses by, for instance, organizing a set of interdisciplinary lessons in which History works in collaboration with a course of 3D graphics, or Archaeology with Web Design, or Art with Digital Audio. Exciting as these possibilities are, there are real-world considerations: teachers need to have good skills in organizing workgroups, the availability of powerful enough computers, the will to devote a greater amount of time than is usually required, and one or more additional supporting tutors. In the absence of these conditions, it must be acknowledged that the risk of failure is high.

Given the objective difficulties in several Italian universities to carry through such an operation, especially in view of the poor incentives provided by the Italian university system for interdisciplinary courses, such a goal will be beyond the reach of many teachers. Interdisciplinary education could be a turning point in term of quality of learning, especially in the Humanities, and the digital world could be in the vanguard of change, but only if cultural, financial and structural investments are forthcoming.

In our experience, Second Life proved to be a good learning environment, owing to:

- The wide creative possibilities available to users in customizing objects, environments and avatars;
- The ability to acquire, for free or at low cost, in-world objects and textures, thereby saving considerable time and energy;
- The possibility to bring together into a single, virtual, communal space several students who may be physically distanced from each other, and thus to enable them to communicate in writing and by voice; in other words, the opportunity inexpensively to create truly international "classes";
- The availability of tools and accessories that make communication and interaction between avatars and between objects and avatars easier.

Second Life has, however, also problematic aspects. First it is not a particularly "intuitive" environment, given that it requires to users to learn skills even to navigate the world – mouse and keyboard commands become "natural" only after hours of use – much less to create content. In order to become a successful "resident" in Second Life, one needs to overcome a period of "training", which newcomers will find more or less difficult depending on their level of initial skills in related technologies, and the outcomes they wish to achieve. This is why new users in Second Life are normally directed to Welcome Island, where other avatars, guides, panels and notecards help them learn how to walk, watch, chat, stand and sit, fly and teleport from place to

place. The Second Life introductory materials are sufficient to enable students to acquire such basic skills without supervision, but the demands on technical infrastructure – hardware and internet access – and tutors become significant if students are required to use institutional facilities to be in world, especially during class.

It is also noteworthy that very few students are ever likely to number Second Life among their preferred technologies; indeed, when asked if they would continue to use Second Life beyond the duration of the assessed project, the responses of the CCH students were equivocal at best, and more often negative (from student feedback 2009-2010):

...although it does give some important advantages, Second Life seems rather obscure, and I do not think I am very likely to use it after the project's completion.

I have uninstalled SL from my laptop once the MA was over and I don't think I will use it again, the reason being that I do not find it useful for my interests.

I have used it a little bit, mainly just for amusement.

I would never enter SL for social or virtual bonding reasons, however I would be inclined to log in, for educational, informative and observatory reasons.

While SL does have drawbacks as a virtual classroom for the kinds of reasons discussed above, including the considerable cost, in time, of developing course resources or delivering content to SL, it is also true that the power of SL (unlike Skype or Powerpoint, for example) is to integrate a variety of technologies in such a way that they are more than the sum of parts, creating an holistic, interactive, sensory-experiential environment. The question to keep in mind is: what kinds of teaching and learning experiences can be uniquely enabled by the specific capabilities of SL that are also sufficiently distinctive and beneficial that this level of investment is worthwhile?

The truth is that we are still learning, ourselves, what are the unique, and uniquely enabling, properties and possibilities of integrated, virtual experience, and the future is likely to hold many interesting "failures" as well as "successes" in our quest for understanding. In this venture, we will need to remind ourselves, our students and colleagues, that we must define "success" in terms of progress on this shared journey of discovery, rather than as a sum of predictable "outcomes".

So far, early experiments suggest that SL's combination of the perceptual, social and psychological aspects of avatar-based experience; together with SL's facilitation of collaborative content creation, make SL – despite its myriad of constraints and frustrations – can make it a superb learning laboratory wherever spatial and temporal dimensions are important.

ACKNOWLEDGMENT

We thank the British Council and CRUI (the Italian Rector's Council) for financing international exchange (our travels to visit partner institutions), the lecturers and researchers involved (Richard Beacham, Martin Blazeby, Drew Baker, Marco Bani, Beatrice Rapisarda) and the students who volunteered to help beyond their duties (Francesco Genovesi, Elisa Ciregia, Flavia Piscioneri, Francesco Orsi, and Alan Zucconi).

REFERENCES

Alkedo project video-documentary. (2010). Retrieved June 2010 from http://www.cch.kcl. ac.uk/ teaching/madct/projects/ alkedo/Alkedo_ VideoDocumentary.wmv

Alkedo project website. (2009). Retrieved June 2010 from http://www.cch.kcl.ac.uk/ teaching/ madct/projects/alkedo/

Alkedo project wiki. (2009). Retrieved June 2010 from http://www.cch.kcl.ac.uk/ teaching/madct/ projects/ alkedo/wiki/

Bani, M. (2008). *La computer grafica: Strumento per la ricerca, la didattica e la divulgazione storica.* Unpublished master dissertation, supervisors E. Salvatori, R. Beacham & A. Cisternino, University of Pisa, Italy

Beacham, R., Denard, H., & Niccolucci, F. (2006). An introduction to the London charter. *Proceedings of VAST Conference*, (pp. 263-269).

Childs, M. (2009). Theatron 3 final report. In *Theatron3.* Retrieved June 2010 http://cms.cch. kcl.ac.uk/theatron /fileadmin/templates/main/ THEATRON_Final_Report.pdf

Ciregia, E. (2009). *Ricostruzione 3D del processo edificativo della Torre di Pisa.* Master Thesis, University of Pisa.

Dacos, M. (Ed.). (2010). *Manifeste des Digital humanities, proposed by professionals or observers of the digital humanities.* In THATCamp, Paris 18-19 May. Retrieved from http://tcp.hypotheses. org/318

Denard, H. (2005). Visualization and performance documentation editorial. *Didaskalia, 6*(2).

Digital Humanities Island. (2007). Retrieved June 2010 from http://slurl.com/ secondlife/ DigitalHumanities/186/167/28/ ?title=DigitalHumanities%20Island

EPOCH. *The European Research Network of Excellence in Open Cultural Heritage.* (2008). Retrieved June 2010 from http://www.epoch-net.org/

Gütl, Ch., Chang, V., Kopeinik, S., & Williams, R. (2009). *3D virtual worlds as a tool for collaborative learning settings in geographically dispersed environments. Conference ICL.*

Joseph, B. (2007). Best practices in using virtual worlds for education. *Proceedings of the Second Life Education Workshop at the SL Community Convention.*

Kamimo Islands. (2007). Retrieved June 2010 from http://slurl.com/secondlife/ Kamimo_Island/127/148/25, project from http://kamimo-islands. blogspot.com/

Kemp, J., & Livingstone, D. (2006). Putting a Second Life "metaverse" skin on Learning Management Systems. In *Proceedings of the Second Life Education Workshop at SLCC.* Retrieved June 2010 from http://www.sloodle.com/ white-paper.pdf

Molka-Danielsen, J., & Deutschmann, M. (Eds.). (2009). *Learning and teaching in the virtual world of Second Life.* Trondheim, Norway: Tapir Academic Press.

Norman, D. (2002). *The design of everyday things.* Jackson, TN: Basic Books.

Ondrejka, C. (2008). Education unleashed: Participatory culture, education and innovation in Second Life. In Salen, K. (Ed.), *The ecology of games: Connecting youth, games, and learning* (pp. 229–251). Cambridge, MA: MIT Press.

Second Life in DH-Pisa Wiki. (2008). Retrieved June 2010 from http://iu.di.unipi.it/wiki /index. php/IU_Second_Life

TheArketipo blog. (2009). Retrieved June 2010 from http://arketipo-sl.blogspot.com/

The London Charter. (2006). Retrieved June 2010 from http://www.londoncharter.org/

The London Charter in Second Life project. (2009). Retrieved June 2010 from http://iu.di.unipi.it/sl/london/

Wankel, C., & Kingsley, J. (Eds.). (2009). *Higher education in virtual worlds: Teaching and learning in Second Life.* London, UK: Information Age Publishing.

KEY TERMS AND DEFINITIONS

3D Modeling: Building a three-dimensional model of an object or building.

Computer-Based Cultural Heritage Visualization: Visualization of cultural heritage assets by means of computer-based/digital reconstruction and rendering methods.

Interdisciplinary Education: Education spanning several disciplines.

Multi User Virtual Environment: A persistent virtual world, usually accessed over the Internet, allowing a large number of simultaneous users to interact through their 3D counterparts, i.e. their *avatars*.

Second Life: A Multi User Virtual Environment managed by Linden Lab.

The London Charter: A set of internationally-recognized principles ensuring that digital visualization methods are, and are perceived as, intellectually rigorous and robust.

ENDNOTES

[1] Bani, in collaboration with the Museum of London, completed a 3D model and documentary video on the Roman fort of Londinium (Bani, 2008)

[2] An *affordance* is a quality of an object, or an environment, that allows an individual to perform an action.

Chapter 11
Trip to the Virtual Career World

Tom Wunderlich
Old Dominion University, USA

Beverly Forbes
Old Dominion University, USA

Erin Mills
Old Dominion University, USA

ABSTRACT

A Faculty Innovator Grant allowed the Old Dominion University Career Management Center to develop the capability and protocol to take a group of students to an employer site in Second Life (SL) within the context of a one-credit-hour career course. This chapter will discuss the development process and the challenges encountered in preparing a class to visit and productively interact with employers in SL. It will also discuss minimizing development costs and the amount of faculty time and effort necessary to incorporate trips to virtual worlds in their class syllabi. This is an example of "how to" for those interested in taking groups into SL rather than an academic study of the effects of a visit in SL on the students. Therefore citing of research and discussion of educational outcomes is kept to a minimum.

INTRODUCTION

The ability to facilitate mediated experiences via virtual field trips can help reduce barriers and provide situated, cooperative, and experiential learning in a constructive and relevant environment. Established virtual worlds create opportunities for students to gather and interact with a focus on visiting large, otherwise hard-to- approach companies. These organizations are already conducting recruiting, training, and development virtually. This project was developed to help prepare students for the way organizations are doing business by providing insight, both in etiquette and literacy, into appropriate professional networking that is transferrable to both the virtual and real world.

Old Dominion University's Career Management Center (CMC) is a two- time national award winner for innovative career services delivered: live face to face, live via distance synchronously, and on demand via distance asynchronously. CMC provides electronic services to clients world wide 24/7/365. The focal point of this capability is

DOI: 10.4018/978-1-60960-545-2.ch011

the Cyber Career Center[1] staffed by a full-time supervisor and two graduate assistants as Cyber Career Coaches. Old Dominion University is a state university comprised of 24,000 students and each of the university's six colleges has a CMC faculty administrator assigned as the Career Liaison with full service satellite offices operating in Art & Letters, Business, Engineering, and Sciences.

Building upon this expertise, the university awarded a Faculty Innovator Grant allowing the CMC to develop a protocol to take a group of students in the context of a career course to an employer site in Second Life (SL). Students interacted with employer representatives and guided activities in the simulation and returned in the space of a class period. Students documented and reflected on this experience in their final portfolio presentation for the class.

CMC established a private island in SL with facilities, spaces, and vehicles for training staff and students to use avatars and to serve as a tour group gathering and departure point. CMC has developed a trained staff of Cyber Coaches and has created a training protocol to prepare those unfamiliar with SL and avatar usage to be able to function as part of a tour group. As a result, students in both of the CMC taught 200 and 400-level career courses successfully created their avatars and learned to navigate and communicate in SL in preparation for virtual field trips to employer sites.

Note: Table 1 outlines our sections and locations. Two sections from two different level career courses, UNIV 200 and UNIV 400 were successfully taken to IBM during the fall of 2009. Three sections, two from UNIV 200 and one from UNIV 400, were taken to Lockheed Martin in the spring of 2010. Courses included diverse majors and a variety of age groups including non-traditional aged students.

Evaluations were made by surveying the students after each phase of the experience and corrections made to the syllabus and protocol based on that feedback. These revisions have led to expanding the SL capability to include other classes that have a career component in their syllabi. Based on the success and growth potential of this project, this chapter will discuss the development process and the difficulties encountered in preparing a class to visit and productively interact with employers in SL for career development and academic purposes. It will also discuss minimizing development costs and minimizing the amount of faculty time and learning curve to utilize virtual worlds, in order to incorporate this capability in their class syllabi.

Major employers now have elaborate corporate sites developed in SL to support their marketing and personnel recruitment activities and enhance internal collaboration capabilities for their staff. The project discussed in this chapter develops the protocol to prepare a class to take advantage of these employer-based simulations, to gain new experiences, and to interact with people whom they would not normally have access.

BACKGROUND

The value of SL is the ability to "travel" to unique destinations and to move about within the environment, have an exchange of information with others, and interact with resources by sight, text, and audio. The primary goal of this project was to use the technology provided by a virtual world to take students where they could not normally go and gain experiences that would otherwise elude them, addressing the student - employer interaction issue and ensuring a "bridge" between the experience in the virtual world and the actual professional practices students might encounter in the real world. The intent of this project was

Table 1. Course Sections and Locations

Semester	Class Level/Title	Company
Fall	UNIV 200 and UNIV 400	IBM
Spring	UNIV 200 and UNIV 400	Lockheed

to organize guided activities by constructing a training and gathering place in SL, identifying SL employer sites, and developing a training and tour protocol to augment the learning experience in order to:

- Provide enrichment and stimulation to CMC courses and the "bridge" between theoretical classroom and real- world interaction by using virtual world technology and protocol.
- Provide virtual opportunities for groups of students to visit employer sites and interact with employer personnel, events, products and activities which previously were beyond their physical capability to reach.

This approach is supported by research on online gaming and usage of electronic communication by college- age students. Delwiche (2006) suggests that game-based assignments are most effective when they build bridges between the domain of the game world and an overlapping domain of professional practice. According to the the ECAR Study of Undergraduates Students and Information Technology (Smith, Salaway, Caruso, & Katz, 2009), over 50% of students report they like to learn through programs they can control, such as video games and simulations. Additionally, experience with and affinity for games as learning tools is an increasingly universal characteristic among those entering higher education and the workforce. A recent survey conducted by Pew Internet and American Life Project (2009) found that the online game experience is rich, varied, and common among young people, offering opportunity for increased social interaction and civic engagement. The success of game-based learning strategies indicate that active participation and interaction are the center of the experience.

Initial Approach

After following SL discussions on the Second Life Educator Discussion list (SLED) for over a year and attending several of Anders Gronstedt's Train for Success[2] in world meetings and tours, CMC staff decided to apply for a Faculty Innovator Grant from the Old Dominion University Center for Learning Technologies. The grant provided funds to establish a private CMC island in SL in order to further explore the possibilities of developing virtual tours to enhance the syllabus of our CMC Career Courses. The grant, awarded in January 2009, provided enough funds for the initial purchase, set up and operation of a private island for six months. The CMC developed the island with necessary training areas, vehicles, and objects with a goal to minimize the time and money spent on construction. The intent was to create a training sandbox and point for arrival and departure through a "career portal" and not a destination that attracts visitors. Most resources were free or minimally constructed and branded to create an open but highly identifiable CMC area for gathering and preparing student groups. The limited initial inventory provided staff basic training opportunities for participants to develop their SL and avatar skills. The New Media Consortium, NMC Resource Center Island, was an excellent resource for free structures to set up the CMC Island and helped provide free professional avatar clothing for the student classes later on. By using these free resources and readily constructed objects, the CMC Island was completed for only the cost of uploading our logo.

At the same time construction of the CMC Career Portal was underway, the Assistant Dean made contact with Chuck Hamilton, at IBM Center for Advanced Learning, who was a speaker at Anders Gronstedt's Train for Success sessions in May 2008. From this international contact, local IBM contacts were identified and eventually led to working with two IBM volunteer SL representatives, who agreed to host the first

Figure 1. CMC Career Portal Arrival and Departure Point

CMC virtual field trip. The plan for Fall 2009 was to take a class to the IBM simulation to interact with IBM personnel regarding careers at IBM and participate in IBM developed simulations demonstrating what IBM does.

An assignment model was developed and added to the syllabus as follows (See Appendix A):

1. **Homework Assignment 1:** Create SL account, create an avatar and practice basic

Figure 2. Start of CMC Training Sandbox

Figure 3. Aerial View of CMC Career Portal and Training Sandbox

movements and navigation, contact Cyber Coach for assistance if necessary.

2. **Homework Assignment 2:** Meet in the Cyber Career Center (CCC), and under supervision of Cyber Career Coach, professionally dress Avatar, practice navigation

skills and use of communication tools in SL by moving about CMC Site and interacting with a Cyber Career Coach.

3. **Class Assignment 1:** Meet in the CCC, log in with Avatar and meet on CMC's island. Under supervision of instructor receive brief-

Figure 4. Fun Training Objects and Area CMC Training Sandbox

ing and instructions about the visit to the employer SL site. Teleport to site as directed by the instructor and proceed as a group to employer site contact point. After presentation and tour or activity as preplanned by Instructor and employer host, return to SL CMC island site and log out.

4. **Class Assignment 2:** Utilize information and any artifacts gathered to complete and present a final report as part of a portfolio presentation during week of finals.

The class utilized a Quick Start Guide (New Media Consortium, 2010) and two case studies on SL employer use by Linden Lab (2009a ; 2009b) as references when the initial homework assignment was made. The classes also viewed a short YouTube video (http://video.google.com/video play?docid=-2623416574204916957#) to help manage expectations of avatar use and interaction in SL.

Evaluation of First Semester Trips

Trip evaluations were developed and administered to each student after completing the out- of- class phases and after the actual trip to identify issues that needed to be addressed in the protocol, technology, and site experience. The employer hosts were also contacted for feedback and suggestions after each trip.

The students were asked to comment on the following areas:

- Logging into Second Life for the First Time
- Downloading software from Second Life
- Creating the Avatar
- Navigation and Communication practice before the Trip
- Gathering and Departure for the Trip
- Arrival on Employer Site
- Navigation on Employer Site

- Interaction and Communication with site Host Avatar
- Departure from Employer Site
- Arrival and Dismissal from CMC Site

In addition, as part of their final portfolio students were required to reflect on their experiences in visiting a real corporation by virtual means, include any artifacts they obtained and discuss how this affected their career development or plans. Reviewing these presentations provided additional subjective input as to the student satisfaction and effectiveness of the exercise.

The lessons learned from the evaluations fell into three categories: trip organization, employer hosts and student interaction. For the trip organizer, the majority of the coordination efforts were with the employers. Initial access to a private employer island was coordinated by providing to the host well in advance all individual students avatar names. To simplify this process, group membership is recommended for future initiatives to easily grant teleport access for student groups. Time zones and meeting times have to be coordinated carefully as presenters may be from multiple time zones. In the first trip, several presenters missed the tours because the time was not correctly communicated. The coordinating communications have to specify SL time or reference a specific time zone in establishing the time for the tour.

Employer hosts and course instructors must keep the tour moving and engaged in the simulation or have the group participate in an activity. As soon as the tour settled into a normal classroom presentation format, students began multi-tasking, opening other browser windows, completing homework online or checking text messages, while listening to the presenter. Thus, the trip organizer needs to work with the employer host to keep the tour moving and have hands-on activities for the students to engage in or view from different perspectives. An article by Erica and Sam Driver (2009) entitled *End Death By Lecture: Tours, Not*

Speeches, is a very helpful reference for organizing the non-lecture component of the experience.

Lessons learned for student preparation were eye opening for the trip organizers. Student encountered very few problems with establishing accounts in SL. The instructions provided by SL were sufficient, making some of our initial in-house documentation unnecessary. Students utilized the Quick Start Guide (New Media Consortium, 2010) to augment the online instructions provided by SL.

One of the students' major challenges became modifying and dressing their avatar. Students asked for assistance most often and expressed the most frustration in this area. Navigation and communication was not difficult; and most students could master it in one session with a Cyber Coach. Cyber Coaches determined a list of activities that were necessary to ensure each student demonstrated reasonable proficiency in all areas of navigation and communication. When interacting with the host presenters instructors concluded that more preplanning with the students was necessary regarding the types of questions they could and should ask. In addition to the normal hesitancy to ask questions, as in a real world class, the employer host was not allowed to answer or discuss some questions due to company policy about their use of virtual worlds. Necessary preparation mirrored that of informational interviews including development of preplanned questions. Class discussions addressed the type of questions to ask and who should ask them. This must be discussed in advance with both the employer host and the students in order to develop a communication exchange. It was also determined that it would be beneficial to take the class on a practice "shopping trip" prior to the actual trip to the employer site. This would give the group practice in teleporting to an unfamiliar location, and selecting and changing into professional business clothing. It would give the tour organizers practice in teleporting a group and moving the group around a simulation. This shopping trip and the requirement of the avatars to

be dressed professionally helped reinforce the need to dress appropriately when meeting prospective employers. However, professional dress is not generally a requirement when taking a class on tours to other venues such as museums; so this step is not essential in all SL tour preparations.

Modification of Approach and Second Trips

The Spring Semester 2010 trips were expanded to two sections of UNIV 200 and one section of UNIV 400/500, a total of 41 students. These trips were to a different employer site, Lockheed Martin. Extensive contact was made with representatives who would be the hosts for our trip during the early part of the semester. Several preliminary visits were made to the Lockheed Martin Center for Innovation, private site by CMC and Lockheed Martin staff avatars. Student questions were collected and submitted in advance and input was received from Lockheed Martin staff regarding the parameters of the discussion. Other interactive activities, including driving vehicles to the runway to view the aircraft exhibits, were discussed. An additional class period was devoted to a "shopping trip" as previously discussed. Navigation and communication signage was acquired from NMC and posted on our island to assist in the navigation and communication training as well as implementing a more structured training regimen by the Cyber Coaches. Note cards with the link to the employer site and a link back to the CMC site were placed in boxes on the reception desk in the CMC area of the island. Students had to direct their avatars to pickup these note cards to obtain access to teleport. This allowed the students to practice picking up an artifact and provided temporary access to the private employer site.

Evaluation of Second Trips

Upon logging into SL, the avatar returns to its last location. The shopping trip exercise demonstrated the need for avatars to be returned to the CMC SL Island before logging out to ensure they would be in the proper place to start the class trip the next time. Several students were unable to identify where they were when they logged in and required instructor assistance to return their avatars to the CMC Island for class. Because we are taking groups of students who are not familiar with SL and do not use SL on their own, it was found to be important to have all the students physically in one room so that the instructor can monitor, and address any technological problems. Those students who did attempt the trip from another location were late, lost, or encountered communication and navigation problems which degraded the experience for them.

Non-traditional students reported no difficulties with the technology although some initially expressed misgivings before attempting to set up their accounts. In fact, the non-traditional students asked more insightful questions and engaged the employer host in more communication from which all the students benefitted. Since the majority of the students were located in one computer lab facility for the tour, their communication was limited to chatting questions. They could hear the employer host through the overhead speaker system in the room. Providing multiple headsets and voice communication from each terminal was not attempted in this cycle. The students did not have any difficulty with utilizing the chat mode, particularly since the questions had to be somewhat scripted as discussed previously. As on a real world field trip, there was an obvious difference in maturity level between the sophomores and the seniors in that the sophomores required more supervision. The 200-level class, upon teleporting to the employer site, careened immediately into the fish pond, in the vehicles and wandered about the area unescorted. The seniors arrived in an orderly group, immediately recognized the employer host, and gathered on their own to start the tour.

Impact of Project

Many existing resources in SL have been identified through this process, and the CMC has dedicated centralized expertise to integrate this virtual world experience across the curriculum of all six colleges in the university, building on coursework and capabilities already in place. The protocol, CMC launch and recovery site in SL, and trained Cyber Coaches developed by this project can be used by multiple classes to visit employer sites, museums, events, and other virtual activities, as appropriate for the topic of the class, with minimal individual instructor knowledge of SL or virtual technology.

In times of budget cuts and a lean economy, it is more feasible to take virtual field trips and directly interact with individuals to gain a sense of company culture, than to attempt a physical visit. SL not only addresses physical barriers, it bridges the gap by taking what students are doing socially through Web 2.0 and virtual communication media and gaming and brings it into an educational context. While initial experiences will be synchronous, knowledge transfer and community connections may pave the way for asynchronous initiatives, both in SL and through more traditional means for the students to follow through with employer contacts, and by reflecting on what they have experienced, contribute to the overall goals of this project and the student's academic and career development.

FUTURE DIRECTIONS

The Dean of the College of Engineering and Technology has agreed to include these trips in the syllabus of the Freshman Engineering project classes in the Fall of 2010. The trips will be integrated into a career module as part of the syllabus of the course with the module being taught by the CMC Liaison to the College. Each CMC liaison is identifying appropriate introductory courses in each major where a career-relevant SL trip could be considered value added to the syllabus. The Cyber Center Supervisor is also identifying SL sites that would be appropriate to support those visits and coordination with hosts from selected sites is underway. The intent is to be able to offer virtual trips to the career world in which the CMC Liaison would coordinate with a faculty member and then with the Cyber Center Supervisor and Cyber Coaches to provide all of the SL aspects of the trip and student preparation. The faculty member would only have to assign the trip as part of the syllabus and observe the trip from the CMC Cyber Career Center.

The Engineering Early Advantage Program for Women is a summer interaction program for entering female engineering students. This program includes an engineering work experience in an off- campus employer location and will incorporate SL visits in the summer of 2010 as part of its syllabus, supplementing the students' project work in modeling and simulation at the Virginia Modeling, Analysis and Simulation Center. Incorporation of this methodology into the syllabus of a funded NSF grant project for high school students and teachers entitled MarineTech with the College of Engineering and Technology is currently underway to be implemented in Fall 2010. Additional grant proposals are being submitted to expand this capability to other high school enrichment and outreach programs by the university; particularly in the Science, Engineering, Technology and Mathematics (STEM) fields.

CONCLUSION

The virtual trips to the career world have been successfully integrated into the syllabus of all 200- and 400- level career courses taught by CMC. The protocol and SL facilities developed and controlled by CMC will enable CMC to become more integrated in the academic curriculum of majors in each of the university's six colleges while providing an academic and career-related value added dimension to those courses, with minimal effect on the faculty member's work load.

ACKNOWLEDGMENT

This project was supported in part by a grant from the Old Dominion University Center for Learning Technologies. All of the staff members identified above were Co-Principal Investigators and participated significantly in the development and delivery of the project described in this chapter. Laura Czerniak, Career Management Center, Old Dominion University, was also a Co-Principal Investigator and provided technical assistance to this project. A special thanks to Dr. Charles Wilson, Dean, University College, Old Dominion University, for his encouragement and support of this project and his review of this chapter. Recognition should also be given to our employer partners, Chuck Hamilton, Patti Davis, and Robert Muhlestein of IBM and John Dannon, Diane Love, and Charles Hargraves of Lockheed Martin. In addition, thanks to Anders Gronstedt for his Train for Success Program in Second Life and personal communications that led to the employer contacts, making this project possible.

REFERENCES

Delwiche, A. (2006). Massively Multiplayer Online Games (MMOs) in the new media classroom. *Journal of Educational Technology & Society*, *9*(3), 160–172.

Driver, E., & Driver, S. (2009). End death-by-lecture: Tours, not speeches. *ThinkBalm*. Retrieved May 2010, www.thinkbalm.com

Linden Lab. (2009a). *Simulation training and prototyping in virtual worlds: Northrop Grumman in Second Life*. Linden Research, Inc. Retrieved November 2009, http://work.secondlife.com

Linden Lab. (2009b). *How meeting in Second Life transformed IBM's technology elite into virtual world believers.* Linden Research, Inc. Retrieved November 2009, http://secondlifegrid.net/

New Media Consortium. (2009). *Quick start guide.* Retrieved November 2009, http://sl.nmc.org/join/%20Second Life Registration Pew Internet and American Life Project. (2009). *Pew Internet.* Retrieved May 2010, www.pewinternet.org

Smith, S., Salaway, G., Caruso, J., & Katz, R. (2009). The ECAR study of undergraduate students and Information Technology. *EDUCAUSE Center for Applied Research*, 6, 61.

ENDNOTES

[1] Cyber Career Center – For a complete description of the Cyber Career Center Concept see www.odu.edu/cmc under the pull down menu for About.

[2] Anders Gronstedt's Train for Success – Monthly Online Seminars in Second Life, http://gronstedtgroup.com/

APPENDIX

Figure 5.

UNIV 200/400 Spring 2010 Schedule

Week of	UNIV 200 Mon 11:00	Presenter	UNIV 200 Weds 2:00	Presenter	UNIV 400 Weds 3:00	Presenter
1/11-1/15	Welcome & Intro	Erin	Welcome & Intro	Bev	Welcome & Intro	Tom
1/18-1/22	MLK HOLIDAY	Off	Career Planning Experiential Ed	Bev	Career Planning Goal Setting	Tom
1/25-1/29	Career Research Intro SL	Erin	Career Research Intro SL	Bev	Career Research Intro SL	Tom
2/1-2/5	Resumania & Resumes	Erin	Resumania & Resumes	Erin	Resumania & Resumes	Erin
2/8-2/12	Job Search Strategies	Erin	Job Search Strategies	Bev	Job Search Strategies	Tom
2/15-2/19	Networking/30 Sec Commercial	Pam	Networking/30 Sec Commercial	Pam	Networking/30 Sec Commercial	Pam
2/22-2/26	How to Work a Career Fair	Randy	How to Work a Career Fair	Randy	How to Work a Career Fair	Randy
3/1-3/5	SPRING CAREER FAIR	Off	SPRING CAREER FAIR	Off	SPRING CAREER FAIR	Off
3/8-3/12	SPRING BREAK	SPRING BREAK	SPRING BREAK	SPRING BREAK	SPRING BREAK	SPRING BREAK
3/15-3/19	Second Life	Erin	Second Life	Bev	Second Life	Tom
3/22-3/26	Interview Skills	Bev	Interview Skills	Bev	Interview Skills	Bev
3/29-4/2	Evaluating a Job Offer	Penny	Evaluating a Job Offer	Penny	Evaluating a Job Offer	Penny
4/5-4/9	Second Life Employer	Erin	Second Life Employer	Bev	Second Life Employer	Tom
4/12-4/16	Prof Comm/Cash Course	Erin	Portfolio Presentations	Bev	Portfolio Presentations	Tom
4/19-4/23	Portfolio Presentations	Erin	Portfolio Presentations	Bev	Portfolio Presentations	Tom
4/26-4/30	Portfolio Presentations	Erin	READING DAY		READING DAY	

Chapter 12
Web Based Authoring for Virtual Worlds Using PIVOTE

David Burden
Daden Limited, UK

Andrew Jinman
Daden Limited, UK

ABSTRACT

When educators started to use virtual worlds such as Second Life to create learning exercises, the natural approach was to script these exercises using the in-world tools. However, experience with this approach highlighted a number of significant issues including the high level of skill required to create and maintain the exercises, problems of scaling, longevity and accessibility. As part of the PREVIEW project, the authors of this chapter had the opportunity to consider a new approach – where all the non-3D elements of the exercise were defined and managed on the Web.

This chapter starts with a description of the "traditional" approach to MUVE exercise design, while presenting an assessment of the problems inherent in this approach. Following is a description of the PIVOTE system from a technical, author and user point of view, including future developments and expectations. This chapter also presents two case studies of how PIVOTE has been used by different institutions.

BACKGROUND

The "Traditional" Approach to MUVE Exercise Design

Virtual worlds have led to a huge increase in the use of MUVEs for education and learning, since they make the building and scripting readily accessible to the eLearning enthusiasts and professionals within education. Often educators needed little more skill than that required to write and script a web page.

The result has been an explosion in in-world built and scripted learning experiences. These typically have one or more of the following features:

DOI: 10.4018/978-1-60960-545-2.ch012

- Custom scripts in each object causing the object to perform the desired action(s) (e.g. give a note card, say some text etc.)
- Custom communications (e.g. text messages, IM, in-world email) were used to pass information/action between objects in the exercise
- Large amounts of text displayed via note cards or as images created using out-of-world tools such as Photoshop, MS Paint or PowerPoint.

Problems with the "Traditional" Approach

Whilst this "traditional" approach has been widely adopted and indeed has enabled the explosive use of MUVEs for vLearning; it is not without problems. For instance:

- A high level of skill is required to create and maintain the exercise
- Maintaining complex exercises becomes increasingly difficult
- The exercise is not necessarily available to those without access to the MUVE
- There is a dependency on that particular MUVE, and the investment in the exercise may be wasted if the institution moves to another MUVE
- The exercise operates in isolation from the organisations Learning Management System (LMS) or Virtual Learning Environment (VLE).

Let's look at each of these in turn.

1. Skill Level

Whilst scripting languages are relatively simple by programming language standards, they are still undoubtedly computer languages. The coder has to be aware of issues such as:

- Defining and typing variables
- Flow control
- Command key words and line structure
- Line terminating characters
- World unique functions
- States and subroutines

As such, they are not going to be easily learned by those without an interest in, or aptitude for, computer programming.

Even the process of creating (and maintaining) scripts and note cards takes a certain understanding of the way that the world works. For instance in Second Life, each object holds its own instance of each script and note card so you must update each individually. In worlds such as the now defunct Metaplace, scripts and similar resources were centrally referenced.

Even simple text displays can be hard to create in some worlds. For instance ActiveWorlds has a relatively simple script command to place text on a prim; there is no such simple method in Second Life. While users can create "floaty text" in a single font above a prim, to place text on a prim requires either the use of: a texture created in Photoshop or other similar graphics software, media and shared media streams, or Xytext (prim based alphanumeric character displays), none of which are intuitive to the average educator.

While learning to build in a world like ActiveWorlds or Second Life is considerably easier than using a package such as 3D Studio Max, it is also something that takes a while to learn, and even more time to become proficient at. It is, in theory, possible to share learning exercises created in Second Life, however the vagaries of that world's permissions and grouping systems mean that this rarely happens with other than the most simple of builds.

2. Maintenance

It is one thing to create an exercise in a virtual world, but quite another to maintain it over the weeks, months and potentially years as problems are spotted and fixed, and syllabuses and technology change. By having all of the structure and content stored in, and distributed through, tens or even hundreds of in-world objects, trying to find the right object to change and then make amendments can become a major issue.

It does not take much imagination to see how hard it might be to make a fundamental change to the structure and content of the exercise, especially if the changes are being made after a long period of time after the original exercise was built. In fact it may be easier to just recreate the whole exercise from scratch, with all the lost time and resource implications that implies.

3. MUVE Access

All of us who work with virtual worlds are aware of the challenges of arranging access to our chosen virtual world from institutional PCs. At the very least this is likely to involve:

- Ensuring that PCs have sufficient graphics power to run the world
- Ensuring that the network has sufficient bandwidth to support potentially 50 or even 100 concurrent virtual world sessions (maybe even more)
- Negotiating with the IT department for the relevant ports in the firewall to be opened up (or even installing a virtual world server in the IT department!)

Few institutions that we are aware of are in the privileged position of being able to run a virtual world from every PC on campus. This immediately restricts the potential access of students to the exercises, particularly if they come to see them as valuable personal revision tools as well formal group learning activities. Access limitations don't stop at the campus firewall either. What about access for students from their homes, internet cafés or even mobile devices? How about

remote learners who may be operating with PCs and internet connections which are well below campus (or urban student) standards?

If we create a valuable learning experience and then cut students off from it for a lot of the time, then aren't we failing to take full advantage of what the learning has to offer?

By embedding the structure and content of the exercise in a virtual world, we are doing just that. If we want to make the same experience available to other PC users, and especially to mobile users, then we will have to re-write it on another platform thus adding to the cost of the whole project. And then we face the challenge of trying to keep changes in each version synchronized.

4. MUVE Dependency

Institutional organizations have a different take on the issue of embedding so much content in a single platform; they see it as risk. What happens if the virtual world provider closes the world? (As happened with Metaplace, There.com and to an extent Wonderland between late 2009 and early 2010). Is the whole exercise lost? Is there money to re-create it? Or what happens if it becomes clear that the institution has backed the wrong project and their chosen virtual world is falling by the wayside, whilst all their peers are trumpeting their work on some other more successful platform?

Increasingly IT organizations are moving to standards based systems that protect their investment. This applies to data more than anything else. If data is in a proprietary format then it is at risk (the BBC's Domesday video disc being a classic example). If the data is held in an open standard, then whatever happens to the platform, there is a good chance that it can either be deployed directly onto another platform, or at least transcoded into another form.

As institutions create more and more content for virtual worlds, they will become increasingly sensitive to the risks that they are introducing if they do not have the exercises defined in an open, standards-based, way.

5. LMS/VLE Integration

Most educational institutions now use some form of LMS/VLE to manage their (2D) educational content. This is undoubtedly a good move, but by hand-crafting learning applications within a virtual world, we are creating an island of learning that stands outside of the LMS/VLE ; with all the issues of student record keeping, assessment and performance management that that implies.

It is perfectly possible to interface a virtual world based learning application with an LMS/VLE but this does depend on a number of factors:

- The LMS/VLE must offer some sort of Application Programming Interface (API), ideally as a web service
- The virtual world must support some form of Application Programming Interface (API), ideally as a web service
- The exercise developer must have sufficient programming skills to develop both the virtual world and possibly web-services interfaces between the two – and this is not for the faint hearted.

One example of how this can be accomplished is through the SLOODLE system (www.sloodle.org). SLOODLE was developed as a Second Life interface for the MOODLE LMS/VLE. However since MOODLE did not have its own web services interface, SLOODLE needs an additional module to be installed on the MOODLE server to work. Once this module is installed then objects in Second Life can make use of some of the MOODLE functionality, such as: registering a user onto a course/assignment, sharing chat room discussions or accessing simple quizzes.

But SLOODLE only solves the problem for MOODLE. There are also solutions around for other LMS/VLEs, but we end up with a series of point solutions rather than a common approach – and the focus is again on developing unique code within each virtual world.

Authoring Tools

If we look back at the development of other e-Learning technologies then we should not be surprised that similar problems have been encountered (and solved) in the past through the development of authoring systems. For instance:

- Educational (and game) cartridges and CD-ROMs used to be created at the code level, until developers created higher level abstractions of the content and "authoring tools" to enable quicker content creation by more educationally focused staff, and to allow software to run on different technology platforms (PCs, Macs, and before that BBC Micros, Amigas, Ataris and even ZX Spectrum's)
- Web development has been through a similar cycle, moving from hand crafted HTML and JavaScript to authoring tools that can create content optimized for different browsers and bandwidths, and now even for different mobile phones.

An authoring tool can be defined as an application which does one or more of the following:

- Abstracts the structure and content of a learning exercise to a level above the specifics of a single platform
- Does not require programming skills in order to create exercises
- Can generate the learning exercise on more than one platform
- Enables sharing & re-use of content at the abstraction level between content developers

173

- Enables developers to draw on a library of "learning objects"

It was to provide just such a system for virtual worlds that the open-source PIVOTE application was developed. Initially it was as a solution for one specific v-Learning project, but PIVOTE has become a very flexible authoring tool for virtual worlds learning.

Having been intimately involved with the development of PIVOTE, we believe that it is a powerful and flexible system, and so worthy of being used here as an example of a v-Learning authoring system.

However the analysis that follows should be taken as being representative of how any authoring system for virtual worlds could work, and others are more than free to take the concepts discussed and use them to create their own authoring tools (although of course we'd rather you joined the PIVOTE open-source community).

The PREVIEW Project

The genesis of PIVOTE was in the PREVIEW project (Conradi, 2008). PREVIEW – Problem Based Learning in a Virtual World – was a UK Joint Information Systems Committee (JISC) funded project which ran from Feb 2008 to Mar 2009 to examine different styles of problem-based learning within virtual worlds. A key requirement was to develop some paramedic assessment scenarios for use at St George's Hospital, University of London. Daden Limited (a UK based virtual world's solution provider) was the technical partner for the project, and had previously worked with the University of Coventry, one of the other PREVIEW partners.

Daden could have developed the project in the traditional manner using embedded content, but during their discussions with St George's, they were introduced to the concept of a "virtual patient", and more particularly the Medbiquitous Virtual Patient (MVP) XML standard (http://

groups.medbiq.org/medbiq/display/VPWG/Home) (Ellaway, Poulton, Fors, McGee, & Albright, 2008; Triola et al., 2007).

In the medical world a Virtual Patient has nothing to do with virtual worlds (Ellaway, Candler, Green, & Smothers, 2006). It is simply a description of a learning exercise involving a patient. The exercise could be manifest as nothing more sophisticated than photocopied sheets of information, questions and options. For Example:

Mrs Bloggs walks into your surgery room. She is looking tired and pale. Do you:
a. Tell her to take two aspirin and go away
b. Give her a cup of tea and ask about the kids
c. Reach for your stethoscope

Virtual Patients have existed as eLearning materials for some time (e.g. Labyrinth from the University of Edinburgh) (Pouton, Conradi, Kavia, Round, & Hilton, 2009), and are a natural for the web; as a series of media rich screens joined by option links. As more Medical Schools created web based virtual patients, it became obvious that there would be advantages if Schools could share their virtual patients, and run them on each other's systems. The Medbiquitous Consortium, made up of leading Medical Schools from across the globe, set up a working group in 2005 to create a standard for the interchange of virtual patients – the result was the open Medbiquitous Virtual Patient (MVP) standard, which recently became an ANSI standard (ANSI/MEDBIQ VP.10.1-2010).

The most important aspects of MVP are that it:

- Provides a way of representing the structure and (2D) content of an exercise in a completely neutral way
- Uses XML, the most flexible and interchangeable of computer data formats (partly through being both machine and human readable)
- Supports several medical specific data types but has enough key generic data

types, and an XtensibleInfo data format, to allow it to be used to model almost any "task" type training and learning exercise.

The PREVIEW team recognized that if MVP could be used as the basis of the virtual world exercises, then not only would there be a point solution to the needs of PREVIEW, but the architecture would also overcome the limitations of in-world development (as listed in the first part of this chapter), and be applicable to almost educational and learning organization and exercise.

Daden developed the original PREVIEW MVP system during Feb 2008 – Apr 2008, and delivered it to St George's for trials (Burden e al, 2008). St George's carried out technical and user trials during the summer term 2008, feeding back changes to Daden, and the system went live in the Autumn Term 2008, with project reporting and evaluation in the Spring of 2009. One of the conclusions of the PREVIEW project team was that the MVP system showed considerable promise as a general tool. Under the terms of the JISC project the team was mandated to make the software available free-of-charge to UK education. Rather than just do this, the team applied to JISC for some additional benefits realization funding, and this enabled the MVP player – now christened PIVOTE – to be released into open source through Google Code and a GPL Version 3 license.

PIVOTE: WEB-BASED AUTHORING FOR VIRTUAL WORLDS

PIVOTE Overview and Technical Design

As previously discussed PIVOTE (www.pivote. info) is an authoring system for virtual worlds. In fact, it can also be used to author exercises for the web, and even mobile phones. PIVOTE consists of 7 main elements:

- Exercise Definition
- PIVOTE Editor
- PIVOTE Player
- Web Interface
- Virtual World Interface
- Virtual World Objects
- Student Performance Data

An outline of the architecture is shown in Figure 1, and each element is described in more detail below:

Figure 1. PIVOTE Architecture. (© 2010, Daden Limited. Used with permission.)

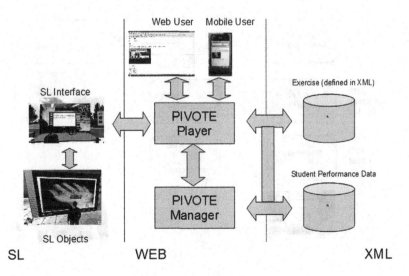

Exercise Definition

The definition of the exercise is stored in the Medbiquitous Virtual Patient (MVP) XML format.

With PIVOTE we have implemented most of the common features of the MVP standard (a compliance table is on the PIVOTE wiki), and are contributing to a working group on developing a Virtual World Profile for MVP (i.e. guidance on how to implement the standard in virtual worlds.)

MVP has a three-tier data model (see Figure 2):

- **Activity Nodes (AN):** which define the structure and flow of an exercise, and high level rules
- **Data Availability Nodes (DAM):** which link each activity node to one or more asset nodes
- **Asset Nodes:** principally text-based Virtual Patient Data nodes, but also Xtensible Info and Manifest (media) nodes, which define non-3D content and actions to be presented to the user

In practice we are finding that almost all exercises only have a 1:1 relationship between Activity Nodes and Data Availability Nodes (DAM), although most DAM nodes will link to more than one Asset Node. This flexibility in linking Asset and DAM nodes supports a high degree of re-use since any piece of text or action need only be defined once yet used multiple times.

There are only two areas where we have departed from the MVP specification, and we are seeking to have these changes incorporated into future versions of the specification:

- A "device" parameter at the DAM-Asset link level, so that a particular asset can be routed to a particular virtual world device.
- Variable-based rules at the DAM-Asset level (copying the AN level rules which already exist), so that a DAM can show one piece of information if a variable has one value or range, and a different piece of information for another value (e.g. different heart beat recordings based on the value of the heart-rate counter, or additional hints if a user has a high attempts counter)

The MVP specification also allows for the storage of meta-data including a description of the exercise and parameters that can be used to

Figure 2. MVP 3 Tier Model. (© 2010, Daden Limited. Used with permission.)

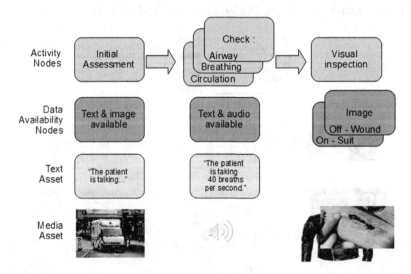

filter a set of exercise (e.g. in the medical case by age/sex/complaint of patient).

PIVOTE Editor

The PIVOTE editor is a web-based application used to create, edit and maintain the MVP cases. By navigating through and completing a set of web forms the author can:

- Create whatever nodes are required (AN, DAM and asset nodes)
- Link AN/DAM nodes to asset nodes
- Establish variables (e.g. score, heart-rate, attempts taken etc.)
- Define rules governing access to activity nodes (e.g. must visit node A before B)
- Establish links between Activity Nodes (e.g. as a flow through an exercise or as options in a quiz, although in virtual world simulations we usually have no hard-coded links since the user is interacting with objects based on their own training and decision making, not through an artificial path)
- Define DAM level rules for asset node access

The Editor is currently text only, although we are hoping that the community will create a graphical editor. The Editor also lets authors export the XML data to their hard-drive, and import XML from other authors.

The editor supports user accounts, and sharing and editing privileges so that multiple authors can work through the same instance of the editor program. Figure 3 shows examples of the PIVOTE Editor screens.

PIVOTE Player

The PIVOTE player is the heart of the system. This is again implemented as a web based program, and in fact is primarily operated as a web-service. This means that the user does not typically interact with it directly from a web page – although a web front-end does exist to support authors with testing and as an access method for last resort by users.

The web-service waits for a call from an interface module (e.g. the Virtual World interface). The call will give details about the user (e.g. avatar name), which exercise they are accessing, a session ID, the node they are activating (e.g. if they have just pressed a light switch in the virtual

Figure 3. PIVOTE Editor Screens. (© 2010, Daden Limited. Used with permission.)

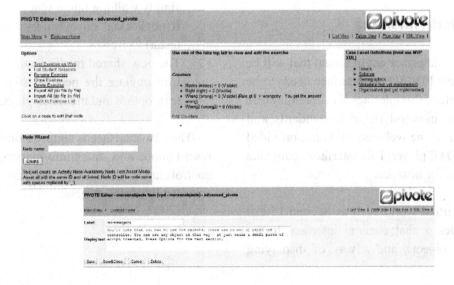

world they might be triggering the "light on" node in the exercise), and any user data which is relevant (e.g. position or something they have just said – particularly relevant if they are accessing a chat node – see below).

The player will then:

- Access the exercise definition
- Find the node that has been activated
- Check the node rules to make sure the user can access the node
- Apply any variable changes and rules
- Retrieve the response data from the asset nodes (applying any rules), and associated device IDs
- Update the student session log
- Send all the data back in an XML packet to the calling interface as the response to the web service.

In addition to this main path, the player will also:

- Create a web page representing the output and available options – used mainly for debugging or as an access route of last resort
- Create a simple web page suitable for viewing in a virtual world with text, images or other media being fed back

Virtual World Interface

For each user interface environment that will be used to access PIVOTE an interface needs to be built. The role of this interface is to communicate between the in-world devices, standards and languages, and the web service being provided by the PIVOTE player. This interface could take many forms, for instance:

- In a virtual world such as Second Life it provides a chat channel interface to in-world objects, and a way of displaying

the virtual world friendly web pages being generated by the player

- In another virtual world it might convert between the web service and the in-world scripting language (e.g. Java in Open Wonderland, LUA in Vastpark)
- In a web browser it might convert between the web service and Flash, or even HTML

The original Second Life interface was a relatively large affair since as well as providing the web service interface, it also provided a media screen to display the web pages, a set of command buttons to control key functions, and a set of soft buttons for choosing options.

Our experience since then has led us to considerably simplify the interface. This has been due to factors such as:

- Those setting PIVOTE up found that configuring the media screen caused the most problems – yet it is used less and less in PIVOTE cases
- Users typically only used the screen and controller at the beginning and end of a session – and it was otherwise a distraction and intrusion into the simulation
- Most exercises are now started just by pressing a large "START" button, or by simply walking into a space
- If not locked down students could easily restart exercises
- The new shared media features of Second Life obviate the need to switch between text, option and media displays.

The new interface is simply a black box with reset buttons and status information. Any other controls and displays required are created as standard PIVOTE objects.

Virtual World Objects

The key to any PIVOTE virtual world exercise are the objects. To us the whole point of using a virtual world is that you can simulate real-life, so the user should just be able to interact with virtual versions of the real life objects they would encounter in the scenario. Any object in Second Life (or probably any other virtual world) can become a PIVOTE object by embedding a simple script in it.

At its simplest (e.g. for a button) the script will:

- Detect an event (e.g. touch_start for a button, but could also be a collision, or some chat, or a timer etc.)
- Read its node/device ID (usually stored in the Description field for easy configuration)
- Send a message to the PIVOTE interface (on the private PIVOTE chat channel in Second Life) comprising information such as: node ID being triggered (usually derived from device ID and action), avatar that triggered the action, any additional information – such as any chat heard

- Listen for a response from the Interface, checking against its device ID and then taking any required action (e.g. display or chat data, open/close, move, reset etc.)

The key point is that the objects (and even the interface) have no exercise dependent logic or content in them. They are just recording and communicating that an event has occurred, and then waiting for the web-based PIVOTE system and MVP exercise definition to tell them (and other elements of the scenario) how to respond. This simple message passing is shown in Figure 4.

The beauty of PIVOTE objects is that they are usually very generic, and so can be used not only multiple times in a given exercise, but also shared between exercises and even organizations. All that is needed is to possibly change the device/node ID (so it is unique), and to ensure that the MVP exercise definitions (which can also be shared) are edited to create the response required for that exercise.

Some of the generic objects which we have created (and which are all available for free in Second Life and through the PIVOTE web site) include: Simple Touch button, Door, Invisible

Figure 4. PIVOTE Message Passing. (© 2010, Daden Limited. Used with permission.)

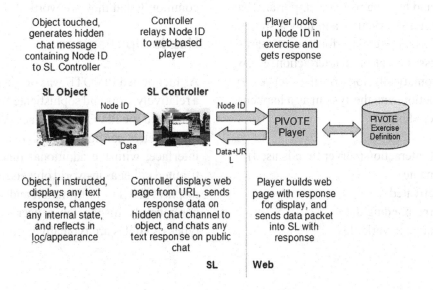

Figure 5. Some typical PIVOTE objects. (© 2010, Daden Limited. Used with permission.)

Barrier, URL Giver, Inventory Giver, Two-way vehicle radio, Telephone, Computer, ID Badge etc.

In addition the original PREVIEW project created 20 to 30 medical devices as used by UK Paramedics, and these were also placed into Open Source and are available in the PIVOTE Information Centre on St George's island in Second Life. Figure 5 shows some typical PIVOTE objects.

Student Performance Data

In academic and training use, it is important that there is evidence of whether and how a student has undertaken an exercise: for course marks, evidence for assessment, or for after-action review. PIVOTE automatically logs on the web every student interaction with the system as it happens. These log files show:

- Time of interaction (server time is used)
- Avatar name
- Node activated
- Any corresponding data
- Any change in variables

The logs can be viewed by the tutor through the PIVOTE Manager, and can also be exported as XML or text to hard disc, or made available as XML through a web service for import into an LMS/VLE.

Other PIVOTE Components

Whilst the above elements describe the essential components of a PIVOTE system, there are some other elements that we have found are used so commonly that they are worth describing here.

Heads-Up Displays

As mentioned PIVOTE was originally used with a relatively large and sophisticated controller that contained the PIVOTE Interface. We have found that a better configuration is a simpler, hidden, interface, with the additional functionality distributed either as in-world objects, or as heads-up displays (HUD - information and buttons which permanently display on a user's screen). Two types of HUDs are typically used:

- **Tutor's HUD:** This lets tutors start the exercise, see which Node a student is on, and optionally trigger actions within the scenario (e.g. different customers coming into a shop during a retail training scenario)
- **Student's HUD:** This provide student with access to information which does not typical sit within the immersive environment, this may include things link status buttons, menu options, close-up images, support videos, hints and mentor videos. The HUD can also be used for other purposes, such as to record any user chat, track their location, show their score or elapsed time, and to provide them with a task aide-memoire or check list.

An example of a student HUD is shown in Figure 6.

Non-Player Characters (Bots)

Most PIVOTE scenarios require the user to interact with another character. Whilst in some cases the character can be played by another user one of the whole reasons for using eLearning is so that the user can learn without using additional staff, and at any time. For this reason most characters are actually what gamers call Non-Player Characters (NPCs), or "bots" for short.

These bots operate completely under computer control, and in this case under PIVOTE control. The defining features of a bot object in PIVOTE are that:

- It can listen to and respond to text chat (such as when the user asks it a question)
- It can move around and undertake other typical user actions – such as giving or receiving objects, showing URLs, interacting with other objects etc

A standard bot script is available through the PIVOTE web site and in Second Life, and example bots are shown at Figure 7.

Within the PIVOTE Editor we have a special data format that we use to define the chat capabilities of the bot – how they respond when spoken to. This uses the XtensibleInfo format in MVP. For each chat node (usually, but not necessarily, one per bot) we can create a number of input/output/actions triples which define:

Figure 6. Example User HUD. (© 2010, Daden Limited. Used with permission.)

Figure 7. Different Bot types. (© 2010, Daden Limited. Used with permission.)

- **Input:** what key words we are (or are not) looking for to trigger this response
- **Output:** what words the bot will say in response
- **Action:** what action the bot will also take (e.g. move, say something else, give etc.)

When the bot hears some text it passes it through the Interface to the relevant chat node, where the PIVOTE player scores each triple based on the keywords to see which best matches the input, and then sends the appropriate output and action responses. If no triple matches, there is also a default triple which defines the response – which may be to say and do nothing, or say something like "Sorry, I don't understand".

The chatbot component of PIVOTE has been drawn from Daden's own Discourse chatbot engine (Burden, 2008). Users who need a more sophisticated chatbot than PIVOTE can provide, could consider using that, and then interfacing it into PIVOTE (which Daden can provide).

PIVOTE AUTHORING

Having described the components of PIVOTE we can now look at how they are used to create a particular scenario.

Planning the Scenario

The key challenge we have found is in getting authors to think in "object" terms. Typically when developing a training exercise the author might create a flow-chat of the activity – giving the student different choices at each stage. These choices may reflect one-off options (e.g. do you switch the light on or off), or options of sequence (e.g. do you switch the light on first, or open the door). Unless we are at the very earliest stages of training we typically do not want our virtual world exercises to be so controlled. Instead we just want to put the student into an environment with (in this example) a light switch and a door and then let them choose (based on their training) which they do, and in which order.

In order to achieve this, what we have to do is identify from an initial document, such as a flow chart or a use-case diagram, what the objects are that are pertinent to the exercise, and what the actions are that the user can take with each object. Some actions might be negative (or even dangerous), some objects might be implied (e.g. walking into a room is actually "entering" the "room" object). Spending a good amount of time at this stage mapping out each object and its associated actions into a detailed table is vital to the creation of the exercise.

Transferring to PIVOTE

Transferring the table to PIVOTE is actually a relatively straightforward process, using the Node Wizard to create the basic node triples (AN-DAM-Assets), and then adding specific rules and extra assets as required.

Once we have the exercise in PIVOTE we can use the web editor to check any logic flows and responses, but usually people want to dive straight back into the virtual world.

Building the Objects

We can now start building our objects. In many cases these will be built from scratch and the PIVOTE code is then easily embedded into them. You will have to ensure that the script generates the right device-action Node IDs for each possible user interaction, and that it is listening for and responding to each action instruction it might be given by PIVOTE. The large number of example PIVOTE scripts will give you a good start.

As you build the PIVOTE objects and the general immersive environment, you will begin to get a far better idea of how the exercise should flow, and you begin to enter an iterative develop-test-refine process moving between the virtual world and the browser based PIVOTE editor (which of course with Second Life Shared Media you can actually access from in-world).

Testing

It is vitally important that once you complete testing to your satisfaction you start testing it on colleagues, tame students and then volunteer live students. Virtual Worlds, simulation and chatbot development are all very iterative – and PIVOTE usually involves all three. During this testing you might want to do additional data capture – including full text and audio recording, SL and RL video recording, user tracking etc. so as to augment the PIVOTE logs in your analysis.

Narrative, Drive, Objectives and Pedagogy

We have deliberately not talked here about topics such as what the aim of the exercise is, what pedagogical approach you are using and what results you expect. That is because PIVOTE can be used in a wide variety of different ways; from simple quizzes to fully immersive life-and-death simulations.

However, since we are principally using PIVOTE for simulations, and even serious-game based simulations, we need to think about some of the "game" and "story" elements than we do for simple quizzes. In particular the scenario will need some sort of narrative, and in particular narrative drive. Because PIVOTE typically presents an open ended space where the user *could* do what they want we need to find ways of encouraging them to stay on the "plot path" of our simulation. There are both carrots and sticks we can deploy to help encourage this.

Layers and Variations

With PIVOTE it is easy to create variations once you have a basic scenario. This is because most variations only need changes to the exercise through the PIVOTE editor, rather than in-world. For instance when we developed the first Paramedic scenario it took about 4 to 5 days of effort.

The second scenario took an afternoon, as all we had to change was the feedback for each relevant treatment.

Since PIVOTE inherits MVP's clear distinction between structure and content it also means that it is possible to have the same structure for an exercise, but with different content – all that is needed is a control variable to switch between the two. So for instance a scenario could operate:

- In "teaching" mode where students are given additional information and references back to their teaching before each step
- In "revision" mode where there are hints available if the learner is struggling (measured by a low "right answer" variable)
- In "assessment" mode where no additional information is available

Another opportunity is to use the same basic scenario and environment but to explore it from different viewpoints, for instance as the electrician, plumber and manager in a maintenance example.

PIVOTE User Experience

So how does all this feel from a user point of view? Let's take a typical scenario, say a maintenance call on a piece of equipment.

- If the user if not familiar with an environment like Second Life they should be given the opportunity to get used to it. However, if all they are doing is this learning exercise (and ones like it) there is no need to overplay the familiarization – they are using it as a tool, not a social experience
- Then they need to be briefed on the scenario – just as in Real Life this could take place in a meeting room – or better still a "crew room" that resembles their normal work environment

- They get changed into basic "work" clothes – although ideally the avatars will already be in that state
- The scenario is then started by one of:
  - The tutor pressing a control on their HUD
  - The user pressing a START button on the wall
  - The user just walking through a door
- A first challenge might be put on the appropriate Personal Protective Equipment (PPE). This could be hinted at by a "Hat and Boots" sign, and the objects could be available in a locker. Opening the locker, taking the hat and boots and wearing them could all be PIVOTE actions.
- Walking through the gate onto the site can be a hidden check for PPE – if they aren't wearing any, a PIVOTE controlled foreman NPC shouts at them to get dressed and the gate (may) stay locked.
- When they approach the equipment they can enter a "point and click" period as they examine the equipment and any external controls (e.g. power feeds etc.). Each touch is detected by PIVOTE and PIVOTE feeds back what they see. If detail is required this may come up as a separate image in a HUD. They can also use the HUD to call up items such as maintenance manuals and circuit diagrams – again each action is tracked and facilitated by PIVOTE
- To create some sense of drive the students may be given a time limit, or have to deal with constant interjections (e.g. boss asking how they are doing), or have a checklist to work-through – again each can be generated and managed by PIVOTE
- Once they have assessed the situation, PIVOTE may give them some options as to the problem – so as to see what their diagnosis is. PIVOTE can lock down any direct manipulation with the equipment until this is completed

- The user might need to have a third party make a change before they can work safely – e.g. tripping an isolator. PIVOTE can simulate a radio or phone, and use the chatbot function to simulate a plain language conversation to get power switched off. Power state is also tracked by PIVOTE through a variable.
- Now the user can start work. Touching each object can bring up a menu of actions (switch on/off, unscrew, disconnect etc.). Each action is enabled and tracked by PIVOTE, and local scripting animates the objects accordingly
- With each action PIVOTE will check its rules and variables to see what feedback to give. For instance if the user didn't isolate the local supply but relied on the remote isolation then the scenario may say that power is still live as there is an alternate route – so if they touch the live wire they get a shock and the scenario is over.
- We find it useful if each activity is rated Red/Amber/Green (RAG) based on how important/dangerous it is through a PIVOTE variable, and also what the real time duration of each task would be (again a PIVOTE variable that could feed a HUD based clock)
- Once the user has finished the task and confirmed all is OK they can head back to the staff room and the scenario stops automatically and feedback is given either as they walk through the door, clock-off, or similar.

PIVOTE can be configured to give the user a summary of their work (dependent on the pedagogy in use) – using the RAG node ratings, a score, or any other variables.

Remember also that it is easy for other students to follow the learners actions remotely within the virtual world (using manual or automatic camera control), or for the tutor to create a video screen-capture of the whole proceedings.

CASE STUDIES

To give you some idea of the scope of projects in which PIVOTE has been used we present here two short case studies: one of the original PREVIEW project at St George's, University of London, and one from South Lanarkshire Council.

St George's University of London (SGUL)

St George's University of London (SGUL) decided to explore the value of using virtual worlds to deliver Problem-based Learning (PBL) for paramedic students. The intent was to look at how the 3D immersive virtual world environment could offer to simulate scenarios that are difficult to replicate meaningfully in the classroom setting.

An Island was bought in the virtual world Second Life, and various environments were developed – including a hospital, a high street, a residential home and an Underground station. The PIVOTE system was used to implement the scenarios written by the Paramedic tutors. In each scenario the students collaborated in the assessment and management of a patient at an accident scene, finishing with a handover at the hospital. The sessions were facilitated by a tutor.

To inform the development process and evaluate the scenarios as learning resources, tutor/student feedback surveys/focus groups were conducted. Some key findings are summarized in Table 1.

Almost all students were first-time users of SL, and 75% agreed that "it is easy to collaborate in the SL scenarios". Student comments included: "Communicating with others helped assess the situation… gave better understanding" and "It's much better to be able to actually perform treatments rather than just talk about it." One tutor

Table 1. Paramedic Student Perceptions of PIVOTE driven Second Life scenarios

Paramedic Student perceptions (n=20)	Strongly Agree	Agree	Neutral	Disagree	Strongly Disagree
SL is relevant resource for field/clinical work preparation	5	15	0	0	0
I can access SL scenarios at my own convenience	7	13	0	0	0
SL scenarios will enable me to analyze my own clinical performance	2	10	4	2	2
SL is valuable for my revision for my practical examination	3	12	4	1	0
SL scenarios will help me to manage patients with similar conditions	4	12	4	0	0

commented: "the open nature lends itself very strongly to creating a rich and valuable decision-making exercise."

SGUL's experiences showed that the SL environment appears to engage students effectively in learning, with few technology barriers. Students believed Second Life could provide a more authentic learner environment than classroom-based PBL, but did not want it to detract from classroom teaching time. It was concluded that virtual worlds can offer effective teaching spaces, as long as the activity takes advantage of the unique features and strengths of the platform, such as the visual presence of the space.

SGUL have now developed a scenario for medicine, again using PIVOTE and building on the work with the Paramedic scenarios. This is to be delivered in Problem Based Learning tutorials from May 2010.

South Lanarkshire Council, Core Connex Project

South Lanarkshire Council wanted to explore the possibilities, opportunities and potential of Teen Second Life (TSL) as a learning resource for young people as well as develop high quality resources within the environment designed collaboratively with the target audience.

The project was contracted to Twofour Learning where Daden Limited assisted and developed

the learning resources, implementing the learning activities using PIVOTE.

Essentially the learning resources used PIVOTE as a back-end system to drive Role-playing scenarios in the Immersive virtual world of TSL. The scenarios tackled cultural sensitive subjects such as Territorialism, Sectarianism and Knife Crime. The young people become characters within the scenarios playing through "situations" where they encounter a simulation of the described anti-social behavior. The aim being to complete the activities and unlock rewards, access to new zones and receive in-depth knowledge of these problems in Scottish society.

Created in an urban environment (resembling Glasgow) the young people play through the three simulated situations. Once engaged in the activity the young people discover information in the form of: notecards, dialogue with NPC's (non playing characters), web links and images.

Territorialism

Learning Outcome: *better understanding of territorialism (why it appeals, what are the problems) what alternatives there might be to this type of behavior (where/how else can they get the same outcome of protection / friendship / status).*

In Scotland there are certain areas of towns that some young people can't visit because they would be at risk of violence or abuse because they come from the "wrong" area. In the TSL simulation this is replicated, you find there are two different areas of town red/yellow hills; during your exploration of the area you are denied access to the cinema, talk with NPC's who explain the situation and either help or subject you to abuse. Reaching the community center, a neutral safe haven, an employee gives you further information, including a real example case in 2006, where a young person was beaten to death by neighboring youths from another part of town.

Sectarianism

Learning Outcome: *understand the impact of sectarian behavior.*

In west Scotland this is a particular issue; especially religion associated with football. In the simulation the young people are put in a situation where they are the recipient of intolerance. Discovering a society divided by the type of shoes people wear. By interacting with a variety of NPC's the user discovers this divide shapes their behaviors, beliefs and emotions, spanning over decades of their history. Once complete the users gain further information on sectarianism in Scotland and gain access to the Cinema which was previously off limits!

Knife Crime

Learning Outcome: *better understanding of the impact / consequences of carrying a knife. Costumes, props and information will be provided throughout this scenario.*

During the participation of this experience users cross the street to see two youths arguing in an ally, suddenly one produces a knife and your told to run! One of the youths pushes you towards the park where a doctor describes "his story". The doctor then divulges that on many occasions he has experienced the results of knife crime in Glasgow and as a reward he continues to tell his story of his experiences via audio clips.

Outcomes, Benefits and Observations Found

Safe / protective environment: The simulations were found to be safe and protective for the young people to explore such sensitive subjects such as knife crime. In the real world, simulating a "knife attack" maybe deemed impractical, insensitive and rather inappropriate for young people. In TSL the seriousness of the situation can be easily portrayed to the user without putting these people at risk.

Support and advice available when required: As part of the delivery of this project each user (young person) was given a "Safety HUD" allowing access to telephone support numbers and email addresses. Additionally if any situation occurred in-world which was found to be unsettling users would push there "panic buttons" allowing them to submit a quick report of the incident. This was found to be reassuring for many users of the environment.

Geographically diverse: Universal Connections facilities that provide access to TSL allowed multiple users to log on and take part in the scenarios. This was found to be of great importance and allowed the council to run fewer sessions without the need to run multiple sessions at multiple centers, making it extremely cost affective to deliver.

THE FUTURE OF PIVOTE

To us the current iteration of PIVOTE is just the start. Our ultimate aim is for it to grow into a cross-platform virtual world authoring tool – which will let teachers and tutors create engaging, immersive experience without needing any low-level knowledge of the platform they are writing for – and to enable their students to access the learning from as many devices and environments as possible.

These are few of the things that we (and others) are working on to add to PIVOTE over the next few months and years:

- The ability to create web based forms accessed by the user from inside the virtual world (e.g. using the new Second Life Shared Media), and having PIVOTE respond appropriately to the completed form
- A 2D editor to control the layout of the 3D environment – whereas PIVOTE is currently concerned only with the structure and non-3D content of the learning this would extend its scope to the 3D environment as well (and in a cross-platform way)
- A graphical drag and drop flow chart type editor for PIVOTE cases
- Extension into other virtual worlds and environments (eg Open Wonderland, Vastpark)

One key issue that needs to be addressed is what PIVOTE actually is. One way of looking at it is as an application – but to us that may be too restrictive. We'd love other people to write the equivalent of the PIVOTE system in other computer languages (e.g. C# or PHP), and write a better user interface – so it doesn't even *look* like our PIVOTE. What really makes it "PIVOTE" though is:

- The use of the MVP standard – and particular the emerging Virtual World schema and our XtensibleInfo and other additions – to define, store (and of course exchange) the exercise definitions
- The use the APIs we have developed for:
  ○ Web to Second Life (and other virtual world) communications with the SL Interface
  ○ Object to Interface communications within Second Life

It is these two things that, to us, actually define what a "PIVOTE compliant" (or "PIVOTE inside") system is – alongside the aspiration for a platform independent virtual world authoring tool.

Getting Involved

PIVOTE is an open-source project – this means that it is dependent on the community for its future development. The PIVOTE web site (www.pivote. info) includes a Governance document that shows how PIVOTE is managed, and more importantly how people can get involved in a variety of ways within the project – such as providing user case studies, helping other users, sharing content and objects, helping to create new features, developing interfaces to other virtual worlds, and improving documentation (efforts are already underway to translate PIVOTE documentation into Italian and Spanish).

CONCLUSION

We hope that this discussion of PIVOTE has given you an insight into a more scalable approach to developing virtual world learning and training systems. The aim is to move as much of the data, structure and functionality out of the virtual world and onto the web as possible – making cross-platform operation and maintenance easier – and also significantly reducing the skill level needed to get involved with creating virtual world exercises.

Whether you use PIVOTE or not, hopefully the ideas described here can help inform the learning systems you do use and build. But if you do decide to go down the PIVOTE route (and we hope you do), then please join the community and help PIVOTE grow.

REFERENCES

Burden, D. (2008). *Deploying embodied AI into virtual worlds*. BCS SGAI Conference.

Burden, D., Conradi, E., Woodham, L., Poulton, T., Savin-Baden, M., & Kavia, S. (2008). *Creating and assessing a virtual patient player in Second Life*. Researching Learning in Virtual Environments Conference.

Conradi, E. (2008). *Innovations in online PBL: A virtual world case study*. 13th Ottawa International Conference on Clinical Compliance.

Ellaway, R., Candler, C., Greene, P., & Smothers, V. (2006). *An architectural model for MedBiquitous virtual patients*. MedBiquitous.

Ellaway, R., Poulton, T., Fors, U., McGee, J., & Albright, S. (2008). Building a virtual patient-commons. *Medical Teacher, 30*(2), 170–174. doi:10.1080/01421590701874074

Poulton, T., Conradi, E., Kavia, S., Round, J., & Hilton, S. (2009). The replacement of paper cases by interactive online virtual patients in problem-based learning. *Medical Teacher, 31*(8). doi:10.1080/01421590903141082

Triola, M. M., Campion, N., McGee, J. B., Albright, S., Greene, P., Smothers, V., & Ellaway, R. (2007). An XML standard for virtual patients: Exchanging case-based simulations in medical education. *AMIA Annual Symposium Proceedings,* (pp. 741-745).

KEY TERMS AND DEFINITIONS

MUVE (plural MUVEs): Refers to online, multi-user virtual environments, sometimes called virtual worlds.

PIVOTE: An open-source authoring system for learning in virtual worlds. Created by Daden Limited.

PREVIEW: A project acronym for: Problem-based learning in virtual interactive educational worlds.

Problem-Based Learning (PBL): A student centered instructional strategy in which students collaboratively solve problems and reflect on their experiences.

Second Life (SL): A virtual world developed by Linden Lab that launched on June 23, 2003, and is accessible on the Internet.

Virtual Learning Environments (VLE): Are a set of teaching and learning tools designed to enhance a student's learning experience by including computers and the Internet in the learning process.

Virtual Worlds: A genre of online community that often takes the form of a computer-based simulated environment, through which users can interact with one another and use or create objects.

Web Authoring: A category of software that enables the user to developing an application using simple web tools.

Chapter 13

Immersive Education Spaces Using Open Wonderland:
From Pedagogy through to Practice

Michael Gardner
University of Essex, UK

Adela Gánem-Gutiérrez
University of Essex, UK

John Scott
University of Essex, UK

Bernard Horan
University of Essex, UK

Vic Callaghan
University of Essex, UK

ABSTRACT

This chapter presents a case study of the use of virtual world environment in UK Higher Education. It reports on the activities carried out as part of the SIMiLLE (System for an Immersive and Mixed reality Language Learning) project to create a culturally sensitive virtual world to support language learning (funded by the UK government JISC program). The SIMiLLE project built on an earlier project called MiRTLE, which created a mixed-reality space for teaching and learning. The aim of the SIMiLLE project was to investigate the technical feasibility and pedagogical value of using virtual environments to provide a realistic socio-cultural setting for language learning interaction. The chapter begins by providing some background information on the Wonderland platform and the MiRTLE project, and then outlines the requirements for SIMiLLE, and how these requirements were supported through the use of a virtual world based on the Open Wonderland virtual world platform. The chapter then presents the framework

DOI: 10.4018/978-1-60960-545-2.ch013

used for the evaluation of the system, with a particular focus on the importance of incorporating peda-gogy into the design of these systems, and how to support good practice with the ever-growing use of 3D virtual environments in formalized education. Finally, the results from the formative and summative evaluations are summarized, and the lessons learnt are presented, which can help inform future uses of immersive education spaces within Higher Education.

INTRODUCTION

Judging by the growing interest in virtual world environments as reflected in computer-assisted language learning international conferences such as WorldCALL and EuroCALL, these applications are part of a group of emerging technologies that have great potential for foreign/second language learning. The shift in the use of the web from static to more interactive uses (the so-called Web 2.0) is reshaping the way we learn (Alexander, 2006). However, there is virtually no research to date to provide evidence of the specific traits and characteristics of technological applications such as virtual world environments that might contribute to the learning of second and foreign languages (L2).

In this chapter we present the findings from the SIMiLLE project. The problem we aimed to address in this project relates to the need to enrich foreign language learning experiences for over-seas students who wish to study in a UK Higher Education Institution (HEI). By studying in the UK the students have the advantage of being im-mersed in the culture, but traditional classroom methods rarely take advantage of the cultural context to control the learning content (classroom learning by definition removes students from the 'real' world). Whereas outside of the classroom, students often cluster together forming linguistic or cultural islands, which are often isolated from their immediate cultural surroundings.

This chapter provides some background information on the technology platform used (Wonderland) and our previous project MiRTLE (Gardner, Scott, & Horan, 2008; Callaghan, Shen,

Gardner, Shen, & Wang, 2010). We then describe the SIMiLLE project in more detail including the requirements for the project and how we intended to support best practice in L2 teaching and learning. This is followed by an overview of the design of the SIMiLLE systems and the evaluation frameworks used. We then provide a summary of the key findings from the different evaluation phases employed by the project. The ultimate objectives of this work were to improve the design of immersive education spaces, to assess and validate the effectiveness of different pedagogical approaches, and inform best practice in this emerging field. We hope to demonstrate that the lessons learned from the SIMiLLE trials go towards achieving these objectives.

BACKGROUND

The Use of Virtual Worlds in Education

In 2005, the international student population worldwide was 115 million, growing at a rate of approximately 15% per annum (Perkinson, 2006). Education is increasingly important in modern knowledge-based economies (Clarke & Callaghan, 2007) where learning is rapidly becoming a lifelong process. China is a good example of this rise in demand: it now has the largest higher education system in the world, awarding more university degrees than the US and India combined (Baker, 2007); university admissions in China have risen from under 10% of young people in 1998 to 21% in 2005 (Wang,

2007). This increase is equivalent to a growth rate of 30% per year since 1999 (Li, Whalley, Zhang, & Zhao, 2008).

The worldwide rise in demand for education, coupled with the rapid evolution of information technology, has led to new ways of learning and providing education. ELearning has been promoted by most education institutions and numerous corporations to facilitate better learning and teaching. Learning management platforms, such as Moodle[1] and Blackboard[2], have been in use for several years. Many on-line higher education institutions, such as the UK Open University[3] and the Hong Kong Open University[4], have developed and deployed their own eLearning platforms and infrastructure to provide adaptive and efficient eLearning services. ELearning has become learner-centered, emphasizing pervasive and personalized learning technologies (Thomas, 2008). As both traditional classroom learning and Web-based learning offer strengths and suffer from limitations, there is now a trend for eLearning systems to combine the strengths of the two into blended learning[5] (Kim, 2007). "Computer support for multifaceted communication can improve student learning when students use 3D chat rooms, blogs, and such interactive environments such as virtual worlds" (Dickey, 2005).

There is a great deal of interest in applying immersive virtual worlds to teaching and learning. Much of this interest has been caused by the success of commercial platforms such as the World of Warcraft (WoW)[6] for on-line gaming, and Second Life[7] for on-line social networking and e-commerce. These environments have a high level of realism and associated levels of engagement, as well as supporting and encouraging social interaction. The most commonly used virtual world used by educators seems to be Second Life, though several others are aimed at this sector, including Open Wonderland[8], Metaplace[9], Whyville[10] and Activeworlds[11]. Other virtual worlds, such as gaming worlds like WoW, have also been used for education. Examples of the use

of virtual worlds in education include: Harvard Law School, running simulated law court rooms[12]; Hong Kong Polytechnic University School of Hotel & Tourism Management[13]; Edinburgh Masters course on eLearning[14]; Imperial College London Polyclinic[15]. To date, more than 100 HEIs are registered on Second Life.

Open Wonderland

Open Wonderland is a cross-platform, open-source toolkit that provides a client-server architecture and set of technologies for building virtual- and mixed-reality environments. The toolkit is built on several technologies, including the Project Darkstar game server[16], jVoiceBridge[17] for adding spatially realistic immersive audio, and jMonkeyEngine[18] (JME) to generate a scene. There is an existing and growing tool chain around JME, including a Collada[19] loader—this is a benefit to Wonderland content developers, as it allows users to easily import 3D objects such as can be found on Google Warehouse[20]. Additional objects and components in the Open Wonderland toolkit (such as a camera device to record audio and video seen from a client) make use of other technologies, such as the Java Media Framework[21].

Open Wonderland provides a rich set of objects for creating environments, and supports shared software applications, such as word processors, web browsers, and document-presentation tools. For example, one or several users can draw on a virtual whiteboard and view PDF documents and presentations. A user, represented by an avatar, can communicate through the avatar to others in the world by means of a headset or microphone and speaker or by the use of a dedicated chat window for text messages. The scene generated by an Open Wonderland client can be viewed from a first-person or several third-person perspectives.

Figure 1 shows the Wonderland Server Architecture. It conforms to the Representational State Transfer (REST) style of architecture. A Wonderland client is run on a user's local PC.

Figure 1. Wonderland Server Architecture

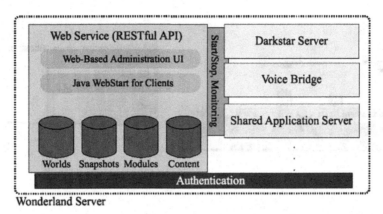

This is achieved using Java WebStart[22], which (so long as the user has Java already installed) allows a user to access a web page to initiate the download and execution of the Wonderland client. The server may also be administered via the same web page. This enables the initial world to be selected, snapshots of the current world state to be taken and modules to be added and removed. Modules may be code that extends the core system's functionality such as an SVG Whiteboard, or artwork such as being developed for the worlds used by the SIMiLLE project. The administrative facilities also allow the Darkstar Server, Voice Bridge and Shared Application Server to be stopped and started together with their properties being set. The Darkstar server is an online games engine and the Voice Bridge provides the audio capabilities in world via Voice over IP with a selectable range of audio qualities. The Shared Application Server allows the in-world sharing of X11 applications such as Firefox and OpenOffice.

The development of the original Wonderland platform by Sun Microsystems was originally conceived as a tool to support collaborative working by Sun employees (Yankelovich et al., 2004). As such it had several clear design goals appropriate for our project:

- Focus on social interaction, formal and informal

- Strong sense of social presence, allowing for discussion of sensitive topics
- Spontaneous, unplanned interactions, particularly socializing before and after planned events to build trust
- Enhance communication during formal interactions
- Design for collaboration
- Seamless document sharing with no need to switch contexts
- Extreme extensibility
- Allow developers to add any sort of new behavior

As such the key strengths of the Open Wonderland toolkit can be characterized as:

- Live application sharing
- Integration with business data
- Internal or external deployment
- Darkstar scalability: from very large to very small implementations
- Open and extensible: 100% Java
- Cross platform: Windows, Mac OS X, Linux and Solaris
- Open source, open art path
- Audio (spatial) as a core feature with extensive telephony integration

Figure 2. MiRTLE. Lecturer's View of Remotely Located Students and Student's View of Lecture

a
b

Wonderland is often compared to the Second Life platform. The Wonderland platform is primarily intended to be tailored and integrated by organizations within their own infrastructures, whereas Second Life is a publicly accessible online service with very large numbers of users who can make use of a virtual economy to organize their lives. Second Life has already been used extensively by teaching institutions to carry out online teaching (for example see [Robbins, 2007]). There is no doubt that Second Life has been used very successfully to support online teaching and learning. However, it does have several issues around its use, particularly concerned with the privacy and security for participants taking part in online sessions, and whether there are sufficient controls in place for organizations to use it as part of their formal teaching infrastructure.

MiRTLE

The objective of the MiRTLE project (Mixed Reality Teaching & Learning Environment) was to provide a mixed reality environment for a combination of local and remote students in a traditional instructive higher education setting. Figures 2a and 2b illustrate the virtual classroom from an early version of MiRTLE. The environment augmented existing teaching practice with the ability to foster a sense of community amongst remote students, and between remote and co-located locations. The mixed reality environment linked the physical

world of the classroom with a virtual world for remote learners. MiRTLE was deployed across all the major server architectures, including Windows, Mac OS X, Solaris and Linux (Ubuntu). The key achievement was the successful demonstration of the concept of combining physical and virtual worlds into a single practical service. This was validated in several deployment scenarios and the final version of MiRTLE has been adopted by others around the world.

From the initial evaluations of MiRTLE at the University of Essex, a number of valuable issues were highlighted that have implications for future uses of this technology. It particularly highlighted potential social issues, such as the impact on student motivation and perceptions of crowding and jostling for position in the virtual classroom. The trial showed that there was potential for naturalistic and spontaneous social interaction between virtual and physically present students, which may increase a sense of presence for all involved. Teachers also recognized the potential value of this approach, and that, once students are logged on and settled, the MiRTLE environment had a minimal impact on normal learning patterns. A key finding was that spontaneous social interaction between virtual and physically present students was possible. It implies that MiRTLE facilitated a breaking down of the barriers between the virtual and the physical, allowing impromptu and naturalistic exchanges that are likely to increase a sense of presence for all involved.

SIMiLLE

The MiRTLE project was very much about emulating current teaching practice by modeling and augmenting existing teaching or lecture rooms. The SIMiLLE project took a different approach in that it looked to exploit one of the key features of virtual worlds, that of being able to simulate new and existing environments, which can enable effective teaching and learning to take place. One of the aims of the SIMiLLE project was to investigate the technical feasibility and pedagogical value of using virtual environments to provide a realistic socio-cultural setting and content for second/foreign language (L2) learning. It is recognized that optimum language learning occurs when the learner is immersed in the host culture. However, if students are given language-learning tasks to complete in the real (host culture) world, it is difficult for teachers to observe and assess progress. On the other hand, the traditional approach is for students to act out their simulations or role-plays in a classroom setting that is removed from the everyday cultural milieu. The problem for English as a Second Language (ESL) learners based in their home country on distance learning programs is even greater, with no access to the cultural milieu at all. In both sets of circumstances a virtual world that reflects features of the host cultural environment and supports a range of potential everyday language learning interactions could provide a valuable medium for achieving ESL teaching and learning outcomes.

The SIMiLLE project explored the technical viability and pedagogical value of such an approach by building a virtual world for L2 language learning using the Open Wonderland platform.

Requirements

User needs for SIMiLLE were gathered through several workshops and discussions with key stakeholders. As one aim of the project was to evaluate the pedagogical value of virtual worlds for language learning, it was important that the system and processes envisioned in the scenarios were based on specified teaching and learning outcomes drawn from the Common European Framework of Reference for Languages: Learning, Teaching, and Assessment[23] (CEFR). It was also important that the system supported real-world classroom practice. This implied the need to elicit both the dynamics of classroom practice; for example, how simulation and role play activities are embedded in the class format, how many students are in a typical class, how many students each activity involves, how long the activity lasts for, the teachers role in the activity etc.; and, the pedagogical perspective: the types of teaching and learning objectives the activity is designed to achieve, how the activities are developed, documented and assessed, what standards it is based upon, what type of virtual world activities are useful and help to develop the desired language competence.

The resulting SIMiLLE scenarios reflect three different user perspectives. Scenario 1: the teacher perspective, considers the practicalities of creating and managing virtual world activities that meet specified teaching and learning objectives. It includes proposals for documents and processes, such as the Activity Plan and the Role Outline, that support in-world simulation activities for a class of around 16 students. Scenario 2: the classroom learner perspective, considers the experience of the student taking part in the in-world activities designed by the teacher. This includes being briefed about the roles s/he will play within the activity. Finally, scenario 3: the distance learner perspective, considered the experience of learners enrolled on on-line courses from remote locations.

Supporting Practice

To support the use of SIMiLLE in everyday classroom practice, it was necessary to provide a framework to help teachers define the learning outcomes for the Virtual World (VW) activities they design. The framework produced was based

Figure 3. SIMiLLE Concept

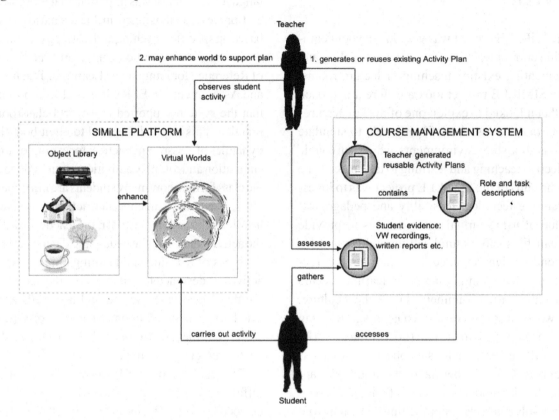

on discussions with teaching staff and details drawn from both the CEFR and related local syllabus documents.

At the conceptual level SIMiLLE is envisaged as an open and flexible platform containing multiple resources for teachers to develop and refine their own learning scenarios; enhance virtual worlds with supporting objects; and observe student interactions. It is language independent allowing the creation of multiple worlds to reflect various cultural contexts. Students are able to access the virtual world to carry out tasks, assume roles, make recordings and/or produce written evidence according to teacher instruction. As simulation or role-play activity is embedded within classroom practice, SIMiLLE is seen as working in conjunction with Course Management Systems (CMS) such as Moodle, which support document handling and student-teacher commu-

nication. Figure 3 provides an illustration of the overall concept.

The process of developing learning activities within the virtual world starts with the teacher generating an Activity Plan (similar to a lesson plan) based on their desired teaching and learning outcomes. A new learning activity/scenario may imply the need for new objects in a particular virtual world. For example, if the scenario required students to post a letter and no post box object existed in the specified world, the teacher would be able to access the object library and update the world with a suitable virtual artifact. Activity plans are stored on the CMS making them available for reuse or modification.

The Activity Plan contains task and role descriptions for groups of students (possibly for the whole class). As part of the project we produced templates for these documents to enable teachers to easily plan for new teaching activities using the SIMiLLE platform. When the activity is due to take place, the students access their task and role descriptions on the CMS and then enter the world to carry out the activity. The teacher may be in the virtual world at the same time observing student interactions and making in-world recordings. Similarly the students may be required to record some or all of their activities as evidence or for personal reflection. Alternatively they may be required to produce written reports as evidence. Any such files would be stored on the CMS allowing the teacher to assess progress.

The SIMiLLE concept has the potential to address three different contexts of use:

1. As part of a classroom activity involving all class members with a teacher present in both the real and virtual worlds
2. Outside the classroom but with the teacher present in–world
3. As a space for independent activity with no teacher presence

Design

The Virtual World requirements for SIMiLLE were realized using the Open Wonderland toolkit version 0.5. The toolkit provides the capability to build a world that has immersive audio and provides the ability to share desktop applications. It is an extensible system enabling users and developers to create their own worlds and add new features to the worlds in the form of modules. The virtual world supports a range of language learning competences and skills (e.g. listening and spoken interactions) as well as providing a realistic and meaningful representation of British life within the capabilities of the technical platform. Representations of British life are provided by offering a variety of contexts in which interactions can take place. These contexts include a coffee shop, a train station, a travel advice center/travel agents, a bank and a post office. Within each of these contexts a

number of objects were required to facilitate the learning activities. Teachers and Students have the ability to adopt a particular persona as required by the learning activity. Example personas identified in the project scenarios included:

- Bank Teller
- Post Office Teller
- Ticket Sales Clerk
- Train Travel Information Advisor
- Travel Agent

In addition, the Moodle Content Management System (CMS) at the University of Essex was used as a repository for all the support resources required for the project trials. These included:

- Activity Plans
- Role outlines
- Teaching support material
- Online help and support materials for the SIMiLLE users (e.g. user guides)

For the trials the use of the Wonderland virtual world was scheduled as part of a planned teaching activity, which was described and supported on a Moodle course page. Hyper-links were used to allow users to seamlessly launch the Wonderland virtual world from a link embedded on an activity description on Moodle, with all staff and students taking part in the SIMiLLE trials being provided with account login information to allow them to access the core Moodle course website.

One of the strengths of the Wonderland platform is the ability to drag content (documents) from the PC desktop into a Wonderland world. These documents are then presented as objects within the 3D world. Any Collada compliant object can be imported and viewed within the world. This feature supported one of the scenarios identified in the requirements, which was the ability for teachers to customise the virtual world with new objects. A useful repository for publicly available Collada content is the Google Sketchup 3D warehouse[24], which contains thousands of freely available content objects.

The virtual world was constructed using a collection of 3D objects. These were uploaded into the world and positioned where required. Also shared applications were placed in world to support the local context or task requirements (e.g. a web browser was used to access a crossword that was completed collaboratively by the students). The initial models for the world were created using Google SketchUp. These were then exported into either Collada format as .dae files or Google Earth format as .kmz files, which Wonderland can import. The world itself consists of a village and a representation of part of the University campus. The village contains a Railway Station, Post Office and Restaurant. The campus contains a Post Office, Bank, Shop, Travel Agent, Restaurant and Lecture Theatre.

Figures 4 and 5 illustrate screens from SIMiLLE with an avatar firstly standing in the virtual University of Essex campus and then in the Village.

EVALUATION

The framework for the evaluation of SIMiLLE was underpinned by theoretical and methodological considerations reported in research on related fields such as general education, e-learning, computer-assisted language learning (CALL), and more specifically, computer-mediated communication (CMC). In this context, a core goal of the SIMiLLE project was to contribute to the body of research aimed at identifying and exploring the specific traits and characteristics of technological applications such as Virtual World environments that might contribute to the learning of second and foreign languages.

The importance of providing instructed L2 learners with opportunities to engage in interaction and activities that can prepare them for 'real-life' communication has long been recognized by language educators. For the last 30 years, computer applications have increasingly permeated and transformed L2 learning and teaching by providing a new dimension and opportunities for students

Figure 4. SIMiLLE Virtual University of Essex Campus

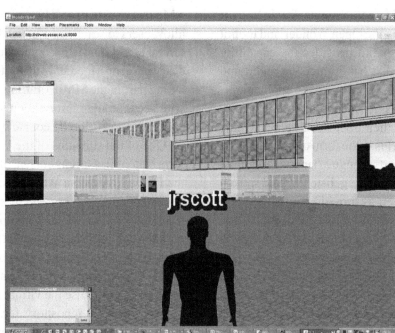

to interact and communicate with other learners and with native speakers. Furthermore, "there is a substantial body of data that indicates that student perceptions of CALL are on the whole positive" (Felix, 2008: 156). However, the nature and complexity of this field can result in a tendency to shape pedagogical practice driven by technology, which might have not been adequately researched. We are therefore, challenged "to integrate technology appropriately into our practice... and this requires reflection, research, and innovation" (Gillespie, 2008: 122).

As outlined in previous sections of this chapter, the problem we aimed to address in this project related to the need to enrich foreign language learning experiences for overseas students who wish to study in a UK HE institution. Second language acquisition (SLA) research indicates that certain conditions need to be met for L2 learning to be successful (Ellis, 1994, 2005), for example:

- Learners need to be exposed to the target language, i.e., comprehensible, rich, and varied input.
- Learners must have opportunities to produce the target language, e.g., comprehensible output.
- Learners need to be able to negotiate meaning and use the target language in a social, authentic context.
- Intercultural and pragmatic aspects have to be addressed in order to help L2 learners become competent L2 users since language is embedded in specific cultural and communication contexts.

A key issue, therefore, for materials designers, foreign/second language tutors, and SLA researchers alike is to establish the extent to which specific CALL applications can support the above conditions. CALL evaluation, however, has historically lacked 'methodological rigor' (Reeder et al., 2004, p. 258), an essential issue we need to address if we want to be able to provide our

Figure 5. SIMiLLE Virtual Village

learners with robust L2 learning materials. To this goal, the SIMiLLE evaluation was informed by data gathered by means of both introspective and empirical techniques. Furthermore, the evaluation cycle of the project included the analysis of processes and outcomes during the formative and summative stages of the virtual environment evaluation, an approach which is not normally adopted in CALL evaluative frameworks despite its importance (Reeder et al. 2004, p. 260).

The two phases – formative and summative cycles – of the SIMiLLE evaluation process addressed two general evaluation criteria:

A. Delivery/interaction issues, i.e. the virtual world environment as such (what participants think about it, their experience, motivation, ease of use, etc.). This type of evaluation primarily used judgmental evaluation methods (e.g. pre and post questionnaires and focus groups).

B. Knowledge gains in terms of content knowledge (e.g. socio-cultural knowledge: life on campus, life in Britain, academic life) and, importantly, in terms of second language learning gains, were assessed by means of micro-genetic analysis of interaction. Data collection methods included observations, in-world recordings, and audio recordings.

More specifically, and taking into account the evaluation criteria highlighted by Chapelle (2001), we aimed to determine the value and potential of SIMiLLE to support L2 learning with respect to: (a) practicality and acceptability issues; in other words, it is necessary to determine the potential of this environment for the implementation of pedagogic tasks designed to enable the type of interaction identified as supportive of second language acquisition; (b) authenticity; this issue involves two fundamental aspects: on the one hand, the interaction between the pedagogic tasks offered by means of the virtual world environment and the type of tasks L2 students need to carry out in non-pedagogical contexts, and on the other hand, the extent to which students are able to see that connection; (c) learner fit; this criterion refers to the appropriateness of the tasks in relation to the students' age, computer experience, needs, and so forth, as well as establishing whether or not the difficulty level of the SIMiLLE tasks is appropriate for the learners to increase their L2 ability; this issue is closely related to (d) L2 learning potential; that is, we need to determine the extent to which SIMiLLE and the pedagogic tasks implemented in this environment provide opportunities for learners to achieve the tasks and L2 learning objectives, e.g. in relation to interaction, collaboration, co-construction of knowledge, focus on form and meaning, etc.; finally, (e) impact, which refers to the overall learning experience undergone by the students and includes the extent to which the environment supports learner autonomy or the ability for students to exercise control over the environment, resources, and language. These five issues were addressed in relation to the virtual world environment, the pedagogic tasks, and the students' performance while carrying out the tasks. The SIMiLLE evaluation cycle comprised of a mixed methods approach to data collection and analysis in order to gather introspective and empirically based information.

Participants

The participants were student volunteers (N =11) and a language tutor recruited at the University of Essex. Five students participated in the formative phase of the evaluation trial. They were all speakers of English as a foreign language at upper intermediate level. The participants' mother tongue included Arabic, Turkish, and Thai.

For the summative evaluation phase, six students and their class tutor volunteered to participate. The students were enrolled in a general English course at intermediate level (level B1 according to the CEFR). The participants' mother tongues included Arabic and Chinese.

All participants were computer literate, but none of them had any prior experience of using 3D virtual world environments.

Data Gathering Instruments and Procedure

Data was gathered in a sequence of three sessions for the formative evaluation phase and four sessions for the summative evaluation trial (see Table 1 – the figures indicate the allotted time in minutes allocated to each task).

Data Analysis Procedure

Data gathered through the sequence of sessions summarized above provided the raw information for analysis. The information gathered by means of the various questionnaires was collated and analyzed primarily to investigate students' perceptions about the environment and their experience while carrying out the tasks. The questionnaires also provided information about the relationship between the students' background and computer familiarity and their personal evaluation of the activity while interacting on SIMiLLE.

Observations of students' interaction while carrying out the tasks (i.e., screen recordings) and the focus groups audio recordings were analyzed qualitatively.

Main Findings

a. *Practicality and acceptability:* SIMiLLE appears to be a suitable environment for the satisfactory implementation of this type of task and the identified drawbacks did not have a substantial effect on the participants' views about the environment.

b. *Authenticity as perceived by the participants:* Some students described SIMiLLE as a "realistic environment" and some said

Table 1. Summary of data collection procedure and timing for the formative evaluation (FE) and the summative evaluation (SE)

Session A	Timing	
	FE	SE
(1) Consent forms	5'	5'
(2) Biodata and computer use/CALL/elearning/VWs experience/history questionnaire	10'	10'
(3) Task (1): SIMiLLE familiarity training provided by (a) written instructions sheet; and (b) training task	90'	40'
(4) Training feedback questionnaire to gather information about 3a and 3b	15'	10'
Session B		
(5) Participants carried out Role-play task – their interactions were recorded using screen capture software.	45'	45'
(6) Post-task questionnaire	12'	10'
Session C		
(7) Participants carried out Treasure Hunt task – their interactions were recorded using screen capture software.	N/A	30'
(8) Post-task questionnaire	N/A	10'
Session D		
(9) Focus group session – audio-recorded	42'	35'

The sessions took place in a computer lab where participants were able to log in to SIMiLLE. The researchers were present during the sessions and technical support was available when needed.

that the tasks carried out in-world could "prepare them for real-life interaction" in similar situations. Nonetheless, a student identified certain disadvantages of interacting in SIMiLLE such as increased difficulty in turn-taking since body language and facial features which normally empower face-to-face interaction are difficult, if not impossible, to simulate.

c.   *Learner fit:* Students found both tasks "useful", "good for variety", "useful for practice and vocabulary" and to "increase their confidence in speaking". Nonetheless, pedagogical tasks must be carefully fine-tuned to students' L2 learning needs and linguistic ability in order to provide students with an adequate level of demand and challenge to maximize opportunities for L2 learning. This is particularly important in an environment such as SIMiLLE where learner autonomy is an important factor for students to feel at ease while completing their language tasks.

d.   *L2 learning potential:* The tasks provided learners with opportunities to practice listening, speaking, reading and writing in the L2 as well as opportunities to work on vocabulary. Participants also engaged in negotiation of meaning; they had opportunities to pose questions, make requests, ask for information, clarification, and practice functions such as agreeing and disagreeing. Importantly, the participants considered the experience in SIMiLLE highly relevant for their L2 development. Furthermore, the video recordings provide specific examples of language related episodes (Swain & Lapkin, 1995) such as work on vocabulary items, e.g., spelling the word 'dungeon' and collaboration to help a partner get to a place by giving directions in the L2.

e.   *Impact:* Participants felt very comfortable interacting and using SIMiLLE and praised their overall experience with the environment. They found their work during the

trials very relevant for their L2 learning. On the negative side, the students listed the following as some problematic issues which need to be addressed: prolonged delays, e.g., waiting for avatars to download and/or move; limited number of places to visit in-world; and the visual quality of the world. These limitations were mainly due to the Beta quality of the Wonderland toolset being used and external project constraints.

In conclusion, the participants identified the following characteristics as contributing to a positive experience:

- The training documents were useful and helpful in enabling independent use of the world.
- SIMiLLE has the potential to help students learn about UK cultural aspects.
- Both tasks were perceived by the participants as activities that can prepare them for their stay in the UK.
- The environment has the potential to simulate real places.
- They found the opportunity to use in-world applications such as sticky notes and the Web browser motivating and potentially useful.
- They also considered the 'sharing' of those applications an asset to promote interaction.
- The use of avatars might help 'shy' students to interact more freely than in a face-to-face situation.
- The use of avatars can help individuals to 'explore different identities'.

Aspects which still need to be improved include:

- Training documents need to be enhanced by increasing the use of visual support, for example by producing videos demonstrating the basics of using SIMiLLE and interacting in this 3D virtual world environment.

- A 'trouble-shooting' sheet could be prepared to support teachers.
- It is essential that teachers are aware of the options available to them to follow and monitor students as effectively as possible since this is of paramount pedagogical importance.
- Visual aspects of the world can be enhanced.
- Work on the delivery of a more stable platform.
- Improve downloading time.

The Teacher's Perspective

With regard to SIMiLLE as a teaching environment, the participating teacher considered it a potentially useful tool to help language tutors increase interest levels and modify the pedagogic approach in the L2 classroom. She also thought that working in this kind of environment might help increase motivation levels which, in turn, can make the target language more memorable for students. Importantly, she felt that the students were freer in their speaking and were able to focus on communication to a greater extent because the use of avatars decreased the potential stress associated with making errors. In other words, anonymity would give students more confidence and be more adventurous while communicating in the L2. She considered the fact that body language and facial expressions are very limited in SIMiLLE might prove to be an asset because students would need to be more accurate with their language – particularly pronunciation – to be understood by their partners.

The only drawback reported by the teacher was the issue of monitoring. She found the world a restrictive environment for this task and reported that finding students was not always easy. Finally, the fact that students can be located in different parts of the 3D world, might hinder the ability to help all students. This can be particularly important with large numbers of students.

CONCLUSION

This chapter has described work on the SIMiLLE project using a virtual reality environment (Open Wonderland) to support teaching and learning for second language learning. This was built on previous work on the MiRTLE project that explored how the same platform could be used to augment existing (generic) teaching practice (i.e. lectures). The approach we took in designing the SIMiLLE immersive education space was rooted in the clear pedagogical needs of teaching second and foreign language learners. The role of the virtual world in this instance is to provide a rich environment for learners to practice their skills in a variety of realistic settings, and allow teachers and learners to configure the environment and to record and playback their experiences for further reflection and review. A key issue we addressed was in supporting the best practice and processes involved in using this new type of environment. As part of this we have developed template activity plans and role outlines which teachers could use to structure their teaching sessions, and we integrated this and the virtual world within the University of Essex course management system (Moodle). We also described a range of formative and summative evaluation activities, which have been used to assess the effectiveness of this approach, and to validate the pedagogical approach being used, and inform best practice in this emerging field. Overall the outcomes from the SIMiLLE trials were very positive. This is particularly encouraging considering the relative immaturity of the virtual world tools being used. With the support of the open source community we hope to see drastic improvements in the reliability, scalability and usability of these systems in the future. What we hope to have demonstrated by this work is the need for a clear pedagogical framework that informs the usage of these virtual world tools. This needs to include the development of appropriate tools to support the design of effective learning activities (for example, activity plans and role outlines), and be underpinned by effective training and support materials. We believe that this is critical to the successful use of and ultimate widespread adoption of virtual worlds within formalized education in the future.

ACKNOWLEDGMENT

The SIMiLLE project was funded by the Joint Information Systems Committee (JISC), in the UK. The MiRTLE project was funded by Sun Microsystems. We would also like to thank all the participants who kindly took part in the evaluation trials and process.

REFERENCES

Alexander, B. (2006). Web 2.0: A new wave of innovation for teaching and learning? *EDUCAUSE Review, 41*(2), 32–44.

Baker, M. (2007). *China's bid for world domination*. Retrieved from http://news.bbc.co.uk/1/hi/education/ 7098561.stm

Callaghan, V., Shen, L., Gardner, M., Shen, R., & Wang, M. (2010). A mixed reality approach to hybrid learning in mixed culture environments. In Wang, F. L., Fong, J., & Kwan, R. (Eds.), *Handbook of research on hybrid learning models: Advanced tools, technologies, and applications* (pp. 260–283). Hershey, PA: IGI Global. doi:10.4018/978-1-60566-380-7.ch016

Chapelle, C. A. (2001). *Computer applications in second language acquisition: Foundations for teaching, testing and research*. Cambridge, UK: Cambridge University Press.

Clarke, G., & Callaghan, V. (2007). Ubiquitous computing, informatization, urban structures and density. *Built Environment Journal, 33*(2), 196–212. doi:10.2148/benv.33.2.196

Dickey, M. (2005). Three-dimensional virtual worlds and distance learning: Two case studies of active worlds as a medium for distance education. *British Journal of Educational Technology, 36*(3), 439–451. doi:10.1111/j.1467-8535.2005.00477.x

Ellis, R. (1994). *The study of second language acquisition*. Oxford, UK: OUP.

Ellis, R. (2005). *Instructed second language acquisition. A literature review*. New Zealand: Ministry of Education.

Felix, U. (2008). The unreasonable effectiveness of CALL: What have we learned in two decades of research? *ReCALL, 20*(2), 141–161. doi:10.1017/S0958344008000323

Gardner, M., Scott, J., & Horan, B. (2008). *Reflections on the use of Project Wonderland as a mixed-reality environment for teaching and learning*. ReLIVE 08 Conference.

Gillespie, J. (2008). Mastering multimedia: Teaching languages through technology. *ReCALL, 20*(2), 121–123. doi:10.1017/S0958344008000128

Kim, W. (2007). *Towards a definition and methodology for blended learning*. International Workshop on Blended Learning 2007 (WBL 07).

Li, Y., Whalley, J., Zhang, S., & Zhao, X. (2008). *China's higher education transformation and its global implications*. Retrieved from http://www.voxeu.org/index. php?q=node/1066

Perkinson, R. (2006). *International higher education*. Plenary Address Going Global2, The UK's International Education Conference. Retrieved from http://www.whitneyintl.com/ documents/ Innovation_and_International_Responsibility.pdf

Reeder, K., Heift, T., Roche, J., Tabyanian, S., Schlickau, S., & Golz, P. (2004). Toward a theory of E/Valuation for second language learning media. In Fotos, S., & Browne, C. M. (Eds.), *New perspective on CALL for second language classrooms* (pp. 255–278). Mahwah, NJ: Lawrence Erlbaum.

Robbins, S (2007). *Using a Multi-User Virtual Environment (MUVE) for education: One instructor's adventure in Second Life*. 360 Report on Games and Education.

Swain, M., & Lapkin, S. (1995). Problems in output and the cognitive processes they generate: A step towards second language learning. *Applied Linguistics, 16*, 371–391. doi:10.1093/applin/16.3.371

Thomas, S. (2008). Pervasive scale: A model of pervasive, ubiquitous, and ambient learning. *IEEE Pervasive Computing / IEEE Computer Society [and] IEEE Communications Society, 7*(1), 85–88.

Wang, Y. (2007). Chinese higher education on an overpass of fourfold transitions. *Journal of Higher Education Research in China, 8*.

Yankelovich, N., Walker, W., Roberts, P., Wessler, M., Kaplan, J., & Provino, J. (2004). Meeting central: Making distributed meetings more effective. *Proceedings of CSCW '04*.

ENDNOTES

1   http://moodle.org/
2   http://www.blackboard.com/
3   http://www.open.ac.uk/
4   http://www.ouhk.edu.hk/
5   Blended learning is the process of incorporating many different learning styles that can be accomplished through the use of 'blended' virtual and physical resources.
6   http://www.worldofwarcraft.com/
7   http://www.secondlife.com/
8   http://www.openwonderland.org/
9   http://www.metaplace.com/
10   http://www.whyville.net/
11   http://www.activeworlds.com/
12   http://slurl.com/secondlife/Berkman/69/54/24/
13   http://slurl.com/secondlife/Polyusotel/114/158/26/
14   http://slurl.com/secondlife/Vue/205/53/30
15   http://slurl.com/secondlife/HealthLands/94/109/31/
16   RedDwarf is the official community fork of Project Darkstar: http://www.reddwarf-server.org/
17   http://jvoicebridge.dev.java.net
18   http://www.jmonkeyengine.com/
19   https://collada.org
20   http://sketchup.google.com/3dwarehouse/
21   http://java.sun.com/products/java-media/jmf
22   http://java.sun.com/javase/technologies/desktop/javawebstart/index.jsp
23   http://www.coe.int/t/dg4/linguistic/CADRE_EN.asp
24   http://sketchup.google.com/3dwarehouse

Chapter 14
Teaching and Learning in Second Life:
A Case Study

Jiuguang Feng
Towson University, USA

Liyan Song
Towson University, USA

ABSTRACT

Various advantages of Multi User Virtual Environment (MUVE) have been identified in literature. However, MUVEs have not been widely adopted in educational settings due to technical and pedagogical challenges. This chapter discusses a qualitative case study that examines how Second Life, as a MUVE, was diffused on a university campus. Both instructors and students' perspectives were examined using interviews, observations, and survey data collection methods. The theory of diffusion of innovation was used as a theoretical framework in both the design of the study and the analysis of the data. The findings from the study indicate that although the future application of MUVE can be promising, various challenges exist for instructors to adopt Second Life in their instruction.

INTRODUCTION

The Multi- User Virtual Environment (MUVE) is not a new concept and it has been discussed in literature for almost two decades (Cobb & Frazer, 2005). However, its application has only started gaining popularity over the last 5 years, with around 180 virtual worlds at present available or under development (de Freitas, 2008). The emergence of virtual learning environments have led to many social, pedagogical, institutional, and technological challenges and opportunities for the learning and teaching community (de Freitas, 2008). The unique nature and characteristics of MUVEs and its application, introduce further complexities regarding the impact and implica-

DOI: 10.4018/978-1-60960-545-2.ch014

tions of virtual worlds for teaching and learning. The advantages of MUVEs seem to be obvious. However challenges remain in widely implementing MUVEs in education. Some of the challenges are technological and others are more conceptual.

It is important to highlight that the nature of technology has an impact on how a technology is used in educational spheres. However, the actual use of technology is not completely determined by the technology itself, but rather shaped by sociocultural forces (Veletsianos, 2009). Although empirical results from the most of the studies are promising that the use of MUVEs would bring a powerful pedagogical change towards constructivist learning, the adoption of technology innovation has been slow. Further exploration on how a technological innovation is adopted or diffused in education is needed. The purpose of this chapter is to discuss the diffusion of MUVEs in education. Specifically, we investigated how Second Life, as a technological innovation, was diffused on a university campus in our case study. We first review the literature on the various advantages of MUVEs and introduce the diffusion of innovation theory as well as classifying a MUVE as an innovation. Next, we present the case study with findings and discussions. Finally, we conclude the chapter with implications on future research.

ADVANTAGES OF MUVES

MUVEs can support students' constructivist learning (Bronnack, Riedl, & Tashner, 2006; Dede, Whitehouse, & Brown L'Bahy, 2003; Dickey, 2005), and help build a community of learners (de Freitas, 2010). Research projects have taken a social constructivist approach to learning in virtual worlds (Dede, et al., 2003; Dickey, 2005; Bronnack, et al., 2006). Specifically, MUVEs can support experiential learning, collaboration, and inquiry-based learning.

MUVEs support experiential learning. Educational MUVEs are synthetic worlds that have the capability of providing learners with experiential learning. For example, in Braman, Vincenti, Arboleda, and Jinman's research (2009), the instructors used SL in an introductory computer science course where students learned to build objects and practiced repeatedly. Their findings suggested that the expressive power and creative nature of SL enabled students to extend conceptualized versions of themselves and their work into creative virtual spaces. The interactive and expressive nature of MUVEs can also help support students to learn foreign languages. For example, in Wang, Song, Stone, and Yan's research (2009), students in China met with students in the United States in SL where they exchanged ideas through both oral and written communication. The authentic communication between them helped improve their foreign language skills.

MUVEs support online collaboration. In Childress and Braswell's (2006) study, SL was integrated into an online graduate level course to strengthen students' sense of community and to provide better communication between instructors and students. A three-story office building was built as the study space for the class where students could come for academic reading and social interactive. They could also leave messages for the instructors. Students had come to this environment to work on their group projects because the interactivity and immersion of SL would make it a rich environment for cooperative learning activities (Childress & Braswell, 2006). It was further stated that the applications of MUVEs could help increase realism and interactivity, thus blurring the line between the face-to-face learning environment and the online virtual earning environment (Childress & Braswell, 2006).

MUVEs support inquiry-based learning. It is hard to design and implement scientific inquiry due to limited resources (National Research Council, 2005). The emergence of MUVEs presents an opportunity for educators to conduce inquiry-based learning in virtual environments. One example of simulated, inquiry-based learning in educational MUVEs is the River City Project (Clarke & Dede, 2005). The River City MUVE Project was created and developed by Harvard University. It is usually a 2-4 weeks long curriculum designed to help improve middle school students' scientific inquiry skills. In the River City project, students were asked to work in teams to develop a hypothesis for the cause of a disease. Their quest included various engaging activities such as interviewing citizens of River City, reading relevant documents, visiting the hospital, and reviewing photographs. Agents were available to provide guidance, but the students choose their own approaches to the inquiry. The purpose of this project was to help students to learn both science concepts and inquiry (Nelson & Ketelhut, 2007). A research on this project showed that students were intrinsically motivated by the curriculum, and actively engaged in what they described as realistic inquiry, and they said that they felt like scientists (Clarke & Dede, 2005).

DIFFUSION OF INNOVATION

An innovation refers to a new idea, practice or object in a social system (Rogers, 1995). According to Rogers (2003), innovation diffusion is a process through which innovations spread by communication channels between members and groups in a social system. The Innovation theorists believe that certain characteristics determine the rate at which an innovation is adopted by a social system, and these characteristics include relative advantage, compatibility, complexity, trialability and observability of the innovation (Rogers, 2003). Relative advantage is the extent to which innovations will increase someone's job performance. Compatibility refers to the congruence of the innovations with the existing set of values and past experiences. Complexity is the ease with which innovations can be learned and comprehended by potential users. Trialability is the degree to which innovations can be piloted on a small scale to

test their efficacy. At last, observability refers to positive outcomes one sees from implementation of the innovation (Rogers, 2003). Rogers noted that the constructs of the innovation attributes is interrelated. Due to the fact of the interrelated characteristics among these five constructs, some researchers have focused on certain attributes or certain groups of attributes of the perceived attributes (Demir, 2006).

Diffusion theory has potential application to information technology ideas and techniques, and has been used as the theoretical basis for a number of research projects on information systems (Clarke, 1999) because teachers and schools are regularly exposed various new and innovative technologies. The theory of innovation diffusion has been incorporated into the instructional technology field to increase the adoption of instructional technologies because of a growing realization that innovative instructional products and practices have suffered from a lack of utilization (Surry, 1997). The Diffusion of Innovation Theory is valuable to the field of instructional technology because instructional technology is an innovation-based discipline and many of the technological products represent radical innovations in the form and delivery of instruction (Surry, 1997). By better understanding factors that influence adoption of an innovation, instructional technologist, teachers and organizations will be better prepared to adopt the innovation.

Diffusion research investigates how the major elements of diffusion and various other factors interact to facilitate or impede the adoption of a specific product or practice among members of a particular adopter group (Surry, 1997). Some instructional technology diffusion research has focused on the perceived attributes of innovation (Rogers, 1995) and other research investigated the factors that influenced students' attitude toward the innovation based on Rogers' theory of the diffusion of innovations (Demir, 2006). More research in this area is needed, especially ones that focus on the process of innovation diffusion.

MUVEs as an Innovation. MUVEs are a socially, pedagogically, institutionally, and technologically complex environment (Feng & Song, 2010). According to Nelson and Ketelhut (2007), "Educational MUVEs have emerged in recent years as a form of social constructivist and situated cognitive based educational software" (p. 269). This area of research and practice presents the teaching and learning community with real challenges. Meanwhile, these environments offer potential such as providing broader capabilities for a learner-centered classroom, increasing students' engagement and motivation, and opening up a new space for learners to explore (de Freitas, 2010).

The Complexity of MUVE. Complexity refers to the degree to which an innovation is perceived as relatively difficult to understand and use (Rogers, 1995). As a matter of fact, any new idea can be classified on the complexity-simplicity continuum. Some innovations are easier for potential adopters to use whereas others are more complicated. Rogers (1995) further suggested that the complexity of an innovation, as perceived by members of a social system, was negatively related to its rate of adoption. On the complexity-simplicity continuum, MUVE falls into the higher complexity category. However, there are multiple meanings of the complexity and they are technical complexity, social complexity, and pedagogical complexity.

- **Technical Complexity:** The technical complexity of MUVEs has been shown from at least two levels. First, the technical problems associated with MUVEs are caused by computers lacking certain capabilities such as dedicated graphic cards, and constant computer software updates. Secondly, a 3-demensional world is an interface that requires time for people to get used to the view and navigation.
- **Social Complexity:** The social complexity of teaching and learning within MUVEs mainly refers to the variety of social capa-

bilities of MUVEs. All possible kinds of social activities, such as marriage, shopping, dating and selling and buying real estates, can be conducted. The complexity of MUVEs can be one of the barriers for teachers to adopt because they might feel intimidated to enter into the complex environment.

- **Pedagogical Complexity:** Due to the fact that a MUVE is a technically and socially complex world, teachers need to make pedagogical adjustments. Simply transferring traditional classroom pedagogy to a virtual environment would not work.

In summary, the literature has identified various advantages of MUVEs. However, a MUVE is still not well diffused despite of its advantages. In the following section, we present our case study on the diffusion of Second Life as a MUVE on a university campus.

TEACHING AND LEARNING IN SECOND LIFE: A CASE STUDY

The purpose of the study was to understand how MUVE was diffused in a mid-Atlantic metropolitan university. Specifically, we examined how Second Life as a MUVE, was diffused on a university campus. The study adopted a qualitative research method approach using interviews and observations as data collection methods. To help provide a more comprehensive view on the relative advantages of SL, we surveyed the students who had classes in SL about their perceptions. The triangulation of different sources of data helps generate more valid and robust descriptions and explanations (Stake, 2000).

The research context was a mid-Atlantic Metropolitan University (referred to as X University). The Second Life campus of the university was built in October 2008. Since then, various activities have been conducted on the SL campus. Different virtual objects have been built and some instructors have taken advantage of the virtual campus and extended their classes in SL. However, there are only a few instructors who have used SL in their instruction. Despite the various workshops on the use of SL in education, SL is still not widely adopted on this campus. Our case study investigated on the diffusion of SL on this campus, attempting to identify why SL is not well adopted.

Participants

Participants in the study include instructors and students from four undergraduate and graduate classes. Pseudonyms will be used for the participants in the study. Since there were a limited number of instructors who had taught with SL on campus, the sampling selection method was an exhaustive one where all members of the SL core team were invited to participate in the study. Due to the current availability of the instructors, the participants included three instructors and one instructional technologist: Tim, Laura, Jena, and Nicole. Tim had taught several courses with SL and was a member in the SL core team. Laura had held office hours in SL. Jena is a professor who had taught a 3-D design course in SL. Nicole was an instructional technologist and had assisted instructors who wanted to start teaching with SL, and she was also a member in the SL core team.

Data Collection

This qualitative study included observation reports of various workshops in the university and four interviews with three instructors and an instructional technologist. The workshops were not only to teach teachers and students on how to use SL (e.g., getting around and building things), but were also showcase of various teaching and learning activities that the instructors and students had conducted in Second Life on campus. Observations were conducted on multiple workshops from 2009 to 2010.

Four semi-structured interviews were conducted with the instructors and the instructional technologist. The open-ended semi-structured interviews would allow researchers to add additional questions during the interview in a more prompt manner and give participants opportunities to express their emerging ideas (Merriam, 1992). Students in those instructors' classes were surveyed regarding students' perceptions on the relative advantages of SL. The following analysis is based on the four interviews, formal and informal observations and from the students' survey.

Findings: How SL was Diffused on Campus

The Attributes of SL as an Innovation

The theory of perceived attributes of an innovation is based on the notion that individuals will adopt an innovation if they perceive that the innovation has the following attributes: (1) the innovation must have some relative advantage over an existing innovation or the status quo; (2) it is important that the innovation be compatible with existing values and practices; (3) the innovation cannot be too complex; (4) the innovation must have trialability, which means the innovation can be tested for a limited time without adoption; and (5) the innovation must offer observable results (Rogers, 1995). In our study, we mainly examined the complexity and the relative advantage of SL used in teaching and learning.

The Complexity of SL

Technical Complexity: Some of the technical difficulties that students had experienced included unfamiliarity with the 3-D world such as navigation and building avatars. On the campus where the research was conducted, most of the computers do not have SL software and the users are not allowed to install software without the administrators' permission. This created challenges for instructors to utilize SL more frequently in their instruction because they had to update the SL software with administrator's permission because they sometimes run into problems when doing this update on their own (Laura and Nicole).

Social Complexity: When asked to give suggestions about what experience or knowledge teachers should have before exploring SL for their classroom, Tim and Nicole both pointed that overcoming the culture barriers in SL was more important than overcoming the technical barriers for instructors who want to start teaching with SL. Tim thought the first thing for instructors to do was to explore SL for a while to see how people interact and to learn the norms of the environment; teachers should really take the time to explore and to understand the culture of SL. Nicole also thought that the first barrier was being able to wrap your mind around SL and being able to understand what SL is. If you were open to explore, then you could apply this in a learning environment: that was half of the battle. The others, such as how to walk, fly, and learning about the technology will come overtime. The X University has a SL Core Team with which other faculty members can connect to ask for help with technical problems. Simply, understanding what SL is about is the first major task according to the participants.

Social factors also influenced the instructors' connection with communities outside the university. All three instructors have been to various SL sites and have been involved in other SL social activities. As a SL new resident, Laura first heard of SL by reading an article about the Vassar College having a recreation of Sistine Chapel in their SL area in a newsletter about technology and education. She was immediately fascinated by the idea and became a resident and went to the site. She thought that it was a great implication and it would be the immersion experience without the cost of actually traveling to somewhere, and without the risk. The social aspects seem to always fascinate the instructors to explore more

opportunities to utilize SL in teaching, and to add complexities for instructors who want to use a simple instructional tool.

SL is more socially complex than many other instructional tools because it can serve as a virtual social community to link the instructor to some other professionals and help them join some professional organizations. One of the exceptional examples that Nicole mentioned was that one faculty member in the Art Department, Jenny, actually had an artist from New York come to critique her students' work in SL. It offered instructors and students the opportunities to really communicate with professionals that they may not have the opportunity to do in real world due to lack of time, lack of funding and so on. Tim said in the interview that there were many fantastic research groups in SL and he belongs to several on virtual learning, artificial intelligence, programming and design.

In Roger's diffusion of innovation theory, the complexity of the innovation is always negatively related to the diffusion process (Rogers, 1995). The findings from our study supported Roger's statement. The technical complexity was found negatively related to the instructors' adoption of SL in our study. The 3-D virtual world can be intimidating for many new participants and scare away many instructors and students. However, the social complexity can be both positively and negatively related to people's adoption of SL since it both presented challenges and provided opportunities for instructors. On one hand, many instructors who are not familiar with the SL culture and who have less skillful with computers might feel intimidated to enter into the complex virtual world. On the other hand, the social complexity, the rich context also provides valuable opportunities for instructors to engage in professional development activities. Nicole has been to a place where people can act in Shakespeare's play, Hamlet. That is just one of the many examples that those interviewed mentioned about how the social complexity of SL can be utilized in teaching.

The Relative Advantage

Nobody had come for the office hours last semester. It usually took my students a long time to figure out how to get to the place where the office hours were held and how to set up their avatars. If they want to talk to me, they can simply call me. -**Laura**

You designed it, you manufactured it, you have it in Second Life. I don't know why you are not going to put an amount of dollars beside it and start making money of what you have just produced. It is right there, it is that easy. You are right at the door! -**Jena**

The relative advantage of innovation means that the degree of which the innovation is better than the idea or it supersedes (Rogers, 1995). The true relative advantage of an instructional tool is that it can be utilized to improve students' learning. In the actual application, the three instructors' experiences vary greatly in terms of pedagogical effectiveness. Laura said that nobody had come for the office hours last semester while Tim and Jena have not only used SL as a tool but also an environment for students' collaboration and link them to other professionals in the field. In Laura's situation, it usually took her students a long time to figure out how to get to the place where the office hours were held and how to set up their avatars. If they really had a question and they wanted it to be answered, they would just have come to see her physically and the course was not an online one. The contrast is interesting as well as reasonable because the three instructors (Laura, Tim and Jena) have used SL in different ways and their students are very different regarding their computer skills. Towards using certain technology, it is important for instructors to avoid the tendency of using technology for its own sake, and they need to consider the effectiveness of using it as a tool. Since the purpose of Laura's situation was not to use SL but to communicate, to train students how to use SL would be waste of precious time in a full course when time was limited and they could choose more effective and appropriate tools in this specific situation. In contrast, the purpose of Tim's class was to show SL as creative applications of computers, similar in Jena's situation, SL could be a useful tool for students who are majored in 3-D design, so it was certainly not a waste of time to train their students before they used SL. Despite the differences, both of their experiments should be encouraged since we do not know what the relative advantage of certain emerging technologies have unless we try them. We should encourage experimentation and at the same time consider pedagogical issues. Laura thought that she would train the students next time, if the class is about emerging technologies. Therefore, the relative advantage is not only perceived as what other people could do and have done, but the true relative advantage to improve teaching and learning is to experiment with it as a tool.

From the students survey (see Table 1), we can see that SL not only shares common advantages with other online tools, but also has some unique advantage as a MUVE. For example, "Not having to physically be in class" is a shared advantage of any online tools, but "To travel to different virtual places" is a unique characteristic for MUVE. Furthermore, "People who are shy may benefit from SL" might also be a shared advantage with other online tools since some students who feel shy in the face-to-face class feel more comfortable in online discussion by using any online tools, such as Discussion Board, or Wiki, while "It is the same as real life" is definitely a unique characteristic and an obvious advantage of MUVE. The implications of the shared and unique advantages of SL in students' perception for educators are that we should not only take advantage of SL as a common online tool to deliver instruction from

Table 1. The Advantages of SL from Students' Responses

The Unique Advantages of SL	SL Shared advantages with other online tools
It is a lot more fun and interactive to be in a SL classroom setting.	It is easier to show up for a class in SL than it is in the real world. People who are shy may benefit from SL.
It is very interesting to travel to different virtual places.	Not having to physically be in class.
It is the same as real life.	You can do it from the comfort of your own room
Meeting new people.	No need to go to the classroom and discuss with others anytime

distance or to encourage students' cooperation and participation. More importantly, we should take advantage the unique advantages of MUVEs and provide students unique and productive learning experiences.

Adopter Categories and Opinion Leader

Venturesomeness is almost an obsession with innovators (Roger, 1995. P282)

Two categorizations are generally accepted as valid in diffusion theory. First, within this distribution five basic adopter categories are posited to exist: innovators (first 2.5 percent of the population to adopt), early adopters (12.5 percent), early majority (34 percent), late majority (34 percent) and laggards (final 16 percent) (Rogers, 1995). The second major categorization paradigm used in adoption theory concerns personal influence. A basic assumption of diffusion theory is that some individuals within a given social structure are influential in persuading others to adopt products. However, the attempts to identify the characteristics of these opinion leaders do not completely apply to the diffusion of innovative instructional technology on campus.

All instructors had excellent computer skills (except for Laura) in the SL core team. Although the adoption of the technology is closely related to the teachers' attitudes towards technology as attitude constitutes various dimensions. Some examples of these are perceived usefulness: computer

confidence (Rovai & Childress, 2002), training (Tsitouridou & Vryzas, 2003), gender (Sadik, 2006), knowledge about computers (Yuen, Law & Chan, 1999), anxiety, confidence, and liking (Yildirim, 2000). From the case study, we can see that knowledge about 3-D worlds seems to be a decisive factor for innovators. It is an interesting fact that they tended to underestimate the technical complexities of MUVEs and they assumed that when instructors began to think seriously how to use SL in their teaching, half of the battle was done.

The three instructors (except Laura) have met students and other faculty members regularly in SL. Their students could talk with them about the interface and they also have taught the students some practical skills such as SL building. In addition to the four instructors as innovators and opinion leaders, the president of X university also successful held two Study Breaks on SL campus. To some extent, the president also served as both a innovator and opinion leaders in the diffusion process due to his influence in the university. Some students did not know about SL at all, but they set up Avatars and became familiar with the environment because they wanted to talk with the president.

We can see that even the diffusion process seemed to be stuck in the innovator stage and did not move to the "early adopter" stage (Rogers, 1995); it was actually still moving slowly. By the end of the study, we have heard that more professors started to use Second Life. It will be interesting to keep exploring the diffusion process.

Solutions and Recommendations- Is MUVE for Everyone?

Just like I said, SL is not for everyone. I fully understand that many of the instructors are not interested in MUVEs at all. -**Jena**

SL has not reached the peak, because as educators we have not reached the peak of how we can apply it. The novelty may reach its peak, and then instructors are going to do serious pedagogical work and empirical research to apply MUVE into their class and embed it in their class. – **Nicole**

Is MUVEs for everyone? The answer is: it depends. Based on the analysis of the case study, there are several suggestions about the adoption and use of SL.

First, generally speaking, social complexity and technical difficulties are negatively related to the teachers' adoption of teaching with SL since SL is a multi-faceted virtual reality and relatively newer and more complex technology. However, the social complexity can be positively related to the future adoption of SL or other MUVEs because it provides various opportunities for simulations and role-play and to apply what students have learned in a seemingly real world setting. Therefore, instructors can take advantage of the complexity of SL, which is a unique characteristic of SL as an innovation, spend some time in SL to become more familiar with SL and take advantage of its social complexity.

Second, teachers' adoption of SL has been justified by their perceptions of SL and is based on their pragmatist beliefs on whether SL can be used in their subjects effectively. In Roger's (1995) Diffusion of Innovation Theory, it was defined as relative advantage. For Tim's' course, students were using SL as a professional tool where they could make tangible benefits in the future when they would be able to use SL programming, the

relative advantage is very tangible. In Laura' situation, although she had some ideas about teaching with SL, she was not sure that it was actually going to happen. As much as she thought SL was fun, she did not want to take time away from the other things they had to do in the class. Moreover, the office hours had turned out to be not very productive, since none of her students came and they had alternative ways to communicate with their instructor such as making phone calls and sending emails. In other words, they tended to choose the way that they were familiar with. It is a completely justifiable reason for instructors to choose tools for the sake of effectiveness. That has illustrated Roger's (1995) theory that relative advantage is positively related to the adoption of an innovation.

Third, although the "innovators" and "opinion leaders" (Rogers, 1995) have emerged during the SL diffusion process, it seemed that the process was stuck in the 'innovators" stage and was getting extremely slowly to the "early adopter' stage in the university since we have heard that some of professors in the college of business had also begun to use it. We will keep exploring how the SL innovation would be continually diffused on campus. Meanwhile, we would also like to propose a "SL Cooperative Model", which should be joint efforts from the Office of Technology Services, the instructors who want to initiate teaching with SL, and the innovators. The detailed process is illustrated in Figure 1.

From Figure 1 we can see that in the case study, the observed university has gone through the first two stages but the process has been significantly slowed down in the application stage. As Nicole pointed out, the so called "peak' of SL is novelty wise, but SL has not reached the peak in its application. For the current situation in the case study, it is essential to keep promoting SL on campus and the cooperation between the innovators and other instructors.

Figure 1.

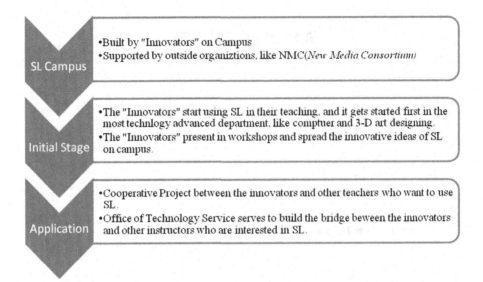

FUTURE RESEARCH DIRECTIONS

As a new learning environment or an emerging instructional technology, the types of instructional models should be defined in order to create effective learning environments for students. For example, some courses offered by the university in SL are to teach how to use SL itself as a professional tool in computer science and interactive multimedia courses. SL can also be used as a communication tool since teachers can hold office hours in SL to meet with their students. However, it is equally advantageous to use SL as platform for role playing and a synchronous online system in teaching because the richness of its self-constructed environment. In this study, SL has been only used as a communication tool and professional tool. Therefore, the importance of the examination of how SL is used in teaching is that it can provide a generic framework to develop SL instructional models to guide and assist educators to develop their own courses more effectively and in less time. In addition, when a new technology emerges, it usually takes a long time for educators to research and understand the optimal way of using it. During the research and experiments,

it is reasonable there are both opportunities and challenges about the new learning tool. As it was shown in the study, the responses from the students about SL used in teaching were related to how instructors used them instead of how advantageous SL was as an instructional technology. Therefore, it is important to examine teachers' and students' perception about educational MUVE.

MUVE are a complex social environment. The social factors also have been shown as important besides teaching; all the instructors in the study have been to various SL sites and been involved in other SL social activities. There are many educators using SL in many different ways and they are always willing to share ideas. MUVEs can open up the boundaries of learning and professional development for instructors, and help students apply what they have learned in class. The social aspects seem to always fascinate the instructors to explore more opportunities to utilize SL in teaching, and add complexities for instructors who want to use a simple instructional tool. Therefore the social aspects of MUVEs need to be further explored and investigated.

Furthermore, in universities and colleges, the wide adoption of certain instructional technology

Figure 2. MUVE Adoption

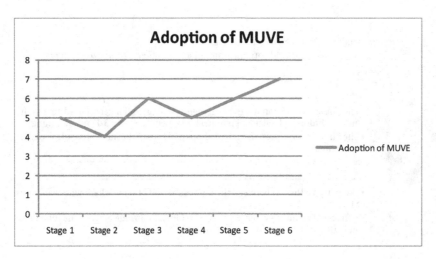

usually takes long time as Roger (1995) illustrated in the S Curve. It starts slowly in the beginning, then it gets steeper when the idea is more wildly recognized and accepted, when the adoption rate is saturated, there is no longer very noticeable increase. However, the adoption sometime does not work that way for how teachers adopt certain instructional technology, there is a more zigzag way even accompanying with occasionally going backwards. For example, in the study, Laura had stopped using SL since the office hour did not work well. As shown in Figure 2, the adoption of SL is more like a zigzag curve than an S curve (Roger, 1995). In the first stage, 4 instructors started using SL, than one teacher stopped using it, and then more instructors joined the group. For long term, although we can be optimistic about the general trend of rising in adoption, the rising path is not always that smooth.

CONCLUSION

In summary, the implementation of SL involves a number of decisions that are difficult to make. There are certain difficulties associated with SL used in teaching such as technical problems, social factors of SL, and pedagogical issues. The analy-sis of the teachers' interviews and observations helped raise additional questions with respect to the characteristics of SL currently favorably discussed in the literature, such as interactivity, accessibility, self-constructed environment by SL residents, active engagement as well as intrinsic motivation of learners. However, to teach with SL remains a hard decision for instructors to make, since they need to take into account various variables such as the social complexity, diffusion of innovation models, technical difficulties of SL and pedagogical effectiveness when SL is used in their specific course. Finally, how MUVEs as an innovation diffused on a university campus is an interesting phenomenon to explore further.

REFERENCES

Braman, J., Vincenti, G., Arboleda, A., & Jinman, A. (2009). Learning computer science fundamentals through virtual environments. *Proceedings of the 3rd International Conference on Online Communities and Social Computing: Held as Part of HCI International 2009*, (pp. 423-431).

Bronack, S., Riedl, R., & Tashner, J. (2006). Learning in the zone: A social constructivist framework for distance education in a 3D virtual world. *Interactive Learning Environments, 14*(3), 219–232. doi:10.1080/10494820600909157

Childress, M., & Braswell, R. (2006). Using Massively Multiplayer Online Role-Playing Games for online learning. *Distance Education, 27*(2), 187–196. doi:10.1080/01587910600789522

Clarke, J., & Dede, C. (2005). *Making learning meaningful: An exploratory study of using multi-user environments (MUVEs) in middle school science*. American Educational Research Association Conference.

Clarke, R. (1999). *A primer in diffusion of innovations theory*. Australian National University. Retrieved from http://www.anu.edu.au/people/Roger.Clarke/SOS/InnDiff.html

Cobb, D., & Fraser, D. (2005). Multimedia learning in virtual reality. In Mayer, R. (Ed.), *The Cambridge handbook of multimedia learning* (pp. 525–548). Cambridge, UK: Cambridge University Press.

de Freitas, S. (2008). *Serious virtual worlds: A scoping study*. Bristol, UK: Joint Information Systems Committee.

de Freitas, S. (2010). Editorial: Crossing boundaries: Learning and teaching in virtual worlds. *British Journal of Educational Technology, 41*(1), 3–9. doi:10.1111/j.1467-8535.2009.01045.x

Dede, C. Whitehouse, P., & Brown L'Bahy, T. (2003). Designing and studying learning experiences that use multiple interactive media to bridge distance and time. In C. Vrasidas, & G. V. Glass (Eds.), *Distance education and distributed learning*. London, UK: Eurospan.

Demir, K. (2006). Rogers' theory of the diffusion of innovations and online course registration. *Educational Administration: Theory & Practice, 47*, 386–392.

Dickey, M. (2005a). Three-dimensional virtual worlds and distance learning: Two case studies of active worlds as a medium for distance education. *British Journal of Educational Technology, 36*(3), 439–451. doi:10.1111/j.1467-8535.2005.00477.x

Feng, J., & Song, L. (2010). Teaching in Second Life: Students and instructors' perceptions. *Proceedings of the Society for Information Technology & Teacher Education International Conference (SITE)*.

Merriam, S. B. (1992). *Qualitative research in education*. San Francisco, CA: Jossey-Bass Inc.

National Research Council (NRC). (2005). America's lab report: Investigations in high school science. In M. L. H. Susan, R. Singer, & H. A. Schweingruber (Eds.), *Board on science education, center for education, division of behavioral and social sciences and education*. Washington, DC: The National Academies Press. Committee on High School Science Laboratories: Role and Vision.

Nelson, B., & Ketelhut, D. J. (2007). Scientific inquiry in educational multi-user virtual environments. *Educational Psychology Review, 19*(3), 265–283. doi:10.1007/s10648-007-9048-1

Rogers, E. M. (1995). *Diffusion of innovations*. New York, NY: Free Press.

Rogers, E. M. (2003). *Diffusion of innovations*. New York, NY: Free Press.

Rovai, A. P., & Childress, M. D. (2002). Explaining and predicting resistance to computer anxiety reduction among teacher education students. *Journal of Research on Technology in Education, 35*(2), 226–235.

Sadik, A. (2006). Factors influencing teachers' attitudes toward personal use and school use of computers: New evidence from a developing nation. *Evaluation Review, 30*(1), 86–113. doi:10.1177/0193841X05276688

Stake, R. E. (2000). Case studies. In Denzin, N. K., & Lincoln, Y. S. (Eds.), *Handbook of qualitative research* (2nd ed., pp. 435–454). Thousand Oaks, CA: Sage Publications Ltd.

Surry, D. W. (1997). *Presentation at the Annual Conference of the Association for Educational Communications and Technology* (AECT).

Tsitouridou, M., & Vryzas, K. (2003). Early childhood teachers' attitudes towards computer and Information Technology: The case of Greece. *Information Technology in Childhood Education Annual, 1*, 187–207.

Veletsianos, G. (2009). The impact and implications of virtual character expressiveness on learning and agent-learner interactions. *Journal of Computer Assisted Learning, 25*(4), 345–357. doi:10.1111/j.1365-2729.2009.00317.x

Wang, C. X., Song, H., Stone, D. E., & Yan, Q. (2009). Integrating Second Life into an EFL program in China: Research collaborations across the continents. *Tech Trend, 53*(6).

Yildirim, S. (2000). Effects of an educational computing course on pre-service and in-service teachers: A discussion and analysis of attitudes and use. *Journal of Research on Computing in Education, 32*(4), 479–495.

Yuen, H. K., Law, N., & Chan, H. (1999). Improving IT training for serving teachers through evaluation. In Cumming, G., Okamoto, T., & Gomez, L. (Eds.), *Advanced research in computers and communications in education* (*Vol. 2*, pp. 441–448). Amsterdam, The Netherlands: IOS Press.

KEY TERMS AND DEFINITIONS

Complexity: Complexity refers to the degree to which an innovation is perceived as relatively difficult to understand and use (Rogers, 1995).

Diffusion of Innovation: An idea, practice or object that is perceived as new by members of a social system (Rogers,1995).

Educational MUVE Innovators: The first group of people who use MUVE in their teaching and sometimes who also serve to disseminate the innovative ideas about educational MUVE.

Educational MUVE: Multi-user virtual environments in which teaching and learning activities have been conducted.

MUVE Diffusion of Innovation Model: The model how MUVE is diffused in the educational settings, especially in a higher educational institution.

MUVE Technical Difficulties: The difficulties that caused by the uniqueness of 3-D virtual, people who have never experienced the 3-D world might experience certain level of difficulties when they get into the brand new environment.

Relative Advantage: The relative advantage of innovation means that the degree of which the innovation is better than the idea or it supersedes (Rogers, 1995).

Social Complexities: The unique characteristic of MUVE where residents can interact with each other and conduct other social activities, such as joining a professional organization and conducting virtual tours together.

Section 3
MUVEs in the Classroom:
Experiences, Lessons and Applications

Chapter 15
Science through Second Life:
A Case Study of MUVE's in an Urban 9th Grade Classroom

Elizabeth Wellman
Educational Consultant, Los Angeles, USA

Cathy Arreguin
San Diego State University, USA

ABSTRACT

The purpose of this chapter is to provide educators with a case study of the design, development, and implementation of a Multi User Virtual Environment as a core medium in a high school based blended learning system. Science through Second Life focuses on the opportunities and challenges encountered by educators in the creation and realization of a series of virtual learning environments in Teen Second Life on the topic of environmental sustainability. This chapter considers instructional approaches to support scientific literacy and thinking, the optimal use of multiple media for supporting media literacy growth, and the use of the blended environment to motivate students, gain their attention, and foster a longer term interest in science. Specific examples of learning activities, supportive instructional materials and the pedagogical reasoning are woven into a larger narrative detailing a semester long, 9th grade science class. By reporting the design and development process and the subsequent course of implementation of instructional activities, this chapter provides pre- and in-service teachers and instructional designers with a model of instructional design and practical considerations for developing MUVEs in a blended instructional environment.

DOI: 10.4018/978-1-60960-545-2.ch015

INTRODUCTION

Incorporating technology into classroom practice is a significant process for teachers. There is the practical issue of having convenient access to the technology. There is also the need to have some flexibility in the curriculum as well as to meet state and school district mandated standards for content curriculum. Teachers need to be adequately prepared both technically and in strategies for the use of technology to support disciplinary learning. Finally for optimal implementation of technology for learning, many believe that the teachers need to hold constructivist pedagogical beliefs (Ertmer, 2005 after Becker, 2001). It is these last two points – designing MUVEs to support disciplinary learning and designing blended MUVE and classroom environments grounded on social constructivist learning principles - which we will focus on.

This is a case study of the design, development and implementation of a MUVE in a 9th grade urban science classroom. As instructional designers who collaborated on this MUVE we are interested in examining how the availability of a MUVE as an integral aspect of the learning environment impacts the instructional and virtual environment design. As an integral part of our examination of our process, we will look at how the Science through Second Life MUVE supported science learning through the manifestation of social constructivist principles. We will do this through the presentation, discussion and analysis of four learning modules that embody social constructivist instructional approaches. We will describe and analyze how those instructional approaches manifested themselves in the design and deployment of the MUVE, and the student activity, which resulted.

Unlike a research study, the goals here are to capture, describe and illustrate specific learning moments to better understand the shared impact of design, instruction and learning. These moments are exemplified through narrative and vignettes to:

- Portray the essence and feel of learning and teaching in a MUVE.
- Relate these descriptions to the impact of the MUVE on the instructional design process.
- Identify how the MUVE supported disciplinary learning.
- Identify how social constructivist principles were manifested.

BACKGROUND

Instructional Design is the process of systematically developing learning materials through the analysis of learner needs, content structure and available media. (Culatta, 2010). In general, the instructional design for this science based MUVE is based on social constructivist principles and learning theories such as authentic learning. Lemke (1990, in Palincsar, 1998) suggests examples of the social construction of science understanding includes: observing, describing, comparing, classifying, analyzing, discussing, hypothesizing, theorizing, questioning, challenging, arguing, designing experiments, following procedures, judging, evaluating, deciding, concluding, generalizing, reporting and writing in and through the language of science. Palinscar goes on to posit that this involves the use of tools and discourses. Through engagement with these processes students identify themselves with scientific activity.

The Science through Second Life (StSL) curriculum concentrated on sustainability concepts and scientific thinking, applying these to local and global concerns. We saw scientific thinking as students engaged in scientific inquiry to understand interrelationships, using a scientific process and applying scientific understandings to local and global problem solving (Bransford, 2000).

Learning for these students took place in an authentic context. Authentic implies a realistic situation with students actively involved in cognitive, physical and social realms (Grabinger,

1996). A core assumption for authentic learning is that skills and understanding are best acquired actively within realistic contexts.

To optimally support these contexts, we see the use of media and the MUVE as significant and influential. The idea that technology, content knowledge and pedagogy are complexly interrelated (Mishra & Koehler, 2006), supports the use of the MUVE as an environment which can in and of itself influence the pedagogy and the content knowledge addressed. Our use of the MUVE for authentic learning is an example of this. Dede discusses the concept of mediated immersion which refers to students engaging in pervasive experiences within a "digitally enhanced context" (Clarke, Dede & Dieterlee, 2005) with the advantage of being able to participate in experiences in the classroom that otherwise would not be possible. Nearly all of our instructional design immersed students in experiential learning that wasn't possible in a traditional classroom.

Approaches

There are four different pedagogical approaches that were used in this curriculum.

1. Establishing identity in the learning environment, in this case a MUVE.
2. Establishing authentic learning experiences for the students.
3. Asking students to model being a scientist and to do this while interacting with scientific models.
4. Utilizing experts from outside the classroom environment to model scientific activity for the apprentice scientist.

The Program

Russell hurried into his science class, grabbed a laptop from the cart and slid into his seat, eager to begin before the bell rang. As his teacher prepared to take roll, he logged into the class space in Teen

Second Life; his avatar appearing on the roof of the house he and his partner had been carefully detailing the day before.

Across the classroom, his partner, Andre, was doing the same. Andre had quickly found out that missing a day of this science unit was difficult to make up. Every day counted. Even being late meant falling behind. As a result, the teacher had noticed that the class as a whole was noticeably less tardy than the semester before. In fact, one student, while on suspension, had insisted on logging into their virtual world environment each day from home in order to keep up with his assignments.

Next to Andre, Monica was peering at her laptop screen, intently exploring the area next to the student houses. Over the weekend, the environment had changed. The class had recently finished analyzing environmental problems in a European city. Now, it seemed, they would be looking at the impacts of fossil fuels in Alaska and other natural environments.

The bell rang. 8:30am. Another day in Science through Second Life.

(The account above synthesizes observed experiences of several actual students. All names have been changed.)

Science through Second Life (StSL) was a series of learning modules, which utilized a classroom/MUVE blended environment for student interaction. It was commissioned in the winter of 2008 by Global Kids, Inc., an independent non-profit organization located in New York City, educating and inspiring urban youth to become successful students, global citizens and community leaders by engaging them in academically rigorous, socially dynamic, content-rich learning experiences (Global Kids, Inc., 2010). Funded by a Motorola Innovation Generation grant designed to inspire students towards science related careers,

StSL was implemented at the High School for Global Citizenship (HSGC), a Global Kids, Inc. partner (Motorola, 2010). Located in Brooklyn, New York, the HSGC is an innovative, small urban high school whose mission is to create a community of active learners who are engaged participants in the democratic process, who understand the connections between local actions and global events and who have a heightened awareness of the current issues facing the global community (HSGC, 2010).

As an urban school, HGSC provided the Science through Second Life project an opportunity to better understand how urban students – students with high poverty, low achievement, and highdropout rates - would respond in terms of motivation and engagement in science as well as achievement (Russo, 2004). A third party evaluator focused efforts on examining these parameters as discussed in the chapter section Project Evaluation/Student Outcomes.

The four sustainability science modules - Housing, Solid Waste, Fossil Fuels, Green Energy - created for this blended classroom/MUVE learning, met both New York Learning (content) Standards (2008) and the HSGC goals of creating active learners and global citizens. The 19 students (10 female, 9 male) came from the surrounding urban African-American cultural community and greatly varied in their literacy, science and computer familiarity levels (Turkay, 2008).

Initial Technological Conditions and Considerations

Since 2006, Global Kids, Inc has had a pioneering presence on the Second Life Teen Grid. Used primarily for online leadership development, their multi-region space was already well used by teens in current Global Kids programs. In January 2008, Global Kids added an additional region (an island) as the virtual location for the StSL project. To promote possible future scalability, all MUVE activities were designed to take place on one-eighth of the island. Half of this space was the students' virtual homes, their base of operations. The other half rotated between three other learning modules for students to investigate and explore. As the learning proceeded, this space limitation required an instructional designer to have the virtual world skills to both take up and build out the specific learning scenarios designed for each module in very short periods of time to accommodate the instructional schedule.

Beginning in January 2008, students spent significant time over six weeks in Second Life participating in skills training. The remaining ten weeks of the spring semester were devoted to the sustainability science modules. Each module lasted between 2-3 weeks and was taught using a blended format of "live" classroom activities, online web-based research, and the exploratory Teen Second Life MUVE. Classroom activities centered on science related discussions, synthesizing concepts and written reflections. Students recorded and analyzed data, maintained their scientific journals which contained observations, hypotheses, analyses and conclusions, and posted responses to inquiry questions on an online public blog. In contrast the MUVE provided authentic and discovery learning, a space for collaboration and an environment to both model science processes and provide digitally produced three-dimensional science models.

Because the MUVE was both persistent and open to the rest of the Teen Grid, learners were able to log on outside of class time. In addition, they were able to visit other parts of the Teen Grid on their own. Several class members did so, as evidenced by additional inventory items and specialized knowledge not offered in class. Learners, however, varied greatly in their after school access to computers. As such, all mandated computer related work (both Second Life and other online sources) was completed during class time.

Figure 1. The Scientific Method in StSL

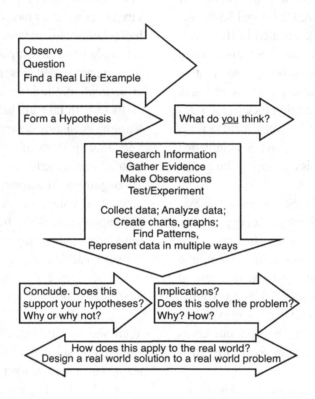

Four Core Instructional Design Questions

As we designed this environment, we found that four questions repeatedly arose. These questions were at the core of the learning.

1. How do we want the students to learn?

To ground the overall instruction we established a few global principals for the students' learning process. Most importantly, we wanted them to 'be' scientists; to model scientific behavior. Students were engaged in observation, investigations, explorations, hypothesizing, gathering data, structuring and analyzing data, drawing, concluding, presenting and defending their conclusions and making suggestions for future action. Figure 1 illustrates the process that the students were explicitly asked to engage in. A more colorful

and motivating version of this figure was placed on a billboard in a prominent central area of the MUVE for student reference. To ensure that they would never be without it, they also received paper copies for their scientific journals. Based on this, our concern as the instructional designers was to conceptualize the design of the MUVE as a problem in designing an environment that is a scientific model, scientifically valid and supports activities that utilize the scientific method at an appropriate level for these students. The students engaged in learning by modeling the scientific method while engaged with the scientific model.

2. What do we want the students to learn?

Foremost and most practically, we wanted the students to learn the science – in this case, scientific sustainability concepts mandated by the school, district and state. We also wanted them to learn how to learn using the scientific method. Second, we wanted them to develop a socio-cultural understanding of sustainability, both on the local scale, in their homes and neighborhood, and on a global scale. This means that students would be investigating the human effects of non-sustainable practices and the difference when sustainable practices are employed. Comparing and contrasting, the development of empathy for others waskey for students to develop this socio-cultural understanding. The instructional design problem was to provide authentic opportunities to explore sustainability issues on both the local and the global levels.

3.   How do these students learn?

Our best indicators of how these students learned were based on their academic work in the classroom during the first semester of the year. This project was implemented in the second semester. In the first semester the students were in a traditionally structured classroom with didactic learning methods using predominantly text-based materials. In contrast, the StSL instructional design focused on providing students with an array of information and media options for the students resulting in expanded learning opportunities and pathways.

4.   Which blended learning environment options will optimize learning?

This question focused on the media available and the way the media available were used, both independently and as a network or system of information. The instructional designers' concern was how best to utilize the strengths of the different media, project how the students might use this system of information and scaffold their use of it especially in regards to supporting student use of the scientific method. In a nutshell, it was through an understanding of the science, understanding of the audience and understanding of the possibili-

ties in the MUVE/blended environment that the instructional designer could affect an optimal realization of an effective learning environment.

The four instructional modules that were developed -- Green Housing, Solid Waste, Fossil Fuels and Alternative Energy -- were chosen based on the HSGC's curriculum plan and NY State Standards. Each module manifested a different approach to the problem of how to use a classroom/MUVE environment to teach sustainability.

1.   In the first module, Green Housing, the emphasis was on students establishing identity and agency in the MUVE.
2.   In the second module, Solid Waste, the emphasis was on establishing an authentic global problem modeled in the MUVE and asking students to seek solutions to it using the scientific method.
3.   In the third module, Fossil Fuels, the emphasis was on establishing a MUVE, a three-dimensional digital environment where students learned by exploration and using the scientific method.
4.   In the fourth module, Alternative Energy, students learned through interactions with real scientists, extending the MUVE environment beyond the classroom. Specifically, these interactions were with 3D models of sustainable technologies and with a visiting scientist.

It is important to note that none of the modules were exclusively the form of instruction delineated above. Rather, all modules contained many of these elements. The distinction being made here is the pedagogical emphasis in the instruction based upon the characteristics of particular instructional units.

Using Teen Second Life (TSL) as the MUVE environment, the Green Housing module was the first module built and used. It anchored – visually and instructionally - the subsequent activities.

Figure 2. Student Homes

Green Housing Module: A Closer Look

Setting student identity and agency in the MUVE was a critical initial step. For students to have ownership of the content they needed to also establish themselves as scientists and science thinkers in the MUVE (Clarke & Dede, 2005). In this case, we were interested in the students establishing an aspect of their real-life personas in-world as well as establishing their role in-world as that of a scientist.

Students started the first module "Green Housing', not in the MUVE, but in their own homes, gathering data on their own carbon footprint. The students brought the data to the classroom and used one of many carbon footprint calculators, an analytic tool on the Internet. They calculated their personal carbon footprint in four areas - at home, transportation, food, and waste and recycling. This data analysis brought up questions for them - Why is my footprint so high? What can I do to lower it? In this first activity students used the scientific method, setting a pattern of usage for the rest of the unit.

Students had practiced their skills in TSL prior to the introduction of the unit, so were comfortable entering the MUVE for the first time. Students found a built environment in place, including a generic house for each team consisting of two students. It was their responsibility to customize these virtual houses, and to make them their virtual homes. Students modified, some extensively, their virtual houses using their own real life homes as models and creating new ones (See Figure 2).

Logging in early to the MUVE, the instructional designers were astonished, and pleased, to see that, overnight, the house belonging to Russell and Andre had been transformed. Instead of one floor, there were two, complete with a sun deck on the roof. Students had changed the building materials of both the inside and outside of the building and added furniture. The showcase of their efforts, however, was the addition of a garage and a driveway, primarily to display a motorcycle they had enterprisingly acquired.

Russell and Andre were creating their home in the MUVE. This experiential connection gave them both an identity in the MUVE and a sense of pride in their virtual world work. Russell and Andre were concerned about the details of their roof, both aesthetically and in terms of the way it reflects their real life carbon footprint. With the home, they created their own environment within the MUVE, one that other students talked about and wanted to enter. This was a clear declaration and validation of their identity in the MUVE. When the homes were completed, the range of identity and individuality expressed was compelling (see Figure 2). Throughout the 10-week unit, Russell and Andre were able to use their virtual home as a base and make changes to it both as directed by the curriculum and as they desired. These homes, located in a cluster on the MUVE created physical community and provided an anchor point in the instruction for the student that directly related to the science they were exploring, both in the virtual space and in real life. With an established identity in the MUVE, students initiated relationships with other members of the community - the virtual instructional support person, the instructional designers and with each other. These relationships both mirrored and expanded their real life relationships.

These homes were also the starting point for their scientific investigations. The students reflected the natural resource and energy data, and carbon footprint for their real homes as signs throughout their homes in the MUVE. These signs, provided templates for different natural resource and energy data modified by the students, reflected and displayed the data they gathered from their real life homes and analyzed in the classroom. When touched in-world, these signs gave information about the students' carbon footprint --including information about water and power use, garbage and recycling, and food products.

Solid Waste (Naples) Module: A Closer Look

Authentic learning provides the student with meaningful learning, learning both within a realistic context and by asking the student to engage in realistic processes. In the MUVE, maintaining a high level of credibility and accuracy in the activities and resources was crucial to providing an authentic learning experience to the students. Each of the four modules modeled an authentic sustainability situation. The Solid Waste unit's reliance on this approach to explore global understandings was central. Authenticity was critical to facilitate valid investigation of global understandings.

In the second module 'Solid Waste', students engaged in activities focused on identifying, analyzing and providing solutions to the trash problem that the people of Naples, Italy are currently experiencing. Students were asked to use scientific methods to generate a global understanding of this sustainability issue and apply this understanding to develop a scientifically valid, culturally aware solution.

Unlike the 'House' module, the 'Solid Waste' module began with the students as avatars entering a model of Naples in the MUVE. This model incorporated buildings, roads and a plaza built to elicit the look and feel of the real Naples. Students were free to explore and learn about this virtual city, its people, its history and its culture using MUVE tools such as flying, zooming, taking photos and 'speaking' with the inhabitants. Gathering data started with observation of the environment. Fires burned and trash was piled up, there were bad smells (cued in the chat box), cockroaches and rats. Students needed to ask questions about what they observed and answer them through an extended information gathering process.

Students learned about the viewpoints of citizens by interviewing chatbots, scripted objects tied to online artificial intelligence databases programmed to reflect the actual attitudes and perceptions of various representative citizens of Naples who had differing and sometimes contradictory perceptions of the problem. Content for the chatbots consisted of authentic researched opinions, quotes and descriptions drawn directly from newspapers, videos and other accounts of the garbage problem in Naples.

Russell and Andre's avatars ran into Naples and promptly stopped in front of a young man waving a sign. They briefly debated who he might be before they clicked on the chatbot for information. Satisfied that he was a street protestor, angry about the garbage, they flew up for a birds-eye view of the city. "Over there!" Andre moved towards the

Figure 3. Scientific Survey of a Virtual Naples Garbage Dump

back of a building. "All right! A fire!" Russell exclaimed as he dove towards the crackling flames.

Unlike the real Naples, clicking on posters and paintings in the rooms of the city led students to specified pages on the internet, extending their information gathering beyond the MUVE, yet, significantly, accessing it through the MUVE, within the context of the problem solving environment. In another more fanciful feature, the center fountain spoke to the students as they passed by, giving them information on what the problem was they were to investigate. Including these fanciful or fantasy elements is well accepted as a motivational method (Malone, 1981).

Like the real Naples, and any town or city, a scientific survey could be conducted of the garbage dump (Figure 3). In virtual Naples, a garbage dump lay around a corner, cued by its large size and the vermin periodically running around it. Here groups of students could conduct a scientific survey and place a virtual pole, marking a data line to record the garbage that was actually there. Using the camera tool, students could get a close enough view of the garbage to record a chart of the data of the types of garbage in their scientific journals. To enhance the authenticity of the activity the student avatars were required to don safety and protective clothing and equipment, providing active visual reinforcement that they were scientists. The opportunity to virtually travel abroad and participate in research gave students a unique view of a compelling and timely real life problem and gave them a basis to draw conclusions and make culturally sensitive, scientifically based recommendations.

Fossil Fuels Module: A Closer Look

Utilizing the MUVE environment to create a model of the science and to provide an environment for students to engage in scientific thinking captured one of the strengths of the blended environment - the ability for instructional designers to create three-dimensional models of scientific realities and provide an active space for students to model the scientific process.

In the third module, students investigated the effects of Fossil Fuels by using the scientific method. Two paths that fossil fuels take from ore to home were created in the MUVE - one from a coalmine to a refinery to a power plant to the houses and second from an oilrig in the Arctic Ocean through the pipeline to the refinery to the power plant to the houses. The homes that the students created were linked visually and scientifically into the paths of the fossil fuel. Modeling the fossil fuel process from extraction to the power in their own virtual homes, reflected by the data that they had posted from their real homes, this three-dimensional interactive immersive environment learning experience was created both by the

Figure 4. Overview of Tableau for the Fossil Fuels Module

instructional designers and by the students for the students' learning. The authenticity was grounded in the students' homes in real life being modeled in the MUVE. Critical to the successful instructional implementation of an environment such as this, were scientifically valid representations specifically tailored to the students. In addition, a plethora of thoughtfully chosen and strategically located resources were placed in the MUVE for students to discover and explore.

When entering the MUVE, students were free to explore. We found that providing a subtle guide in the form of a pathway encouraged students to scaffold though information. Using a revised version of Annie Leonard's 'The Story of Stuff' (Leonard, 2008) as the structuring content for the science, students started by investigating a virtual coal mine. In the mine, helmets had to be donned by the avatars, several canaries indicated levels of dangerous gases at different points in the mine, touching signs led to web-based resources, and a chatbot miner helped students understand the human side of working in the mines.

Monica and Tamara approached the entrance to the mine and put on their mining helmets, ready to scientifically investigate the effects of coal mining. Passing by a singing caged canary, Monica speculated that the consequences of coal mining were mainly "digging up the ground". As

they entered the cave, however, Tamara remembered something about "black lung disease."

Deep in the mine, they split up, each intent on exploring the data surrounding them. Monica clicked on a map, bringing up a web page featuring data on American coalmines, and began to take notes. Tamara clicked on a nearby chatbot miner, listening carefully to stories of digging the rock and breathing coal dust.

As they continued further in the mine, they noticed another caged canary - silent and lying still at the bottom of its cage.

Surfacing from an immersive experience, our students frequently found themselves with more questions than when they started. This experience models one of the cornerstones of practicing science - observing and formulating questions. We believed that one of the strengths of the MUVE was our ability to front-load an environment ripe for student question formation and then supportively designed for students to seek out and answer their questions.

Outside the mine, learners took water samples to understand how mining affects the health of streams and rivers. At the Arctic oilrig, students looked at the effects of oil extraction; chatting with an oil spill researcher, and learned how various arctic animals are impacted by oil spills, later

Figure 5. Water Treatment Plant

recording their observations for both human and environmental impacts. The oil refinery allowed students to explore the process of energy production - beginning to form a basis from which to compare sustainable forms of energy production in a future unit.

The class also looked at greenhouse gases, using 3D capabilities to teleport up into the atmosphere and sample and compare different levels of several greenhouse gases. In this activity, the technology provided the instructional designers with another opportunity to model and explore scientific information in ways that would be impossible without the MUVE. The additional motivation and engagement that the students experienced in being able to teleport to scientific stations, as well as the opportunity to have them gather and record historical data at different locations on the earth, created an active and immersed activity, inherently different from researching data on the internet.

Alternative Energy

The MUVE also provides opportunities to expand the classroom by its inherent ability to allow people who are remote to the classroom to log in and, as an avatar, interact with the students. There are motivational as well as learning advantages.

Zev Paiss, a scientist from Boulder, CO was interested in interacting with the students on issues of sustainability. In particular, he had built a virtual model of a sustainable water treatment plant appropriate to use for student tours and as a contextual basis for a discussion of broader sustainability issues. In the MUVE it was possible to copy a large object like the water treatment plant and rebuild it temporarily in a new location, in this case, for a day. These capabilities gave students the opportunity to work one on one with a scientist, reinforcing that they are participating in a global community.

Arriving in world one day towards the end of the unit, Monica and Tamara found a huge obstruction in the middle of the island. It hadn't been there before – however with confidence they moved their avatars into it to explore. Tamara chatted to other student avatars as they walked and flew in, creating a sizable gathering. An avatar named Zev, balding with white hair, introduced himself and explained that they were going to go on a tour of this water treatment plant. Monica started to use her camera controls to see the detail. She asked Zev questions – it was evident that he knew what he was talking about.

Zev's visit was highly motivational for the students and was cited by them as the most interesting experience of the project. A scientist from out of state bringing science to them, interacting with them, in their environment was a new learning experience, and was inconceivable in this classroom except in a MUVE.

The Alternative Energy unit was shorter than the others. The students spent the rest of their time scientifically investigating interactive 3D models of windmills, solar panels, sustainable houses and geothermal energy. By correlating the information in their visual environment to linked information beyond the MUVE they began to correlate it to their own lives. This culminated in the identification of a specific problem in sustainable energy for their final projects.

Other Design Considerations: Daily Planning

A structured yet flexible manner of implementation was necessary. With several people working collaboratively and with the time inherent in building the environment, it was critical to structure the development of the instruction, the MUVE and the learning. For the teacher unfamiliar with the MUVE, a detailed, structured framework was essential to conduct classroom activities. To accomplish this, the instructional designers wrote a daily lesson plan for the team with details and specifics on the continuity of the activities. It contained learning goals, standards, media and how to use it, learning activities, inquiry questions, homework, assessment and "Techtips" informing the teacher of specific technical aspects in using the MUVE. Taken together, the daily plans provided a coherent, in-depth curriculum for the 10-week unit. The table below uses Day 2 of the second unit (Solid Waste) as an illustration. Previous to this lesson, students had entered a model of present day Naples on TSL, which, as reflected in the simulation, has a substantial and alarming trash problem. During the course of this unit, students

eventually explored the city, talked with the citizens, conducted a scientific survey and gathered observations and information about Naples and its trash problem. Learners hypothesized, gathered and analyzed data, drew conclusions, proposed remediation and projected the results as a continuation of their activities on Day 1.

- Section 1 identifies the media that will be used on this day, the materials the students need to complete their objectives for the day, and the material the teacher needs to prepare for the environment -- all designed for effective intermediation supporting student thinking as a scientist, developing and implementing the scientific method.
- Section 2 addresses the activities that lead to student learning.
- Section 3 delineates closure activities and assessment measures for the day.
- Section 4 communicates between the instructional designers and the teacher.

Table Notes:

- URL's are not complete. Some are proprietary; others are no longer active links.
- Standards: In the U.S., Standards for most courses are mandated at the state level and explicitly described in most curricula. We used New York City standards as this was implemented in Brooklyn, a borough of New York City. Implementation policies mandated delineating NYC standards for *each* of the 50 individual days of instruction.
- Assessment took many forms throughout the 50 days. While most assessments were primarily written, others were verbal or image-based. These multiple modalities: blogs, Teen Second Life, paper, online texting, presentation and chat, all contributed to assist the teacher in forming a well-

Table 1. Model of a Daily Plan

Day 2	Science Through Second Life – Unit 2 – Solid Waste			
Section 1: Media & Materials				
Media	Internet: text, images	Blogs	TSL: 3D representations	Print
Materials	Student Resource Folder: Handouts Notes Observations Journal		Links for Science Notebooks http://..._SolidWaste_mission.doc http://...SolidWaste_observations.doc	
MUVE (Teen Second Life) (see Figure 3)	Chatbot Scripts; Mayor, Activist, Mother, Shopkeeper, Scientist Naples Environment: Buildings, trash, fires, random garbage, pier, fountain, citizens, tourism office, cafe, officials, landfill, sticks/safety gear		Links for Hanging Pictures in Mayor's office: http://www.portanapoli... http://volcano. ... http://www.naples... http://en.wikipedia.org/wiki/Naples...	
Section 2:Standards New York City Department of Education				
STANDARD E:	"Students should be able to identify new problems or needs. "			
STANDARD F: NATURAL RESOURCES	"Human populations use resources in the environment in order to maintain and improve their existence. Natural resources have been and will continue to be used to maintain human populations. "			
STANDARD F: NATURAL AND HUMAN-INDUCED HAZARDS	"The earth does not have infinite resources; increasing human consumption places severe stress on the natural processes that renew some resources, and it depletes those resources that cannot be renewed. Human activities can enhance potential for hazards. Acquisition of resources, urban growth, and waste disposal can accelerate rates of natural change. "			
Section 3: Activities				
Pre-Class	All students should: Have an electronic or paper copy of the materials. Be able to access the internet. Have their science notebook.			
Aim	Inquiry Question: Daily Prompt: Respond in science journals. Discuss: How does the way information is illustrated on maps affect how you think about that information?			
Goals/Objective	The students will:Gather information, Critically observe. Develop skills for analyzing information.			
Motivation, Warm-Up	Daily Thought Question (Blog): As a scientist how would you investigate ecological problems?			
Main Activity	Objective		Activity	
	2.2.1 (Scientific Observation) Using the snapshot option, report back on three important facts that they have learned on their initial scouting trip.		Break up into your groups from yesterday. Go into TSL and "buy" Unit 2 Student Resources box. Each group has 10 minutes to walk around TSL Naples and make observations in their scientific notebooks using the format provided in the student packet. They are not expected to observe everything in this time. At the conclusion students will send a virtual postcard to "Headquarters" (the teacher) with a summary of what they have found.	
	2.2.2 (questions) In groups in their science notebooks.		Students review observations and list questions that arise as a result of these observations.	
Section 4: Wrap Up				
Closure Activity	Blog Prompt: Based upon your observations, what do you think is Naples problem? What questions did you raise?			

continued on the following page

Table 1. continued

Assessments (Written)	Each student will:
	  Record observational evidence in their notebook.
	  Report back on evidence with a TSL postcard.
	  Record in their notebooks questions they had while engaged in observations and conversations w/ their group.
	  Analyze in their blog observations and questions they have.	

Homework	Science Notebook: Do you know of any place that has a problem like Naples? Describe it. Why do they have it?	
TechNotes	This unit uses observation skills in a MUVE. Students discover that many items are "clickable". Some students will find clicking on objects will lead them to different URLs, or give themobjects or notecards fortheirinvestigations. Students should click on the info cube at the entrance to Naples.	Chatbots are scripted 2D objects that respond to specific questions typed in chat. In this unit, chatbots demonstrate the varying opinions of different citizens in Naples. Just as when "real" people are interviewed, chatbots may vary their answers each time they are asked a question. All answers are accurate and taken from actual accounts of the Naples problem. As different groups compare data later, they may gain additional insights from differences.

Figure 6. A Student Project using Comic Life in the MUVE

rounded assessment of each individual student.

Student Evaluation

Students were regularly assessed in multiple ways. The assessments were designed to take advantage of the strengths of either the classroom, online or in-world environments. Assessments included a science journal – answering questions, thinking and speculating about science, worksheets which guided some of the learning process, labs which used in world environments, the use of comic strip software to express concepts (Figure 6), expressing sustainability adjustments to their in world homes iteratively as they progressed, a cumula-

tive in world poster presentation and blogging on science inquiry questions which reflected global and local concerns. These blogs were posted to the Global Kids website.

These assessment methods provided the students with a variety of media to express their understandings. They also provided students with a variety of environments to demonstrate their understandings. Interestingly, many of these environments –in particular the MUVE blogging, - provided an opportunity for people beyond the teacher-student dyad to view and comment on their work. The evaluative activities that were between the teacher and the student were exclusively conducted in the classroom.

Figure 7. Final in-world Projects Presentation

During the 10-week project students were asked to complete two large in world projects – their homes and the final poster presentation in the center area of the world (see Figure 7). Both of these involved a synthesis of science knowledge and MUVE skills. This final poster presentation was also presented verbally in the classroom, using the MUVE as a presentation tool. This multiplicity of evaluations in multiple environments gave students a range of opportunities to express their understandings.

Solutions and Recommendations

As the last student left her classroom, Tracy sat down in front of her computer and logged into Skype to discuss recent observations and possible curricular modifications with the rest of the design and development team. These meetings were crucial. Although the entire team routinely observed the students from within the virtual world environment, in reality, they were distributed across three different states and two countries. Only Tracy had direct classroom insight.

The development cycle for this project was tight. As one module was being taught, others were still in development.Although appropriate learning theory and transferable features of exemplary

works had been carefully considered for each activity and environment, the actual implementation of the curriculum always indicated needed changes.

Tracy listened as the in-world teaching assistant, Kate, a Scottish educator, suggested the addition of a created example of an upcoming assignment for students to reference. Students were combining their in-world building skills with a comic strip creator. While not strictly science related, these skills would later be needed to complete the final science project. As Kate offered to mock up a demo, Beth and Cathy, virtual world educators and instructional designers, voiced their own concerns. Beth asked for feedback as to how the literacy level was working for these specific students. Cathy had observed students working in the current science environment and noticed students missing certain in-world cues. She suggested different virtual environment strategies that might help students be more successful in discovering important contextual science information.

Despite the needed modifications, all agreed that students were engaged and that activities were taking longer than anticipated. For both students and the team, this curriculum was becoming, as someone had said, ''hard fun''.

What Worked and Why? The Benefits of using a MUVE

In reflecting on this project, we are acutely aware of aspects we feel were quite successful, as well as those needing further revision and redesign.

Student Homes

We were aware of the role of the avatar - in particular, *customizable* avatars - as a powerful tool for learner engagement. However, we underestimated the motivational force of a customizable, personal, persistent *space*. Giving students a "Homebase" from which to express both personal scientific data and their own individual and team personalities motivated learners to quickly "own" their learning environment and in-world deliverables. We observed this persistent learning context being accessed and modified outside of classroom hours far beyond course requirements.

Students who were new to virtual world environments also felt "at home" in a consistently familiar visual and spatial environment. Modification of student homes was a visual metaphor for new knowledge and higher level thinking students were experiencing. Knowledge and ideas expressed in neighboring homes could be compared and contrasted easily.

A Blended Approach

The novelty effect of a virtual world environment cannot replace the intentional design of platform appropriate activities. As designers, we strategically matched the activity or task with the most appropriate learning environment. If a learning activity was "NPIRL" (Not Possible In Real Life), we most likely chose the virtual world environment. In our case, we choose activities that were too expensive, impractical, dangerous or physically impossible to do in a physical classroom.

Other activities (online research or blog post reflections) were best done outside of an immersive environment. In these cases, the classroom teacher could verbally facilitate the higher level thinking skills needed. Websites could be more authentically accessed, leading to a greater likelihood of a broader transfer of online research skills.

By capitalizing on the affordances (strengths) of each environment - immersive, online and classroom - we were best able to engage the learner in instruction most likely to maximize learning.

Rotational Multi-Day Activities

As with many schools, computer access and Internet connectivity was limited. In addition, student absences could quickly hamper team projects. Designing multi-station, multi-class session activities allowed for fewer students "in-world" at one time - maximizing both computer and bandwidth limitations. While some team members researched online or reflected in journals, others could gather in-world and experience in-world data. For example, the Fossil Fuels module contained stations about stream pollution, coal mining and oil extraction and processing. Over the course of several days, students had room to fully explore each mini-environment without feeling crowded or waiting their turn. This set-up also allowed for learner choice.

What Didn't Work? Considerations for Future Projects

Pushed vs. Pulled information

In a rich, immersive environment, we found students missing visual and auditory cues and vital information that was chatted, or "pushed" out to them. For example, in the Solid Waste module, students entered via a town square. As they explored the square, a fountain would whisper facts about water quality when students walked nearby. Because students were overwhelmed with new visual and auditory information, they tended to miss the chat - which quickly faded away. Learners didn't even know they had missed vital information and lacked the cue to "back up and review". A more successful design strategy was to create interactive objects, such as a poster, that responded to student mouse clicks, allowing students to "pull" information out of the environment.

Time Frame

Our observation is that, in general, active virtual world learning takes more time than traditional classroom based activities. For this project, planned two-week modules actually took two and a half to three weeks to complete. While technical difficulties may have played a small role, a more important factor was the nature of exploratory learning the students were experiencing. In Naples, for example, students actually simulated a garbage dump string survey, rather than merely looking at a data table.

Single Learner Experiences Instead Of Multi-Learner Realities

In designing learning environments and activities, the designer was often pre-testing as an individual user. However, in reality, these environments were experienced more often with *groups* of students. Occasionally, scripted objects (objects that responded to avatar interactions) did not function correctly and were overwhelmed when multiple students attempted to access them at one time. For example, chatbot objects representing Naples town citizens were "mobbed" by multiple students and could not respond with programmed responses. This led to student frustration, confusion and, in some cases, a belief that the chatbot "did not like me"!

Project Evaluation/Student Outcomes

The purpose of the evaluation was to look for positive changes in students' attitudes, confidence engaging in science and increased media literacy.

As specified by the granting agency, the emphasis of the primary evaluation instruments was to measure levels of student engagement in science and motivation to continue to pursue science related work. Concurrently, changes in content knowledge were observed.

That said, several interesting outcomes were noted:

1. Students' attitudes towards science-related careers changed positively with the StSL curriculum.
2. Students' self-efficacy and self-confidence in their abilities to do science-related work increased.
3. Compared to the traditional science curriculum, the number of students reporting being overwhelmed by science class fell by 50%
4. Low achieving students' grades improved significantly compared to the previous semester.
5. Students' collective intelligence skills improved throughout the semester. More students reported that they felt more comfortable working with others to get something done using digital media in the post survey (Turkay, 2008).

These results were similar to a pilot study by Ketelhut (2006). She believes, and we concur, that new measures of self-efficacy in science are needed in response to the new learning environments.

The third party project evaluation for the granting agency was not designed to focus on measuring changes in content knowledge. The emphasis on student engagement and motivation in science was specified by the granting agency and appropriate for the emphasis Global Kids places on its projects. A primary goal of the grant was to support student engagement in science and motivation to continue to pursue science related work.

CONCLUSION/FUTURE DIRECTIONS

We were fortunate to have the opportunity to work on a project that specifically focused on the development of a virtual environment for a specific classroom for a specific curriculum. It brought up for us a number of questions about the development and use of a MUVE in high school classrooms.

A primary concern is the issue of scalability. With four educators developing this over several months, it is difficult to imagine an on-going situation in a school that could support this effort. Several alternatives are possible. Environments can be developed for use by several classes or schools concurrently. In some MUVE platforms, pre-developed instructional environments can be packaged and distributed for immediate classroom use. In classrooms that do not have one-to-one computing capabilities, a MUVE could be used as a presentation tool oras part of small group work. Another possibility we would encourage is a paradigm in which students both create the environment and engage in it for learning. Students creating the environment as an integral part of their learning isa powerful model.

An area we would like to see explored more formally in research studies is longitudinal student outcomes across domains. Are there measureable short and long term gains in the areas of science, global issues, sustainability and the scientific process? How do these attitudes and understandings affect decisions that these students make about the direction of their lives both now and as they become adults? Measuring these is a complex undertaking yet essential to understanding how best to use MUVEs in science education.

The questions of social interaction are also wide open. The possibilities of classroom interaction, texting in the MUVE, responding to blogs online, as well as communicating with voice, video, and student MUVE pictures opens up many pathways for social constructivism that cannot exist in the classroom alone.

From a learning perspective, MUVE projects like Science through Second Life hold promise for supporting the kinds of learning activities that promote media literacy skills, science literacy, inquiry and critical thinking.

Tamara logged into the class blog site for one last post. Her teacher had asked them for a final reflection describing their virtual world experiences.

"...One thing I learned about science in Second Life is that science is really not that hard. I always thought, "I can't do this," but now I have learned so much. I learned about sustainability and how I can help to make our earth better.

I never knew I was this smart ..."

- Student blog post. Name changed for privacy. (Global Kids Digital Media Initiative, 2008).

REFERENCES

Becker, H. J., & Ravitz, J. L. (2001). Computer use by teachers: Are Cuban's predictions correct? *Proceedings of the 2001 Annual Meeting of the American Educational Research Association.*

Bransford, J., Brown, L., & Cocking, R. C. (2000). *How people learn: Brain, mind, experience, and school.* Washington, DC: National Academy Press.

Clarke, J., & Dede, C. (2005). Making learning meaningful: An exploratory study of using multi-user environments (MUVEs) in middle school science. *Proceedings of the American Educational Research Association Conference.*

Clarke, J., Dede, C., & Dieterle, E. (2008). Emerging technologies for collaborative, mediated, immersive learning. In Voogt, J., & Knezek, G. (Eds.), *The international handbook of technology in primary and secondary education* (pp. 901–910). New York, NY: Springer-Verlag. doi:10.1007/978-0-387-73315-9_55

Culatta, R. (2010*). Instructional Design.*Retrieved from http://www.instructionaldesign.org

Ertmer, P. (2005). Teacher pedagogical beliefs: The final frontier in our quest for technology integration? *Educational Technology Research and Development*, *53*(4), 25–39. doi:10.1007/BF02504683

Global Kids. (2010). *Our mission.* Retrieved from http://globalkids.org/

Global Kids Digital Media Initiative. (2008). *Teen's comment on their SiSL experience.* Retrieved from http://olpgglobalkids.org/science_in_second_life/

Grabinger, R. (1996). Rich environments for active learning. In Jonassen, D. H. (Ed.), *Handbook of research for educational communications and technology* (pp. 665–692). New York, NY: Macmillan.

HSGC. (2010). *Mission statement.* Retrieved from http://hsgc.org/mission_statement.jsp?rn=9256881

Ketelhut, D. J. *(2006).* Assessing scientific and technological self-efficacy: A measurement pilot. Proceedings of the American Educational Research Association.

Lemke, J. (1990). *Talking science: Language, learning, and values.* Norwood, NJ: Ablex.

Leonard, A. (2008). *The story of stuff.* Retrieved from http://www.storyofstuff.com/

Malone, T. W. (1981). Toward a theory of intrinsically motivating instruction. *Cognitive Science*, *5*(4), 333–369. doi:10.1207/s15516709cog0504_2

Mishra, P., & Koehler, M. J. (2006). Technological pedagogical content knowledge: A framework for integrating technology in teacher knowledge. *Teachers College Record*, *108*(6), 1017–1054. doi:10.1111/j.1467-9620.2006.00684.x

Motorola. (2010). *Innovation generation grants.* Retrieved from http://responsibility.motorola.com/ index.php/society/comminvest /education/igg/

Nelson, B., Ketelhut, D. J., Clarke, J., Bowman, C., & Dede, C. (2005). Design-based research strategies for developing a scientific inquiry curriculum in a multi-user virtual environment. *Educational Technology*, *45*(1), 21–27.

New York Learning Standards. (2008). *The living environment: Core curriculum.* Retrieved from http://www.p12.nysed.gov/ ciai/mst/pub/livingen.pdf

Palinscar, A. (1998). Social constructivist perspectives on teaching and learning. *Annual Review of Psychology*, *49*, 345–375. doi:10.1146/annurev.psych.49.1.345

Russo, P. (2004). *What makes any school an urban school?* Retrieved June 2010 from http://www.oswego.edu/~prusso1/ what_makes_any_school_an_urban_s.htm

Turkay, S. (2008). *Global Kids, Inc's Science Through Second Life curriculum evaluation.* Retrieved from http://www.webstrategies.com/NPC/StSLEvaluation.pdf

KEY TERMS AND DEFINITIONS

Blended Learning Environments: Usually refers to learning environments that consist of both face-to-face interaction and online interaction. This increases the learning options for the instructor and the student.

Instructional Design: A creative process which references the state and needs of the students, the resources available, nature of the content and learning theory to develop and produce a learning experience.

Social Constructivism: The learning theory that learning inherently occurs in relationship to other people and cultures, and that knowledge is constructed through this interaction.

Authentic Learning: A learning approach that posits that student learn more deeply if their learning is attached to a meaningful experience. Students tend to engage in exploration, inquiry and discourse with this method.

Science Literacy: Science Literacy is the evolving ability of students to engage in the process of the scientific method and thinking and their capacity for extending this engagement to social, cultural and life decision making.

Sustainability: Sustainability is the capacity of an ecology to remain balanced over time. Many natural ecologies are currently deemed unsustainable and in crisis.

Urban: An urban environment is one with a density of population, with low income and frequently with a diverse cultural mix. Many social attributes tend to arise in urban environments such as increased crime and violence, single parent families, lowered literacy rates and decreased health.

Chapter 16
Virtual Worlds – Enjoyment, Motivation and Anonymity:
Environments to Reengage Disaffected Learners with Education

Marc Thompson
Cambridge Education @ Islington, UK

ABSTRACT

This chapter considers the effectiveness of virtual worlds as environments in which disaffected or "failed" learners can be reengaged with education. The premise is that virtual worlds allow learners to "play" with their identity and potentially reinvent themselves as better learners. This idea is supported by research which shows virtual worlds as engaging, motivating, fun places to learn. The topics of "identity in virtual worlds," "identity and learning," and "education in virtual worlds" are examined. One hundred 13 to 17 year old pupils were observed working in the Second Life teen Grid which is a virtual world restricted to young people between 13 and 17 years old. Written feedback from 68 of these pupils was analyzed. This is supported by in excess of 1500 hours of participant observations in the adult Second Life virtual world.

INTRODUCTION

This chapter explores how the concept of virtual worlds can be used to support the learning of disaffected pupils. The hypothesis is that disengaged

DOI: 10.4018/978-1-60960-545-2.ch016

or disaffected learners can experience success and become more effective learners by creating a new learner identity in a virtual world.

Craft (2007, p. 206) states: "As virtual worlds are a recent phenomenon, the body of relevant academic literature is still nascent". However Craft (2007, p. 210) goes on to point out that since the works of Plato and Aristotle, philosophers have questioned how humans respond to simulations and images of behavior (although Craft focuses on immoral behavior), and how such images make the behavior more likely in the viewer. Although the concept of learner identity in virtual worlds is new, the underlying question is old.

People, young and old can construct whole new characters with associated identity issues and live (and possibly learn) through them in a virtual world environment. Being able to learn as Another Self anonymously or what I refer to as Anonymous Self has huge benefits for the shy, scared or embarrassed. In 2006 I ran a teaching assistant training course for men; older men reengaging with learning. They were nervous and confessed to having many fears. These confessions usually surfaced after four or five weeks of the ten week course. They had bottled up their fears hiding behind their strong masculine outward facades. Most had little success in learning and had bitter experiences of school. Once they shared their fears they started again with a new set of expectations and a willingness to seek help and guidance. It occurred to me that being able to construct a new façade to try out new skills and acceptably show weakness would have allowed them to explore and experience learning as a different and possibly more successful learner earlier in their lives.

Local Authorities (LAs) in the UK have a duty to provide educational services to any pupils or students who cannot attend a mainstream school. Reengaging learners requires more flexibility in attitude to the curriculum and therefore more scope for new approaches. It may require new methods of online delivery, support and activities. The Department for Children Schools and Families (DCSF) e-strategy (Harnessing technology: transforming learning and children's services, 2005) has the reengaging of disaffected learners and using Information and Communication Technology (ICT) to reach all learners as major themes.

The British Educational Communications and Technology Agency (Becta, 2005, p. 1) categorizes students requiring alternative provision as:

- those excluded for a period of more than fifteen days from school
- those not able to attend mainstream school for an extended period owing to medical reasons
- those who are members of a traveler community

These students are more likely to have lower literacy and numeracy skills, exhibit disruptive and challenging behavior and will need a focus on developing key skills for improving self-control and self-esteem.

Bradford and Crowe (2006, p. 330) point out that "gaming sites" are perceived as "cool places" to hangout and Second Life, where my project was hosted, is often confused with a regular gaming environment which may give it kudos with younger learners. Of course it is not a game, there are no rules of play and you can't win. For example, Habbo hotel is the most popular teen virtual world with 124 million registered users and 11 million visits to its site every month.

Internet time has replaced television time in the United States and Europe isn't far behind in this trend. The next step is the development of internet browsing on your television using the remote control. So, televisions may get a new lease of life but traditional programming is losing the battle with the internet.

Even if we put aside all the physical and technological benefits of learning in and through virtual worlds, simply being able to learn as "another self" has many benefits for both capable learners and for previously unsuccessful or unfulfilled learners. Learners can enhance their learning skills or become learners for the first time.

IDENTITY IN VIRTUAL WORLDS

In a virtual world both the external factors, the environment and community and the internal factor, of personality, can be altered and modified. In 1995 Sherry Turkle summed up the impact of the internet on society as … "Changing the way we think, the nature of our sexuality, the form of our communities, our very identities". (Turkle, 1995, p. 9). This view is certainly now part of accepted thinking. Yes, the internet has profoundly changed the lives of most people particularly in more developed countries but there are still areas where the exact nature, depth and potential impact are still unclear. "We are able to step through the looking glass. We are learning to live in virtual worlds". (Turkle, 1995, p. 9).

Turkle (1995) aligns this debate about the multiplicity of identity in virtual worlds with the postmodern French theorists of the 1960s and early 1970s such as Lacan, Foucault, Deleuze and Guattari. Their post modern theories use terms such as non-linear and decentred; things are hard to pigeon hole and define which suits multifaceted complex virtual worlds. They contrast with logical linear explainable modernist theory. She acknowledges the pressure on the individual to be "unitary" but concludes by saying, "In my computer-mediated worlds, the self is multiple…" (Turkle, 1995, p. 15).

Castronova (2007, p. 27) cites the work of Reeves and Nass (1996) who concluded that the brain evolved in an environment without media and so it responds to images as it would the real thing. Seeing a tiger on TV it responds to a "tiger" not a "TV tiger". The brain inherently suspends disbelief. So we are inherently predisposed to responding naturally within virtual world environments.

Turkle (1995, p. 138) explores Freud's idea of the super ego and how later psychoanalysts question the concept of an overriding control centre and suggested a mind full of "inner agents". It is the changing relations between these agents that generate the self. As the relationship between these agents change, they generate a different self or multiple selves.

Virtual worlds allow the user to experiment with and modify these relationships to form new identities, initially fixed in the world in which they were created but in time able to move into and influence behavior and attitudes in the real world.

Ligorio and Talamo (2000) discuss dialogical construction of self which refers to the development of identity through conversation. However to analyze this they had to provide avatars which they refer to as "visual embodiments" for their participants. Students between 9 and 15 years were selected from Italy and the Netherlands to inhabit a virtual world called 'Euroland'. Participants had to build three dimensional houses in this basic virtual environment through collaboration and consensus. Their research showed that; 'Identities in cyber space are co-constructed, situated, not stable, occasioned and indexed' Ligorio and Talamo (2000, p. 16). They noted that discourse was more important in this process than shape alone.

Turkle (1995, p. 258) wonders how we can be multiple and coherent although Jungean theorists encourage individuals to become acquainted with their whole range of personae. Could redefining a character in a virtual environment exacerbate the real world issues experienced by learners? Could it open a door to darker aspects of one's personality? Turkle (1995, p. 259) poses a crucial question, "What is the self when it divides itself between its constituent 'alters'?".

Above all it is important to remember that behind every avatar there is a real person. "Users are harmed when others… betray their trust online" Craft (2007, p. 216). Educators need to remember this in their development and planning of virtual world lessons.

IDENTITY AND LEARNING

For Etienne Wenger (2002, p. 4), learning is central to human identity. Crossnan, Field, Gallacher and Merrill (2003, p. 56) cite the Chicago School's use of "career" as a metaphor for the social course of the individual which is mediated by institutional structures and everyday life (Barker, 1989; Becker, 1963 in Crossnan et al., 2003).

Individual, subjective experiences influence attitudes and their development as a certain type of person. These experiences affect changes that may occur to the person's role both positive and negative, and their perceptions of themselves.

The learner therefore can change. What Bloomer and Hodkinson refer to as the learning career (in Crossnan, 2003, p. 56) based on the Chicago School's use of the term "career", can be influenced by external factors and redirected. Situated learning can be modified for the better.

Crossnan et al (ibid) go on to point out that Bloomer and Hodkinson's work stops at adolescence. They take this analysis of learning careers in to adulthood. Adults can have their learning career altered by positive experiences of learning including informal learning.

Their previous life experiences have often given them little confidence about engaging in the process of learning and indeed in some cases ... resulted in hostility towards educational institutions. (Crossnan et al., 2003, p. 58).

With such fragility it is possible that tension may be alleviated in an alternate reality. Why then can't the use of an alternative identity not only allow but positively encourage experimentation and progress to a more positive learner identity?

Crossnan et al cite the experience of one adult, who left school as soon as she could,

I was so shy at school... I hated being singled out. My face would go bright red. I hated it and I remember one teacher humiliating me... I re-

member that to this day. I was always afraid of getting it wrong. Crossnan et al. (2003, p. 62).

This learner did return to learning but tentatively as the idea of a campus still scared her. As her identity as a learner became stronger, so her fear of formal education lessened. These types of feelings are shared by many school refusers, excluded pupils and disaffected learners. She stresses she did not become someone but found her own identity. Virtual worlds can ease this process ironically by actually allowing the learner to be someone else if they so choose. She pointed out that the first few steps are hard ... practicing in a virtual world can make those steps much easier.

EDUCATION IN VIRTUAL WORLDS

There is "a significant body of Second Life activity in UK higher and further education, with just over 40 universities actively involved to varying degrees" Bayne and Littleton (2008, p. 1). The Office for standards in Education (OFSTED) in the UK, are yet to offer thoughts on virtual world technology but they have examined the use of "Virtual Learning Environments" (VLE), often referred to as "Managed Learning Environments" (MLE).

The crucial features provided by VLEs are off-site access, discussion forums, audio visual conferencing, e-mail and messaging - all of which seem relatively primitive compared to the functions afforded by virtual world environments.

Security fears are the first issue to deal with in educating young people through virtual worlds. Peggy Sheehy (2008 podcast) opened Ramapo Island in Teen life for 300 middle school students. She set about reassuring her principle and superiors, a route I had to mirror:

I once again reiterated the difference between the teen grid and the main grid. The teen grid only allows thirteen to seventeen year olds, with adults not allowed in without a fairly extensive background check and, even then, they need to be associated with and locked down to the education presence that they are working on (Sheehy, 2008).

The quality of the virtual world is important. Ash, Dede, Loftin and Salzman (1999, p. 8) suggest that learners must find it believable if they are to suspend disbelief and immerse themselves in the virtual environment. They further point out that levels of motivation increase in well designed immersive worlds.

Much of the learning environment in a virtual world can and should be generated by the learners themselves. What better way to ensure learners have pride in their environment. "Centralized top down planning fails …because users prefer to design their own culture and artifacts" (Dede, 1996, p. 2).

This powerful aspect of virtual worlds is recognized by Becta. These resources can easily focus on local issues and the functionality of the tools in many virtual worlds is intuitive in their use.

The Department for Children Schools and Families (DCSF) in the UK promote the use of teaching and learning strategies from what they refer to as the "social and constructivist family" with the learning objectives of, "Constructing knowledge, addressing misconceptions, solving problems and reasoning empathetically"(DCSF, 2007, p. 7).

In virtual worlds, learners can create and manage their learning environment. While the ground area of sims (simulated virtual islands) in Second Life for example are set to 64000 m2, there is no limit to the height of construction. Sky platforms can be stacked and allocated to individuals to populate and manage.

Bronack, Riedl and Tasher cite Vygotsy (1978) who demonstrated that learning occurs first on the social level and next on the individual one. This is a crucial consideration in trying to reengage with disaffected learners. What sort of community could lure the disaffected and disengaged to learn?

Fun is a huge attraction. With learning as fun a priority for many practitioners, Castronovo (2007, p. 103) offers a definition of fun. Fun is a pleasurable sensation attributed to an activity when:

1. The activity causes the co activation of motivational system
2. The activity is (possibly metaphorically) related to survival [I would suggest this may include the need to pass a test or succeed in an academic pursuit].
3. The individual's choices promote survival, and
4. The situation is known to be play.

As picture one and two illustrate, fun is easily had in virtual worlds directly linked to underlying learning outcomes.

The "Schome project" from the words school and home (The Schome community, 2007) avoided "challenging students", choosing to select its pupils from the National Association of Gifted and Talented Youth (NAGTY).

149 students were given access to Schome Park on the Teen Life grid of Second Life. These students were called "Sparkers".

The team discovered strong evidence that those students that participated fully with the project enhanced their communication, teamwork, leadership and creativity skills; referred to by the project group as 'knowledge age skills (The Schome community 2007, p. 4).

Sparkers found that their experiences on Schome Island were impacting on their real world confidence.

Global Kids is a project on the Lower East side of New York. Rik Panganiban explained that Global Kids has been able to motivate and inspire urban public school students, many of whom have been labeled at risk of school dropout (2009). Becta suggest using online technology to engage with disaffected learners by choosing subjects which have a high interest for learners themselves. Among Global Kids' successes is the "Tanzania Dig" project where students talked directly to archaeologists in Africa as they were excavating a site and replicated the dig in the virtual world. They have also published some powerful video shorts such as the 'Child Soldiers' video about the experiences of children in Uganda which can be found on YouTube. The key principles for a successful virtual world site, which apply equally to an education based world, are the five C's: Creativity, Competition, Collection, Community and Caring.

Dede (1996, p. 3) suggested that the skills afforded by virtual worlds are tantamount to magical powers and their impact on learning is only just emerging. He further suggests that the fluidity of identity is in itself an opportunity for learning. To truly induce immersion in virtual environments, the content must be as real as possible as viewed from outside (exocentric) and from within as a user (egocentric) which may explain the obsession with the quality of the graphics when presenting a virtual world for the first time. Dede (2004, p. 11) cites the work of Salzman (2000). He likens the two 'frames of reference' (FOR) as being like a human looking at a doll's house from the outside (exocentric) compared to a dolls perspective of experiencing the doll's house from the inside (egocentric).

An egocentric view generates a greater sense of immersion but it is further reinforced if it is believable from outside. A "bicentric" view combines the strengths of both frames of reference which I hoped to achieve on Islington's islands.

Joly (2007) quotes John Lester from Linden Lab who run Second Life. It is no surprise to him that educational institutions are using Second Life, he states:

Second Life gives both students and faculty a new medium for exploring things like distance learning, experiential learning, simulation, and scientific *visualization in a fundamentally collaborative environment, John Lester in July (2007).*

MY METHODOLOGY

I used questionnaires (both general open questions and a lykert scale statement list), validation group interviews and in-world ethnographic observations. My questionnaire was quite short, only using seven questions and qualitative in nature but carried values which could be totaled for analysis using a lykert scale. The data is ranked. The most positive responses scoring the highest for analysis. These questionnaires made up the bulk of my research. Observations were also made of the students as they worked and played in the teen Second Life grid. In terms of ethics they knew they were being observed. I also gathered information and opinions from teachers involved in the project or those I trained to work in Second Life.

My experience and observations in the adult Second Life grid began in July 2007 following a presentation by Professor Jillian Salmon from Leicester University and is essentially an ethnographic study. Ethnography usually involves the study of the culture of groups or societies. It is carried out primarily by engaging in fieldwork which involves studying people in their natural settings. In my case it involved the study of avatars in their virtual world.

My avatar "Barnsbury Blanco" recently celebrated his third birthday. I spent 1500 hours submersed in Second Life. In comparison, for example, McKeon and Wyche (2005) based their research findings on 30 – 40 hours each in Second Life. I adopted a very informal approach as a participant primarily in 'role play simulations which run on a theme e.g. Roman Britain or Post Apocalyptic America. It would be fair to say that over the three year period I became completely immersed often referred to as "going native".

My research with students who completed evaluation questionnaires took place between

Table 1. Student Groups

Group	Number of students on role	Number completing feedback	Reason for selection	Gender
1) Spanish Language Class Year 10 (14/15 years) Girls	14	14	Non purposive	Female
2) HG 1 Year 9 (13/14 years) Girls	19	17	Non purposive	Female
3) HG 2 Year 9 (13/14 years) Girls	8	6	Non purposive	Female
4) Challenging Boys Year 9 (13/14 years). 14 spoke English as an additional language. 9 students on 'School Action' under the SEN register.	17	11	Purposive	Male
5) MT1 Year 10 (14/15 years) ICT Girls	19	14	Purposive	Female
6) MT2 Year 10 (14/15 years) ICT Girls	15	6	Purposive	Female
Pilot Group. Pupil Referral Unit Local Authority. Year 10. Provision for excluded pupils.	Maximum seen 4	0	Purposive	Mixed
Out of Borough. Provision for teens out of education looking work distance.	4	0	Purposive	Mixed
Totals	100	68		

February 2009 and December 2009. However I was able to pilot my research as early as January 2008 with a group of excluded pupils attending the Local Authority's key stage 4, pupil referral unit (14-17 years old). The findings from this early effort are presented in my results.

My case studies involved a small accessible, high interest group. I used a total of eight groups from four school settings all within the 14 to 17 age range. I recorded feedback from 65 students although there were more students involved owing to absence and other commitments not all students were available on the final session when questionnaires were given out.

I made it very clear to my students that there was no right or wrong answer to the questions; they simply had to select the statements which most accurately matched their own thoughts and feelings. There were certainly no answers that would

please or displease me more than others (which I think disappointed some). I had two follow up group interviews to validate my findings through the questionnaire. The students were randomly selected by the regular class teacher.

My group were non random in as much as I wanted students between 14 to 17 years old, the age range for using the Second Life teen grid. Although only three of the surveyed groups were probability sampled i.e. I wanted groups who were interested in ICT and would be potentially highly motivated (groups MT1 and MT2 in Table 1) and I wanted a group of challenging pupils showing signs of disaffection or withdrawal from education (the boy group). The two groups from the pupil referral units were obviously purposive and non random, being my main focus. The other groups were non purposive (except of course they were in the age range) and were to provide a sample of general attitudes to virtual worlds. As a convenience sample, I was limited by the number of schools and teachers willing and able to provide a group of students to teach that met my interest criteria.

My research focused on young people because of the nature of my work. However I believe my findings are relevant to adults as well, the fact that young people are so responsive to influences on their identity was an additional benefit.

I considered identity to be something that includes a person's view of themselves and is multiple and changeable, particularly as it develops in the young. In theory a younger group should be more responsive to the opportunity to experiment with 'alternative selves' than older users of virtual worlds. Adolescent identity is subjected to multiple external forces as opposed to younger children who can dream of being whatever they want.

We live in a society where concepts of self, community and "what is right and wrong" are constantly changing. This makes it particularly challenging for young people to construct a sense of self and identify their most cherished values (Bers, 2001, p. 365).

I overlooked the fact that the last week of each half term often clashes with school activities. This reduced pupil numbers. The worst affected group was MT2 shown in Table 1, where over half the group went on an offsite visit on the final week of the project.

The "Out of Borough Provision" (Group 2: Table 1) was a government funded project for young people and adults, geared towards helping people back into/move forward in work or training. One of the courses is for young people 16-18yrs who are currently not in education, employment or training (NEET). All students from the unit had at least basic Information Technology (IT) skills and could work comfortably with Microsoft Office or equivalent. I never actually met any of these students face to face nor did I meet their tutor other than 'in world' and over the telephone.

I have presented the data as graphs and tables and used average scores for each statement. I tried median and mode analysis but found the results offered no new insights due to the size of the cohorts involved. What did help with analysis was comparing the responses when rounded off to whole numbers and when rounded off to two decimal places. I did not analyze the data by gender primarily due to the small number of boys involved. Nor did I break down the data by age. I don't believe comparing year 10 and year 9 pupils would have added significantly to my findings.

TEACHING THE STUDENTS AND THE CURRICULUM ADOPTED

The Schome (School Home) project team (The Schome Project, 2007) state that there is a steep learning curve to fully access the teen life grid. I am unsure what the benchmark is for this statement. Yes students learn quickly and there is a lot to learn. However many of the skills are already practiced in other forms of e-learning e.g. chat, text, voice, cut and paste and saving documents and other forms of internet engagement such as gaming e.g. walking, flying, taking and placing objects and editing characters.

I taught my students how to function in Second Life and gave them a project to complete to demonstrate their new skills. My students and teachers developed significant competence with just an average of four hours tuition. They acquired to varying degrees 38 of the 44 Second Life key skills highlighted by the Schome team (Figure 1). They did not cover writing script, video machinima, using Huds, uploading sounds, uploading images and setting preferences all of which I consider advanced skills.

I originally planned to use the Global Kids curriculum as the outline for my sessions estimating I could cover two sessions per lesson over

Figure 1. Students having fun wearing "nuclear power stations" (How to wear an object from inventory)

Figure 2. Students enjoying a row boat race. (How to use and drive an object)

Table 2. Schome report (2007) skills set for second life

Allow edit	Editing Objects	Resizing	Using Chat
Changing Appearance	Flying	Retrieving Objects	Using Friends
Changing Clothes	Force Sun	Right Click Pie	Using Full Map
Changing Textures	Give Items	Rotating Objects	Using HUDs
Controlling Camera	Instant Message	Setting Preferences	Using Inventory
Creating Folders	Joining Prims	Shopping	Using Minimap
Creating Objects	Landing	Sitting Down	Using Notecards
Creating Prims	Movement	Taking Photographs	Using Search
Dancing Gestures	Moving Objects	Teleporting	Video Machinima
Deciding Chat	Opening Inventory	Uploading Images	Walking
Driving Vehicles	Recording Chat	Uploading Sounds	Writing Script

four weeks, leaving two weeks for a project. The Global Kids curriculum is composed of nine sequential "levels." Each level is composed of modules which include individual lesson plans or "missions". In total there are 163 missions.

The nature of the environment made all my students want more than a sequential step by step curriculum could offer. In fact the Global Kids team suggests that their materials could be used in any order to support learners.

A change of approach was quickly required. The first group immediately got distracted by their own desire to learn, they wanted skills in batches and made their requirements clear. In a true social constructivist manner students demanded knowledge about their new environment and blocks of skills were negotiated. We dealt with walking, flying, talking and instant messaging together. Brief instructions followed by periods of practice, then a recap before moving on to the next batch of skills.

The beginning of each lesson began with establishing a learning contract for that session. I would deliver knowledge or facilitate learning; they would go away and practice. Imagine a shoal of fish suddenly washed up on land and finding themselves with all the physical attributes of humans including intelligence but with no instruction manual. The learning demands would be similar to those expressed by the students.

Of course some of the skills are quite intuitive particularly for experienced online gamers. I learned from the students. In the pilot project

one student immediately began running towards the horizon. "Wow I said how do you know the 'Control R' command?"

"I don't sir just hit the forward arrow twice, same on all games" he replied.

The lesson outlines began to follow the same pattern which students found reassuring.

1. Negotiate things to be learned and record agreed aims.
2. Demonstrate the skills required.
3. Students practice one or more of the skills through a task.
4. Students recap what they have learned and record it on a note card (Picture 3. Similar to the notepad facility in windows) and send the note to the tutor.

Each lesson involved negotiation so no two groups had the same lessons; a flavor of lesson content is shown in Table 3. Lessons averaged one and a half hours. An example of a "project sheet is attached in Figure 4 "Making a car".

The following figures illustrate the learner's experience. Students in default avatar guise meet for their first lesson (Figure 5) and are supported by direct access to the Global Kids curriculum through an object in-world (Figure 6).

After acquiring key skills they complete projects in teams, initially simple tasks such as building bridges (Figure 7), leading to more complex projects such as putting on a fashion show (Figure 8).

Figure 3. Note card shown on the users screen before being passed to the tutor

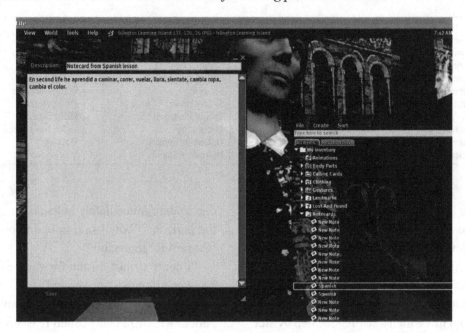

Table 3. Lesson outlines

Week 1 Skills Use Inventory, Walk, Talk, Fly, Change environment settings (make it sunny), Receive and use a Teleport invitation, Edit Appearance, Using note cards	Activities Map the island Change your avatars appearance and clothes
Week 2 Skills Add friends to your list, Join a group, Send teleport invitation, Buying objects and putting contents in your inventory ,Basic building skills	Activity Treasure hunt Make a bridge
Week 3 Skills Using voice, Editing clothing, Guest speaker logging in: making clothes, Using textures	Activity Make shirt and trousers/skirt for your avatar
Week 4 Skills How to put a script in an object Putting sounds in an objects	Activity Make a basic door that opens and shuts Introduce projects see week 5
Week 5 and 6 Skills All of the previous skills employed	Group Activity Make a stage and prepare a portfolio of clothes for a fashion show Or Build a basic car and prepare to race.

Figure 4. Making a Car

Your Task

Build a car which can carry two people. You will race your car against other cars around a track.

Here is a very basic example.

Note it has a steering wheel and steering column which are just for show.

The key parts are

1) A body (the dark grey section on the example). This is the Root Prim and must contain the script 'Realistic car' AND 'car seat' script.   WHEN JOINING THE PIECES OF THE CAR TOGETHER THIS MUST BE THE LAST PIECE YOU SELECT BECAUSE IT IS THE ROOT PRIM.

ALSO the X axis which is the red arrow must point to the BACK OF THE CAR. You really need to remember this !!!!!!!!!

2) Wheels (light grey), you may use 2 or 4 wheels. This example has 2 wheels. The front wheels can contain 'Front Wheel' script and the rear wheels can contain 'Rear Wheel' script (if you dont put script in the wheels it still drives but doesnt look as good). Select glass as the material for your wheels in 'edit' object tab at the bottom 'material'. For some reason the car will go faster as glass has the lowest drag in secondlife .

3) The passenger seat. (The yellow box on the example) shouldnt need a 'Car Seat' script. Experiment with sitting on it, once attached to the car you want the passenger facing the same way as the driver. Only the passenger can sit here, you to control the car.

So

Build your car (not too big please)
Drag and drop all the scripts into the relevant pieces of the vehicle
Select all the pieces making sure you select the root prim (car body) last
Link all the parts (either tools link or ctrl L)

PREPARE TO RACE

Figure 5. New arrivals in default avatar form

Figure 6. The "Object Link" to the Global Kids Curriculum Book

Figure 7. Building Bridges

Figure 8. Preparing for the Final Show

Figure 9. Lykert Scale statements

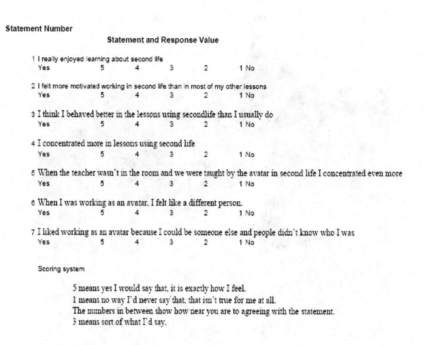

Statement Number

Statement and Response Value

1 I really enjoyed learning about second life
  Yes   5   4   3   2   1 No

2 I felt more motivated working in second life than in most of my other lessons
  Yes   5   4   3   2   1 No

3 I think I behaved better in the lessons using secondlife than I usually do
  Yes   5   4   3   2   1 No

4 I concentrated more in lessons using second life
  Yes   5   4   3   2   1 No

5 When the teacher wasn't in the room and we were taught by the avatar in second life I concentrated even more
  Yes   5   4   3   2   1 No

6 When I was working as an avatar, I felt like a different person.
  Yes   5   4   3   2   1 No

7 I liked working as an avatar because I could be someone else and people didn't know who I was
  Yes   5   4   3   2   1 No

Scoring system

  5 means yes I would say that, it is exactly how I feel.
  1 means no way I'd never say that, that isn't true for me at all.
  The numbers in between show how near you are to agreeing with the statement.
  3 means sort of what I'd say.

Figure 10. Results for all Students

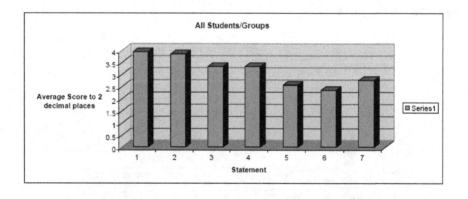

RESULTS CONCLUSION AND FUTURE

Figure 9 shows the content of the questionnaire. The graphed results follow in Figures 10, 13 and 14. Tables are shown in Figures 11 and 12.

I was surprised and initially disappointed by some of the results particularly the feedback on behavior and being an avatar.

Findings from questions 1 and 2: I really enjoyed learning about Second Life and I felt more motivated working in Second Life than in most of my other lessons.

All the graphs show that enjoyment and motivation were high; behavior was good. Even the most negative groups scored 4 (yes I would agree) for enjoyment and behavior.

Figure 11. Result Tables for All Students, ICT students and Challenging Students

| Statement | Group/number students | | | | | | Total per question | Average | | Rounded |
| | Points per statement | | | | | | | Total students | | |
	G1/14	G2/17	G3/6	G4/11	G5/14	G6/6				
1	48	57	30	45	61	27	268	68	3.94	4
2	49	54	30	48	53	28	262		3.85	4
3	50	52	19	43	41	22	227		3.33	3
4	46	51	11	46	50	23	227		3.33	3
5	37	36	12	32	39	19	175		2.57	3
6	30	33	10	32	36	19	160		2.35	2
7	35	38	19	38	38	20	188		2.76	3

| ICT groups G5 to 6 | | | Total per question | Average | | Groups |
Statement	G5/14	G6/6		Total students	Rounded	
1	61	27	89	20	4.4	4	
2	53	28	83		4	4	Group 1 Spanish Girls
3	41	22	66		3.15	3	Group 2 H1 Mainstream Girls
4	50	23	77		3.65	4	Group 3 H2 Mainstream Girls
5	39	19	63		2.9	3	Group 4 Challenging Boys
6	36	19	61		2.75	3	Group 5 M1 Mainstream Girls
7	38	20	65		2.9	3	Group 6 M2 Mainstream Girls

| Statement | Challenging Groups G1 to 4 | | | | Total per question | Average | | Rounded |
	G1/14	G2/17	G3/6	G4/11		Total students		
1	48	57	30	45	180	48	3.75	4
2	49	54	30	48	181		3.77	4
3	50	52	19	43	164		3.41	3
4	46	51	11	46	154		3.2	3
5	37	36	12	32	117		2.43	2
6	30	33	10	32	105		2.19	2
7	35	38	19	38	130		2.7	3

All students enjoyed the project, and felt they were more motivated and behaved better than most other lessons.

The non purposive groups had a more typical attitude towards the learning; they did the tasks and engaged in the processes but were conscious of their peers and careful not to look too enthusiastic.

Findings from questions 3 and 4: I think I behaved better in the lessons using Second Life than I usually do and I concentrated more in lessons using Second Life.

Much of the information gathered here seems dependant on the perceived behavior of the students. It would have been beneficial to ask students how they felt they behaved in classes before the project began.

Group 1, the "Boys" group, and group 2, the nine girls (HG1), were aware of the challenging nature of their behavior and this was reflected in their high scores. The other groups were either well behaved and motivated so improvement would be considered minimal such as groups 5 and 6 or they were simply delusional about their behavior, considering themselves well behaved and focused such as groups 2 and 3.

Findings from question 5: When the teacher wasn't in the room and we were taught by the avatar in Second Life I concentrated even more.

Group 5, the year 10 ICT girls (MT1) were unique in that they received two lessons through a teacher in world and yet they rated this approach less favorably than those asked to imagine this scenario.

They also stated that they didn't particularly find being trained by the 'avatar on screen more engaging and yet the teacher said they were

Figure 12. Results by Group

Statement	G1/14	Ave	Rounded
1	48	3.43	3
2	49	3.5	3
3	50	3.57	4
4	46	3.28	3
5	37	2.64	3
6	30	2.14	2
7	35	2.5	2
total ave		21.06	
totals		3	3

	G2/17	Ave	Rounded
	57	3.35	3
	54	3.18	3
	52	3.06	3
	51	3	3
	36	2.12	2
	33	1.94	2
	38	2.24	2
		16.89	
		2.7	3

	G3/6	Ave	Rounded
	30	5	5
	30	5	5
	19	3.2	3
	11	1.83	2
	12	2	2
	10	1.67	2
	19	3.17	3
		21.87	
		3.12	3

Statement	G4/11	Ave	Rounded
1	45	4.09	4
2	48	4.36	4
3	43	3.9	4
4	46	4.18	4
5	32	2.9	3
6	32	2.9	3
7	38	3.45	3
total ave		25.78	
totals		3.7	4

	G5/14	Ave	Rounded
	61	4.36	4
	53	3.78	4
	41	2.93	3
	50	3.57	4
	39	2.78	3
	36	2.57	3
	38	2.71	3
		22.7	
		3.24	3

	G6/6	Ave	Rounded
	27	4.5	4
	28	4.67	5
	22	3.67	4
	23	3.83	4
	19	3.17	3
	19	3.17	3
	20	3.33	3
		26.34	
		3.8	4

Groups

Group 1 Spanish Girls
Group 2 H1 Mainstream Girls
Group 3 H2 Mainstream Girls
Group 4 Challenging Boys
Group 5 M1 Mainstream Girls
Group 6 M2 Mainstream Girls

transfixed when I took a lesson from home using 'voice' to aid my teaching.

I observed and helped this same group when I arranged for a guest speaker from the US to show them how to edit and make clothes …the levels of concentration were cranked up and off task chat although normally acceptable was minimal.

The 'Out of Borough Unit' went very well, although attendance was disappointing. The young people in such provision do have an unusual number of external factors bearing down on them and observations from the teacher in the classroom were very positive. Given easier access to ICT.i.e. home access and some form of incentive to attend, I believe this group would have benefitted more from the program but in the end they only managed three sessions. It must be noted that their attendance was voluntary not only for my project but for the units provision as a whole.

The more motivated students, groups 5 and 6, rated the avatar identity experience positively as did the disaffected boys group; the project seemed to grab their imagination. The more challenging groups were not convinced by the 'avatar experience' and were unwilling to suspend disbelief, although teacher comments and observations suggest that this negativity may well be influenced by their general negative attitude to learning or adverse peer pressure. Some of these students were obviously engrossed in certain aspects of the project which was not reflected in their feedback.

Findings from questions 6 and 7: When I was working as an avatar, I felt like a different person and I liked working as an avatar because I could be someone else and people didn't know who I was.

Groups 5 and 6 had more time in world which helped their ability to suspend disbelief in fact all groups with six sessions had three of these

Figure 13. Graphs by Group

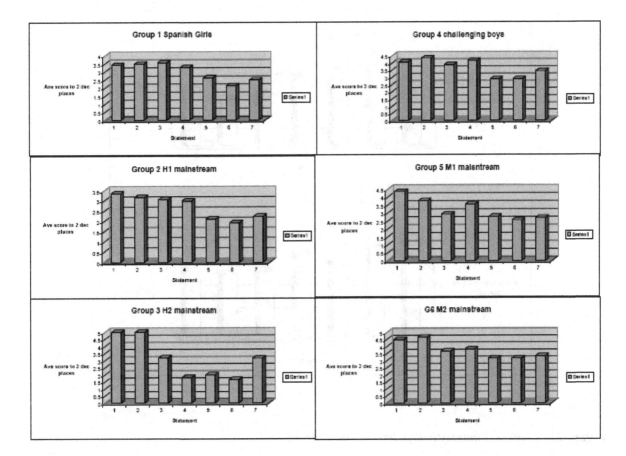

dominated by group or pair activities which allowed them to fully explore this new approach to learning. These students rated the anonymity of working as an avatar higher than others.

Group 1 (Spanish lesson girls) were also very positive about the anonymity of working as an avatar. The boys group (group 4) all opted for grand avatars most choosing cartoon or super hero designs such as spawn or spider man which were part of a collection of free objects I gave them in their inventories (Figure 15).

Group 6 (ICT girls) were the most positive although still only rating it just above the three average points score. This was possibly as I allowed this group more time to edit the appearance of their avatar although they may have been more excited.

Statements 6 and 7 pose very similar questions for participants so that I could check that they had been clear about my line of research ; had they suspended disbelief and become absorbed by the avatar as a new self?

The non purposive groups (1, 2 and 3) were less impressed with being avatars. The lowest scores for question 6 were recorded by group 3 (mainstream girls non purposive) 1.67 a strong disagree however question 7 doesn't support this score and suggests a lack of engagement with the feedback process and possibly the whole program.

During the follow up interviews group 5 were very positive about the experience. They backed up their statement choices in the interview and suggested a variety of uses for Second Life such

Figure 14. Graphs of ICT students and Challenging students

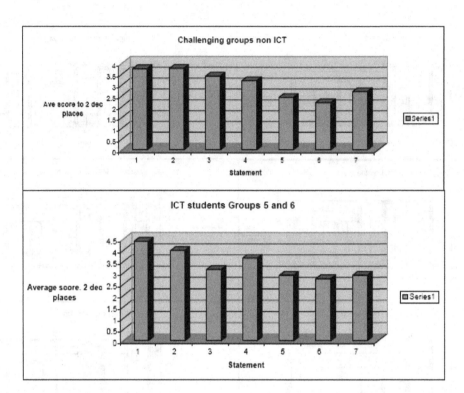

Figure 15. A boy as a fantasy character with the teacher

as Design and Technology, Drama, Media studies and English.

I pressed group 2 to validate the suggestion that they felt completely disengaged from the avatar and saw it only as a doll which they used for the purpose of the lesson. Interestingly five of the six students interviewed said they tried to make the avatar look like themselves, "At first I just dressed it as a dolly but after a while I tried to make it look more like me and dressed it the way I would like to dress…" Tamara (Year 9).

The group from the local Pupil Referral Unit did engage but a mountain of difficulties and setbacks made this impossible to get off the ground in any meaningful way. Rather than sound negative about this situation I recorded my findings and experiences and translated that into a series of 'must haves' for a successful project in school which I applied successfully to the distance learning program at the out of borough unit and are listed in my conclusions.

The "borough" and "out of borough unit" groups all said they enjoyed working in Second Life but they had so little time in world, two only having two hours, one having four hours and the out of borough group having six hours. I was also unable to get direct feedback at the end of each program for a variety of reasons so relied on recorded comments during the training on which to draw conclusions and make observations.

They all behaved immaculately in world and were more polite than the mainstream classes. The following comments were quite surprising; ''Thank you very much I really enjoyed that.'', ''Excellent look forward to next week.''

One senior consultant was very impressed by the way students were using Second Life at the local pupil referral unit. She was particularly taken by the virtual café one had set up and congratulated me on my work. I had to point out that I had in fact failed miserably in my attempts to work with students there and my legacy was

Figure 16. Students from the Out of Borough Unit

simply a link on the desktop which obviously students had discovered and embarked on their own journey of discovery. Clearly the attractions and uses of virtual worlds go beyond the scope of traditional teaching methods.

Another indication that pupils may have held back on their praise for the project were the comments of other teachers. I certainly believe they were more engaged in the work than feedback suggests. Two teachers, one a qualified inspector commented on the excellent behavior and motivation of group 1 and group 3. These students were known to the teachers and they were amazed by the level of concentration and engagement they saw.

Based on four questions teachers gave feedback on their experiences of working in the virtual world. They found the experience enjoyable and challenging. They felt it had good potential as a tool to engage disaffected learners and most commented favorably on being able to hide behind the avatar; one particularly enjoyed being a man. The summary is presented in Figure 17.

CONCLUSION

I believe it is important to remember that in general, people inherently don't like work, they like to play. They are obliged to attend school by

Figure 17. Teacher Comments

Nine teachers were asked to comment on the following areas.

1) The level of engagement second life offers ... (did you enjoy it?)

All teachers thoroughly enjoyed the experience and were happy to consider collaborating in a second life project.

2) How you felt being able to interact as an avatar with other avatars especially when you didn't know who was behind the avatar. Any potential uses that spring to mind?

"It allowed a freedom or even a blank slate. I could behave out of character with impunity," stated one. Others shamelessly enjoyed misbehaving whilst some struggled with the experience.

"I was very busy trying to get my avatar to do what I wanted - I felt that I was a mixed ability group and I was on the SEN table."

When under pressure one confessed, "When I built I talked to my colleagues next to me, rather than communicating Avatar to Avatar!"

3) Potential for working with disaffected and/or difficult pupils using a virtual world. Do you think it would improve behaviour motivation and engagement possibly even achievement?

Their was broad appreciation of this suggestion.

"seems to be very engaging and motivating." Although seeing its p[potential in other curriculum areas was more challenging.

Appropriate skills were mentioned, one teacher commented that it could work,

"As long as they (pupils) felt able to operate the avatars - that they were not failing or frustrated with it as well as everything else."

The need for good management and planning was also mentioned.

4) Anything else you want to say?

Most notable here was one female teacher that really enjoyed being a 'man'.

the state. To hook students there needs to be a domain of shared interest (Wenger, 1998). People go to fun sites and enjoy fun tasks. An interest such as Star Trek is easier to harness than school work for challenging students and so the learning environment in itself must be of interest initially to engage the individual. This is the strength of virtual worlds for pupils, particularly disruptive pupils: the environment can be engaging in itself before content or usage comes into play.

David Wortley from the "Serious Games Institute" in the UK (Syedain, 2008, p. 21) observed that when people are looking at avatars sitting around a table they are more committed than they are when taking part in a web seminar. He also observed that meetings are more focused and business like and there is noticeably less chit-chat. Having said this, Wortley then devalues these important factors and says he is unsure that virtual worlds offer a lot more than older technologies such as web conferencing which I hope I have shown to untrue. Dawson (2006) mentions the key factors affecting motivation: poor expectations, low self confidence, previous experience of bullying and the lack of a relevant curriculum. I believe my research has shown that we can alleviate or eliminate some of these by educating students within a virtual world.

Time in world is clearly a factor. My research has shown that adults can easily spend eleven hours or more in world in a day and my groups only had a maximum of twelve hours most only experiencing six to eight hours. Based on such a short time I am pleased with the overall feedback about "feeling like another person or character and enjoying the idea of being someone else" (Question 7). The average score for all participants was 2.76 rising to 3.45 for group 4 which interestingly was the all boy group who chose the fantasy figure avatars.

In reengaging failed learners it is important to encourage a positive 'can do' environment so the avatar doesn't take on all the negative attributes developed by the user and appeal to the audience

in their tried and trusted manner as disruptive and challenging. I don't believe these students actually like being disengaged or disruptive; it is an opportunity for a fresh start. More likely is the good student acting out a desire to be naughty and disruptive, something they never do in real life. Here the core self soon takes control as a sense of purpose develops in the work they do.

Not only do virtual worlds cater for individual issues of identity and experiences but they cater for new ways of learning. My students were blessed with these skills. Their learning styles require, "seeking, sieving, and synthesizing" Dede (2004, p. 7 in Abraham et al., 2007, p. 92).

The technology involved in the user interface of less complex tools such as virtual learning environments (very different from virtual worlds) are no easier than those required for accessing virtual worlds and, as Ash et al. (1999) go on to state; new learning experiences that are highly perceptual are possible. "Entering a college… should create a sense of excitement about learning" (JISC, 2006, p. 8).

Students teleporting in to our learning island are greeted by a 15th century Spanish galleon (Figure 18); a constant source of excitement matched only by students' first lesson in the space station simulation orbiting earth, or any other selected planet from the menu (Figure 19).

What Bloomer and Hodkinson (in Crossnan 2003) refer to as situated learning can be changed and the whole learner identity can be reconstructed in virtual worlds. Does attitude change because the virtual world provides a good environment or is it in fact the very possibility of change that the virtual world offers that encourages the desire to change for the better? Complete anonymity is possible and the idea of a 'new self' can be explored. We have seen how virtual world users can suspend disbelief and the sense of interaction is far greater than via a chat room. The option to try learning again and control this learning I would argue are key drivers. Reducing the pressure on the individual to conform and learn

Figure 18. View of "Learning Island"

Figure 19. A building seminar in the space station

encourages engagement in the learning process. What could be more devoid of pressure than using an anonymous identity to engage with learning for the first time?

Discipline is relatively safe. Avatars can be frozen, muted or blocked in addition to normal verbal and or a written warning …but it is all in a non-real virtual environment, so the damage to the ego of the real person is at least once removed.

Failure can be disassociated from the person behind the new identity (the avatar) and apportioned wholly on the character invented for this new identity itself. I believe that through a simple selective process the successful aspects of this new identity can be filtered out and owned by the creator to positively affect his or her real life learning career. Meadows refers to the avatar as a 'device for social fiction' (2008, p. 78). It is not fiction in the mind of the user and users are not always engaged in fiction, but more importantly acquiring new knowledge and new skills. Rather than take over, as Meadows (2008, p. 82) suggests, the avatar may just affect the real person; the real person with a non linear personality in which "we are many personalities".

People may well "prefer their avatar personas to their real ones" (Meadows, 2008, p. 83), but this may lead to a more positive more effective more pleasing persona in real life.

Often colleagues say, "Ah so the characteristics developed in the virtual world transfer into the real world?" Well, actually, no. They are already there in the real world. If we follow the thinking of Jung, where identity is not linear; the real world and virtual world facilitate the development of aspects of the core personality that are present in different ways. The whole concept for me is utterly liberating: Governments in China, South Korea and Vietnam are trying to limit internet access for teens (Meadows, 2008, p. 122) without first considering whether this is actually the problem or in fact the solution to a real world issue faced by teens.

We get what we ask for and the development and success of virtual worlds is a result of that (increasingly global) democratic process. What Thompson et al (1999) refer to as a "technomorphic" phenomenon is a place educators need to be. What Boellstorff (2008) refers to as 'techne' must apply to educators, who should be shaping these new and exciting learning environments and influencing the characters within them.

My colleagues and I are not "neo-millennials" or "millennials", however we are all digitally literate sometimes more so than the students we teach and we are regular users of the internet. We do not shirk our responsibility to guide younger users in the most appropriate and safest way to use evolving technology simply because we had to make do with books, analogue TV, pen and paper and telephones attached to the house. We do however recognize the inherent advantages students have today, growing up in a technologically rich environment and hope to exploit that to the full. The accessibility of virtual world environments across the globe facilitates what for Sheehy (2008) is the foundation for 21st century learning, global collaboration. She hopes to see the development of a global curriculum for learning in Second Life, which with basic training could be accessed by all students in the UK whether on school role or not.

In the US, post secondary education has been the main area of expansion for virtual world based education. 18 million students are expected to be enrolled in post secondary education in 2010 (Bonack et al., 2006, p. 1). Most of these students will have access to distance education. Most of this is internet based asynchronous training. Nearly half of the colleges adopting distance learning employed synchronous technology such as virtual worlds.

While Becta has four areas of focus for a successful virtual world project I have ten. As a result of my pilot study at the local unit and supported by my further observations I would suggest the following as the basic factors required to successfully run and deliver training in a virtual world,

1. Access to ICT equipment.
2. Well managed, fit for purpose ICT equipment.
3. A good broadband connection (minimum 5 MB ideally 10 MB and upward)
4. A named person to manage the ICT equipment and to deal with network issues and firewalls.
5. Enthusiastic staff on the ground willing to accept minor setbacks and push on.
6. Direct involvement of the Leadership team.
7. Staff with some awareness of virtual world technology.
8. Staff, not necessarily teaching staff, preferably two, willing to run the project in the classroom whilst trainers work remotely through the Second Life platform if remote training is required.
9. Staff that appreciate that this is a new and exciting experiment and that there will be glitches, failures and teething problems.
10. Staff willing to explore the levels of literacy support required both in the real classroom and in Second Life and develop/pilot resources and strategies to that end.

Whilst the skills required to teach and learn in virtual worlds require a steep learning curve, it costs a fraction of the budget currently invested in building schools for the future in the UK and constructivist pedagogy is implicit in the training and skills required for educating in virtual worlds.

There are human limits to how far "users" can divorce themselves from the avatar experience which I have observed in my research. As mentioned discussing identity in virtual worlds, there are real people behind avatars and I noted that people will give up trying in any endeavor if they repeatedly fail.

The same rules apply in Second Life as in real life. I found that whilst behaviors are far more extreme in many role play islands, feelings are the same. In fact the more extreme the roles play the more people demand the rules are respected. If you go outside the rules or push peoples' limits of tolerance people react the same as in real life; they withdraw, complain get upset and sometimes leave altogether. I noted at least three long term users of Second Life completely withdraw from the environment due to failed romances and I suspect the same would be true of learners if learning was unsuccessful. I think the human spirit could probably tolerate one possibly two failures and no more. After this the idea of identity construction or anonymity would then be linked with failure and the "driver" (of the avatar) would give up. These real life/second life tolerances provide a vast area for study. Whatever the future holds all users would do well to note the following quote from a wise (Anonymous) person in Second Life, quoted as written;

'I am a real life person behind this Avi (avatar) and I have RL (real life) feelings. if you don't have RL feelings and think that this is only a game and I'm only a cartoon then we will have nothing serious, simple. I'm tired of being played and lied to and hurt people. Wake up there are RL people behind these avi's and they have hearts and feelings and emotions …'

REFERENCES

Abraham, D. C., Johnson, N. A., Junglas, I. A., Loughlin, P. M., & Steel, D. J. (2007). Identity formation, learning styles and trust in virtual worlds. *The Data Base for Advances in Information Systems, 38*(4).

Anonymous. (2009, April 3). Second Life credited with boost to academic ability at Plymouth school. *Plymouth Herald*.

Anonymous wiki. (2009). *Identity and virtual world avatars Web identity: Exploring identity, privacy, & anonymity online*. Retrieved from http://webidentity.wikidot.com/ identity-and-virtual-world-avatars

Ash, K., Dede, C., Loftin, R. B., & Salzman, M. (1999). Using virtual reality technology to convey abstract scientific concepts. In Jacobson, M. J., & Kozma, R. B. (Eds.), *Learning the sciences of the 21st century: Research, design, and implementing advanced technology learning environments.* Hillsdale, NJ: Lawrence Erlbaum.

Bayne, S., & Littleton, F. (2008, February 28). Virtual worlds in education. *The Higher Education Academy Newsletter, 10.*

Becta. (2005). *Developing content for pupil referral units and alternative provision.* Retrieved from http://www.becta.org.uk

Becta. (2006). *Designing digital resources for PRUs and alternative provision.* Retrieved from http//www.becta.org.uk

Becta. (2007). *Harnessing technology review 2007: Progress and impact of technology in education.* Retrieved from http//www.becta.org.uk

Bers, M. U. (2001). Identity construction environments: Developing personal and moral values through the design of a virtual city. *Journal of the Learning Sciences, 10*(4), 365–415. doi:10.1207/S15327809JLS1004new_1

Boellstorff, T. (2008). *An anthropologist explores the virtually human: Coming of age in Second Life.* Princeton, NJ: Princeton University Press.

Bonack, S., Riedl, R., & Tahser, J. (2006). Learning in the zone: A social constructivist framework for distance education in a 3-Dimensional virtual world. *Interactive Learning Environments, 14*(3), 219–232. doi:10.1080/10494820600909157

Bradford, S., & Crowe, N. (2006). Hanging out in Runescape: Identity, work and leisure in the virtual playground. *Children's Geographies, 4*(3).

Castronova, E. (2007). *Exodus to the virtual world: How online fun is changing reality.* Hants, UK: Palgrave Macmillan.

Craft, A. J. (2007). Sin in cyber-Eden: Understanding the metaphysics and morals of virtual worlds. *Ethics and Information Technology, 9*(3). doi:10.1007/s10676-007-9144-4

Crosssan, B., Field, J., Gallacher, J., & Merrill, B. (2003). Understanding participation in learning for non-traditional adult learners: Learning careers and the construction of learning identities. *British Journal of Sociology of Education, 24*(1). doi:10.1080/01425690301907

Dawson, G. (2006). *Education committee: Pupil motivation inquiry right track response.* Retrieved from http://www.scottish.parliament.uk/business/committees/education/ inquiries/pmi/Right%20Track.pdf

DCFS. (2005). *Harnessing technology: Transforming learning and children's services.* Retrieved from http://www.dcfs.gov.uk/ publicatiuons/e-strategy

DCSF. (2007). *Trends in further education.* Retrieved from http://www.dcsf.gov.uk/trends /index.cfm?fuseaction=home.s howChart&cid=4&iid=20&chid=77

DCSF. (2009). *The national strategies: The five components of personalised learning.* Retrieved from http://www.standards.dcsf.gov.uk /NationalStrategies

Dede, C. (1996). The evolution of constructivists learning environments: Immersion in distributed, virtual worlds. In Wilson, G. B. (Ed.), *Constructivist learning environments: Case studies in instructional design.* Englewood Cliffs, NJ: Educational Technology.

Dede, C. (2004). *Planning for Neomillennial learning styles: Implications for investments in technology and faculty.* Cambridge, MA: Harvard Graduate School of Education.

Joint Information Systems Committee (JISC). (2006). *Designing spaces for effective learning: A guide to 21st century learning space design.* Retrieved from http://www.jisc.ac.uk/ media/ documents /publications /learningspaces.pdf

Joly, K. (2007). *A second life for higher education? University business solutions for higher education.* Retrieved from http://www.universitybusiness. com/ ViewArticle.aspx?articleid=797

Ligorio, M. B., & Talamo, A. (2000). *Identity in cyberspace: The social construction of identity through online virtual interactions.* Retrieved from http://www.activeworlds.com/ edu/research/ identity.pdf

McKeon, M., & Wyche, S. (2005). *Life across boundaries: Design, identity and gender in SL.* Retrieved from http://www.mattmckeon.com / portfolio/ second-life.pdf

Meadows, M. S. (2008). *I, avatar: The culture and consequences of having a Second Life.* Berkeley, CA: New Riders Press.

OFSTED. (2009). *Virtual learning environments: An evaluation of their development in a sample of educational settings.* Retrieved from http://www. ofsted.gov.uk/ content/download/8797/95679 /file/VLE%20an%20evaluation %20of%20 their%20 development.pdf

Panganiban, R. (2009). *Do virtual worlds support or hold back marginalized youth?* Retrieved from http://www.holymeatballs.org/ virtual_worlds/ second_life/ curriculum_development

Sheehy, P. (2008). *The great leveller- Second Life in middle school.* Retrieved from http://olpglobalkids.org/rezed/

Syedain, H. (2008, April 17). Out of this world. *People Management.*

The Schome Community. (2007). *The Schome-NAGTY teen Second Life pilot final report.* Retrieved from http://kn.open.ac.uk/public/ document.cfm?docid=9851

Thompson, M., Tranvik, T., & Selle, P. (1999). *Doing technology (and democracy) the Pack-Domkey's way: The technomorphic approach to ICT policy.* Retrieved from http://www.sv.uio. no/mutr/ publikasjoner/rapp2000 /rapport9.htm

Turkle, S. (1995). *Life on the screen: Identity in the age of the internet.* New York, NY: Simon & Schuster.

Vygotsky, L. (1986). *Thought and language.* Cambridge, MA: MIT Press.

Wenger, E. (1998). *Communities of practice: Learning, meaning, and identity.* Cambridge, UK: Cambridge University Press.

Chapter 17
Why Videogames are not Teacher–Proof:
The Central Role of the Teacher when Using New Technologies in the Classroom

Melissa Gresalfi
Indiana University, USA

Jacqueline Barnes
Indiana University, USA

Patrick Pettyjohn
Indiana University, USA

ABSTRACT

This chapter considers the crucial role that the teacher plays in supporting successful use of immersive technology in the classroom, focusing particularly on the use of an interactive, online, multiplayer videogame called Quest Atlantis. This chapter presents an account of successful strategies for integrating immersive technologies into teaching practice, such that the game does not replace the teacher, nor the teacher replace the game, but rather the two are integrated in their mutual support of student learning. The authors focus specifically on two distinct roles that teachers can play in leading whole-class discussions: attuning students to important concepts and connections in the game, and deepening opportunities to learn beyond what is afforded in game design. For each role, the authors present two contrasting cases with the goal of illuminating the central role that a teacher can play when integrating complex technologies into the classroom. Differences in the ways that teachers support their students while using games like Quest Atlantis are not trivial; it is argued that differences in teachers' support of whole-class conversations can create dramatically different opportunities for students to learn.

DOI: 10.4018/978-1-60960-545-2.ch017

INTRODUCTION

The Pew Report (2008) documented the increasing popularity of videogames for children and young adults, finding that 97% of teens between the ages of 12-17 play some form of computer or videogame. Despite their popularity and the growing agreement of the potential of videogames for supporting engagement, interest, and learning (Barab et al., 2007; Gee, 2003; Hickey, Ingram-Goble, & Jameson, 2009; Shaffer, 2006; Squire, 2006; Steinkuehler, 2006), schools have been slow to harness the potential of this new medium. Furthermore, the obstacles and benefits associated with using technology in classrooms have not been explored. Thus, little is known about how teachers integrate immersive technologies such as interactive, online, multiplayer videogames in the classroom, and, more specifically, what role the teacher must play in classrooms that integrate these technologies. An assumption motivating this chapter is that there is a need for detailed analyses of effective use of immersive technologies in classrooms and a need to better understand the kinds of teaching practices that support successful technology integration. As a field, we lack robust examples of successful and deep integration of technology that can support an emerging vision for practicing teachers.

In this chapter, we begin to address this gap by considering the crucial role of the teacher in supporting successful use of immersive technology in the classroom. This chapter presents an account of successful strategies for integrating immersive technologies into teaching practice, such that the game does not replace the teacher, nor the teacher replace the game, but rather the two are integrated in their mutual support of student learning. We present contrasting cases from two different curricular units being taught in the context of an online multiplayer videogame called *Quest Atlantis* (www.questatlantis.org). Quest Atlantis (QA) is an international learning and teaching project that uses a 3D multi-user environment to immerse children (ages 9-16) in educational tasks. Although disciplinary content can differ significantly among QA units and activities, the structure, goals, and narratives of the units overlap considerably and are all designed to foster an experience of *transformational play* (Barab, Gresalfi, & Arici, 2009). Briefly, transformational play describes an experience that a person can have while engaged in game play, which involves taking on the role of a protagonist who must employ conceptual understandings to interrogate and ultimately make choices that have the potential to transform a problem-based fictional context. Positioning students in this way sparks their interest, but even more importantly, can lead to deeper engagement with content.

We focus on Quest Atlantis because it represents a kind of game (narratively rich, situationally complex, and allowing for exploration) that is well entrenched outside of school, but only beginning to gain popularity inside classrooms. Despite the potential of games like Quest Atlantis for supporting learning, integrating the game into traditional classroom contexts creates novel challenges for students and teachers. QA is best understood as an immersive project-based-learning curriculum, rather than a traditional "drill and practice" computer game of the type commonly used in schools. Because the game is so different from curricula typically used in classrooms, implementing the game effectively requires that students and teachers change some of their common practices. For teachers accustomed to using instructional techniques that are more aligned with drill and practice, using immersive games like Quest Atlantis requires learning more about inquiry teaching methodologies and guiding students rather than leading them through activities. Even for teachers familiar with more inquiry-based projects, the videogame can create new and unusual demands (for example, students might play the game at very different speeds, or need help focusing on content amidst the exciting narrative) (c.f. Cross, Gresalfi, & Hudson, under review).

In this chapter we present contrasting cases that have been chosen because they illuminate the central role that a teacher can play when integrating complex technologies into the classroom. Differences in the ways that teachers support their students while using games like Quest Atlantis are not trivial; here we argue that differences in teachers' support of whole-class conversations can create dramatically different opportunities for students to learn. We focus specifically on two distinct roles that teachers can play in leading whole-class discussions: *Attuning students* to important concepts and connections in the game, and *Deepening opportunities* to learn beyond what is afforded in game design.

THE ROLE OF NEW TECHNOLOGIES IN CLASSROOMS

Although immersive technologies such as videogames have demonstrated potential for supporting student learning (Barab et al., 2007; Hickey, Ingram-Goble, & Jameson, 2009; Squire, 2006), they also create new and unique challenges for teachers. One challenge stems from the fact that students usually play videogames individually and reach different points in the game at different times, making whole-class conversations difficult to structure. This personalization of game experience may act as both a benefit and a challenge to student engagement. Additionally, teachers are often unsure about how to support students to share their thinking without the traditional artifacts of worksheets or overhead projectors. As a consequence, the mismatch between current pedagogical practice and the practices afforded (or demanded) by new technologies creates barriers to integration into classrooms (Ertmer, 2005; Straub, 2009). Integrating immersive technologies appears to be significantly different than adopting more superficial forms of technology, such as word processing or spreadsheets. These superficial additions are frequent and common, as the technical

supplements can easily be added or removed without altering content. More permanent, irreversible changes require a commitment to profoundly change one's practice (Cuban, 1993; Ertmer, 1999, 2005). As a consequence, integrating immersive technologies into schools is not simply a matter of making those technologies available. Instead, like every other reform that has the potential to change classroom practice, it will be important to work closely with teachers and school communities in order to develop a vision of what successful integration in classrooms looks like.

The new forms of expertise demanded by new technologies have been referred to as *Technological Pedagogical Content Knowledge* (TPACK). Mishra and Koehler (2006) define TPACK as "the knowledge of the existence, components, and capabilities of various technologies as they are used in teaching and learning settings" (p. 1028). Differing from technology experts like technicians or engineers who need to have an understanding of technologies themselves, teachers are additionally required to possess knowledge of how their *teaching* can be altered or enhanced with the various technological affordances. The idea of Technological Pedagogical Content Knowledge builds from the work of Shulman (1986), who clarified that teachers need to use several different knowledge bases simultaneously in order to teach effectively. He illuminated the difference between content specific knowledge (i.e., mathematics, biology, grammar) and pedagogical knowledge (i.e., classroom management, curriculum design, instruction), and observed that several teacher education programs focused on either pedagogy or content, but not their intersection. Troubled by this dichotomy, Shulman established the concept of Pedagogical Content Knowledge (PCK) in order to highlight the complex ways teachers transform content so that it can be comprehensible for others and useful for teaching. As 21st century technology education initiatives have allowed for technology to be easily accessed in classrooms, it became clear that technology added a new dimension to teachers' pedagogical content knowledge, thus motivating the development of the construct of TPACK.

As mentioned above, the use of new technologies in the classroom creates a fundamental shift in traditional pedagogical practice. Traditional methods of teaching, such as giving lectures and reading from textbooks, often produce a linear experience, while immersive games are designed to support a non-linear individual trajectory. When using immersive games, the teacher is no longer the only source of information. Teachers must adapt their style of teaching to guide students and provide them with tools to explore, while attuning students' attention to meaningful features within the game environment and within the classroom (Baylor & Ritchie, 2002; Wheeler, 2001). It is important to note that technologies in the classroom do not diminish the importance of the teacher; educational games alone, because of their complexity, benefit tremendously from teacher support. Indeed, simply using new technologies does not always generate deep understandings, as the actions of a teacher are vital to maximizing the potential of any new technology in the classroom. Teachers must help students engage with the technology, but also understand its relation to the greater context in which it is situated (Squire et al., 2001). In the case of immersive games, the teacher must help students engage with the narrative and content of the game, but also connect game play to real world contexts. In this way, teachers can promote reflection on game-play experiences, critical thinking skills, and collaboration, to prepare children for their lives outside of school.

If videogames require such dramatic changes in classroom practice, one might ask why introducing them in the classroom is worthwhile. Immersive educational games create several opportunities for student engagement that are frequently lacking in traditional schooling. Commercial games have been documented to support rich discussions and complex strategy use among players, the development of productive new in-game identities,

and opportunities for intense collaboration (Gee, 2003; Shaffer, 2006; Steinkuehler, 2006, Squire, 2006). In particular, the immersive context can embed students' inquiry in contexts that can have consequence, thus transforming targeted concepts from rules to be remembered to tools that can be applied. Immersive virtual games seek to offer a form of participation similar to that found in the real world, in that in order to successfully use content such as measures of center, one must be a competent statistician, but also have a rich contextual knowledge base in knowing *when* and *how* to use that content knowledge. Instead of filling out worksheets or completing story problems, content in immersive games is embedded in rich problematic story lines, which is extracted as the students interact with non-player characters and other embedded objects.

In addition, the fantasy of online videogames can serve as legitimate feedback for students' thinking; rather than having to look to a teacher for whether one's solution is accurate, the situational context can change in response to students' decisions, thus pushing back on students' thinking and actions. To be successful, students will not be able to simply fill out answers on worksheet, but must become an active participant playing within the rules of the game so that they may effectively discern how content knowledge maybe used as a tool in resolving the conflict (Barab & Roth, 2006; Salen & Zimmerman, 2004). In immersive games, students take on particular roles and engage various plot lines, which can evolve and change based on the choices that they make. Overall, games allow people to create and recreate new identities or roles, which can result in powerful motivation and deep learning (Gee, 2003).

OVERVIEW OF THE CASES

In what follows, we present two sets of contrasting cases; one that draws from two classrooms using a persuasive writing unit called *Modern*

Prometheus, and a second that draws from two classrooms using a mathematics activity about coordinate plotting called *Crypto Coordinates*. Both activities take place within the immersive videogame *Quest Atlantis*.

Our analysis considers videotapes of whole-class discussion and focuses particularly on the ways that conversations engaged both the content and context of the activities. In particular, we have attended to the kinds of *opportunities to learn* (Greeno & Gresalfi, 2008; Gresalfi, 2009) that are afforded through the whole-class discussions, and have chosen teacher cases that offer illuminative contrasts in terms of those opportunities. With the goal of trying to understand the role of whole-class discussions in mediating the experience of the videogame, we have chosen exchanges that represent both more and less productive examples of whole-class discussions. In selecting these episodes, our goal is not to make a claim about particular teachers being more or less effective overall, but rather to illuminate teacher moves that can serve to enhance student learning in the context of using immersive videogames.

In analyzing these cases, we first transcribed the episodes, including both teacher and student utterances. We then looked at the content of exchanges between students and the teacher, leveraging methods of discourse analysis (Gee, 1999). The goal in this fine-grained analysis was to more closely examine how the whole class discussion in general, and the teachers' orchestration of it in particular, created opportunities to learn the content targeted by the curriculum. Below we present first contrasting cases from the *Modern Prometheus* unit, and then cases from the *Crypto Coordinates* unit. We discuss the differences between the kinds of opportunities to learn presented in these cases, and then discuss successful practices that could be seen across the specific curricula.

Attuning Attention in the Modern Prometheus Unit

Videogames have both the benefit and drawback of being extremely complex – they offer players unparalleled freedom to test contextual boundaries, and opportunities to try on different roles or creatively navigate though non-linear trajectories to accomplish in-game goals. In other words, there's a lot to see, and many interesting things to explore anywhere that an avatar can go. Part of the purpose of videogames is to support and celebrate this exploration, as it is a key element of problem solving. This is one reason why immersive games are so appealing and entertaining for students. On the other hand, these very features of game play, if not constrained, can be a pedagogical and instructional nightmare for teachers. Specifically, this complexity can create an opportunity for students to, at times, overlook key ideas that could serve to structure their game play more effectively. Due to the complexity and diversity of action afforded in immersive videogames, it often helps if teachers don't simply set students free in the game without first orienting them to some key actions and ideas that they might want to keep in mind. When this is done well, an opening discussion does not become a set of instructions, but rather serves to set an intention for the students, helping to frame their upcoming activity.

Teachers can play a significant role in *attuning* students to particular aspects of the game that are especially relevant for their learning. The notion of attunement is drawn from ecological psychology. Gibson (1979) theorized that individuals perceive problems or opportunities for action (affordances) in relation to their ability to act upon those opportunities (effectivities). In order for action occur, the individual will initially have to perceive how the context is bidding for action while simultaneously perceiving how he/she can use their available effectivities to act upon the context. The act of perceiving an affordance requires the individual to discern, within a com-

Figure 1. Image of Ingolstadt from the Modern Prometheus Unit

plex situation, which contextual information is useful and which information insignificant. On the other hand, if an individual has the relevant effectives to act within a particular context, but fails to perceive a need for action, then no action will occur (Barab & Roth, 2006). Attunement can therefore be understood to be the process by which an individual comes to be able to act on affordance-effectivity pairings.

In the following section, we will discuss the importance of teachers attuning students to particular affordances in complex immersive game contexts. The cases below illustrate how two teachers leveraged curriculum materials and whole class discussions differently to attune their students to aspects of the game that have pedagogical significance. The cases come from a 4th grade and 7th grade classroom that were using an activity about persuasive writing, called *Modern Prometheus*. Both teachers had previous experience using Quest Atlantis, although the Modern Prometheus unit was new to both teachers.

Background on the Modern Prometheus Unit

In the Modern Prometheus unit, inspired by Mary Shelley's *Frankenstein*, students are presented with issues concerning medical ethics and consider concepts such as whether the ends justify the means and the nature of human existence as they explore a town affected by a disastrous plague (see Figure 1 for an image of Plague World). Questers come to Ingolstadt as investigative reporters and learn that the town is not only suffering from the terrible effects of a plague, but is divided over an issue of medical ethics. A character named Dr. Frank is working hard to find a cure and save the town, but his methods are thought by some to be unethical and immoral. Questers are soon drawn into this conflict when they are asked to investigate the problem and write a persuasive article for the local paper. Students learn the techniques of persuasive writing and how to construct a 5-paragraph essay during their explorations, and those skills will be put to the test when the fates of the doctor and his creation depend on their decision.

The Modern Prometheus unit includes embedded persuasive writing scaffolds which serve as progress check-points throughout the game. To simulate real-world investigative reporter activity, students are asked to navigate throughout the entire town of Ingolstadt and collect evidence from fictional characters that will support their thesis. The purpose of this activity is for students to make connections between the evidence they are collecting and how it might support their argument. What is complex about this activity is that students are not bound by a step-by-step trajectory; students can explore the town however they would like, and can easily get involved in the aesthetics of the game without thinking carefully about different perspectives that the townspeople might have. It is for this reason that students are positioned as investigative reporters—to help structure their exploration through Ingolstadt—but this positioning can easily be lost in the complexity of the immersive experience. It is useful therefore if teachers help to attune students to opportunities to act within their role of investigative reporter, help locate non-player characters that they can interview, and navigate through the 3D space.

Example 1: Launching the Unit

The launch of an activity is the first key element of supporting and attuning student engagement. The launch sets the tone of the activity, and creates a set of expectations for what students will need to do. In the following launch of Modern Prometheus, the teacher asked the students to read the opening letter (an excerpt can be found in Figure 2). She then held a discussion that helped the students attune to and define their role in the game storyline: to act as investigative reporters (as opposed to other enjoyable but unproductive activities, such as playing tag with other avatars). What is important to note in the excerpt below is the way the teacher used the discussion to attune students to their role as investigative reporters, and

more specifically, what playing that role would require (i.e., "search for a reason to a problem…" "someone who finds clues…"). In this way, the discussion established a purpose for students' engagement, and helped them determine how to proceed in the game.

Ms.S: Now from reading this, you should be able to understand role you're going to take once you enter the world of Ingolstadt. What role are you going to play?

St1: Maggie?

Ms.S: No.

St2: The son?

Ms.S: What?

St2: The son?

Ms.S: No… What role are going you going to play? What is your job? (Immediately, several student's hands are raised, and can hear them making "ooooh" sound.) What's your job?

St3: You're umm writing a letter, um your going to talk to the people about and helping Dr. Frank with the ingredients and then your going to write a letter to mom about what's happening and umm… that's all.

Ms.S: Ok, if you could come up with a, come with a job description or a title of a particular job you are going to be fulfilling what would it be? St4?

St4: An investigator?

Ms.S: An investigator, very good. What does an investigator do? What does it do…St5?

St5: He investigates

Ms.S: Well yeah, well you can't answer a question with the same word. What does that mean? What does that mean to investigate?

St6: Look for clues.

Ms.S: Look for clues.

St7: You have to find clues in order to find out what people are talking about.

Ms.S: You're going to search out the reason why there is a problem. Yes. Who else? Who

Figure 2. Excerpt of introductory letter from Modern Prometheus unit

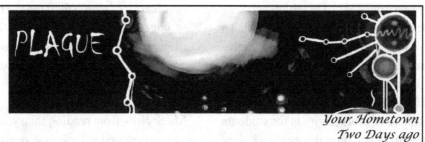

Your Hometown
Two Days ago

My Dear Child,
As your mother, I have seen you grow into a thoughtful person who makes good choices. I am so proud that you have decided to become an investigative reporter—your skills in gathering facts, examining the evidence, and writing persuasive articles to convince others will help so many people. You will need to use all of these skills when you complete your journalism course in Ingolstadt. You will be making some very tough decisions that will affect an entire village—one that means a lot to me. Oh dear, I am getting ahead of myself. I should first tell you what I know about the troubles in this village!
......
When you wrote and told me you would be finishing your apprenticeship as an investigative reporter by writing about the plague in Ingolstadt, I was so relieved, because I have become very worried about Victor— especially since his last letter to me. I have included the letter for you to read. There is something in it that worries me....Dr. Victor Frank saved your life... this is our chance to repay him! However, you must of course use your own good judgment and your ability to evaluate different points of view—I don't want to influence you too much. I have contacted several people in the town to be on the lookout for you and to help you gather information for your article. Please be safe, and remember that your opinions and how you write the article may help the entire village of Ingolstadt!
Watch for my letters, darling. With all of my love,
Mom

else? Other side of the room? What does an investigator do?

St8: Um, somebody who finds clues and tries to piece together mystery

Ms.S: Ok, could be people who find clues and put together a mystery. Alright. Good…Yes.

Ms.S: … You've been given a letter, two letters that will help you identify what your purpose is. Does this help you? When you go into the world and as you get started? You think maybe? Why St3?

St3: Your mom had had some people helping.

Ms.S: Ok, so you know there is already some people within the world who will help you, who are your friends. Right? Does it help to know what it is you're supposed to be doing before hand?

Sts: Yes.

Through this discussion the teacher defined the role that students were to play as they entered Ingolstadt, and attuned them to their purpose in the game: to be investigative reporters who "look for clues," "search for reasons to the problem," and "…piece together a mystery." Such attunement does not define how students will engage the game upon entering the world, but helps to frame the kinds of activities that they are likely to try, how they are likely to explore, and how they will regulate their own behavior. In this way, the game can become not simply an opportunity to have fun and be entertained, but also to begin to engage content-specific ideas (in this case, building an argument based on your investigation of a situation, and leverage that argument in order to persuade others of your opinion). Indeed, when interviewed, students described their intention and position in the game as people who were on a mission to help change Ingolstadt. When explicitly asked, "What's going in on in Ingolstadt?" students often described the conflict or situation in terms of a first person role, as a protagonist, who was there to fulfill a mission with the goal of finding a cure to stop the plague.

Jared: I'm pretty much there to find a cure and stop people from dying.

Alejandro: Um there's like this plague and people are getting sick and possibly dying and we're trying to go and um like people to stop the plague.

Emily: Well, I want the whole town of Ingolstadt to be better because I want him to find a cure…

Simone: I'm an investigative reporter, and my mother's name is Maggie, and she lived in the town where I was raised. So everybody knows me because of my mom know where I work at in the big city and all that junk. So, I come here and meet Scoop, and he's like the head of the newspaper and basically what I'm learning from this is persuasive writing.

Example 2: Supporting the Unit

Teachers can also help attune students to key ideas in game play by reflecting on experiences they have had. When such support occurs in the midst of students' game play, it can help students

to notice key ideas or events that might have otherwise passed them by. In this way, discussions that occur in the midst of the unit can help students to make sense of some of the complexity that they are experiencing. The following excerpt comes from a whole-class conversation that took place after the students had read the introductory letter and had some time in the game to explore the world and meet some of the characters.

Ms L: …So we're going to have a conversation about it. So, over here we have the children who have chosen con and over here we have pro and we're going to be talking about the story. Before we know what pro and con stand for, let's have somebody tell the story. Now, here is how I want to do it. I don't want somebody talking for a half-hour, because you could, couldn't you? We're going to have somebody make one statement so you want to think sequentially. One statement and opening statement about what the story is about. Then the next person I call needs to be listening very carefully to what the first person said and build on what they said. Don't repeat it, and don't jump so far ahead that you leave big gaps. You know what I am saying? Try to say the next step…Ok, tell me the opening statement, what is this story about? St1, start for us.

St1: Well our Mom, Maggie, sent us to Ingolstadt to complete a mission.

Ms. L: Next step. Next step St2.

St2: There's a plague and the whole town is affected, and were supposed to find out more about the antidote.

Ms. L: Good, next step. St3.

St3: Umm, so we go there and we investigate around there.

Ms L:: Go and investigate, good. You're really good at this. Alright, next step after you investigate then what happens? (Indicates to a boy that he had the floor)

St4: Well, um you talk to some of the people about the plague and um we talk about our thesis.

Ms L: Ok, you talk to some of the people about the plague and then you talk about the idea of a thesis. Ok, what's next.

St5: Um, then you talk to Scoop (NPC) about not teaching fish how to swim.

Ms L: Ok, now Scoop comes in. Who's Scoop? Lyle who's Scoop?

St6: The editor of the newspaper.

Ms. L: He is the editor of the Bugle newspaper. Why does Scoop want to talk to us? What does he want to talk to us about? Rachael?

St8: Because his writer is sick and he wants us to help him finish the other writer's article.

Ms. L: Ok, he needs some help and apparently we are what?

St9: Investigative reporters.

Ms. L: Investigative reporters. So we've talked to people about the plague, and we've heard something about a pro and con thesis, and then what? Eva.

St10: So then we decide which side we want to be on, and around the village and gather evidence to support your thesis.

Ms. L: Ok, when she says which side you want to be on. What does she mean by that? When she says, "What side do you want to be on?"

St11: Um, there's two sides and the sides are um, the first one is con, and the con side is if, the doctor has a creation and on the con side they want you to stop the experiments on the creation because the creation has rights and its pretty much like a human being. It's just treated wrong because it doesn't look like a human being. And the second side is pro, and is to keep the doctor working on his experiment to cure the plague.

Ms. L: Ok, so, you've done a really good job summarizing the background how we got there and what we did once we got there and we talked a little bit about our role as investigative writers and make a thesis decision. Everybody got all that?

This whole-class conversation occurred after the students spent some time in Ingolstadt, and had an opportunity to become immersed in the narrative of the unit and explore the world. At this point, the teacher called the students together for a whole-class discussion to review what they had done so far, and in particular, to help them think about and process what they had learned. The teacher began the discussion by framing its purpose: to talk about the point of view (pro versus con) that the students have chosen to take in terms of the argument they want to advance. The teacher first ensured that the students had met key characters (the editor of the newspaper who has given them the assignment, other characters in the space). She then attuned the students to the purpose of their investigation, which is to form an opinion and then convince others of the reasonableness of that opinion. In so doing, the discussion served two purposes: to ensure that all students have access to the main ideas of the game, a form of procedural attunement, and to ensure that students understand why they are in Ingolstadt, and use that information in order to complete the assignment, a form of conceptual attunement.

Building on Opportunities to Learn in the Crypto Coordinates Mission

A good game is designed to include multiple opportunities to learn particular skills and procedures as well as strategies and new conceptual understandings. However, game elements alone do not provide all possible opportunities for learning; the teacher plays a significant role in pulling out and emphasizing significant ideas that might get lost, overlooked, or misunderstood in the midst of game play. Class discussions allow students to informally share their experiences in the game, debate with their classmates, and interrogate aspects of the content they are learning. Further, classroom discussions involve the entire class, making the information potentially available to any student who is listening. Teachers may use class discussions to pull out the big ideas from the game by pushing on content understanding and connecting game experiences to the real world.

Opportunities to learn only become opportunities if they are *recognized* and *realized*. The previous section focused on the role of the teacher in helping students to *recognize* particularly significant elements of the game through the process of attunement, helping students to take on a role that would shape their game play in meaningful ways. Realizing opportunities to learn requires more than simply recognizing them, however—one must also be able to act on them. As an example, an activity like Modern Prometheus that invites students to use persuasive writing as a means of convincing others is only effective if students are able to understand and use the tools of persuasive writing. This opportunity to learn is often embedded in the game. However, the teacher plays a significant role in pulling out opportunities to learn and helping students to realize and act on those opportunities. In addition, class discussions connect opportunities to learn in game world to those that might be found in the real world. As students learn content within the game narrative, they may connect the same information to the larger context of the real world (promoting transfer to that larger real world context). While it is true that some students construct this link for themselves (by relating game choices to their real life), the teacher may help construct this link for other students, or further strengthen this link for everyone.

In the following section, we discuss the importance of teachers' use of whole-class discussions to help students to realize opportunities to learn in the game context. The cases below illustrate how two teachers leveraged classroom discussions to pull out opportunities to learn in the game. These cases come from two 6th grade classrooms that were using an activity about coordinate plotting, taught in the context of archeology and navigation of a magical island. The two teachers presented

here are 6th grade math instructors in the same junior high school. Neither teacher had used Quest Atlantis previously, but the teachers attended the same Quest Atlantis training sessions. In addition to teacher training, both classes had a member of the Quest Atlantis team visit their classroom to help model teaching with Quest Atlantis.

Background on Crypto Coordinates Mission

Crypto Coordinates is an activity designed to teach students about coordinate plotting. The game takes place in the context of an archeological dig on a magical island, and begins with a message in a bottle from an archeologist named Dr. Leopold who has been trapped by the island. Students must take action, using coordinate plotting as a means of successfully navigating though the island's magical jungle in order to rescue Dr. Leo, before its too late. Students are introduced to the mathematical rules of coordinate plotting, and the protective restrictions of the magical island. They must make choices as they continue through the jungle. For example, students must choose whether to take artifacts (earning money in the game), or leave the artifacts in their place (gaining the island's trust). Mathematically, the quester must plot the location of any artifact they find using a map, and use the same map to navigate within a winding path to avoid angering the island (see Figure 3 for an image of Cryptojungle).

Opportunities to learn were designed into the game in multiple ways. First, each character either emphasized a key idea relating to coordinate plotting, created an opportunity for students to practice coordinate plotting, or highlighted the relevance of plotting in other contexts. As an example, the first character that the students encounter, Archie, introduce them to the idea of coordinate plotting by first explaining why he finds it useful (in the context of archeology, to be able to mark precisely where artifacts are found), and second by introducing them to the procedures associated

Figure 3. Image of the island from the Crypto Coordinates unit

with coordinate plotting. Later characters contrast the conventions of coordinate plotting with other plotting conventions (for example, navigating using the directions of north, south, east, and west), thus creating an opportunity for students to consider how such rules allow people to communicate with each other. Still other characters (like Luka, discussed below) afford opportunities for students to use coordinate plotting as a tool for accomplishing desired ends.

Examples 3 and 4: Contrasting Opportunities to Learn

As previously mentioned, the non-linear game experience creates challenges for teachers structuring whole-class discussions. Many teachers think it is important to "take the pulse" of the class to see where students are in the mission (teachers can determine this information from the teacher toolkit associated with QA, but many prefer to assess this more informally). However, learning about where students are in the mission can become either a procedural task to ensure that people are moving along, or an opportunity for future discussion and immersion into the narrative. Below, we contrast two whole-class discussions, both of

which begin by asking students about what point they've reached in the game. However, what is distinctive is how the two conversations unfold: the first stays firmly in the area of procedural engagement, while the second becomes an opportunity for deeper discussion about the content.

Example 3: This excerpt is of a conversation that occurred at the end of the second day of class. The teacher (Ms. B) opened the discussion with a bid for someone to summarize the activities of the day. The tasks that the students mention are listed on their "mission page"; a guideline for what needs to be accomplished in the game (see Figure 4). One student responded to this question by reporting on her specific activities, although not the meaning of those activities. The teacher took up this response and began to take a poll about the point that students have reached during that day's work.

Ms. B: What'd you guys do today on the computer? Erin?

S1: I was at the part where I had to talk to the owl. I did one wrong and I had to go back and fix it and then I had to turn it off.

Ms. B: So, you had to turn it off just now? (student nods) So, you've talked to the owl.

Figure 4. Mission Page from the Crypto Coordinates Unit

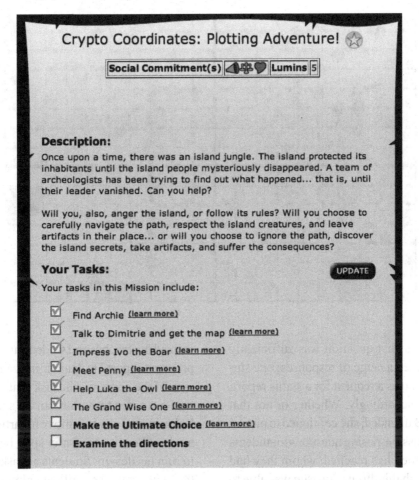

How many of you have talked to the owl? [Students raise hands]

S2: I'm talking to him right now.

Ms. B: You're talking to him right now? How many of you have gotten to the boar? Pig? [Students raise hands]

Ms. B: He's hard to catch….A little fast. How about the skunk? Have you all talked to the skunk?

S3: Yeah, I'm trying to find the Grand Wise One.

Ms. B: Oh, wow. Who's going to find the Grand Wise One? [Students raise hands]

S4: I'm heading there now.

Ms. B: Just a few. Yes?

S5: I found a little doll.

Ms. B: You found a doll? Have you guys been finding artifacts?

S6: I found this talking statue.

Ms. B: Have you encountered the talking tree? How many of you were kicked out of the jungle? [Students raise hands]

Ms. B: Well, tomorrow, we're going to be working on the same thing. And, like I said earlier, we might be finished with this by Friday, which is a lot faster than I thought we would, and it's possible that some of you may be finished sooner. So, I'll let you go back and do the OTAK ones when you've finished. Very good job.

Figure 5. Shifting berry task from the Crypto Coordinates unit

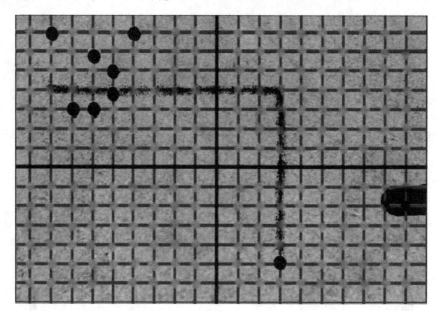

The teacher's first question was sufficiently open that it invited a range of responses; one student interpreted it as a request for a status report, and responded accordingly. Whether or not that was what Ms. B intended, she continued to pursue this line of discussion, posing questions to students about how far they had reached, whom they had met, etc. Through this discussion, she was able to determine roughly how far students had progressed through the mission, and ensured that no one was hopelessly confused, but otherwise did not highlight additional information that students might have encountered in the game. On the one hand, the game itself is quite narratively rich, and thus the teacher might have felt that she did not need to engage additional discussions with the students in order to support their reasoning. However, in limiting her discussion with the students to their progress in the game, significant opportunities to learn were missed.

Example 4: In contrast, another teacher, Mr. K, organized a similar conversation quite differently, although he also opened the discussion by asking "where people are." However, the conversation did not remain at the level of status updates, and instead the teacher and students used the students' progress reports to launch into a deeper discussion of the content. The task that the teacher and students refer to below can be seen in figure 5; Luka the owl wants to move his artwork (a portrait made of berries) to a safer spot, but doesn't want to ruin his design. Students are asked to use what they know about coordinate plotting to move the design and ensure that it looks identical in its new location.

Mr. K: Ok, just listen, please. Before you open the computers, so, we've been working on this for 3 days. On our fourth day, I'm curious to know where people are. Isaac told me he's talking to the owl. What's the owl's name? Do you remember? Luka, right? So, is anybody else to the owl, or has already seen the owl?

[Students raise hands].

Mr. K: Ok, so a handful of people. What does the owl want you to do?

S1: Fix his artwork and put it under the tree.

Mr. K: Yeah. Fix his artwork. So, he's got this arrangement of some sort of berries and he wants them moved to a different location based on specific rules. What were the rules?

S2: You have to keep them in the same place, move them by 11, and down by 9.

Mr. K: Ok, so the one thing it wanted you to do, and I don't remember it's something like this (draws some berry arrangement on the board) that has to be moved down here. And, how far did you say they had to move?

S2: 11 across, 9 down.

Mr. K: 11 across and 9 down (draws approximate location). Did anybody figure out a different way to go about moving these? I don't know if I talked to anybody in here about this. Let's say it was like this, to make it easier to draw (makes the picture just two dots). Anybody figure out a different way to move them without having to count 11 across and 9 down? Like, let's say this berry is this one right here. And, you've got the grid lines (draws them in). Any other ideas on how you could move this? How would you know where to put it? First of all, I don't have the grid lines. I just drew this up really quickly, but I don't need to count 11 across and 9 down. If I know this one is here, where does this one have to go?

S3: Right above it.

Mr. K: Right above it?

S3: Yeah. If you look on that, it has to be one up, I mean two up.

Mr. K: Yeah, so there were certain things where you just had to compare the location. If this one is located there, no matter where it is, this one is always going to be two above it. So, some people realized that you could just count and make sure they're in the same arrangement. That ended up being 11 across and 9 down for everything. As long as they are moved the same amount of spaces, they're going to end up in the same arrangement.

Mr. K launched the whole class discussion with a similar question to Ms. B by asking "where

people are." However, unlike Ms. B, he didn't stop after determining the students' progress; he extended the discussion by asking about elements of the task (in this case, what Luka the owl wants the students to do). Mr. K first reviewed the Luka activity by drawing a grid on the board and reviewing the rules Luka provided. In so doing, he emphasized an opportunity to learn that was present in the game, but which might have been confusing or unclear to the students. Specifically, students needed to calculate where a berry would be located once it had moved a set number of spaces. It is important here to contrast the move that Mr. K made in this discussion with how the discussion in Ms. B's classroom unfolded. In Ms. B's classroom, if students were confused about Luka, the purpose of the assignment, or the logistics of the task, they would have had to ask questions of clarification—Ms. B did not create opportunities for students to learn beyond elements of the game. In contrast, Mr. K reviewed the activity and presented it in a different way, thus enhancing the opportunity to learn that was present in the game.

Additionally, Mr. K created a new opportunity to learn that was only implicit in the assignment, which he initiated by asking "did anybody figure out another way to go about moving these?" In what followed, Mr. K introduced an alternative to solving the Luka problem, which involves realizing that the relative positions of the berries will not change if they are all moved the exact same amount, and therefore students do not have to count eleven spaces across and nine spaces down for each berry. Rather, they can look at the starting picture to determine where each berry will go, relative to the first berry that was moved. Although some students discovered this relative positioning for themselves, for others, Mr. K's intervention created a novel opportunity to learn about unchanging relative positions of the berries as they are moved across the grid.

CONCLUSION AND RECOMMENDATIONS

The examples of whole-class discussions within this chapter illustrate the important role that teachers must continue to play in supporting student learning, even as educational technology becomes increasingly sophisticated and complex. As videogames enter the classroom, an enormous potential exists for new types of learning and engagement. Games create vast activity systems with their own rules, constraints and affordances. As students interact within these systems, they experience real consequences and legitimate feedback within game play. However, as games provide new types of experiences and learning for students, teachers must fill new roles in supporting new types of engagement. Our goal has been to illustrate that, although complex technologies create significant new learning experiences, they do not replace the role of the teacher in the classroom. Indeed, we have argued that the teacher's presence and active guidance when using complex technologies is essential for supporting high-quality learning. Thus, teachers' roles in classrooms using complex technologies is in no way diminished, but instead, must change.

It should be clear that teachers in the examples shared do not determine or control students' engagement with the game, but rather, they support and enhance it. In the examples shared from the context of the *Modern Prometheus* curriculum, we highlighted the ways that teachers can *attune* students to significant aspects of the game both before the game begins, and while students are playing. These acts of attunement help students to understand the role that they play within the game, and can frame their participation so that they can be purposeful and intentional as they move through the complex game space. Notably, in the examples shared above, both teachers' discussions were embedded in the context of the game narrative itself—neither teacher attempted to focus on content only, therefore turning the narrative of the game into a secondary part of students' engagement. Instead, they leveraged the game narrative in order to create a purpose for students' play; a purpose that could then serve to frame students' content engagement.

We also highlighted the important role of the teacher in enhancing and extending opportunities to learn that are built into the game design. In the example above, Ms. B asked students to share their experiences within the game, but did not push the conversation further. She relied on the game to teach the important concepts, while providing only minimal support. In contrast, Mr. K used the game only as a conversational prompt, pushing the conversation forward by clearing up mathematical misconceptions and extending opportunities to learn. The difference between what students are likely to learn in these two classrooms is significant; although students in both classrooms benefit from the designed opportunities to learn in the game, it is when teachers take on the curriculum as their own that learning can really take off.

The examples of whole-class discussions shared in this chapter were particularly artful in that teachers did not pit themselves against the game (asking students to ignore the context, or focusing only on content in discussions). Instead, teachers used the context of the game to leverage content understanding. In this way, the teacher and the whole-class discussions together contribute to an integrative experience that involves the immersive videogame and elements of the real world, thus helping to form links between in-game play and out-of-game learning.

REFERENCES

Barab, S. A., Gresalfi, M. S., & Arici, A. (2009). Transformational play: Why educators should care about games. *Educational Leadership, 67*(1), 76–80.

Barab, S. A., & Roth, W. M. (2006). Curriclum-based ecosystems: Supporting knowing from an ecological perspective. *Educational Researcher*, *35*(5), 3–13. doi:10.3102/0013189X035005003

Barab, S. A., Zuiker, S., Warren, S., Hickey, D., Ingram-Goble, A., Kwon, E., Kouper, I., & Herring, S. (2007). Situationally embodied curriculum: Relating formalisms and contexts. *Science Education*.

Baylor, A., & Ritchie, D. (2002). What factors facilitate teacher skill, teacher morale, and perceived student learning in technology-using classrooms? *Computers & Education*, *39*, 395–414. doi:10.1016/S0360-1315(02)00075-1

Cross, D., Gresalfi, M. S., & Hudson, R. A. (Manuscript submitted for publication). Building bridges between content and context in mathematics classrooms. *Mathematics Teaching in the Middle School*.

Cuban, L. (1993). Computers meet classroom: Classroom wins. *Teachers College Record*, *95*, 185–210.

Ertmer, P. A. (1999). Addressing first- and second-order barriers to change: Strategies for technology integration. *Educational Technology Research and Development*, *47*(4), 47–61. doi:10.1007/BF02299597

Ertmer, P. A. (2005). Teacher pedagogical beliefs: The final frontier in our quest for technology integration? *Educational Technology Research and Development*, *53*(4), 25–39. doi:10.1007/BF02504683

Gee, J. P. (1999). *An introduction to discourse analysis: Theory and method*. London, UK: Routledge.

Gee, J. P. (2003). *What video games have to teach us about learning and literacy*. New York, NY: Palgrave/Macmillan.

Gibson, J. J. (1979). *The ecological approach to visual perception*. Boston, MA: Houghton Mifflin.

Greeno, J. G., & Gresalfi, M. S. (2008). Opportunities to learn in practice and identity. In Moss, P. A., Pullin, D. C., Gee, J. P., Haertel, E. H., & Young, L. J. (Eds.), *Assessment, equity, and opportunity to learn* (pp. 170–199). New York, NY: Cambridge University Press.

Gresalfi, M. S. (2009). Taking up opportunities to learn: Constructing dispositions in mathematics classrooms. *Journal of the Learning Sciences*, *18*, 327–369. doi:10.1080/10508400903013470

Hickey, D., Ingram-Goble, A., & Jameson, E. M. (2009). Designing assessments and assessing designs in virtual educational environments. *Journal of Science Education and Technology*, *18*(2), 187–208. doi:10.1007/s10956-008-9143-1

Mishra, P., & Koehler, M. J. (2006). Technological pedagogical content knowledge: A framework for teacher knowledge. *Teachers College Record*, *108*(6), 1017–1054. doi:10.1111/j.1467-9620.2006.00684.x

Report, P. (2008). Teens, video games and civics. Retrieved from http://pewresearch.org/pubs/953/

Salen, K., & Zimmerman, E. (2004). *Rules of play*. Cambridge, MA: MIT Press.

Shaffer, D. W. (2006). Epistemic frames for epistemic games. *Computers & Education*, *46*(3), 223. doi:10.1016/j.compedu.2005.11.003

Shulman, L. (1986). Those who understand: Knowledge growth in teaching. *Educational Researcher*, *15*, 4–14.

Squire, K. D. (2006). From content to context: Videogames as designed experiences. *Educational Researcher*, *35*(8), 19–29. doi:10.3102/0013189X035008019

Squire, K. D., McKinster, J. G., Barnett, M., Leuhmann, A. L., & Barab, S. A. (2001). Designed curriculum and local culture: Acknowledging the primacy of classroom culture. *Science Education, 87*(4), 468–489. doi:10.1002/sce.10084

Steinkuehler, C. A. (2006). Massively multiplayer onine video gaming as participation in a discourse. *Mind, Culture, and Activity, 13*(1), 38–52. doi:10.1207/s15327884mca1301_4

Straub, E. T. (2009). Understanding technology adoption: Theory and future directions for informal learning. *Review of Educational Research, 79*(2), 625–649. doi:10.3102/0034654308325896

Vygotsky, L. S. (1967). Play and its role in the mental development of the child. *Social Psychology, 5*, 6–18.

Wheeler, S. (2001). Information and Communication Technologies and the changing role of the teacher. *Journal of Educational Media, 26*(1). doi:10.1080/135816500120069292

Chapter 18
Constructing an Experience in a Virtual Green Home

Mary Ann Mengel
Pennsylvania State University, USA

ABSTRACT

Undergraduate students in an environmental science course learned to make environmentally-conscious decisions by visiting a virtual green home in Second Life (SL). One group of learners was immersed in a virtual field trip experience where they viewed evidence of green decisions in a virtual home. Another group studied the same content through a static website. Pre-test and post-test results for both groups demonstrate significant differences in scores after instruction. Results suggest a virtual world can provide an instructionally effective medium if instructors allow ample time and training for students to become familiar with the environment. Feedback from SL participants suggests that learners felt they had participated in an "experience." Instructional design considerations which focus on creating an educational experience involving active tasks and social interactions might best maximize the educational usage of a virtual world.

INTRODUCTION

Two sections of an undergraduate environmental science course participated in a study which compared instruction in Second Life with a static Web-based delivery method. One section studied green homes by visiting a Web site where

DOI: 10.4018/978-1-60960-545-2.ch018

they read descriptions and viewed photographs (control group, N=51). Their experience was grounded in decidedly Web 1.0 methodologies. The other section visited a virtual green home in SL and participated in related instructional activities (experimental group, N = 58). Pre-test and post-test data indicates that both groups showed significant differences in scores after instruction. When comparing the results of the two groups

Figure 1. Comparison of pre-test and post-test scores in experimental and control group

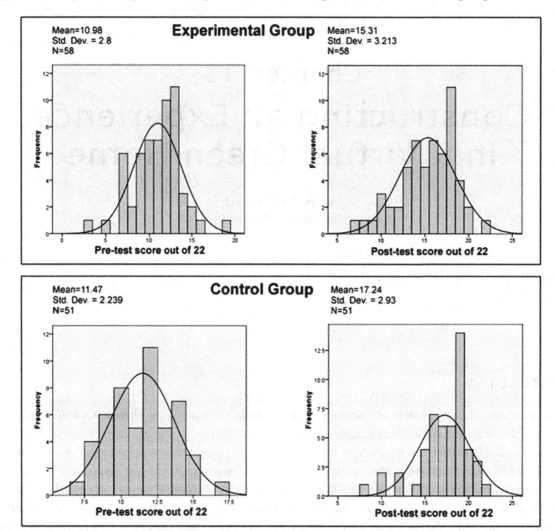

to each other, there was a statistically significant difference between the two groups' performances on pre-test and post-test scores, with the control group showing a greater difference.

The sample for this study consisted of undergraduate students enrolled in Biological Science 003, an introductory environmental science course, which fulfills a natural sciences general elective requirement. This course had previously been delivered in a traditional face-to-face format; although after adding the new online elements described in this chapter, the delivery method might be categorized as web-enhanced. The

level of outside-of-class online activities does not constitute the label of a hybrid course. Two sections of Bi Sc 003 were randomly assigned as the experimental group and control group.

Considerations for Site Design

Creating educational environments and activities within a 3D virtual world necessitates the exploration of new approaches within the field of instructional design—a paradigm shift from the conventions presented by standard models. At this point in history, there is not yet a large

Figure 2. Students visit the virtual green home

repository of best practices to guide early innovators, nor is there a common understanding among instructional designers regarding how to maximize instructional opportunities in a virtual world.

As educators venture into virtual worlds, sharp contrasts with traditional instruction become clear. Unlike traditional instruction delivered through a textbook or lecture where a voice of authority transmits the content to the student, 3D virtual worlds inherently allow content to be discovered and explored—creating an experience in which learners participate. The learners can be, in a virtual sense, physically immersed within their content, with the content surrounding them and becoming part of their environment. As the environment is explored, learners make choices about what to look at, where to move, who they will talk to, and how they will react to what is occurring around them. In the process, memories of experiences are formed, impressions are constructed, and reactions to the subject matter are generated. In response, learners select new directions to pursue based upon what has occurred. In a dynamically changing, interactive environment, learners are continually faced with an array of decisions regarding how they will choose to encounter the situations in which they are immersed. The sensation of being

physically, albeit virtually, immersed within the content can, by default, expand the realm of how knowledge might be assimilated. This ability to become immersed in the content differentiates the virtual world experience from the traditional classroom; likewise, the learners' distinct sense of a physical presence alongside remote classmates is unique when compared with other forms of online education, as well.

Defining the Objectives

This SL instructional activity and a corresponding instructional Web site were designed to expose students to ideas related to making green decisions in their own home. Learning objectives are for students to recognize the implications of their ecological footprint on the planet, to identify the lasting environmental implications of their decisions, and as a result to identify wise environmental choices related to building, decorating, maintaining and operating a home. These objectives, which parallel a growing global interest in green and sustainable living, are met by venturing beyond the traditional content of the course into a virtual environment.

To enhance the undergraduate environmental science course, a course-specific instructional site, in the form of a virtual green home, was designed, built and deployed in SL. During the course of the site's deployment, visitors were observed as they participated in the educational experience at the virtual home. Qualitative feedback on the mode of instruction was gathered through a survey of participants in both the experimental and control groups. Informal discussion with participants provided further insight into their impressions and reactions.

This engaging outside-of-class learning experience allows students to explore ideas related to green considerations and choices for their home by taking a virtual field trip to a green home. Rather than reading about choices that contribute to a green home, such as bamboo flooring and recycled glass countertops, which the control group did through an instructional Web site, students in the SL group wander through a three-dimensional green home where they search for and discover green solutions. In the process, they observe 3D visual representations of these solutions implemented in a home.

The introductory environmental science course is offered to two or three sections of students each semester. Each section consists of approximately 60 students. Most of the students fall into the age range of traditional undergraduates; however, several non-traditional aged students often take the course. The learners in this study represent a variety of majors and their pre-existing knowledge in the area of computer skills, gaming, and virtual worlds is varied. Within the experimental group, 11.8% of the learners had prior experience with online multi-player role playing games; 22% had heard of SL; only 6.9% had explored SL prior to this project. In the control group, 19% had prior experience with online multi-player role-playing games; 27% had heard of SL; and none had previously explored SL.

BACKGROUND

Perhaps the most fundamental benefit of using a virtual world for education is the provision of a shared venue where students at dispersed geographic locations can participate in synchronous instruction (Kemp & Haycock, 2008). However, in this situation, the students were not geographically dispersed from one another; therefore distance between participants was not a motivator for the chosen approach. In contrast, the distance between the campus and a real-world example of a green home and the time associated with a field trip could have contributed to the decision to develop a virtual site. An online visit conducted outside of class addressed logistical considerations. However, beyond logistics, the educational benefits afforded by an online multi-user virtual environment such as SL are much more far-reaching.

The potential educational value of virtual worlds emerges when geographically dispersed students and their instructor can visualize their own presence in relation to their peers and the environment, and the actions and reactions of online classmates are made visually apparent (DeLucia, Francese, Passero, & Tortora, 2009). Downes (2008) states, "learning... is a process of 'becoming' rather than a process of 'acquiring'" (¶ 55). As a result of virtual experiences, students can actively seek and assimilate the subject matter, rather than hope to have it transmitted to them through the efforts of an instructor or through words they read in a textbook.

To fully appreciate the potential advantages of the virtual world platform, it is valuable to consider factors which can contribute to student engagement in online learning in general. Alley and Jansak (2001) identify several factors which might impact student engagement in an online environment. The virtual world platform provides for several of these contributing elements to occur naturally. Learners construct knowledge through the act of exploration. Students are responsible for choosing their pathway through a learning experience which is unique to them. The array of choices and options can be intrinsically motivating. Each student chooses their own course of action during each individual visit to the site. The environment can provide for either social interaction or private exploration. During subsequent visits, the learner can choose an alternate pathway or elect to interact with a new group of concurrent visitors.

Childress and Braswell (2006) contend that a 3D virtual world such as SL allows for "highly collaborative learning opportunities anchored in real-world experiences" (p. 189). The level of interaction between users is enhanced because residents can see and understand their proximity to other avatars and objects. Rather than engaging in game play, visitors to SL participate in "open-ended opportunities for exploration and invention" (Kemp & Haycock, 2008, p. 91), creating new and seemingly limitless possibilities for learning experiences based on 3D technology. Not long ago, the prospect of creating instructional opportunities in a virtual world was not within the realm of possibilities for most educational institutions. Although the technology is now available, the best way to utilize this technology can be elusive for some instructional designers, yet the potential benefits are boundless.

Early adopters have found that a 3D virtual world can accommodate experiential activities that "not only helped to achieve learning outcomes but also… surpass course objectives" (Jarmon, Traphagan, & Mayrath, 2008, p. 166). In today's schools, concepts are often abstracted and removed from the situations to which they are relevant. Facts themselves are studied as self-contained entities (Barab, Hay, Barnett, & Squire, 2001). Within an immersive virtual world, facts can "exist" in the domain to which they pertain; the content does not need to be separated from the context. Students visually observe their avatar in a relation to the task in which they are participating. Learner interactions are not disembodied but visible to all participants (Kapp & O'Driscoll, 2007).

This intermingling of the learning content within its environment has fascinating implications for creating rich learning environments. Gaimster (2008) states, "It is the sense of presence, of feeling as if you are actually within the world that sets these environments apart from other web-based forms of communication" (p. 191). Prasolova-Førland (2008) states, "The proper balance between the atmosphere and functionality varies depending on the purpose, i.e. the former is more important in the worlds focusing on art and creativity while the latter is more crucial in the systems facilitating work and information retrieval" (p. 195). In this instructional context, it was critical that learners explore the entire virtual home and surrounding grounds to retrieve all relevant instructional content. The environment did not need to evoke aesthetic sensations; instead, the display and function of green elements drew comparison with their real-world counterparts.

Because a thorough tour of the site was required, learners are gently guided by visual cues which provide hints to assist with choosing an appropriate pathway. Subtle suggestions such as sidewalks, rock pathways, and doors guide learners; and more direct suggestions of a possible path, such as signs, automatic text chat messages, and an interactive map, help insure that learners discover all pertinent content.

Through a visit to a virtual world, learners create a level of understanding based upon the experiences in which they choose to participate. They construct their interpretation of the subject matter around the perceived reality of this experience. Downes (2008) contends that what we believe is real is something we have constructed—an artifact that we have created as a result of our experiences. He states, "the 'virtual' is every bit as real as the 'real' except that it's not physical" (¶ 20).

Figure 3. Students search for learning stations

BUILDING AN EXPERIENCE

Constructing an Activity

What does SL—or any multi-user 3D virtual environment—bring to course content that a traditional textbook and lecture cannot provide? At the most basic level, a multi-user virtual world removes the content from the textbook and makes it part of an "experience" in which the learner participates. As we live our lives, we remember our experiences as a series of snapshots, impressions, sounds, interactions, and conversations that become part of our memory. When we participate in an educational process rooted in "experience" we create new memories. The premise that learners will link these virtually-created memories and experiences with the new instructional content they discover in-world to construct their own perceptions and recollections of the subject matter provides a strong basis for the 3D approach.

In a virtual world, the environment could consist of a very simple setting in which care-fully designed learning activities will take place. The environment could have little to do with the content, but might simply be the designated space where the learners meet to participate in an activity. In many cases, the specific appearance of the environment, or at precisely which location a class meets in-world, is not a primary contributor to the learning experience. Knowledge is gained through some type of participation and interaction with other visitors.

In this case, the environment relates specifically to the instructional content, since it simulates the appearance of a real-world home with an array of green features. Yet, in order to engage the learner in a memorable experience, a prescribed activity for the location was developed—a virtual scavenger hunt. The activity insured that visitors would wander throughout the entire site, locate and identify each of the features that contributed to a green home, visually observe those elements, read and save a detailed description of each green component for future review. In this case, learners are interacting with elements in the environment.

Each green aspect to be studied was visually depicted in the 3D home. A high level of photo-realism was not required. By providing the minimum amount of detail necessary to allow visitors to draw a parallel between an object's virtual portrayal and its real-world counterpart, the environment provided sufficient cues to enable learners to visualize how the object would be utilized in a real home. Understanding the usage and function of the green components was more important than seeing and recalling intricate details of the physical appearance of the green components.

There are twenty-two green concepts illustrated and described throughout the site. The defined goal is to locate all twenty-two concepts, which are represented by blue discs. Each blue disc denotes a learning station, which appears adjacent to the corresponding green element. By clicking on a blue disc, learners reveal more details about the element--delivered as text through an SL note-card. Learners are instructed to read and save the notecards in their SL inventory for future review. Learners are also encouraged to copy and paste the content of the notecards to a Word document, creating a study guide for offline review.

A virtual scavenger hunt, in which learners search for and locate the green elements, sets the learners in motion by providing a task and a goal—to find all of the learning stations. Learners may choose to participate on their own, or they can work side-by-side with other avatars. The ability to see and interact with classmates who are engaged in the same activity provides an additional channel of information and feedback to guide a learner's journey through the site. Some choose to become either followers or leaders, depending upon their personality and level of comfort with the technology.

As learners explore the site, they encounter objects that add to their feeling of immersion and engage them in interactions. Some of the green features incorporate sound effects, movement, or clickable components. These environmental effects and interactive elements help build the sense of being engrossed in a setting where one's actions impact the surrounding world and where memorable events occur. Visitors click on objects in order to initiate actions such as a wall rolling away to reveal insulation; and they observe green home solutions in motion, such as a compost tumbler.

In front of the home, an interactive mailbox allows visitors to leave a note documenting their visit to the site. Many of the learners opt to also include positive comments and suggestions regarding their SL learning experience.

Communicating Expectations

Very few of the learners had prior experience with SL or virtual worlds. This is currently a common situation and must be addressed prior to sending learners in-world. In order to plan for a successful experience at this site, participants must be comfortable with basics such as teleporting, walking, flying, instant messaging, opening notecards and saving objects to inventory.

Many quality videos that describe common SL tasks are readily available on YouTube. Links to several selected videos and instructions for locating the SL site were assembled in a PDF document, which was placed in the Learning Management System (LMS) for the course. In preparation for their virtual visit, students were asked to review the document and the associated instructional videos. The videos provided an overview of many of the prerequisite skills for an effective site visit, such as how to walk, fly, teleport, chat, and save a notecard. In addition, a brief overview of SL was presented during class time, with demonstrations of conventions such as flying, walking, and teleporting.

The PDF document posted in the LMS served as a container for all necessary instructions, links, images, and documentation related to the site visit. This document can be prepared and tested by an instructional designer to insure that all necessary information is up-to-date and clearly communicated to the students in preparation for their site visit. The instructor needs to post only one document in the LMS for each course section. This simplifies the preparatory process and ensures that all necessary instructions are adequately communicated. In this case, the task of reading the preparatory document was assigned to the class the week prior to the planned site visit.

Both in the introductory document, and again through signage posted at the entrance to the virtual site, learners are informed of the expectations for their participation. They are instructed to search for and locate each of 22 learning stations, to read the associated content, and to save each notecard to their inventory for later review. Several virtual modifications to the visual metaphor for a real-world green home assist in leading learners to the content. At the end of the home's sidewalk, an interactive map identifies and geographically orients all twenty-two learning stations. Visitors can click a station on the map to teleport directly to the associated station. Several teleport pads are scattered throughout the home and the grounds to assist in locating concealed or easy-to-miss areas such as the basement or the roof. The strategic location of informational signs and the automated generation of chat messages at important junctures provide additional feedback to guide a visitor's journey. The roof of the home is partially open to allow learners to easily fly in, out, and around the site.

Navigating through a virtual world is not intuitive to many learners. One of the tasks that proved most difficult for participants was to find the green home after entering SL. The concept that SL is a world with many possible destinations was new and somewhat confusing to some participants. Understanding the structure of the SL environment and how to leverage the conventions of teleporting and flying takes practice and experience before instruction can be maximized. Even with the provision of a direct SLURL, helping the learners to find the desired location was one of the largest hurdles to overcome. In spite of efforts to provide clear instructions, some participants experienced difficulties. In subsequent semesters, open computer lab times were scheduled, during which time an assistant was available to guide any participants in their entry to the site. Future enhancements might include creating an introductory video with site-specific instructions to be included in the LMS.

Planning for Interaction

In addition to the task of simulating a real-world environment, there are social considerations to consider in a 3D world. Unlike the process of reading a textbook—a solitary activity—the process of discovering content within a virtual world takes place alongside other learners. If learners have questions about what is expected of them, they can pose their question to a nearby avatar. Learners can discuss the content they are studying with others who are simultaneously exploring the same concepts. Fostering opportunities to encourage interaction among visitors should be an important consideration in designing the learning experience.

In an attempt to plan for interaction among visitors, the virtual green home features an outdoor campfire surrounded by benches, which is meant to be a gathering place for participants to gather, interact, and possibly reflect upon the green elements incorporated into the home. This usage is suggested through signage. Few students utilized this space for discussion purposes with other learners. Through casual observation, it appeared that the participants were focused on accomplishing the assigned task—to locate the blue discs. In general, they did not seem interested in lingering for discussion. In order to generate further discussion and consideration of the subject matter, an assigned activity could be designed which would encourage each visitor to converse with another visitor about a particular green feature.

Based on casual observation of students who visited, some learners preferred to explore the site on their own and avoided contact with other avatars. Some approached others and initiated conversation about what they were to do, or shared information about where the blue discs were located.

In a follow-up survey and informal discussion, some learners reported feeling uncomfortable with the idea of encountering strangers in SL. Learners who ignored or had difficulty with the direct SLURL to the green home found themselves immersed in the chaos at Orientation Island, which added to this impression. Some students arrived at Orientation Island expecting to find a green home amidst the bedlam.

Many of the students in this study were new to SL, having created their account specifically for this assignment. Observation of the learners indicated that many were cautious about interaction with avatars they didn't know. Upon being approached, some participants walked away. However, some attempted to start a conversation through the SL text chat feature. A common icebreaker was, "BiSci 3?" which allowed for affirmative identification as co-members of the same class. This was often followed up with questions or comments regarding how to proceed with the task at hand—the scavenger hunt.

Avoiding the distraction which can be created by unwanted visitors and arriving at unanticipated destinations is an important consideration in creating a safe and effective learning environment. Although the green home site is public, it is generally visited only by those who have been invited, providing a comfortable educational environment—after the learner arrives.

Beyond asking learners to participate in the scavenger hunt activity, providing opportunities to reflect on what they have learned could enhance the site's effectiveness. The addition of an interactive quizzing feature, which would allow visitors to self-test their understanding of green concepts, is a planned area of improvement. The lure of friendly competition between classmates could entice learners to engage in an interactive multi-player quizzing game—a type of interaction which might be perceived as safe. This would not only help reinforce the instructional concepts, but also add an additional layer of social contact to the site.

What the Learners Said

The reaction of the students to the virtual learning experience was largely positive. One participant stated "I liked it because the material I learned was not only informative, but I felt like I got to experience it first hand, since I could see it in the home." Another stated, "I liked it because it was sort of like experiencing a green home." One participant said, "Learning in a virtual green home was an effective way to interact and learn because I got a chance to see firsthand what everything was and its functions." Another student stated that the educational experience was effective "because as we were walking around, we got to see what aspects of the house we were learning about."

The ability to physically move throughout a virtual environment and to choose a unique path through the environment was viewed favorably by students. One participant stated that a feature which helped with learning was "being able to fly and teleport. Since I could fly, I could easily move around the site." Similarly, another student cited flying as important saying, "Being able to fly around,… I got to see what all the house had to offer." These thoughts were echoed in the comment, "Flying [was important to my learning] because I could move freely and explore where I wanted first."

Regarding the ability to participate within the environment, a student stated, "This was an interesting way to get us to learn about green homes. I like that it's interactive and it's easier to learn and remember things when you have this kind of visual." This student's comment speaks to the premise that designing activities which allow for

Figure 4. Learners assist each other through text chat

students to both act and react will enhance their ability to remember their virtual experiences and consequently build knowledge.

In spite of having received instructions for participation in the scavenger hunt activity, both in the LMS and on signage posted throughout the site, many visiting students asked each other, "What are we supposed to do?" Perhaps this was a disguised method to initiate discussion, or perhaps it was a true indication of lack of clarity regarding expectations. Nonetheless, classmates were willing to assist each other by providing direction and suggestions through text chat.

While some learners experienced initial confusion, this student's comments summarize the experience for most, "After I figured this out, I actually found this to be quite interesting. It took a while to arrive to this site, but once I did, collecting the facts was simple. I printed them out to make a study guide."

Areas of Concern

Some opponents of educational uses of virtual worlds—and SL in particular—contend that today's young generation already spends too much time playing video games, and that attempting to create instruction within this venue supports what some view as a societal problem. This idea is based upon the fallacy that virtual worlds are simply another computer game. It also ignores the explosive societal trend toward online delivery of education, which positions a new generation of learners in front of a computer screen rather than interacting in face-to-face classrooms.

According to Allen & Seaman's report on online education (2010), "Over 4.6 million students were taking at least one online course during the fall 2008 term; a 17 percent increase over the number reported the previous year" (p. 1). Growth in technology has enabled new online educational models to leverage a variety of tools--such as virtual worlds--to effectively meet learning objectives. Because of the exponential growth of online education, business as usual no longer suffices. New delivery methods require the exploration and development of innovative tools, techniques, and methodologies in order to not only keep pace with the change, but to forge the pathway for the future of education.

Some critics voice concern regarding the variety of adult content which has been prolific in SL as a reason to ignore any potential benefits of this approach. Through careful planning and positioning of virtual instructional sites in private or limited access areas of SL, or by using one of several alternative virtual world platforms, this potentially problematic issue can effectively be minimized or avoided.

As with any new technology, some oppose this new approach simply because they cannot envision the potential benefits until they have seen examples of successes. In fact, a few of the participants in this study indicated that they prefer textbooks or lectures as opposed to online activities.

There is, of course, validity to the views of some naysayers. Time will tell how these concerns are addressed. As the result of experimentation and discovery, it is likely that the educational value of the virtual world platform and the unique innovative approaches it accommodates will become more broadly understood and widely implemented. As online learning continues to become more widely accepted and becomes an expected alternative to traditional classrooms, virtual worlds can provide a unique venue in which to create dynamic interactive learning experiences that are in no way limited by geographic constraints. Further exploration of instructional opportunities within this realm certainly merits future exploration in order to conceive, develop, and understand methodologies for maximizing the social and interactive affordances which are unique to this environment.

Solutions and Recommendations

Based upon the deployment of this virtual educational experience, it became obvious that several logistical, technical, and administrative issues must be addressed by the instructional designer to successfully deploy this type of educational experience. When implementing a 3D virtual learning experience for traditional undergraduate students, careful consideration must be given to preparing the learners for the instructional experience.

If, as in this case, a virtual world experience is utilized to supplement a traditional face-to-face course, proper preparation of the learners may necessitate devoting a block of valuable class time to a demonstration of how to access and navigate a virtual world. In addition, learners might be asked to review introductory materials that cover common prerequisite tasks. It can be assumed that most participants will not have previously visited SL and will not have an existing account. As a result, the process of preparation includes creating an account, selecting an avatar, and adding some level of customization to the avatar, if desired. When making the decision to pursue educational usages of a virtual world, these logistical and administrative requirements and the associated time investment should be considered. Before proceeding with the selection of a virtual world as an appropriate instructional technology, it should be clear that the benefits of the 3D approach can potentially outweigh the cost of participation in preparation time and acquisition of prerequisite knowledge. There should be a clear connection between the benefits this approach can offer and the process of attaining the course's learning objectives.

To ease the learners' entry to the virtual world, it can be helpful to offer open computer lab times during which a lab assistant is available to assist students with their first visit. In the case of a traditional classroom, it is possible to organize such a gateway to ease entry to the world. Naturally, this would not be feasible in the case of an online course with no face-to-face component.

When using SL, if at all possible, learners should be provided instructions which direct them to bypass Orientation Island and arrive at an alternate orientation activity. The potential chaos at SL's main portal can be a huge distraction. Learners should be allowed time and opportunities to practice basic SL skills prior to taking part in any instructional activities. When they are deemed ready to proceed, clear expectations for their participation in the virtual world activities should be communicated. This introduction might occur at a private orientation area developed specifically to complement the course content. Explanatory documents, videos, and self-tests on basic skills can help ease learners up the steep learning curve of prerequisite knowledge.

Another potential difficulty may arise because of the hardware requirements necessary to run SL or other 3D virtual worlds. Throughout the course of this project, most students have been able to run SL on their own computer; however, in a few cases a student chose to work with a classmate because of the limitations of their personal computer. Providing access to a properly equipped campus computer lab facility can help address this issue, but brings with it several related issues.

In a campus setting, lab computers are often updated at the beginning of the semester, with the expectation that they will not require further updates by local IT support until the semester ends. Typically, students do not have administrative privileges for lab computers. Because Linden Labs releases frequent updates that are often required in order to run SL, there is the potential this situation could become a maintenance headache or even prevent students from accessing SL according to the desired schedule. This may be difficult to overcome, but awareness of the potential problem can allow for advance planning which could circumvent the issue. Beyond the obvious need to address logistical and technical concerns, the primary focus of the instructional designer becomes how to design an engaging, interactive experience for the learner, which will result in the student attaining the identified learning objectives.

Some types of instructional content are especially suited to SL or virtual worlds. When learning objectives relate to social experiments, practice of foreign language skills, experimenting with economic scenarios, or practicing methods for dialogue or interaction with colleagues, SL provides low-cost access to a microcosm where these areas can be explored—often without the need to own or develop a custom site, but rather by engaging with the existing in-world community. In these situations, it can be relatively easy to envision an appropriate instructional activity because the learning objectives already call for engagement in a particular series of tasks that relate directly to in-world scenarios.

When learning objectives do not involve an inherent social or verbal element, the determination to pursue delivery in a virtual world may be less concrete. As in this project, if the objectives relate to experiencing an otherwise inaccessible environment, a virtual world can be a good fit. This could involve creating and developing an environment that does not exist in the real-world—such as altering the proportions and scale of the real world, or recreating a historical site that no longer exists. In other cases, rendering a replica of an existing location that students cannot otherwise visit could be a reason to pursue this approach. In these situations, designing the participatory activities may require a great deal of creativity. The design and development of the virtual environment for this type of instructional site could potentially be much more comprehensive, time consuming, technically challenging and expensive than designing socially-based activities which could take place in almost any virtual location.

Table 1. Paired samples for pre-test and post-test scores in experimental group

			95% Confidence Interval of the Difference				
			Paired Differences				
Mean	Std. deviation	Std. error mean	Lower	Upper	t	df	Sig. (2-tailed)
-4.328	3.125	.410	-5.149	-3.506	-10.545	57	.000

Table 2. Paired samples for pre-test and post-test scores in control group

			95% Confidence Interval of the Difference				
			Paired Differences				
Mean	Std. deviation	Std. error mean	Lower	Upper	t	df	Sig. (2-tailed)
-5.765	2.826	.396	-6.559	-4.970	-14.570	50	.000

What the Data Tells Us

The many unique qualities of the virtual world platform point to great potential as an educational tool. But, how effectively can students learn through participation in a virtual world experience? To investigate, a control group viewed content via a static Web site and an experimental group explored content through an SL visit. Both groups participated in a pre-test and post-test. There was a significant level of difference between the pre-test and post-test scores of the experimental group ($t(57) = -10.545$, $p = .00$) as illustrated in Table 1.

Likewise, there was also a significant level of difference between the pre-test and post-test scores of the control group ($t(50) = -14.570$, $p = .00$), as illustrated in Table 2.

These findings indicate that participants in both groups achieved a significantly higher test score through participation in their assigned instructional activities. However, the difference between pre-test and post-test was greater for the control group ($M = 5.765$, $SD = 2.826$) than for the experimental group ($M = 4.328$, $SD = 3.125$). Demographic factors may have contributed to the greater difference between test scores in the con-

trol group. However, the data shows that both groups achieved significant differences in scores.

When comparing the demographics of participants in the two groups, some notable differences emerge. Within the experimental group, only 5.2% of participants listed their major within a category related to science, technology, or engineering; and 65.5% of participants reported a general or strong interest in environmental science. The experimental group consisted primarily of traditionally aged undergraduate students, with only 5% of participants listing their age as 21 or older. The experimental group was predominantly female (58.6%). The participants had limited prior experience with online instruction with only 8.6% having previously taken a course offered completely online.

In contrast, within the control group, 19.6% of the participants listed their major within a category related to science, technology, or engineering; and 86.3% of participants indicated they had a general or strong interest in environmental science. The control group consisted of a more mature sample with 22% of participants listing their age as 21 or older. The control group was predominantly male (55%). The participants in this group had more prior experience with online instruction than the

Figure 5. Comparison of Demographics in Experimental and Control Group

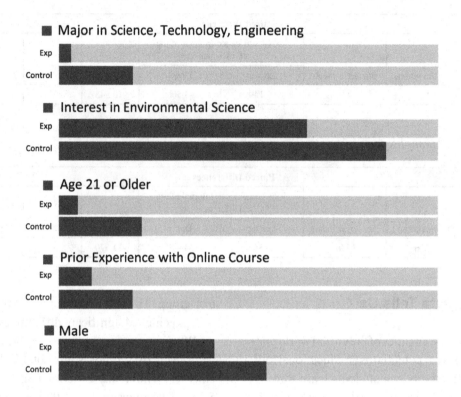

experimental group, with 19.6% having previously taken a course offered completely online.

Although the results of this study show a significant difference in learning between the experimental and control group, the results also show that both groups achieved significant differences between pre-test and post-test scores. Since there were notable demographic differences between the two groups, the control group's greater difference in scores from pre- to post-test might be partly attributed to the composition of the groups. Further research would be necessary before results could be generalized to a larger population.

Spending a greater amount of time in SL increased the likelihood that participants in the experimental group would receive a higher test score by 14.8%; and having prior experience with SL increased the likelihood that participants in the experimental group would receive a higher test score by 11.5%. It is possible that, had there been a longer time period in which to become familiar with SL prior to the instructional activities, the post-test scores for the experimental group would have been higher. For most participants in this study, this was their first venture into a virtual world, yet significant differences in pre-test and post-test scores were attained. If learners entering a virtual instructional site were already familiar with virtual world navigation and communication techniques or if they had a longer period of time to become proficient, the learning outcomes could potentially be quite different.

Perhaps because the course for which this site was developed is an introductory elective course, few students appeared to exhibit an innate curiosity related to the subject matter or a desire to go beyond simply fulfilling the requirements of the assignment. Almost one quarter of the learners in the experimental group reported they had little or no interest in environmental science. Through observation of visitors and comments from students, it appeared that the goal of the majority of participants was to complete the prescribed activities to the degree that would allow them to receive a satisfactory grade. Learners were looking for a concrete prescription for successful participation—and nothing more. Adding additional interactive elements for learners to explore, both on their own or collaboratively with others, might begin to engage students in higher order thinking skills.

A very interesting pattern emerges when examining comments from the participants. Qualitative feedback on the green home unit was gathered from both groups. When asked why the instruction in which they participated was or was not effective, comments from the experimental group included words and phrases such as: hands-on, activity, visual learner, real-life experience, new, exciting, engaging, interact, see firsthand, walk, and explore. These phrases seem to describe aspects of an *experience* in which the visitors felt they had participated. In contrast, comments from the control group included words and phrases such as: interesting, own pace, use of computer, read from Web site, easy to access, broken into sections, enjoyment of reading online texts, easy to follow. Unlike the phrases from the experimental group, these terms primarily describe the organization and delivery of information.

FUTURE RESEARCH DIRECTIONS

If, by asking students to engage in well-designed educational activities in a virtual world, educators can create within those students a sense of physical immersion within the subject matter, and assist those students in forming lasting memories of experiences which are centered on the instructional content, perhaps a new, enhanced foundation for online education may emerge. The development and testing of instructional design models that will guide course designers to maximize the immersive qualities of the virtual world experience is an area that warrants further exploration.

The first step in designing an educational site in a virtual world should be to envision the world as a setting in which an activity will take place, rather than a destination. The degree to which a virtual world environment is conducive to *uniquely* enabling learners to participate in an activity which aligns with identified learning objectives is a suggested measure of whether this approach is appropriate for a particular course or unit. Future research might further explore types of in-world activities that can enhance interactive 3D learning sites and build upon the unique experiential nature of a virtual world.

CONCLUSION

Both instructional approaches utilized in this study were effective, but the learning processes which the participants experienced and described was quite different. The SL visitors seemed to describe aspects of an experience, while the group that used an instructional Web site noted aspects of the organization and delivery of text.

Instructional design considerations which center on expanding the depth of memories and experiences constructed by learners could potentially engage learners in a unique, effective and appealing educational environment. Recommendations to maximize the educational affordances of a 3D virtual world include designing learning activities which encourage competition with self or others, call for collaboration with and interaction among visitors, or engage visitors in "physical" activity with elements of the environment. By providing for the unfolding of scenarios where learners are asked to discover new knowledge and physically (albeit virtually) interact with course content, course designers can create an educational experience which might allow learners to build memories constructed around an experience with the course content.

For some types of instructional content, a 3D virtual world is not appropriate due to the high learning curve involved in preparing learners for participation. The approach followed for this unit is not always a wise solution because of the time required to prepare the learners, the potential for insufficient availability of properly equipped computer labs, or the design and development time associated with building a custom virtual site.

In spite of these cautions, a virtual world can uniquely provide opportunities for exploration, interaction, collaboration, and discovery. Not an end in itself, a virtual world is a venue in which learning can occur. Designing effective and appropriate activities to take place within that venue is the charge of the forward thinking instructional designer. Considerations for instructional design should capitalize on the unique characteristics of a 3D world. The unique capabilities include but are not limited to the ability to:

- See oneself personified in relation to other learners
- Choose a unique, individual pathway of exploration
- Observe 3D objects from any angle, or at greatly enlarged or reduced scale
- Participate in learning activities with geographically dispersed classmates while experiencing a unique sense of physical presence in a group of learners
- Create lasting memories based upon perception of an experience
- Interact with the environment and/or subject matter through deliberate actions
- Participate in social experiences and activities

Designing the provisions for an educational "experience" in a virtual world such as SL can effectively engage students in the learning process. After learners work through any technical hurdles, most report that they enjoy virtual 3D learning activities. Results of a pre-test and post-test indicate that students can effectively learn through participation in a virtual world, and responses from SL participants reflect a sense of having engaged in an experience which helped them to learn. The affordances of a 3D virtual world provide for a degree of presence amongst geographically dispersed online students that would otherwise be difficult to attain. Learners generate memories and build knowledge in a manner that appears unique to the 3D mode of delivery. As a result, a virtual 3D educational experience can either add depth to an online course or enhance a traditional face-to-face course.

REFERENCES

Allen, I. E., & Seaman, J. (2010). *Learning on demand: Online education in the United States, 2009*. Babson Park, MA: Babson Survey Research Group.

Alley, L. R., & Jansak, K. E. (2001). The ten keys to quality assurance and assessment in online learning. *Journal of Interactive Instruction Development, 13*(3), 3–18.

Barab, S. A., Hay, K. E., Barnett, M., & Squire, K. (2001). Constructing virtual worlds: Tracing the historical development of learner practices. *Cognition and Instruction, 19*(1), 47–94. doi:10.1207/S1532690XCI1901_2

Childress, M., & Braswell, R. (2006). Using massively multiplayer online role-playing games for online learning. *Distance Education, 27*(2), 187–196. doi:10.1080/01587910600789522

DeLucia, A., Francese, R., Passero, I., & Tortora, G. (2009). Development and evaluation of a virtual campus on Second Life: The case of Second-DMI. *Computers & Education, 52*(1), 220–223. doi:10.1016/j.compedu.2008.08.001

Downes, S. (2008). *The reality of virtual learning.* Presented to the Defense Learning Academy, DNDLearn Conference, Cornwall, Ontario, January 30, 2008. Retrieved May 29, 2010, from http://halfanhour.blogspot.com/ 2008/02/reality-of-virtual -learning.html

Gaimster, J. (2008). Reflections on interactions in virtual worlds and their implication for learning art and design. *Art. Design & Communication in Higher Education, 6*(3), 187–199. doi:10.1386/adch.6.3.187_1

Jarmon, L., Traphagan, T., & Mayrath, M. (2008). Understanding project-based learning in Second Life with a pedagogy, training, and assessment trio. *Educational Media International, 45*(3), 157–176. doi:10.1080/09523980802283889

Kapp, K., & O'Driscoll, T. (2007). Escaping flatland: The emergence of 3D synchronous learning. *Guild Research 360° Report on Synchronous Learning Systems,* 111-153.

Kemp, J. W., & Haycock, K. (2008). Immersive learning environments in parallel universes: Learning through Second Life. *School Libraries Worldwide, 14*(2), 89–97.

Prasolova-Førland, E. (2008). Analyzing place metaphors in 3D educational collaborative virtual environments. *Computers in Human Behavior, 24,* 185–204. doi:10.1016/j.chb.2007.01.009

ADDITIONAL READING

Kapp, K., & O'Driscoll, T. (2010). *Learning in 3D: Adding a new dimension to enterprise learning and collaboration.* San Francisco, CA: John Wiley and Sons, Inc.

KEY TERMS AND DEFINITIONS

Avatar: A 3D graphic representation of an individual that is often customized in appearance.

Experience: In the context of this article, an experience is a group of instructional activities in a virtual world which involve interaction with the environment, objects in the environment, or other visitors. The experience and related actions are reactions become part of the visitor's memory.

Notecard: An object containing text, which can be saved within a SL visitor's inventory.

Orientation Island: The default entry point for new Second Life users, which is noted for providing beginners with instructions and for being frequented by visitors who harass newcomers.

SLURL: A Second Life URL is a hyperlink from a Web page that directs visitors to a specific location within Second Life.

Teleport: A method of travel within Second Life that allows visitors to quickly move from their current location directly to another specific location.

Teleport Pad: An object in Second Life—usually a disc on the ground—which when clicked will take a visitor's avatar directly to another location.

Chapter 19
Teaching Project Management with Second Life

Marc Conrad
University of Bedfordshire, UK

ABSTRACT

Project Management is a field of intellectual and pragmatic enquiry that is inherently inter-disciplinary. It typically involves the integration of areas such as: project scoping, time, cost, and human resource management, whilst the management of effective inter-team communication, project risk, and procurement aspects are all central to the discipline. To try to cover all of these areas within a single university assignment presents somewhat of a challenge. This chapter demonstrates that the deployment of a Multi User Virtual Environment can indeed encompass these areas in an effective manner, both from learning objectives, realism, and assessment points of view. The chapter has emerged from the experience of three years deployment of Second Life as an integral part of a unit on Project Management, offered as part of both undergraduate and postgraduate courses within the Department of Computer Science and Technology at the University of Bedfordshire. Examples illustrate the work that has been produced by the students of these courses.

INTRODUCTION

The Project Management Institute (PMI) defines Project Management as "the application of knowledge, skills, tools, and techniques to project activities to meet project requirements" (PMI, 2008).

DOI: 10.4018/978-1-60960-545-2.ch019

A keystone is the successful balance of scope, time and cost - the so called triple constraint: an increase of scope can be addressed by allowing more time, but it may increase the cost. As part of a university assignment, this balancing act can only be simulated up to a certain extent. For instance strict deadlines are prescribed by submission dates that do not leave any leeway for balancing and cost management needs to be simulated as there are typically no resources from the university or the students themselves to provide money that could be spent for real. Other knowledge areas defined by the PMI are quality (sometimes seen as part of scope management), risk, human resources, communication and procurement. In addition, the knowledge area of integration serves to tie together the different tools and techniques used to address the demands from the other areas. To setup an assignment that encompasses all those areas in a realistic way is not straightforward and need to be crafted carefully.

At the University of Bedfordshire two units, one in the final year of undergraduate level, the other on postgraduate level, utilize Second Life for teaching Project Management. Conceptually the structure follows Wilson (2002) in that "the assessment in this unit was designed as a simulation of an activity that they [the students] were likely to be involved in real life". With this in mind, the assessments aim to encompass the characteristics of situated learning identified by Herrington and Oliver (2000), namely: authentic context, activities and assessment; expert performances; multiple roles and perspectives; collaborative construction of knowledge; reflection and articulation; and finally coaching and scaffolding. The authenticity in context, activity and assessment in particular are areas where the use of virtual worlds such as Second Life provides significant improvement compared to traditional approaches. It allows to pursuit a real, i.e. authentic, project from within the lab environment of an educational institution: students build a *real* showcase in Second Life, not a simulation. Other characteristics of situated learning such as multiple roles, collaboration or scaffolding clearly have to be part of this approach to make the assignment successful and relevant for this level of teaching. However, with the overall scope of this book in mind, we focus on those aspects of teaching Project Management that are particularly enhanced by the use of Second Life.

BACKGROUND

At the University of Bedfordshire, UK, Second Life had been used in 2008 for the first time to address the Project Management knowledge areas as learning outcomes within a unit on the postgraduate level. Since then, the assignment has been repeated with slight variations both on the postgraduate and final year undergraduate levels. The more experimental experience from the first year has been published elsewhere (Conrad, Pike, Sant, & Nwafor, 2009) where the focus was on the suitability of Second Life to be used for an assignment of that kind (which is by now established, also in view of many other teaching and learning activities within virtual worlds including those discussed in other chapters of this book). Also, in that paper, a particular emphasis was made on the aspect of large student numbers of up to 800 that needed to be accommodated. The main findings were that institutional support is essential (still, many teachers have to put pressure on their IT departments to allow access to Second Life from within their institution) and that students do appreciate the use of Second Life in teaching or at least do not object to this. In particular the 'steep learning curve' that students have to master in order to get an avatar and to work within Second Life does not seem to constitute a real problem. If at all, issues are rather with Second Life itself as it does not scale well to large student cohorts. In the long vision an integration of virtual worlds within a virtual learning environment such as Blackboard or Moodle, as it is for instance piloted in the SLoodle project (Kemp & Livingstone, 2006), might therefore be desirable and is henceforth recommended.

In this chapter we leave these issues aside and focus on the particular aspects of teaching Project Management. The units Social and Professional Project Management (on the undergraduate level) and Professional Project Management (on the postgraduate level) are taught across a number of awards within the field of Computing at the

University of Bedfordshire. These include awards in Computer Science, Networking, Security, Computer Graphics, as well as Information Systems. It can hence be assumed that all participants of the assignments are computer literate.

While the exact details of the assignments given to the students vary slightly from year to year and between postgraduate and undergraduate level, the basic structure is typically as follows: students are assigned to project teams (the size varies from 3 to 10 or more) and are given a variety of artifacts to be produced, including the Second Life showcase. Other artifacts used in the previous years include a PowerPoint presentation, booklets, podcasts or videos. In addition, guidance is given on the use of PRINCE2® as a project management methodology and templates are provided. At certain dates the submission of project documentation is required (such as highlight reports) that allow the tutors to provide formative feedback. The students are marked according to their individual contribution. To illustrate this, here is an excerpt of the assignment brief that has been given to the postgraduate students in the Academic Year 2009/2010:

[...] You are working as a group of 10 individuals who need to come together and work as a team. You will be using the PRINCE2® project management methodology to run a real-life project. As part of an educational advisory team you have been asked to create an educational showcase. The area that you look at must be directly related to the pathway that you are studying, but may cover any aspect of technology within this area. As part of this project you will have to deliver a number of products. Just like in any real-project there are a set of deliverables and a set of deadlines – these are non-negotiable and any late deliverables will be zero marked (non submission).

As a team you must produce the following, and meet the specified deadlines [...]

An educational showcase in the Second Life Island of the University of Bedfordshire [...]

Resources that are provided to the students regarding Second Life consist of a web link to an introduction on how to create an avatar and first steps to use the avatar within the virtual environment (Penfold, Ma, Choy, & Lav, 2008) and several links into Second Life (slurl's) that can be explored with an avatar. For instance in the Academic Year 2009 / 2010 a slurl to the Caledon Oxbridge virtual university (Shang, 2006) and two links to public sandboxes have been provided where students were able to experiment and explore building. Because of the ever changing nature of Second Life these links need to be verified each time before the assignment starts. Also a slurl that directs the students to the area where they are expected to build the showcase is given. Figure 1 shows a screenshot that has been given to the postgraduate students in 2010. This allows the students to recognize the building area in-world. The following is an excerpt from the instructions given on the postgraduate course 2009/2010 that also provides the constraints:

This is a link to the island where to build your showcase. In the North-East corner is the dedicated area where to build your showcase. Please find the 5m x 5m space with the name of your group on it. Your showcase must not exceed 20 prims and must fit into the 5m x 5m space. The maximum height is 8m. The cost for the showcase (upload of textures, externally bought scripts) must not exceed L\$1000 (at the current rate this is less than £3).

In order to be able to build in this area you must be a member of the group [...]. Please send an email to [...] containing your real name, your student number, your avatar name and the name of your group. Then a group invitation will be send to you that you must accept.

Figure 1. Screenshot presented to the 2009/10 postgraduate course that illustrates the location where the students are to build the showcases. Each of the dedicated 10m x 10m areas accommodates space for four groups. The name of the group (the groups have been given the names of the US states) is written on the floor of each showcase. The back walls show the logo of the University of Bedfordshire and the unit code (CIS011-6)

Please note:

- Avatars who 'rezz' more than 20 prims in the showcase area might be removed from the group without warning and their prims will be deleted.
- Prims outside the dedicated 5m x 5m group area may be removed without warning and their owner might be removed from the group.

In the following we shortly introduce each of the knowledge areas of project management and discuss how they have been instantiated within Second Life in the course of the assignment at the University of Bedfordshire. Many of these observations generalize to other Multi User Virtual Environments. In the definition of the knowledge areas we follow Schwalbe (2010), an essential reading text for the course that is itself based on the PMBOK® framework (PMI, 2008).

PROJECT MANAGEMENT KNOWLEDGE AREAS AND SECOND LIFE

Project Scope Management

Project Scope Management involves defining and controlling the work that is included in a project. Scope definition is often deliverable oriented. Indeed there are two types of deliverables: the actual products, here in particular the Second Life showcase, and the project documentation. Key documentation are the work breakdown structure (a break down of the work into discrete tasks often graphically visualized in the form of a hierarchy), highlight reports and documentation for initiating and closing the project. PRINCE2® templates for these documents are provided by the course team.

The product 'Second Life Showcase' is specified by both quantitative and qualitative constraints. Qualitatively the showcase is constrained by its purpose. It must "educate the general public"

Figure 2. Showcase area in the AY 2008 / 2009 for the undergraduate course after completion

on a relevant topic. The topic must be related to the student's pathway but is otherwise determined by the students themselves. For instance students on the Networking award may discuss the difference between various wireless standards; students on a Computer Science award may discuss recent topics such as Cloud Computing. If not all of the students share the same award the group chooses some middle ground, for instance a mixed group with students from Security and Networking would work on Network Security. The aim is that all students of a group are able to contribute content-wise.

Another qualitative constraint given to the students is the requirement for the showcase to be 'interactive' and 'visually appealing'. Here the students need to proactively reason how these can be met. Quantitative boundaries are the size of the showcase and the number of primitives (the basic building blocks of any Second Life object, also called 'prims'). These quantitative constraints naturally originate from the fact that resources on a Second Life island are limited. The price of any piece of land within Second Life is directly related to the number of prims supported by the land. Hence the students are led to investigate

Internet resources on prim efficient building – a topic discussed in various Second Life related blogs or tutorials. Constraints that have been used for the showcase were 50 prims on a 10m x 10m space, 10 prims on a 5m x 5m space and 20 prims on a 5m x 5m space. Examples can be seen in Figures 2 through 4. It seems indeed that the exact number of the prim limit given to the students does not seem to matter too much for the feasibility and success of the assignment. Indeed a constraint limiting the showcase to a small number of prims such as 10 is useful to highlight to students the importance of understanding what is *not* a constraint. For instance many groups feel that their showcase must resemble a 'real' building with walls and roofs. However these features are nowhere specified – a fact that becomes clear only under the pressure to build prim efficient. On the other hand allowing a larger number of primitives enhances the creative potential of the teams.

Project Time Management

Time Management includes the task of scheduling the activities, often in a diagrammatic way. Milestones are defined. A visible output of student

Figure 3. Showcase in the AY 2008 / 2009 for the postgraduate course after work has been completed

Figure 4. Showcase in the AY 2009 / 2010 for the undergraduate course (in the sky). Below on the ground is the showcase area for the postgraduate students

work is a Gantt chart that students submit as part of the project documentation portfolio. As the assignment is part of a university course, certain time constraints are prescribed with defined milestones. For the postgraduate course the assignment has been distributed in the first week of teaching and a total of 11 teaching weeks was given for

the production of the deliverables. Milestones are given by three PRINCE2® style Highlight reports that must be produced in regular intervals. After completion of the products two more weeks are given to write a reflective final project report. The assignment for the undergraduate students follows a similar pattern, but is stretched over a year-long course of 24 weeks.

The students are required to professionally schedule all necessary activities. In particular, time must be scheduled to familiarize oneself with the Virtual Environment! In Second Life this is for instance the creation of an avatar and learning how to build. Often there is a tacit (and sometimes voiced as a critique) assumption that the students have to 'learn' Second Life so that they are able to do the assignment. Indeed the opposite is the case, and this needs to be communicated clearly: if the project team doesn't have the necessary skills for a certain task (such as using an avatar in Second Life), the acquisition of these skills needs to be scheduled: resources need to be allocated *as part of the project.*

Project Cost Management

Developing good cost estimates in real projects is often based on previous experience or quantifiable parameters. In a university assignment the situation is hence complicated as any previous experience with similar projects cannot be assumed. Also, neither the students nor the university (in the role of the project sponsor) typically have sufficient funding for a project budget that could be used for real. Second Life with its in-world currency allows some budgeting using Linden Dollars. Indeed, the showcase requires images to convey information. Students need to produce these images (for instance PowerPoint slides exported as jpg's are often used) and upload the images into Second Life so that they can be used as textures for primitives. The upload of one texture is currently priced as L$10 and the assignment brief limits the total project budget to L$1000. The budget can be freely used. For instance scripts or eye catching sculptures can be purchased to enhance the showcase as long as it is balanced against the cost of the projected number of the necessary textures.

The exchange rate from Linden Dollars to real money of currently L$1000 = $6.19 USD (as of May 2010) means that while some 'realistic' budgeting can be done using the currency of the virtual world, the real costs are low and insignificant compared to other costs of student life such as the purchase of books.

Project Quality Management

The International Organization for Standardization defines quality as the degree to which a set of inherent characteristics fulfill requirements (Schwalbe, 2010, p. 183). Key to quality planning is the identification of quality standards that are relevant to the project. Some of the standards for the Second Life showcase are a direct consequence of the scope definition. Others are less tangible, for instance an appropriate 'look and feel' of the final product. Given the creative potential that is inherent to building in a virtual environment this 'look and feel' aspect is of particular interest. In order to achieve best results students need to conduct market surveys within Second Life, for instance by visiting exhibitions or professional business showcases for inspiration. Indeed the question of 'how real should the showcase be' may lead to some discussion. In a virtual world, such as Second Life, items can fly or hover, change color or move around by themselves. Physical laws such as gravity are often optional. Still, anecdotal evidence from the student's work shows a certain bias to mirror the real world: there are walls and a roof; posters or slideshows are hanging on the walls. Students may reason if a more creative use of the possibilities of Second Life that allow non-realistic builds is 'qualitatively' better. While on one hand it could be argued that non-realistic features like hovering objects are more attractive, on the other hand, the use of the realistic metaphor in constructions may be more appropriate for the intended audience of the showcase (the 'public'). Quality here is driven by customer expectations, which means that part of the quality management is the clarification of these expectations (for instance with a small scale customer survey).

Main tools and techniques for quality planning are checklists and metrics. These may include:

- The number of primitives used in the showcase. For the novice user the mechanism of counting the primitives in a Second Life build is often not transparent and something to get used to. However the limitation on a number of primitives is ubiquitous to Second Life. Any purchase of land within Second Life is associated with the number of prims that can be used on this land. Hence tutorials and other documentation that address the issue to build 'prim efficient' are widely available on the Internet. Rather than giving the students a direct means to count their primitives they are given general advice on how to acquire this knowledge.

- Building within the boundaries. The students were given a space of 10m x 10m (undergraduates) or 5m x 5m (postgraduates) on which they can build their showcase. It needs to be emphasized to the students that they need to work within this area. Even more, the showcase areas have been setup so that they are adjacent to each other. So any group building outside their boundaries is in danger to interfere with the builds of their peers. Any such interference must be dealt with professionally. That means that when a group finds an alien object on their own area they establish the owner of this object and contact him or her and ask them to remove the object. Only if this approach is not successful the problem must be escalated to the project board (who are the tutors of the course) who should try to mediate first (for instance by speaking with the owner of the unwanted object face-to-face). The removal of misplaced objects by the course tutor directly should only be the last resort if any approach to resolve the conflict via mediation was unsuccessful.

- The showcase must convey certain information. It must be made sure that the information presented is accurate and related to the topic the group has chosen.

- The quality of the textures used is of importance. Any editing software that is able to export images of type jpg or png can be used. For instance Microsoft Power Point is fine for this aspect. Measurable quality aspects are font size and general readability. Also preservation of the aspect ratio, i.e. the ratio between width and height of the texture is a quality issue as overly stretched images may look unprofessional.

- The showcase typically will contain scripts, i.e. small pieces of software that perform functionalities, such as progression from one slide to the next on an in-world slide show, or the opening of a door when touched. There may also be more sophisticated features. Hence the project contains an aspect of software quality assurance as well, at least on a small scale. Basic strategies should be developed to ensure proper software testing.

- The importance of the 'look and feel' has been discussed already. Should the 'general public' (who serves here as the customer) think, smile or both? What would be the intended reaction and how can it be measured?

Finally, prim count can be used to illustrate the concept of data visualization in quality management. Pie charts can demonstrate how many primitives are used for structure, furniture, posters etc. A control chart may visualize the number of prims used while building the showcase.

Project Risk Management

A project risk is defined by the PMI as an uncertainty that can have a negative or positive effect on meeting the project objectives. In particular those risks with negative effects need to be addressed explicitly. In order to address risk management as a learning outcome the students are exposed to certain risks that need to be managed by the team. In the context of Second Life contingency plans should for example address the following situations:

- Availability of Second Life on the client side: There are several risks in this context. Second Life may not be available for an individual team member, e.g. when working from home with a slow Internet connection. (However it is not the project team's responsibility that Second Life is accessible from within the university premises – this needs to be established before the start of the course). Contingency plans may include the redistribution of work to other team members, or the use of a public Internet cafe for certain particular tasks.
- Availability of Linden Lab as a service provider: The worst case scenario is obviously Second Life being no longer available. For instance, if for some reason the contract with the educational institution and Second Life terminates early, or that Linden Lab defaults into administration. These risks need to be addressed primarily by the course team and cannot realistically be relied on the students to resolve. However the possibility of these risks should be included in the project documentation as well.
- Availability of the building area: There are two risks that need to be managed by the project team: the unavailability because the Second Life island is overcrowded, or a temporary unavailability due to mainte-

nance by the owner of the island or Linden Labs.
- Similar to the risk of non-availability of the building area due to overcrowding is the general risk of interference with other groups. Primitives and objects may be misplaced and impact other groups' structures. In such events the situation needs to be managed (typically by contacting the owner of the misplaced object, see also the discussion within the 'quality' section in this chapter) and the action needs to be properly recorded.
- Other risks are the accidental deletion of Second Life objects, the unavailability of the avatar due to lost passwords or problems caused by software bugs in Second Life itself (such as data base problems that lead to lost items).

The course team needs to ensure proper assessment and grading if any of these risks materialize. For instance if some desirable features of the showcase are missing as part of a contingency plan that has been put in place to address problems of unavailability of Second Life, this should be rewarded as proper management. In contrast, an unfinished structure that cannot be explained by the project team is not acceptable. It is however not the role of the course tutors to minimize risks other than those that impact the assessment as a whole. Any action by the course team (for instance removing misplaced objects or to eject / restrict avatars from the island to ease overcrowding) should only be carried out as a response to a formal request of the project manager to the project board (the course tutors typically assume the role of the project board).

Human Resources

Staff development has two objectives: The acquisition of necessary skills and the strengthening of team coherence through team building.

Individual skills include the ability to build in Second Life, knowledge on how to use scripts and general knowledge about avatars. It is necessary to highlight that the acquisition of these skills is part of the project. Knowledge of Second Life is not a prerequisite for the assignment, but the gaining of the knowledge must be managed as part of the project.

The project teams are typically pre-assigned by the course tutors: students cannot choose their team members and have to work with peers who are not necessarily their friends. A professional attitude is necessary and also team building activities, such as a meeting in the local coffee shop, are encouraged as part of the project. If the project team is locally distributed they may experiment with a virtual team building event. Second Life offers a plethora of recreational events such as concerts or exhibitions and the team may decide to share such an experience virtually. It is then a matter of reflection and evaluation in what way such an event is useful and can replace events in the real world.

The role of ethics and professional conduct in Project Management can also be translated into virtual environments. Professional bodies such as the PMI or the British Computer Society (BCS) provide guidance in form of a 'Code of Conduct' (aimed to projects in real life) and the project teams are encouraged to define their own instantiation of a Code of Conduct within the virtual environment. This then may include items such as not to rezz objects that are in the way of other people, a dress code that may range from 'no nudity' to 'professional suit' or a restriction to a maximum of avatars that are logged in concurrently so as to avoid overcrowding.

Project Communication Management

It is often said that Project Managers spend 90% of their job communicating (Schwalbe, 2010, p. 194). Hence there is a strong argument that communication must be managed professionally.

Communication may range from spontaneous to scheduled meetings, can be informal and ad hoc or formal and minuted. Virtual worlds such as Second Life add another dimension to communication: meetings can be hold in-world or in the real world. The assignment has no formal requirement of any communication in-world. However students are encouraged to try this. The different communication channels available in Second Life such as voice, Instant Messages (IM's) or open chat can be explored for suitability. An advantage of Instant Messaging is the traceability of discussions. That feature can be highlighted to the students as a reason to use it. The project team may also decide to use special tools that facilitate communication such as voting boxes for group decisions.

Students may reflect on the difference and effectiveness of communication through avatars, given that much of communication in real life is made via body language or the way, how things are said. Also more philosophical questions can be raised, in how far an avatar represents the real person and how real world relationships translate into the virtual environment.

Project Procurement Management

Procurement Management includes the acquisition of goods and services for the project from outside the organization. The use of Second Life allows the possibility to include procurement as part of the assignment. The project team is limited by a budget of L$1000 and this can be used to purchase items that may enhance the look and feel of the showcase. However this must be balanced against the need to upload textures that carry information on the subject as discussed in the 'cost' section.

There are also many free objects available that can be used for building and decisions need to be made if it is better for the project team to 'hunt' for such freebies or to build the desired object from scratch. The students have to make a professional make-or-buy analysis where this is relevant. It is necessary to communicate clearly to the students that the use of externally procured objects is allowed, if the purchase is properly managed. The mechanisms of Second Life allow for the identification of the creator of any object, which helps to identify externally sourced objects. Any such object needs to be related to the project teams' procurement management processes.

When discussing procurement as part of the underpinning teaching it is highlighted to the students that there is an important external provider already, namely Linden Lab for the provision of Second Life itself. Indeed when the avatar is created the project team is constrained by Linden Labs' terms and conditions. Issues such as forgotten passwords or certain technical problems need to be addressed directly with this 'external supplier' of the project.

Project Integration Management

Project Integration Management serves to coordinate the various activities related to the eight other knowledge areas (Scope, Time, Cost, Quality, Human Resources, Communication, Risk and Procurement). In the assignment, the Project Management Methodology PRINCE2® is used for that purpose. PRINCE2® is well established, championed by the UK government and hence became the de facto standard of projects in the United Kingdom. The students are asked to submit the following documents as part of the PRINCE2® driven project portfolio (and which are used, together with an individual reflective report for marking purposes):

- The Project Brief and Project Initiation Document (in methodologies other than PRINCE2® these are often known as statement of work or project charter) need to be produced at the beginning of the project. Typically students receive immediate, formative, feedback on the Project Brief so as to address any potential issues in the subsequent Project Initiation Document.

- Highlight reports in regular intervals, typically every three to four weeks that serve as status reports and give an overview on the progress of the work to date.
- A lessons learned report that evaluates any issues (resolved or otherwise) and good practices that have occurred during the project and that formerly closes the project.

PRINCE2® Templates for each of these reports are provided by the course tutors and those have to be used by the project teams. The approach of PRINCE2® is product based. Starting from the Second Life showcase (and the other products that must be developed) the necessary work such as for instance research, design issues or familiarization with Second Life are derived. A Product Breakdown Structure that goes hand in hand with a Work Breakdown Structure is useful.

Part of Project Integration Management is also project initiation. In particular the students should perform a stakeholder analysis so that they are encouraged to identify the various roles of the people related to the project. In the case of the Second Life showcase clearly the project manager, the project team and the tutors (in the role of the project board) are stakeholders. Other stakeholders are identified as the potential 'consumers' of the showcase and the owner of the Second Life Island (as a resource provider, or functional manager).

At project closure, the students typically demonstrate their showcase while meeting the project board in real world. One or more team members make a walk through with their avatar showing the various features. In a distance learning course it may be possible to accommodate this closing process within Second Life as an in-world meeting. In addition, the showcases are evaluated by the course tutor with their own avatar in-world to inspect the fulfillment of the constraints (number of prims used), the visual appeal, suitability for the 'general public' and the use of scripts. It should be emphasized that the final product, i.e. the showcase, is only a minor element in the marking process. The emphasis is rather on the proper project management as such. Information on this is drawn from the project documentation such as the highlight reports and the lessons learned report together with a personal reflection by the student.

Example Showcases

Figure 2 shows the showcase area of the undergraduate students of the Academic year 2008 / 2009. Platforms of 10m x 10m size have been provided and a maximum of 50 prims was allowed. The platforms were disconnected from each other and did float in the sky on two levels. That year a clear message was given to the students to make use of the creative potential of Second Life. A link to a Second Life exhibition, the 2009 Education Faire, was given so that the students may get inspired on how to build showcases. Still many groups did build 'houses' (with walls and a roof), but some preferred more open structures. One group build a car to illustrate smart technologies used in automotive industry.

The area used by the postgraduate students in that year is shown in Figure 3. Resource constraints on the University's Second Life island meant that the showcase was restricted to 10 prims and a 5m x 5m space was provided for each group. Platforms that accommodate four showcases each, as can be seen in Figure 1, have been provided on ground level. Because of the large number of more than fifty groups in that year a similar area has been setup on an adjacent island. Because of the prim limit most groups used slideshows, i.e. scripts that change images on a prim surface (when clicked or automatically after a certain delay) to convey information. A more architectural interesting structure can be seen in the foreground with a floating ball on top presumably to symbolize 'cloud' computing.

Figure 4 shows the showcases constructed during the undergraduate course in the Academic Year 2009 / 2010. Two parallel floating platforms that are connected by two bridges ac-

commodate in total 24 showcases of size 10m x 10m each. Although the builds of the previous year were available for the students to see and get ideas from, it seems that again house-like structures have been the preferred option. On the ground the area for the postgraduate students can be seen (compare with Figure 1) where building has just started.

FUTURE DIRECTIONS

While the assignment makes central use of Second Life as a platform it is not strictly used as a *remote* collaboration tool. The students are typically full time students having regular face to face meetings in real life. However, given how the task has been setup it should be possible to use this type of assignment in a pure online course, where students are locally distributed and only have contact with the tutor and each other remotely. Currently the Department of Computer Science and Technology at the University of Bedfordshire does not offer a remotely delivered course where Project Management is part of the syllabus, so it was not (yet) possible to test this option in practice.

The students doing the unit on Project Management were enrolled in computing related courses such as Computer Science, Networking or Computer Graphics. Hence a general affinity towards the use of computers and familiarity with user interfaces can be assumed for the student cohort discussed in this chapter. Indeed, Project Management is a generic skill applicable in many areas. It remains to be explored however if a Second Life based assignment for courses unrelated to computing, such as business, media or social studies would be similarly appropriate and successful. Anecdotal evidence suggests that users of Second Life (the 'residents') come from a wide range of social and educational backgrounds so it may well be the case that students without knowledge in computing may engage with the assignment easily and without any signification problems.

Another aspect is the technology advance within the Second Life platform or other virtual worlds. The new Second Life viewer 2.0 that allows to stream web contents on the surfaces of prims (shared media) provides new opportunities to extend the scope of the assignment. For instance a video production might be required as part of the assessment that could be integrated into the showcase. Clearly this would have a direct impact on the scope definition of the project and the subsequent quality management.

It should also be constantly monitored if indeed Second Life is the best virtual world for the purpose of this assignment. For administrative and budget purposes it may be advisable to move to a university owned world, for instance driven by the OpenSim platform. However this has a direct impact in relation to cost management (where the currency of L$ is used for budgeting) and procurement management (where the students have to deal with an external provider, namely Linden Labs) and it needs to be carefully reviewed if the benefits of a change away from Second Life to a different provider or software solution outweighs the potential loss of these features.

CONCLUSION

Virtual worlds offer new possibilities in the educational sector and we have shown how Second Life in particular can help to teach students the essential concepts of Project Management. Indeed areas that are difficult to address in 'conventional' assignments, such as cost, risk or quality management can be addressed in a very natural way within a multi user virtual environment. In addition, any practical assignment in Project Management should have some relevance to the student's degree and henceforth has to strike a balance: it needs to be challenging enough so that proper management is necessary, but on the other hand should not require the student to acquire knowledge unrelated to their pathway of study. The use of Second Life as it has been discussed in this chapter offers an approach that addresses these requirements based on the model of situated learning. Even more, in view of the technological advance and given that virtual environments may well play a more prominent role in society in the near future, this type of assignment provides useful, transferable skills that prepare students for work in a distributed and virtual environment.

REFERENCES

Conrad, M., Pike, D., Sant, P., & Nwafor, C. (2009). Teaching large student cohorts in Second Life. *International Conference on Computer Supported Education 2009, 1*, 11-18.

Herrington, J., & Oliver, R. (2000). An instructional design framework for authentic learning environments. *Educational Technology Research and Development, 48*(3), 23–48. doi:10.1007/BF02319856

Kemp, J., & Livingstone, D. (2006). Putting a Second Life "Metaverse" skin on Learning Management Systems. *Proceedings of the Second Life Education Workshop at SLCC, San Francisco*, (pp. 13-18).

Penfold, P., Ma, H., Choy, C., & Lav, N. (2008). *Handbook – orientation programme to Sl for PolyU students*. Retrieved May, 16, 2010, from http://www.scribd.com/doc/4612700/Handbook-Orientation- Programme-to-SL-for- PolyU-Students

PMI. (2008). *A guide to the Project Management Body of Knowledge (PMBOK® Guide)*. Newtown Square, PA: Project Management Institute.

Schwalbe, K. (2010). *Introduction to project management* (3rd ed.). Hamel, MN: Kathy Schwalbe LLC.

Shang, D. (2006). Caledon Oxbridge University. Retrieved May, 16, 2010, at http://slurl.com/sec-ondlife/ Caledon%20Oxbridge /92/197/27

Wilson, W. (2002). *Lessons in reality: Teaching project management, professionalism and ethics to third year IT students. Informing Science, InSITE - Where Parallels Intersect*. Informing Science Institute.

KEY TERMS AND DEFINITIONS

Human Resources: a term used to describe the individuals who comprise the workforce of an organization. In Project Management the two primary objectives of Human Resources Management are to ensure that the team has or acquires the necessary skills and to achieve team coherence.

PMBOK®: the Guide to the Project Management Body of Knowledge (PMBOK® Guide) is the de facto standard on defining Project Management. It is published by the Project Management Institute, a global organization that aims to represent the Project Management profession.

PRINCE2®: (Projects in Controlled Environments) is a process-based Project Management methodology. Because it is championed by the UK government it became the de-facto standard for project management in the United Kingdom.

Procurement Management: denotes the management of resourcing products or services externally (in contrast to having them developed by the project team directly).

Project Management: the discipline of planning, controlling and managing resources in order to achieve a successful completion of a project.

Project Scope Management: defined as the processes in Project Management that ensure that all (and only) the work required to complete the project is included in the course of planning and executing the project.

Project: temporary endeavor undertaken to create a unique product or service.

Quality: the degree to which a set of inherent characteristics fulfill requirements.

Situated Learning: a model of learning that takes place in the same context in which it is applied.

Chapter 20
Virtual Team Role Playing:
Development of a Learning Environment

Bjoern Jaeger
Molde University College, Norway & Curtin University, Australia

Berit Helgheim
Molde University College, Norway

ABSTRACT

Working in a virtual world creates new opportunities for both students and teachers. In particular, virtual team role play provides excellent support for collaborative learning approaches in a cost efficient manner. The purpose of this chapter is to describe experiences developing a virtual team role play learning environment in Second Life® over a period of three years. Theoretical justification for bringing role playing into a virtual world is provided. The chapter outlines the role play, its setup in both real and virtual world, and describes how it has evolved from a setup at one university, to a distributed case involving several locations. Experiences from role playing sessions are presented for each year.

INTRODUCTION

This chapter summarizes our experiences of developing a learning environment for virtual team role playing in Second Life. The development was carried out in the spring semesters of 2008, 2009 and 2010 in management information systems classes at Molde University College, Norway and at Curtin University of Technology in Perth, Australia. The role play selected is frequently used in information systems and business classes worldwide for addressing the complex issue of buying, implementing and using a particular type of information systems called Enterprise Resource Planning (ERP) systems. Students are introduced to various ERP-system characteristics in an engaging way by letting them act as a buyer in a purchasing team or a seller in a sales team. This chapter focuses on the establishment of a virtual learning environment in Second Life and the corresponding real world learning environment from which students login to Second Life. The

DOI: 10.4018/978-1-60960-545-2.ch020

combined setup of the two environments appeared to be a challenging task. We describe our efforts leading to recommendations while recognizing that the potential for improvements is still high.

Role Playing

A leading principle for us in creating learning environments is that it must increase student involvement, since according to Astin (1985), the effectiveness of any educational policy or practice is directly related to the capacity of that policy or practice to increase student involvement. In role playing, students actively participate in learning activities. Role play used for educational purposes has been a characteristic of the student-centred learning environment (Bloom, 1956; Aldrich, 2005; De Freitas, 2006). Through role play students engage in stories that are either open-ended or defined by a manuscript or a combination as is often the case in learning situations like ours, where students demonstrate their knowledge by filling in open parts. Role play is a social activity in which players act or take on specific roles presented to them. In doing so, players express their ideas, arguments and feelings, in their effort to convince others. Through the interaction, players get the opportunity to both share their knowledge and to extend their knowledge by learning from others. Role play has a high learning value in educational domains where skills such as critical thinking, group communication, debate and decision making are of high importance. Business education and information systems management are two such domains. In classes where the emphasis is upon choices, role play exercises focusing on decision making are ideal for supporting an educator's training needs (De Freitas, 2006). Recent developments of virtual worlds like Second Life have enabled the design of more sophisticated online role play environments which both mimic real world environments more closely than before, and which go beyond what is possible in real world domains (Aldrich, 2005; Jones, 2007).

Role playing in a virtual world setting have several advantages compared with a classroom setting. For example creating a business environment is difficult in a classroom compared to doing it in a virtual world regarding the appearance of the students and the creation of a modern business conference room. Also, a virtual world gives flexibility for off-campus guests and students to participate from office or home. Further; inviting off-campus guests to a virtual world session is cost efficient and easy.

In this role play there are three learning dimensions:

1. Students will gain knowledge of different ERP-systems;
2. Students will gain insight on selection criteria when purchasing information systems; and
3. The training aspects in acting in a simulated business environment, either as sales representatives or in a purchasing team

The Role Play Case

The role play selected is Response to Request-For-Proposal for an ERP-system. This is a well-developed and much used role play worldwide in business and management information systems classes described in the book *Enterprise Resource Planning* by Mary Sumner (2004). The context of the role play is a fictional mid-sized manufacturing company, Wingate Electric that has a set of computer applications handling their information management needs. Their applications have become fragmented over time and costly to operate and maintain; consequently the company is considering buying a new ERP-system to solve these problems. The new system should have functions supporting financial and accounting processes including general ledger and accounts payable/receivable, with the option of adding modules for production planning and manufacturing later on. The company develops a request-for-proposal which describes their needs of a new system. There

Table 1. Example of Role Play Setup for 30 Students

Set 1	Team 1: Purchasing	4 students
	Team 2: Sale vendor A	4 students
	Team 3: Sale vendor B	4 students
	Team 4: Sale vendor C	4 students
Set 2	Team 1: Purchasing	4 students
	Team 2: Sale vendor A	4 students
	Team 3: Sale vendor B	3 students
	Team 4: Sale vendor C	3 students
Total: Two sets	8 teams	30 students

Table 2. Example of Minimal Role Play Setup Involving 3 Students

Set 1	Team 1: Purchasing	1 student
	Team 2: Sale vendor A	1 students
	Team 3: Sale vendor B	1 students
Total: One set	3 teams	3 students

are three competing ERP-vendors who respond to the request-for-proposal; Oracle, Microsoft and SAP. After a presentation by each vendor, Wingate goes through a decision process to decide upon a winner. A class using the role play is organized into several sets of four teams; one sales team with four members for each of the three vendors and one purchasing team with four members representing a panel of managers from Wingate Electric. In this way 16 students participate in each set. The number of participants in each team can be adjusted from one to more than four according to the class size. For example a class with 30 students can be set up as:

The number of vendors represented by a sales team can also be adjusted with minimal effort. Thus, the setup is very flexible regarding the number of students and roles played. A minimal configuration consists of three students; two sales teams with one sales manager each and one purchasing team with a purchasing manager.

During the preparations, each team has to complete a literature search and eventually other actions like contacting the vendors in order to gather information and to develop specific deliverables to be used during the role play. This preparation phase is considered to be important for the learning outcome related to the specific topics studied (i.e. characteristics of ERP systems). The role playing activity in itself is considered a strong motivational factor for the preparation.

Deliverables for the purchasing team is a scorecard developed based on a set of selection criteria and a scoring method for evaluation of alternative ERP-systems. Each sales team develops a sales presentation. The teams are given the company background of Wingate Electric together with team directions, a list of roles with job titles, the background of each role and pointers to literature. In the role playing act, each sales team presents their ERP-system while the purchasing team from Wingate Electric asks questions and use the scorecard to record their marks. When all sales have completed their presentations the purchasing team uses scores given to decide upon a winning vendor. Before announcing the winner they provide feedback to each sales team in regards to how effectively each presentation addressed the selection criteria. The amount of work assigned for the role play can easily be adjusted depending on the focus of the class and the time available. The preparation part can be comprehensive requiring the students to do all the preparations themselves, or it can be minimal by handing out pre-made sales team presentations and pre-made scorecards for the purchasing team to complete.

In the remainder of the chapter we provide a theoretical justification and an outline of our development methodology. This is followed by a section describing our development efforts over the last three years, and a section that summarizes our recommendations for future improvements.

THEORETICAL JUSTIFICATION AND DEVELOPMENT METHODOLOGY

Explicit and Tacit Knowledge

In practice purchasing decisions are made based on both explicit and tacit knowledge. The purpose of the role play is to introduce students to basic characteristics of ERP-systems together with an introduction to the purchasing decision process including the importance of teams and the use of explicit and tacit knowledge. Giunipero, Dawley and Anthony found that approximately equal amounts of formal data and tacit knowledge were used in buying decisions made by purchasing managers (1999). Tacit knowledge relates to personal experiences, it represents knowledge that is used in evaluation, points of view, commitments and decisions. This type of knowledge is difficult to articulate or codify. Introducing a team-oriented role play to convey tacit knowledge requires a rich medium like Second Life capable of conveying multiple cues expressing this knowledge. A simulated business environment in Second Life can be used for training students to act in real business environments. Further, by recording the sessions in Second Life students can review their performance.

In contrast to tacit knowledge, explicit knowledge is knowledge that has been codified. Explicit knowledge in the form of vendor websites, online library resources, trade publications and marketing publications only takes a purchase manager half the way to make a decision. Students and inexperienced purchase managers typically break social norms and misunderstand subtle cues that experienced buyers take for granted. When teaching we would like to introduce students to the importance of tacit knowledge in making purchasing decisions. Role plays have been found to be a useful technique in teaching people-facing skills including training purchasing and sales people.

Role Playing in Second Life

Second Life being a non-gaming virtual world imagined and created by its users can be used for role play. The primary interaction object in Second Life is an avatar which is a representation of a user. The term was made popular by Neal Stephenson (1992) in his novel *Snow Crash,* but the word originates from the Sanskrit word Avatāra which means descent. An avatar in Second Life has human characteristics, including speech and facial expressions which enables the transfer of expressions in the affective domain.

In the section below we present three arguments to justify bringing role playing from the real world into the virtual world. The first argument is actually a set of arguments that follows from Media Richness Theory from the management information systems field described below, the second is cost efficiency which includes an increased opportunity to use external guest experts from real companies in the role play, and in the third argument we claim that virtual worlds are superior to video conferencing for role playing.

Media Richness Theory Arguments

The researchers Daft and Lengel proposed that communication media have varying capacities for resolving ambiguity and facilitating understanding (Daft & Lengel, 1984). Although some researchers question parts of the theory, it has been successfully used to describe the suitability of a communications medium to communicate certain tasks, and we find that it provides useful insight in the characteristics of virtual worlds. The main assumptions of Media Richness Theory are that individuals, groups, and organizations process information to reduce uncertainty and equivocality, and that some communication media process information in a more suitable way than others for a given task.

Uncertainty is the difference between the amount of information required to perform the

319

task and the amount of information already possessed. By increasing the amount of information uncertainty can be reduced. Equivocality is defined as the ambiguity inherent in the task caused by conflicting interests and expectations. It cannot be reduced by increasing the amount of information. It is handled by negotiations and risk assessment which incorporate the inherent uncertainty and provide a foundation for management decisions involving equivocality together. It is closely related to the tacit knowledge of the manager.

Richness is characterized by four properties:

1. Multiplicity of cues;
2. Ability to provide feedback;
3. Ability to provide personal focus; and
4. Capability of language variety.

When tasks entail processing highly equivocal information, as is required for example in the negotiation process in purchasing, then the medium that supports communications and information processing must be rich. For the task of processing unequivocal information such as performing a standard business transaction or filling out a standard form then a less rich medium is suitable. A face-to-face meeting is rich because gestures, facial expressions, surrounding contexts, and other sensory cues provide rich supplementary information beyond spoken or written words.

The four properties of Media Richness Theory are seen to support the use of Second Life for role play as follows:

1. *Multiplicity of cues*: Cues can steer participants towards issues that help make real progress in a role play, and away from distracting ones. Cues can inform the avatar in action (purchaser or vendor) where they are in the process i.e. what has been delivered and what remains. Cues can monitor and report reactions of the purchaser to the vendor, and vice versa. The avatar appearance is a cue that can help to create realistic role plays (Jones,

2007), as can the group memberships of an avatar. Group membership is a fundamental social structure in Second Life stored in the avatar's profile shown by right-clicking on the avatar.

Cues in the real world where students log in to Second Life must be considered since these can also be used to help participants focus on issues that make real progress, and away from distracting ones. Important issues here are what kind of environment the workstation is in (PC lab, office, living room, bedroom, kitchen or office at home), how many others are co-located in the same room, if others are co-located; what do they do, are they connected to Second Life), and what other visual and audible sources are affecting the person participating in the role play.

2. *Feedback capabilities* are supported in two ways in Second Life. First, the virtual environment supports instant feedback from other avatars and from constructs within Second Life. Secondly, feedback can be supported by using recordings. Second Life, being a mediated technology via a PC, inherits the intrinsic property of mediated technologies that they can be recorded, stored and played back with little effort and small costs. Recording is not an option in Second Life, but one can use screen recording programmes that record all activities including sound into a movie file. Popular recording tools are Camtasia (2008) and Fraps (2008). Recording and playback enables a post-exercise reflection of the virtual-experience and a debriefing of the experiences which is important for the learning outcome (De Freitas, 2006). In addition, and of high practical value, is that it provides valuable feedback to the teachers and the learning environment designers.

3. *Personal focus* is supported by the use of avatars together with instant text messages or voice chat that can be used for all users,

a group of users or between two users. This separation of channels is not possible to do in a real classroom environment or in video conferencing. Personal focus is also supported by the feeling of presence users experience when acting via their avatar in virtual worlds (Gorini, Gaggioli, Vigna, & Riva, 2008).

4. *Capability of language variety*: This is the range of meaning that can be conveyed by language in a broad sense. For example numbers and formulas provide precision, while natural speaking language conveys broader meaning with more uncertain and equivocal messages. This can be denoted as multiplicity of communication forms which is supported in Second Life through facilities like voice chat and instant messages.

Cost Efficiency Argument

Second Life has the capability to create a wide range of learning environments in a cost efficient way compared with real life environments. A real life role play would be substantially more expensive due to the costs of co-locating participants, allocating or renting professional meeting rooms, changing the appearance of the academics into a business style, and setting up studio recording capabilities. A promising opportunity is the possibility to invite guest experts from other organizations and businesses at virtually zero monetary cost. Professionals being experts in their field can give guest lectures, advise students and participate in interactive discussions and role plays. It makes it possible for students to interact directly with experts. The few studies that have reported involvement of virtual guest experts in mediated teaching environments found that students were excited by the opportunity of holding discussions with the guest hosts, and vice versa; the guests were positive about spending time doing the interaction (Kumari, 2001; Wearmouth, Smith,

& Soler, 2004). We see it as an additional factor for motivation.

Virtual Worlds are Superior to Video Conferencing Argument

Video conferencing is a common technology in distance education. At Molde University College, various forms of video conferencing are used in several classes (web-based by Elluminate and Marratech, in a dedicated studio by Tandberg). Video conferencing does not support distributed/virtual teams who would like to meet in a common virtual place even if each participant is located on a separate geographical location. Making efficient team presentations, performing negotiations, showing group membership and coordinating activities is hard in this environment. Virtual worlds, on the other hand offer the possibility to create a common virtual place to meet. One can create realistic environments familiar to the participants, participants can easily express team membership by grouping themselves together much in the same way as in real life. At the same time they can utilize the range of communication facilities like private and group conversations.

Methodology

We base our development of the learning environment on principles of design science in information systems research. It is a problem-solving paradigm that seeks to create innovations using information systems (Simon, 1996) where design is seen as both a process and a product. The learning environment is the design product and our design process consists of the activities design, run and evaluate as illustrated in Figure 1. The evaluation provides feedback and a better understanding of the learning environment in order to improve both the environment and the role play assignment. This design-run-evaluate sequence is repeated each semester. It goes on as long as the role playing takes place to incorporate

Figure 1. Continuous Development of the Learning Environment in a Design-Run-Evaluate Loop

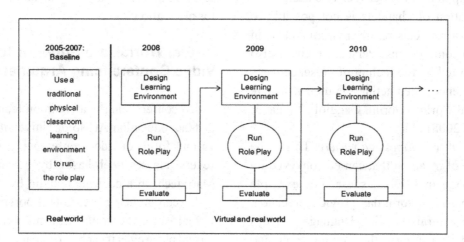

technological innovations and lessons learned in each semester.

DEVELOPMENT OF THE LEARNING ENVIRONMENT

Background

Role play had been used at Molde University College in a traditional on-campus classroom environment for three years (2005–2007) when a need emerged to use role play in a class given simultaneously in three cities by video conferencing. Video conferencing has inherent characteristics that make it unsuitable for multi-party role playing with parties in several physical locations (see section above) leading us to consider Second Life for running the role play. Our experiences with Second Life from other projects were promising and the virtual campus provided just what we needed: a common place for geographically distributed participants to meet (Creelman, Richardson, & Petrakou, 2008; Molka-Danielsen, Carter, Richardson, & Jæger, 2009). Thus we decided to use Second Life for the course with students in three different cities. The setup has been gradually improved and used in various classes in 2008, 2009

and 2010 as we describe in the next sections and as illustrated in Figure 1.

Baseline Real World Role Play Environment 2005–2007

Role play is frequently used in information systems and business classes for addressing the complex issue of buying, implementing and using ERP systems. The role play was created by Prof. M. Sumner from Southern Illinois University Edwardsville, USA who used it in a seminar series when visiting Molde University College in 2005, 2006 and 2007. The role play is described in Sumner's book *Enterprise Resource Planning* (2004) in the case "Response to Request-For-Proposal for an ERP-system". The elements of the role play were described in Section "The Role Play Case". This is a highly simplified description of the process of selecting an ERP-system. Real organizations typically spend several months making a decision. The classroom was set up for the role play by letting the four members of the purchasing team from Wingate Electric sit at a panel table at the top right of the classroom. The four members of a sales team gave their presentation at the PC connected to the video projector at the top left of the classroom. The students who did not take an active part in the role play watched the presentations from the desks in the classroom. They were asked to give their marks on a scorecard provided by the selection committee to keep all students in the class engaged.

Role Playing in Second Life 2008

Since we had no experience in running a distributed role play in Second Life we needed technical equipment, time for training participants, and time to make the learning material. It became clear that running a full-scale role play in Second Life would be a highly risky attempt, thus we decided to do initial investigations by running a Pilot Study in March 2008 to test logistics and gather information prior to the full-scale test to be done in March 2009.

The role play was used in the courses LOG505 Purchase Management and BØK700 Enterprise Resource Planning (ERP) with SAP at Molde University College. LOG505 is delivered to three cities simultaneously via video conferencing, while BØK700 is on-campus in Molde. A detailed description of the setup, questionnaires used and results are described in our technical report/ working paper (Jæger & Helgheim, 2008). Here we will highlight the major aspects.

Design 2008

Environment to Conduct the Role Play

As were described in Section "The Role Play Case" this type of meeting is typically held in a high-end executive conference room since buying an ERP-system is often the single largest investment a company makes in a time horizon of 10–20 years. We wanted an executive board room in Second Life to make the role play realistic. DnB NOR, Norway's largest bank/financial services group had their own island with business environments including executive meeting rooms as shown in Figure 2 (2008). DnB NOR were willing to lend us the room.

The meeting room was perfect for our needs, it was located in a business building, it had a large conference table suitable for the role play, a reception area for participants to meet, and a business lounge to relax during breaks.

Avatar Dress Code

Avatars should be dressed formally in a typical executive style to be aligned with the formal real world environment. Avatar appearance is one cue from the real world that can be mimicked in the virtual world. We assume that the first impression largely defines "who" an avatar is – the three-second-first-impression – just like in the real world. However, since none of the students had any previous experience with Second Life, and since we were on a strict time schedule with no time for training, we chose not to focus on avatar appearance in the pilot role play. The students were asked to create their avatars and preferably be dressed in an executive style.

Real World Setup to Log On to Second Life

A new setup for three locations connecting via Second Life was required. We had no experience in running Second Life in three locations simultaneously with several students at each location. We needed technical equipment, time for training participants, and time to make the learning material. A full-scale role play in Second Life would be a highly risky attempt, thus we decided to do initial investigations by running the pilot study in March 2008 to test logistics and gather information. PCs that could run Second Life were allocated, as well as headsets with microphones at each of the three locations in Molde, Ålesund and Kristiansund. The Internet firewalls at the three locations were configured to allow Second Life with voice chat. Each of the three educational locations was equipped with computer labs or auditorium with video projector and loudspeakers connected to a PC running Second Life.

This year, participating in the role play in Second Life was voluntary. Students who did

Figure 2. Snapshot of Second Life virtual team role playing in the board room of DnB NOR. The Wingate Electric purchasing team is on the right hand side and the Oracle sales team is on the left hand side. At the near end of the table is an invited guest expert from DnB NOR and a course instructor

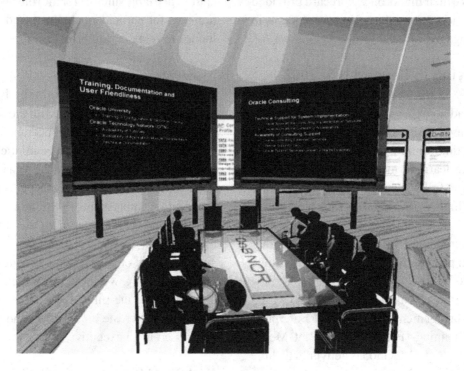

Figure 3. The three cities of role play participants were Kristiansund, Molde and Ålesund where instructors and students log on to Second Life from a PC in a campus classroom or PC-lab. The guest expert logs in from his business office in Oslo

not participate in the role play observed the session on a large screen via a video projector and loudspeakers connected to a PC in the computer lab/classroom.

Run 2008

Running the role play was organized in three steps. First, we had a briefing session in which students were informed about the nature and purpose of the role play and they were give a 30 minute introduction to Second Life. Second, the role play was run. Third, when all sales teams had finished a debriefing session was held in which the purchasing team provided feedback to each sales team with respect to how effectively each presentation addressed the selection criteria before they announced the winner. The debriefing ended with a discussion of the experiences at each site.

Invited Guest Experts

Four professionals in four Norwegian companies were asked to participate in the role play. All of them were enthusiastic and would do the guest appearance pro bono for the course. The professionals had experience of using ERP-systems and of buying and selling large complex software systems. The four companies asked were: DnB NOR, Ernst and Young, The Norwegian Labour and Welfare Administration (NAV) and Wise Consulting. The professionals were excited to be using Second Life to be in direct contact with students. Reasons mentioned were: it might help in recruiting new employees, enable new innovative business opportunities, and use Second Life as a collaborative tool for team work. Due to the limited scope of our pilot study we only used an expert from DnB NOR. The purpose of having a professional present was also to enhance the feeling of a real life experience for the students, and to get feedback from professionals on student performance and role play content.

Evaluation 2008

The evaluation method was a combination of informal discussions with teachers and students and a questionnaire. The major findings are reported here, details are given in Jæger & Helgheim (2008).

Student Perceptions

12 students participated in the role play, 26 were observers. The students were asked questions with a five-point scale were 5 is the highest score. Note; in this pilot study we did not focus on the perceived learning outcome but rather on the technical implementation of the role play and likewise the setup and handling of the questionnaire. 6 of 12 participating students answered the questionnaire, and all the 26 observing students. The major findings were:

- For observers who followed the role play on the large screen with audio from loud speakers the session soon became hard to follow. This was caused by a number of distracting cues. A major one being that they first heard the person representing the avatar speaking in real life, then a fraction of a second later the same voice came from the loud speakers. The delay is due to the fact that the Second Life servers are in California and clients in Europe. Furthermore the slides displayed in Second Life were too small to be seen properly on the large screen.
- Participants in Second Life must have a specific set of Second Life-skills needed for the play for it to run smoothly with as few distracting cues as possible, such as: handling the toggle to talk button and other voice controls, using the presentation tools, entering and leaving the meeting room in a proper way, learning how to open the meeting and introduce themselves.

Figure 4. An executive meeting room at the Kamimo virtual campus was created and used since it simplified access right management. Kamimo is owned by Molde University College

Other Findings:

- Students were immersed in their roles: even when one of the observing avatars was bored and started flying naked over the conference table (!) the players kept on with their presentation and discussion.
- Even with minimal introduction in Second Life the players adopted well to their roles in a realistic way. This was evident by senior managers taking the lead, and area specific managers asking proper questions for their role. The sales representatives made up their own sales stories in addition to the ones handed out to improve their presentation.

Role Playing in Second Life 2009

The role play was used in the courses LOG702 Purchasing and Supply Chain Theory at Molde University College. These students had no knowl-

edge of ERP-systems. As an introduction to the role play the students were given a three-hour lecture of ERP-systems. They were also shown an example of a real ERP system from SAP.

Design 2009

Real World Setup: This year the role play was conducted on a single campus with students logging in to Second Life from two separate classrooms/PC-labs. The sales team in one and the purchasing team in the other room. The teacher controlled that only one student was speaking at a time.

Avatar Dress Code
As can be seen from the screen below the dress code for avatars was still an issue to address.

Run 2009

The role play in 2009 was done for a single class in a single campus but with students in separate

Figure 5. Avatars from the Purchasing team 2009. On the left hand side we see the CEO as a human and the financial manager as a gorilla. On the right hand side we see the sales team from Oracle

rooms. The sessions were recorded using Fraps. Based on the more than three hours of video we made a four minute long summary video. The video is available on You Tube: http://www.youtube.com/watch?v=bqwjNB4-skc

Evaluation 2009

The evaluation method was a combination of informal discussions with teachers and students and a questionnaire as in 2008.

Student Perceptions

The students were asked questions with the same five-point scale as in 2008; 10 of 20 students answered the questionnaire. Here we report on three major findings.

- The students rated both the learning outcome of doing the role play in Second Life as an alternative to a classroom, and the influence of being in a simulated real life meeting room environment as somewhat better in Second Life than traditional role playing in classrooms.
- On the question of whether the role play had any learning effect related to the theory in the course, the students rated this as somewhat higher than average. This indicates that the students were able to use the

theoretical aspects on purchasing learned in the course in a practical situation.

- The learning outcome regarding ERP-systems was rated as low. This was probably due to the fact that the students only had the three hour lecture on ERP-systems as a basis. For such students, the introduction to ERP-systems should be extended for the role play to be effective in this regard.

Role Playing in Second Life 2010

Design 2010

We used the same meeting room as in 2009. In 2010 we extended the role play to an international setting where students from one class in Molde, Norway and one class in Perth Australia participated in the same role play forming true virtual teams. A virtual team is defined as a group of people who interact through inter-dependant tasks guided by common purpose and work across space, time and organizational boundaries with links strengthened by webs of communication technologies (Lipnack & Stamps, 1997).

Run 2010

The students in Norway and Australia did not know each other which made the virtual team role play

Figure 6. Presentation by the Sales Team from SAP Business ByDesign (Molde, Norway)

Figure 7. Examples of Avatars with a Business Appearance

more realistic. Doing the role play in Second Life was voluntary; the students not participating had to do it in a classroom. All 22 students in Molde volunteered for Second Life while 6 of 24 students in Perth joined giving a total of 28 students. The students in Perth formed two sales teams. The other teams were in Molde.

Avatar Dress Code

This year we required the avatars to follow a business dress code. We provided them with

several suitable business wardrobes for them to select from both for women and men. Examples are shown below.

Evaluation 2010

The method used was, as in 2008 and 2009, a combination of informal discussions with teachers and students and a questionnaire. Here we report on the major findings.

Student Perceptions

This year we used a seven-point Likert scale together with the opportunity to give comments as free text; 18 of the 22 students in Molde answered the questionnaire. All 6 students in Perth answered the questionnaire.

The results in Molde and Perth were nearly identical so we present the combined results.

- The students considered the role play as useful and that it could be used by real businesses (average: 5.1).
- The students perceived that they got a feeling of presence / got a good feeling of presence (average: 4.4)
- They considered the amount of work required for doing the role play in Second Life as about the same or less as doing the role play in real life.

Additional comments on the open-ended questions were:

- I learnt something useful this way. My attitude towards Second Life is quite positive.
- It (Second Life) has many advantages and provides a good feeling of presence, as it is 3D.
- Gives a feeling of presence and of real life. A very good experience.
- No stage fright to worry about. So easier to time presentation precisely.
- I did not have any faith in it when we made our Avatar but was impressed when we did our presentation.
- It was efficient and real-time business decision making.
- Feeling of distance was less than expected.
- You don't have the feeling of seeing the person and his/her facial expressions.
- Need better internet connection. Sometime it does not work because of the distance.

- Bad sound and fast talking presenters – I had problems to get everything that was said.

RECOMMENDATIONS

The environment is clearly an interesting arena for running virtual team role plays, yet we still see potential for improvements. Some recommendations are given in this section.

1. Let Each Participant be Alone in a Separate Physical Room

This will reduce the number of distracting cues and help students to get a feeling of presence in the virtual environment. We used classrooms, PC-labs, and offices.

2. Provide Business Clothing for Avatars

This will reduce the number of distracting cues and help to create an immersive situation.

3. Make Sure Voice Chat Works and that Participants are Trained to Handle the Voice Features

Voice is an important communication channel. The voice service in Second Life is not a straight forward plug-and-play service. Special considerations must be taken for the setup of the PCs used, the headsets and the voice configuration in Second Life. The management of all students and coordination of setup needs special attention. The basic procedure used to set up and test the sound was:

a. Test the network connection and loud speakers by playing a You Tube video.
b. Test microphones and headsets by using Skype and its call-back function.

c. Test voice in Second Life by:
  i. Teleporting the Avatar to the Voice Test site in Second life. This site has a similar functionality as the call back functionality in Skype;
  ii. Teleporting to the virtual board room to be used in the role play, arrange to meet others and talk to them. Adjust voice settings.

4. Record the Second Life Role Playing Sessions

a. Use an external recording tool like Camtasia or Fraps.
b. A standard PC with one sound card one cannot talk in Second Life at the same time as voice chat is recorded.
c. Use a separate PC and avatar for this, or buy a sound card with multiple I/O channels.

5. Further Improvements

a. Consider using a set of pre-made avatars as role models given to the students.
b. Scale the virtual meeting room by making the presentation screens larger and the conference table and chairs smaller.
c. Let the conference table be in a separate room with no other avatars than the participating ones (and possibly the ones recording).
d. Make guidelines for external experts on technical issues like how to connect, where and how to meet in Second Life, and guidelines on how to act in Second Life, where to sit, what is expected/wanted behaviour.
e. Each run should consist of briefing, running and debriefing

CONCLUSION

Our experiences are that the students have adopted both tacit and explicit knowledge by participat-

ing in the virtual team role play in Second Life. A thorough and comprehensive preparation is required by the students in order to gain a successful learning outcome.

In general the technical operation of Second Life is not a problem. The students handled the environment well (moving around, operating menus, appearance, etc.) after 30 minutes of training. However, there were two major barriers that were constant challenges. One was getting voice chat to work and maintaining it over time. The other was that the Second Life client only runs on PCs with certain types of graphic card. We consider these two issues to be a result of the contemporary technology used and that these issues will be of a lesser problem as the technology evolves. Lastly we observed that by bringing in participants from other organizations (external experts or students from other universities) the atmosphere became more formal, more focused and more like in a real business environment.

REFERENCES

Aldrich, C. (2005). *Learning by doing*. San Francisco, CA: Pfeiffer.

Astin, A. W. (1985). Involvement: The cornerstone of excellence. *Change, 17*(4), 35–39. doi:10.108 0/00091383.1985.9940532

Bloom, B. S. (1956). *The taxonomy of educational objectives: Classification of educational goals handbook 1: The cognitive domain*. New York, NY: McKay Press.

Camtasia. (2008). Retrieved 15 September, 2008, from http://www.techsmith.com/

Creelman, A., Richardson, D., & Petrakou, A. (2008). *Teaching and learning in Second Life - experience from the Kamimo project*. Online Information Conference, London, UK.

Daft, R. L., & Lengel, R. H. (1984). Information richness: A new approach to managerial behavior and organizational design. In Cummings, L. L., & Staw, B. M. (Eds.), *Research in organizational behavior* (pp. 191–233). Homewood, IL: JAI Press.

De Freitas, S. (2006) *Learning in immersive worlds*. Joint Information Systems Committee (JISC) e-Learning Programme, UK. Retrieved 15 September 2008, from http://www.jisc.ac.uk/media/documents/programmes/elearninginnovation/gamingreport_v3.pdf

DnB NOR. (2008). *DnB NOR*. Retrieved 15 September 2008, from: https://www.dnbnor.com

Fraps. (2008). Retrieved 15 September, 2008 from http://www.fraps.com/

Giunipero, L., Dawley, D., & Anthony, W. P. (1999). The impact of tacit knowledge on purchasing decisions. *The Journal of Supply Chain Management*, 35(1), 42–49. doi:10.1111/j.1745-493X.1999.tb00055.x

Gorini, G., Gaggioli, A., Vigna, C., & Riva, G. (2008). A Second Life for e-health: Prospects for the use of 3-D virtual worlds in clinical psychology. *Journal of Medical Internet Research, 10*(3), e21. Retrieved 10 October, 2008 from http://www.jmir.org/2008/3/e21/

Jæger, B., & Helgheim, B. (2008). *Results from a role play exercise in Second Life for LOG505 and BØK700*. (Working Paper/Arbeidsnotat 2008:11), Molde University College, Norway.

Jones, S. (2007). Adding value to online role plays: Virtual situated learning environments. *Proceedings of Ascilite, Singapore 2007*.

Kumari, D. S. (2001). Connecting graduate students to virtual guests through asynchronous discussions – analysis of an experience. *Journal of Asynchronous Learning Networks*, 5(2), 53–63.

Lipnack, J., & Stamps, J. (1997). *Virtual teams*. New York, NY: John Wiley and Sons, Inc.

Molka-Danielsen, J., Carter, B. W., Richardson, D., & Jæger, B. (2009). Teaching and learning effectively within a virtual campus. *International Journal of Networking and Virtual Organisations*, 6(5), 476–498. doi:10.1504/IJNVO.2009.027392

Simon, H. A. (1996). *The sciences of the artificial* (3rd ed.). Cambridge, MA: MIT Press.

Stephenson, N. (1992). *Snow crash*. New York, NY: Bantam Spectra Books.

Sumner, M. (2004). *Enterprise resource planning*. Upper Saddle River, NJ: Prentice Hall.

Wearmouth, J., Smith, A. P., & Soler, J. (2004). Computer conferencing with access to a guest expert in the professional development of special educational needs coordinators. *British Journal of Educational Technology*, 35(1), 81–93. doi:10.1111/j.1467-8535.2004.00370.x

KEY TERMS AND DEFINITIONS

Avatar: An avatar is a representation of a user. It originates from the Sanskrit word Avatāra which means descent.

ERP-system: A digital information system that seamlessly supports and automates business processes by integrating functional areas and sharing data across an organization.

Explicit Knowledge: Knowledge that has been codified.

Learning Environment: The place and setting where learning occurs; it includes the characteristics of the setting.

Role Playing: A social activity in which players act or take on specific roles presented to them.

Tacit Knowledge: Knowledge that relates to personal experiences, it represents knowledge that is used in evaluation, points of view, commitments and decisions.

Virtual Team: A group of people who interact through inter-dependant tasks guided by common purpose and work across space, time and organizational boundaries with links strengthened by webs of communication technologies (Lipnack & Stamps, 1997).

Chapter 21
Cross–University Collaborative Learning:
Extending the Classroom via Virtual Worlds

Anne P. Massey
Indiana University, USA

Mitzi M. Montoya
Arizona State University, USA

Valerie Bartelt
Indiana University, USA

ABSTRACT

Over the last two decades, communication and collaboration tools to support student project work have evolved significantly, with an expanding array of options. Most recently, 3D virtual worlds (VW) have emerged. This chapter explores the use of collaborative tools in a cross-university course where student ("virtual") teams engaged in a multi-week project. The student project teams had access to a collaborative toolkit that included Web 1.0 (traditional) and Web 2.0 tools, as well as collaboration spaces in a VW. Findings suggest that more successful student teams were better able to match Web 2.0 and VW collaborative technologies to project activities, while other lower performing teams defaulted to more familiar Web 1.0 technologies. The VW played a key role in facilitating relationship building in the collaborative learning process. The findings are particularly relevant to instructors seeking to integrate and use VWs in the classroom for collaborative project work and distance learning settings.

DOI: 10.4018/978-1-60960-545-2.ch021

INTRODUCTION

The concept of collaborative learning has been widely researched and is generally accepted as beneficial for critical thinking, student satisfaction, learning enhancement and performance (David, 1993; Gokhale, 1995). Collaborative learning involves social (interpersonal) processes by which a small group of learners work together on a problem-solving task (Alavi, 1994; Dillenbourg, 1999). The concept itself is based on premises of effective learning, including active learning and the construction of knowledge (Wittrock, 1978); cooperation and teamwork (c.f., Glaser & Bassok, 1989); and, learning "by doing" (Massey, Ramesh, & Khatri, 2006).

Over the last two decades, whole new opportunities for collaborative learning have emerged as new communication and collaboration tools have become available, particularly in the context of distance education. As of 2009, according to the U.S. Department of Education[1], over 65% of two and four-year colleges in the U.S. offered college-level distance education courses. Yet, even with the array of communication and collaboration technologies, a specific challenge facing distance education is how to get distributed students to collaborate in teams in a way that is efficient and effective (Guth, 2006).

Email, document repositories, telephone/ teleconferencing, and web/video-conferencing, among technologies characterized as more "traditional", are still widely used to support distance learning (Bates, 2005). Recently, we have been witnessing the integration of Web 2.0 tools such as wikis, blogs and social networking applications into learning environments (Sigala, 2007). And today, while still in a nascent phase, three dimensional (3D) virtual worlds (VWs) are emerging as new learning platforms. A VW is a computer simulated 3D environment where users relate using visual representations of themselves known as avatars. Participants can meet and interact with others and with the content and objects of the VW (Bartle, 2004). Avatars can communicate using text, audio/video, and gestures (Benford, Greenhalgh, Rodden, & Pycock, 2001). Because several people can affect the same environment simultaneously, the world is considered shared or multi-user. As of late, there is growing interest in using VWs to support collaborative distance education (Ritzema & Harris, 2008).

Collectively, traditional media ("Web 1.0"), Web 2.0 tools, and VWs (e.g., *Second Life, Open Wonderland*) can offer a collaborative toolkit for distance learners. Ultimately, however, students and instructors select collaborative tools for a variety of reasons. For example, some students may have different access to, experience with or preference for particular tools. While both Web 2.0 and VWs offer the potential to enable and enhance the efforts of distributed student teams, evidence from the organizational research literature suggests that team members tend to default to tools they are most familiar and comfortable with (Montoya, Massey, Hung, & Crisp, 2009; Lassila & Hendler, 2007), regardless of whether or not the particular tool is a good "fit" to the project activities.

In this chapter, we explore the use of collaborative tools by cross-university ("virtual") student teams engaged in a multi-week course and innovation project. The student teams had access to a collaborative toolkit that included three types of tools: Web 1.0 (email, document repository, telephone/teleconferencing), Web 2.0 (wiki, text-chat), and collaboration spaces in *Second Life*, a VW developed by Linden Lab. We observed the teams as they worked and captured feedback upon completion of their projects in order to understand how various types of tools were deployed in support of their class projects. Upon completion of the course, we examined the relative importance of each tool type to project activities, and also how team-level choice of tools was related to project performance. We were particularly interested in understanding the role a VW could play in supporting distance education-based collaborative learning.

BACKGROUND

Collaborative Learning and Task-Technology Fit

Teamwork enables collaborative learning by allowing participants to improve their mental models of a particular domain during the problem-solving process (i.e., while working together on an academic task). Enabling and achieving the benefits of collaborative learning through technology-support (and other means) requires, however, an understanding of underlying team functions and behaviors.

Group communication research suggests that teams perform various simultaneous functions as they work toward goals, including: *production* (performance of the task), *team well-being* (relationships among team members), and *member-support* (relationships with others) (McGrath, 1991; Fjermestad & Hiltz, 1998). While team interaction can be conceptualized in different ways, it broadly includes behaviors in support of team functions and task activities.

Specifically, past research identifies three categories of team behaviors underlying the three functions: *informational behaviors, decisional behaviors,* and *interpersonal behaviors* (Briggs, Nunamaker, & Sprague, 1997; Marks, Mathieu, & Zaccaro, 2001). Information exchange behaviors refer to the efforts made by team members to *convey* data, information, and knowledge. Decision-making behaviors involve team members critically examining others' contributions with the goal of *converging* to a common understanding such that a decision can be reached or problem solved. Team decision-making behaviors also include *coordination* or process/project management efforts, such as the establishment of operating procedures and how the team will proceed. Both information exchange

and decision-making behaviors directly support the production function of a team (Marks, Mathieu, & Zaccaro, 2001; McGrath, 1991). Finally, *social/relational* behaviors involve managing relations among team members as well as relations between individual members and the team. The development of relational ties is associated with team member support and team well-being functions. Interpersonal processes often involve interactions not germane to the focal performance task, e.g., socializing, personal or interpersonal discussions (McGrath, 1991; Warkentin, Sayeed, & Hightower, 1997).

In order to enable the necessary team functions and underlying behaviors, distributed teams – in this case, virtual student teams – should have appropriate collaborative infrastructures available to them (c.f., Duarte & Synder, 2006; Beise, 2004). The concept of "fit" between the capabilities of collaborative tools and student team behaviors is essential to team interactions and ultimately collaborative learning and project performance (Massey, Montoya, & Hung, 2003).

Generally, face-to-face work sets the standard for communication – it is the basis of comparison when evaluating a collaborative technology. By comparison, a collaborative tool may be described in terms of three highly related dimensions: *richness, interactivity,* and *social presence* (Daft, Lengel, & Trevino, 1987; Zack, 1993; Short, Williams, & Christie, 1976). Richness is the extent to which a collaborative tool can be used to transmit both verbal and nonverbal cues. Interactivity is the extent to which rapid feedback is allowed. Social presence is the degree to which a sense of others is felt. As an example, email is considered lower on all three dimensions than videoconferencing, and face-to-face would be highest on all three dimensions. Collaborative technologies may also be categorized according to whether or not the enable synchronous (same time) or asynchronous (different time) communications. Synchronous tools include such things as text-chat, video/audio-conferencing, and VWs.

Asynchronous tools include such things as email, document repositories, and wikis.

Given their immersive and interactive nature, VWs have the potential to transform collaboration by offering not only very high levels of richness, interactivity, and presence, but also capabilities not previously possible, including movement within and between virtual spaces, and the overall enrichment of experience.

It is important to note, however, that simply making collaborative technologies available to student teams does not necessarily lead to use. In addition, availability of a collaborative toolkit does not insure appropriate technology use or fit relative to team behaviors and project activities. Ultimately, any given technology either enables or hinders a team member's ability to exchange informational content and cues, as well as the ability of that information to change understanding or behavior of other team members within a time interval. Successful collaboration requires effective and efficient information exchange and absorption.

In order to better understand how virtual student teams use various collaborative tools, especially given the introduction of Web 2.0 and VWs into the mix of enabling technologies, we explored the following questions:

1. Are there different patterns of collaborative tool use relative to project activities? That is, are some tools better suited to particular activities than others?
2. Do different patterns of use of collaborative tools relate to differential levels of student team performance?
3. What specific role does a VW play in supporting project activities?

CONTEXT OF EXPLORATION

The context of study involved a cross-university course focused on technology-enabled Service Innovation. A total of 42 students from the authors' respective institutions worked in 11 virtual student teams (3 or 4 students/team) using a variety of collaboration tools, including a VW. The course was motivated by transformations occurring in the global service economy. Specifically, growth in the service economy is occurring as businesses convert products into services and enhance traditional products with information service components. New collaborative tools (including wikis, blogs, and VWs) are being used to support service innovation efforts in industry. Successful technology-enabled service innovation requires integration of business opportunity and technology capabilities. Achieving this kind of cross-disciplinary integration requires collaborative development of solutions. As such, this course was an appropriate platform to learn about service innovation and simultaneously experience the realities of working in distributed environments.

In addition to webinar-based lectures, the course involved a team-based learning component and an associated industry-sponsored case competition. Specifically, over a period of 7 weeks, each team developed a business case for a service innovation that could be delivered by the corporate sponsor in the VW *Second Life*. The course culminated in a virtual case competition, in which each team made its case for its proposed service innovation.

Collaborative Environment

The collaborative toolkit enabled engagement between faculty, students and project sponsors throughout the course. Indiana University's Oncourse Collaboration and Learning (Oncourse CL) platform, based on Sakai open-source software, provided supporting Web 1.0 (e.g., email and document repositories) and Web 2.0 (e.g., wikis, text-chat) tools for both faculty-to-class and student-to-student (virtual team) interactions. A class portal was used to share course-related presentations, URLs of interest, and announce-

Figure 1. VW Collaborative Meeting Space

ments. Formal class meetings were delivered and recorded using Adobe Connect. Individual team portals, with similar tools and capabilities, enabled team level project-related work. Student teams could use whichever communication and collaboration tools they preferred. In each portal, usage statistics, team interactions and content were captured. If desired, teams could use telephone or web-conferencing, but had to log use and purpose of use.

In addition to the collaborative tools, a virtual meeting space was provided on NC State University's DELTA campus in *Second Life.* Here, students could access small pods for team meetings as shown in Figure 1. Faculty met with each team on DELTA and the project sponsors met with the student teams on their respective VW islands.

Data Collection

Following completion of the course, students were asked to reflect on their experiences and complete a questionnaire. The questionnaire captured perceptions of the importance of each collaborative tool to work processes and outcomes. Again, the three types of collaborative tools included:

- Web 1.0 (email, document repositories, telephone/web conferencing)
- Web 2.0 (text-chat, wiki)
- Virtual World (*Second Life*)

First, the following question was asked in order to gain some sense of the overall importance of each tool: *"During this course, you had several collaboration tools available to you. Please indicate how important each tool was to your team collaborations."* Students could rate the tool on a 5-point scale from "Not used" (0) to "Essential"(5).

Second, based on the earlier discussion regarding team functions and underlying behaviors, students were asked to weight the use of the various collaborative tools for the following team activities:

- Exchange Information (e.g., store and retrieve documents, URLs etc.) [*convey*]
- Solve Problems or Make Decisions [*converge*]
- Project Management (e.g., schedule, assign work, track status etc.) [*coordinate*]
- Socialize and Build Team Relationships [*social/relational*]

Figure 2. Distribution of Importance of Tool to Overall Collaborations

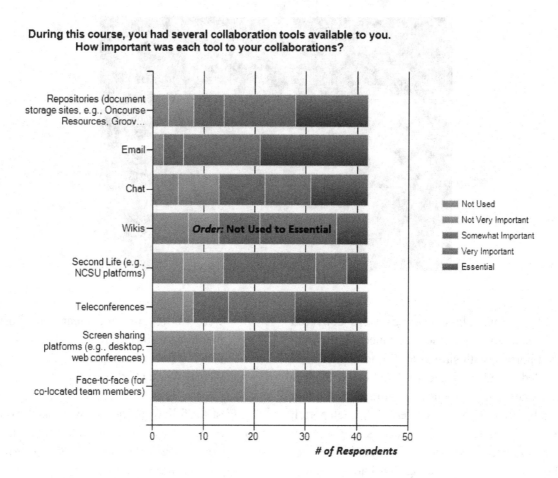

That is, in order to gain a deeper understanding of the use of various tools relative to these activities, students were instructed to: *"Think back on your team project in terms of the various collaboration tools and team activities. For each activity, allocate 100 points across the various tools to indicate your degree of use of the different tools for the activity".*

Lastly, in terms of performance, each team's final project was evaluated by the industry sponsor and independently assessed by faculty raters. Each project was scored on three dimensions (range, organization, and depth) using a scale from 1 (very low) to 7 (very high). An overall performance score was created for each team by averaging the three dimensions. Performance ranged from a low

of 2.89 to a perfect score of 7.0, with a mean of 4.98 and standard deviation of 1.45.

RESULTS

"Fit" between Tools and Collaborative Activities

Figure 2 summarizes the distribution of student responses for the survey question regarding the importance of each tool to <u>overall</u> collaborations. As shown, email was perceived to be the most important (with thirty-six of the students noting it as very important or essential), followed by wiki, document repositories, and teleconferencing.

Figure 3. Relative Importance of Tools to Conveyance

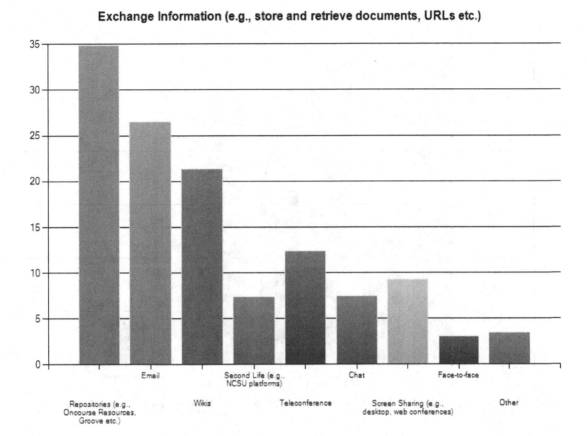

Conversely, twenty-eight of the students deemed the VW as somewhat important and another ten as either very important or essential to supporting collaborations.

However, as discussed earlier, collaboration consists of multiple activities (i.e., conveyance, convergence, etc.) and thus deeper insight is offered by examining the relative importance (or weighting) of the tools to each of these activities. Figure 3-6 illustrate, by collaborative activity, the average weighting (i.e., 0 to 100) of the importance of each tool as perceived by the individual students.

As shown in Figure 3, for conveyance, document repositories, email and wiki were reported (i.e., weighted) as the top three used tools. The exchange of information (e.g., documents, URLs etc.) does not require immediate feedback or high interactivity, thus these asynchronous tools "fit" the activity at hand. Here, synchronous tools (VW, teleconferencing/web-conferencing, and chat) were used to a much lesser degree.

Figure 4 shows that, for convergence, while email was weighted as the most used tool, three synchronous tools were also highly weighted–VW *Second Life*, teleconference, and text-chat. Prior research (c.f., Montoya et al. 2009) has shown individuals often default to the least common denominator and most familiar tool – here, likely email. However, these results suggest that students did, in fact, deploy richer and more interactive media for solving problems and/or making deci-

Figure 4. Convergence

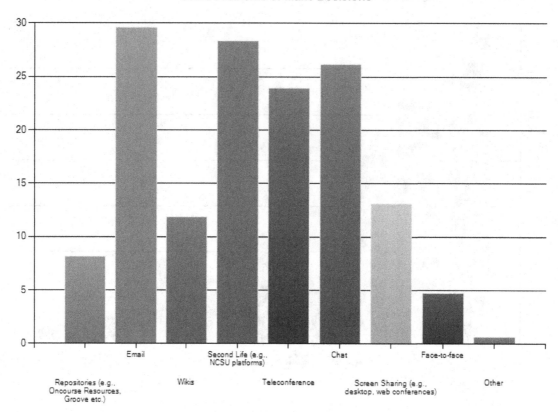

sions regarding the team project, with the VW leading the way.

In Figure 5, email predominates as the tool of choice for coordination or project management related activities. In this course, since no specific calendaring or scheduling tool was provided, the easiest means to coordinate work may have been via email.

Lastly, Figure 6 illustrates the relative importance of each tool to social/relationship-building interactions. As in most distance education settings, students had no history with team members at the other university. And, as discussed earlier, socialization is essential to team functioning, satisfaction, and ultimately performance. Here, we see the key role that the VW *Second Life*,

played in supporting relationship building. Teleconferencing and text-chat were deemed as next two most important tools in this regard. Compared to these tools, however, the VW would be characterized as richer, more interactive, and the one providing the greatest sense of presence to users.

Performance Patterns

Finally, to examine how *each team* used the three types of collaborative tools (Web 1.0, Web 2.0, VW) we ordered the 11 student project teams from worst to best performance to look for patterns of use. Table 1 summarizes the overall percentage usage of Web 1.0, Web 2.0, and the VW (based on the weightings of the members of each team) in

Figure 5. Coordination

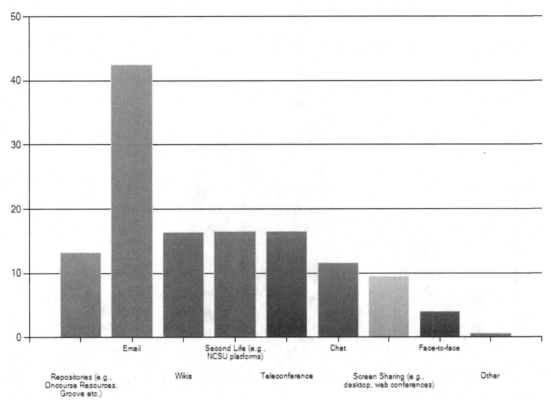

Coordination (e.g., schedule, assign work, track status etc.)

support of each team's project work. We conducted Spearman tests of correlation to examine whether the use of the various types of collaborative tools was related to performance. The results indicate that a *greater* reliance on Web 1.0 technologies was *negatively* related to project performance.

As Table 1 shows, there were different patterns of collaborative technology use across the 11 virtual teams. It appears that some teams continue to rely heavily on traditional Web 1.0 tools, reporting overall use of greater than 50%, i.e., Team 5, 6, 7 and 10. Within the Web 1.0 category of tools, very few teams reported use of telephone/web-conferencing; rather, they tended to use asynchronous tools such as email and document repositories.

On the other hand, the results indicate that newer collaborative technologies (Web 2.0 and the VW) were incorporated into overall use patterns, i.e., 7 of the 11 virtual student teams reported using these (in combination) more than 50% of the time.

To gain deeper insight into the drivers of performance we take a closer examination of the worst and best performing teams (Teams 1 and 11). Specifically, how they each used the collaborative tool types for various team activities, including the writing of team deliverables. As shown in Figure 7, the best team (Team 11) tended to use newer collaborative tools (Web 2.0 options and the VW *Second Life*) for *all* task activities more than the worst performing team. The worst performing team (Team 1) relied more heavily on

Figure 6. Social/Relationship Building

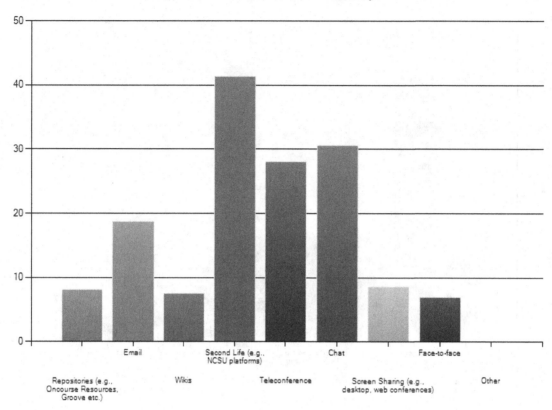

Table 1. Usage % of Collaborative Tool Type by Team

Team # Worst to Best Performance	Web 1.0	Web 2.0	VW *Second Life*
1	.47	.33	.20
2	.34	.21	.45
3	.41	.37	.22
4	.24	.41	.35
5	.71	.19	.10
6	.61	.03	.37
7	.54	.34	.13
8	.28	.69	.04
9	.48	.24	.28
10	.52	.19	.29
11	.22	.34	.44

Figure 7. Best and Worst Performing Teams

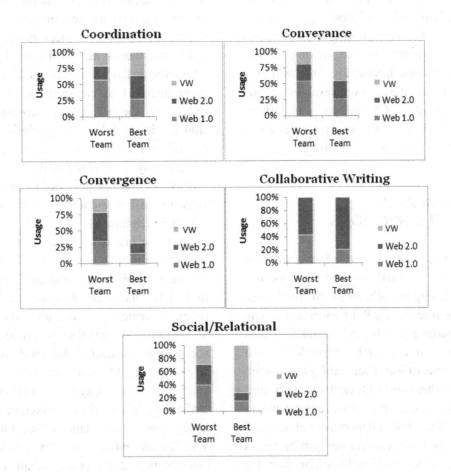

traditional Web 1.0 tools, particularly email and document repositories. The Web 1.0 tools used by Team 1 were asynchronous and, as noted earlier, are considered to be lean, low interactivity, and low in social presence. Conversely, for each task activity, the best performing team appears to have successfully appropriated the capabilities of Web 2.0 and the VW *Second Life* relative to its collaborative activities. This is not to suggest that email and document repositories were irrelevant; rather, Team 11 was able to use these tools in complementary and appropriate ways.

Overall, the results in Figure 7 suggest that the best performing team was able to successfully match ("fit") the capabilities of tool types to the needs of the various team activities. For

this team, use of the VW played a key role in facilitating the development of relationships between team members. Social interactions that help develop team relationships are critical to team performance because they engender trust and commitment. This may partially explain the best performing team's results.

In addition to the findings presented in Figure 7, we examined the content of the team portals to gain deeper insight into tool use. In terms of coordination, the best team used the VW *Second Life* and text-chat (both synchronous tools) to discuss project management, and then create a schedule in the wiki (an asynchronous tool). For conveyance (sharing of ideas) and convergence (decision-making) activities, they relied most heavily on the VW *Second Life* (again high in richness, interactivity, and social presence) where they held regularly scheduled team meetings. Once this team moved into production (i.e., writing/editing) of team deliverables, they deployed the wiki tool, ultimately moving the final deliverables into the document repository. Overall, team 11 reflects good use of tools in light of task activities and a logical progression of work over time.

DISCUSSION AND RESEARCH DIRECTIONS

In this chapter, we have reported on a study of how distributed ("virtual") student teams use traditional and emerging collaborative technologies, including the role that a VW like *Second Life* can play in supporting team behaviors and activities. In particular, our exploration provides insight into the patterns of use where *multiple* tools are available simultaneously. Overall, our study suggests that more successful teams are better able to match Web 2.0 and VW collaborative technologies to task activities, while lower performing teams defaulted to more traditional/familiar Web 1.0 technologies. Our findings suggest that Web 2.0 and VW collaborative tools may begin to address the missing component of human interaction that has plagued virtual work. For example, in our study, the VW was a good venue for developing and building team relationships and for holding decision-making discussions. Other tools, such as wikis and document repositories, complemented the capabilities of the VW by providing the means to write, edit, share, and store project-related documents.

From our perspective, the VW played a key role in enabling collaboration and developing relationships between geographically dispersed team members. As an immersive and interactive space, it also made project work more interesting and motivated learning. For example, while in the VW *Second Life*, teams visited different locations to learn about what other companies were doing, particularly from a services perspective. Over half of the students agreed or strongly agreed that interacting in the VW was fun and interesting and contributed to their engagement with the project. In addition, the sense of presence created for the students in the VW is a capability simply not possible with other collaborative technologies. Here, nearly 60% of the students indicated that the VW *Second Life* provided them with a strong sense of realism and a feeling of connectedness with their teammates.

In some instances, team members also had the opportunity to engage in ad hoc real-time communication with company representatives in the VW. One corporate sponsor, a Fortune 500 financial services firm, already had a presence in *Second Life*. Student team members were given access to the sponsor's island and invited to visit so that they could learn more about the company and talk with company representatives in world. Ordinarily, this kind of interaction opportunity is not possible in distance education settings. A VW like *Second Life* can clearly help overcome distance, time, and access constraints, opening up new opportunities for distance learners.

Yet, without understanding how and why students use collaborative technologies relative to team activities, academic institutions may support and/or invest in ineffective tools and platforms. Our results indicate that simply making collaborative technologies available did not lead to use. Several teams in our study did not take advantage of the Web 2.0 or VW tools. Past research has shown that usefulness and ease of use drive intentions to adopt any new technology (e.g. Davis, 1989; Venkatesh & Davis, 2000). Organizations, including academic institutions, must work to engender positive attitudes toward existing and/or new technologies to influence use. Mechanisms such as training and use testimonials can be used to clearly illustrate the usefulness.

Actively influencing attitudes is particularly pertinent when a new technology – such as a VW – is intended to replace (or complement) traditional tools with which individuals are more familiar and comfortable. Importantly, when attempting to engender positive attitudes, training programs will need to go beyond knowing the technical nuances, i.e. "how it works", to knowing *why* and when a technology is useful (Montoya et al., 2009).

The limitations of our current study offer several avenues for future research. First, our sample (11 teams consisting of 42 students) is small and the students were fairly heterogeneous, particularly with regard to demographics and relatively novice experience with VWs. Future research is needed to explore the learning curve associated with a VW as well as usage patterns of more experienced users. From a practice perspective, this insight will help academic institutions understand what the start-up costs will be to transition (even some aspects) of distance education to a VW. Second, research is also needed to examine alternative VWs, in particular those that explicitly collaborative support features. In this study, we expect different VW usage patterns (and perhaps performance) might have emerged if the VW platform, for example, allowed for (easy) document sharing or editing. Increasingly, VWs are being explicitly designed with collaboration in mind (e.g., *Protosphere, Open Wonderland*). Third, while this course allowed for an examination of team behaviors and activities, it was not intended to be a controlled experiment. Thus, while our efforts provide foundational insights, future research involving controlled experiments as well as continued field explorations is needed. For example, past research strongly suggests that as distributed team members become more experienced with a collaborative tool, each other, and task activities, they are better able to leverage tool capabilities. This type of longitudinal and controlled examination should facilitate deeper insights.

CONCLUSION

New communication and collaboration technologies have fueled the growth of distance education. Simultaneously, they have created new opportunities for collaborative learning. Collaborative learning involves social processes by which a small group of learners work together on a problem-solving task. Learners can benefit from interaction and collaboration with others who are typically more diverse than would be found in any one course. Traditional media (Web 1.0), Web 2.0 tools, and VWs present distance learners with the means to overcome boundaries such as geography and time. However, while technology is a necessary enabler, technology alone will not drive successful collaboration. As in traditional classroom settings, distance educators are faced with the challenge of how to get distributed students to collaborate in ways that are efficient and effective.

This study examined how cross-university student teams deployed traditional and emerging collaborative technologies – Web 1.0, Web 2.0, and the VW *Second Life* – to support team-based project activities. We were specifically interested in how various types of tools supported team activities (information exchange, problem solving/decision making, project management, and the development of social relationships) *and* how use related to team performance. We were also interested in gaining a deeper understanding of how students used the VW. Overall, our results suggest that better performing teams were able to successfully match the capabilities of tool types to the needs of the various team activities. For example, teams that used the wiki for collaborative writing of project deliverables performed better than those who used email attachments. We also found that team use of the collaboration spaces in the VW facilitated the development of relationships between students on the various project teams. Overall, these findings are relevant to academic institutions seeking to integrate and use VWs for distance education and, in particular, to enable collaborative learning. Proactively dealing with the challenge of moving beyond traditional ways of working will be essential to leveraging and capitalizing on investments in collaborative tools.

REFERENCES

Alavi, M. (1994). Computer-mediated collaborative learning: An empirical evaluation. *Management Information Systems Quarterly*, *18*(2), 159–175. doi:10.2307/249763

Bartle, R. (2004). *Designing virtual worlds*. Indianapolis, IN: New Riders Publishing.

Bates, A. W. (2005). *Technology, e-learning and distance education*. New York, NY: Routlege.

Beise, C. M. (2004). IT project managers' perceptions and use of virtual team technologies. *Information Resources Management Journal*, *17*(4), 73–88. doi:10.4018/irmj.2004100104

Benford, S., Greenhalgh, C., Rodden, T., & Pycock, J. (2001). Collaborative virtual environments. *Communications of the ACM*, *44*(7), 79–85. doi:10.1145/379300.379322

Briggs, R. O., Nunamaker, J. F., & Sprague, R. (1997). 1001 Unanswered research questions in GSS. *Journal of Management Information Systems*, *14*(3), 3–21.

Daft, R., Lengel, R., & Trevino, L. (1987). Message equivocality, media selection, and manager performance implications for Information Systems. *Management Information Systems Quarterly*, *11*(3), 355–366. doi:10.2307/248682

David, B. (1993). *Tools for teaching*. San Francisco, CA: Jossey Bass.

Davis, F. D. (1989). Perceived usefulness, perceived ease of use, and user acceptance of Information Technology. *Management Information Systems Quarterly*, *13*(3), 319–340. doi:10.2307/249008

Dillenbourg, P. (1999). What do you mean by collaborative learning? In Dillenbourg, P. (Ed.), *Collaborative learning: Cognitive and computational approaches* (pp. 1–19). Bingley, UK: Emerald Group Publishing Limited.

Duarte, D., & Snyder, N. (2006). *Mastering virtual teams: Strategies, tools, and techniques that succeed*. San Francisco, CA: Jossey-Bass.

Fjermestad, J., & Hiltz, S. R. (1998). An assessment of group support systems experimental research: Methodology and results. *Journal of Management Information Systems*, *15*(3), 7–149.

Glaser, R., & Bassok, M. (1989). Learning theory and the study of instruction. *Annual Review of Psychology*, *40*, 631–666. doi:10.1146/annurev.ps.40.020189.003215

Gokhale, A. (1995). Collaborative learning enhances critical thinking. *Journal of Technology Education*, *7*(1), 22–30.

Guth, S. (2006). Discovering collaborative e-learning through an online writing course. *Innovate*, *3*(2).

Lassila, O., & Hendler, J. (2007). Embracing Web 3.0. *IEEE Internet Computing*, *11*(3), 90–93. doi:10.1109/MIC.2007.52

Marks, M. A., Mathieu, J. E., & Zaccaro, S. J. (2001). A temporally based framework and taxonomy of team processes. *Academy of Management Review*, *26*(3), 356–376. doi:10.2307/259182

Massey, A. P., Montoya, M. M., & Hung, Y. T. C. (2003). Because time matters: Temporal coordination in global virtual project teams. *Journal of Management Information Systems*, *19*(4), 129–155.

Massey, A. P., Ramesh, V., & Khatri, V. (2006). Design, development, and assessment of mobile applications: The case for problem-based learning. *IEEE Transactions on Education, 49*(2), 183–192. doi:10.1109/TE.2006.875700

McGrath, J. E. (1991). Time, interaction, and performance (TIP): A theory of groups. *Small Group Research, 22*(2), 147–174. doi:10.1177/1046496491222001

Montoya, M. M., Massey, A. P., Hung, Y. T. C., & Crisp, C. B. (2009). Can you hear me now? Communication in virtual product development teams. *Journal of Product Innovation Management, 26*(2), 139–155. doi:10.1111/j.1540-5885.2009.00342.x

Ritzema, T., & Harris, B. (2008). The use of Second Life for distance education. *Journal of Computing Sciences in Colleges, 23*(6), 110–116.

Short, J. A., Williams, F., & Christie, B. (1976). *The social psychology of telecommunications.* New York, NY: Wiley.

Sigala, M. (2007). Integrating Web 2.0 in e-learning environments: A socio-technical approach. *International Journal of Knowledge and Learning, 3*(6), 628–648. doi:10.1504/IJKL.2007.016837

Venkatesh, V., & Davis, F. D. (2000). A theoretical extension of the technology acceptance model: Four longitudinal field studies. *Management Science, 46*(2), 186–204. doi:10.1287/mnsc.46.2.186.11926

Warkentin, M. E., Sayeed, L., & Hightower, R. (1997). Virtual teams versus face-to-face teams: An exploratory study of a Web-based conference system. *Decision Sciences, 28*(4), 975–996. doi:10.1111/j.1540-5915.1997.tb01338.x

Wittrock, M. C. (1978). The cognitive movement of instruction. *Educational Psychologist, 13*, 15–29. doi:10.1080/00461527809529192

Zack, M. (1993). Interactivity and communication mode choice in ongoing management groups. *Information Systems Research, 4*(3), 207–261. doi:10.1287/isre.4.3.207

ENDNOTE

[1] IES National Center for Education Statistics, U.S. Department of Education Institute of Education Sciences http://nces.ed.gov/fastfacts/display.asp?id=80.

Chapter 22
Object Design in Virtual Immersive Environments

Jan Baum
Towson University, USA

ABSTRACT

The ubiquity of digital technology and the pervasiveness of the Web have led to a paradigm shift in life and work. Never before have so many tools for communication, contribution, and collaboration been so globally interconnected. The Object Design program at Towson University engages the network effect of emergent technologies developing pedagogy to keep pace with global developments. Students learn 21st century skills as they engage virtual immersive environments as a digital design tool, for iterative prototyping, as a virtual presence augmenting traditional studio practice, to engage new economic platforms, and as a virtual learning environment for global dialogue and collaboration. Steady growth in virtual immersive environments support a burgeoning virtual goods market and further exploration for learning, training, and innovation across social sectors: enterprise, education, and government in the evolution of society.

INTRODUCTION

The objectives for this chapter are to illustrate the investigation into the emergent field of virtual immersive environments (VIEs) and 3D learning environments (3DLEs) within the Interdisciplinary Object Design (IOD) program at Towson University. The two terms, VIEs and 3DLEs are used interchangeably here, are distinct from MMORPGs, and emphasize an educational intention rather than a gaming intention. The VIE used by Towson University is Second Life, (SL) so all references to our work in VIEs is accurate for SL but may not hold true for other VIEs.

From the outset, there are several unique factors of SL that make it a compelling technology

DOI: 10.4018/978-1-60960-545-2.ch022

for investigation: it is a highly engaging simulated 3-dimensional environment, it is accessible worldwide, it relies on user-generated content and is dependent on an open culture, and it is free. The IOD program uses SL as a digital design tool, to augment our tangible, real world studio practice with a virtual presence in a virtual world, and as a collaborative workspace. The IOD program is infused with an entrepreneurial spirit and continually explores and adapts new technologies, tools, methodologies, and pedagogies keeping pace with global developments. The majority of courses engage a hybrid methodology of blended learning formats and traditional design studio instructional formats, as well as emergent formats such as just-in-time teaching and peer-to-peer learning.

Future Directions explores object design within VIEs as a component to the sustainable design movement and examines the growing interest by venture capital firms in the rapidly rising virtual goods market. Additionally, Future Directions examines the ways in which VIEs are poised to change learning in the 21st century and ways they can be further utilized to develop business models and marketing strategies for creative entrepreneurship by preparing leaders of the future workforce.

BACKGROUND

The Pervasiveness of Digital Technology

Digital technology has changed our lives and how we work: it is accessible, pervasive, easy to use, and lowers barriers. Digital design technology has also significantly become more accessible and easy to use and has contributed to the dissolution of discipline specific boundaries traditionally drawn along material and dimensional lines and erode individual-centric making. We are in a new era with new tools and new ways of working. There has been a paradigm shift. For most of us, we have been holding the tiger by the tail. First we

began to use the web as a primary information source albeit in a static read-only form. Moving to a decentralized dynamic flat web where users generated content through peer production methods, with information flowing in all directions, we began participating in email listservs, blogs, Flickr, and Facebook, contributing information and looking for the most current information in these places. We started aggregating information socially through wikis and sites like Del.ici.ous and networking socially online through Facebook, LinkedIn, Ning, and Twitter; and all the while discovering new ways of working, knowing, collaborating, and co-creating, through an ever increasing variety of Web 2.0 tools. These tools come together exponentially with the emergent and dynamic immersive web. Through VIEs we have highly engaging, cost-effective, postgeographic, collaborative ways of working that afford synchronous and asynchronous learning opportunities. The ubiquity of digital technology have ushered in an era in which social production is king and collaboration is key.

The Immersive Environment

VIEs are fully engaging *because* they simulate 3-dimensional space and host hundreds of users simultaneously who engage non-static objects, activities and multiple channel conversations. Time flies by as users are engrossed. SL mimics the real world as users sense the person behind the avatar and shared experiences form emotional social bonds (Figure 1). People are fascinated by this aspect of VIEs. "The paradox of a virtual world is that it adds human interaction to the online experience (Clendaniel, 2007, 79). Virtual world expert Edward Castronova said recently, "People still act like people even when they are wearing a bunny suit" (2010). Although SL is still graphically simple, users find themselves engaged and grasp the essence of the VIE and the potential it offers. Educational institutions, private enterprise and government agencies are

Figure 1. Students in Second Life. VIE Users Experience Social Bonds through Shared Experiences

exploring VIEs for this potential. The scalable, 360 degree 3-dimensional environment is applicable to myriad scenarios. SL's accessibility to a global audience is an especially appealing feature having the potential to extend the learning environment in unprecedented ways. A primary goal in utilizing SL, as an educational platform at Towson University, was creating and facilitating a broad, national and international dialogue within specific disciplines, but also transcending disciplines.

21st Century Learning

In comparison to other sectors of society, it is argued that education has not evolved at the same rate, seriously falling behind, and thereby failing our citizens and society. Our lives have changed significantly over the last twenty years as we have adapted to the pervasiveness of the web. The web is cited as a disruptive technology akin to the printing press and the steam engine marking significant changes in economic, social, and political systems. If we look at developments in each of these areas over the last two years alone

the evidence is plentiful. Historically, significant changes in the educational model are attributed to the invention of the printing press moving from the master-apprentice system to the teacher-student classroom model (Kapp & O'Driscoll, 2010). As Thomas Friedman illustrates in *The Lexus and the Olive Tree* (Friedman, 2000) and *The World is Flat* (Friedman, 2005) our world is getting smaller and flatter making competition stiffer as we are more and more dynamically interconnected. We must innovate and find new ways of working in this emergent global society. Education is not exempt and ought to be at the forefront.

In the realm of online immersive media, Karl Kapp and Tony O'Driscoll as well as Clark Aldrich advocate the integration of emerging digital media with education. All advocate for a way of learning that is more innate to human beings, learning by doing, which is tried and true. Kapp and O'Driscoll in *Learning In 3D* outline two primary learning types: productive learning and generative learning. Productive learning teaches people what we already know, is focused on productivity, and maintains the status quo. Based on the classroom-centric model, professors attempt to pour information into students' heads. It is passive and does not encourage or require individual thinking. Generative learning is based on growth. It is active and dependent on the individual taking initiative, and learning by doing. Generative learning occurs when we are challenged with learning about tasks that are new and different, the results of which lead to the emergence of knowledge. The participatory web ushered in an era of user-generated content with information flowing from all directions as people entrepreneurially engage open–ended digital technologies. Learning is becoming decentralized as formal learning fails to fulfill learning needs and "…learners leverage the web to learn from each other…" (Kapp & O'Driscoll, 2010, p.35) initiating peer-to-peer learning. Educators can either resist students who are engaging multiple channels in class or they can engage this new way of learning and working. Today, "books are dead trees with old ideas," (Kapp & O'Driscoll, 2010). New tools pose new questions and provide new opportunities when we apply open-ended methodologies and develop new pedagogies. "The ability to learn and adapt into perpetuity is becoming a core capability…" (Kapp & O'Driscoll, 2010, p. 27). Aldrich (2009a) contrasts 19th century learning by knowing and 21st century learning by doing. Learning by knowing is passive, linear, and can be epitomized as a Powerpoint presentation. Life is not linear and we learn by practicing many times on the job, the hard way. Adlrich (2009b) argues that learning by doing via simulations is active, non-linear, and provides multiple perspectives on one scenario. Attention (not enough) is paid to acquiring 21st century skills and proponents of VIEs advocate that working within VIEs allows students to learn transferable skills. VIEs encourage interaction, fostering communication, connection, collaboration, and permit cross-pollination with a decentralized open-culture based on user-generated content leading to innovation. Lawrence Lessig in *Free Culture* (2004) outlines a strong argument for the essential role of openness to an innovative society.

Thomas Friedman in an interview with Charlie Rose says all he is thinking about these days is how ideas make the difference to a free market, democratic society: "We are creating suboptimal solutions to our problems. We are in gridlock. Our system is broken (Rose & Vega, 2009).

The Towson Innovation Lab

The exploration of the new digital frontier of VIEs within the IOD program started with an individual initiative with Second Life in 2006. In 2008, a team of four Principal Investigators from the Department of Art + Design, Department of Computer Information Sciences, and the Center for Advancement in Instructional Technology was awarded a Teaching Innovation Grant to establish the Towson Innovation Lab [TIL], Towson University's island in Second Life (Figure 2). The TIL is inherently collaborative with each of the four PIs working together to establish the design of the island, best practices, and university events. The island serves as a virtual campus where faculty, staff, and students can access an international audience exploring various aspects of 3d immersive learning environments for educational purposes: lectures, meetings, course activities, and original research. The center of the island and one quad is available for general use in the university and the remaining three quads are program specific.

Virtual Immersive Environments and Interdisciplinary Object Design

Integration of VIEs into the IOD curriculum began in the fall of 2008 designing specific projects for scheduled courses. Initial interest in SL was as an extension of the tangible world of the studio classroom offering new possibilities rather than engaging a popular preconceived notion as a kind of alternate existence. Our foray into VIEs was as a 3DLE. The Object Design quad is an extension of the design studio learning environment but it does not imitate the actual physical environment

Figure 2. Towson Innovation Lab in Second Life. An Aerial View of the Island, (top); Sample Building, (bottom)

of the studio or the campus but rather engages the new medium of VIEs (Figure 3). The purpose of education is inquiry and the pursuit of knowledge with which to evolve society. It is from this perspective that educators engaging new technologies and endeavors are successful. Advancement fails when current methodology and pedagogy is simply laid on top of new mediums. Practicing just-in-time teaching, open-ended problems are designed for VIEs and students are encouraged to arrive at independent, individual solutions based on their understanding of SL.

Initially our workflow was tangible to virtual meaning our work was focused in the traditional studio learning environment and we imported digital versions of the tangible objects into the virtual environment exploring how the virtual environment could enhance traditional work. Very quickly we discovered a range of unimagined opportunities that VIEs offer and not just for our studio design practice. Immediately students became social producers within SL, shaping the Object Design quad and creating its content. User-created content in SL is a feature that dis-

Figure 3. Interdisciplinary Object Design Quad

tinguishes VIEs from MMORPGs and why SL is the most prominent VIE in use today.

The accessibility of SL affords many opportunities for users. SL is free to join and inhabit, and requires a minimal amount of time to become familiar with the interface. Once in SL there are many "freebies" available and of course building is free users just need build permissions. The IOD program director has a premium membership,

which earns 1,500 Lindens, the SL currency, a month. Lindens are distributed to students and faculty as needed mainly for image uploads but for anything that encourages the exploration of VIEs. The cost of working in SL for our students is zero, which provides certain freedoms such as the opportunity to design highly creative objects and environments and practice the iterative design process.

Second Life as Digital Design Tool

The ubiquity and accessibility of digital design tools and digital manufacturing opportunities are profoundly changing the design field. Most significantly, specific discipline boundaries traditionally drawn along material and dimensional lines are dissolving, as are the barriers to entry. Digital design tools allow young designers to envision designs much more quickly than traditional, pre-digital tools and outsourcing bureaus make tangible results a reality complete with material charts from which designers can choose. Digital designers watch form evolve before their eyes and envision material application as they apply textures to form. With each click of a mouse design variables are adjusted and the next iteration of the design is visualized, allowing the designer to test form and material combinations to find iterations worth prototyping. For the object design student the design process encompasses an overwhelmingly broad range of considerations from form to materials. Digital design tools make envisioning those choices easier and faster allowing students to move though a variety of design decisions quickly to test scale, proportion, color, texture, density, material choices, etc.

The 3D modeling tools in SL are one set of digital design tools that we use in the IOD program. The immersive environment allows for comparative scale and movement around the created object or within a created space as opposed to rotating the object on a screen and having to adjust or recall issues of scale. While more sophisticated software exists which combines the use of an avatar with designed form and material properties, such as Drexel University's Digital Museum Project (Martin, 2010), the build tools in SL offer a fundamental introduction to 3D digital design vocabulary and methodology. The nature of the technology supports an iterative design process within a scaled, 3-dimensional environment.

Second Life as Visualization Tool

Students use SL as a visualization tool. In *ART 422 Designing for Production*, students create simulations of trade show presentations for the product lines they designed and manufactured for the course. After familiarizing themselves with the SL interface, learning basic building skills and how to import images, they practiced the iterative design process working through iterations of their simulations. This group of students studied product branding earlier in the semester and were encouraged to integrate branding concepts into their simulations. Without real world constraints of money and time, as in the money and time it would take to actually create a 3-dimensional trade show presentation, students are free to design and explore highly creative, innovative custom presentations that market brand identity (Figure 4).

Once IOD students are granted access to build on the island, the island is available to them 24/7 which advances the university initiative. Students take advantage of this opportunity creating gallery-type environments, which showcase specific collections of work such as computer-aided design work, sustainable design work, and explore how various design decisions can best present different types of work. In preparation for a gallery exhibition in tangible life, students prototyped installation solutions in SL, adjacently laying out iterations and inviting feedback from colleagues and professors. VIEs are a great tool that is unparalleled (Figure 5).

Augmenting Tangible Life

The TIL provides the students and IOD program with a virtual presence accessible worldwide, 24/7. Senior portfolios line the perimeter of the island framing the Object Design quad, select trade show simulations remain installed, a gallery showcases the current collaborative project and our work in rapid prototyping and digital manufacturing, and new gallery-style structures pop up intermit-

Figure 4. Examples of Trade Show Simulations

tently to highlight special initiatives like social and sustainable design and the Honors students' exhibition in downtown Baltimore, Maryland.

A Virtual Presence, in a Virtual World

In the spring of 2009, students in ART 497 Senior Project, a capstone course, installed their portfolios on interactive presentation boards in SL (Figure 6). Next to the boards they installed interactive drop boxes where visitors could leave note cards

providing feedback on their portfolios. The program director facilitated the feedback process for colleagues visiting the island who were new to the SL environment. Some students elected to create a scripted note card that was given to visitors when visitors clicked on their presentation boards. Students in the ART 422 Designing for Production course also utilized drop box and scripted note card features in conjunction with their trade show simulations. Senior Project students delivered an artist/designer talk both in-world and

Figure 5. Examples of Student Created Galleries

in tangible life. For their in-world presentations students used their interactive presentation boards. For the in-world presentations the class met in a computer lab while individual presenters cycled through a single computer station in the design studio classroom providing everyone the opportunity to experience giving a lecture through the SL interface and observing their peers' lectures in SL. The program director invited national and international colleagues, some attending from as far away as the University of Dundee in Scotland.

Students in the ART 499 Honors Project course created a hybrid replica of Jordan Faye Contemporary, a downtown gallery in Baltimore, Maryland where this group of honors students mount-

ed an exhibition of their year-long projects. The gallery simulation portrayed the local Baltimore architectural style and flavor while showcasing the individual aesthetics and collections of work.

Students in ART 422 Designing for Production were encouraged to explore VIEs as an economic platform. They designed and manufactured product lines throughout the course of the semester, studied branding, created a web presence using Web 2.0 tools, and installed their product lines in SL via simulated trade show presentations. Students were encouraged to view SL as a microcosm test-marketing strategies for their product lines and to adjust the properties on their virtual objects making them available for sale within SL.

Figure 6. Interactive student presentation boards

Augmenting Realities

The blurry boundary line between tangible life and virtual life and the conduits connecting them is intriguing and worthy of exploration as illustrated by the movie Tron in 1982; it was one of the first suggestions of a blended experience of the physical and the virtual. Clicking on an object in SL can open up a real-life webpage within the SL interface augmenting the virtual immersive environment. Likewise a SLurl posted on Twitter can transport someone from tangible life to the virtual immersive environment. There is total fluidity connecting the flat web and the immersive web. Students in ART 422 Designing for Production bridge the looking glass, as monitors are sometimes referred, between trade show simulations and product-specific blogs and websites with scripted links allowing the SL visitor to view a wider spectrum of information about the brand, products, and designer/maker. IOD students are well versed with a broad range of Web 2.0 tools, which are integrated throughout the IOD curriculum. In their final presentations, at the end of the program, students are proud to be able to say, "You can find me on Facebook, follow by blog [gives blog address], see my work in SL and friend me in SL [gives avatar name and TIL SLurl], or follow me on Twitter [gives twitter feed]. Many of these channels are linked to their SL presence. The fluidity between the flat web and immersive web contribute to the augmented realities of our lives regardless of the direction of the information flow: GPS on our handhelds or the web in our immersive environment. Our lives are real, virtual, and augmented (Figure 7).

A Collaborative Workspace

From its inception the TIL has been a collaborative project and space. The faculty of the SL team holds weekly in-world office hours where they practice just-in-time teaching and model peer-to-peer learning. Students attending these office hours are exposed to cross-disciplinary teamwork, team work across faculty/staff and faculty/student lines, and gain an understanding of the different groups of students from a variety of programs and disciplines that are involved in the TIL. The TIL has made immersive learning available to at least three other institutions of higher education by virtue of partnerships with colleagues worldwide. The permeable borders of SL are readily apparent extending the classroom exponentially.

Figure 7. Interactive Presentation Boards Showing Images in Tangible Life

Global Design Collaboration

HOME   ABOUT THIS PROJECT   AVATAR NAMES   HYPE!   PRESS

RESEARCH + PRESENTATIONS   WHERE YOU CAN FIND ME

The ubiquity and accessibility of digital technology connects us as much as we want to be connected and allows for spontaneous interactions. One evening while working in SL from home helping ART 422 Designing for Production students with their trade show simulations, I noticed a colleague from NY state was online via the green button on his Gmail account. Having multiple computers running, I instant messaged him inquiring if he was 'in' SL. He confirmed, so I emailed him the TIL SLurl and he joined us for a critique. VIEs are an amazing tool: accessible, cost-effective, post-geographic.

Formal Collaboration: The Propaganda Project

The seeds for collaboration between Towson University and Winthrop University were planted at a meeting of the CADLaboration group, a consortium of institutions of higher education organized in an effort to foster education and substantive collaboration among artists working with digital technologies and their integration into arts curricula (Mission Statement, 2006). In the spring of 2009 professors from Towson and Winthrop co-authored a design brief and visual presentation titled the Propaganda Project, which was assigned to students in digital modeling courses.

The TIL was used as a virtual classroom and final projects were installed in the gallery on the TIL. Each piece had a drop box/note card feature and students were required to provide constructive criticism for their peers. The Propaganda Project was a pilot project.

Formal Collaboration: The Global Design Collaboration

The Global Design Collaboration (GDC) project was launched in the spring of 2010 with a call for partners via a number of national and international email listservs. The response was strong yielding interest from the New Media Studies Department at Charles University in the Czech Republic, masters students from The Stockholm School of Economics in Stockholm, Sweden, and art and design students at Asian University in Thailand, as well as a number of institutions and range of programs from the USA. The students involved in the first version of the GDC were from Towson University, Winthrop University, and the University of Dundee, Scotland drawing on faculty from these institutions as well as faculty from Penn State Altoona (Pennsylvania, USA), The Art Institute of Philadelphia (Pennsylvania, USA), and York Technical College/3D Systems (South Carolina, USA).

The GDC was integrated into current course offerings: ART 307 & ART 507, Materials: Concept and Process, ART 361 & ART 515, Digital Object Design I, ARTS 483 and 584, Digital Modeling and Advanced Digital Modeling. The curricula and students were unified with a common problem to solve: the Hype! Project. The GDC was structured to include the following in-world activities: scheduled cross-cultural dialogue, in-progress design reviews of design research (including concept sketches and bubble maps), guest lectures, guest critiques, and access to regularly scheduled office hours. As an ice-breaker students were asked to team up creating interactive boards in-world sharing examples of exciting design and excellent examples of Hype! After initial in-world dialogue and design reviews students would self-select cross-institutionally for collaborative work documenting collaborative efforts. Several communication technologies were set-up in support of the GDC. A blog, http://globaldesigncollaboration. wordpress.com, (Figure 7) catalogs the various parts of the project: the design brief, participants and their avatar names, technical requirements, and press. A Ning group was created in lieu of access to a content management system that all participants could access.

In addition to the Hype! Project several advanced students were asked to engage in a true digital design collaboration as a facet of the GDC. These students were charged with the task of co-designing and co-creating an object, a bracelet, which was rapid prototyped in a variety of materials. The assignment was presented openly, with only a few requirements: that the object/s be designed and created as a collective group effort, and the communications surrounding the work be documented (Baum, Starrett, & Voigt, 2010).

The GDC students installed their work on interactive presentation boards in the center of the Object Design quad for assessment by faculty and review by outside jurors. Faculty provided specific parameters for the boards to make the workload manageable. Faculty from 3D Systems University/

York Technical College and The Art Institute of Philadelphia juried the work selecting twenty-one pieces for the in-world exhibition. Remote faculty from Penn State Altoona and The Art Institute of Philadelphia served as guest critics reviewing the interactive presentation boards and critiquing the exhibition in real-time (Figure 8). The majority of students from the different schools attended the in-world critique from common classrooms. Due to schedule constraints some students logged in remotely to participate.

Network Effect

The network effect is the exponential value of numerous people being connected via a network whether social, academic, professional, etc. Aldrich (2009a) describes it this way: "...if five people are on a network, the power is not five times greater than one person, but 2 to the fifth (2 X 2 X 2 X 2 X 2= 32) because you realize the value of each connection" (p.378). Working collaboratively, several events were facilitated during the GDC project by engaging various audiences. The SL team hosted a university lecture in the Department of Art + Design by artist Jeff Lipsky of Massachusetts, "Filthy Fluno: An Artists' Life in Second Life". Lipsky, a.k.a. Filthy Fluno, was featured in the NY Times magazine in March 2009 as an artist who had created a successful professional artist life in a VIE. The event was widely advertised and in attendance were students and faculty from throughout Towson University, the GDC partner institutions, as well as a cadre of Jeff Lipsky's and Filthy Fluno's colleagues. The lecture was simulcast in SL permitting SL residents to watch the lecture happening at the University in real-time, across time zones through the VIE of SL thereby augmenting numerous realities from numerous directions. The GDC faculty team also organized a lecture in SL by Kara Rodriguez, from her home in NYC, "From Art School to Industry" in which Rodriguez discussed the evolution from an object design program in college to her work

Figure 8. Guest Critics in-World

for commercial jeweler David Yurman. These events, held within SL along with the outside jurors and guest critics, contribute to the network effect within education.

PROBLEMS, SOLUTIONS, RECOMMENDATIONS, REFLECTIONS

Virtual Immersive Environments and Interdisciplinary Object Design

There was some student resistance to SL based on negative preconceived notions of MMORPGs.

Some students responded saying, "I don't have time for my first life, how can I have time for a second life?" and commenting that they would rather spend time with their friends in tangible life than time in a virtual reality. A faculty champion communicating a vision for how a VIE like SL might be used academically, and professionally is necessary. Partnering with other educational institutions and bringing in guest critics and speakers also facilitated greater acceptance and engagement. Students from one institution allied themselves when interacting in the immersive environment with groups of students from other institutions whereas before the collaborative partnership there was more student resistance. Faculty with more experience with both SL and teaching, facilitated SL events like Q + A sessions with guest lecturers which contributed to a network effect.

The IOD program has incorporated VIE projects into existing curriculum and courses adding it on top of the current course load. A combination of efforts could make VIE integration a better experience for students such as introducing SL at the beginning of the program as students are gaining familiarity with other kinds of online tools and implementing a schedule in which students use the VIE within the various courses as they move through the program. Incorporating VIE projects into existing curriculum is a natural way to begin and one that is disarming. In addition new courses could be developed to specifically utilize the new opportunities VIEs provide.

A Virtual Presence and a New Economic Platform

After students learn the culture of VIEs and the nature of the medium, exploration and development of methodologies can occur. For example, how VIEs can be used to market objects, test traditional marketing strategies, and develop medium-specific strategies. Likewise, much work is still needed to be done with regard to using VIEs to create a virtual presence for tangible studio practice.

The Global Design Collaboration

The largest obstacle in obtaining full integration of the GDC was that the launch time did not allow adequate planning time between participants, especially international partners. Semester calendars were set and course requirements specified. In some cases the integration of initiatives was possible and in other cases the conversation became tangential. A few interested parties discovered they were over-committed and could not integrate this project at this time but expressed interest in future collaboration. In addition, working with different calendars, even in the USA, shortened and disrupted the project preventing key activities from occurring in an ideal form. If the project were planned further in advance and possibly on a calendar year basis greater integration and collaboration would be possible.

The various courses had students with different levels of SL experience having respective advantages and disadvantages. For students with limited or no experience with SL, a more structured implementation strategy would be helpful in getting students up to speed. Even for students familiar with SL interest levels varied indicating it would be prudent to conduct short, regular sessions in SL at the beginning of the semester to give students maximum time to engage the interface on their own. Pairing students up within a course as well as small teams between schools could facilitate collaboration and peer-to-peer learning. Faculty members could tailor the GDC to courses while maintaining sufficient common ground and calendars to facilitate levels of engagement and collaboration.

There was some difficulty integrating beginning 3d modeling and a SL component. We started with the 3d modeling software, which was greater in complexity than the build tools of SL. Our digital natives were a bit overwhelmed by learning two interfaces concurrently. A strategy to address this might be to introduce 3d modeling via the build capability of SL, where aspects of 3d modeling such as primitives are clearly illustrated, creating a foundation for and common language between the two digital media. Orienting students in an immersive environment as a secondary focus, they may discover SL is a fun, new environment.

For broader cross-disciplinary collaboration more dialogue earlier on is required in order to arrive at a central project that can be structured to work across multiple disciplines. How might masters level students from an economics and entrepreneurial strategy program dovetail with object designers? How can students from a new media studies program contribute to an art and design problem? The variety of digital communication technologies available makes cross-disciplinary collaboration a more achievable reality (Baum, Starrett, & Voigt, 2010). The shortened time frame did not allow for such discussions and development.

Getting an array of faculty and guests up to speed with SL required a variety of activities and opportunities. All participants were welcome to attend the SL team's weekly in-world office hours. One of the initial four PIs trained GDC faculty partners, who in turn trained guest critics, primarily through remote sessions in SL but also via Skype and the telephone. Activities ranged from navigating the interface and immersive environment to sharing SL etiquette and best practices for student participation. Headsets were purchased for guests to make the in-world critiques a more fluid conversation with practice sessions and dry runs held prior to scheduled events. For the in-world jurying, a GDC team member was on call.

The Collaborative Design Project

Many students feel some hesitation when first beginning to familiarize themselves with SL and when they start a collaborative project. Initial contact and establishing rapport between collaborators is key. It was clear that the students had realized the need to more clearly define their own intentions for the direction of the project. They quickly assessed the strengths of all collaboration participants and began to play to their strengths accepting each other's competencies and deficiencies. The following are some excerpts from the student reflections:

Throughout this collaborative experience, I found myself to be more forgiving with the design and allowing for more readily made changes. I became less controlling about the actual design and found myself thinking how, I believe, my professors have been trying to get me to think since I came here; "what happens if..." I begin taking this attitude

to more of my work I will be more successful, and that [doing] this collaboration has brought to my attention [that] about myself. What I learned about my fellow collaborators is that they can bring very different intriguing ideas to the table that I would have never thought to explore. This makes for a more interesting and successful piece. I would definitely consider this collaboration to be successful. - Kaylyth Harris, Winthrop University

I think that Second Life is a really great tool to use as a means for critique. It's an easy, free and efficient way to include people from across the world in what we're doing at Towson and it allows us to be involved with other art programs. In terms of the collaboration, I think it was a really great exercise. We could have used the primitive style building to get visual ideas across (quickly) that we could not express through e-mail or on the phone and that were too difficult/time consuming to try and work out in CAD. If we were to meet in Second Life, that 'person-to-person' contact could have been a little more personable. Even looking at an avatar makes things not as awkward because there is some essence of the person you're communicating with in their avatar. - Rachel Timmins, Towson University (Baum, Starrett, & Voigt, 2010)

FUTURE RESEARCH DIRECTIONS

In 2001 the estimated number of people who were participating in virtual worlds was between three to four million worldwide. In 2007 the number of users was estimated at thirty to forty million (Castronova, 2007). Guest (2007) suggests that as of "April 2007, Stanford-based Gartner, Inc. technology analysts predicted that by the end of 2011, 80% of Internet users....would have a "second life" although not necessarily in Second Life" (p. 23). This points to a number of directions that are worthy of further exploration: the virtual goods market, VWs as a microcosm for new business models and creative entrepreneurship, and developing pedagogy for the 21st century.

The trajectory of the burgeoning virtual goods market parallels that of participation in VWs and is fed by virtual social worlds, VIEs, and MMORPGs. There are annual virtual goods summits and a quick Google search reveals Virtual Goods Insider, Virtual Goods News, Techcrunch has something to say about virtual goods as does Media Bistro. Anshe Chung was featured on the June 2006 cover of Business Week magazine as the first millionaire in SL, a title earned by her thriving virtual real estate business. Another example includes Rivers Run Red, the UK branding company, which works with companies such as Reebok, Disney and the BBC in SL. Number fifty-seven on Fast Company's "The Hundred Most Creative People in Business in 2009" is Susan Wu, the CEO of Ohai. Wu is the first venture capitalist to focus on virtual goods-products that don't exist off-line, such as everything your avatar needs in Second Life. Fast Company cites Wu as the doyenne of this growing niche. Her start-up has earned millions of dollars in funding (Allen, 2009). Economist Edward Castronova puts the virtual goods business at $6 billion. He predicts that when VW users gets to one hundred million, two hundred million, or one billion, the economic activity will be significant enough that people will start paying attention whether you play or not (Castronova, 2007, p. 7).

Rising awareness of social issues around the world has led the emergent field of social design, which encourages creative thinkers from a variety of disciplines to identify and address social issues through new means. While some people are addressing social issues in SL they are probably not aware of the emerging social design movement and this is a testament to the accessibility and the cross-pollination potential of SL. The IOD program at Towson University engages both social and sustainable design agendas. Issues surrounding sustainable design have to do primarily with raw material sourcing and the life of those materials as

our landfills are filling up and first world nations dump debris in third world nations but also include global ethical issues. Virtual objects alleviate these problems. Creating viable business models within VWs for object designers could be a new frontier in sustainable design providing designers with the opportunity to participate in a new economic platform augmenting their performance in the existing economy. There is a track record of people wanting digital versions of creative products, and creatives are engaging digital media and releasing versions of their products their way leading to new business models (Elstrom, 2009). A good visual arts case study is Jeff Lipsky, a.k.a. Filthy Fluno who quit his day job, after opening an art gallery in tangible life that was augmented by his professional endeavors in SL. He is engaged in selling both tangible and virtual art. Customers arrive through both the front door and virtual door for either tangible art or virtual art; he sells tangible paintings through SL to people all over the world as well as selling virtual paintings to people all over the world via SL: one endeavor, two outlets, two revenue streams. The virtual economy, as it turns out, is not so virtual. As the object design field feels the same competitive pressure and shrinking markets as enterprise everywhere, object designers also need to look to emerging economic platforms, develop new business models based on new media, apply relevant theories, and engage entrepreneurial thinking.

SL is a microcosm of life; it mimics tangible life while offering new unforeseen opportunities in myriad forms from socialization to education and enterprise to personal enrichment. SL has already proven its potential in these arenas as well as its status as a new frontier for further development. What we have not yet seen is the network effect among interoperable digital media. In a special section on social networking The Economist states, "This is just the beginning of the global era of connectedness" (2010, p. 5). In "Atoms are the New Bits," Chris Anderson (2010) examines the next industrial revolution citing the last ten years were about Facebook, Twitter and other forms of open social media the next ten years will be about applying 'post institutional social models on the web' to real life: "This is how industries are reinvented" (p.62-63). The social aspects of VIEs require active participation as well as many unique individual choices about representation and interaction. These aspects in combination within the simulated environment make 3d social networking a powerful element of VIEs. Jay Cross, author of *Informal Learning: Rediscovering the Natural Pathways that Inspire Innovation and Performance, Work Smarter, and Implementing eLearning* and chair of the Internet Time Alliance, suggests that we rethink learning as optimizing our networks (Kapp & O'Driscoll, 2010). Kapp & O'Driscoll go on to advocate that human networks create meaningful context (2010). Aldrich's work centers on interactivity with the acronym *Hive* serving as both a moniker and a metaphor. Creating a culture of interactivity in the learning environment is an example of pedagogy that is emerging from new forms of technology. Doing leads to learning, interactivity leads to higher rates of learning, and experience leads to conviction (Aldrich, 2010). Users learn a wide array of transferable skills just by participating in VIEs. One of the greatest attractions of SL is that it is essentially risk-free; time is the only casualty. Users from all sectors can test methodologies from traditional to entrepreneurial and develop new methodologies originating from VIEs.

Digital technology has inherently changed how we work, bringing people into closer proximity worldwide. Leapfrogging has helped developing nations begin to access the progress of the 20th and 21st centuries although the playing field is not yet level. We have never had so much information, so many ways of communicating and so many innovative tools with which to work. *What* we do with this new paradigm is yet to be determined. The point of education is investigation and discovery, the pursuit of knowledge in order to evolve society. The educational sector is behind in terms

of integrating emerging media into learning methodology. Often advancements are discovered by hands-on investigating, experimenting, and playing. Online digital game designers have practiced the iterative design process in honing their games keeping users well engaged by giving players constant feedback and introducing activities in specific increments. VIEs share many of these accomplishments but with goals of discovery, collaboration, and innovation which has a broad range of enterprises engaged: Reuters, Intel, IBM, Electric Sheep, Ernst & Young, Think Balm, The Holocaust Museum, etc. VIEs incorporated into educational institutions with a 21st century pedagogy developed with students and enterprise may lead to new solutions for today's challenges and unforeseen opportunities for the future. Some disciplines will naturally fall away but those that engage myriad emerging technologies will surface with a new place in the game making a contribution to the evolution of society. Educating tomorrow's world citizens through global platforms and collaboration is our best bet. Virtual worlds are gigantic, diverse, and persistent.

REFERENCES

A Special Report on Social Networking. (2010). *The Economist, 394*(8667), 1-20.

Aldrich, C. (2009a). *Learning online with games, simulations, and virtual worlds: Strategies for online instruction.* San Francisco, CA: John Wiley and Sons, Inc.

Aldrich, C. (2009b). *The complete guide to simulations and serious games: How the most valuable content will be created in the age beyond Guttenberg to Google.* San Francisco, CA: Pfeiffer, a Wiley Imprint.

Aldrich, C. (2010). *Simulations, games, and virtual worlds: The unifying view for deployment.* Federal Commission on Virtual Worlds.

Allen, W. (2009). The hundred most creative people in business in 2009. *Fast Company, 136,* 106–107.

Anderson, C. (2010). Atoms are the new bits. *Wired, 18*(2), 58–65.

Baum, J., Starrett, C., & Voigt, K. (2010). *Methods for collaboration in virtual realms*. The Athens Institute for Education and Research Conference.

Cadlaboration. (2006). *Mission statement*. Retrieved 13 July, 2010, from http://cadlaboration. wikispaces.com /Project+Vision

Castronova, E. (2007). *Exodus to the virtual world: How online fun is changing reality*. New York, NY: Palgrave Macmillan.

Castronova, E. (2010). *Studying beehives, not bees: Virtual worlds policy analysis*. Federal Commission on Virtual Worlds.

Clendaniel, M. (2007). Get a life. *Good, 7,* 76–81.

Elstrom, P. (2009, July 10). The increasing value of free. *Business Week,* 81-82.

Friedman, T. (2000). *The Lexus and the olive tree: Understanding globalization*. New York, NY: Knopf Doubleday Publishing Group.

Friedman, T. (2005). *The world is flat, a brief history of the twenty first century*. New York, NY: Farrar, Straus and Giroux.

Guest, T. (2007). *Second lives, a journey through virtual worlds*. New York, NY: Random House.

Kapp, K., & O'Driscoll, T. (2010). *Learning in 3D, adding a new dimension to enterprise learning and collaboration*. San Francisco, CA: John Wiley and Sons, Inc.

Lessig, L. (2004). *Free culture, the nature and future of creativity*. New York, NY: Penguin Group.

Martin, K. (2010). *A virtual fashion design research tool*. The Athens Institute for Education and Research Conference.

Rose, C., & Vega, Y. (2009). *Charlie Rose*. New York, NY: Public Broadcasting System.

Chapter 23

Instructional Design of an Advanced Interactive Discovery Environment:
Exploring Team Communication and Technology Use in Virtual Collaborative Engineering Problem Solving

YiYan Wu
Syracuse University, USA

Tiffany A. Koszalka
Syracuse University, USA

ABSTRACT

This chapter examines the instructional design of, and reports on research conducted within, a multiuser virtual environment created for a distributed Collaborative Engineering Design (CED) course. The course's Advanced Interactive Discovery Environment (AIDE) provided a variety of synchronous online tools and communication devices to support SameTime virtual team collaboration and problem-solving within the course. The research helped to unpack (1) which tools team members engaged with during collaborative learning activities, (2) how and why they used or did not use provided online features to support their individual learning and enhance team productivity, collaboration, and communication, and (3) how team members communicated socially. The research also describes how different team social communication patterns may be related to the patterns of team technology use. Relevant theoretical frameworks including social learning, media stickiness, cognitive imprinting, and recommendations on how different tools can be effectively integrated into multiuser virtual environments to facilitate learning are discussed.

DOI: 10.4018/978-1-60960-545-2.ch023

INTRODUCTION

Dieterle and Clarke (2005) advocated that the best learning environments for students are those that are authentic, situated, and distributed across internal and external sources. With advances in computational technologies and network connectivity, Multiuser Virtual Learning Environments (MVEs) and Computer-Supported Collaborative Learning (CSCL) have become more integrated into instructional environments to provide learners with the tools to communicate synchronously in virtual ways. Simultaneously, authentic problem-solving experiences incorporating simulations and sharing applications like electronic whiteboards also began to be integrated into these new multiuser virtual learning environments to create a real-world situated learning experience. Educational environments were thus beginning to be designed to engage learners in the complex distributed collaborative activities experienced by practicing engineers and scientists (Shuman et al., 2002). Such environments can provide learners with dynamic, interactive multiuser virtual spaces in which they are able to engage in rich hands-on learning experiences, apply new content knowledge to legitimate problems, collaborate in problem solving, and use the emerging technologies of their practice.

Geer and Barnes (2006) suggested that with the rapid development of emerging technologies and virtual environments educators face a predicament of deciding which technologies are best suited to support expected learning. Given a lack of knowledge of emerging technologies and lack of pedagogical guidance about integrating technologies for collaboration and communication, educators are often left with mounting dilemmas and confusion about which technology-based

resources are most effective for given pedagogies and learning expectations. In addition, the lack of understanding about how students learn in complex distributed collaborative activities and how their cognitive processes operate within synchronous virtual learning environments inhibits the design and implementation of effective and appropriate CSCL environments. As Pellegrino (2006, p.3) stated:

...most current approaches to curriculum, instruction, and assessment are based on theories and models that have not kept pace with modern knowledge of how people learn. They have been designed on the basis of implicit and highly limited conceptions of learning. Those conceptions tend to be fragmented, outdated, and poorly delineated for domains of subject matter knowledge.

In addition, little research has been provided that clarifies the role of communication in multiuser technology use, learning, and problem solving within synchronous computer-mediated learning environments. Limited research has focused on observations of team members becoming more task-oriented and developing clearer role expectations among themselves in online learning communities, with little focus on content or process learning (Jonassen & Kwon, 2001). Numerous researchers who study such multiuser virtual environments have found no conclusive evidence that these environments work, and when and most importantly why they do or do not work (Kirschner et al., 2004). Therefore, additional theories and confirming research are needed to better inform the instructional design (ID) of multiuser virtual environments that facilitate learning of subject matter and appropriately incorporate emerging technologies in pedagogically sound ways.

THEORETICAL FOUNDATON: SOCIAL COMMUNICATION, COGNITIVE IMPRINTING, MEDIA STICKINESS AND THEIR IMPLICATIONS TO ID

Social Communication to Learning in Multiuser Virtual Environments

From social constructivist perspectives, learning is observed to be a social process by which knowledge is generated through a network of collaborative interactions and is distributed among humans and tools that interact (Lowyck & Poysa, 2001). Collaborative learning theories suggest that effective learning requires learners with various types and levels of knowledge to work together toward a common knowledge development goal (Gokhale, 1995). Peers are key players in the human learning process as working together can be beneficial in helping each gain better understanding by 'tossing around' diverse ideas, considering the strengths and weaknesses of each idea, and revising their current knowledge and beliefs in light of new evidence and insights from others (Ormrod, 2008). During social interactions each learner constructs his or her own knowledge and skills and contributes to team member learning (Panitz, 1996).

A learner's cognitive growth can be promoted by peer interactions. Such interactions also tend to stimulate the learner's affect or feelings and motivations. For example, many learners find interactive collaborative learning sessions highly motivating, in part, because such environments address their social needs while they are studying subject matter (Ormrod, 2008). As Chen (1994) observed, students who felt uncomfortable in an educational communication environment avoided social interaction, were less argumentative, and were less willing to advocate their position or challenge other students on controversial issues. Fåhræus (1999) found communication pattern differences among productive and unproductive

groups, specifying that the content of productive groups' messages contained higher frequencies of greetings, personal descriptions of participants' professional, social, technological context and questions, and feedback among group members.

Rourke and Anderson (2002) warned that although a moderate amount of social communication created a productive climate for learning, social communication that overtook critical discourse exasperated some learners. Learners welcomed interpersonal interaction during online collaborations. However, if the collaboration became too social and moved away from the task-orientation, learners became very dissatisfied. Thus, social-collaborative learning activities, focusing on learning tasks with a non-disruptive level of informal social communications, are impacting the learners' affective domain (e.g., feelings, emotions) and support cognitive development (learning).

Virtual multiuser environments involve complicated social patterns and communication strategies that often require multiple synchronous communication channels (e.g., voice, video, document sharing, whiteboard features) to engage learners in collaborative tasks and learning. Rourke and Anderson (2002) and others (e.g. CSCL researchers) suggested that further investigation should be made into the nature of these relationships between social communication and learning, especially in synchronous multiuser educational environments where little research has been shared.

Several factors have been identified in prior research that mediate a virtual team's communication, interaction, and its learning process. These factors include learners characteristics, prior content knowledge, cultural differences, provision of a CMC coach, and content of the course (Geer & Barnes, 2007; Hron & Friedrich, 2003; Prinsen, Volman, & Terwel, 2007; Ross 1996; Solimeno et al., 2008). To disclose and understand team communication within virtual multiuser learning environments, this study examined four social communication variables identified as important to synchronous CSCL team communications including the: (1) level of team member participation (Kapur & Kinzer, 2007; Prinsen, Volman, & Terwel, 2007; Ross, 1996); (2) amount of team socialization – time in off-task activities (Rourke & Anderson, 2002); (3) amount of in-team time on-task (Jonassen & Kwon, 2001); and (4) team communication [strategy] differences (Cho et al., 2007; Nussbaum et al., 2004). This data was considered with the team members' overall evaluation of their synchronous collaborative communication experiences and studied in light of the types of technologies provided during individual and collaborative learning activities.

Cognitive Imprinting Theory

Cognitive imprinting (Geer, 2005) accounts for a tendency of multiuser virtual learning groups to repeat early patterns of communication, which can indicate their cognition levels, as they collaboratively solve a problem as a team. Learner initial communication patterns were shown to be powerful in determining subsequent interactive behaviors in synchronous multiuser learning communities. Kapur and Kinzer (2007) found that inequities in team member participation patterns exhibited a high sensitivity to initial exchange and patterns tended to get locked-in early in the discussion, ultimately lowering the quality of discussion and, in turn, the group performance. Furthermore, Geer and Barnes (2007) suggested that the notion of cognitive imprinting can be taken as a means of characterizing the serially consistent cognitive behavior of the students within technology-facilitated learning environments, and further may reflect desired learning outcomes.

Technology Implementation: Media Stickiness Theory

Huysman et al. (2003) suggested the concept of media stickiness to explain the tendency of individuals or groups to maintain early choices

of technologies despite the introduction of more useful and value-added technologies. Although distributed virtual teams exhibited distinctly different patterns and preferences for communication, collaboration, and learning technology choices, their choices were generally found to be made early in project work and remained the preferred practice throughout the project.

Both cognitive imprinting and media stickiness imply that team communication and technology adoption patterns rely on student initial cognitive behaviors. Once these cognitive behaviors became habitual the chance of changing patterns was limited. This may in turn constrain student learning of new concepts, skills, and knowledge, especially in creativity and higher order cognition development. Both theories seem to conflict with Rogers' theory of innovation adoption. Rogers (1983) suggested that adopting innovations, like new technology tools, concepts, or skills, is a process of passing from an initial stage of knowledge of an innovation, into a stage of forming an attitude toward the innovation, into a stage of making a decision to adopt or reject the innovation, into a stage of implementing (using) the new innovation, and into a final stage of making a decision to adopt [or not] the innovation.

To support adoption of synchronous multiuser collaboration tools, for example, training should help students develop knowledge and practice using the new technologies. Training should also provide instruction in technology-based collaborative communication skills (e.g., team management strategies) while encouraging students to experiment with the new communication technologies within the virtual environment. As Grabowski and Koszalka (2002) suggested, continuously engaging students with new technologies and repeating such activities helps students form knowledge and attitudes toward innovations that bring them value and aid in adoption.

However, knowledge and practice are not always sufficient in supporting the adoption process. As to technology adoption, it is still not clearly understood whether a lack of knowledge and attitude toward a new technology or a failure in the implementation (use) of a new technology is to blame for lack of adoption. More specifically, no empirical data was found that indicates sticking to an initially chosen technology is a failure in knowledge of a new technology or were there data found that indicate in which stage of the innovation-decision process it is most likely where technology adoption failures may occur. In addition, the concept of habitual inertia (inaction), implied in both the cognitive imprinting and media stickiness theories, is valuable in describing contexts where a constant and repetitive performance is expected to be developed. Therefore, examination of students' team learning processes and understanding of instructional and learning needs will help in understanding when learning inertia may occur, whether it needs to be maintained or stopped, and what instructional interventions may be appropriately designed and implemented to support technology adoption choices.

RESEARCH CONTEXT

A collaborative engineering design (CED) course was created to engage distributed teams of engineering students in a multiuser, blended synchronous and asynchronous, virtual environment to learn about and solve authentic engineering design problems. The CED incorporated a virtual multiuser work environment, the Advanced Interactive Discovery Environment (AIDE), to engage learners with a variety of tools that supported synchronous distributed, interdisciplinary, collaborative engineering design tasks. This environment allowed multiple learners entry into this virtual space to participate synchronously in live lectures and discussions to learn about and apply engineering concepts. Learners were able to employ a variety of communication and analysis tools in a virtual large class setting or in small team activities. While inside the AIDE,

learners were able to share ideas and explore solutions orally and visually through audio and video conferencing, shared writing and drawing spaces, and data analysis application sharing. Dietele and Clarke (2005) identified that "...multiuser virtual environments enable multiple simultaneous participants to be able to access virtual contexts, ... communicate with other participants, ... and take part in experiences incorporating modeling and mentoring about problems similar to those in real world context". The CED AIDE SameTime environment created a significant, interactive, virtual collaboration learning experience by offering innovative instructional ways to students for knowledge sharing and decision-making tasks.

CED COURSE DESIGN

The Study Context, Instructional Design Foundations, and Multiuser Virtual Environments

Instructors from two universities collaboratively taught the semester-long CED course directly to the students from their home institute and synchronously through the AIDE at a distance for those at the partnering institute. Participating students from both universities simultaneously attended course lectures either in-person at their home institute or through multiuser virtual environment synchronous tools depending on which of the two professors was responsible for the session content. Students were assigned to distributed design teams with 50% from the local and 50% from the distance university. Each received instruction in the foundational engineering content and necessary technology skills to participate in the course activities. For several weeks however, the students were split into one of two engineering content learning tracks. Thus students, for the sake of a culminating activity, had different engineering expertise from which to collaborate on a resolution for a given engineering design problem, which

Figure 1. Distance learning classroom. (a) Student view. (b) Faculty view

(a)   (b)

required students to create a preliminary design of a thermo-structural system for a specific location on a hypothetical second-generation reusable launch vehicle (RLV) for NASA space missions. Each distributed team therefore had a mix of students from both universities and each of the two engineering content tracks. These distributed engineering design teams thus had to bring together different types of engineering knowledge to collaboratively solve a design problem in an authentic engineering working environment, that is, as distributed interdisciplinary teams working to solve complex engineering problems. The course instructors acted as project managers and mentors to help the teams be successful at their tasks.

The Advanced Interactive Discovery Environment (AIDE) for Engineering Education was developed in partnership between the faculties of the two universities. The AIDE integrated and advanced the best features of virtual, collaborative engineering environments, state-of-the-art simulation tools, and advanced learning management systems (Davidson et al., 2002). Pedagogical approaches, including generative, problem-based, and collaborative instructional strategies formed the structure of the course to fully engaged learners with the AIDE to learn content and learn how to resolve engineering design problems.

The course was also designed to promote skills development in using leading-edge technologies, working on distributed teams, writing project reports, and giving oral presentations. Teamwork was a critical aspect of the course design thus several team building exercises were presented. Early in the semester *best practices* labs were conducted to help students build productive teams using the collaboration technologies available in the AIDE.

Course Technology

The course infrastructure was built with four main components: (1) distance learning classrooms (DLC) equipped with video conferencing system for the synchronous full class instruction – See Figure 1, (2) IP-based web-conferencing to satisfy the needs of multiple simultaneous partial-class events and synchronous team collaboration, (3) asynchronous online information management and communication system provided a platform to document course materials, exchange files, and store engineering discipline-related resources, and (4) a physical design studio and individual tablet-pc provided a suite of technology tools for the students. See Table 1.

The provided multiuser synchronous communication features (SameTime [ST]) included video and audio, interactive shared whiteboard,

Table 1. Summary of provided classroom and virtual tools

Location	Tools	Description / Key features
Distance Learning Classrooms	• Video conferencing equipment,	Facilitate delivery of instruction and 2-way communication and interaction
	• Projection equipment and electronic white board (facilitate local and distance education)	Facilitate 2-way communication and interaction
	• SmartBoard	Facilitate presentation, document, etc. sharing, communication, and interaction
Design Studio	• Physical lab (at each site) with computer stations	Engineering and analysis software loaded stations to facilitate computation and design activities; supports communication
Course hardware	• Tablet PC for individual students	Provide 24/7 access to AIDE ST for all students
Virtual (AIDE ST)	***Synchronous communications***	
	• Video / audio	Real time (taped/stored) video conferencing
	• Interactive shared whiteboard	Collaborative space where teams can draw, type, color, highlight, etc., all see and edit together
	• Screen sharing	Ability to show all team members an application or document, one person demonstrates and edits
	• Meeting Room Chat	Text-based communication, all can add and see comments posted
	• Polling	Ability for team members to vote in response to posted questions during meetings. question must be posted before a ST meeting session begins
	• Send Web Page	Ability to open and share a Web Page, one person implements and others can see
	• Hand raising	Ability for any team member to take control of talking (audio sharing) during ST session
	Asynchronous Communications	
	• Course announcements	Information, notices, reminders posted by instructors
	• Team work storage spaces	Storage space open only to specified team members
	• Student drop boxes	For submission of each student's assignments
	• Threaded discussion board	Traditional discussion board
	• Team project management tools	Templates to help teams management their progress and report to course managers

application sharing, chats, instant messaging, document posting, and presence-awareness. The DST lectures and learners' team meetings were conducted through SameTime. The asynchronous AIDE services (e.g., course announcement, team work spaces, student drop-boxes, threaded discussion board, and team project management tools) also provided supports for team communication and learning activities. See Figure 2.

RESEARCH QUESTIONS

An initial data analyses suggested the course design fostered engineering content learning, CED problem-solving, collaborative technologies knowledge, and development of collaboration skills (Koszalka & Wu, 2008). However, two significant instructional design themes emerged from this initial analysis: designing effective uses of technology resources during collabora-

Figure 2. Sample of Web-based synchronous meeting and discussion screen. Participants can see the current speaker, share applications, use chat, and markup whiteboard during the discussion

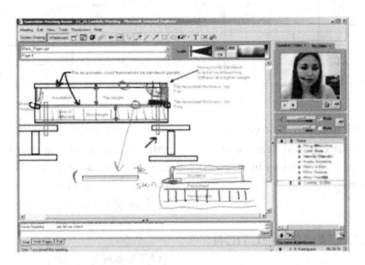

tive activities and supporting team collaboration strategies. Learners reported that they were not aware of the value some of the provided AIDE tools, how to use them effectively in their collaborative work, or even about the existence of particular tools until late of the semester (Koszalka & Wu, 2008). This feedback appears to support Kirschner et al. (2004) conjectured that learners sometimes participated in online environments very enthusiastically, but often used the tools in a perfunctory way. Learners also tended to display different understandings of team participation and often reported that their team work suffered because of a lack of a team management planning and team structure in the virtual environment. It was not known whether the issue was in the design of the learning environment, the types of technology tools and resources provided, training on the technology tools, or instruction in team collaboration and the use of the technology tools during collaborative design activities.

The instructional goals of multiuser virtual environments were to equip learners with cognitive skills through which they learn how to be successful lifelong learners and problem-solvers when they are situated in different contexts facing challenges from new technologies, new people, and new problems. Hence, learners unable to use technologies or to effectively learn in a virtual multiuser CED environment may not yet have obtained the skills and knowledge to be successful in such complex and authentic environments. They may also lack the collaboration skills necessary to participate effectively in collaborative problem-solving activities. Based on these conjectures, the four research questions for this study included:

- Which AIDE SameTime (synchronous multiuser) web-conferencing technology tools did the teams use most often during the CED project? How and why do they use these tools?
- Are there different patterns between the two teams in learning and / or adopting of technologies during the team's AIDE SameTime synchronous web conferencing meetings?
- What type of technology-based communication patterns did each team display?

Table 2. Descriptive information of analyzed team communication videos

Team	Sept. 12	Sept. 15	Sept. 21	Oct. 5	Oct. 27	Oct. 31	Nov. 5	Nov. 14	Nov. 29	Total video minutes
Alpha	1		1	1		1		1		484
Gamma		1		1	1		1		1	371
Subtotal	**1**	**1**	**1**	**2**	**1**	**1**	**1**	**1**	**1**	**855**

• Was there a relationship between team communication pattern and team use of AIDE SameTime (synchronous multiuser) technologies during meetings?

METHODS AND DATA COLLECTION

This was a mixed methods exploration of a virtual multiuser collaborative engineering design course with a focus on how learners engaged with the provided synchronous communication tools. A stratified random sample of the synchronous multiuser AIDE SameTime team recorded meetings was identified to ensure that data represented sessions held at the beginning, middle, and end of the course, representing all four units in the course.

The sampled videos were reviewed using a structured video review protocol. A SameTime Video Review Sheet (protocol) was composed of three parts developed from a combination of existing data analysis and demographic protocols and a synthesis of the literature and similar studies on social learning activities (Geer & Barnes, 2007; Huysman et al., 2003; Ross, 1996; Rourke & Anderson, 2002). Part I of the review protocol was a Technology / Media Use & Computer Tools Competence Table, adapted from Huysman et al.'s (2003) team media-use pattern table. Part II was a SameTime Tech-mediated Team Communication protocol created through the synthesis of the literature on variables of social collaboration that affect learning during distributed learning activities. Part III was a series of evaluative and

demographic questions to provide descriptive information about the teams and their members. Each video was reviewed by two coders who used the SameTime Video Review Sheet to gather a variety of qualitative data.

DATA ANALYSIS

One-hundred and forty-two SameTime team meetings were recorded during the course, 83 were usable as data. A stratified random sampling technique was used to select ten videos, five each from two CED teams. The videos represented both teams and all time periods over the course. The ten videos represented approximately 855 minutes of team interactions. See table 2.

Three doctoral students were recruited and trained as coders. Each sampled video was reviewed by two coders. The inter-rater reliability of the coding was 89.96%. All data was imported into QDA Miner software for coding. Seventy-two sub-codes were produced under four major categories: (1) demographics, (2) technology use, (3) team communication, and (4) reflection.

RESULTS

Overall, the data suggested that the two teams had different technology use patterns and communication strategies. Specific results for each research questions are presented below.

R. Q. 1: Which AIDE SameTime (Multiuser Synchronous) Web-Conferencing Technology Tools Did the Team Use Most Often during the CED Project? How and Why Do They Use These Tools?

Major SameTime Tools Used

It was observed that audio, video, interactive whiteboard, window chat room and screen sharing were the five major SameTime multiuser tools most frequently used in the sampled synchronous meeting videos.

Interactive whiteboard: The WB was used when the team members collaborated on the team project. The most frequently used Whiteboard features included the pen, presenting, changing slides, and eraser. The two teams seemed comfortable using different editing and communicating features provided by the interactive whiteboard. They used these tools to review team documents, take notes, brainstorm, visualize their thoughts through writing or drawing, and cooperate on scheduling and team logistics, or to merely scrawl for fun.

Window chat room: This feature was frequently used to (1) backup to audio for brainstorming, (2) express an opinion, inform, comment, send out a query, or respond without interrupting the audio, or (3) joke, give a salute or acknowledge to team-mate without interrupting the audio.

Screen sharing: The AIDE SameTime Screen Sharing features were used regularly by the Alpha team. The screen sharing does not allow multi-editors. The person sharing the screen took notes on his or her screen during team discussions and the other team members ensured that all changes were recorded correctly as they read the shared screen. As was observed, uploading the screen sharing document was time consuming and running the screen sharing tool slowed the performance of other SameTime tools (e.g., audio, video). The

screen sharing feature was used less frequently by the Alpha team toward the end of the semester.

Computer audio and video: The audio and video features were the most commonly used synchronous communication features of the AIDE SameTime.

R. Q. 2: Are there Different Patterns Between the Two Teams in Learning and / or Adopting Technologies during the Team's AIDE SameTime Synchronous Web Conferencing Meetings?

Team Differences in Multiuser Technology Uses

At the beginning of the semester, both teams were observed practicing different technologies and tools to a certain level within the SameTime meeting environment. The two teams presented different technology use patterns and these differences included:

Number of tools used: The Alpha team members were observed using ST tools extensively while the Gamma team members were observed using only the basic meeting features, such as presenting documents and pen tools that the interactive whiteboard supports. Among the 14 mini-features of the interactive whiteboard, the Alpha team experimented and used 13 while the Gamma team only used 7 (see tables 3 & 4). In addition, Gamma team was rarely observed using screen-sharing and send-web-page features in the sampled SameTime videos.

Use frequency of major tools: The Alpha team used interactive whiteboard 3 times more often and the window chat room 10 times more often than the Gamma team. In addition, the Alpha team used the screen sharing application four times while the Gamma team never used it (see figures 3 and 4).

The window chat room was the technology reported most commonly used by the students in

Table 3. Team Alpha tech use frequency

		Alpha Sep12	Alpha Sep21	Alpha Oct05	Alpha Oct31	Alpha Nov14	Total
Interactive Whiteboard	Arrow	1	0	0	0	0	1
	Changing slides	7	2	2	9	1	21
	Circle	0	0	1	0	0	1
	Colors	9	0	18	6	0	33
	Creating a New Slide	0	0	1	1	1	3
	Eraser	1	0	21	10	11	43
	Line	1	0	0	0	0	0
	Pen	10	2	42	49	26	129
	Presenting/Uploading	3	1	2	8	2	16
	Rectangle	2	0	7	0	0	9
	Refreshing	0	0	2	0	0	2
	Selection	0	0	1	0	0	1
	Thickness	0	0	0	0	0	0
	Typing	4	0	9	1	7	21
	Total	**38**	**5**	**106**	**103**	**48**	**300**
Screen Sharing		**0**	**3**	**0**	**1**	**0**	**4**
Send Web Page		**0**	**0**	**0**	**0**	**0**	**0**
Window Chat Room		**6**	**29**	**58**	**15**	**103**	**211**

Table 4. Team Gamma tech use frequency

		Gamma Sep15	Gamma Oct05	Gamma Oct27	Gamma Nov05	Gamma Nov29	Total
Interactive Whiteboard	Arrow	0	0	0	0	0	0
	Changing slides	4	25	0	0	6	35
	Circle	0	0	0	0	0	0
	Colors	2	1	0	0	4	7
	Creating a New Slide	0	1	1	1	1	4
	Eraser	1	4	1	0	2	8
	Line	0	0	0	0	0	0
	Pen	5	38	9	9	13	74
	Presenting/Uploading	1	5	1	1	2	10
	Rectangle	0	0	0	0	0	0
	Refreshing	0	0	0	0	0	0
	Selection	0	0	0	0	0	0
	Thickness	1	1	0	0	5	7
	Typing	0	0	0	0	0	0
	Total	**0**	**75**	**12**	**11**	**0**	**98**
Screen Sharing		**0**	**0**	**0**	**0**	**0**	**0**
Send Web Page		**0**	**0**	**0**	**0**	**0**	**0**
Window Chat Room		**7**	**8**	**0**	**0**	**7**	**22**

Figure 3. Team Alpha technology use pattern (four major tools used)

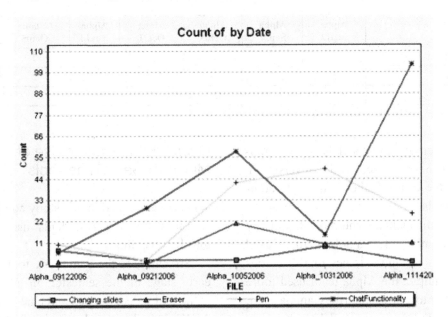

Figure 4. Team Gamma technology use pattern (four major tools used)

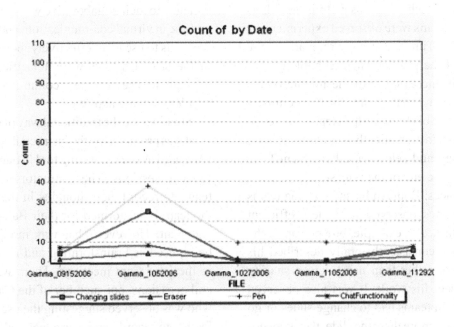

their daily life routines outside of classes; therefore, it was presumed that students felt more comfortable using chat than other SameTime technologies. Data suggested that the Alpha team used chat very commonly throughout the entire semester while the Gamma team was observed using the chat feature less often. The chat was used as the major salutation tool by the Gamma team when someone accessed the meeting late. As the Gamma team became more familiar with

Table 5. Technology issues encountered by each team

Team	Alpha Sep12	Alpha Sep21	Alpha Oct05	Alpha Oct31	Alpha Nov14	Gamma Oct05	Gamma Nov29
Audio / Video issues	5	13	8	3	6	2	1
Other tech issues	5	2	0	0	1	2	0
Total	43					5	

the SameTime environment and the audio equipment, they generally used oral conversation, rarely using the chat or other SameTime communication tools.

Issues and difficulties: The more frequently and higher number of technology tools used during sessions the more issues or difficulties arose. For example, the Alpha team used more different tools, more often, than the Gamma team. The Alpha team also encountered 43 technology issues, 8 times more than those encountered by the Gamma team. See table 5.

Patterns of technology use: Both the Alpha and Gamma teams were observed experimenting with the SameTime technology regularly at the beginning of the project. Their technology uses continuously increased until the middle of the semester. Pen and chat became the two dominant collaboration tools for the Alpha team. However, the Gamma team dramatically decreased their use of technology and seldom used the SameTime tools toward the end of the semester.

Tool choices: Both Alpha and Gamma teams were sometimes observed using less efficient tools for a task. For example, one person in the Gamma team consistently orally described his analysis work rather than using screen sharing tool to present his work. It was also observed that when both teams had to change slides or go back-and-forth more than one slide, they kept going slide-by-slide rather than using the dropdown menu to go directly to the desired slide. These choices decreased the productivity of the meeting.

Overall Evaluation of Use of Multiuser SameTime Tools

The data generated in this study confirms media stickiness existing in students' use of technologies by revealing:

Stickiness to the SameTime tools used at the early stage of the semester: In addition to the audio and video, the pen and chat were two new AIDE SameTime technologies that both teams stuck with throughout the semester. This suggests that the team members identified these tools as valuable to their collaborative work, easy to learn and use in virtual communication, and developed the skills to use them effectively; but found some of the provided tools were not efficient, or too difficult to use for their communications and problem solving activities.

Stickiness to the traditional way of using tools: Chat was promoted by the instructors and required to be used as brainstorming tool in one of the Best Practice sessions. The instructors required the teams to record their thoughts in the chat when the team brainstormed for their Ball-in-pipe assignment. However, chat was rarely observed being used as brainstorming and recording tool in the later team meetings. There was, on several occasions, one member of the Gamma team who was observed suggesting the use of the chat feature to record key ideas generated in the team discussions but his proposal was never accepted by other team members.

Traditional technologies used for communication outside of the SameTime environment: Additional data was gathered suggesting that students from both teams continued to use text messaging, cell phone, and emails most frequently outside of the ADIE to exchange documents or to inform each other of scheduling changes or other emergencies. This suggests that the student were comfortable with these everyday tools, saw value in them for communicating with their teammates, and perhaps were not as comfortable with using only the provided AIDE tools.

TEAM COMMUNICATION

R. Q. 3: What type of Technology-Based Social Communication Patterns did Each Team Display?

Team Participation

Alpha team: At the start of the semester, the moderator[1] of the meeting tended to take more initiative and be more expressive during virtual meetings. The moderator usually dominated the conversation and ensured that the team was on track. In general, the interaction among team members was well-balanced and participation of the team members was generally equal. It was often observed that two students would take one side of an issue or argument and the other two members would support a different idea or approach. After AF[2] joined the Alpha team (mid-semester) the team dynamics were observed to change. AF appeared to have a good grasp of the content knowledge and be very focused on tasks. AF began to lead and dominate many of the discussions in a majority of the meetings.

Gamma team: In general, participation was roughly equal for members GL, BZ, and BK. MW[3] was observed to have a fair level of engagement at the semester start; however, MW's participation became less toward the semester end. BZ and GL were often observed taking over as leaders and polarizing the discussion. BK was not central to the group suggestions but his contributions were

thoughtful suggesting he was listening and waiting for appropriate times to contribute. It is worth noting that when GL was not attending a meeting, the team dynamics changed slightly. BK and BZ took over as conversation leaders and BK became well conversed.

On-Task Performance

Both Alpha and Gamma teams appeared to be task-oriented and deadline driven during their synchronous virtual meetings. They each had specific tasks to accomplish in every session. The meeting usually started with technology normalization checking that all team members had the SameTime set-up and ensured proper SameTime functioning. Depending on tasks, meeting time was sometimes separated into individual work and team collaboration periods. During individual work time, each member worked on his own solution to a common problem and then the team collaborated by exchanging, discussing, and comparing individual thoughts. At the end of the meeting, the teams usually scheduled the next meeting time and discussed team logistics. Although common collaboration routines were used by both teams, on-task performance and communication patterns were different.

Alpha team: Alpha team meetings and working structures were relatively loose. Team members were observed having food or beverage during meetings, being late, stepping away in the middle of the discussion, or chatting casually. There did not appear to be a team management strategy and the team productivity was low. Feedback from one of the instructors suggested that the Alpha team had a weak plan for their design project, without specifics as to who was to complete each task and by when. The Alpha team did not have an effective scheduling process – they spent much longer in their scheduling phase than was necessary, leaving them less working time for their design project. The team spent up to 35 minutes at the meeting start trying to schedule the next session yet could not reach consensus on a time that fit everyone's schedule. After 15 minutes of content discussion, the team returned to discuss scheduling finally identifying a tentative schedule.

Content related jokes were generated during team conversations. The Alpha team members were occasionally observed teasing their team members. The jokes created by the team were entertaining and may have helped them relax. However, the jokes may also have been distracting to team productivity. It was observed that after joking around it sometimes took long periods of time to refocus on the meeting goals.

Gamma team: the Gamma team was strongly focused on project content and tasks. When the meeting started, team members briefly checked the technologies and greeted their peers. They quickly moved onto tasks. Based on the feedback from one of the instructors, the Gamma team had a reasonably good plan for their design project with dates, specific tasks, and assignments.

Socialization and Off-Task Time

Major reasons causing the team to get off-task included: waiting for other team members to login in, encountering technology problems, such as someone's voice was cut off, waiting for the screen sharing application to open, team members needing to step away, and frustration from the lack of focus during team discussions. The Alpha team was observed being off-task more than ten times. Meanwhile, it was rarely observed that the Gamma team was off task.

Team Dynamics and Communication Differences

Personality vs. Teamality: Every student appeared to react differently to a particular problem perhaps due to their personality differences. However, when the students worked as a team, every team started forming its communication characteristics,

or we may name it *teamality*, regardless the diversity its team members' personalities appeared.

Alpha team examples: The five team members in the Alpha team sometimes appeared to behave differently. For instance, MA appears to like the role as moderator, often taking charge and making decisions quickly. AB appeared more detached, not participating very often, and seeking the most straightforward solutions. LS, in contrast, was observed using technology more and really wanted to tackle the solution by sticking to his own thoughts and plan. JR preferred a more pragmatic approach while settling for a feasible solution, if possible. AF joined the team late and showed excellent content knowledge among all the team members. However, the students together formed some unique team characteristics. The Alpha members appeared to have strong interests in exploring the ST technologies and therefore practiced most of the tools at the beginning of the semester. The ST tools, especially the Whiteboard features, were used as collaboration tools and also used for fun activities. For instance, team Alpha members sometimes use color pens to draw cartoon images or play games (e.g., tic-tac-toe) during the off-task periods. Therefore, compared to the Gamma team, they were observed to be able to choose more effective tools or use multiple tools in their practice. For example, they used rectangle tool to build tables or used color tools to differentiate or highlight key points. At another side, the team appeared to easily lose focus and their meetings therefore resulted in low productivity. This may be explained by: (a) more technical issues encountered by the team increased the average meeting time which may bring up meeting fatigue; (b) side-talks, off-track conversations, or jokes that distracted the team attention and delayed work progress.

Gamma team examples: Personality differences among the Gamma team members may explain their different levels of participation. GL and BZ seem to be more talkative and social. They usually appeared to dominate most of the team conversation and maneuvered the direction of the meetings. BK seems to be very confident in the content knowledge and he was very conversant when he started talking about the content and his analysis work. It was difficult to make any judgment about MW because he rarely spoke during the meetings. Although every person was observed having distinctive personalities, the Gamma team appeared to have different *teamality* from the Alpha team. The team was very task-focused. Members were rarely observed in side-talks or joking. The team seemed satisfied with basic communication features (e.g., audio). Therefore, the team used fewer AIDE features, encountered much fewer technology issues, and appeared to have more efficient and effective meeting sessions and produced higher-quality performance.

Other Differences

Two other factors seemed to contribute to the team dynamics and may have influenced team communication pattern: content and institutional differences.

Content knowledge differences: The students who had better content knowledge appeared to engage more in team conversations. Although these students may show different personalities, they appeared to be more confident, conversant, and prepared, often raising good questions about particular points and, in most situations, dominated in the entire meeting. For instance, AF in the Alpha team appeared to be a good leader steering the team in proper directions. BK in the Gamma team always participated at the key times providing insightful thoughts, clarifying explanation and ideas. These students were observed less engaged in the off-task activities and chatter. This trend was observed throughout the entire semester.

Institutional differences: The institutional differences were distinctive between the Gamma team members. The two CU students focused more on problem solving, searching and utilizing more resources outside of the course to help with

their analysis process. Meanwhile, the two SU students were more concerned about the timeline of completing the design project and appeared to have more team management skills. Skills from students from the two universities contributed to the success of the team performance.

Overall Evaluation of Team Communication

Overall, three major team communication themes emerged from the data analysis. First, different personalities, institutional cultures, content knowledge and skills contributed to the dynamics of each team. Second, data suggested from the cognitive imprinting theory perspective (Geer, 2005), a team's initial communication patterns were powerful predictors in determining subsequent interactive behaviors. However, the data also suggests that the team's communication pattern may change when the team dynamics change. For example, when the GL was not present, BK became conversant. He and BZ were observed dominating the conversation. Third, an explanation for AF's minor engagement in meetings still remains mystery at this point. Data collected from the sample archival video data do not suggest rationale for his limited engagement. However, when GL and BZ called MW several times asking for his thoughts about the design project MW rarely was able to provide a complete answer. Perhaps MW did not have sufficient content knowledge or he was not motivated to participate. There were also several occasions when MW was not in the meetings and GL criticized his low quality work commenting that this was 'the crappiest work he had ever seen.' Other members did not make specific comments, however, seemed to agree with GL. Thus, dynamics of the team, cognitive and initial media preferences, and unidentified individual characteristics were related to communication effectiveness and team productivity.

CONCLUSION

Team Communication vs. Team Technology Use and Adoption

This study helps extend the media stickiness theory by discovering that a person's choice of a particular technology within a virtual multiuser learning environment and sticking to its use relies primarily on needs related to communication, socialization, or problem solving. This perspective aligns with Geer and Barnes' (2007) suggestion that "…high levels of creativity through collaboration … are not always necessary to their immediate goals … the learning of participants needs to be considered." (p. 135). When a team's communication needs are satisfied, motivation for using other new tools is limited therefore tools deemed useless are eventually dropped suggesting the team does not see the necessity of using the tool regardless of how well it was designed to meet a communication need. For example, the Gamma team was observed sticking to the pen tool to draw tables rather than using the rectangle tool. This may be explained by the fact that the pen was sufficient and easy to use and use of the rectangle tools was more time consuming. Changing to a new way of working required a cost-benefit analysis (Huysman et al., 2003) suggesting that the cost of using the rectangle tools was more than using the pen tool in this case. Students' communication needs played a major role in the variation of tools they use and how long they continue to use each tool.

Adopting particular technologies and sticking to their use are not simply a team or any particular individual's decision. A team's selection of specific technologies tends to have the following characteristics: technologies frequently used in team members' daily life are more often adopted by the team and personal interests in technologies intrigue members into practicing additional new technologies but does not necessarily lead to the adoption of a particular new technology. The second characteristic may conflict with what Huys-man et al. (2003) suggested that "lack of internal communication process was one potential source of media stickiness in virtual teams" (p. 432). JD in the Alpha team suggested using the typing tool instead of pen writing at the beginning of the semester. Some of the team members followed him using the typing tool, however typing was eventually dropped while pen writing remained a common activity. External feedback does not seem to promote students' adoption of particular tools either. The two instructors commented several times that neither team appeared to use the SameTime technology adequately although they had sufficient technology competences. However, the feedback criticizing these teams' habitual way of working did not have enough power to make a permanent change in both teams' technology use.

Two possible explanations for the media stickiness observed in this study are: 1) students may realize that use of more tools causes more technical issues and 2) using many tools reduced the teams' productivity and ability to meet assignment deadlines. Due to the busy schedule of the team members, the teams usually had one hour meeting times in which they needed to accomplish multiple tasks including technology normalization, scheduling, team logistics, and content discussion. Therefore experimenting with different new tools may have been deemed a low priority on the team's task list.

Team's technology use may relate to the team's communication characteristics. It was observed that the Alpha team, who practiced more technologies and encountered more technology issues, had lower productivity. While the Gamma team, using few technologies and rarely encountering technology issues, had much higher productivity and performed better in team management. This possible connection may suggest that the Alpha team did not have good team management skills to prioritize tasks. This also suggests that if the students face multiple learning goals (e.g., learning technology and learning content knowledge), they may not be able to do well in every goal if the task load is beyond their ability. As some of the students suggested that the course should be designed as one-year course because there were too many concepts to learn. Therefore, two instructional interventions to consider in the future course design include: 1) providing constant feedback in terms of team management including topics such as how to prioritize tasks and 2) balance instructional goals, student learning load, and the time allowed for completing the course.

Various factors contributed to team dynamics, which results in the formation of a team's 'personality' – or its *teamality*. A team's teamality may suggest a team's communication pattern, its technology choices, and the team management strategy. These patterns would remain consistent and / or grow stronger (e.g., MW in the Gamma team appeared to participate less and less in the meeting throughout the semester) as the theory of cognitive imprinting suggests. However, the data in this study also implies that when the team dynamics are altered due to some change in the team (e.g., more members joined the team, or someone is not present in the meeting), teamality would also change, which hence impacts the team's communication patterns and team productivity. For example, the Alpha team was observed becoming more productive after AF joined. In the future instructional design, it may be important to switch team members at the beginning of the course (e.g., in the Best Practices sessions) to help students learn about different personalities and communication patterns in virtual teams. Hence, they may be able to more quickly fit into a team collaboration culture and to develop more mature and insightful thoughts about how to learn with a team.

This study has revealed very specific details about how two distributed teams worked within a synchronous multiuser environment. The video analysis, surveying, and document analysis have allowed an intimate investigation of how and why learners use system and non-system technology based tools to collaborate, problem solve, and learn. These data suggested a 'teamality' variable influenced by the team dynamics, technology choices, and individual members' characteristics. Further unpacking of this concept may help in designing more powerful synchronous virtual learning environments and tools that help learners engage in deep learning and develop the competencies to be successful in multiuser virtual environments.

REFERENCES

Chen, G. (1994). Social desirability as a predictor of argumentativeness and communication apprehension. *Journal of Psychology Interdisciplinary & Applied, 128*(4), 433–439. doi:10.1080/00223980.1994.9712749

Cho, H., Gay, G., Davidson, B., & Ingraffea, A. (2007). Social networks, communication styles, and learning performance in a CSCL community. *Computers & Education, 49*(2), 309–329. .doi:10.1016/j.compedu.2005.07.003

Davidson, B. D., Davidson, R., Gay, G., Ingraffea, A., Miller, M., & Nozick, L. … Rath, C. (2002). Collaborative distance design of aerospace structures. *Proceedings of the 32nd ASEE/IEEE Frontiers in Education Conference,* Boston, Massachusetts.

Dieterle, E., & Clarke, J. (2005). Multi-user virtual environments for teaching and learning . In Pagani, M. (Ed.), *Encyclopedia of multimedia technology and networking* (2nd ed.). Hershey, PA: Idea Group, Inc.

Fåhræus, E. R. (1999). Tutoring group learning at a distance. *Proceedings of Society for Information Technology & Teacher Education International Conference, 1999,* 152–157.

Geer, R. (2005). *Imprinting and its impact on online learning environments.* Australasian Society for Computers in Learning in Tertiary Education.

Geer, R., & Barnes, A. (2006). Media stickiness and cognitive imprinting: Inertia and creativity in cooperative work & learning with ICTs. *Proceedings of the World Computer Congress*, (pp. 55-64).

Geer, R., & Barnes, A. (2007). Beyond media stickiness and cognitive imprinting: Rethinking creativity in cooperative work & learning with ICTs. *Education and Information Technologies*, *12*, 123–136. doi:10.1007/s10639-007-9036-6

Gokhale, A. (1995). Collaborative learning enhances critical thinking. *Journal of Technology Education*, *7*(1), 22–30.

Grabowski, B., & Koszalka, T. (2002). Helping educators harvest Internet resources: The development of technology integration support tools. *Proceedings of the IADIS International Conference WWW/Internet 2002.*

Hron, A., & Friedrich, H. (2003). A review of Web-based collaborative learning: Factors beyond technology. *Journal of Computer Assisted Learning*, *19*(1), 70–79. doi:10.1046/j.0266-4909.2002.00007.x

Huysman, M., Steinfield, C., Jang, C. Y., & David, K., Huis In 'T Veld, M., Poot, J., & Mulder, I. (2003). Virtual teams and the appropriation of communication technology: Exploring the concept of media stickiness. *Computer Supported Cooperative Work*, *12*(4), 411–436. doi:10.1023/A:1026145017609

Jonassen, D. H., & Kwon, H. (2001). Communication patterns in computer mediated versus face-to-face group problem solving. *Educational Technology Research and Development*, *49*(1), 35–51. doi:10.1007/BF02504505

Kapur, M., & Kinzer, C. K. (2007). Examining the effect of problem type in a synchronous computer-supported collaborative learning (CSCL) environment. *Educational Technology and Development*, *55*(5), 439–459. doi:10.1007/s11423-007-9045-6

Kirschner, P., Strijbos, J. W., Krejins, K., & Beers, P. J. (2004). Designing electronic collaborative learning environments. *Educational Technology Research and Development*, *52*(3), 47–66. doi:10.1007/BF02504675

Koszalka, T. A., & Wu, Y. (2008). *Evaluation of a cross-institutional collaborative distributed engineering educational environment*. 12th Global Chinese Computer and Communication Conference.

Lowyck, L., & Poysa, J. (2001). Design of collaborative learning environments. *Computers in Human Behavior*, *17*(5-6), 507–516. doi:10.1016/S0747-5632(01)00017-6

Nussbaum, E. M., Hartley, K., Sinatra, G., Reynolds, R., & Bendixen, L. D. (2004). Personality interactions and scaffolding in on-line discussions. *Journal of Educational Computing Research*, *30*(1-2), 113–136. doi:10.2190/H8P4-QJUF-JXME-6JD8

Ormrod, J. E. (2008). *Human learning* (5th ed.). Upper Saddle River, NJ: Pearson.

Panitz, T. (1996). *A definition of collaborative vs. cooperative learning*. Retrieved January 2, 2010, from http://www.city.londonmet.ac.uk/ deliberations/collab.learning /panitz2.html

Pellegrino, J. W. (2006). *Rethinking and redesigning curriculum, instruction and assessment: What contemporary research and theory suggests*. Retrieved February 24, 2010, from http://www.skillscommission.org/ pdf/commissioned_papers/Rethinking%20and%20 Redesigning.pdf

Prinsen, F., Volman, M. L. L., & Terwel, J. (2007). The influence of learner characteristics on degree and type of participation in a CSCL environment. *British Journal of Educational Technology*, *38*(6), 1037–1055. doi:10.1111/j.1467-8535.2006.00692.x

Rogers, E. M. (1983). *Diffusion of innovation* (3rd ed.). New York, NY: Macmillan.

Ross, J. A. (1996). *Computer communication skills and participation in a computer-mediated conferencing course*. Annual Conference of the American Educational Research Association.

Rourke, L., & Anderson, T. (2002). Exploring social communication in computer conferencing. *Journal of Interactive Learning Research, 13*(3), 259–275.

Shuman, L. J., Atman, C. J., Eschenbach, E. A., Evans, D., Felder, R. M., & Imbrie, P. K. … Richard, L. G. (2002). The future of engineering education. *Proceedings of the 32nd Annual ASEE/IEEE Conference on Frontiers in Education*.

Solimeno, A., Mebane, M., Tomai, M., & Francescato, D. (2008). The influence of students and teachers characteristics on the efficacy of face-to-face and computer supported collaborative learning. *Computers & Education, 51*(1), 109–128. doi:10.1016/j.compedu.2007.04.003

ENDNOTES

[1] Team members took turns as the team moderator. The responsibilities of the meeting moderator included: (a) scheduling meetings and notifying the team (b) checking the ST technology to ensure it was functioning normally before the meeting; (c) uploading meeting agendas, assignments, and relevant documents to ST meeting before the meeting; (d). recording the meeting; (e). closing the recording and meeting.

[2] The Delta team was dismissed because three students dropped from the course. The composition of each team was reshuffled and AF was assigned to the Alpha team.

[3] GL and MW were from SU and BZ and BK were from CU.

Chapter 24
Towards Usable Collaborative Virtual Reality Environments for Promoting Listening Comprehension

Miguel A. Garcia-Ruiz
University of Colima, Mexico

Arthur Edwards
University of Colima, Mexico

Raul Aquino-Santos
University of Colima, Mexico

Jay Tashiro
University of Ontario Institute of Technology, Canada

Bill Kapralos
University of Ontario Institute of Technology, Canada

ABSTRACT

This chapter investigates whether an educational virtual environment can be developed to practice listening comprehension skills that meets second language student needs, complies with usability criteria, and is motivating to use. The chapter also investigates whether the usability of virtual reality(VR) technology positively affects language learning listening comprehension. It provides background research and information in Computer Assisted Language Learning (CALL), VR, and second language methodology. It then presents a technical and qualitative description of Realtown, a virtual environment designed to promote listening comprehension. This chapter also describes a usability study of Realtown. Student errors, motivation, and ease of use, among other features, were positively measured on listening comprehension activities in Realtown. Future work includes longitudinal studies on learning issues, first-person, and collaborative experiences in VR, including the impact of VR on learning and knowledge transfer when combined with traditional instruction.

DOI: 10.4018/978-1-60960-545-2.ch024

INTRODUCTION

Technology has been used to teach the four language skills (reading, writing, listening comprehension and speaking), and listening comprehension has sometimes represented the most difficult skill in which to achieve competence. Although CD-ROM/DVD-ROM-based technology and multimedia software provide comprehensible input, the relationship of sound and visuals in their video materials do not parallel the real world given the lack of user interaction (Bush & Terry, 1997, p. 95).

Consequently, the use of virtual reality technology for providing listening comprehension practice presents students an environment in which they can interact actively within a computer interface where they can, in fact, "perform actions" represented by an avatar, interacting with the interface using various sensory channels. Performing actions in response to commands forms the basis of the James Asher's Total Physical Response Method (Asher, 1977).

Although virtual reality (VR) was first introduced in the 1960s, it became more widely used in educational settings in the 1990s, where most of the research and development was in the areas of chemistry and medicine (Youngblut, 1998). For example, Park, Yoon, Kim, Lee and Han (2007) presents a virtual simulation system for a total knee replacement. Their system is based on mechanical computer-aided design (CAD) software and implemented using basic CAD functionality such as shape modeling, assembly, automation, etc., allowing surgeons to determine important surgical parameters prior to the operation itself. Ting, Lin, Chen, Lee and Chang (2003) describe a virtual reality system for unicompartmental knee replacement surgery training using a typical PC-based system and low-cost, six-degrees of freedom (motion) and three-degrees of freedom (force/resistive) manual manipulator. They model both the soft and skeletal tissue of the knee (based on computerized tomography scans) in addition

to an assortment of surgical tools. Using the manual manipulator, trainees are able to interact with the model, performing the surgical steps comprising the unicompartmental knee replacement procedure.

The application of VR to second language instruction has been a much more recent development. One of the most important investigations is the Zengo Sayu Project (Rose & Billinghurst, 1996), which is an immersive educational environment for learning Japanese. The Zengo Sayu Project examined whether students could learn spoken Japanese using the Zengo Sayu VR system, how the System compared to traditional instruction in terms of learning gain, and whether the Zengo Sayu approach had a positive effect on student motivation and attitudes towards learning Japanese. However, conclusions from the study are inconclusive.

Recently, Internet-based 3D social networking environments such as Linden Labs' Second Life (SL) have been used for second language learning. SL is an online virtual world where millions of Internet users have been registered to primarily socialize, but they can also contribute to SL by developing and uploading graphical objects, buildings, etc. and thus customize the environment. Its users can interact as virtual personifications called avatars, and users can communicate with each other using gestures, text messages, and their voice using voice over IP (VoIP). SL can be accessed via the following URL: http://secondlife. com. In general, SL graphics and many of its features can be personalized. The ability to personalize the SL environment is considered a fun and compelling feature. There are two versions of SL, one for adults and one for users between 13 to 17 years of age, called Teen Second Life. The SL virtual environment, often referred to as the "metaverse" contains many "islands" (also called "sims") that can be purchased and owned for a fee from Linden Lab or from other SL residents. Once purchased, the user can opt for using his/her island for their desired purposes. SL applications are primarily intended for entertainment purposes, but their use in educational settings is increasing. Education and general training are not opposed to providing fun and entertainment. For instance, in foreign language learning, fun and humor are ways to lower the "affective barrier." By lowering the affective barrier to learning, one also lowers anxiety and other negative feelings towards a learning experience (Krashen, 1982, 1988). There are already a number of educational islands that are owned by universities and private firms around the world, where courses are being taught. In addition, some educational institutions provide virtual facilities to their students, such as virtual classrooms, laboratories, and libraries (Gollub, 2007). SL also boasts virtual museums that can be used in educational activities as well.

There are presently several educational institutions offering second language (L2) classes in SL, including the internationally recognized Instituto Cervantes of Spain. This cultural institution has also developed a virtual library in SL containing books in Spanish, Spaniard, and memorabilia, and a virtual expo hall. The website is: http://secondlife.cervantes.es/ (in Spanish). Other efforts to support L2 have emerged, such as English Town, a web portal containing free SL resources for language teachers and learners (http://slenglish.ning.com/), including the development of a SL sim for learning English as a second language (ESL). Other efforts include Carter and Elseth (2008), who described a usability study of SL for teaching ESL. Results demonstrated high student motivation when using SL.

In addition to SL, recently there has been a big push for the application of virtual reality and videogame-based technologies in general for learning and training, fueled in part by the technological savvy of today's generation of learners (the "millennials"). Traditional teaching-and-learning environments are often quoted by the millennial generation as "boring" and they do not address the unique learning needs of this generation (Hanna, 2003). Millennials see technology as a necessity,

both in life and in learning (Mangold, 2007). They do not appreciate or learn as much from passive learning which most often occurs in lecture style teaching, but instead prefer to be actively involved (Sinclair & Ferguson, 2009). This high level of interactivity is not easily captured in traditional teaching/learning environments. However the more recent use of simulations through virtual reality and videogame-based technologies have been noted as one of the most effective means of promoting interactivity and active involvement in learning (Cowen & Tesh, 2002).

In contrast to traditional teaching environments where the teacher controls the learning (e.g., *teacher-centered*), gaming and interactive simulation environments support *learner-centered* education whereby learners are able to actively work through problems while acquiring knowledge through interactive practice learning thereby allowing the player to learn via an active, critical learning approach (Stapleton, 2004). By designing the scenario appropriately, a problem-based learning approach can be realized (Savery & Duffy, 1995). These experience-based methods incorporate more complex and diverse approaches to learning processes and outcomes; allow for interactivity; allow for cognitive as well as affective learning; and perhaps most importantly, foster active learning (Ruben, 1999; Squire, 2008). Video games and virtual environments provide students the opportunity to learn to appreciate the interrelationship of complex behaviors, sign systems, and the formation of social groups (Lieberman, 1997). They inherently support experiential learning by providing students with concrete experiences and active experimentation (Kolb, 1984). By designing the scenario appropriately, a problem-based learning approach can be realized (Savery & Duffy, 1995). As an aside, *serious games* is a term that has been used to describe video games that have been designed specifically for training and education (Annetta, 2010).

The Federation of American Scientists and the American Association for the Advancement of

Science (AAAS) Invention and Impact Conference provided convincing evidence for exploring the use of advanced educational technologies and serious games for education. In particular, advances in artificial intelligence algorithms as well as new programming and graphics strategies for game and simulation development provide many opportunities to develop educational materials that can lead to improved learning and skills development. In fact, there is a growing interest in the use of video game-based technology for education and training (Durkin, 2010). Yet, we are still faced by the oddity that there is still insufficient research in the area of VR and/or serious games and their application to CALL to firmly establish its potential and limitations. Garcia-Ruiz, Tashiro, Kapralos and Vargas Martin (2010) noted some of the critical gaps in our knowledge about what "really works" in simulations and serious games: (1) how does a simulation or serious game enhance disposition to engage in learning; (2) what are the relationships between the level of realism in a simulation or game and learning outcomes; (3) how does one define the threshold of experience within a game or simulation that leads to measurable learning outcomes; (4) what are the cognitive processes developed during learning while working within a game or simulation; (5) in what knowledge domains is learning being retained and how stable is the retention; (6) what is the disposition to act on the knowledge gained during work within a simulation; (7) how well can the knowledge gained within a game or simulation be transferred; and (8) what are the differences in learning that manifest as conceptual competencies and performance competencies. Garcia-Ruiz et al. (2010) concluded that we need sophisticated research vehicles that are themselves virtual environments (VEs) and that allow collection and analysis of data to bridge these gaps in our knowledge. Certainly, it is a daunting task to build and validate a virtual environment that combines teaching-learning-assessment with research engines.

However, the authors have completed work on an online virtual environment called Realtown, which was designed to allow students to practice listening comprehension. Reviewing the knowledge gaps listed above, it should be clear that the usability of a virtual environment will impact how students engage within an immersive environment and how they sustain engagement to a threshold of learning something. In this chapter, we explore research on Realtown and examine this type of system as a teaching-learning-assessment environment that can be used as a research platform. We will focus on studies of the usability of Realtown. We note that Realtown was evaluated according to general usability parameters of user satisfaction, ease of use, efficacy and efficiency of the Realtown virtual environment (Le Peuple & Scane, 2003; Tromp, Steed, & Wilson, 2003) within the field of Human-Computer Interaction (HCI), which concerns the way to make pleasant, efficient, easy-to-use and safe computer interfaces (Preece et al., 1994).

The International Organization for Standardization (ISO) norm 9241 part 11 defines usability as "the extent to which a product can be used by specified users to achieve specified goals with effectiveness, efficiency, and satisfaction in a specified context of use" (ISO 9241, 1998). Nielsen and Landauer (1993) pointed out that usability has five quality-of-use components: Learnability (how users learn to use the computer interface), efficiency (how users perform tasks at the interface), memorability (after returning to use the interface, what users remember about its usage), errors (user errors performed at the interface, and how to recover from them) and satisfaction (the subjective experience of comfort and motivation about using an interface). There are trends in the literature that claim that if an educational computer program has a high degree of usability, it will support learning more effectively and will positively impact student extrinsic motivation about its use (Zaharias, 2004, 2006; MacFarlane, Sim,

& Horton, 2005). This is also consistent with the results obtained by Virvou and Katsionis (2008).

Essentially, our research focused on whether an educational virtual reality environment could be developed to practice listening comprehension skills that meets student needs, meets usability criteria, and is motivating to use. We were especially interested in the impact the usability of virtual reality technology has on listening comprehension as an important component of language learning. Consequently, we wrote this chapter to unfold in six sections. First, we provide background research and information in computer assisted language learning (CALL). Next, we extend the concept of CALL into models for building effective VR, and second language methodology. Thirdly, we present a technical and qualitative description of Realtown, a collaborative virtual environment designed to promote listening comprehension, created with the Distributed Interactive Virtual Environment (DIVE) platform. Fourth, we turn to detailed analysis of the importance of usability studies in the development of environments such as Realtown, with a discussion of employing the methods of the Think Aloud Protocol and post-questionnaires, conducted as a preamble to subsequent studies employing collaborative listening comprehension. Fifthly, we examine important areas of misconception development and student errors, motivation, and ease of use, among other features, during their work within Realtown, including a discussion regarding the usability guidelines emanated from our usability studies on collaborative virtual worlds for second language learning.

Finally, we look to the future, the use of evidence-based models of instructional design, and the need for longitudinal studies of learning issues, particularly with respect to first-person and collaborative experiences in virtual environments. A particular focus of this section of our proposed chapter is a discussion of models for combining VR with more traditional instruction as a transition that does not dramatically increase faculty workload while they learn how to engage in new methods and materials for instruction. Discussions of future work also will include: (1) studies comparing different graphical representations of aerial views of a city for promoting listening comprehension, as well as related learning issues and first-person actions and experiences in collaborative virtual environments; (2) how traditional listening comprehension can be promoted using virtual environments; (3) the need to create new systems that solve problems related to how much of the actual listening "comprehension" is attributable to the user's situated experience in an immersive world, particularly in the contest of the value of collaborations with peers and instructors.

BACKGROUND RESEARCH IN COMPUTER ASSISTED LANGUAGE LEARNING (CALL)

Computer Assisted Language Learning

A simple and direct definition of CALL is "the search for and study of applications of the computer in language teaching and learning" (Levy, 1997). During the last four decades, CALL materials have evolved from very basic text processing, gap-filling tasks, and simple programming to interactive multimedia presentations that include sound, animation, and full-motion video (Beatty, 2003). CALL, therefore, to a great degree, reflects technological development, and it evolves to incorporate new technologies and teaching methods. However, it is certain that computer-assisted language learning will continue to develop in the areas of speech production and recognition, as well as intelligent systems and virtual reality (Chapelle, 2001).

Since the 1970s, with the advent of electronic bulletin board systems (BBS) accessed by modem, and more recently the Internet, people have been able to carry out informal synchronous and asynchronous communications, by sending text messages among peers using network services, such as Telnet, and access remote databases mounted on a server, all this with a specific purpose, for example, to play in a multi-user role-playing game. This was dubbed multi-user domain or MUD (Haynes & Holmevik, 1998). It was also referred to as multi-user dungeon and multiple undergraduate destroyer, due to their application in role-playing computer games such as Dungeons and Dragons. Moreover, a MOO (MUD object-oriented) is a multiple-user and text-based online system where users and the system describe three-dimensional objects, scenarios (also called "rooms") and actions, based on the object-oriented programming paradigm (Curtis & Nichols, 1994). MOOs are direct descendants of MUDs. Due to general participants' high levels of engagement and interaction seen in early MOO applications, among other characteristics, educators have considered their use as tools for CALL. Turbee (1996) reported the application of three specialized MOOs for second language learning: schMOOze University, MundoHispano, and MOOfrançais, for learners of English, Spanish, and French, respectively.

The most significant development in the last decade of the 20th century was the proliferation of the Internet, which has provided students an almost limitless source of information and learning activities. Tools such a chat, e-mail, discussion forums, instant messaging, etc. are today commonly exploited by educators. These tools, although not created to teach languages *per se*, have proven to be very effective in assisting students learn languages because of the communicative and collaborative value of the interactions they provide (Soloway et al., 2000; Hudson & Bruckman, 2001).

However, more recently, increased computational processing power and speed, as well as algorithms to compact and stream data, audio, and visual elements, now permits virtual reality to be increasingly used in educational applications. Furthermore, new, more versatile and powerful

programming tools allows developers to create new CALL software, affording language learners the opportunity to use VR, artificial intelligence, expert systems, voice recognition, and interactive multimedia applications in DVD format to provide students a greater variety of activities and presentation of content (Levy, 1997).

Virtual Reality and CALL

Currently, virtual reality (according to Sherman and Craig (2003), the highly interactive and multi-sensorial computer-generated 3D environments) involves relatively new technologies that may have significant applications in the area of CALL. Although different aspects of online language learning have been studied, its possible application in conjunction with VR represents a relatively new area of investigation. Virtual reality may prove to have a significant role in language instruction in the future.

According to Youngblut (1998), "presently, many researchers and educational practitioners believe that VR offers strong benefits that can support education. For some, VR's ability to facilitate constructivist learning activities is the key issue. Others focus on the potential to provide alternative forms of learning that can support different types of learners, such as visually oriented learners. Still others see the ability for learners, and educators, to collaborate in a virtual class that transcends geographical boundaries as the major benefit." There is also evidence indicating that VR can contribute to raising both interest and motivation in students and effectively supporting knowledge transfer. This is true, according to Dede et al. (1996), because learning can be settled within an experiential framework. However, more research is needed to explore the practical potential of this tool, and there is little published work on the application of VR in CALL literature.

Today, VR technology comprises a computer-generated graphical 3D space (also commonly referred to as a "virtual environment", or "virtual world" despite some subtle differences), where users can interact with it using specialized input/output devices (Sherman & Craig, 2003). The virtual environment senses the position and orientation of the participants, which are represented by an avatar similar to the one shown in Figure 1.

The use of input devices for interacting with the virtual environment produces a physiological effect called "immersion", generated with the participants' senses. The psychological effect of being immersed in a virtual environment (the perception of actually "being there," within the virtual environment) is called "presence" (Burdea & Coiffet, 2003; Kalawsky, 2000). Another characteristic of virtual environments is that they can convey tactile (haptic), auditory, or visual information to their respective human sensory channels simultaneously, that is, they have the ability to be multi-modal. According to Dede et al. (1996), both immersion and multimodality in VR are important because students receive different sensory stimuli within a virtual environment, which promotes learning according to both stimuli and constructionist theories.

VR can be classified as semi-immersive or fully-immersive. The former consists of a desktop computer where the virtual environment is shown on the monitor, generally seen in stereo, and the participant can navigate using a special device or the conventional mouse (also known as "fish-tank" VR). Generally, the desktop computer can sense the position and orientation of the participant, which is reflected in the virtual environment. In a fully-immersive virtual environment, the participant can interact with the virtual environment with almost all his/her senses using special input-output devices, such as data gloves, a head-mounted display (HMD), headphones, etc. The degree of immersion and presence varies in both types of systems, although the desktop virtual reality system is enough to produce an acceptable immersion for many applications including education (Robertson, Czeminski, & van Dantzich, 1997).

Figure 1. A virtual personification (avatar) of a participant

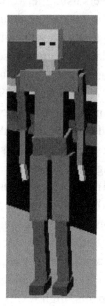

Virtual reality has been applied in education mainly for training technical skills and teaching abstract or complex concepts, where students use their sensory channels to interact with the virtual learning environment, with the object to support the learning process and to foster competences and abilities (Antonietti, Imperio, Rasi, & Sacco, 2001; Dalgarno & Lee, 2010; Dede et al., 1997; Youngblut, 1998; Su & Loftin, 2001; Zajtchuk & Satava, 1997).

In addition, VR technology recreates situations or concepts that can be difficult to present in a real environment (Dalgarno & Lee, 2010; Dede et al., 1997; Sherman & Craig, 2003). For example, in chemistry, students can explore a virtual atomic structure with virtual protons and electrons moving around its core (Byrne, 1996). As Winn (1993) explained, scientific information can be presented in a different scale, facilitating comprehension of micro and macroscopic concepts. In relation to this, literature has identified four main assumed benefits of virtual reality in education:

- Reification. A virtual environment can make concepts more explicit and concrete (Winn, 1993).
- Transduction. A virtual environment can contain information that is not present in one sensory channel (Winn, 1993).
- Scale manipulation. As (Winn, 1993) discusses, scientific information can be presented in a different scale, facilitating comprehension of micro and macroscopic concepts.
- Intrinsic and extrinsic views. Users can observe the virtual environment from many perspectives and angles, thus providing them with additional details to better inspect specific problems presented within different contexts (Dede et al., 1997).

Language Teaching Methodology

The Communicative Approach (CA) outlines most of the principles that guide second language instruction and materials development. Introducing VR into second language instruction, according to Larsen-Freeman (2000) is consistent with several premises of the CA, including:

- Language acquisition is promoted by "authentic language" introduced within a real-world context, and students should be given opportunities to develop strategies for interpreting language as it is actually used by native speakers.
- Communicative interaction (communication with purpose) encourages collaboration among students. It also provides students with the opportunity to work on communicative strategies, including negotiating meaning and pragmatics. Language use is based on linguistic functions and each linguistic function can have many different forms.
- Some virtual environments incorporate gaming-type elements and games share

certain features with real communicative events, and in particular, they provide a reason for exchange. They also provide immediate feedback from the listener on whether or not he/she has successfully comprehended.

Although a virtual environment (VE) cannot approximate the real world insofar as language learning is concerned, VR environments can provide users listening experiences that employ "authentic language," such as the following transcript of actual instructions: "Certainly, go straight down Bush Street until you reach the corner of Bush and Clinton." Figure 2 shows a student steering an avatar in Realtown, following the instructions.

In addition, according to constructivist psychology, the focus of learning should be on how individuals interact with, and learn from the world that surrounds them. Constructionists view learning as a product of an individual's interaction with the environment dynamically. Consequently, learning is a process of constructing knowledge and instructional practices should provide the learner what they need in order to accomplish this. Therefore, it follows that the richer the context in which learning takes place, the more effective it can be (Laurillard, 2002). Thus, an educational virtual environment should provide a rich, multi-sensorial and first-person experience for a student, where he/she can interact with the virtual environment, to explore it at his/her own pace (Winn, 1993). This is also in agreement with a situated learning approach whereby the learning environment is modeled on the context whereby the knowledge is expected to be applied (Brown, Collins, & Duguid, 1989; Dalgarno & Lee, 2010).

Since Realtown is intended to provide a low-anxiety space for practicing listening comprehension skills, the fact that its interactions are not based on "real-life" is an advantage as its users are not exposed to social or performance variables that can lead to anxiety (Harris, Kem-

Figure 2. A student steering an avatar (a virtual persona of the student), following the preceding instructions

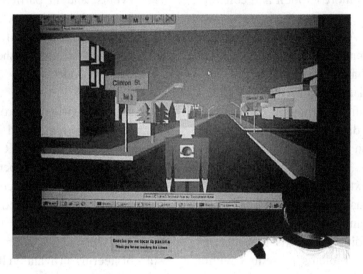

merling, & North, 2002). With respect to second language learning, "it has been shown that anxiety negatively affects performance in the second language. In some cases, anxiety provides some of the highest simple correlations of attitudes with achievement" (Ellis, 1994).

Moreover, regarding learning anxiety, Larsen-Freeman (2000) described many governing principles of James Asher's Total Physical Response, including:

- Meaning in the target language is often conveyed through actions and carrying out physical activities help activate memory.
- The imperative is an important linguistic device to direct behavior.
- Students can learn through observing actions as well as by performing them.
- Feelings of success and low anxiety facilitate learning.
- Students should not be made to memorize fixed routines.
- Students must develop flexibility in understanding a new language that is presented in chunks, rather than individual words or exact sentences.

Since the Realtown virtual environment offers close to 30 locations (an aerial view of Realtown is shown in Figure 3), in addition to an equal or greater number of objects, and since given that the students listen to instructions that are provided randomly, students can participate in the activity for a substantial period without listening to a repeated set of instructions given that students listen to instructions that are provided randomly, students can participate in the activity for a substantial period without listening to a repeated set of instructions. This is important as it provides many novel language and situational combinations, since given that students listen to instructions that are provided randomly, students can participate in the activity for a substantial period without listening to a repeated set of instructions. Finally, because language, theoretically, should be presented naturally and in "chunks" in a low-anxiety environment, students should be exposed to language that is richly contextualized within more extensive discourse that is just slightly above their actual comprehension, providing what Krashen (2004) calls comprehensible input ($i + 1$). According to Krashen (2004) "a strong affective filter (e.g., high anxiety) will prevent comprehensible input

Figure 3. An aerial view of Realtown. The street and building names were placed as guidance for this chapter only

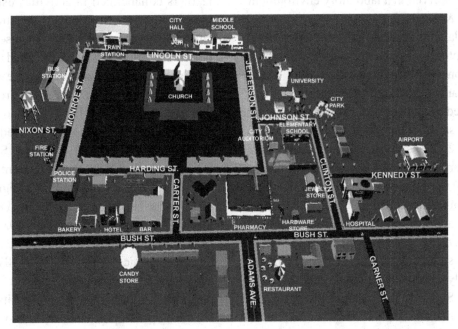

from reaching those parts of the brain that do language acquisition."

CALL into Models for Building Effective VR, and Second Language Methodology

The study we present in this chapter was conducted following the usability method called Think Aloud Protocol (Preece et al., 1994; Preece, Rogers, & Sharp, 2002), which is a special speech protocol. In it, the user that tests the computer interface (Realtown) is asked to speak aloud what he/she thinks and feels about the interface while carrying out a task. The experimenter has to encourage the user to keep him/her talking. Qualitative data is generally collected using direct observations, note taking, a post-questionnaire on usability, and video recordings.

The Think Aloud protocol has been regarded by human-computer interaction researchers as one of the most practical and effective methods for obtaining qualitative data about the usability

of a computer interface, which also has been successfully used for testing the usability of virtual environments (Smith & Hart, 2006). Advantages of the Think Aloud method include:

- It is possible to obtain good quality qualitative data.
- The experimenter is able to obtain a better understanding of the user's mental model of the interface.
- Experimenters can obtain the user's terminology to later incorporate it into the interface.
- The Think Aloud Protocol is very effective to obtain immediate feedback on the user interaction
- It is effective in analyzing user needs and expectations regarding the interface.

Nevertheless, a disadvantage of this method is that it may generate qualitative data that can be difficult to analyze and take long time to interpret. Another disadvantage is that user attitudes, interactions, and opinions may change if they are tested and observed in a laboratory environment (Le Peuple & Scane, 2003).

To validate the results of the study described in this chapter, we conducted a methodological triangulation with qualitative data from video recordings and note taking. Quantitative data was also obtained by applying a questionnaire for user interaction satisfaction, or QUIS (Shneiderman & Plaisant, 2005) as a post-test. In addition, user errors performed within the virtual environment and the time were registered. Further refinements of our virtual environment will be based on their findings. In addition, future usability studies with more participants are being planned to obtain statistically significant data, as Realtown is being continuously improved by employing usability results and Software Engineering life cycle development methods.

Previous Work

Rose and Billinghurst (1996) developed Zengo Sayu, one of the first applications of virtual reality to second language learning. Zengo Sayu is a virtual environment created for teaching spoken Japanese language (basic nouns, sentence structure, colors and prepositions of place) to children. Although the comparison of this teaching method with conventional methods of Japanese teaching was not statistically significant, the students were able to learn with Zengo Sayu. In addition, the authors report that students were in control of learning at their own pace, and explored the environment by themselves as active participants. This exploratory application paved the way for future VR applications applied to foreign language learning.

Milton and Garbi (2000) developed and tested Internet-based virtual environments with virtual representations of a zoo, towns, and a shopping center, for foreign language teaching of primary school students. In the virtual environments, learners collaborated in activities using avatars (graphical personifications of the students) and chat rooms to communicate. The researchers reported that students who participated in activities within the virtual environments were doing it in a "relatively naturalistic way," as in ordering food in a virtual restaurant. It was also noted that the student communication was unforced.

The Rapid Tactical Training System for Learning Arabic is another important attempt to incorporate VR into second or foreign language instruction. This project, funded by Defense Advanced Research Projects Agency (DARPA), is in response to the need of the United States military to provide basic communicative skills in foreign languages and cultures to its onsite land-based personnel. It is designed to assist military personnel develop a rapport with locals in order to help them accomplish a variety of missions, including post-war reconstruction. The system consists of a simulated village that provides intelligent agent coaches that accompanies each learner through a variety of situations and corresponding speech acts. This virtual aid provides feedback on learner performance within a multimodal interface that provides a contextually rich setting to help motivate and engage learners. In a preliminary technical report published in 2004, the authors report that although the system had only been used briefly, they report having made significant progress in combining pedagogical agents, pedagogical drama, speech recognition, and game technologies in support of language learning. A formative usability evaluation of eight new learners, each participating individually in a single two hour session, indicates that the learners found the VR environment to be fun and interesting. Participants were also confident with the practice and felt that they would be able to master the "game" (Johnson et al., 2004).

Figure 4. A view of a typical public building

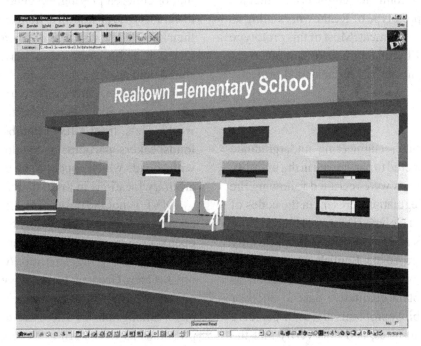

THE REALTOWN RESEARCH PROJECT

Based on the theories and research reviewed in this chapter, a virtual environment is being developed according to Software Engineering techniques, following the prototyping software development method (McConnell, 1996), which is designed to minimize errors and promote good software design of the virtual environment. In addition, usability methods are being applied to enhance the ease of use and "look and feel" of the virtual environment interface, such as the Think Aloud Protocol, which is carried out with end users, in this case students, and the Heuristic Evaluation, done by usability and Software Engineering experts (Le peuple & Scane, 2003; Nielsen & Mack, 1994; Preece et al., 1994).

The virtual environment was developed using the Distributed Interactive Virtual Environments (DIVE) program (Carlsson & Hagsand, 1993; Frecon & Stenius, 1998). DIVE is a virtual environment browser that can run on various versions of the Unix, Linux, Windows, and Solaris operating systems. A DIVE virtual environment can be distributed (can run on an intranet or the Internet) using a peer-to-peer multicast architecture, but a DIVE proxy and a server must be installed prior to its use. Participants in a distributed environment are represented as avatars, and they can communicate with each other by speaking over a microphone through Voice over Internet Protocol (VoIP), using an instant-messenger window, or by gesturing using the avatar.

Realtown content is modeled after a typical United States town and includes a variety of public and private buildings including a city hall, police and fire stations, schools, etc., as well as a supermarket, bank, pharmacy, hardware store, etc. Figure 4 shows a typical public building of the Realtown virtual environment.

Usability Study Description

As a preamble for further virtual reality in CALL studies, a Think Aloud Protocol usability study was conducted with computer engineering students using the first prototype of Realtown, running as a standalone environment. Most of this prototype was developed by undergraduate computer engineering students as part of their final projects.

Participants

Nineteen computer engineering undergraduate students volunteered to participate in the usability study. The students were recruited following the current ethics regulations present in the codes of the University of Colima. Their ages ranged from 20 and 22 years and all of them had successfully completed intermediate English courses. With respect to prototype testing, 19 participants is sufficient to obtain qualitative data to uncover most of the usability problems that users perceive in computer interfaces, and thus verify that the objective of the virtual environment is being accomplished, and make further corrections and adaptations to the prototype if needed (Nielsen & Landauer, 1993). In addition, the participants are representative of the end users of Realtown. A demographics questionnaire was administered prior to the test. In it, most of the participants reported having played video games recently for at least one hour per week. This question was asked since it has been suggested that video game exposure can affect how virtual environments for learning are used (Fassbender et al., 2006; Losh, 2006). None of students reported visual or hearing problems.

Materials

The Realtown virtual environment, developed using the Distributed Interactive Virtual Environments (DIVE) platform, was used for the study. Background sounds were incorporated into the virtual town, and were played through hi-fi loudspeakers to help increase realism. Some of these sounds included background traffic noise as well as competing foreground noises such as dogs bark-

ing, or children playing. Students received three different types of stimuli to help them incorporate their knowledge: visual, auditory, and kinesthetic. DIVE has the capacity to play monophonic, stereo, and spatial (3D) sounds both locally and in a distributed virtual environment, contributing to a more accurate representation of the real world. Thus, from a fixed number of stationary loudspeakers participants could be presented with sounds which appear to be emanating from arbitrary locations in three-dimensional space.

DIVE is not the only application that can run collaborative virtual environments. There are other open source programs and programming libraries, for example VR Juggler (http://www.vrjuggler. org/), Open Croquet (http://www.opencroquet. org), and Open Simulator (http://opensimulator. org/), among others. There are commercial applications as well, such as Second Life, but we wanted to use an open source virtual environment application for our studies to avoid paying fees for their use, because one of our intentions is to further apply our research in developing countries where educational institutions possibly cannot afford paying for virtual environments software. Although Konstantinidis, Tsiatsos and Pompostsis (2009) describe a guidance approach about selecting a collaborative virtual environment for learning, our decision to choose a particular virtual environment platform was based on two main reasons: Its technical features and the usability of its interface. DIVE was chosen for this project because, compared to other collaborative virtual environment platforms, it is relatively easy to install and program, it does not require a large memory, a powerful graphics card, and a fast microprocessor to run, it is free for non-commercial applications, it runs on multiple operating systems, and allows the integration of VRML code, it can run as a stand-alone collaborative virtual environment without the need of Internet connection, and the programs written for DIVE are highly portable among DIVE's versions of operating systems. Other important technical features of

Figure 5. A student using the keyboard to navigate the avatar in Realtown

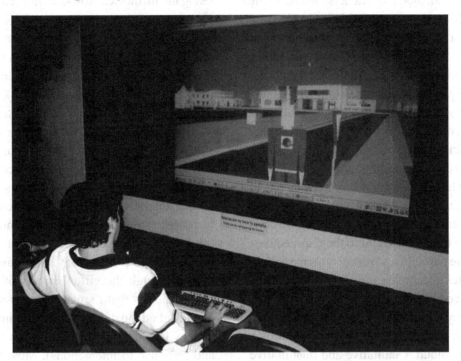

DIVE include real-time 3D sound rendering, and stereoscopic visualization of virtual environments with active shutter glasses in some computer platforms. Steed and Frecon (2005) describe in more detail technical features about the design and features of DIVE. In addition, we have seen in previous usability studies that participants who used DIVE felt confident using DIVE's navigation tools, and participants' navigation skills in DIVE improved quickly (Garcia-Ruiz, Edwards, Aquino-Santos, & El-Seoud, 2008). However, DIVE documentation is limited.

The virtual environment projected using a 2000-Lumen data projector on a large screen (over a surface within the screen of about 2 × 2 meters). The virtual environment was installed on a personal computer with 2 Gb of main memory, and a graphics card with 256 Mb of graphics memory and 200 Mhz of Graphics Processing Unit (GPU) speed. It is important to note that most of the computers and laptops currently available in the market meet the minimal hardware require-

ments to run Realtown. All of the participants were video recorded while performing the test, and a usability questionnaire with some of the questions related to evaluating multimedia were taken from the Questionnaire for User Interface Satisfaction (QUIS) (Shneiderman & Plaisant, 2005), was also used. A student using Realtown is shown in Figure 5.

Procedure

The usability study was based on the Think Aloud Protocol (Preece et al., 1994). Each student participated in the usability study separately, and was asked to sit in front of the projected virtual environment, at a distance of approximately three meters from the screen. Students were placed at a point within the virtual town in the created virtual environment. The task was to move (navigate) the avatar from point A to B. Specifically, the student had to reach the elementary school in Realtown, according to the following oral instructions in

English that included distracters and real-life sounds: "Go straight down Bush Street until you reach the corner of Bush and Clinton. You'll pass a pharmacy and a hardware store. Then, take a left on Clinton Street in front of the hospital. After that go straight on Clinton Street until you see the elementary school on the *left, right* in front of the park." The consecutive use of the words "left" and "right" exemplifies how using authentic language provides very interesting, but sometimes confusing word use. The instructions were played by one of the experimenters on a different computer from the study. Students used the arrow keys of a wireless keyboard to direct the avatar to the required destination. The participants were given a maximum of 15 minutes to complete the navigation task and were allowed to listen to the instructions as many times as they requested. Students were asked to express their actions and feelings about Realtown by speaking aloud. Qualitative and quantitative data was collected using direct observations, a post-questionnaire on usability (QUIS), and video recordings. We consider that the pedagogical scenario of Realtown is based on the constructivist learning philosophy (Winn, 1993; Youngblut, 1998), and it supports students' cognitive goals of understanding and knowledge-building according to past and recent real-life experiences, improving a sense of accomplishment, providing motivation, and focusing on listening comprehension skills (Federation of American Scientists, 2005).

Results

Prior to the usability study with the 19 student participants, we wanted to gauge which input device was most effective for navigating in the Realtown virtual environment. Five engineering students (which did not participate in the usability study) informally tested various input devices, such as a gaming joystick, a conventional mouse, a wireless mouse, a conventional keyboard and a wireless keyboard. We found that the latter was comfortable enough for the students to easily

navigate in the Realtown virtual environment. However, students had many difficulties with the wireless mouse, especially for navigating the avatar and holding the mouse in the air (this mouse has a rolling ball to move the computer pointer, and the user has to grasp it), since their arms became tired after a few minutes.

Qualitative results of the Think Aloud Protocol study show that participant reactions were very favorable. Video analysis of the recorded study and data from post questionnaires showed that participants never mentioned or showed frustration or boredom with the system, and most of them felt immersed in Realtown. None of the participants reported feeling dizzy when navigating the avatar through the virtual streets of Realtown. This indicates that the virtual environment was displayed adequately and with minimal (if any) latency (the delay in the 3D graphics rendering and response to interactions). Most of the participants declared that the sound effects helped them navigate and find their way in the virtual environment, which is cause for concern as many of the effects were added as distracters. Seventy percent of participants could correctly follow the pre-recorded instructions after hearing them just once or twice.

Figure 6 depicts the average of some of the opinion scale results of the QUIS questionnaire administered to the participants (1=strongly disagree, 9=strongly agree). All were general student reactions regarding the virtual environment. It can be seen that all their responses were positive. Moreover, all the students felt immersed in the virtual environment. This is important, since immersion promotes learning according to constructionist and stimuli theories.

The usability questionnaire also included opinion scales on the main elements of the virtual environment. Figure 7 shows the average of each of the scales used by the participants (1=strongly disagree, 9=strongly agree).

After analyzing the video recordings and the student comments made during and after the tests,

Figure 6. Some opinion scale results on student reactions about Realtown

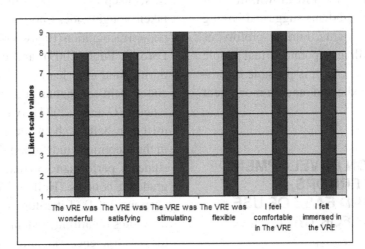

Figure 7. Main elements evaluated in the virtual environment

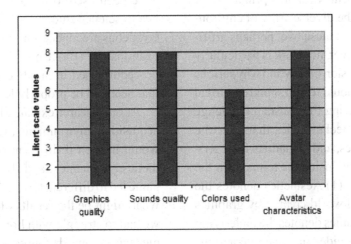

a number of usability problems were encountered. The main problems are described as follows:

- Although the buildings and the streets were convincing representations, students reported that the colors and appearance of the virtual buildings of Realtown were not realistic enough. In further prototype versions, we will enhance building façades by adding textures to them (real images of buildings).

- A couple of times, students steered the avatar through buildings and trees as if they were not solid; however, this was not a problem that impeded them from completing the task. We noticed that all the participants predominantly kept on the virtual streets, and no one used this navigation problem for taking "short cuts". To avoid this in the future, it is possible to program collision detection feature in Realtown.

- Most of the students were expecting to see virtual people walking on the streets, as well as moving cars in Realtown. In addition, one of the students suggested having working traffic lights. Further prototypes of Realtown will incorporate virtual people and working cars, as it is possible to program both periodic and random movement in them.

MISCONCEPTION DEVELOPMENT AND STUDENT ERRORS, MOTIVATION, AND EASE OF USE REGARDING VR FOR CALL

Becker (2010) describes some of the distinctions between environments designed primarily as games and environments designed primarily for learning, as well as the diverse array of environments that fall between these two, perhaps artificial, polarities. However, her work is particularly important in its discussion of how and why serious game development should rest on sound empirical foundations while facing the constant challenge of rapidly changing technologies that alter the Aesthetics, Mechanics, and Dynamics for a serious game. Here, we are using the terms from the literature on gaming: (1) Aesthetics denotes the sense of the fictional world created by graphics and sound; (2) Mechanics denotes the underlying programming that provides fictional interactions within the virtual setting; and (3) Dynamics is a term used to capture the potential interactions possible in a game and the emergence of end user's engagement within such interactions.

Our work in the area of serious games for health care education led us to explore a number of issues in the literature that raise concerns about possibilities of health sciences students developing misconceptions while working within certain types of instructional modalities. Some of these misconceptions could have deadly consequences as these students progress into positions of health care providers and become engaged in patient care.

Misconceptions can be defined as students' mistaken thoughts, ideas, notions, an underdeveloped pattern recognition (Balkissoon, Blossfield, Salud, Ford, & Pugh, 2009), and can develop before, during, and after learning, leading to erroneous concepts in conceptual and performance competencies (Ozmen, 2004). A number of students' mistaken beliefs about the sciences are present in the incoming student population, which affect students' performance in undergraduate and even graduate courses (Halloun & Hestenes, 1985; Ozmen, 2004). Literature describes a number of studies regarding students' misconceptions in the health sciences, including students' erroneous concepts, such as in respiratory physiology (Michael et al., 1999). Emerging computer simulations have been used to uncover and address serious health science students' misconceptions, such as erroneous preconceptions in clinical digital rectal examination (Balkisoon et al., 2009), a critical procedure used in the detection of colon cancer that needs to be properly learned and practiced.

As our research expanded to examine language acquisition environments, we began to ask what would happen if different combinations of aesthetics, mechanics, and dynamics for a serious game led to different types of reasoning, and if so, what might be the results of such reasoning. So, we had to struggle with how and why aesthetics, mechanics, and dynamics could shape learning and development of cognitive processes leading to patterns of students' reasoning. In particular, we began to focus on what types of misconceptions might evolve within different types of learning environments developed as serious games or educational simulations.

During the past year, we synthesized a better understanding of what we do not know about "what really works" in educational simulations and serious games (Garcia-Ruiz et al., 2010). Our review of a broad literature revealed there are important gaps in our knowledge about effective use of educational simulations and serious games:

1. How does a simulation or serious game enhance disposition to engage in a learning process?
2. What are the relationships between the level of realism in a simulation or game and learning outcomes?
3. How do you define the threshold of experience within a game or simulation that leads to measurable learning outcomes?
4. What are the cognitive processes being developed during learning while working within a game or simulation?
5. In what knowledge domains is learning being retained and how stable is the retention?
6. What is the disposition to act on the knowledge gained during work within a simulation?
7. How well can the knowledge gained within a game or simulation be transferred?
8. What are the differences in learning that manifest as conceptual competencies and performance competencies?

The results of this literature review led us to conclude that, in general, serious games/virtual simulation developers have an underdeveloped understanding of how misconceptions might be inculcated in student users. Certainly a major problem is that many studies of simulations and serious games reporting improved learning and skills development had methodological flaws. We also found research designs in which the sample sizes were often small and limited attention was focused on the multitude of variables shaping learning, and how so many of these variables are confounded. As we continued to explore simulation and serious game environments, we could not escape the gnawing uncertainties about what is being learned in such environments, how learning progresses, and what opportunities there are for following tangents to the educational objectives that lead to inculcation of misconceptions, some of which could be quite dangerous in health-related

disciplines. Of course, we don't have any illusions about more traditional methods and materials of education being free of potential for developing misconceptions. Even so, the tremendous emphasis on simulation and serious game usage in education ought to be tempered by the same kinds of standards for evidence-based practice used in health care, which led us to promote the idea of evidence-based learning.

Indeed, we are still faced with the uncomfortable question of "what really works" to improve higher order thinking without instilling misconceptions. For example, even given the propensity of millennial students (perhaps because of the propensity) to engage in new models of instructional environments, how do we know if misconceptions are developed. What are the potentials for embedded interactions to lead students on tangents in their development of cognitive schema? Such cognitive schema may have flaws in pattern recognition and so lead to misconceptions. Misconceptions can lead to incomplete understanding of complexity in many discipline areas. Health care training environments that result in misconceptions could lead to the possibility of adverse medical effects and possible death of patients when health sciences students become health care practitioners. Language training in which students develop misconceptions may also cause a number of problems, especially in language and cultural sensitivity training for military personnel who have to quickly distinguish between friend and foe during military interventions in a combat zone populated by people speaking a different language than the military personnel (Barret & Johnson, 2010).

An important issue is that each serious game or simulation has its own idiosyncrasies in the construction of how and why the developers mimicked elements of the real world and the interactions that occur in the real world. At the very least, then, we need to contextualize "what really works" within the situated learning experience of each different type of serious game.

Barret and Johnson (2010) provide insights on the instructional design process used to create certain types of language acquisition environments. They point out that design of serious games for language training requires careful attention to, and a broad as well as deep understanding of learning, cognitive processes during learning, motivation, emotions, and play within the situated experience of a language acquisition environment. Their approach combines different theoretical frameworks, including situated cognition and language learning, constructivism, task-based language learning, cognitive flexibility theory, and sociocultural theory. They argue that there are important factors in teaching-learning-assessment environments for language acquisition that tend to center around learner control in technology-mediated environments, the types and quality of feedback provided to learners, and factors shaping motivation to stay engaged in a learning process nested within a serious game environment.

These arguments are not new, but Barret and Johnson add an analysis of key facets in the design of the educational elements. Specifically, they examine task-based frameworks that are then expanded into dialogue models, speech recognition, the use of believable virtual humans as non-playing characters (NPCs) within a serious game language training environment, learner models for correct and incorrect usage of relevant linguistic patterns situated within a cultural and task-based experience, and the integrating threads of effective narrative developed and continuously revised by use of new types of content authoring systems. This approach deepened our understanding of the critical role of usability studies for Realtown and how Realtown could evolve to study misconception development in language learning and listening comprehension, and, as Realtown's capacities are more fully developed,

to study misconception development in speaking, reading, writing, listening and as well as listening comprehension.

First, we recognized that dialogue models could be based on a variety of taxonomies that would allow keying of the most common language usage pattern mistakes. Secondly, we began studies of artificial intelligence systems that had more sophisticated speech recognition capacities. Consequently, we could examine how to increase requirements for accurate pronunciation without discouraging engagement for beginners while guiding users to improved accuracy as their skills developed.

Thirdly, we had been studying the impact of realism on learning and expanded this work to look at the relative importance of realism in design of NPCs who were given instructional roles as they interacted with student players. Certainly, humans are very attuned to nonverbal cuing during communications, so at some level of proficiency such cueing would have to be enabled in NPCs. However, such additional information is the situated experience of a student learner would have to be driven empirically in order to avoid swamping the learner with too much detail and discouraging continued engagement in the teaching-learning-assessment environment. Not unrelated to the use of believable virtual humans as well as to dialogue models and AI systems, a fourth critical areas was the development of learner models that recognized the variation in acceptable language usage patterns while building an environment in which student players moved sensibly towards an understanding of correct and incorrect usage of relevant linguistic patterns situated within a cultural and task-based experience.

The fifth critical area of focus emerged in our work as we thought through how to design environments that combined teaching-learning-assessment capacities with research capacities to study the complexities of the learning processes in the context of authentic measures of what was learned, how long learning was retained, and the patterns of misconceptions that had developed both individually and in groups of student learners. Certainly, Barrett and Johnson (2010) touched on the issues around integrating threads of effective narrative developed and continuously revised by use of new types of content authoring systems. However, Garcia Ruiz and colleagues (Garcia-Ruiz, et al., 2010) expanded the conceptual framework of serious games to include four engines: (1) a virtual world generator (including authoring sub-engines as well as catalogues of renderings to create different levels of realism and interactivity); (2) a system for following and recording key variables in users' choices and interactions within the virtual world; (3) a sophisticated authentic learning outcomes assessment engine based on cognitive taxonomies; and (4) a data mining engine allowing collation of data from the other engines and analysis of the complex relationships among teaching-learning variables in each situated experience possible within the virtual world.

The work reported in this chapter on Realtown is part of our ongoing study of simulation and serious games environments. We have many uncertainties about what is being learned in such environments, how learning progresses, and what opportunities there are for students to engage in and follow tangents to the educational objectives, and that may lead to development of misconceptions. However, we emphatically note that more traditional methods and materials of education are certainly not free of the potential for students to develop misconceptions. Even so, our new models of teaching-learning-assessment-research environments provide an opportunity to shift education to a more evidence-based framework and to be more thoughtful about and critical of educational methods and materials as faculty members and students become increasingly interested in simulation and serious game usage in education.

FUTURE WORK AND CONCLUDING REMARKS

Realtown has been designed to present language and provide a language learning environment consistent with many of the most fundamental second language methodological principles of the communicative approach, which is presently the principal methodological second language teaching approach, as well as many basic principles of Curran's Community Language Learning, (Larsen-Freeman, 2000), and Krashen and Terrel's Natural Approach (Krashen & Terrel, 1983), although the most applicable in the case of Realtown, is Total Physical Response (Asher, 1977; Larsen-Freeman, 2000).

Although Realtown was initially tested as a stand-alone virtual environment, it can run as a distributed environment in its current state. Further participants can access Realtown from a local network or through the Internet. To function properly, a DIVE server, which is a small software application, needs to be installed on a computer dedicated to run this application.

It has been proposed that VR can function to teach languages as it permits the student to use visual, auditory and kinesthetic stimuli to place the learner closer to "real-life" contexts, and since language is best learned when used in low-anxiety "real-world" contexts, it would appear that VR may contribute significantly to second language instruction in the future.

Although fully-immersive virtual reality is very effective for providing realistic and multi-sensorial immersion to participants, its associated cost is very high and sometimes difficult to maintain. For these reasons, an open source program (DIVE) and a personal desktop computer are being employed for doing research and development as virtual environment for learning, which corresponds to the current infrastructure of some developing countries. This research shows that relatively modest computer equipment is sufficient for usable and functional virtual environments in CALL.

We found that the Think Aloud Protocol and the QUIS questionnaire usability methods, combined with video recordings and note takings, were very useful for analyzing the extrinsic motivation of the students that participated in our study, as well as the overall usability of the desktop virtual environment system.

Future work will include studies comparing different graphical representations of aerial views of a city for promoting listening comprehension, as well as related learning issues and first-person actions and experiences in virtual environments. Immediate research, however, will focus on how traditional listening comprehension can be promoted using virtual environments. Most exercises in common textbook series present a two-dimensional aerial perspective of a city based on a regular grid system. Many commercial CD-ROMs only transfer the same listening comprehension exercises to a digital format. Because the traditional view of the city does not approximate what a person would perceive at street level, and because most city schematics are based on a regular grid pattern, it is difficult to determine how much the student has actually comprehended. The question of how much of the actual listening "comprehension" is attributable to the user's knowledge and application of grid coordinates in resolving the comprehension exercise thus arises. Future studies will compare student listening comprehension of an exercise based on a traditional two-dimensional aerial view of a regularly patterned city, with an exercise involving an irregularly patterned three-dimensional street-level perspective.

ACKNOWLEDGMENT

Company and product names are trademarks or registered trademarks of their respective companies. Miguel A. Garcia-Ruiz participated in the preparation of this chapter while he was a Visiting Professor at the Faculty of Business and IT, University of Ontario Institute of Technology, Oshawa, Canada, and acknowledges partial support from the National Council of Science and Technology (CONACYT) of Mexico. Jayshiro Tashiro acknowledges the financial support of grants from HealthForceOntario and the Social Sciences and Humanities Research Council of Canada. The financial support of the Natural Sciences and Engineering Research Council of Canada (NSERC) in the form of a Discovery grant to Bill Kapralos is gratefully acknowledged.

REFERENCES

Annetta, L. (2010). The I's have it: A framework for serious educational game design. *Review of General Psychology, 14*, 105–112. doi:10.1037/a0018985

Antonietti, E., Imperio, C., Rasi, C., & Sacco, M. (2001). Virtual reality and hypermedia in learning the use of a turning lathe. *Journal of Computer Assisted Learning, 17*(2), 142–155. doi:10.1046/j.0266-4909.2001.00167.x

Asher, J. (1977). *Learning another language through actions: The complete teacher's guidebook*. Los Gatos, CA: Sky Oaks Productions.

Balkissoon, R., Blossfield, K., Salud, L., Ford, D., & Pugh, C. (2009). Lost in translation: Unfolding medical students' misconceptions of how to perform a clinical digital rectal examination. *American Journal of Surgery, 197*, 525–532. doi:10.1016/j.amjsurg.2008.11.025

Barrett, K. A., & Johnson, W. L. (2010). Developing serious games for learning language-in-culture. In Eck, R. A. (Ed.), *Gaming and cognition: Theories and practice from the learning sciences* (pp. 281–311). Hershey, PA: Information Science Reference.

Beatty, K. (2003). *Teaching and researching computer-assisted language learning*. London, UK: Pearson Education Limited.

Becker, K. (2010). Distinctions between games and learning: A review of current literature on games in education. In Eck, R. A. (Ed.), *Gaming and cognition: Theories and practice from the learning sciences* (pp. 22–54). Hershey, PA: Information Science Reference.

Brown, J. S., Collins, A., & Duguid, S. (1989). Situated cognition and the culture of learning. *Educational Researcher, 18*(1), 32–42.

Burdea, G. C., & Coiffet, P. (2003). *Virtual reality technology* (2nd ed.). Hoboken, NJ: Wiley.

Bush, M. D., & Terry, R. M. (Eds.). (1997). *Technology-enhanced language learning.* Lincolnwood, IL: National Textbook Company.

Byrne, C. M. (1996). *Water on tap: The use of virtual reality as an educational tool.* Unpublished PhD thesis, University of Washington, Department of Industrial Engineering.

Carlsson, C., & Hagsand, D. (1993). *DIVE - multiuser virtual reality system.* VRAIS '93, IEEE Virtual Reality Annual international Symposium.

Carter, B., & Elseth, D. (2008). The usefulness of Second Life for language learning. In de Cássia Veiga Marriott, R., & Lupion Torres, P. (Eds.), *Handbook of research on e-learning methodologies for language acquisition* (pp. 443–455). Hershey, PA: IGI Global. doi:10.4018/9781599049946.ch027

Chapelle, C. (2001). *Computer applications in second language acquisition, foundations for teaching testing and research.* Cambridge, UK: Cambridge University Press.

Cowen, K. J., & Tesh, A. S. (2002). Effects of gaming on nursing students' knowledge of pediatric cardiovascular dysfunction. *The Journal of Nursing Education, 41*(11), 507–509.

Curtis, P., & Nichols, D. (1994). *MUDs grow up: Social virtual reality in the real world* (pp. 193–200). COMPCON.

Dalgarno, B., & Lee, M. J. W. (2010). What are the learning affordances of 3D virtual environments? *British Journal of Educational Technology, 41*(1), 10–32. doi:10.1111/j.1467-8535.2009.01038.x

Dede, C., Salzman, M., & Loftin, B. (1996). ScienceSpace: Virtual realities for learning complex and abstract scientific concepts. *Proceedings IEEE Virtual Reality Annual International Symposium (VRAIS '96).*

Dede, C., Salzman, M., Loftin, R. B., & Ash, K. (1997). *Using virtual reality technology to convey abstract scientific concepts.* Hillsdale, NJ: Lawrence Erlbaum.

Durkin, K. (2010). Video games and young people with developmental disorders. *Review of General Psychology, 14*, 122–140. doi:10.1037/a0019438

Ellis, R. (1994). *The study of second language acquisition.* Oxford, UK: Oxford University Press.

Fassbender, E., Richards, D., & Kavakli, M. (2006). Game engineering approach to the effect of music on learning in virtual-immersive environments. *Proceedings of the 2006 International Conference on Game Research and Development.*

Federation of American Scientists. (2005). *Harnessing the power of video games for learning.* Retrieved July 19, 2010, from http://www.fas. org/gamesummit/Resources/Summit%20on% 20Educational%20Games.pdf

Frecon, E., & Stenius, M. (1998). DIVE: A scalable network architecture for distributed virtual environments. *Distributed Systems Engineering, 5.*

Garcia-Ruiz, M. A., Edwards, A., Aquino-Santos, R., & El-Seoud, S. A. (2008). Collaborating and learning a second language in a wireless virtual reality environment. *International Journal of Mobile Learning and Organization, 2*(4), 369–377. doi:10.1504/IJMLO.2008.020689

Garcia-Ruiz, M. A., Tashiro, J., Kapralos, B., & Vargas Martin, M. (2010). Crouching tangents, hidden danger: Assessing development of dangerous misconceptions within serious games for healthcare education. In Hai-Jew, S. (Ed.), *Virtual immersive and 3D learning spaces: Emerging technologies and trends*. Hershey, PA: IGI Global.

Gollub, R. (2007). Second Life and education. *Crossroads*, *14*(1), 1–8. doi:10.1145/1349332.1349334

Halloun, I. A., & Hestenes, D. (1985). The initial knowledge state of college physics students. *American Journal of Physics*, *53*, 1043–1055. doi:10.1119/1.14030

Hanna, D. E. (2003, July/August). Building a leadership vision: Eleven strategic challenges for higher education. *EDUCAUSE*.

Harris, S. R., Kemmerling, R. L., & North, M. M. (2002). Brief virtual reality therapy for public speaking anxiety. *Cyberpsychology & Behavior*, *5*(6), 543–550. doi:10.1089/109493102321018187

Haynes, C., & Holmevik, J. R. (1998). *High wired: On the design, use, and theory of educational MOOs*. Ann Arbor, MI: University of Michigan Press.

Hudson, J. M., & Bruckman, A. (2001). Effects of CMC on student participation patterns in a foreign language learning environment. *Proceedings of CHI '01*.

ISO 9241-11. (1998). *Ergonomic requirements for office work with visual display terminals (VDTs) – part 11: Guidance on usability*. International Organization for Standardization.

Johnson, W. L., Beal, C., Fowles-Winkler, A., Lauper, U., Marsella, S., & Narayanan, S. ... Vilhjálmsson, H. (2004). Tactical language training system: An interim report. (LNCS 3220), (pp. 336-345).

Kalawsky, R. (2000). The validity of presence as a reliable human performance metric in immersive environments. *Proceedings of 3rd International Workshop on Presence*.

Kolb, D. (1984). *Experiential learning: experience as the source of learning and development*. Englewood Cliffs, NJ: Prentice-Hall.

Konstantinidis, A., Tsiatsos, T., & Pomportsis, A. (2009). Collaborative virtual learning environments: Design and evaluation. *Multimedia Tools and Applications*, *44*(2), 279–304. doi:10.1007/s11042-009-0289-5

Krashen, S., & Terrell, T. (1983). *The natural approach: Language acquisition in the classroom*. Hayward, CA: Alemany Press.

Krashen, S. D. (1982). *Principles and practices in second language acquisition*. New York, NY: Prentice-Hall.

Krashen, S. D. (1988). *Second language acquisition and second language learning* (2nd ed.). New York, NY: Prentice Hall.

Krashen, S. D. (2004). *Applying the comprehension hypothesis: Some suggestions*. 13th International Symposium and Book Fair on Language Teaching.

Larsen-Freeman, D. (2000). *Technique and principles in language teaching*. Oxford, UK: Oxford University Press.

Laurillard, D. (2002). *Rethinking university teaching, a conversational framework for the effective use of learning technologies* (2nd ed.). London, UK: Routledge and Falmer. doi:10.4324/9780203304846

Le Peuple, J., & Scane, R. (2003). *User interface design*. Exeter, UK: Crucial.

Levy, M. (1997). *Computer-assisted language learning: Context and conceptualization*. Oxford, UK: Oxford University Press.

Lieberman, D. (1997). Interactive video games for health promotion: Effects on knowledge, self-efficacy, social support and health. In Gold, R. L., & Manning, T. (Eds.), *Health promotion and interactive technology* (pp. 103–120). Norwell, NJ: Lawrence Erlbaum Associates.

Losh, E. (2006). Making things public: Democracy and government-funded videogames and virtual reality simulations. *Proceedings of the 2006 ACM SIGGRAPH Symposium on Videogames.*

MacFarlane, S., Sim, G., & Horton, M. (2005). Assessing usability and fun in educational software. *Proceedings of the 2005 Conference on interaction Design and Children.*

Mangold, K. (2007). Educating a new generation: Teaching baby boomer faculty about millennial students. *Nurse Educator, 32*(1), 21–23. doi:10.1097/00006223-200701000-00007

McConnell, S. (1996). *Rapid development.* Redmond, WA: Microsoft Press.

Michael, J. A., Richardson, D., Rovick, A., Modell, H., Bruce, D., & Horwitz, B. (1999). Undergraduate students' misconceptions about respiratory physiology. *Advances in Physiology Education, 22*(1), 127–135.

Milton, J., & Garbi, A. (2000). *Collaborative virtual reality approaches for very young language learners.* EDEN Research Workshop Papers, European Distance Education Network.

Nielsen, J. (1994). *Usability engineering.* San Francisco, CA: Morgan Kaufmann.

Nielsen, J., & Landauer, T. K. (1993). A mathematical model of the finding of usability problems. *Proceedings of ACM INTERCHI '93 Conference.*

Nielsen, J., & Mack, R. (Eds.). (1994). *Usability inspection methods.* New York, NY: John Wiley and Sons.

Ozmen, H. (2004). Some student misconceptions in chemistry: A literature review of chemical bonding. *Journal of Science Education and Technology, 13*(2), 147–159. doi:10.1023/B:JOST.0000031255.92943.6d

Park, S. H., Yoon, Y. S., Kim, L. H., Lee, S. H., & Han, M. (2007). Virtual knee joint replacement surgery system. *Proceedings of the International Conference on Geometric Modeling and Imaging,* (pp. 79-84).

Preece, J., Rogers, Y., & Sharp, H. (2002). *Interaction design: Beyond human-computer interaction.* New York, NY: John Wiley and Sons.

Preece, J., Rogers, Y., Sharp, H., Benyon, D., Holland, S., & Carey, T. (1994). *Human-computer interaction.* Wokingham, UK: Addison-Wesley.

Robertson, G., Czeminski, M., & van Dantzich, M. (1997). Immersion in desktop virtual reality. *Proceedings of UIST '97.*

Rose, H., & Billinghurst, M. (1996). *Zengo Sayu: An immersive educational environment for learning Japanese.* Final Report to The Washington Technology Center, University of Washington.

Ruben, D. (1999). Simulations, games, and experience-based learning: The quest for a new paradigm for teaching and learning. *Health Education Research. Theory into Practice, 30*(4), 498–505.

Savery, J., & Duffy, T. (1995). Problem based learning: An instructional model and its constructivist framework. *Educational Technology, 35*(5), 31–38.

Sherman, W. R., & Craig, A. B. (2003). *Understanding virtual reality.* San Francisco, CA: Morgan Kauffman.

Shneiderman, B., & Plaisant, C. (2005). *Designing the user interface* (4th ed.). Reading, MA: Addison-Wesley.

Sinclair, B., & Ferguson, K. (2009). Integrating simulated teaching/learning strategies in undergraduate nursing education. *International Journal of Nursing Education Scholarship, 6*(1). doi:10.2202/1548-923X.1676

Smith, S. P., & Hart, J. (2006). *Evaluating distributed cognitive resources for wayfinding in a desktop virtual environment*. IEEE Symposium on 3D User Interfaces (3DUI 2006), (pp. 3-10).

Soloway, E., Norris, C., Blumenfeld, P., Fishman, B., Krajcik, J., & Marx, R. (2000). Log on education: K-12 and the Internet. *Communications of the ACM, 43*(1). doi:10.1145/323830.323838

Squire, K. D. (2008). Video game–based learning: An emerging paradigm for instruction. *Performance Improvement Quarterly, 21*(2), 7–36. doi:10.1002/piq.20020

Stapleton, A. (2004). Serious games: Serious opportunities. *Proceedings of the 2004 Australian Game Developers Conference*, (pp. 1-6).

Steed, A., & Frecon, E. (2005). Construction of collaborative virtual environments. In Sanchez-Segura, M. I. (Ed.), *Developing future interactive systems* (pp. 235–268). Hershey, PA: IGI Global.

Su, S., & Loftin, R. B. (2001). A shared virtual environment for exploring and designing molecules. *Communications of the ACM, 44*(12). doi:10.1145/501317.501344

Ting, Y., Lin, S. D., Chen, C. H., Lee, S. S., & Chang, Y. F. (2003). Development of a virtual reality surgical platform for unicompartmental knee replacement. *Proceedings of the IEEE International Conference on Systems, Man and Cybernetics, 3*, (pp. 2932-2937).

Tromp, J. G., Steed, A., & Wilson, J. R. (2003). Systematic usability evaluation and design issues for collaborative virtual environments. *Presence (Cambridge, Mass.), 12*(3), 241–267. doi:10.1162/105474603765879512

Turbee, L. (1996). *MOOing in a foreign language: How, why, and who?* Retrieved on November 26, 2007, from http://web.syr.edu/ ~lmturbee/itechtm.html

Virvou, M., & Katsionis, G. (2008). On the usability and likeability of virtual reality games for education: The case of VR-ENGAGE. *Computers & Education, 50*, 154–178. doi:10.1016/j.compedu.2006.04.004

Winn, W. (1993). *A conceptual basis for educational applications of virtual reality*. Human Interface Technology Laboratory, University of Washington. (Report No. TR-93-9).

Youngblut, C. (1998). *Educational uses of virtual reality technology. (Technical report IDA Document D-2128)*. Alexandria, Virginia: Institute for Defense Analyses.

Zaharias, P. (2004). Tutorial: Usability and e-learning: The road towards integration. *eLearn Magazine, 6*, 4.

Zaharias, P. (2006). A usability evaluation method for e-learning: Focus on motivation and learning. *Proceedings of CHI 2006*.

Zajtchuk, R., & Satava, R. M. (1997). Medical applications of virtual reality. *Communications of the ACM, 40*(9). doi:10.1145/260750.260768

ADDITIONAL READING

Churchill, E. F., Snowdon, D. N., & Munro, A. J. (Eds.). (2001). *Collaborative virtual environments*. Heidelberg, Germany: Springer-Verlag.

Deubel, P. (2007). Virtual worlds: A next generation for instruction delivery. *Journal of Instruction Delivery Systems, 21*(2), 6–12.

Hodge, E. M., & Collins, S. (2010). Collaborative efforts: Teaching and learning in virtual worlds. *EDUCAUSE Review, 45*(3), 62–63.

Rubens, W., Emans, B., Leinonen, T., Skarmeta, A. G., & Simons, R. (2005). Design of web-based collaborative learning environments. Translating the pedagogical learning principles to human computer interface. *Computers & Education*, *45*(3), 276–294. doi:10.1016/j.compedu.2005.04.008

Stevens, V. (2006). Second life in education and language learning. *TESL-EJ*, *10*(3), 1–4.

KEY TERMS AND DEFINITIONS

Collaborative Virtual Reality: A shared virtual world using a local network or the Internet as a communication medium, where its users interact to work, learn, train, and carry out other activities together.

Computer Assisted Language Learning (CALL): Computer-based learning technology that promotes student-centered learning, and is intended to facilitate the language learning process.

Listening Comprehension: Cognitive process in which the listener constructs meaning by understanding speech (spoken words), and it can be described in levels.

Misconception: In the area of education, erroneous student's understanding or mistaken notion of a scientific or technological concept or phenomenon.

Usability: Usability studies and assesses how efficiently and satisfactorily people uses a user interface in order to achieve a particular goal in a particular context of use.

Virtual Environment: A computer-generated 3D space, also called virtual world, where 3D graphical objects and sounds reside. Its user is represented in the virtual environment by an avatar (a graphical personification) and can interact with the virtual objects and its environment.

Virtual Reality: Computer technology capable of generating a three-dimensional space called virtual environment, which is highly user interactive, multimodal, and immersive.

Chapter 25
Second Language Teaching in Virtual Worlds:
The Case of European College Students under the ERASMUS Program

Paulo Frias
University of Porto, Portugal

Ricardo N. Fernandes
University of Porto, Portugal

Ricardo Cruz
University of Porto, Portugal

ABSTRACT

This project is a proposal for a case study that aims to describe and understand communicative and pedagogical processes involved in Second Life® (SL™) in a context of second language learning, by modelling in-world lessons of Portuguese as a second language for ERASMUS students[1] arriving in Portugal. The purpose is to provide examples of situated e-learning driven activities and perceive how an immersive context stimulates learning by involving students in a virtual reality situation, where real life language context situations are provoked and where 'not possible in real life' learning routines happen. This will allow experiencing the advantages of this platform compared to physical life teaching and learning contexts, through the inherent characteristics of this medium, such as the synchronous and simultaneous use of voice and text.

INTRODUCTION

Modernity has brought changes to our society and all citizens that are living and growing in this new age of knowledge feel the new canons of an incoming age (Loureiro & Bettencourt, 2009). Education, an important area of social and civilization development, cannot disregard those new changes, and may not be disconnect from ongoing changes in teaching and learning theories and practices since the last century. For that reason, teachers have being challenged to

DOI: 10.4018/978-1-60960-545-2.ch025

develop new strategies of teaching and learning, in order to accomplish the requirements of a networked society and improve the know-how of their students, in a digital age. Nowadays, we are living in the age of the "digital native" (Grewal & Harris, 2009), and due to the advantages of the social web, students "have a lot of practice of e-mailing, blogging, Googling, chatting, gaming (...) (Bekkers, 2009). They are multitasking, just like the new paradigms of education requests.

Students are no longer simple information collectors. They are now more active and reactive users. They develop and share contents and information. In fact, each of us are content builders, which is shared by a new type of communicator. However, Web 2.0 is, nowadays, an old-fashion paradigm. We are, today, in the presence of what some academics call the Web 3.0 (Loureiro & Bettencourt, 2009). This concept is related to virtual environments, interactive 3D dimensional universes that are experienced by the user with avatars, and that enable sharing, co-creation and communication to a next level in education. A new era of a real collaborative web is being explored, where "humans become more linked together (...) more networked (...) and the Internet has no limits or borders" (Veen & Vrakking, 2006, cited by Loureiro, 2009).

According with the Web 3.0 assumptions, Second Life, having itself MUVEs (Multi-User Virtual Environment) characteristics, may have huge possibilities if used for education and teaching purposes.

Our target group, for this e-learning project, are the ERASMUS college students. The ERASMUS Program was established in 1987. It is a mobility program among universities of member states of the European Union, and also of other associated states, that involves students and teachers, and allows the former to study in another country for 3, 6 or 12 months. The main goal of the program is to encourage and support students and teachers' academic mobility inside the European Union,

and other European countries such as Norway, Iceland, Turkey or Liechtenstein.

In the ERASMUS program, students need to be exposed to the language of the foreign country before their period of studying abroad. This takes time and effort for languages that are recognized as being difficult. Thus, proficiency in a foreign language can explain the difference between moving students and non-moving students. Students will accept very easily to learn English and probably other widely spoken languages, but they will be more reluctant to learn other languages unless they are motivated by specific reasons (Fuller et al., 2005). SL may allow an immersive experience, and keep students motivated and focused to learn a foreign language. We have perceived that "education began, slowly, to realize that many of the attributes of great game playing, from the intellectual challenge to the provision of multiple learning styles had an immediate part of to play in learning" (Freitas & Neumann, 2009).

In this study, our focus group is the ERASMUS students who come to Portugal for studying.

THE E-LEARNING CONTEXT IN SECOND LIFE

In recent years, some educators come up with ideas of transforming existing platforms to provide rich multimedia experience, together with open-ended content creation and large global communities, the MUVEs (Kapp & O'Driscoll, 2010). The aim is to use MUVEs as an immersive learning environment to provide a new perspective of implementing situated learning or other methods through the use of new technology.

Multi-user virtual environments provide opportunities for students to explore authentic learning environments. The process of internalization results of multiple sensory inputs such as visual, auditory and tactile (Perez, 2009) because learning is embedded within the activities, the context and a specific culture. Social interaction is a critical component of situated learning, as learners become involved in "the community of practice" (Lau & Wong, 2009). Second language acquisition may be a challenging task, specially for busy young adults. It requires the repetition of communicative meaningful interactions with balanced input and output situations, so that the learner may acquire as much language functions, vocabulary, syntax, and grammar in context as possible. The most effective process to achieve this is by providing a learning objective in different contexts, specially through a task-based approach. Interaction and building upon existing knowledge is the usual learning routines in virtual learning environments. Students collaborate in most cases and build together their knowledge. This is also referred to as problem-solving learning. This happens due to the interactive nature of the MUVEs, as well as a collaborative approach to the acquisition of new concepts and a high level of engagement (Perez, 2009). One way of targeting this is by the use of simulations, because they provide a learning by doing routine, which replicates elements of the real situation and put the learner in the center of the process (Castronova, 2005). A project-based scenario approach is also a good process to deal with the technological limitations that students may have with the interface, since it is possible to organize activities for the first sessions that ease the difficulties associated with the immersive experience (Baudrillard, 2001). The three-dimensionality enabled by a virtual world promotes the sense of presence and interactiveness, which facilitates the learning experience, compared to other non-immersive e-learning routines. An experiential simulation such as this virtual environment provides the basis for empathic understanding, facilitating collaboration and reducing the affective filter caused by the negative emotional responses of the learner, when exposed to a foreign language (Garcia, 1994).

It is possible to apply different learning strategies considering the versatility of this environment (Leonard, Sherblom, & Withers, 2009). The differ-

ent socialization patterns, the loss of identity and the isolation due to the language barrier can be also addressed in this environment. The theoretical context for this study is based on constructivism, a cognitive approach, the multiple intelligences theory and communicative skills. In the virtual world it is assumed the role of the teacher as a mediator of wishful awe-inspiring rich linguistic and cultural information, that can also be found in real-life experiences. Learner's diverse learning styles (e.g.: auditory, kinetic, etc) could be met by providing a multimedia context in which a mirror of physical life is obtainable but presents organized and resumed information This multi-directional communication model is the framework where these theories are applied, in the virtual world. It is possible to assess fully interactivity by observing instant messaging among students and between them and the teacher. Cooperative working relationships are also observable by interaction of students through objects and note cards sharing (Brown, Hobbs, & Gordon, 2008). In this paradigm, the teacher becomes a facilitator, integrating tools into the teaching process, and assisting students in the tasks (Chodos, Naeimi, & Stroulia, 2009).

SOCIOLOGICAL PERSPECTIVE OF VIRTUAL WORLDS

A phenomenological interpretation of the social concept could provide a new analysis about virtual worlds, based on social relationships (Schutz & Luckmann, 1971). That is, we only understand, in an efficient way, what we experiment, in our daily routines, in our social life. One of the reasons why this is particularly challenging for instructors is because of the nature of the conceptualization of learning. The social nature of virtual worlds is build upon the dialogic model (Kahai, Carroll, & Jestice, 2007). Sociology says that social is not just defined as interactions between individuals and groups, but also the relations between individuals and the spaces they co-construct around themselves. The act of building and producing becomes, this way, a powerful training and teaching tool, supporting socialization and extending opportunities for conceptual thinking and exploration.

Nowadays, the mass communication *media* are creating a "global village", because people, all over the world, see the globalization of events (McLuhan, 1964). In this SL project, we have explored the concept of "hyper-reality" (Andersen, 2002), in the cyberspace way. The composition of the virtual world environment helps to make an appropriated guide to the technological education. Second Life is a new world of opportunities in this subject: it can enhance learning skills, motivating students to engage more actively in teaching and learning activities. In such a pedagogical environment, SL can facilitate different kinds of processes, such as searching for information, presenting information, producing and organizing materials, and coordinating the different tasks in the work process, with more detail. In a social point of view, this method will bring a "new all relationship between computer interaction, social interaction and other forms of everyday practices" (Drotner, 1999). SL is a mixed environment that can be situated in an area known as "educational entertainment" (Cotton & Oliver, 1994). Edutainment is a neologism composed of the words education and entertainment. This term has its origin based on printed *media*, such as textbooks, encyclopedias and children's books, which present a rich combination of textual information and images, in order to better exemplify the matter presented. According to Cotton and Oliver (1994), based on the changes caused by information technology, educators now have a new role to play, because education is becoming part of the virtual business as SL. This is part of a new model of education for the information age, based on learning theories, especially within a socio-cultural perspective, and results from educational research, that combines practice and action research, in areas more in vogue such as motivation and the management of change.

THEORETICAL PROPOSAL

Objectives

The goal of this proposal is to understand communicational processes in Second Life in a context of second language learning, aimed at ERASMUS students. It conceptualizes and applies certain activities with a focus group of students. The learning language (L2) is Portuguese. This proposal should contribute to the explanation of how SL, as a virtual reality immersive tool, empowers the teaching and learning of a second language. This may occur due to two main reasons. On the one hand, the distance effect present in traditional e-learning tools such as *Moodle* or *Joomla* is eliminated. Distance learning becomes much more feasible when students from around the world can log in and interact as if they were next to each other (Fuller et al., 2005). On the other hand, the use of this platform suggests the reformulation of the teaching and learning paradigm. The educational experiences of virtual worlds do not exist inherently within these worlds, but rather within the ways in which the users engage their ideas within these worlds. Therefore, the curricula of virtual worlds includes what happens as well as when, how, with whom, and why (Carpenter, 2009).

As said before, our target group for this e-learning project is the Erasmus students. The University of Porto has an active participation in this program. In 1990, it has received 31 foreign students, and, in 2008, 589. Figure 1 illustrates the evolution of the number of students involved each year:

This mobility of foreign students motivates the emergence of this study, aimed at testing a virtual learning environment for Portuguese non native speakers students.

Figure 1. Evolution of student mobility - Erasmus out & in 1990/91 - 2008/09 (University of Porto, 2009)

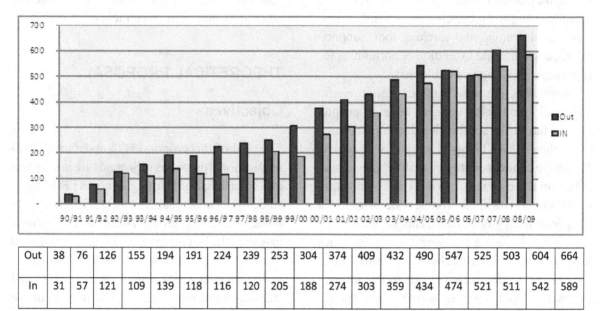

Out	38	76	126	155	194	191	224	239	253	304	374	409	432	490	547	525	503	604	664
In	31	57	121	109	139	118	116	120	205	188	274	303	359	434	474	521	511	542	589

Hypotheses

The best way to conduct an orderly and precise organization of a research is around working hypotheses, without sacrificing the spirit of discovery and curiosity that characterizes all intellectual effort. In addition, a work cannot be considered a real investigation if it isn't structured around one or several hypotheses.

First of all, a hypothesis means, by definition, a spirit of discovery that should characterize any scientific investigation. Supported by a theoretical reflexion and previous knowledge of a studied phenomenon, it seems like a presupposition about the real behavior of the real studied objects. "In many forms and processes, the investigations present themselves always like shuttle movements, between a theoretical reflexion and an empiric work. The hypotheses are the main actors of this movement: provide them the range and assure coherence between the work parts" (Quivy & Campenhoudt, 2003).

This proposal presents the following hypotheses:

- Students can learn a foreign language in a virtual world immersion context – Second Life;
- Students can overcome cultural limitations and expectations usual in traditional classrooms.

Methodology

As in other experiments with learning in VWs, the methodology used merges features of a case study and a quasi-experimental design (Twining & Footring, 2010). In this study, we gathered European students located in Porto and managed to experiment two lessons with a focus group. Focus group research involves organized discussion with a selected group of individuals to gain information about a topic. In this case, we gathered ERASMUS students to figure out how sustainable it is to teach a foreign language in virtual worlds. We have built a questionnaire to apply after the focus group sessions in Second Life. Considering the universe of students that may participate in this case study, a preliminary questionnaire was applied in order to characterize the students as far as computer technology is concerned: hardware, Internet habits, and attitude towards technology. The pos-questionnaire, although not used, was built to apply after the focus group and is based on evaluation categories about the aftermath immersion and learning experiences.

The lessons were devised taking into account a computer-mediated communication (CMC) paradigm. The goal is not to reproduce activities in-world that could equally be done in real life. We also took into consideration the fact that the use of this technology for the novelty factor is a misuse that can be demotivating for all (Teeler & Gray, 2000; Windeatt, Hardisty, & Eastment, 2000). Thus, we first identified a pedagogy and assessed the possibilities of the platform. Then, we designed the learning experience and implemented it. The final stage will be the analysis and evaluation.

Due to technological limitations associated with network heavy traffic, it was impossible to succeed in the usage of voice in-world. However, we have already tried some experimental lessons. However, the survey built to apply after the immersive learning experience has not been applied yet. That will be the future direction of this study.

Preliminary Pre-Questionnaire Analysis

The preliminary questionnaire was applied in order to characterize the students as far as computer technology is concerned: hardware, Internet habits, and attitude towards technology. The questionnaire was applied to 27 ERASMUS students whose mother tongue was non romanic. This trait is particularly important, since the more distant the native language (L1) is from the learning language (L2) the more relevant is the students' learning.

The social-demography variables are: age, gender, and nationality. As far as age is concerned, the mode is 22 years-old, although there are students with 33 years-old, which means that the range is

considerable. 63% of the students are male and 37% are female. Countries vary from Belgium, Poland, Germany, USA, and Greece, among others. The presence of non-European nations is explained by the extension of the ERASMUS program to non-European countries.

Of the 27 students, 37% have brought their laptop computer to Portugal, but 63% don't have a laptop computer. This may hinder the usage of information technology, and also the participation in a study such as this one.

A significant value is the one related to the time spent online weekly for recreational, work or studying activities. So, 40,7% answered that they are more than 9 hours a week, approximately, on the Internet. As far as online activities are concerned, 38,5% of the universe uses instant message daily and 63% uses text message daily, and 29,6% uses voice over Internet daily too. This may be explained by the fact that these students are far from their homes and friends or that they are using this communication tools to build new social networks in the community where they are inserted. Not surprisingly, 70,4% of the students inquired never play online multi-user computer games and 88,9% never use virtual worlds. This could suggest a low level of incidence of 3D online environments. This is directly related to the need of powerful hardware and broadband connections to use these platforms.

Pedagogy and Applicability

As said, in this proposal, the applied pedagogy was holistic with a constructivist approach and a task-based model. This means that the learning process involves individual understanding and performance of tasks as well as group activities. Frequent feedback must be provided and the learning is based on stages of personal and social constructs. Students first conceptualise, then construct, and finally apply by engaging with others (Slone, 2009).

Many companies are known to be using Second Life as a meeting space, a research environment and an educational area, considering the vast amount of possibilities that it offers, specially contextual and authentic social interactions, including role plays and simulations (Peachey, Gillen, & Ferguson, 2008). Similar environments that potentiate ludic-driven learning are video games and multiplayer game worlds. Krashen, an important methodologist in second language acquisition, refers that "the major function of the second language classroom is to provide intake for acquisition" (1981: 101). This statement disregards the necessity of providing opportunities for output by the learner. However, his observations and conclusions at the time are also applicable to the process of online learning and teaching through 3D virtual worlds, as noticed too by Grant (2008). Krashen (1981) mentions the necessity of stimulating fluent outputs based on active meaningful communication rather than controlled and conscious utterances. Second language acquisition must balance moments of controlled output and informal unstructured production that can be provided by immersion of the learner in the linguistic environment of the target language. However, the learners must be directly and actively engaged in a meaningful communication situation, where the target language is being regularly and actively used. 3D virtual worlds such as Second Life may provide such an environment that allows and stimulates students to produce output utterances, and most importantly, allows, at the same time, for tutors to provide correction, and guide learners to conscious learning of the language without interrupting the linguistic process and the student's engagement. This happens due to the functionalities of the software. The use of this platform allows the use of voice streams by the teacher and the students in a regular interaction. During the students' utterances, the teacher may use text chat to guide or correct some structures. This is possible also in an input activity. As the teacher speaks, he or she may write some of the structures

used, or some words, to allow the phonetic and graphemic association by the students. This will provide two simultaneous language inputs for students: listening and reading. Other possible application for the usage of voiced and texted interactions is the possibility of dialogs between the teacher and the students, and among students (or even among students and native speakers of the target language) - role played or spontaneous - be recorded and analyzed in a ulterior moment (Wilhelm, Ross, & Love, 2009). Students, this way, realise they are not passive receivers of information, but actively build the language structures as needed, and, most importantly, without breaking the communication flow, which is a situation not possible in a classical learning environment or even in a casual language communication flow. A 3D immersion virtual environment that combines text and voice allows for these combined informal and structured language outputs that may be associated to relevant and meaningful communication situations. This provides a 3D learning experience (3DLE). Besides, it facilitates an individualised instructional context, by providing targeted feedback to individual students, through private text chat or private talk (Haughton & Romero, 2009). This is of utmost importance, because a virtual presence reduces fears and embarrassment that the learner may feel. He or she may actually interact with other under the supposition of using an alter ego, allowing confidence levels to rise (Henderson et al., 2009). In Figure 2, adapted from Haughton and Romero (2009) explains the importance of knowing the students' motivations, so that the instructor may adapted the curricula to meet their needs and goals. The contents of our proposed lessons take into consideration the aspirations and needs of foreign European students that are bound to arrive in a different European country where a different language is spoken. One of their first endeavours is to find appropriate lodging. That is the reason why one of the lessons is focused on parts of the house, types of houses and describing city environments.

Figure 2. Relationships between student's inputs, outcomes and the instructor (Haughton & Romero, 2009, adapted)

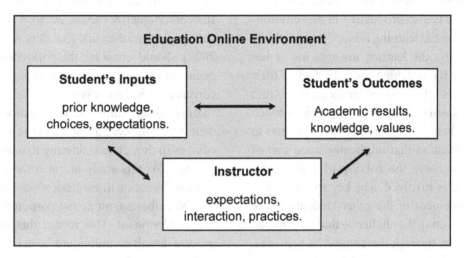

Many educators fall in the trap of replicating a traditional class-based approach (Brown et al., 2008). A field trip to other places in the simulator, role plays, guided tours or scavenger hunts are part of a more efficient model in terms of taking advantage of the virtual environment. Students and educators should not expect to behave in a similar way as in a traditional educational setting (Kapp & O'Driscoll, 2010). If this happens, the value of a 3D classroom is not perceived. Learners must be in a context where interaction with the environment and each others is important, which means that moving around is important. In the words of Kapp and O'Driscoll: "The replication of a existing classroom environment brings no value to the learning experience." (2010:323). The lessons were devised taking into account the medium where they would occur, under a computer-mediated communication (CMC) paradigm. It allows a diversity of the language learning process and a change on the linguistic focus of the proposed tasks, incrementing the motivation levels: "we need to vary as many aspects of the learning process as possible... we can vary the linguistic focus of the tasks... the main language skills file that the tasks activate" (Dörnyei, 2001). There are several learning theories applicable in

the context of education in virtual worlds. Moschini has put forward a description of some of them: constructivism, situated learning, experiential learning, problem-based learning and digital game-based learning (Moschini, 2010). Constructivism is learner centered and focuses on the construction of the knowledge through an interaction with other learners and the environment. Here, the teacher's role is different: a facilitator. Second Life is an excellent medium where a constructivist pedagogic approach may be adopted. In a top level activity, students will be building their own materials, interacting with each other, and actively engaging in language situations, without realizing the rationale behind the activity. The skills needed to complete the tasks are acquired in the virtual environment and considered part of the activity. This task-based learning framework also allows for students to acquire skills in different areas, according to their needs, by their access to resources and experiences at their own pace. The interactions also promote peer-to-peer learning, as students assume a tutoring role and disseminate skills and knowledge acquired in the virtual environment (Brown et al., 2008). In situated learning, the student tries to solve a problem posed by the tutor, whose role is to supervise the activity. Since there is a practice of mutual help for new users in virtual worlds, this approach is also productive in this environment. Experiential learning is based on an attitude of reflexion by the learner, towards his or her experiences. By watching the activities of their peers, learners reflect on the language inputs and outputs and learn by mimicking. A problem-based approach is based on the ability of the learner to analyze a situation that implicates some sort of strategy to achieve the solving of a particular problem that is involved. The key to this model is the involvement of the other students in the process of meeting the challenge that is being put by the teacher, through the context he provides. Finally, a digital games-based learning strategy uses games for educational purposes. Second Life is not a game, as it does not have a purpose on its own. However, it is possible to build games within the environment where learners actively engage in interactions with virtual objects or with each other, following routines defined by the rules of the game.

Regardless of the pedagogy theory applicable, the environment where the lessons take place is of great importance, especially in language learning, considering that culture is the bedrock where any language is built (Moschini, 2010). In virtual worlds, language must be acquired and taught embedded in a constructed cultural environment, where the target language actually exists. In this proposal, the third lesson challenges the students to describe city landscapes of the city of Porto, in Portugal. They become surrounded by an imagery that truly exists and where Portuguese e truly used as a native language. The immersive social environment combines a sense of physical co-presence with linguistic interaction (Henderson et al., 2009). Henderson et al. state that it also promotes collaborative group work, similar to language classroom interactions, where groups can be create and rearrange groups according to pedagogical needs and social dynamics. In this proposal, the applied pedagogy was constructivist.

Some scholars suggest a problem-based learning, as they consider it the most effective in engaging students (Bignell & Parson, 2010). A constructivist pedagogical framework (Sanders & McKeown, 2007) should consider the following: learning occurs in a group; students' knowledge is socially constructed, in a process of action learning, where sharing, collaboration and participation are permanent. Students were involved in the learning process, even though, considering that the proposed students for this study are at a threshold level, some information transmission was implemented too. Nonetheless, an active participation model was predominant. This means that the learning process involves individual understanding and performance of tasks. Frequent feedback, under these circumstances, had to be provided and the learning must be based on stages of personal and social constructs. Students first conceptualize, then construct and finally apply by engaging with others (Slone, 2009). These were the guidelines by which we implemented the activities. The use of this platform allows the use of voice streams by the teacher and the students in a regular interaction. As previously explained, while the teacher speaks, he or she may write some of the structures used, to facilitate the understanding. This will provide two simultaneous language inputs for students: listening and reading. A simultaneous automatic chat translator may also be used by the teacher, which may be useful in a vocabulary input activity. English may be used as the working language between L1 and L2. Another possibility may be for students to ask questions through text while the teacher uses voice. The text or voice dialogs between the teacher and the students - role played or spontaneous - may be recorded and analyzed in an ulterior moment (Wilhelm et al., 2009). To allow this, all avatars should be within a range of 20 meters of the speaker. Students and teacher may listen to the dialogues and the teacher may comment on the structures, providing hints, and giving positive feedback. The platform also allows the distribution of handouts in the form of personal note cards as well as billboards. The role plays and the use of holodecks where similar to real life context is given allow the students to assume social roles where the L2 is needed. This would be very difficult to achieve in a traditional classroom. Students are not passive receivers of information but they actively build the language structures as needed. These role plays are used according to the students' needs, during their staying in the country: shopping in the city, public offices attendance, a visit to the hospital or health center, night life, museums, a bank and other social contexts where L2 is needed with specific functions, collocations and vocabulary (Schuurink & Vries, 2009).

Contents

The use of simulations in education brings a new variable which is the sense of enjoyment and pleasure in learning, favouring the overcome of emotional blocks (Pereira, 2009).

The lessons contents were designed taking in consideration the target population. The first lesson involves a migration from physical life to the virtual world. It is a hybrid plan between real life and inworld interaction. At the beginning of the lesson the students are given several instructions and explanations about the investigation. Then, the user accounts are created and the students log into the virtual world and learn the first steps. The "first hour" learning stage is crucial (Dudeney & Howard, 2009). That's the reasoning that supports the activities planned before entering the virtual world in the first lesson plan, and before entering the simulation. Students will first meet in the The Virtual Ability, Inc. sim (http://virtualability.org/default.aspx). It provides a friendly space to start the experience in the Second Life. During the first moments in the simulation, there is an identification process with the avatar. Each individual looks for familiar references and tries to understand his or her identity. The avatar appearance is an important part of this process. That

Figure 3. Students editing their avatars in the first lesson

is why the language topic for this first lesson is people's appearance and clothes.

Students edit their avatars, acquire an identity and learn to describe someone's appearance and name the clothes items. Figure 3 illustrates students editing their avatars, at the beginning of lesson no. 1. Figures 4 and 5 illustrate students acquiring vocabulary and structures so that they can later describe their own avatars. Initial moments in the virtual environment demand little interaction of the student with the environment so that he or she does not feel challenged by it. Figure 7 illustrates a virtual presentation with language input about the avatars appearance. Students need just to cycle through the presentation in other to learn the vocabulary. The teacher may read each word and provide a context for it. This way, we may conclude that the contents were chosen following a subject-centred and a student-centred approach (Palomäki, 2009).

Lesson plan no.1 (see section at the end) describes the activities and contents focused on the identification of the avatar.

The second and third lessons focus less on the individual and more on the world around. In the second lesson the topic is homes, parts of the house and different areas in a house. The third lesson is focused on the description of landscapes, and the interaction associated with a role play where the

Figure 4. Students learn how to describe their clothes

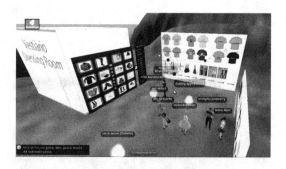

Figure 5. The teacher suggests a matching game focused on clothes items

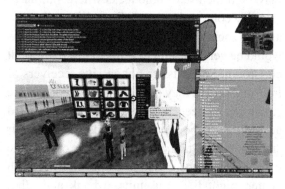

Figure 6. A detail of the matching game

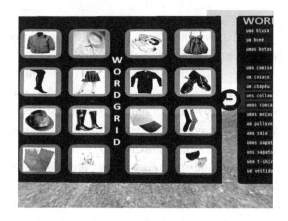

Figure 7. A virtual presentation with vocabulary

students simulate a hotel check-in. A discussion group takes place first, allowing students to gather vocabulary, and only after they feel confident with the structures and vocabulary needed, they move to the holodeck (Moschini, 2010). The idea is to reach the students linguistics needs and use this strategy as a motivation procedure.

Lesson plan no.2 and no.3 (see section at the end) describe the activities and contents focused on parts of the house and the description of landscapes, as well as a role-play in a hotel lobby.

Discussion

With respect to the compatibility of virtual environments to existing learning styles, we believe that today's virtual worlds have multiple channels that favour the learning styles of the newest generation (Junglas et al., 2007; Henderson et al., 2009). Following Turkle's description of the digital native, flexibility and multiplicity is the new paradigm of the self: "we are encouraged to think of ourselves as fluid, emergent, decentralized, multiplicious, flexible, and forever in process" (1995: 263). Second Life users describe their in-world experiences as having a great social presence (Berge, 2008). This meets the multiuser interaction paradigm that characterises theses environments. The immersive nature induces users to be near each other, which means that the environment replicates social practices and forms of collectivity (Panteli, 2009). Most of all, VWs promote high levels of intrinsic motivation - wonder, surprise, exploration, creativity (Brown et al., 2008) - due to the enjoyment and fun that

Figure 8. A virtual book with the lesson contents, that students may browse at their will

Figure 9. A role play in a holodecks where students interact with each other or with the teacher

the experiences should provide (Chandra, Theng, O'Iwin, & Shou-Boon, 2009).

This e-learning technology can reduce costs, compared to the traditional classroom systems, and also eliminates students' transportation costs. It is also an opportunity for promoting education adapted to current demands. There are no restricted rules as far as space, class attendance, time and rhythm requirements are concerned. Besides, the sense of physical proximity and the group synchronous communication (by text or voice) allows students to explore their identity in the context of language practice (Peachey et al., 2008).

Since communicators using a virtual world need to be present at the same time, virtual worlds also differ in terms of the interactivity and the preparation of the messages that individuals produce. For instance, collaborators using the voice channel in a virtual world have a very limited ability to rehearse their messages before transmitting them (Kahai et al., 2007), (Garcia, 1994). This provides a spontaneous communicative environment which means, in other words, true language use in context.

This model also has some disadvantages, such as voice usage limitations, absence of interaction or the learning curve associated with the platform. Some investigators describe the first moments in Second Life as annoying and frustrating, intimidating the user (Carr, Oliver, & Burn, 2010).

If students aren't used to the application, the first in-world experiences may be focused on the creation of a personal identify. In a worst case scenario, the complexity of the interface may reduce the experience to a shallow, one-time engagement with the environment (Dudeney & Howard, 2009).

Students will pay attention to changing their clothes and their appearance until they start to identify with their avatar. Besides, this stage is dedicated to learn how to interact with the environment: how to move, how to use the camera and how to interact with text and voice.

Expected Results

The results of this case study are dependent mostly of the application of the questionnaire after the students have attended the lessons. It is one possible way of finding out the opinion of the learner. Nevertheless, it is always possible to evaluate the students' learning level by engaging in a conversation with him or her about the focused topic. At this time, we can only anticipate and suppose that the students may benefit from the use of this platform and engage in superior levels of interactions, and assimilate in a more efficient way what otherwise would be taught in a classical traditional environment. Engagement, that is, the willingness of a student to spend time learning, is expected to increase, because the platform develops reciprocity and cooperation, and encourages active learning. It promotes a social presence, avoiding the disconnected feeling that most students have in an e-learning platform. By feeling a member of a community of learners, the impact on retention and students' perception of success increases. The collaborative perspective will increase engagement and facilitate a friendly and agreeable learning environment.

CONCLUSION

Education is dealing with a reform of its paradigm. Emerging Internet technologies are permeating our social and organizational life. A consequence of these traditional developments is the way in which they erode traditional learning styles, as evidenced by changes in the ways that the today's generation of students learn. Second Life, in this particular case, provides a potential universe, for students, to develop process-based skills through media with which they are familiar (Grewal & Harris, 2009).

According to the results of the preliminary questionnaire, an empathy and familiarity with the Internet technologies was shown by the students, which allows us to have confidence on a future application of this paradigm of teaching.

Applying this model to European students who want to study in the University of Porto is based on several reasons: financial, technological, educational, and increased effect on students learning.

In a future work, beyond the scope of this one a well structured syllabus could be built with sound scientific background about the teaching of Portuguese as a second language in virtual worlds combined with a humanistic and constructivist approach.

REFERENCES

Andersen, T. F. (2002). *Signs of learning in computer cultures - proposal for a cultural approach to the study of learning and information technology*. Impact.

Baudrillard, J. (2001). *Selected writings*. Cambridge, UK: Polity.

Bekkers, C. (2009). *Teaching & learning in SL: Figuring out some variables*. Retrieved on May 29, 2010, from http://cleobekkers.wordpress.com/2009/01/28/teaching-learning-in-sl-figuring-out-some-variables/

Berge, Z. L. (2008). Multi-User Virtual Environments for education and training. A critical review of Second Life. *Educational Technology Magazine, 48*(3), 27–31.

Bignell, S., & Parson, V. (2010). *Best practice in virtual worlds teaching*. Retrieved from http://previewpsych.org/ BPD2.0.pdf

Brown, E., Hobbs, M., & Gordon, M. (2008). A virtual world environment for group work. *International Journal of Web-Based Learning and Teaching Technologies, 3*, 1–12. doi:10.4018/jwltt.2008010101

Carpenter, S. B. (2009). Virtual worlds as educational experience: Living and learning in interesting times. *Journal of Virtual Worlds Research, 2*(1).

Carr, D., Oliver, M., & Burn, A. (2010). Learning, teaching and ambiguity in virtual worlds. In Peachey, A., Gillen, J., Livingstone, D., & Smith-Robbins, S. (Eds.), *Researching learning in virtual worlds* (pp. 17–30). Lancaster, PA: Springer. doi:10.1007/978-1-84996-047-2_2

Castronova, E. (2005). *Synthetic worlds: The business and culture of online games*. Chicago, IL: University of Chicago Press.

Chandra, S., Theng, Y. L., O'lwin, M., & Shou-Boon, S. F. (2009). *Proposed theoretical framework for virtual world adoption.* SLACTIONS 2009 International Conference: Life, imagination, and work using metaverse platforms.

Chodos, D., Naeimi, P., & Stroulia, E. (2009). An integrated framework for simulation-based training on video and in a virtual world. *Journal of Virtual Worlds Research, 2,* 3–28.

Cotton, B., & Oliver, R. (1994). *The cyberspace lexicon.* London, UK: Phaidon Press, Ltd.

Dörnyei, Z. (2001). *Motivational strategies in the language classroom.* Cambridge, UK: Cambridge University Press. doi:10.1017/CBO9780511667343

Drotner, K. (1999). Unge, medier og modernitet - pejlinger i et foranderligt landskab. *København.*

Dudeney, G., & Howard, R. (2009). *Overcoming the entry barriers to Second Life in higher education. Higher Education in Virtual Worlds Teaching and Learning in Second Life.* Bingley, UK: Emerald Group Publishing Limited.

Freitas, S. D., & Neumann, T. (2009). The use of exploratory learning for supporting immersive learning in virtual environments. *Computers & Education, 52,* 343–352. doi:10.1016/j.compedu.2008.09.010

Fuller, U., Amillo, J., Laxer, C., Mccracken, W. M., & Mertz, J. (2005). Facilitating student learning through study abroad and international projects. *ACM SIGCSE Bulletin, 37,* 139–151. doi:10.1145/1113847.1113892

Garcia, A. L. (1994). *Educación a distancia hoy.* Madrid, Spain: UNED.

Grant, S. (2008). *Immersive Multi-User Virtual Environments: A new platform for foreign language teaching and learning.* Biennial Conference of the Asian Studies Association of Australia in Melbourne.

Grewal, S. K., & Harris, L. (2009). Learning virtually or virtually distracted? The impact of emerging Internet technologies on pedagogical practice. In N. Panteli (Ed.), *Virtual social networks* (18-35). Hampshire, UK: Palgrave Macmillan.

Haughton, N. A., & Romero, L. (2009). The online educator: Instructional strategies for effective practice. *Journal of Online Learning and Teaching, 5,* 570–576.

Henderson, M., Huang, H., Grant, S., & Henderson, L. (2009). *Language acquisition in Second Life: Improving self-efficacy beliefs.* Ascilite Auckland.

Junglas, I. A., Johnson, N. A., Steel, D. J., Abraham, D. C., & Loughlin, P. M. (2007). Identity formation, learning styles and trust in virtual worlds. *SIGMIS Database, 38,* 90–96. doi:10.1145/1314234.1314251

Kahai, S. S., Carroll, E., & Jestice, R. (2007). Team collaboration in virtual worlds. *SIGMIS Database, 38,* 61–68. doi:10.1145/1314234.1314246

Kapp, K. M., & O'Driscoll, T. (2010). *Learning in 3D: Adding a new dimension to enterprise learning and collaboration.* San Francisco, CA: Pfeiffer.

Krashen, S. (1981). *Second language acquisition and second language learning.* Oxford, UK: Pergamon Press Inc.

Lau, N., & Wong, B. (2009). *Multimedia design manipulation using Second Life in education.* SLACTIONS 2009 International Conference: Life, imagination, and work using metaverse platforms.

Leonard, L. G., Sherblom, J. C., & Withers, L. A. (2009). *Communication challenges and opportunities for educators using Second Life. Higher Education in Virtual Worlds Teaching and Learning in Second Life.* Bingley, UK: Emerald Group Publishing Limited.

Loureiro, A., & Bettencourt, T. (2009). *Building knowledge in the virtual world – influence of real life relationships*. SLACTIONS 2009 International Conference: Life, imagination, and work using metaverse platforms, (pp. 111-116).

McLuhan, M. (1964). *Understanding media*. London, UK: Routledge and Kegan Paul.

Moschini, E. (2010). The Second Life researcher toolkit - an exploration of inworld tools, methods and approaches for researching educational projects in Second Life. In Peachey, A., Gillen, J., Livingstone, D., & Smith-Robbins, S. (Eds.), *Researching learning in virtual worlds* (pp. 31–51). Lancaster, PA: Springer. doi:10.1007/978-1-84996-047-2_3

Palomäki, E. (2009). *Applying 3D virtual worlds to education*. Helsinki University of Technology.

Panteli, N. (2009). Virtual social networks: A new dimension for virtuality research. In Panteli, N. (Ed.), *Virtual social networks* (pp. 1–17). Hampshire, UK: Palgrave Macmillan. doi:10.1057/9780230250888

Peachey, A., Gillen, J., & Ferguson, R. (2008). *Fluid leadership in a multi-user virtual environment educational project with teenagers: Schome Park*. Ecologies of Diversities: the developmental and historical interarticulation of human meditational forms: meeting of the International Society for Cultural and Activity Research, (pp. 1-14).

Pereira, M. (2009). *Universidade do Brasil virtual – the use of Second Life to share knowledge in graphic design, game design and visual arts classrooms*. SLACTIONS 2009 International Conference: Life, imagination, and work using metaverse platforms, (pp. 66-68).

Perez, L. (2009). Challenges and opportunities in using MUVEs in K-12 environments. In Tettegah, S., & Calongne, C. (Eds.), *Identity, learning and support in virtual environments* (pp. 45–55). Rotterdam, The Netherlands: Sense Publishers.

Quivy, R., & Campenhoudt, L. V. (2003). *Manual de investigação em ciências sociais, 3ª edição*. Lisboa, Portugal: Gradiva.

Sanders, R. L., & Mckeown, L. (2007). Promoting reflection through action learning in a 3D virtual world. *International Journal of Social Sciences*, *2*(1), 50–55.

Schutz, A., & Luckmann, T. (1971). *The structures of the life-world*. Evanston, IL: Northwestern University Press.

Schuurink, E., & Vries, M. D. (2009). Combining advanced learning technologies in an immigrant educational program. *Proceedings of the 13th International MindTrek Conference: Everyday Life in the Ubiquitous Era*.

Slone, D. J. (2009). A methodology for measuring usability evaluation skills using the constructivist theory and the Second Life virtual world. *Journal of Usability Studies*, *4*, 178–188.

Teeler, D., & Gray, P. (2000). *How to use the Internet in ELT Harlow*. Upper Saddle River, NJ: Pearson Education Limited - Longman.

Turkle, S. (1995). *Life on the screen: Identity in the age of the Internet*. New York, NY: Simon & Schuster.

Twining, P., & Footring, S. (2010). The Schome Park programme: Exploring educational alternatives. In Peachey, A., Gillen, J., Livingstone, D., & Smith-Robbins, S. (Eds.), *Researching learning in virtual worlds* (pp. 53–74). Lancaster, PA: Springer. doi:10.1007/978-1-84996-047-2_4

University of Porto. (2009). *Erasmus statistic report - partnerships and mobility of students, teaching staff and staff training*. International Office.

Veen, W., & Vrakking, B. (2006). *Homo zappiens: Growing up in a digital age*. London, UK: Network Continuum Education.

Wilhelm, W., Ross, S. C., & Love, E. (2009). *Opportunities and challenges for business education in Second Life. Higher Education in Virtual Worlds Teaching and Learning in Second Life*. Bingley, UK: Emerald Group Publishing Limited.

Windeatt, S., Hardisty, D., & Eastment, D. (2000). *The Internet*. Oxford, UK: Oxford University Press.

KEY TERMS AND DEFINITIONS

3DLE: Three-Dimensional Learning Experience. A learning experience in a virtual environment.

Digital Native: someone who grew up surrounded by all sort of digital technology.

Digital Immigrant: someone who adapted to digital technology later in life.

E-Learning: Learning synchronously or asynchronously through the mediation of the cyberspace.

Erasmus: European Scheme for the Mobility for University Students.

Sociology of Virtual Worlds: Ramification of sociology focused on the study of society dimensions, institutions and communities on virtual immersive environments.

Multi-User Virtual Environment (MUVE): Virtual electronic environment where people interact with each other and with virtual objects through representations of themselves called avatars.

Virtual Worlds: Electronic space in which a real experience happens.

ENDNOTES

[1] The ERASMUS Program is named after the Dutch philosopher, Desiderius Erasmus of Rotterdam, known as an opponent of dogmatism, who lived and worked in many places in Europe to expand his knowledge and gain new insights. Later, it was given the backronym *European Scheme for the Mobility for University Students*.

[2] The sign in process is easier and has less steps on this site instead of http://www.secondlife.com.

APPENDIX

QUESTIONNAIRES & LESSON PLANS

1. How old are you? _____
2. Gender:
    2.1. [ ] male
    2.2. [ ] female
3. Where are you from? (country) _____
4. Here in Portugal, do you have a personal laptop computer? If your answer is 'no', please skip to question 4.1. [ ] yes4.2. [ ] no
5. How old is your laptop computer?
    5.1. [ ] Don´t own a personal computer
    5.2. [ ] Less than 1 year old
    5.3. [ ] 1 year old
    5.4. [ ] 2 years old
    5.5. [ ] 3 years old
    5.6. [ ] 4 years old
    5.7. [ ] More than 4 years old
6. Approximately how many hours each week do you spend actively doing Internet activities for school, work, or recreation?
    6.1. [ ] Less than 1 hour
    6.2. [ ] Between 1 and 3 hours
    6.3. [ ] Between 3 and 6 hours
    6.4. [ ] Between 6 and 9 hours
    6.5. [ ] More than 9 hours
7. How often do you do the following for school, work, or recreation?

	Never	Once a year	Once per semester	Monthly	Weekly	Several times a week	Daily
a) Instant message							
b) Text message							
c) Download web-based music							
d) Use college/university library							
e) Presentation software (PowerPoint, etc…)							
f) Social networking websites (Facebook, MySpace, Bebo, Linkedin, etc.)							
g) Online multi-user computer games (World of Warcraft, Everquest, poker, etc…)							
h) Online virtual worlds (Second Life, Forterra, etc.)							
i) Social bookmarking/ tagging (del.ico. us, etc…)							
j) Voice over Internet Protocol (VoIP) from your computer (Skype, etc.)							

8.   Which of the following best describes you? (choose one)
       8.1. [ ] I am skeptical of information technologies and I use them only when I have to.
       8.2. [ ] I am usually one of the last people I know to use information technologies.
       8.3. [ ] I usually use information technologies when most people I know do.
       8.4. [ ] I like information technologies and I use them before most people I know.
       8.5. [ ] I love information technologies and I am among the first to experiment with and use them.

Thank you for your collaboration! This survey will be part of an investigation about virtual worlds. If you would like to know more about this, please contact us: ricardonoronhafernandes@gmail.com and ricardocruz@me.com

     SOURCE: Students and Information Technology, Educause Center for Applied Research Study 6, 2009 (adapted).

Questionnaire Survey

Second Life teaching in virtual worlds – the case of European college students under the Erasmus Programme

1.   Comfort Level with Second Life (first moments)

Please review the following Second Life skills and indicate your comfort level with each item. Don´t think to hard about each one. Answer the questions at your own pace.

Walking

Have not done   Not at all comfortable   Comfortable   Very comfortable

Flying

Have not done   Not at all comfortable   Comfortable   Very comfortable

Teleporting

Have not done   Not at all comfortable   Comfortable   Very comfortable

Chatting

Have not done   Not at all comfortable   Comfortable   Very comfortable

IM'ing

Have not done   Not at all comfortable   Comfortable   Very comfortable

Accessing the Inventory

Have not done   Not at all comfortable   Comfortable   Very comfortable

Using "the wheel" (right click)

Have not done   Not at all comfortable   Comfortable   Very comfortable

Using the MAP

Have not done   Not at all comfortable   Comfortable   Very comfortable

Using the Mini MAP

Have not done   Not at all comfortable   Comfortable   Very comfortable

Using the SEARCH tool

Have not done   Not at all comfortable   Comfortable   Very comfortable

Personalizing the Appeareance

Have not done   Not at all comfortable   Comfortable   Very comfortable

2.   How strongly do you associate the following characteristics with Second Life? Please answer using a 1-5 scale where (1) is "No association" and (5) is "High association."

	1 No Association	2	3	4	5 High Association
Interactive					
Engaging					
Social					
Global					
Easy to use					
Realistic					

3.   Please rate your experience with Second Life on the following attributes. Choose one rating for each using a 1-5 scale where (1) is "poor" and (5) is "excellent".

	1 Poor	2	3	4	5 Excellent
Sign up procedures					
Meeting other people					
Learning how to communicate					
Creating/ modifying the avatar					

4.   **After your experience on Second Life, in your opinion, computer mediated communication (CMC) may help a language learning? Yes or no? Why?**_____

5.   Do you know any words or expressions in Portuguese? How many fo them?

      1 2 3 4 More than 4

6.   Do you consider Second Life similar to real world? Did you feel the effect of immersion?

      I totally agree   I agree   Have no opinion   I disagree   I totally disagree

7.   Comment on the interaction that teacher promoted during lessons.

      _____

8.   Second Life, as a virtual world platform of e-learning, enables a new mechanism of language learning?

      I totally agree   I agree   Have no opinion   I disagree   I totally disagree

9.   Choose the main advantages of the e-learning environment in Second Life:

      (You can choose more than one)

- Second Life, as an e-learning tool, it´s an opportunity for promoting education adapted to current demands
- Students can have formation outside the classroom context
- Students are able to stay on their professional, cultural or family environment
- There are no restricted rules as far as space, class attendance, time and rhythm requirements are concerned.
- The constant bidirectional or multidirectional communication flow ensures a dynamic and active learning of the subjects.

- Students adopt a pro-active attitude towards learning

Source:
New Media Consortium survey: educators in Second Life, Spring 2008.

LESSON PLAN 1

School: University of Porto **Teacher:** Ricardo Cruz and Ricardo Fernandes **Date:**	**Class:** Focus Group – Erasmus Students **Level:** Beginner **Lesson no. 1**
Summary: Introductions. Short explanation about the goals of the investigation. First contact with the virtual environment: sign-up and sign-in. Vocabulary and structures: *aparência – descrição; roupas.*	**Teacher's Purposes:** - To develop Ss' vocabulary and language structures. - To provide Ss with new vocabulary and to lead Ss to use Portuguese in a communicative way.
Assumptions: Ss are computer knowledgeable. **Anticipated Problems:** Some Ss might find some difficulties in understanding some vocabulary. Some Ss may lack some of the vocabulary necessary to engage in a discussion about the topic. Some technical problems may occur during sign-up procedures and during in-word navigation.	**Objectives:** By the end of this lesson Ss will have: Cognitive - identified the main topic of the texts; - selected specific information from a text; - acquired new vocabulary related to the topic; - demonstrated their understanding of the text by: - describing avatars' appearance. - describing avatars' clothes. - developed their speaking skills by participating actively in a discussion. Affective - Participated willingly in the tasks. - Interacted with other Ss. - Showed enthusiasm for the tasks.

CONTENTS

Topic / Context: Describing people. Clothes.	Aids: computers; posters; clothes items; physical and virtual projector; handouts.
Language Work: - vocabulary related to the topic: alto / baixo; estatura media; magro / gordo; estreito / largo; careca; cabelo; cabelo volumoso / comprido / curto; rabo de cavalo; olhos escuros / claros; luvas; cuecas; t-shirt; camisa; camisola; capuz; top; casaco; calças; saia; meias; luvas; smoking; calças de ganga; sapatos; "está na moda"; "é moderno". - new or revised grammar items: stative verbs: ter; estar; vestir; calçar; ser. Adjectives.	Strategies / Activities: **Introducing the topic and motivating Ss:** **Activating Ss' knowledge and anticipating the content of the text** 　　　- change avatars' physical traits and clothes. **Reading comprehension** 　　　- watching images about physical appearance and types of clothes; 　　　- using different clothes and learn their names; **Speaking / Writing** 　　　- describing physical appearance and clothes used.
Evaluation / Assessment: Informal and direct evaluation of Ss' performance.	

Skills	Procedure	Inter.	Aids	Time
L	1. T greets class and explains the purpose of the investigation T directs SS to http://virtualability.org/signup.aspx and invites SS to sign-up to Second Life®. (Figures 1 to 4)	T/WC	Projector computers	20'
L	2. SS are invited to wander around and learn how to use the "viewer". (Figure 5).	T/WC		20'
	T teleports to UP island and invites SS to join him. (Figure 6).			2'
L	T shows SS how to edit their avatar by changing their appearance. (Figure 7).	T/WC		3'
	(At this point T moves to another room and the lesson proceeds exclusively in the virtual world).			
R/L	3. SS are invited to see some images on the projector with an avatar with different physical traits. SS learn the adjective used to illustrate a certain appearance and learn expressions and sentences used to describe the avatar T reads out loud the words and expressions, and writes them, while pointing to them. (Figures 8-11).	T/WC	Mat. 1	
	4. SS are given a handout with the language used. (Figures 12 and 13).			
R	5. SS are now challenged to describe the physical traits of different avatars according to some images projected by the T. T-first demonstrates with one image: "Ela é alta e magra. Tem cabelo claro	T/WC	Mat. 2	1'
S	…	T/WC	Mat. 3	15'
(L)	6. SS are asked to wear some clothes. Each S tries a different item and the teacher names the item and writes it at the same time on the chat bar. Then SS retrieves a notebook with the vocabulary about clothes.			
L/R	7. T names his clothes: "Eu tenho umas calças pretas. Calço sapatos e tenho uma camisola com um capuz"	T/WC	Mat. 4	15'
L	8. SS described what they are wearing.	T/WC		1'
S		T/WC		10'

LESSON PLAN 2

School: University of Porto **Teacher:** Ricardo Cruz and Ricardo Fernandes **Date:**	**Class:** Focus Group – Erasmus Students **Level:** Beginner / Intermediate **Lesson no. 2**
Summary: Homes and buildings. Vocabulary and structures: *casas e edifícios. Partes de uma casa e as divisões da casa.*	**Teacher's Purposes:** - To develop Ss' vocabulary and language structures. - To provide Ss with new vocabulary and to lead Ss to use Portuguese in a communicative way.
Assumptions: Ss are computer knowledgeable.	**Objectives:** By the end of this lesson Ss will have: Cognitive - identified the main topic of the texts; - selected specific information from a text; - acquired new vocabulary related to the topic; - demonstrated their understanding of the text by: - describing homes and buildings; - describing parts of a house; - describing a flat or a house. - developed their speaking skills by participating actively in a discussion. Affective - Participated willingly in the tasks. - Interacted with other Ss. - Showed enthusiasm for the tasks.
Anticipated Problems: Some Ss might find some difficulties in understanding some vocabulary. Some Ss may lack some of the vocabulary necessary to engage in a discussion about the topic. Some technical problems may occur during sign-up procedures and during in-word navigation.	

CONTENTS

Topic / Context: Describing people.	Aids: computers; posters; houses; virtual projector; handouts.

Language Work:
- vocabulary related to the topic:
casa;
prédio;
apartamento;
moradia;
vivenda;
viver;
morar;
elevador;
escadas;
escadaria;
lanço de escadas;
subir; descer;
rés-do-chão;
terceiro andar;
varanda;
vista;
janela;
porta;
telhado;
terraço;
chaminé;
canteiro;
sala de estar;
sala de jantar;
hall;
divisão;
cozinha;
quarto;
quarto de banho / casa de banho;
escritório;
- new or revised grammar items:
Mode and tense: *presente do indicativo* with stative aspectual value.
	Strategies / Activities:
	Introducing the topic and motivating Ss:
	Activating Ss' knowledge and anticipating the content of the text
	    - change avatars' physical traits and clothes.
	Reading comprehension
	    - watching images about physical appearance and types of clothes;
	    - using different clothes and learn their names;
	Speaking / Writing
	    - describing physical appearance and clothes used.

Evaluation / Assessment: Informal and direct evaluation of Ss' performance.	

LESSON PLAN 3

School: University of Porto **Teacher:** Ricardo Cruz and Ricardo Fernandes **Date:**	**Class:** Focus Group – Erasmus Students **Level:** Beginner / Intermediate **Lesson no. 3**
Summary: Landscapes and tourism. Vocabulary and structures: *descrição de uma paisagem. Turismo. No hotel.*	**Teacher's Purposes:** - To develop Ss' vocabulary and language structures. - To provide Ss with new vocabulary and to lead Ss to use Portuguese in a communicative way.
Assumptions: Ss are computer knowledgeable. **Anticipated Problems:** Some Ss might find some difficulties in understanding some vocabulary. Some Ss may lack some of the vocabulary necessary to engage in a discussion about the topic. Some technical problems may occur during sign-up procedures and during in-word navigation.	**Objectives:** By the end of this lesson Ss will have: <u>Cognitive</u> - identified the main topic of the texts; - acquired new vocabulary related to the topic; - applied their understanding of the texts by: - describing a landscape; - role-playing a hotel check-in; - developed their speaking skills by participating actively in a discussion. <u>Affective</u> - Participated willingly in the tasks. - Interacted with other Ss. - Showed enthusiasm for the tasks.

CONTENTS

Topic / Context: Describing people.	Aids: computers; posters; houses; virtual projector; handouts.

Language Work:
- vocabulary related to the topic:
rua;
cidade;
trânsito;
prédios;
pessoas;
ruído;
lojas;
movimento;
trânsito;
stresse;
parque;
árvores;
pedras;
bom tempo;
tempo ameno;
descanço;
ambiente tranquilo;
flores;
paisagem;
pássaros;
passeios;
quarto single
quarto duplo
pensão completa
meia pensão
reserva
fazer uma reserva
fazer o check-in na recepção
recepcionista
- new or revised grammar items:
Mode and tense: *presente do indicativo* with stative aspectual value.
	Strategies / Activities:
	Introducing the topic and motivating Ss:
	Activating Ss' knowledge and anticipating the content of the text
	    - change avatars' physical traits and clothes.
	Reading comprehension
	    - watching images about physical appearance and types of clothes;
	    - using different clothes and learn their names;
	Speaking / Writing
	    - describing physical appearance and clothes used.

Evaluation / Assessment: Informal and direct evaluation of Ss' performance.	

Chapter 26
Teaching Foreign Languages in a Virtual World:
Lesson Plans

Regina Kaplan-Rakowski
Southern Illinois University, USA

ABSTRACT

The author uses her teaching experience, gained both in the real world and in virtual worlds, to convey several potential foreign language activities that could be conducted in a virtual environment. The activities are presented in the form of lesson plans, which teachers should find useful for the preparation of their virtual lessons. The lesson plans follow the conventional format that is used in the USA, however, the lessons themselves are hardly conventional. They take advantage of several affordances of virtual worlds and present activities that are difficult, or even impossible, in a traditional classroom (e.g., traveling in time or traveling in space). Teachers are encouraged to use the lessons as examples of possible activities, which they can modify according to their experience, their preferences and their students' needs.

INTRODUCTION

This chapter provides educators with several foreign language activities that have been developed, tested, and refined specifically for use in a virtual environment. The lesson plans are accompanied with useful hints and practical guidelines for educators for whom teaching in a virtual world is new. The hints and the guidelines are of an applied nature; however, they are written in accordance with cognitive information processing and social cognitive theories, as well as the constructivist epistemology.

DOI: 10.4018/978-1-60960-545-2.ch026

The activities are intended as starting points, which instructors may modify and customize as needed. These needs depend, first of all, on the characteristics of students in the class (their age, background, interests, language level, purpose of study, and preferences). Second, they depend on whether classes are conducted strictly as distance learning, or possibly as hybrid learning, or whether the virtual environment is used as a tool to enhance a traditional classroom (where all the students and the teacher are present in the same real-world room but they all interact in the virtual world). The material should be generalizable to most languages taught at the high-school or undergraduate level, although non-Latin scripts may require software adjustments to enable typing and display on some computers.

It is assumed that before these activities are conducted, the students already have their avatars created and are familiar with basics of *Second Life* (or an alternative virtual environment with similar features). These basics include avatar navigation (moving around, walking, running, flying, sitting down, standing up, etc.) and communication tools management (local chat, instant messenger, voice chat, and logging functions). Further, it would be useful if the students have some basic building skills (making boxes or other shapes, putting textures on those shapes, changing the color of the shapes, and manipulating the shapes).

The lesson plans in this chapter are called: "Time Machine", "Color-Coded Galleries", "Simon Says", "Going to a Restaurant", "Tour Guide", and "Describe Your Creation". Each of these activities takes advantage of several unique features of virtual environments. These features include flexibility regarding geography, time, and physical movement, which is restricted in traditional classrooms. Further, several activities take advantage of various interactivity possibilities, such as student-teacher interactivity, student-student interactivity, and student-content interactivity.

Using virtual environments is increasingly popular for practicing foreign languages. It is not surprising because virtual worlds provide access to native speakers "within a click". Moreover, the meaningfulness of the interactions and the conversations with interlocutors is enhanced thanks to the culturally relevant locations (e.g. talking Italian in a pizzeria), and is further facilitated by useful communication tools (i.e. local chat, voice chat, instant messenger). For ideas of other foreign language activities or/and possibilities of using virtual worlds for language learning, see, for example, Canfield et al., 2009; Cooke-Plagwitz, 2008; Kaplan-Rakowski, 2010a; Kaplan-Rakowski, 2010b; Kaplan-Rakowski & Mizza, 2010; Molka-Danielsen & Deutschmann, 2009; Sadler, 2009; Silva & Larsen, 2010.

Connections with the culture of the target language are especially important for language learning. Therefore several of the activities in this chapter stress the ability of virtual worlds to convey historical or cultural settings that would be difficult to portray in a traditional classroom. These virtual settings may have educational value beyond foreign language instruction, and could be used as well for lessons on geography, cultural studies, anthropology, art, or history.

The lesson plans follow the conventional format used by many teachers in the USA. The plans include an introduction, warm-up, pre-assessment, input, guided practice, independent practice, closure, and assessment based on objectives. Where appropriate, some of these components are purposely omitted, depending on the characteristics of the lesson. The components of each lesson plan also include its title, topic, expected level of the target audience, general description of the lesson plan, lesson objectives, required materials, and estimated time required. Further, at the end of each lesson plan there is a section with additional comments, where the author provides supplemental material, suggestions, and possible modifications to the plan.

LESSON PLANS

Lesson Plan #1

Title: Time Machine

Topic: Historical figures from the culture of the target language

Level: False beginners (then it may be done in the students' native language), advanced (then it may be done in the target language)

Description:

This set of activities provides a unique way to have students not only find out about historical figures from the culture of the language they are learning, but also gives them a chance to identify with the figures. Further, in *Second Life*, there is the possibility for an encounter with historical figures that lived in different times in history.

Objectives: By the end of the lesson, the students should be able to:

• identify several famous figures from the culture of the language they are learning

• situate several famous figures in time and historical context

• identify typical appearance/clothing characteristics of those figures

• list basic achievements of the figures (especially what they became famous for)

Required Virtual Materials:

• virtual clothing of different kinds, especially clothing that would be appropriate to a specific point in history

• a virtual "conference" room for the World Convention

• virtual furniture for the conference room (a big table and chairs, other furniture is optional)

• ambient music (optional)

Estimated Time:

A unit of 3 lessons, 50 min each (lesson 1 – search; lesson 2 – appearance, clothing, and preparing presentations; lesson 3 – the World Convention)

Introduction:

The teacher meets the students as an avatar dressed like Napoleon (if it is a French class, that is. If it is a different language class, then the teacher's avatar should be a representative of the culture of the target language. Please see some suggestions for famous people in different cultures in "additional comments" section). Then the teacher says s/he would like to invite the other historical figures for a World Convention in the avatar's (Napoleon's) mansion.

Warm-Up:

(in the introduction)

Pre-Assessment:

The teacher (Napoleon) asks the students to brainstorm and share with the rest of the class what historical figures (related to the culture of the language they are learning) they have heard of and what they have heard about them.

Input:

(The students create input on their own by searching information themselves. The steps that follow are described in the next section of the lesson plan.)

Independent Practice:

The teacher sends the students a note card with a list of suggestions of historical figures from the culture of the language that they are learning. That list can be the suggestions provided in the "additional comments" section. Alternatively, that list can be enriched with the suggestions that the students made in the pre-assessment brainstorm. Then, the students choose who they want to be. Finally, using the in-world browser or just a regular browser, the students search for information on their chosen figure, focusing on characteristics related to features of both appearance and personality.

[this is where lesson 1 of the unit ends]

Introduction:

The teacher asks the students about how the searches on their historical figures went. S/he then informs the students that they will be customizing their avatars according to the information they have found. The students are also told that the last 20 minutes of the class they will spend on preparing presentations of themselves (i.e. of their chosen figures).

Independent Practice:

The students rely on the information they have found and they change their existing avatars to the historical figure they have chosen to be. For example, if it is a French class and somebody chooses to be Napoleon, we would expect the avatar to be rather short and with the characteristic hat and uniform.

Once all the students look like their chosen figures, they are to explore the way those figures acted, as far as their character is concerned. The features of the character should be displayed by the avatar's attitude, along with the way they talk and interact with the other avatars. For example, again, if somebody is Napoleon, his/her avatar should have the characteristic abrupt motions, narcissistic and domineering behavior, and so forth.

Dependent Practice:

With the help of the teacher, the students prepare a presentation of their historical figure. The students can write their presentations up, or they can jot down the main themes they want to include in their presentation. The teacher makes sure that the students know that in their presentation they need to include: the name of the historical figure, the time period in which s/he lived, and major achievements which the person is famous for.

[this is where lesson 2 of the unit ends]

Introduction:

The teacher invites all the students to the virtual World Convention Center furnished with a table and chairs for all the participants.

Closure:

As the closure for the whole unit, each student (one by one), presents himself/herself (i.e. his/her historical figure). Each student tells the name of the historical figure they are acting, the time period in which s/he lived, and major achievements which the figure is famous for.

Assessment Based on Objectives:

During the presentation, each of the students fill out a form with the information they learn during the presentation. For example:

Name:
Time period:
Major achievements:
Appearance:
Personal characteristics:

Additional Comments:

- If the students are beginners, this class should be done in their native language because the issues may be too complex for beginners to express in the target language.
- This activity is particularly powerful because in real life, it is impossible to have a

meeting/ a convention with most historical figures.

- The whole unit can be expanded to a larger project where students would create whole settings relating to their historical figure, including décor, music, etc., of the time period associated with their historical figure.
- The teacher either asks the students who they want to be, or the teacher prepares in advance a pool of figures that are important for the specific culture. Some suggestions of famous historical people: Italian (da Vinci, Michelangelo, Dante, Galileo Galilei, Garibaldi, Fellini); French (Napoleon, Asterix, Piaf, D'Arc, Dumas, Camus, Monet, Renoir, Debussy); German (Beethoven, Mozart, Nietzsche, Bismarck, Goethe, Hitler); Spanish (Dalí, Cervantes, Gaudi, El Cid, Picasso, Franco); Polish (Chopin, Copernicus, Sklodowska-Curie, John Paul II, Casimir the Great, Mieszko I).

Lesson Plan #2

Title: Color-Coded Galleries
Topic: Grammatical gender, Color-coding approach
Level: Beginners, false-beginners, intermediate

Description:

This activity aims to provide the students with a way to remember the grammatical gender of nouns. The students will do so by building their own vocabulary representations, color-coding them, and creating their own galleries where the word representations will be displayed.

The concept of grammatical gender is hard to grasp by students whose native language does not have such a phenomenon. For example, English speakers struggle to remember that in German, a lamp is feminine (*die Lampe*), a table is masculine (*der Tisch*), but a sofa is neuter (*das Sofa*). Since intuition of which article to use often fails, it is useful to guide the mind with mnemonic cues. In this activity, students use the color-coding of nouns with conventional color associations (feminine objects are colored in pink, masculine objects are colored in blue, and neuter objects are colored in green).

Objectives: By the end of the lesson, the students should be able to:

- create a list of nouns, dividing them into gender groups
- create color-coded boxes and apply to them corresponding word representations (textures)
- distinguish the grammatical gender of vocabulary items
- type the article associated with the grammatical gender of the appropriate noun

Required Virtual Materials:

- Two slide shows (conducted in the virtual space) of pictures of the vocabulary words. Both of the slide shows include the same vocabulary. However, the first one is used for the pre- assessment, while the second one is used for the post-assessment. Other differences are that the second slide show will have the order of pictures altered and they are shown for less time
- note cards with a list of vocabulary to be practiced (the amount of words should be determined by the teacher, who will need to judge the students' level and their learning aptitude)
- virtual "gallery" rooms for students (this could be any rooms with enough space to display the students' artifacts and for visitors to view them)
- images (textures) of the vocabulary from the list (packaged in a box and left in the "galleries")

- a pre-prepared teacher's gallery serving as an example for students to rely on
- one microphone for the presenting group
- headphones for all the students

Estimated Time: 50 minutes

Introduction:

The teacher reads (or writes) a quote: *"In German, a young lady has no sex, while a turnip has."* And asks the students whether they are familiar with this quotation. Then s/he informs the students that it was Mark Twain (1880) who once wrote it, complaining about the difficulty of that language, especially in relation to grammatical gender of German nouns. The teacher then tells the students that during the class the students will try to painlessly master grammatical gender of several nouns.

Warm-Up:

The teacher shows a short slideshow with pictures of the vocabulary items that the class has previously covered. Students are shown each slide for several seconds (the length depends on the difficulty of the words and the degree of familiarity of the vocabulary to the students – the more difficult and the less familiar the vocabulary is, the longer each slide should be displayed) and during that time the students, using instant messenger to address the instructor, need to type the article that goes with the word that the slide represents. For example, if this is a German class and the slide displays "a table", the students will have to type "der" (since it is "der Tisch", a masculine noun).

Pre-Assessment:

(The above-described warm-up activity serves as a pre-assessment. It allows the teacher to immediately see how much the students already know).

Input:

The teacher invites the class to her/his gallery. The gallery contains already prepared boxes with textures representing several selected words from the vocabulary list to be practiced that lesson. Each of the boxes is carefully color-coded according to its grammatical gender. The teacher demonstrates each box in the gallery by pointing to it and pronouncing it, making sure that the articles are made clear. Then the teacher briefly reminds the students how to create a box, how to put texture on it and how to color it. Finally, the teacher announces that the students will create their own galleries with color-coded nouns and that they will demonstrate them to their peers.

Guided Practice:

Students form groups of 2-3 students (this could be done individually, as well). Then they are assigned to their locations ("galleries"). Each location is previously furnished with boxes containing all images (textures) representing vocabulary items that the class is already familiar with.

The teacher sends the students note cards with the vocabulary list. Then, with the teacher's supervision the students sort the nouns into separate gender categories - feminine, masculine, and neuter (if applicable).

Independent Practice:

Having sorted the nouns from the list according to their grammatical gender, the students are asked to furnish their galleries with blocks and apply images (textures) representing vocabulary on those blocks. The main focus then is for students to proceed with the process of color-coding. That is, the students change the colors of boxes (to blue, pink, or green) according to the grammatical gender of the word representations. For instance, the block with "der Tisch" (the table) will be colored in blue since "der Tisch" is a masculine noun.

Closure:

As the wrap-up of the class, showcasing of the galleries takes place. Each group invites the rest of the class to teleport to their gallery. The group then presents each color-coded and textured box by pointing to it and by clearly saying how the word is pronounced. The students need to make sure that the article of the item is clearly heard.

Assessment Based on Objectives:

The teacher displays the same, short slideshow with pictures of the vocabulary items that the class had previously covered and has practiced during the lesson. However, this time the teacher could change the order with which the words are displayed. Moreover, the teacher could shorten the amount of time with which the students are shown each slide. For example, 5-8 seconds for each slide should be enough to time for the students to type the article that goes with the word that the slide represents. This informal "post-test" gives an opportunity to see whether the activity of sorting and creating color-coded nouns improved memory of the grammatical gender of the nouns.

Extensions (For a Homework Assignment, for Example):

Once the teacher is sure that the students are able to handle creating color-coded galleries on their own, the teacher can assign many more items for students to create outside the class.

Additional Comments:

- This activity suggested using images (textures) applied on shapes to represent vocabulary. The reason for using images (textures) is that this is the easiest and the least time consuming method of providing visual representations of words in *Second Life*. However, using 3D representations

of the words could be more powerful and it is suggested that the teachers use those, rather than 2D representations, as long as they have them easily available.

- The students should already have some basic building skills for this activity. For example, they need to know how to create a box and color it; then they need to be able to know how to put a texture on the box. Further, they need to know how to manipulate (move) the box.

Lesson Plan #3

Title: "Simon Says"
Topic: Imperative mode
Level: Beginners, false-beginners

Description:

This activity provides practice for understanding and producing phrases in the imperative mode (i.e. forming commands) in a context of the game known as "Simon Says". While in English the imperative mode is fairly straight-forward, Romance languages (especially Spanish) take rather difficult and non-intuitive forms of the imperative mode that change according to the grammatical number and degree of formality. The flexibility of *Second Life* allows for the performance of numerous actions that can be displayed without inhibition and without physical limitations that are usually present in traditional classroom-based settings.

Objectives: By the end of the lesson, the students should be able to:

- recognize the meaning and form of several command verbs in the target language
- perform the given commands
- make commands by using appropriate imperative mode forms of verbs

Required Materials:

- Animations for the verbs: The amount of the items should be determined according to the students' level. Also, this may depend on the language. If it is Spanish, with its rather complicated imperative construction, then the amount of verbs must be rather small so that cognitive overload would not take place. However, if the language is French, where imperative forms are fairly uncomplicated, then the teacher can allow herself to practice many more verbs.

Estimated Time: 50 min

Introduction:

The teacher informs the students that they will be practicing commands whose forms they learned during the previous lesson. As a refresher on how the command forms are made, the teacher asks the students what they remember about making commands. With the teacher's help, the students restate the rules.

Pre-Assessment:

The teacher sends a note card to students with a list of phrases in the imperative case (see an example in "additional comments" section). Since the imperative case has already been introduced in the previous lesson, the students should be familiar with the phrases but at this point they still need to have some practice with them. For the purpose of the pre-assessment, the students are asked to go through the list of imperative phrases and determine how many phrases they understand and how many phrases they still do not understand.

Input:

(the input has already been given prior to this activity)

During this activity all the students are at the same spot and they are supposed to be doing the same thing (following the commands). Therefore, it is relatively easy to determine whether the objective of being able to follow the orders has been met, or not. The student is instantly aware if s/he is correct, and so is the teacher. (If the teacher notices particular students not being able to follow commands, the teacher should make a special notice of that and consider remedial treatment after the lesson).

Guided Practice:

The teacher asks the students to line up and tells them they are going to play "Simon Says". Then s/he explains the rules of the game: the leader (Simon) tells a command (the commands that are to be practiced are the same ones that the students had been given in the pre-assessment) and the rest of the students need to perform what Simon orders them to do. The students that fail to perform the ordered action drop out of the game and become observers until the next round.

The teacher lets the students briefly (2-3 min) practice animating their avatars (even though they should already be familiar with doing this), then the game begins.

The last student who does not drop out wins. For the award s/he receives $10 Linden and becomes the leader. Then, again, the winner of the next round becomes the next leader, and so forth.

Independent Practice:

(The opportunities of independent practice could be given after the completion of this activity)

Closure:

The students are asked to look again at the command list that the teacher sent to them at the beginning of the lesson. They are asked to self-assess again how many of the commands they think they know and how many they think they still do not know.

Additional Comments:

- An example of a command list: Sit down! Stand up! Turn around! Jump! Run! Fly! Land! Dive! Wave! Smile! Dance! Lie down! Stop flying!
- It is imperative that all the students learn in advance how to animate their avatars and how to do it quickly.
- As an extension to this activity, the teacher can ask the students to choose many other verbs to animate. In addition, they may be asked to create animations on their own.

Lesson Plan #4

Title: Going to a Restaurant
Topic: vocabulary related to foods, restaurant phrases
Level: intermediate, advanced

Description:

In this activity, the students are situated in a virtual restaurant where they can practice skills related to ordering food, reading menus, and experience the culture of the target language. This activity takes advantage of the relative ease of creating relevant settings in virtual worlds where students can participate in role-playing.

Objectives: By the end of the lesson, the students should be able to:

- display a mastery of food vocabulary

- appropriately use vocabulary related to food
- read menus
- order food in a restaurant
- express appropriate restaurant behavior

Required Virtual Materials:

- slideshow conducted in the virtual world containing pictures of foods learned in a previous lesson
- a virtual building resembling a restaurant (for freebies in *Second Life*, check, for example Newbie World - Trifolii (138,25,25), YadNis Junkyard - Leda (210,28,54))
- virtual tables with a minimum of two chairs
- virtual menus (a flat prim with a texture of a menu in the target language)
- virtual candles and ambient music (optional)
- real-world microphones and real-world headphones for all the students (optional – this depends whether the focus of the class is practicing speaking skills, or writing skills)

Estimated Time: 50 minutes

Introduction:

The teacher informs the students that they will be going to a restaurant but before they go, they will review food vocabulary that they had been introduced to in the previous class. S/he then shows the students a slideshow with the pictures of food (for example, bread, cheese, tomatoes, potatoes, rice, beans) and asks the students to type the name of the food they see. The students type the words in the instant messenger to the teacher's avatar (in this way the teacher has access to the students' performance, which will further facilitate the feedback process).

Warm-Up:

The teacher asks the students if they like going out to eat. S/he then asks what they like to eat. Next, the teacher asks what the students know about typical foods from the country/countries where their target language is spoken.

Pre-Assessment:

(the slideshow in the introduction serves as a pre-assessment)

Input:

(this lesson aims at practice of the input that has been previously obtained)

Guided Practice:

The students are divided into three groups: group A, group B, and waiters/waitresses. Then one student from group A is assigned to one student from group B. Next, that pair is assigned to one waiter/waitress (there is one waiter/waitress per two students). The teacher reminds the students that all the conversations are to take place in the target language. The conversations are to be written using instant messenger (addressing the partner, or both the partner and the waiter/waitress when appropriate). Here is a list of further procedures (the teacher may want to send/print the list of the procedures to the students; in this way, the pairs/groups can work time-independently from each other):

- Student A sends a message to Student B asking Student B to go out to eat (all the conversations can either take place in the instant messenger, or via voice chat).
- Student B agrees and suggests meeting at the "Bon Appetite" restaurant.

- In the meantime, the waiters/waitresses need to dress up in appropriate waiter's clothes (provided by the teacher).
- Pairs of students A and B teleport to the front of the restaurant. The waiters/waitresses teleport to the restaurant too and they attach menus to their hands (the menus are provided by the teacher).
- As in real life, the waiters/waitresses approach their guests, take them to the table, show them the menu, and ask what they wish to order.
- The guests (student A and B) discuss the menu in pairs. Alternatively, they ask the waiter/waitress for recommendations.
- Students A and B order food. The waiter/waitress brings the food and the students "eat" it.
- At the end, the students A and B ask for the check. The waiter/waitress brings it to them.
- Students A and B thank each other and say 'good-bye'.

Independent Practice:

Since all the conversations that are produced by the students are saved in their conversation logs, after the lesson is over, the students send the logs via email to the teacher. The teacher then is able to access the conversations and provide feedback to the students.

Closure:

In order to make sure that the objectives of the class have been met, the students are asked to briefly report to the class about their time in the restaurant and about what they have "consumed".

Assessment Based on Objectives:

Even though the teacher guides the students during the class and is able to monitor their work and progress, it is impossible for the teacher to make sure how well all the students are producing the language until the teacher goes through the dialogues after the class.

Additional Comments:

*   As a connection to the cultural component of the target language, it would be appropriate to provide restaurant décor relating to the culture of the target language. For example, if it is an Italian class, maybe a typical pizzeria would be best. A French class may go to a bistro bar. A Japanese class may go to a sushi bar with low tables and no chairs.
*   If this class is not completely at distance and the students are actually present in a real classroom/lab during the virtual world session, it would be nice for the teacher to bring some snacks. It can be a torturing experience to talk about food for the whole class without being able to actually eat something.

Lesson Plan #5

Title: Tour Guide
Topic: Descriptive writing and descriptive narration
Level: Intermediate, advanced

Description:

The purpose of this activity is to provide students with culturally relevant settings in order to increase the meaningfulness of their descriptive writing. Normally, when students are asked to write a descriptive composition, they need to face geographical limitations and are usually told to "imagine you are in Berlin and then describe the Berlin Wall". SL does not have such a limitation so students can virtually be taken to the place

that the teacher wants them to describe, without forcing them to imagine everything.

Objectives: By the end of the unit, the students should be able to:

*   write a description of a culturally relevant setting from the perspective of a guidebook, using 300-500 words.
*   present orally the same culturally relevant setting from the perspective of a tour guide in 10 minutes (this may vary, depending on the level of the students, on how much time the teacher can allocate for this activity, and on how many students there are in class).

Required Virtual Materials:

*   virtual culturally relevant settings (see "additional comments" for suggestions)
*   a real-world microphone and headphones for each student
*   relevant virtual attire provided by the teacher (optional)

Estimated Time:

A unit of three lessons (50 minutes each): Lesson 1 - descriptive writing practice; Lesson 2 – descriptive narration practice; Lesson 3 – showcase

Introduction:

The teacher tells the students that for the next three lessons they will be working on a contribution to a guide book that the class will write collectively. For this purpose, each student will choose a famous location in the country where the target language is spoken. Then they will write the description of that place in the target language with as much detail as possible. Finally, they will present the place to the rest of the class, acting as a tour guide of the site.

Warm-Up:

The teacher asks the students whether they had a chance to visit various sites in the country of the target language. Then s/he asks what these places were and what they were like.

Pre-Assessment:

(included in warm-up)

Input:

Even though prior to this lesson the students should have already been instructed on how to handle descriptive writing, the teacher provides the students with a quick review of this genre of writing. Next, in order to give an example of how the students will need to present their work, the teacher takes the students to her/his chosen site and she sends them a note card with a written description of that site, prepared in advance. The students read the description on their own while being present at the site.

Finally, the teacher orally presents the site to the students. The teacher may choose either to read a pre-prepared written description, or can say it out with her own words.

Guided Practice:

The students choose the places they want to describe and they teleport to the place (see suggestions in the "additional comments" section). Then each student is to describe that place in detail. The descriptions should rather rely on what the places are like visually. No less than 300 words and no more than 500 words can be used in the description. The students are allowed to use dictionaries. They are also allowed to seek help from the teacher.

The students continue working on their descriptions until the end of the class.

[That is where lesson 1 of the unit ends]

Independent Practice:

The students that have been able to complete their writing assignment while still in class send their completed descriptions to the teacher for feedback. The students that have not been able to complete their writing assignment during the class finish their descriptions at home and then send them to the teacher for feedback. However, it is necessary that during the writing process, they need to be in the setting of SL. All the students should receive feedback and all the corrections should be made before the next lesson starts.

[That is where lesson 2 of the unit starts]

Introduction:

The teacher thanks the students for their site descriptions. S/he then gives the students several minutes for questions, if any. Next, s/he reminds the students that during this lesson they will work on their oral presentations of the descriptions they have written.

Guided Practice:

For this, again, the students are to teleport to their sites. This time the students need to make sure they know how to pronounce correctly the words they have written in their descriptions. They are allowed to use online dictionaries (preferably accessed though the SL browser) to verify the pronunciation of the words. They are also allowed to ask the teacher for help.

Independent Practice:

The students have the remaining time of the class available for practicing giving a tour of their chosen sight. Also, since the students will act as guides during the next class, they are encouraged to prepare their relevant tour-guide attire (provided by the teacher). That may include typical tour-guide clothing, a microphone, a little flag, on so on.

[That is where lesson 3 of the unit starts]

Closure:

For closure of the two previous lessons, a showcase begins. The first tour guide (i.e. the first student) welcomes the visitors (i.e. the remaining students) and s/he sends them the URL of the location to be described. When all the students have teleported there, the tour guide starts his description of the site.

When this finishes, the next tour guide welcomes the visitors, sends them the URL to the new location, and describes the site to them. This goes on until every student (tour-guide) has described his locations to the visitors.

During each of the tours, the students are encouraged to take notes, take screenshots, or even record the tours using Snapz Pro X, or other software for video capture.

Assessment Based on Objectives:

The written descriptions (both, the version before the teacher's feedback and the version after the feedback) become a part of the students' digital portfolio.

The oral descriptions may be recorded as well and assessed by the teacher. However, an easier and less consuming option could be to ask the students to fill out a short survey. For example:

Site name:_____

Tour guide name: _____

What were the main highlights of this site?

_____

How would you rate this presentation in the scale from 1 to 5 (1 being poor, 5 being excellent)

_____

Additional Comments:

- For this descriptive writing activity, students can use either SL instant messenger (by typing to the teacher's avatar, or typing to their alternative avatars – in this

manner all the writing can be logged). Alternatively, they can use, for example, *Google docs* that they can access through the browser in SL. For the purpose of this particular activity, we discourage using a word processor, such as *Microsoft Word* where typically the whole screen is taken by the document. We want the students to "be there" and have all the visuals available in the same place they have their writing document open.

- This unit, depending on the main focus of the class, may be extended to many more units – even embracing the whole semester of the class. Obviously, instead of this project being done individually, it can be done collaboratively.

- Several suggestions for virtual sites to describe: French (a Bordeaux winery, the Eiffel Tower, Versailles); Italian (Tower of Pisa, the Coliseum, Vatican City, Venice); Chinese (the Forbidden City, Tiananmen Square, the Great Wall). The locations of many of these suggestions are available in *Second Life*. However, since the URLs will likely change by the time the readers will have this chapter available, the author opts to leave the URLs out. The teachers then will need to search for the locations themselves.

Lesson Plan #6

Title: Describe Your Creation
Topic: Information-gap activity
Level: Intermediate, advanced

Description:

The purpose of this information-gap activity is to provide students with opportunities for meaningful exchange of information. Since one student has information that the other student needs but does not have, there exists the motivation for an understandable exchange of information. In this activity, students use the building tools of *Second Life* to create objects that may be difficult, or even impossible to construct in the real classroom.

Objectives: By the end of the lesson, the students should be able to:

- build a virtual piece of art and describe it
- replicate the virtual original piece of art described

Required Materials:

- a virtual box filled with ready-made artifacts (optional)
- real-world microphones and headphones for all the students (if the voice chat option is chosen)

Estimated Time: 50 minutes

Introduction:

The teacher informs the students that they will be creating their own pieces of art. Then, they will describe them to their partners in a way that the partners can recreate the original artifacts.

Warm-Up:

All the students and the teacher go to the virtual world. First, the teacher makes sure that each student is in a separate location (or, at least, at locations where they cannot see each other, nor can they see the teacher). Second, without explaining why (just yet), the teacher tells the students to open their building tool and follow her instructions. Then she says (in the target language): "Create 3 white balls. Make the second white ball bigger than the first white ball, and make the third white ball bigger than the second one. Now, create 2 black cylinders. Make the second cylinder smaller than the first one. Join the cylinders, putting the smaller one on the top of the other (this will look

like a hat). Create eight small black balls and two small green balls. Put the two small green balls on the smallest white ball (one close to the other). Put four of the previously created black balls on the second white ball and put the remaining four black balls on the third white ball. Align the black balls vertically. Stack the three white balls on top of each other (the biggest one on the bottom, the medium one in the middle, the smallest one on top). Create a small orange cone. Stick it in the center of the smallest white ball, in-between the previously-placed small green balls.

Finally, the teacher asks the students to teleport where she is and the students display what they have created according to the teacher's description. If they followed the description correctly, the creations will appear to be snowmen.

Guided Practice:

The teacher tells the students that they will be making creations during the class and, as shown in the example (the warm-up), they will have to describe their creations to their classmates. The teacher reminds the students that there are two important rules in this activity: 1) the students cannot see each other; 2) the descriptions of the students' creations need to be made in the target language.

The teacher might make sure that none of the students are in the same location. This is important because, in fact, seeing other students' creations before they are described and replicated will ruin the whole activity.

The students build their own creations and prepare saying (or writing) the descriptions of their creations. They can refer to the teacher in case any help is needed.

Independent Practice:

Students (A and B) are assigned to work in pairs. However, they still need to stay separated from each other. The activity follows by having Student

A describe her creation to Student B. Student B creates a replica based on the description. Then Student B describes her creation for student A. Student A creates a replica based on the description. Finally, Students A and B show each other their replicas. That is when they are able to see how much they are similar and how much they are different.

Closure:

All the students gather at a spot suggested by the teacher. Each pair of students simultaneously shows the original creation (created by Student A) with its replica (created by Student B). Everybody is able to see how similar or how different the replicas are from the originals. Depending on the language level of the students, one can expect to see some replicas looking noticeably different from the originals. This should not discourage the students. On the contrary, those differences can be a humorous and entertaining factor of the activity.

Additional Comments:

- This activity can be conducted orally with the students using voice chat. Alternatively, the students can simply use the instant messenger to convey the descriptions to their partners.

CONCLUSION AND CONSIDERATIONS

Anecdotes are common about teachers who complain that they got excited about teaching in *Second Life* and were eager to use it. Then, however, the classes were a flop. In the same way that a teacher cannot just go to the classroom, open a text book to a random page and start teaching, a teacher cannot just "take a class to *Second Life*" in an unplanned, spontaneous way. To organize a class in a virtual world requires experience and

planning because the difficulties that an instructor encounters are different from those in a traditional classroom. An instructor who attempts to teach in a virtual world without proper planning is likely to encounter unexpected impediments, as well as to miss out on the many technological advantages of a virtual environment.

It is also important to remember that virtual worlds, as in the real world can be full of danger and trouble, as well as excitement and wonders. In addition to the usual technical considerations that are part of any class using computers, common problems in a virtual world are the risk of being "grieved" (emotionally or verbally harassed by a stranger), exposure to sexually explicit material and inappropriate language, or taken advantage of. As in real life, we want to avoid such situations, especially when obliged to be responsible for our students. Therefore, it is essential to take caution before taking students to the unknown.

There are several ways in which we can increase security for students. First, we can purchase our own virtual land, which will restrict uninvited guests. However, this can be costly and it limits the spontaneity and richness of the virtual world. Second, we can use educational sandboxes (e.g. *Edunation*) where avatars can come and learn. This practice diminishes the risk rate of being bothered; however, such areas are available for a limited time only. Third, the least secure but the most advantageous way is for the teacher to first go and explore the location of interest, and only then let the students teleport to that area.

The problems that are encountered in virtual worlds are generally common to the risks in any open and unregulated social environment. However, this openness also provides these worlds with their vitality and potential. Educators are hoping that in the near future the virtual worlds will be safer for our students and students will be able to fully explore and take advantage of the rapidly expanding possibilities that these environments provide for learners. The lessons in this chapter should help educators to avoid the most common difficulties of virtual worlds as they learn to master the development of their own teaching practices in these environments. The plans provide an introduction to the possibilities of technological and pedagogical tools that will continually improve and evolve.

REFERENCES

Canfield, D. W., Kaplan-Rakowski, R., Sadler, R., Volle, L., & Thibeault, T. (2009). *CALL in Second Life: Instructional strategies and activities for language learning in a virtual world*. Tempe, AZ: Presentation at CALICO.

Cooke-Plagwitz, J. (2008). New directions in CALL: An objective introduction to *Second Life*. *CALICO Journal, 25*(3).

Kaplan-Rakowski, R. (2010a). Foreign language instruction in a virtual environment: An examination of potential activities. In Vincenti, G., & Braman, J. (Eds.), *Teaching through multi-user virtual environments: Applying dynamic elements to the modern classroom* (pp. 306–325). Hershey, PA: Information Science Reference.

Kaplan-Rakowski, R. (2010b). *Teaching a foreign language in a virtual world – connecting theory with practice*. Lexington, KY: Presentation at KFLC.

Kaplan-Rakowski, R., & Mizza, D. (2010). *Using a virtual world for writing skills development*. Washington, D.C.: Presentation at MAALLT / SEALLT.

Molka-Danielsen, J., & Deutschmann, M. (Eds.). (2009). *Learning and teaching in the virtual world of Second Life*. Trondheim, Norway: Tapir Academic Press.

Sadler, R. (2009). Can you build this? Virtual construction for language learning in Second Life. In Stone, L., & Wilson-Duff, C. (Eds.), *Task-based III: Expanding the range of tasks with online resources*. International Association for Language Learning Technology.

Silva, K., & Larsen, J. E. (2010). *Designing interactive speaking activities in Second Life*. Amherst, MA: Presentation at CALICO.

Twain, M. (1880). *A tramp abroad*. Des Moines, IA: Library of America.

Compilation of References

A Special Report on Social Networking. (2010). *The Economist, 394*(8667), 1-20.

Abraham, D. C., Johnson, N. A., Junglas, I. A., Loughlin, P. M., & Steel, D. J. (2007). Identity formation, learning styles and trust in virtual worlds. *The Data Base for Advances in Information Systems, 38*(4).

Activeworlds Inc. (2010). *Active Worlds.* Newburyport, MA: Activeworlds Inc. Retrieved May 26, 2010, from http://www.activeworlds.com

Adams, N. B. (2007). Toward a model for knowledge development in a virtual environment: Strategies for student ownership. *International Journal for Social Sciences, 2*(2), 71–77.

Adams, N. B., DeVaney, T. A., & Sawyer, S. G. (2009). Measuring conditions conducive to knowledge development. *The Journal of Technology, Learning and Assessment, 8*(1).

Alavi, M. (1994). Computer-mediated collaborative learning: An empirical evaluation. *Management Information Systems Quarterly, 18*(2), 159–175. doi:10.2307/249763

Aldrich, C. (2005). *Learning by doing.* San Francisco, CA: Pfeiffer.

Aldrich, C. (2009a). *Learning online with games, simulations, and virtual worlds: Strategies for online instruction.* San Francisco, CA: John Wiley and Sons, Inc.

Aldrich, C. (2010). *Simulations, games, and virtual worlds: The unifying view for deployment.* Federal Commission on Virtual Worlds.

Aldrich, C. (2009b). *The complete guide to simulations and serious games: How the most valuable content will be created in the age beyond Guttenberg to Google.* San Francisco, CA: Pfeiffer, a Wiley Imprint.

Alexander, B. (2006). Web 2.0: A new wave of innovation for teaching and learning? *EDUCAUSE Review, 41*(2), 32–44.

Alier, M., Casany, M. J., & Piduillem, J. (2009). Towards mobile learning applications integration with learning management systems. In Goh, T. T. (Ed.), *Multiplatform e-learning systems and technologies: Mobile devices for ubiquitions ICT-based education* (pp. 182–194). Hershey, PA/ New York, NY: Information Science Reference.

Alkedo project video-documentary. (2010). Retrieved June 2010 from http://www.cch.kcl.ac.uk/ teaching/ madct/projects/ alkedo/Alkedo_VideoDocumentary.wmv

Alkedo project website. (2009). Retrieved June 2010 from http://www.cch.kcl.ac.uk/ teaching/madct/projects/ alkedo/

Alkedo project wiki. (2009). Retrieved June 2010 from http://www.cch.kcl.ac.uk/ teaching/madct/projects/ alkedo/wiki/

Allen, I. E., & Seaman, J. (2010). *Learning on demand: Online education in the United States, 2009.* Babson Park, MA: Babson Survey Research Group.

Allen, W. (2009). The hundred most creative people in business in 2009. *Fast Company, 136*, 106–107.

Alley, L. R., & Jansak, K. E. (2001). The ten keys to quality assurance and assessment in online learning. *Journal of Interactive Instruction Development, 13*(3), 3–18.

Ally, M. (2004). Foundations of educational theory for online learning. In Anderson, T., & Elloumi, F. (Eds.), *The theory and practice of online learning*. Athabasca, Canada: Athabasca University.

Andersen, T. F. (2002). *Signs of learning in computer cultures - proposal for a cultural approach to the study of learning and information technology*. Impact.

Anderson, L. W., & Krathwohl, D. R. (Eds.). (2001). *A taxonomy for learning, teaching, and assessing: A revision of Bloom's taxonomy of educational objectives*. New York, NY: Longman.

Anderson, C. (2010). Atoms are the new bits. *Wired*, *18*(2), 58–65.

Andreas, K., Tsiatsos, T., Terzidou, T., & Pomportsis, A. (2010). Fostering collaborative learning in second life: Metaphors and affordances. *Computers & Education*, *55*(2), 603–615. doi:10.1016/j.compedu.2010.02.021

Annetta, L. (2010). The I's have it: A framework for serious educational game design. *Review of General Psychology*, *14*, 105–112. doi:10.1037/a0018985

Anonymous wiki. (2009). *Identity and virtual world avatars Web identity: Exploring identity, privacy, & anonymity online*. Retrieved from http://webidentity.wikidot.com/identity-and-virtual-world-avatars

Anonymous. (2008). Living a second life online. *Newsweek*, *152*(4).

Anonymous. (2009, April 3). Second Life credited with boost to academic ability at Plymouth school. *Plymouth Herald*.

Antonacci, D. M., & Modaress, N. (2008). Envisioning the educational possibilities of user-created virtual worlds. *AACE Journal*, *16*(2), 115–126.

Antonacci, D. M., & Modaress, N. (2005). *Second Life: The educational possibilities of a Massively Multiplayer Virtual World* (MMVW). EDUCAUSE Southwest Regional Conference.

Antonietti, E., Imperio, C., Rasi, C., & Sacco, M. (2001). Virtual reality and hypermedia in learning the use of a turning lathe. *Journal of Computer Assisted Learning*, *17*(2), 142–155. doi:10.1046/j.0266-4909.2001.00167.x

Argawal, R., Sambamurthy, V., & Stair, R. (2000). The evolving relationships between general and specific computer self-efficacy: An empirical assessment. *Information Systems Research*, *11*(4), 418–430. doi:10.1287/isre.11.4.418.11876

Aronson, E., & Bridgeman, D. (1979). Jigsaw groups and the desegregated classroom: In pursuit of common goals. *Personality and Social Psychology Bulletin*, *5*, 438–446. doi:10.1177/014616727900500405

Aronson, E., & Patnoe, S. (1997). *The jigsaw classroom: Building cooperation in the classroom*. New York, NY: Longman.

Ash, K., Dede, C., Loftin, R. B., & Salzman, M. (1999). Using virtual reality technology to convey abstract scientific concepts. In Jacobson, M. J., & Kozma, R. B. (Eds.), *Learning the sciences of the 21st century: Research, design, and implementing advanced technology learning environments*. Hillsdale, NJ: Lawrence Erlbaum.

Asher, J. (1977). *Learning another language through actions: The complete teacher's guidebook*. Los Gatos, CA: Sky Oaks Productions.

Astin, A. W. (1985). Involvement: The cornerstone of excellence. *Change*, *17*(4), 35–39. doi:10.1080/00091383.1985.9940532

Autodesk Media and Entertainment. (2010). *3D Studio Max*. Montreal, Canada: Autodesk Media and Entertainment. Retrieved May 26, 2010, from http://www.autodesk.com/3dsmax

Baker, M. (2007). *China's bid for world domination*. Retrieved from http://news.bbc.co.uk/1/hi/education/7098561.stm

Balkissoon, R., Blossfield, K., Salud, L., Ford, D., & Pugh, C. (2009). Lost in translation: Unfolding medical students' misconceptions of how to perform a clinical digital rectal examination. *American Journal of Surgery*, *197*, 525–532. doi:10.1016/j.amjsurg.2008.11.025

Bamburg, J. (1994). *Raising expectations to improve student learning*. Oak Brook, IL: North Central Regional Educational Laboratory.

Bandura, A. (1977). *Social learning theory*. Englewood Cliffs, NJ: Prentice Hall.

Bandura, A. (1985). *Social foundations of thought and action: A social-cognitive theory.* New York, NY: Prentice Hall.

Bandura, A. (1979). Self-referent mechanisms in social learning theory. *The American Psychologist, 34*(5), 439–441. doi:10.1037/0003-066X.34.5.439.b

Bani, M. (2008). *La computer grafica: Strumento per la ricerca, la didattica e la divulgazione storica.* Unpublished master dissertation, supervisors E. Salvatori, R. Beacham & A. Cisternino, University of Pisa, Italy

Barab, S., Gresalfi, M., & Arici, A. (2009). Why educators should care about games. *Educational Leadership,* 76–80.

Barab, S., Thomas, M., Dodge, T., Carteaux, R., & Tuzun, H. (2005). Making learning fun: Quest Atlantis, a game without guns. *Educational Technology Research and Development, 53*(1), 86–107. doi:10.1007/BF02504859

Barab, S. A., Gresalfi, M. S., & Arici, A. (2009). Transformational play: Why educators should care about games. *Educational Leadership, 67*(1), 76–80.

Barab, S. A., & Roth, W. M. (2006). Curriclum-based ecosystems: Supporting knowing from an ecological perspective. *Educational Researcher, 35*(5), 3–13. doi:10.3102/0013189X035005003

Barab, S. A., Hay, K. E., Barnett, M., & Squire, K. (2001). Constructing virtual worlds: Tracing the historical development of learner practices. *Cognition and Instruction, 19*(1), 47–94. doi:10.1207/S1532690XCI1901_2

Barab, S. A., Zuiker, S., Warren, S., Hickey, D., Ingram-Goble, A., Kwon, E., Kouper, I., & Herring, S. (2007). Situationally embodied curriculum: Relating formalisms and contexts. *Science Education.*

Barbieri, T., & Paolini, P. (2001). Cooperation metaphors for virtual museums. In Bearman, D., & Trant, J. (Eds.), *Proceedings Museums & Web.*

Barbieri, T., & Paolini, P. (2001). Broadcast and online cultural heritage: Reconstructing Leonardo's ideal city – from handwritten codexes to webtalk-II: A 3D collaborative virtual environment system. *Proceedings of the Conference on Virtual Reality, Archeology, and Cultural Heritage,* (pp. 61-66).

Barchetti, U., Bucciero, A., Mainetti, L., & Santo Sabato, S. (2005). *WebTalk04: A declarative approach to generate 3D collaborative environments.* VAST 2005 6th International Symposium on Virtual Reality, Archaeology and Cultural Heritage, 3rd Eurographics Workshop on Graphics and Cultural Heritage, (pp. 55-60).

Barkley, E., Cross, P., & Howell, C. (2004). *Collaborative learning techniques: A handbook for college faculty.* San Francisco, CA: Jossey-Bass.

Barrett, K. A., & Johnson, W. L. (2010). Developing serious games for learning language-in-culture. In Eck, R. A. (Ed.), *Gaming and cognition: Theories and practice from the learning sciences* (pp. 281–311). Hershey, PA: Information Science Reference.

Barrett, J., & Gelfgren, S. (2009). Spacing creation: The HUMlab Second Life project. In Molka-Danielsen, J., & Deutschmann, M. (Eds.), *Learning and teaching in the virtual world of Second Life* (pp. 167–183). Trondheim, Norway: Tapir Academic Press.

Bartle, R. (2004). *Designing virtual worlds.* Indianapolis, IN: New Riders Publishing.

Bates, A. W. (2005). *Technology, e-learning and distance education.* New York, NY: Routlege.

Baudrillard, J. (2001). *Selected writings.* Cambridge, UK: Polity.

Baum, J., Starrett, C., & Voigt, K. (2010). *Methods for collaboration in virtual realms.* The Athens Institute for Education and Research Conference.

Baylor, A., & Ritchie, D. (2002). What factors facilitate teacher skill, teacher morale, and perceived student learning in technology-using classrooms? *Computers & Education, 39,* 395–414. doi:10.1016/S0360-1315(02)00075-1

Bayne, S., & Littleton, F. (2008, February 28). Virtual worlds in education. *The Higher Education Academy Newsletter, 10.*

Beacham, R., Denard, H., & Niccolucci, F. (2006). An introduction to the London charter. *Proceedings of VAST Conference,* (pp. 263-269).

Beard, L., Wilson, K., Morra, D., & Keelan, J. (2009). A survey of health-related activities on Second Life. *Journal of Medical Internet Research, 11*(2), e17. doi:10.2196/jmir.1192

Beatty, K. (2003). *Teaching and researching computer-assisted language learning*. London, UK: Pearson Education Limited.

Becker, K. (2010). Distinctions between games and learning: A review of current literature on games in education. In Eck, R. A. (Ed.), *Gaming and cognition: Theories and practice from the learning sciences* (pp. 22–54). Hershey, PA: Information Science Reference.

Becker, H. J., & Ravitz, J. L. (2001). Computer use by teachers: Are Cuban's predictions correct? *Proceedings of the 2001 Annual Meeting of the American Educational Research Association*.

Becta. (2005). *Developing content for pupil referral units and alternative provision*. Retrieved from http://www.becta.org.uk

Becta. (2006). *Designing digital resources for PRUs and alternative provision*. Retrieved from http//www.becta.org.uk

Becta. (2007). *Harnessing technology review 2007: Progress and impact of technology in education*. Retrieved from http//www.becta.org.uk

Beise, C. M. (2004). IT project managers' perceptions and use of virtual team technologies. *Information Resources Management Journal, 17*(4), 73–88. doi:10.4018/irmj.2004100104

Bekkers, C. (2009). *Teaching & learning in SL: Figuring out some variables*. Retrieved on May 29, 2010, from http://cleobekkers.wordpress.com/2009/01/28/teaching-learning-in-sl-figuring-out-some-variables/

Benford, S., Greenhalgh, C., Rodden, T., & Pycock, J. (2001). Collaborative virtual environments. *Communications of the ACM, 44*(7), 79–85. doi:10.1145/379300.379322

Bennett, J., & Peachey, A. (2007). Mashing the MUVE: A mashup model for collaborative learning in Multi-User Virtual Environments. *Proceedings of the Interactive Computer Aided Learning Conference* (ICL2007).

Benson, A. D. (2003). Assessing participant learning in online environments. *New Directions for Adult and Continuing Education, 100*, 69–78. doi:10.1002/ace.120

Berge, Z. L. (2008). Multi-User Virtual Environments for education and training. A critical review of Second Life. *Educational Technology Magazine, 48*(3), 27–31.

Bers, M. U. (2001). Identity construction environments: Developing personal and moral values through the design of a virtual city. *Journal of the Learning Sciences, 10*(4). doi:10.1207/S15327809JLS1004new_1

Bignell, S., & Parson, V. (2010). *Best practice in virtual worlds teaching*. Retrieved from http://previewpsych.org/BPD2.0.pdf

Blades, M., & Vermylen, S. (2004). Virtual ethics for a new age: The Internet and the ethical lawyer. *Georgetown Journal of Legal Ethics*.

Blizzard Entertainment. (2010). *World of Warcraft*. Irvine, CA: Blizzard Entertainment. Retrieved May 26, 2010, from http://www.worldofwarcraft.com

Bloom, B. S. (1956). *The taxonomy of educational objectives: Classification of educational goals handbook 1: The cognitive domain*. New York, NY: McKay Press.

Bloom, B., & Englehart, M. Furst, E., & Hill, W., & Krathwohl, D. (1956). *Taxonomy of educational objectives: The classification of educational goals. Handbook I: Cognitive domain*. New York, NY, Toronto, Canada: Longmans, Green.

Bodemer, D., & Plötzner, R. (2004). Encouraging the active processing of information during learning with multiple and interactive representations. *Proceedings of the 5th International Workshop of SIG 6 Instructional Design of the European Association for Research on Learning and Instruction (EARLI)*, (pp. 127-138).

Boellstorff, T. (2008). *An anthropologist explores the virtually human: Coming of age in Second Life*. Princeton, NJ: Princeton University Press.

Bogden, R. C., & Biklin, S. K. (1998). *Qualitative research in education: An introduction to theory and practice*. Boston, MA: Allyn & Bacon.

Boland, I. H. (2009a). *Efficacy of the 3D multi-user virtual environment (MUVE) Second Life of learning in cognitive constructivist and social constructivist practices.* (Unpublished dissertation), Capella University.

Boland, I. H. (2009b). Learners' love/hate relationship with 3D worlds. *Learning Solutions*, 10-13.

Bolchini, D., Di Blas, N., Paolini, P., & Poggi, C. (2010). Biological life cycle: A new interpretation for the evolution of ICT applications. *Proceedings of the Educational Design Research Conference: Local Change and Global Impact.*

Bonack, S., Riedl, R., & Tahser, J. (2006). Learning in the zone: A social constructivist framework for distance education in a 3-Dimensional virtual world. *Interactive Learning Environments, 14*(3), 219–232. doi:10.1080/10494820600909157

Bonwell, C., & Eison, J. (1991). *Active learning: Creating excitement in the classroom.* (AEHE-ERIC Higher Education Report No.1). Washington, DC: Jossey-Bass.

Bourke, P. (2008). Evaluating Second Life as a tool for collaborative scientific visualization. *Proceedings of the Computer Games and Allied Technology.*

Bradford, S., & Crowe, N. (2006). Hanging out in Runescape: Identity, work and leisure in the virtual playground. *Children's Geographies, 4*(3).

Braman, J., Vincenti, G., Arboleda, A., & Jinman, A. (2009). Learning computer science fundamentals through virtual environments. *Proceedings of the 3rd International Conference on Online Communities and Social Computing: Held as Part of HCI International 2009,* (pp. 423-431).

Bransford, J., Brown, L., & Cocking, R. C. (2000). *How people learn: Brain, mind, experience, and school.* Washington, DC: National Academy Press.

Briggs, R. O., Nunamaker, J. F., & Sprague, R. (1997). 1001 Unanswered research questions in GSS. *Journal of Management Information Systems, 14*(3), 3–21.

Bronack, S., Cheney, A., Riedl, R., & Tashner, J. (2008b). Designing virtual worlds to facilitate communication: Issues, considerations, and lessons learned. *Technical Communication, 55*(3), 261–269.

Bronack, S., Sanders, R., Cheney, A., Riedl, R., Tashner, J., & Matzen, N. (2008a). Presence pedagogy: Teaching in a 3D virtual immersive world. *International Journal of Teaching and Learning in Higher Education, 20*(1), 59–69.

Bronack, S., Riedl, R., & Tashner, J. (2006). Learning in the zone: A social constructivist framework for distance education in a 3D virtual world. *Interactive Learning Environments, 14*(3), 219–232. doi:10.1080/10494820600909157

Brown, J. S., & Adler, R. P. (2008). Minds on fire: Open education, the long tail and learning 2.0. *EDUCAUSE Review, 43*(1), 16–32.

Brown, J. S., Collins, A., & Duguid, S. (1989). Situated cognition and the culture of learning. *Educational Researcher, 18*(1), 32–42.

Brown, E., Hobbs, M., & Gordon, M. (2008). A virtual world environment for group work. *International Journal of Web-Based Learning and Teaching Technologies, 3,* 1–12. doi:10.4018/jwltt.2008010101

Brown, A. (2009). *A second look at Second Life: Virtual worlds and education.* Paper presented and the annual NECC conference, Washington, D.C.

Bucciero, A., Mainetti, L., & Paolini, P. (2005). Flexible 3D collaborative virtual environment: WebTalk04. *Proceedings of the 11th International Conference on Virtual Systems and Multimedia,* (pp. 669-680).

Burdea, G. C., & Coiffet, P. (2003). *Virtual reality technology* (2nd ed.). Hoboken, NJ: Wiley.

Burden, D. (2008). *Deploying embodied AI into virtual worlds.* BCS SGAI Conference.

Burden, D., Conradi, E., Woodham, L., Poulton, T., Savin-Baden, M., & Kavia, S. (2008). *Creating and assessing a virtual patient player in Second Life.* Researching Learning in Virtual Environments Conference.

Burgess, M. L., Slate, J. R., Rojas-LeBouef, A., & LaPrairie, K. (2010). Teaching and learning in Second Life: Using the community of inquiry (Coi) model to support online instruction with graduate students in instructional technology. *The Internet and Higher Education, 13*(1), 84–88. doi:10.1016/j.iheduc.2009.12.003

Bush, M. D., & Terry, R. M. (Eds.). (1997). *Technology-enhanced language learning*. Lincolnwood, IL: National Textbook Company.

Byrne, C. M. (1996). *Water on tap: The use of virtual reality as an educational tool*. Unpublished PhD thesis, University of Washington, Department of Industrial Engineering.

Cabiria, J. (2008). *A Second Life: Online virtual worlds as therapeutic tools for gay and lesbian people*. (Doctoral dissertation). Fielding Graduate University, Santa Barbara, CA.

Cadlaboration. (2006). *Mission statement*. Retrieved 13 July, 2010, from http://cadlaboration.wikispaces.com / Project+Vision

Caillois, R. (1961). *Man, play and games*. New York, NY: Free Press.

Callaghan, V., Shen, L., Gardner, M., Shen, R., & Wang, M. (2010). A mixed reality approach to hybrid learning in mixed culture environments. In Wang, F. L., Fong, J., & Kwan, R. (Eds.), *Handbook of research on hybrid learning models: Advanced tools, technologies, and applications* (pp. 260–283). Hershey, PA: IGI Global. doi:10.4018/978-1-60566-380-7.ch016

Cameron, D. (2005). The net generation goes to university? *Proceedings of the Journalism Education Association Conference*.

Camtasia. (2008). Retrieved 15 September, 2008, from http://www.techsmith.com/

Canfield, D. W., Kaplan-Rakowski, R., Sadler, R., Volle, L., & Thibeault, T. (2009). *CALL in Second Life: Instructional strategies and activities for language learning in a virtual world*. Tempe, AZ: Presentation at CALICO.

Carlsson, C., & Hagsand, D. (1993). *DIVE - multi-user virtual reality system*. VRAIS '93, IEEE Virtual Reality Annual international Symposium.

Carpenter, S. B. (2009). Virtual worlds as educational experience: Living and learning in interesting times. *Journal of Virtual Worlds Research, 2*(1).

Carr, D., Oliver, M., & Burn, A. (2010). Learning, teaching and ambiguity in virtual worlds. In Peachey, A., Gillen, J., Livingstone, D., & Smith-Robbins, S. (Eds.), *Researching learning in virtual worlds* (pp. 17–30). Lancaster, PA: Springer. doi:10.1007/978-1-84996-047-2_2

Carter, B., & Elseth, D. (2008). The usefulness of Second Life for language learning. In de Cássia Veiga Marriott, R., & Lupion Torres, P. (Eds.), *Handbook of research on e-learning methodologies for language acquisition* (pp. 443–455). Hershey, PA: IGI Global. doi:10.4018/9781599049946.ch027

Carter, B. (n.d.). *Virtual Harlem*. Retrieved on June 14, 2010 from http://www.evl.uic.edu/cavern/harlem

Castronova, E. (2007). *Exodus to the virtual world: How online fun is changing reality*. Hants, UK: Palgrave Macmillan.

Castronova, E. (2010). *Studying beehives, not bees: Virtual worlds policy analysis*. Federal Commission on Virtual Worlds.

Castronova, E. (2005). *Synthetic worlds: The business and culture of online games*. Chicago, IL: University of Chicago Press.

Chandra, S., Theng, Y. L., O'lwin, M., & Shou-Boon, S. F. (2009). *Proposed theoretical framework for virtual world adoption*. SLACTIONS 2009 International Conference: Life, imagination, and work using metaverse platforms.

Chapelle, C. A. (2001). *Computer applications in second language acquisition: Foundations for teaching, testing and research*. Cambridge, UK: Cambridge University Press.

Cheal, C. (2009). Student perceptions of a course taught in Second Life. *Innovate: Journal of Online Education, 5*(5).

Chen, G. (1994). Social desirability as a predictor of argumentativeness and communication apprehension. *Journal of Psychology Interdisciplinary & Applied, 128*(4), 433–439. doi:10.1080/00223980.1994.9712749

Childress, M., & Braswell, R. (2006). Using Massively Multiplayer Online Role - Playing Games for online learning. *Distance Education, 27*(2), 187–196. doi:10.1080/01587910600789522

Childs, M. (2009). Theatron 3 final report. In *Theatron3*. Retrieved June 2010 http://cms.cch.kcl.ac.uk/theatron/fileadmin/templates/main/THEATRON_Final_Report.pdf

Cho, H., Gay, G., Davidson, B., & Ingraffea, A. (2007). Social networks, communication styles, and learning performance in a CSCL community. *Computers & Education, 49*(2), 309–329..doi:10.1016/j.compedu.2005.07.003

Chodos, D., Naeimi, P., & Stroulia, E. (2009). An integrated framework for simulation-based training on video and in a virtual world. *Journal of Virtual Worlds Research, 2*(1).

Chover, M., Belmonter, O., & Remolar, I. (2002). *Web-based virtual environments for teaching*. Eurographics/ACM SIGGRAPH Workshop on Computer Graphics Education.

Ciregia, E. (2009). *Ricostruzione 3D del processo edificativo della Torre di Pisa*. Master Thesis, University of Pisa.

Cities, X. L. (2010). *City Life*. Paris, France: Cities XL. Retrieved May 26, 2010, from http://www2.citiesxl.com

Clark, M. A. (2009). Genome Island: A virtual science environment in Second Life. *Innovate: Journal of Online Education, 5*(6).

Clarke, G., & Callaghan, V. (2007). Ubiquitous computing, informatization, urban structures and density. *Built Environment Journal, 33*(2), 196–212. doi:10.2148/benv.33.2.196

Clarke, J., Dede, C., & Dieterle, E. (2008). Emerging technologies for collaborative, mediated, immersive learning. In Voogt, J., & Knezek, G. (Eds.), *The international handbook of technology in primary and secondary education* (pp. 901–910). New York, NY: Springer-Verlag. doi:10.1007/978-0-387-73315-9_55

Clarke, J., & Dede, C. (2005). *Making learning meaningful: An exploratory study of using multi-user environments (MUVEs) in middle school science*. American Educational Research Association Conference.

Clarke, R. (1999). *A primer in diffusion of innovations theory*. Australian National University. Retrieved from http://www.anu.edu.au/people/ Roger.Clarke/SOS/InnDiff.html

Clendaniel, M. (2007). Get a life. *Good, 7*, 76–81.

Cobb, D., & Fraser, D. (2005). Multimedia learning in virtual reality. In Mayer, R. (Ed.), *The Cambridge handbook of multimedia learning* (pp. 525–548). Cambridge, UK: Cambridge University Press.

Cobb, S., Heaney, R., Corcoran, O., & Henderson-Begg, S. (2009). The learning gains and student perceptions of a Second Life virtual lab. *Bioscience Education, 13*.

Conklin, M. S. (2007). *101 Uses for Second Life in the college classroom*. Elon, NC: Elon University, Department of Computing Sciences. Retrieved May 26, 2010, from http://citeseerx.ist.psu.edu/viewdoc/download?doi=10.1.1.133.9588&rep=rep1&type=pdf

Connolly, T., Boyle, L., & Hainey, T. (2009). Arguing for multilingual motivation in Web 2.0: A games-based learning platform for language learning. *Proceedings from The 3rd European Conference on Games Based Learning*.

Conrad, M., Pike, D., Sant, P., & Nwafor, C. (2009). Teaching large student cohorts in Second Life. *International Conference on Computer Supported Education 2009, 1*, 11-18.

Conradi, E. (2008). *Innovations in online PBL: A virtual world case study*. 13th Ottawa International Conference on Clinical Compliance.

Cooke-Plagwitz, J. (2008). New directions in CALL: An objective introduction to *Second Life. CALICO Journal, 25*(3).

Cotton, B., & Oliver, R. (1994). *The cyberspace lexicon*. London, UK: Phaidon Press, Ltd.

Cowen, K. J., & Tesh, A. S. (2002). Effects of gaming on nursing students' knowledge of pediatric cardiovascular dysfunction. *The Journal of Nursing Education, 41*(11), 507–509.

Craft, A. J. (2007). Sin in cyber-Eden: Understanding the metaphysics and morals of virtual worlds. *Ethics and Information Technology, 9*(3). doi:10.1007/s10676-007-9144-4

Creelman, A., Richardson, D., & Petrakou, A. (2008). *Teaching and learning in Second Life - experience from the Kamimo project*. Online Information Conference, London, UK.

Cross, D., Gresalfi, M. S., & Hudson, R. A. (Manuscript submitted for publication). Building bridges between content and context in mathematics classrooms. *Mathematics Teaching in the Middle School*.

Crosssan, B., Field, J., Gallacher, J., & Merrill, B. (2003). Understanding participation in learning for non-traditional adult learners: Learning careers and the construction of learning identities. *British Journal of Sociology of Education, 24*(1). doi:10.1080/01425690301907

Cuban, L. (1993). Computers meet classroom: Classroom wins. *Teachers College Record, 95*, 185–210.

Culatta, R. (2010*). Instructional Design.*Retrieved from http://www.instructionaldesign.org

Curtis, P., & Nichols, D. (1994). *MUDs grow up: Social virtual reality in the real world* (pp. 193–200). COMPCON.

Dacos, M. (Ed.). (2010). *Manifeste des Digital humanities, proposed by professionals or observers of the digital humanities*. In THATCamp, Paris 18-19 May. Retrieved from http://tcp.hypotheses.org/318

Daft, R., Lengel, R., & Trevino, L. (1987). Message equivocality, media selection, and manager performance implications for Information Systems. *Management Information Systems Quarterly, 11*(3), 355–366. doi:10.2307/248682

Daft, R. L., & Lengel, R. H. (1984). Information richness: A new approach to managerial behavior and organizational design. In Cummings, L. L., & Staw, B. M. (Eds.), *Research in organizational behavior* (pp. 191–233). Homewood, IL: JAI Press.

Dalgarno, B., & Lee, M. J. W. (2010). What are the learning affordances of 3D virtual environments? *British Journal of Educational Technology, 41*(1), 10–32. doi:10.1111/j.1467-8535.2009.01038.x

Danforth, D. R. (2010). Development of an interactive virtual 3-D model of the human testis using the Second Life platform. *International Journal of Virtual and Personal Learning Environments, 1*(2), 46–60. doi:10.4018/jvple.2010040104

David, B. (1993). *Tools for teaching*. San Francisco, CA: Jossey Bass.

Davidson, B. D., Davidson, R., Gay, G., Ingraffea, A., Miller, M., & Nozick, L. … Rath, C. (2002). Collaborative distance design of aerospace structures. *Proceedings of the 32nd ASEE/IEEE Frontiers in Education Conference*, Boston, Massachusetts.

Davis, F. D. (1989). Perceived usefulness, perceived ease of use, and user acceptance of Information Technology. *Management Information Systems Quarterly, 13*(3), 319–340. doi:10.2307/249008

Dawson, G. (2006). *Education committee: Pupil motivation inquiry right track response*. Retrieved from http://www.scottish.parliament.uk/business/committees/education/inquiries/pmi/Right% 20Track.pdf

DCFS. (2005). *Harnessing technology: Transforming learning and children's services*. Retrieved from http://www.dcfs.gov.uk/ publicatiuons/e-strategy

DCSF. (2007). *Trends in further education*. Retrieved from http://www.dcsf.gov.uk/trends /index.cfm?fuseaction=home.s howChart&cid =4&iid=20&chid=77

DCSF. (2009). *The national strategies: The five components of personalised learning*. Retrieved from http://www.standards.dcsf.gov.uk /NationalStrategies

de Freitas, S. (2008). *Serious virtual worlds: A scoping study*. Bristol, UK: Joint Information Systems Committee.

de Freitas, S. (2010). Editorial: Crossing boundaries: Learning and teaching in virtual worlds. *British Journal of Educational Technology, 41*(1), 3–9. doi:10.1111/j.1467-8535.2009.01045.x

De Freitas, S. (2006) *Learning in immersive worlds*. Joint Information Systems Committee (JISC) e-Learning Programme, UK. Retrieved 15 September 2008, from http://www.jisc.ac.uk/media/documents/programmes/elearninginnovation/ gamingreport_v3.pdf

de Jong, T., van Joolingen, W., Scott, D., de Hoog, R., Lapied, L., & Valent, R. (1994). SMISLE: System for Multimedia Integrated Simulation Learning Environments. In de Jong, T., & Sarti, L. (Eds.), *Design and production of multimedia and simulation based learning material* (pp. 133–167). Dordrecht, Netherlands: Kluwer Academic Publishers.

Dede, C. (2007). Reinventing the role of information and communications technologies in education. *Yearbook of the National Society for the Study of Education, 106,* 11–38. doi:10.1111/j.1744-7984.2007.00113.x

Dede, C., Clarke, J., Ketelhut, D., Nelson, B., & Bowman, C. (2005). *Students' motivation and learning of science in a multi-user virtual environment. American Educational Research Association.* AERA.

Dede, C. (2004). *Planning for Neomillennial learning styles: Implications for investments in technology and faculty.* Cambridge, MA: Harvard Graduate School of Education.

Dede, C., Salzman, M., Loftin, R. B., & Ash, K. (1997). *Using virtual reality technology to convey abstract scientific concepts.* Hillsdale, NJ: Lawrence Erlbaum.

Dede, C. (1996). The evolution of constructivists learning environments: Immersion in distributed, virtual worlds. In Wilson, G. B. (Ed.), *Constructivist learning environments: Case studies in instructional design.* Englewood Cliffs, NJ: Educational Technology.

Dede, C. Whitehouse, P., & Brown L'Bahy, T. (2003). Designing and studying learning experiences that use multiple interactive media to bridge distance and time. In C. Vrasidas, & G. V. Glass (Eds.), *Distance education and distributed learning.* London, UK: Eurospan.

Dede, C., Salzman, M., & Loftin, B. (1996). ScienceSpace: Virtual realities for learning complex and abstract scientific concepts. *Proceedings IEEE Virtual Reality Annual International Symposium (VRAIS '96).*

DeLucia, A., Francese, R., Passero, I., & Tortora, G. (2009). Development and evaluation of a virtual campus on Second Life: The case of SecondDMI. *Computers & Education, 52*(1), 220–223. doi:10.1016/j.compedu.2008.08.001

Delwiche, A. (2006). Massively Multiplayer Online Games (MMOs) in the new media classroom. *Journal of Educational Technology & Society, 9*(3), 160–172.

DeMers, M. (2010). Second Life as a surrogate for experiential learning. *International Journal of Virtual and Personal Learning Environments, 1*(2), 17–31.

Demir, K. (2006). Rogers' theory of the diffusion of innovations and online course registration. *Educational Administration: Theory & Practice, 47,* 386–392.

Denard, H. (2005). Visualization and performance documentation editorial. *Didaskalia, 6*(2).

Department of Defense. (2001). *Department of Defense handbook: Development of interactive multimedia instruction (IMI), part 3 of 5 parts.* (MIL-HDBK-29612-3A).

Department of Defense. (2010). *TRADOC revised levels of interactivity.* Retrieved July 1, 2010, from http://www.atsc.army.mil/tadlp/

Deutschmann, M., & Panichi, L. (2009). Instructional design, teacher practice and learner autonomy. In Molka-Danielsen, J., & Deutschmann, M. (Eds.), *Learning and teaching in the virtual world of Second Life* (pp. 27–44). Trondheim, Norway: Tapir Academic Press.

Dewey, J. (1938). *Experience and education.* New York, NY: McMillian.

Di Blas, N., & Poggi, C. (2008). The PoliCultura competition. Introducing media literacy in Italian schools. In Leaning, M. (Ed.), *Issues in information and media literacy* (pp. 93–121). Santa Rosa, CA: Informing Science Press.

Di Blas, N., & Boretti, B. (2009). Interactive storytelling in pre-school: A case-study. *Proceedings of IDC 2009 (Interaction Design and Children),* (pp. 44-51).

Di Blas, N., & Poggi, C. (2008). Can ICT support inclusion? Evidence from multi-user edutainment experiences based on 3D worlds. *Proceedings of the Workshop Marginalized Young People: Inclusion Through ICT, IDC 2008.*

Di Blas, N., Garzotto, F., Paolini, P., & Sabiescu, A. (2009). Digital storytelling as a whole-class learning activity: Lessons from a three-years project. *Proceedings of ICIDS 2009.* (LNCS 5915), (pp. 14-25).

Di Blas, N., Paolini, P., & Sabiescu, A. (2010a). Collective digital storytelling at school as a whole-class interaction. *Proceedings of IDC 2010.* (in print)

Di Blas, N., Paolini, P., & Torrebruno, A. (2010b). Digital storytelling at school: Does the TPCK model explain what's going on? *Proceedings of E-Learn 2010 Conference.*

Dickey, M. (2005). Three-dimensional virtual worlds and distance learning: Two case studies of active worlds as a medium for distance education. *British Journal of Educational Technology, 36*(3), 439–451. doi:10.1111/j.1467-8535.2005.00477.x

Dickey, M. (2005a). Three-dimensional virtual worlds and distance learning: Two case studies of active worlds as a medium for distance education. *British Journal of Educational Technology*, *36*(3), 439–451. doi:10.1111/j.1467-8535.2005.00477.x

Diehl, W. C., & Prins, E. (2008). Unintended outcomes in "Second Life": Intercultural literacy and cultural identity in a virtual world. *Language and Intercultural Communication*, *8*(2), 101–118. doi:10.1080/14708470802139619

Dieterle, E., & Clarke, J. (2005). Multi-user virtual environments for teaching and learning. In Pagani, M. (Ed.), *Encyclopedia of multimedia technology and networking* (2nd ed.). Hershey, PA: Idea Group, Inc.

Digital Humanities Island. (2007). Retrieved June 2010 from http://slurl.com/secondlife/ DigitalHumanities/186/167/28/ ?title=DigitalHumanities%20Island

Dillenbourg, P. (2008). Integrating technologies into educational ecosystems. *Distance Education*, *29*(2), 127–140. doi:10.1080/01587910802154939

Dillenbourg, P. (1999). What do you mean by collaborative learning? In Dillenbourg, P. (Ed.), *Collaborative learning: Cognitive and computational approaches* (pp. 1–19). Bingley, UK: Emerald Group Publishing Limited.

Dircknick-Holmfeld, L. (2002). Designing virtual learning environments based on problem oriented project pedagogy. In Dirckinck-Holmfeld, L., & Fibiger, B. (Eds.), *Learing in virtual environments* (pp. 31–54). Frederiksberg, Denmark: Samfundslitteratur.

Djorgovski, S. G., Hut, P., McMillan, S., Vesperini, E., Knop, R., Farr, W., & Graham, M. J. (2009). Exploring the use of virtual worlds as a scientific research platform: The Meta-Institute for Computational Astrophysics (MICA). *Proceedings of Facets of Virtual Environments (FaVE 2009)*.

DnB NOR. (2008). *DnB NOR*. Retrieved 15 September 2008, from: https://www.dnbnor.com

Dörnyei, Z. (2001). *Motivational strategies in the language classroom*. Cambridge, UK: Cambridge University Press. doi:10.1017/CBO9780511667343

dos Santos, R. P. (2009). Second Life physics: Virtual, real or surreal? *Journal of Virtual Worlds Research*, *2*(1).

Downes, S. (2008). *The reality of virtual learning*. Presented to the Defense Learning Academy, DNDLearn Conference, Cornwall, Ontario, January 30, 2008. Retrieved May 29, 2010, from http://halfanhour.blogspot.com/ 2008/02/reality-of-virtual -learning.html

Driscoll, M. (1994). *Psychology of learning for instruction*. Boston, MA: Allyn & Bacon.

Driver, E., & Driver, S. (2009). End death-by-lecture: Tours, not speeches. *ThinkBalm*. Retrieved May 2010, www.thinkbalm.com

Drotner, K. (1999). Unge, medier og modernitet - pejlinger i et foranderligt landskab. *København.*

Duarte, D., & Snyder, N. (2006). *Mastering virtual teams: Strategies, tools, and techniques that succeed*. San Francisco, CA: Jossey-Bass.

Dudeney, G., & Howard, R. (2009). *Overcoming the entry barriers to Second Life in higher education. Higher Education in Virtual Worlds Teaching and Learning in Second Life*. Bingley, UK: Emerald Group Publishing Limited.

Duffy, T., & Jonassen, D. (1992). *Constructivism and the technology of instruction: A conversation*. Hillsdale, NJ: Lawrence Erlbaum Associates.

Durkin, K. (2010). Video games and young people with developmental disorders. *Review of General Psychology*, *14*, 122–140. doi:10.1037/a0019438

Eck, A., Legenhausen, L., & Wolff, D. (1994). The use of telecommunications in a learner-oriented second-language classroom. In Gienow, W., & Hellwig, K. (Eds.), *Interkulturelle Kommunikation und prozeßorienterte Medienpraxis im Fremdsprachenunterricht: Grundlagen, Realisierung, Wirksamkeit* (pp. 43–57). Seelze, Germany: Friedrich Verlag.

Egidius, H. (1999). *PBL och Casemetodik: Hur man gör och varför*. Lund, Sweden: Studentlitteratur.

Electronic Arts Inc. (2010). *SimCity*. Redwood City, CA: Electronic Arts Inc. Retrieved May 26, 2010, from http://www.ea.com

Ellaway, R., Candler, C., Greene, P., & Smothers, V. (2006). *An architectural model for MedBiquitous virtual patients*. MedBiquitous.

Ellaway, R., Poulton, T., Fors, U., McGee, J., & Albright, S. (2008). Building a virtual patient commons. *Medical Teacher, 30*(2), 170–174. doi:10.1080/01421590701874074

Elliott, B. *(2008). Assessment 2.0.* Proceedings of the Open Workshop of TenCompetence, Empowering Learners for Lifelong Competence Development: Pedagogical, Organisational and Technological Issues.

Ellis, R. (1994). *The study of second language acquisition.* Oxford, UK: OUP.

Ellis, R. (2005). *Instructed second language acquisition. A literature review.* New Zealand: Ministry of Education.

Elstrom, P. (2009, July 10). The increasing value of free. *Business Week,* 81-82.

Endo, J., & Harpel, R. L. (1982). The effect of student faculty interactions on students' educational outcomes. *Research in Higher Education, 16*(2), 115–136. doi:10.1007/BF00973505

EPOCH. *The European Research Network of Excellence in Open Cultural Heritage.* (2008). Retrieved June 2010 from http://www.epoch-net.org/

Ertl, B., Kopp, B., & Mandl, H. (2007). Supporting collaborative learning in videoconferencing using collaboration scripts and content schemes. In F. Fischer, I. Kollar, H. Mandl, & J. M. Haake (Eds.), *Scripting computer-supported collaborative learning* (pp. 213-236). New York, NY: Springer Science and Business Media, LLC.

Ertmer, P. (2005). Teacher pedagogical beliefs: The final frontier in our quest for technology integration? *Educational Technology Research and Development, 53*(4), 25–39. doi:10.1007/BF02504683

Ertmer, P. A. (1999). Addressing first- and second-order barriers to change: Strategies for technology integration. *Educational Technology Research and Development, 47*(4), 47–61. doi:10.1007/BF02299597

Ess, C. (2009). *Digital media ethics.* Cambridge, UK: Polity Press.

Ess, C. & Association of Internet Researchers (2002). *Ethical decision-making and Internet research: Recommendations from the AOIR Ethics Working Committee.* Retrieved October 22, 2009, from Association of Internet Researchers: www.aoir.org/reports/ethics.pdf

Evans, M. (2010). The universities and the challenge of realism. *Arts and Humanities in Higher Education: An International Journal of Theory. Research and Practice, 9*(1), 13–21.

Eyler, J. (2009). The power of experiential education. *Liberal Education, 95*(4), 24–31.

Fåhræus, E. R. (1999). Tutoring group learning at a distance. *Proceedings of Society for Information Technology & Teacher Education International Conference, 1999,* 152–157.

Fassbender, E., Richards, D., & Kavakli, M. (2006). Game engineering approach to the effect of music on learning in virtual-immersive environments. *Proceedings of the 2006 International Conference on Game Research and Development.*

Federation of American Scientists. (2005). *Harnessing the power of video games for learning.* Retrieved July 19, 2010, from http://www.fas.org/gamesummit/Resources/Summit%20on% 20Educational%20Games.pdf

Felix, U. (2008). The unreasonable effectiveness of CALL: What have we learned in two decades of research? *ReCALL, 20*(2), 141–161. doi:10.1017/S0958344008000323

Feng, J., & Song, L. (2010). Teaching in Second Life: Students and instructors' perceptions. *Proceedings of the Society for Information Technology & Teacher Education International Conference (SITE).*

Fjermestad, J., & Hiltz, S. R. (1998). An assessment of group support systems experimental research: Methodology and results. *Journal of Management Information Systems, 15*(3), 7–149.

Fjuk, A. (1998). *Computer support for distributed collaborative learning. Exploring a complex problem area.* Unpublished doctoral dissertation, University of Oslo, Norway.

Flannery, J. L. (1994). Teacher as a co-conspirator: Knowledge and authority in collaborative learning. In Bosworth, K., & Hamilton, S. J. (Eds.), *Collaborative learning: Underlying processes and effective techniques* (pp. 15–23). San Francisco, CA: Jossey-Bass.

Fleming, N. D., & Mills, C. (1992). Not another inventory, rather a catalyst for reflection. *To Improve the Academy, 11,* 137-155.

Forehand, M. (2005). Bloom's taxonomy: Original and revised. In M. Orey (Ed.), *Emerging perspectives on learning, teaching, and technology*. Retrieved June 2, 2010, from from http://projects.coe.uga.edu/epltt/

Fortney, K. (2007). *Using Second Life to provide corporate blended learning solutions*. Second Life Education Workshop.

Fraps. (2008). Retrieved 15 September, 2008 from http://www.fraps.com/

Frecon, E., & Stenius, M. (1998). DIVE: A scalable network architecture for distributed virtual environments. *Distributed Systems Engineering, 5*.

Freitas, S. D., & Neumann, T. (2009). The use of exploratory learning for supporting immersive learning in virtual environments. *Computers & Education, 52*, 343–352. doi:10.1016/j.compedu.2008.09.010

Friedman, T. (2000). *The Lexus and the olive tree: Understanding globalization*. New York, NY: Knopf Doubleday Publishing Group.

Friedman, T. (2005). *The world is flat, a brief history of the twenty first century*. New York, NY: Farrar, Straus and Giroux.

Frischer, B. (n.d.). *Rome reborn*. Retrieved June 16, 2010, from http://www.romereborn.virginia.edu

Fuller, U., Amillo, J., Laxer, C., Mccracken, W. M., & Mertz, J. (2005). Facilitating student learning through study abroad and international projects. *ACM SIGCSE Bulletin, 37*, 139–151. doi:10.1145/1113847.1113892

Gaimster, J. (2008). Reflections on interactions in virtual worlds and their implication for learning art and design. *Art. Design & Communication in Higher Education, 6*(3), 187–199. doi:10.1386/adch.6.3.187_1

Gamor, K. (In press). What's in an avatar? Identity, behavior, and integrity in virtual worlds for educational and business communication. In Proctor, R., & Vu, K. (Eds.), *Handbook of human factors in Web design* (2nd ed.). New York, NY: CRC Press.

Garber, A. (2001). Death by Powerpoint. *Small Business Computing.com*. Retrieved from http://www.smallbusinesscomputing.com/biztools/article.php/684871

Garcia, A. L. (1994). *Educación a distancia hoy*. Madrid, Spain: UNED.

Garcia-Ruiz, M. A., Edwards, A., Aquino-Santos, R., & El-Seoud, S. A. (2008). Collaborating and learning a second language in a wireless virtual reality environment. *International Journal of Mobile Learning and Organization, 2*(4), 369–377. doi:10.1504/IJMLO.2008.020689

Garcia-Ruiz, M. A., Tashiro, J., Kapralos, B., & Vargas Martin, M. (2010). Crouching tangents, hidden danger: Assessing development of dangerous misconceptions within serious games for healthcare education. In Hai-Jew, S. (Ed.), *Virtual immersive and 3D learning spaces: Emerging technologies and trends*. Hershey, PA: IGI Global.

Gardner, M., Scott, J., & Horan, B. (2008). *Reflections on the use of Project Wonderland as a mixed-reality environment for teaching and learning*. ReLIVE 08 Conference.

Gee, J. P. (1999). *An introduction to discourse analysis: Theory and method*. London, UK: Routledge.

Gee, J. P. (2003). *What video games have to teach us about learning and literacy*. New York, NY: Palgrave/Macmillan.

Geer, R. (2005). *Imprinting and its impact on online learning environments*. Australasian Society for Computers in Learning in Tertiary Education.

Geer, R., & Barnes, A. (2007). Beyond media stickiness and cognitive imprinting: Rethinking creativity in cooperative work & learning with ICTs. *Education and Information Technologies, 12*, 123–136. doi:10.1007/s10639-007-9036-6

Geer, R., & Barnes, A. (2006). Media stickiness and cognitive imprinting: Inertia and creativity in cooperative work & learning with ICTs. *Proceedings of the World Computer Congress*, (pp. 55-64).

Gibson, J. J. (1979). *The ecological approach to visual perception*. Boston, MA: Houghton Mifflin.

Gillespie, J. (2008). Mastering multimedia: Teaching languages through technology. *ReCALL, 20*(2), 121–123. doi:10.1017/S0958344008000128

Gilman, R., Tashner, J., Bronack, S., Riedl, R., & Cheney, A. (2007). Crossing continents: Bringing teachers and learners together through a 3D immersive world. *Educators' eZine*, April 2007. Retrieved June 15, 2010, from http://www.techlearning.com/ story/showArticle.php?articleID=196604336

Gilster, P. (2007). *Digital literacy*. New York, NY: Wiley Computer.

Giovanelli, M. (2003). Relationship between reflective dispositions toward teaching and effective teaching. *The Journal of Educational Research, 96*(5), 293–309. doi:10.1080/00220670309597642

Girvan, C., & Savage, T. (2010). Identifying an appropriate pedagogy for virtual worlds: A communal constructivism case study. *Computers & Education, 55*(1), 342–349. doi:10.1016/j.compedu.2010.01.020

Giunipero, L., Dawley, D., & Anthony, W. P. (1999). The impact of tacit knowledge on purchasing decisions. *The Journal of Supply Chain Management, 35*(1), 42–49. doi:10.1111/j.1745-493X.1999.tb00055.x

Glaser, R., & Bassok, M. (1989). Learning theory and the study of instruction. *Annual Review of Psychology, 40*, 631–666. doi:10.1146/annurev.ps.40.020189.003215

Global Kids Digital Media Initiative. (2008). *Teen's comment on their SiSL experience.* Retrieved from http://olpglobalkids.org /science_in_second_life/

Global Kids. (2010). *Our mission.* Retrieved from http://globalkids.org/

Gokhale, A. (1995). Collaborative learning enhances critical thinking. *Journal of Technology Education, 7*(1), 22–30.

Gollub, R. (2007). Second Life and education. *Crossroads, 14*(1), 1–8. doi:10.1145/1349332.1349334

Google Inc. (2010). *Google SketchUp.* Mountain View, CA: Google Inc. Retrieved May 26, 2010, from http://sketchup.google.com

Gorini, G., Gaggioli, A., Vigna, C., & Riva, G. (2008). A Second Life for e-health: Prospects for the use of 3-D virtual worlds in clinical psychology. *Journal of Medical Internet Research, 10*(3), e21. Retrieved 10 October, 2008 from http://www.jmir.org/2008/3/e21/

Grabinger, R. (1996). Rich environments for active learning. In Jonassen, D. H. (Ed.), *Handbook of research for educational communications and technology* (pp. 665–692). New York, NY: Macmillan.

Grabowski, B., & Koszalka, T. (2002). Helping educators harvest Internet resources: The development of technology integration support tools. *Proceedings of the IADIS International Conference WWW/Internet 2002.*

Graf, S., & Beate, L. (2005). An evaluation of open source e-learning platforms stressing adaptation issues. *Proceedings of IEEE International Conference on Advanced Learning Technologies (ICALT2005).*

Grant, S. (2008). *Immersive Multi-User Virtual Environments: A new platform for foreign language teaching and learning.* Biennial Conference of the Asian Studies Association of Australia in Melbourne.

Greeno, J. G., & Gresalfi, M. S. (2008). Opportunities to learn in practice and identity. In Moss, P. A., Pullin, D. C., Gee, J. P., Haertel, E. H., & Young, L. J. (Eds.), *Assessment, equity, and opportunity to learn* (pp. 170–199). New York, NY: Cambridge University Press.

Gresalfi, M. S. (2009). Taking up opportunities to learn: Constructing dispositions in mathematics classrooms. *Journal of the Learning Sciences, 18*, 327–369. doi:10.1080/10508400903013470

Grewal, S. K., & Harris, L. (2009). Learning virtually or virtually distracted? The impact of emerging Internet technologies on pedagogical practice. In N. Panteli (Ed.), *Virtual social networks* (18-35). Hampshire, UK: Palgrave Macmillan.

Grivan, C., & Savage, T. (2010). Identifying an appropriate pedagogy for virtual worlds: A communal constructivism case study. *Computers & Education, 55*, 342–349. doi:10.1016/j.compedu.2010.01.020

Guest, T. (2007). *Second lives, a journey through virtual worlds.* New York, NY: Random House.

Guth, S. (2006). Discovering collaborative e-learning through an online writing course. *Innovate, 3*(2).

Gütl, Ch., Chang, V., Kopeinik, S., & Williams, R. (2009). *3D virtual worlds as a tool for collaborative learning settings in geographically dispersed environments.* Conference ICL.

Halloun, I. A., & Hestenes, D. (1985). The initial knowledge state of college physics students. *American Journal of Physics*, *53*, 1043–1055. doi:10.1119/1.14030

Hanna, D. E. (2003, July/August). Building a leadership vision: Eleven strategic challenges for higher education. *EDUCAUSE*.

Harris, S. R., Kemmerling, R. L., & North, M. M. (2002). Brief virtual reality therapy for public speaking anxiety. *Cyberpsychology & Behavior*, *5*(6), 543–550. doi:10.1089/109493102321018187

Haughton, N. A., & Romero, L. (2009). The online educator: Instructional strategies for effective practice. *Journal of Online Learning and Teaching*, *5*, 570–576.

Hay, A., Hodgkinson, M., Peltier, J., & Drago, W. (2004). Interaction and virtual learning. *Strategic Change*, *13*(4), 193–204. doi:10.1002/jsc.679

Haynes, C., & Holmevik, J. R. (1998). *High wired: On the design, use, and theory of educational MOOs*. Ann Arbor, MI: University of Michigan Press.

Heinrich, B. (1995). Language games in the mathematics classroom: Their function and their effects. In Cobbs, P., & Bauersfeld, H. (Eds.), *The emergence of mathematical meaning: Interaction in classroom cultures*. Abindgon, UK: Routledge.

Helm, C. (2006). The assessment of teacher dispositions. *Clearing House (Menasha, Wis.)*, *79*(6), 237–240. doi:10.3200/TCHS.79.6.237-239

Henderson, M., Huang, H., Grant, S., & Henderson, L. (2009). *Language acquisition in Second Life: Improving self-efficacy beliefs*. Ascilite Auckland.

Hendricken, V. (2004). From teaching to mentoring: Principle and practice, dialogue and life in adult education. *Journal of Distance Education*, *19*(2), 93–98.

Herrington, J., & Oliver, R. (2000). An instructional design framework for authentic learning environments. *Educational Technology Research and Development*, *48*(3), 23–48. doi:10.1007/BF02319856

Hickey, D., Ingram-Goble, A., & Jameson, E. M. (2009). Designing assessments and assessing designs in virtual educational environments. *Journal of Science Education and Technology*, *18*(2), 187–208. doi:10.1007/s10956-008-9143-1

Holden, J., Westfall, P., & Gamor, K. (2010). *An instructional media selection guide for distance learning: Implications for blended learning and virtual worlds* (6th ed.). Boston, MA: USDLA.

Hollander, J. B., & Thomas, D. (2009). Commentary: Virtual planning: Second Life and the online studio. *Journal of Planning Education and Research*, *29*, 108. doi:10.1177/0739456X09334142

Hron, A., & Friedrich, H. (2003). A review of Web-based collaborative learning: Factors beyond technology. *Journal of Computer Assisted Learning*, *19*(1), 70–79. doi:10.1046/j.0266-4909.2002.00007.x

HSGC. (2010). *Mission statement*. Retrieved from http://hsgc.org/mission_statement.jsp?rn=9256881

Hudson, K., & Degast-Kennedy, K. (2009). Canadian border simulation at Lyalist College. *Journal of Virtual Worlds Research*, *2*(1).

Hudson, J. M., & Bruckman, A. (2001). Effects of CMC on student participation patterns in a foreign language learning environment. *Proceedings of CHI '01*.

Hunicke, R., LeBlanc, M., & Zubek, R. (2004). MDA: A formal approach to game design and game research. *Proceedings of the Challenges in Game AI Workshop, Nineteenth National Conference on Artificial Intelligence*.

Huxley, A. (1932). *Brave new world*. London, UK: Chatto and Windus.

Huysman, M., Steinfield, C., Jang, C. Y., & David, K., Huis In 'T Veld, M., Poot, J., & Mulder, I. (2003). Virtual teams and the appropriation of communication technology: Exploring the concept of media stickiness. *Computer Supported Cooperative Work*, *12*(4), 411–436. doi:10.1023/A:1026145017609

Idaho State University. (2007). *Instructional Technology Resource Centre*. Retrieved March 2010 from http://www.isu.edu/itrc/resources/ LMS_FINAL_REPORT_MOODLE.pdf

Illeris, K. (1981). *The pedagogy of counter-qualification*. Copenhagen, Denmark: Unge Pædagoger.

Institute for Learning Styles Research. (2003). *Institue for Learning Styles Research*. Retrieved from http://www.learningstyles.org/

International Society for Technology Education. (2009). *Member networking: ISTE in Second Life*. Retrieved October 21, 2009, from http://www.iste.org/Content/ NavigationMenu/Membership/Member_Networking/ ISTE_Second_Life.htm

ISO 9241-11. (1998). *Ergonomic requirements for office work with visual display terminals (VDTs) – part 11: Guidance on usability*. International Organization for Standardization.

Jæger, B., & Helgheim, B. (2008). *Results from a role play exercise in Second Life for LOG505 and BØK700*. (Working Paper/Arbeidsnotat 2008:11), Molde University College, Norway.

Jamison, J. (2008). *Educators in a strange land: The experience of traditional educators when immersed in the virtual environment of Second Life*. (Doctoral dissertation). Capella University, Minneapolis, MN.

Jarmon, L., Traphagan, T., & Mayrath, M. (2008). Understanding project-based learning in Second Life with a pedagogy, training, and assessment trio. *Educational Media International*, *45*(3), 157–176. doi:10.1080/09523980802283889

Johnson, D. W. (1981). Student-student interaction: The neglected variable in education. *Educational Researcher*, *10*(1), 5–10.

Johnson, J. L. (2000). Learning communities and special efforts in the retention of university students: What works, what doesn't, and is the return worth the investment? *Journal of College Student Retention: Research. Theory into Practice*, *2*(3), 219–238.

Johnson, D. W., & Johnson, F. P. (1996). *Joining together: Group theory and group skills* (6th ed.). Boston, MA: Allyn and Bacon.

Johnson, S. D., Suriya, C., Won Yoon, S., Berrett, J. V., & LaFleur, J. (2002). Team development and group processes of virtual learning teams. *Computers & Education*, *39*, 379–393. doi:10.1016/S0360-1315(02)00074-X

Johnson, B. (2003). *Disintermediation and the museum Web experience: Database or documentary-which way should we go?* Museums and the Web.

Johnson, B. (2005). Place-based storytelling tools: A new look at Monticello. *Museums and the Web*, 173-182.

Johnson, L. (2007). *Why creativity matters*. Second Life Education Workshop.

Johnson, L., Levine, A., & Smith, R. (2008). *One year or less: Virtual worlds*. The 2008 Horizon Report: Australia–New Zealand Edition.

Johnson, W. L., Beal, C., Fowles-Winkler, A., Lauper, U., Marsella, S., & Narayanan, S. … Vilhjálmsson, H. (2004). Tactical language training system: An interim report. (LNCS 3220), (pp. 336-345).

Johnstone, A. H., & Percival, F. (1976). Attention breaks in lectures. *Education in Chemistry*, *13*(2), 49–50.

Joint Information Systems Committee (JISC). (2006). *Designing spaces for effective learning: A guide to 21st century learning space design*. Retrieved from http:// www.jisc.ac.uk/ media/documents /publications /learningspaces.pdf

Joly, K. (2007). *A second life for higher education? University business solutions for higher education*. Retrieved from http://www.universitybusiness.com/ ViewArticle. aspx?articleid=797

Jonaitis, S. (2007). Learner control in undergraduate online learning: Instructor perspectives. (Doctoral dissertation). Michigan State University, East Lansing, MI.

Jonassen, D. H., Peck, K. L., & Wilson, B. G. (1999). *Learning with technology: A constructivist perspective*. Upper Saddle River, NJ: Merrill-Prentice Hall.

Jonassen, D., Davidson, M., Collins, M., Campbell, J., & Haag, B. B. (1995). Constructivism and computer-mediated communication in distance education. *American Journal of Distance Education*, *9*, 7–26. doi:10.1080/08923649509526885

Jonassen, D. H., & Kwon, H. (2001). Communication patterns in computer mediated versus face-to-face group problem solving. *Educational Technology Research and Development*, *49*(1), 35–51. doi:10.1007/BF02504505

Jones, S. (2007). Adding value to online role plays: Virtual situated learning environments. *Proceedings of Ascilite, Singapore 2007*.

Joseph, A., & Payne, M. (2003). Group dynamics and collaborative group performance. *ACM SIGCSE Bulletin Archive*, *35*(1), 368–371. doi:10.1145/792548.612008

Joseph, B. (2007). Best practices in using virtual worlds for education. *Proceedings of the Second Life Education Workshop at the SL Community Convention.*

Junglas, I. A., Johnson, N. A., Steel, D. J., Abraham, D. C., & Loughlin, P. M. (2007). Identity formation, learning styles and trust in virtual worlds. *SIGMIS Database, 38,* 90–96. doi:10.1145/1314234.1314251

Kahai, S. S., Carroll, E., & Jestice, R. (2007). Team collaboration in virtual worlds. *SIGMIS Database, 38,* 61–68. doi:10.1145/1314234.1314246

Kalawsky, R. (2000). The validity of presence as a reliable human performance metric in immersive environments. *Proceedings of 3rd International Workshop on Presence.*

Kamimo Islands. (2007). Retrieved June 2010 from http://slurl.com/secondlife/ Kamimo_Island/127/148/25, project from http://kamimo-islands. blogspot.com/

Kao, L., & Galas, C. (2005). *A totally different world: Playing and learning in multi-user virtual environments.* Digital Games Research Association, Seattle, WA. Retrieved from http://www.cathleengalas.com/papers/4Tot allyDifferentWorldDIGRA05.pdf

Kaplan-Rakowski, R. (2010b). *Teaching a foreign language in a virtual world – connecting theory with practice.* Lexington, KY: Presentation at KFLC.

Kaplan-Rakowski, R., & Mizza, D. (2010). *Using a virtual world for writing skills development.* Washington, D.C.: Presentation at MAALLT / SEALLT.

Kaplan-Rakowski, R. (2010a). Foreign language instruction in a virtual environment: An examination of potential activities. In Vincenti, G., & Braman, J. (Eds.), *Teaching through multi-user virtual environments: Applying dynamic elements to the modern classroom* (pp. 306–325). Hershey, PA: Information Science Reference.

Kapp, K., & O'Driscoll, T. (2010). *Learning in 3D: Adding a new dimension to enterprise learning and collaboration.* San Franscisco, CA: Pfeiffer.

Kapp, K., & O'Driscoll, T. (2007). Escaping flatland: The emergence of 3D synchronous learning. *Guild Research 360° Report on Synchronous Learning Systems,* 111-153.

Kapur, M., & Kinzer, C. K. (2007). Examining the effect of problem type in a synchronous computer-supported collaborative learning (CSCL) environment. *Educational Technology and Development, 55*(5), 439–459. doi:10.1007/s11423-007-9045-6

Kay, J., & Fitzgerald, S. (2007). *Exploring the educational uses of Second Life.* Retrieved October 23, 2009, from http://sleducation.wikispaces.com/educationaluses_page1#distance

Kemp, J. W., & Haycock, K. (2008). Immersive learning environments in parallel universes: Learning through Second Life. *School Libraries Worldwide, 14*(2), 89–97.

Kemp, J. (2006). Putting a Second Life "Metaverse" skin on Learning Management Systems. *Proceedings of the Second Life Education Workshop at the Second Life Community Convention.*

Kemp, J., & Livingstone, D. (2006). Putting a Second Life "Metaverse" skin on learning management systems. *Proceedings First Second Life Education Workshop, Part of the 2006 Second Life Community Convention,* (pp. 13-18).

Kenderdine, S. (2001). 1000 years of the Olympic games: Treasures of ancient Greece. Digital reconstruction at the home of the gods. *Museums and the Web,* 173-182.

Ketelhut, D. J. *(2006).* Assessing scientific and technological self-efficacy: A measurement pilot. Proceedings of the American Educational Research Association.

Kim, W. (2007). *Towards a definition and methodology for blended learning.* International Workshop on Blended Learning 2007 (WBL 07).

Kirschner, P., Strijbos, J. W., Krejins, K., & Beers, P. J. (2004). Designing electronic collaborative learning environments. *Educational Technology Research and Development, 52*(3), 47–66. doi:10.1007/BF02504675

Kolb, A. Y. (1984). *Experiential learning: Experience as the source of learning and development.* Englewood Cliffs, NJ: Prentice-Hall.

Kolb, D. A. (1984b). *Experiential learning.* Englewood Cliffs, NJ: Prentice Hall.

Kolb, D. (1984). *Experiential learning: experience as the source of learning and development.* Englewood Cliffs, NJ: Prentice-Hall.

Kolb, D. A., & Fry, R. (1975). Toward an applied theory of experiential learning. In Cooper, C. (Ed.), *Theories of group process*. London, UK: John Wiley.

Konstantinidis, A., Papadopoulos, P., Tsiatsos, T., & Demetriadis, S. (2010a). (Manuscript submitted for publication). Selecting and Evaluating a Learning Management System: A Moodle evaluation based on instructors and students. *International Journal of Distance Education Technologies*.

Konstantinidis, A., Tsiatsos, T., Terzidou, T., & Pomportsis, A. (2010b). Fostering collaboration in Second Life: Metaphors and affordances. *Journal of Computers and Education*, *55*(2), 603–615. doi:10.1016/j.compedu.2010.02.021

Konstantinidis, A., Tsiatsos, T., & Pomportsis, A. (2009). Collaborative virtual learning environments: Design and evaluation. *Multimedia Tools and Applications*, *44*(2), 279–304. doi:10.1007/s11042-009-0289-5

Konstantinou, N., Varlamis, I., & Giannakoulopoulos, A. (2009). *Using 3D worlds in an educational network*. 13th Pan-Hellenic Conference on Informatics.

Koszalka, T. A., & Wu, Y. (2008). *Evaluation of a cross-institutional collaborative distributed engineering educational environment*. 12th Global Chinese Computer and Communication Conference.

Krashen, S., & Terrell, T. (1983). *The natural approach: Language acquisition in the classroom*. Hayward, CA: Alemany Press.

Krashen, S. D. (1982). *Principles and practices in second language acquisition*. New York, NY: Prentice-Hall.

Krashen, S. D. (1988). *Second language acquisition and second language learning* (2nd ed.). New York, NY: Prentice Hall.

Krashen, S. D. (2004). *Applying the comprehension hypothesis: Some suggestions*. 13th International Symposium and Book Fair on Language Teaching.

Kuh, G. (1995). The other curriculum: Out-of-class experiences associated with student learning and personal development. *The Journal of Higher Education*, *66*(2), 123–155. doi:10.2307/2943909

Kuh, G., & Hu, S. (2001). The effects of student-faculty interaction in the 1990s. *The Review of Higher Education*, *24*(3), 309–332. doi:10.1353/rhe.2001.0005

Kumari, D. S. (2001). Connecting graduate students to virtual guests through asynchronous discussions – analysis of an experience. *Journal of Asynchronous Learning Networks*, *5*(2), 53–63.

Lamport, M. (1993). Student-faculty informal interaction and the effect on college student outcomes: A review of the literature. *Adolescence*, *28*(122), 971–990.

Larsen-Freeman, D. (2000). *Technique and principles in language teaching*. Oxford, UK: Oxford University Press.

Lassila, O., & Hendler, J. (2007). Embracing Web 3.0. *IEEE Internet Computing*, *11*(3), 90–93. doi:10.1109/MIC.2007.52

Lau, N., & Wong, B. (2009). *Multimedia design manipulation using Second Life in education*. SLACTIONS 2009 International Conference: Life, imagination, and work using metaverse platforms.

Laurillard, D. (2002). *Rethinking university teaching, a conversational framework for the effective use of learning technologies* (2nd ed.). London, UK: Routledge and Falmer. doi:10.4324/9780203304846

Le Peuple, J., & Scane, R. (2003). *User interface design*. Exeter, UK: Crucial.

Lechner, M., & Tripp, M. (2010). ARML – an augmented reality standard. *Proceedings from Mobile World Congress, Augmented Reality Summit*.

Lehtinen, E., & Hakkarainen, K. (2001). *Computer supported collaborative learning: A review*. Retrieved April 2010 from http://www.comlab.hut.fi/ opetus/205/etatehtava1.pdf

Lemke, J. (1990). *Talking science: Language, learning, and values*. Norwood, NJ: Ablex.

Leonard, L. G., Sherblom, J. C., & Withers, L. A. (2009). *Communication challenges and opportunities for educators using Second Life. Higher Education in Virtual Worlds Teaching and Learning in Second Life*. Bingley, UK: Emerald Group Publishing Limited.

Leonard, A. (2008). *The story of stuff.* Retrieved from http://www.storyofstuff.com/

Lessig, L. (2004). *Free culture, the nature and future of creativity.* New York, NY: Penguin Group.

Levy, M. (1997). *Computer-assisted language learning: Context and conceptualization.* Oxford, UK: Oxford University Press.

Li, Y., Whalley, J., Zhang, S., & Zhao, X. (2008). *China's higher education transformation and its global implications.* Retrieved from http://www.voxeu.org/index.php?q=node/1066

Lieberman, D. (1997). Interactive video games for health promotion: Effects on knowledge, self-efficacy, social support and health. In Gold, R. L., & Manning, T. (Eds.), *Health promotion and interactive technology* (pp. 103–120). Norwell, NJ: Lawrence Erlbaum Associates.

Ligorio, M. B., & Talamo, A. (2000). *Identity in cyberspace: The social construction of identity through online virtual interactions.* Retrieved from http://www.activeworlds.com/ edu/research/identity.pdf

Lim, K. Y. T. (2009). The six learnings of Second Life. *Journal of Virtual Worlds Research, 2*(1).

Lin, C. S. (2001). The experiences in running a cyber school in improving study. *Selected Papers of International Conference on Information Technology in Education of Schools,* (pp. 101-113).

Lincoln, Y. S., & Guba, E. G. (1985). *Naturalistic inquiry.* Newbury Park, CA: Sage Publications.

Linden Lab. (2009a). *Simulation training and prototyping in virtual worlds: Northrop Grumman in Second Life.* Linden Research, Inc. Retrieved November 2009, http://work.secondlife.com

Linden Lab. (2009b). *How meeting in Second Life transformed IBM's technology elite into virtual world believers.* Linden Research, Inc. Retrieved November 2009, http://secondlifegrid.net/

Linden Lab. (2010a). *Second Life.* San Francisco, CA: Linden Lab. Retrieved May 26, 2010, from http://www.secondlife.com

Linden Lab. (2010b). *Second Life educators list.* San Francisco, CA: Linden Lab. Retrieved May 26, 2010, from https://lists.secondlife.com/cgi-bin/mailman/listinfo/educators

Linden Research, Inc. (2009a). *Virtual environments enable new models of learning.* Retrieved October 1, 2009, from http://www.guardian.co.uk/education/2009/apr/21/elearning-university-of-london/print

Linden Research, Inc. (2009b). *What is Second Life?* Retrieved September 22, 2009, from http://secondlife.com/whatis

Lipnack, J., & Stamps, J. (1997). *Virtual teams.* New York, NY: John Wiley and Sons, Inc.

Little, D. (1996). Freedom to learn and compulsion to interact: Promoting learner autonomy through the use of Information Systems and Information Technologies. In R. Pemberton, E. Li, W. Or, & H. Pierson (Eds.), *Taking control: Autonomy in language learning.* Hong Kong, HK: Hong Kong University Press.

Liu, C. (2006). Second Life learning community: A peer-based approach to involving more faculty members in Second Life. *Proceedings of the Second Life Education Workshop at the Second Life Community Convention.*

Losh, E. (2006). Making things public: Democracy and government-funded videogames and virtual reality simulations. *Proceedings of the 2006 ACM SIGGRAPH Symposium on Videogames.*

Loureiro, A., & Bettencourt, T. (2009). *Building knowledge in the virtual world – influence of real life relationships.* SLACTIONS 2009 International Conference: Life, imagination, and work using metaverse platforms, (pp. 111-116).

Lowe, C., & Clark, M. A. (2008). Student perceptions of learning science in a virtual world. *Proceedings 24th Annual Conference on Distance Teaching and Learning.*

Lowyck, L., & Poysa, J. (2001). Design of collaborative learning environments. *Computers in Human Behavior, 17*(5-6), 507–516. doi:10.1016/S0747-5632(01)00017-6

MacArthur, V. (2008). Real ethics in virtual worlds. *Proceedings of the Conference on Human Factors in Computing Systems.*

MacFarlane, S., Sim, G., & Horton, M. (2005). Assessing usability and fun in educational software. *Proceedings of the 2005 Conference on interaction Design and Children.*

Makena Technologies, Inc. (2010). *There.* Silicon Valley, CA: Makena Technologies, Inc. Retrieved May 26, 2010, from http://www.there.com

Malone, T. W. (1981). Toward a theory of intrinsically motivating instruction. *Cognitive Science, 5*(4), 333–369. doi:10.1207/s15516709cog0504_2

Mangold, K. (2007). Educating a new generation: Teaching baby boomer faculty about millennial students. *Nurse Educator, 32*(1), 21–23. doi:10.1097/00006223-200701000-00007

Marks, M. A., Mathieu, J. E., & Zaccaro, S. J. (2001). A temporally based framework and taxonomy of team processes. *Academy of Management Review, 26*(3), 356–376. doi:10.2307/259182

Martin, J. P., & Oebel, G. (2007). Lernen durch Lehren: Paradigmenwechsel in der Didaktik? *Deutschunterricht in Japan, 12,* 4–21.

Martin, J. P. (1985). *Zum Aufbau didaktischer Teilkompetenzen beim Schüler. Fremdsprachenunterricht auf der lerntheoretischen Basis des Informationsverarbeitungsansatzes.* (Dissertation). Tübingen: Narr.

Martin, K. (2010). *A virtual fashion design research tool.* The Athens Institute for Education and Research Conference.

Massey, A. P., Montoya, M. M., & Hung, Y. T. C. (2003). Because time matters: Temporal coordination in global virtual project teams. *Journal of Management Information Systems, 19*(4), 129–155.

Massey, A. P., Ramesh, V., & Khatri, V. (2006). Design, development, and assessment of mobile applications: The case for problem-based learning. *IEEE Transactions on Education, 49*(2), 183–192. doi:10.1109/TE.2006.875700

McConnell, S. (1996). *Rapid development.* Redmond, WA: Microsoft Press.

McGrath, J. E. (1991). Time, interaction, and performance (TIP): A theory of groups. *Small Group Research, 22*(2), 147–174. doi:10.1177/1046496491222001

McKeon, M., & Wyche, S. (2005). *Life across boundaries: Design, identity and gender in SL.* Retrieved from http://www.mattmckeon.com /portfolio/ second-life.pdf

McKnight, D. (2004). An inquiry of NCATE's move into virtue ethics by way of dispositions (Is this what Aristotle meant?). *Educational Studies, 35*(3), 212–230.

McLuhan, M. (1964). *Understanding media.* London, UK: Routledge and Kegan Paul.

Meadows, M. S. (2008). *I, avatar: The culture and consequences of having a Second Life.* Berkeley, CA: New Riders Press.

Merriam, S. B. (1992). *Qualitative research in education.* San Francisco, CA: Jossey-Bass Inc.

Merrill, J. (2009). *Identify formation and expression in Second Life: Implications for the use of virtual places in education.* Paper session: Virtual Learning Environments and Geographic Education. Association of American Geographers Annual Meeting.

Michael, J. A., Richardson, D., Rovick, A., Modell, H., Bruce, D., & Horwitz, B. (1999). Undergraduate students' misconceptions about respiratory physiology. *Advances in Physiology Education, 22*(1), 127–135.

Michailidou, A., & Economides, A. A. (2003). E-learn: Towards a collaborative educational virtual environment. *Journal of Information Technology Education, 2,* 131–152.

Milton, J., & Garbi, A. (2000). *Collaborative virtual reality approaches for very young language learners.* EDEN Research Workshop Papers, European Distance Education Network.

Mishra, P., & Koehler, M. J. (2006). Technological pedagogical content knowledge: A framework for integrating technology in teacher knowledge. *Teachers College Record, 108*(6), 1017–1054. doi:10.1111/j.1467-9620.2006.00684.x

Mishra, P., & Koehler, M. J. (2006). Technological pedagogical content knowledge: A framework for teacher knowledge. *Teachers College Record, 108*(6), 1017–1054. doi:10.1111/j.1467-9620.2006.00684.x

Molka-Danielsen, J., & Deutschmann, M. (Eds.). (2009). *Learning and teaching in the virtual world of Second Life.* Trondheim, Norway: Tapir Academic Press.

Molka-Danielsen, J., Carter, B. W., Richardson, D., & Jæger, B. (2009). Teaching and learning effectively within a virtual campus. *International Journal of Networking and Virtual Organisations*, 6(5), 476–498. doi:10.1504/IJNVO.2009.027392

Molka-Danielsen, J., & Deutschmann, M. (Eds.). (2009). *Learning and teaching in the virtual world of Second Life*. Trondheim, Norway: Tapir Academic Press.

Monahan, T., McArdle, G., & Bertolotto, M. (2007). mCLEV-R: Design and evaluation of an interactive and collaborative m-learning application. *International Journal of Emerging Technologies in Learning*, 2(2), 47–53.

Montoya, M. M., Massey, A. P., Hung, Y. T. C., & Crisp, C. B. (2009). Can you hear me now? Communication in virtual product development teams. *Journal of Product Innovation Management*, 26(2), 139–155. doi:10.1111/j.1540-5885.2009.00342.x

Moore, G. C., & Benbasat, I. (1991). Development of an instrument to measure the perceptions of adopting an Information Technology innovation. *Information Systems Research*, 2(3). doi:10.1287/isre.2.3.192

Moschini, E. (2010). The Second Life researcher toolkit - an exploration of inworld tools, methods and approaches for researching educational projects in Second Life. In Peachey, A., Gillen, J., Livingstone, D., & Smith-Robbins, S. (Eds.), *Researching learning in virtual worlds* (pp. 31–51). Lancaster, PA: Springer. doi:10.1007/978-1-84996-047-2_3

Motorola. (2010). *Innovation generation grants*. Retrieved from http://responsibility.motorola.com/ index.php/society/comminvest /education/igg/

National Council for Accreditation of Teacher Education. (2008). *Professional standards for the accreditation of teacher preparation institutions*.

National Research Council (NRC). (2005). America's lab report: Investigations in high school science. In M. L. H. Susan, R. Singer, & H. A. Schweingruber (Eds.), *Board on science education, center for education, division of behavioral and social sciences and education*. Washington, DC: The National Academies Press. Committee on High School Science Laboratories: Role and Vision.

Natkin, S. (2006). *Video games and interactive media*. Wellesley, MA: A. K. Peters.

Nelson, B., & Ketelhut, D. J. (2007). Scientific inquiry in educational multi-user virtual environments. *Educational Psychology Review*, 19(3), 265–283. doi:10.1007/s10648-007-9048-1

Nelson, B., Ketelhut, D. J., Clarke, J., Bowman, C., & Dede, C. (2005). Design-based research strategies for developing a scientific inquiry curriculum in a multi-user virtual environment. *Educational Technology*, 45(1), 21–27.

New Media Consortium. (2007). *The horizon report: 2007 edition*. Austin, TX: New Media Consortium. Retrieved May 26, 2010, from http://www.nmc.org/pdf/2007_Horizon_Report.pdf

New Media Consortium. (2009). *Quick start guide*. Retrieved November 2009, http://sl.nmc.org/join/%20 Second Life Registration Pew Internet and American Life Project. (2009). *Pew Internet*. Retrieved May 2010, www.pewinternet.org

New York Learning Standards. (2008). *The living environment: Core curriculum*. Retrieved from http://www.p12.nysed.gov/ ciai/mst/pub/livingen.pdf

Nicol, D. J., & Macfarlane-Dick, D. (2006). Formative assessment and self-regulated learning: A model and seven principles of good feedback practice. *Studies in Higher Education*, 31(2), 199–218. doi:10.1080/03075070600572090

Nielsen, J. (1994). *Usability engineering*. San Francisco, CA: Morgan Kaufmann.

Nielsen, J., & Mack, R. (Eds.). (1994). *Usability inspection methods*. New York, NY: John Wiley and Sons.

Nielsen, J., & Landauer, T. K. (1993). A mathematical model of the finding of usability problems. *Proceedings of ACM INTERCHI '93 Conference*.

Norman, D. (2002). *The design of everyday things*. Jackson, TN: Basic Books.

Nussbaum, E. M., Hartley, K., Sinatra, G., Reynolds, R., & Bendixen, L. D. (2004). Personality interactions and scaffolding in on-line discussions. *Journal of Educational Computing Research*, *30*(1-2), 113–136. doi:10.2190/H8P4-QJUF-JXME-6JD8

O'Connell, T. A., Grantham, J., Workman, K., & Wong, W. (2009). Leveraging game-playing skills, expectations and behaviors of digital natives to improve visual analytical tools. *Journal of Virtual Worlds Research*, *2*(1).

O'Conner, E. A. (2010). Instructional and design elements that support effective use of virtual worlds: What graduate student work reveals about Second Life. *Journal of Educational Technology Systems*, *38*(2), 213–234. doi:10.2190/ET.38.2.j

Oblinger, D. G., Barone, C. A., & Hawkins, B. L. (2001). *Distributed education and its challenges: An overview.* American Council on Education. ACE.

OFSTED. (2009). *Virtual learning environments: An evaluation of their development in a sample of educational settings.* Retrieved from http://www.ofsted.gov.uk/ content/download/8797/95679 /file/VLE%20an%20 evaluation %20of%20their%20 development.pdf

Ondrejka, C. (2008). Education unleashed: Participatory culture, education and innovation in Second Life. In Salen, K. (Ed.), *The ecology of games: Connecting youth, games, and learning* (pp. 229–251). Cambridge, MA: MIT Press.

Ormrod, J. E. (2008). *Human learning* (5th ed.). Upper Saddle River, NJ: Pearson.

Ozmen, H. (2004). Some student misconceptions in chemistry: A literature review of chemical bonding. *Journal of Science Education and Technology*, *13*(2), 147–159. doi:10.1023/B:JOST.0000031255.92943.6d

Palinscar, A. (1998). Social constructivist perspectives on teaching and learning. *Annual Review of Psychology*, *49*, 345–375. doi:10.1146/annurev.psych.49.1.345

Palomäki, E. (2009). *Applying 3D virtual worlds to education.* Helsinki University of Technology.

Panganiban, R. (2009). *Do virtual worlds support or hold back marginalized youth?* Retrieved from http://www.holymeatballs.org/ virtual_worlds/second_life/curriculum_development

Panitz, T. (1996). *A definition of collaborative vs. cooperative learning.* Retrieved January 2, 2010, from http://www.city.londonmet.ac.uk/ deliberations/collab.learning /panitz2.html

Panteli, N. (2009). Virtual social networks: A new dimension for virtuality research. In Panteli, N. (Ed.), *Virtual social networks* (pp. 1–17). Hampshire, UK: Palgrave Macmillan. doi:10.1057/9780230250888

Paolini, P. Di Blas., N., & Torrebruno, A. (2009). Media & communication literacy in higher education: Learning a foreign language. *Proceedings of World Conference on Educational Multimedia, Hypermedia and Telecommunications 2009*, (pp. 3210-3220).

Park, S. H., Yoon, Y. S., Kim, L. H., Lee, S. H., & Han, M. (2007). Virtual knee joint replacement surgery system. *Proceedings of the International Conference on Geometric Modeling and Imaging*, (pp. 79-84).

Pascarella, E., & Terenzini, P. (1980). Student-faculty and student-peer relationships as mediators of the structural effects of undergraduate residence arrangement. *The Journal of Educational Research*, *73*(6), 344–353.

Peachey, A., Gillen, J., & Ferguson, R. (2008). *Fluid leadership in a multi-user virtual environment educational project with teenagers: Schome Park.* Ecologies of Diversities: the developmental and historical interarticulation of human meditational forms: meeting of the International Society for Cultural and Activity Research, (pp. 1-14).

Pellegrino, J. W. (2006). *Rethinking and redesigning curriculum, instruction and assessment: What contemporary research and theory suggests.* Retrieved February 24, 2010, from http://www.skillscommission.org/ pdf/commissioned_papers/ Rethinking%20and%20 Redesigning.pdf

Penfold, P., Ma, H., Choy, C., & Lav, N. (2008). *Handbook – orientation programme to Sl for PolyU students.* Retrieved May, 16, 2010, from http://www.scribd.com/doc/ 4612700/Handbook-Orientation- Programme-to-SL-for- PolyU-Students

Pereira, M. (2009). *Universidade do Brasil virtual – the use of Second Life to share knowledge in graphic design, game design and visual arts classrooms.* SLACTIONS 2009 International Conference: Life, imagination, and work using metaverse platforms, (pp. 66-68).

Perez, L. (2009). Challenges and opportunities in using MUVEs in K-12 environments. In Tettegah, S., & Calongne, C. (Eds.), *Identity, learning and support in virtual environments* (pp. 45–55). Rotterdam, The Netherlands: Sense Publishers.

Perkinson, R. (2006). *International higher education.* Plenary Address Going Global2, The UK's International Education Conference. Retrieved from http://www.whitneyintl.com/ documents/Innovation_and_International_Responsibility.pdf

Perry, W. G. (1970). *Forms of intellectual and ethical development in the college years: A scheme.* New York, NY: Holt, Rinehart, and Winston.

Petraglia, J. (1997). *The rhetoric and technology of authenticity in education.* Mahwah, NJ: Lawrence Erlbaum.

PMI. (2008). *A guide to the Project Management Body of Knowledge (PMBOK® Guide).* Newtown Square, PA: Project Management Institute.

Poggi, C. (2006). *Bridging the gap between goals and design.* (Doctoral Dissertation). Politecnico di Milano, Milano, Italy.

Pomeroy, S. (1996). Gendered places, virtual spaces: A feminist geography of cyberspace. (Doctoral dissertation). University of California, Berkeley, CA.

Poulton, T., Conradi, E., Kavia, S., Round, J., & Hilton, S. (2009). The replacement of paper cases by interactive online virtual patients in problem-based learning. *Medical Teacher, 31*(8). doi:10.1080/01421590903141082

Prasolova-Førland, E. (2008). Analyzing place metaphors in 3D educational collaborative virtual environments. *Computers in Human Behavior, 24*(2), 185–204. doi:10.1016/j.chb.2007.01.009

Preece, J., Rogers, Y., & Sharp, H. (2002). *Interaction design: Beyond human-computer interaction.* New York, NY: John Wiley and Sons.

Preece, J., Rogers, Y., Sharp, H., Benyon, D., Holland, S., & Carey, T. (1994). *Human-computer interaction.* Wokingham, UK: Addison-Wesley.

Prinsen, F., Volman, M. L. L., & Terwel, J. (2007). The influence of learner characteristics on degree and type of participation in a CSCL environment. *British Journal of Educational Technology, 38*(6), 1037–1055. doi:10.1111/j.1467-8535.2006.00692.x

Quivy, R., & Campenhoudt, L. V. (2003). *Manual de investigação em ciências sociais, 3ª edição.* Lisboa, Portugal: Gradiva.

Radoiu, D. (2008). Virtual organizations in emerging virtual 3D worlds. *Studia Univ. Babes-Bolyai, Informatica, 53*(2).

Reeder, K., Heift, T., Roche, J., Tabyanian, S., Schlickau, S., & Golz, P. (2004). Toward a theory of E/Valuation for second language learning media. In Fotos, S., & Browne, C. M. (Eds.), *New perspective on CALL for second language classrooms* (pp. 255–278). Mahwah, NJ: Lawrence Erlbaum.

Report, P. (2008). Teens, video games and civics. Retrieved from http://pewresearch.org/pubs/953/

Resta, P., & Laferrière, T. (2007). Technology in support of collaborative learning. *Educational Psychology Review, 19*, 65–83. doi:10.1007/s10648-007-9042-7

Reynolds, T. (2007). *Identifying and measuring educator effectiveness dispositions in online teaching.* Paper presented at the meeting of the International Council for Education on Teaching, San Diego, CA.

Rheingold, H. (1993). *The virtual community: Homesteading on the electronic frontier.* Reading, MA: Addison-Wesley.

Ritzema, T., & Harris, B. (2008). The use of Second Life for distance education. *Journal of Computing Sciences in Colleges, 23*(6), 110–116.

Robbins, S (2007). *Using a Multi-User Virtual Environment (MUVE) for education: One instructor's adventure in Second Life.* 360 Report on Games and Education.

Robertson, G., Czeminski, M., & van Dantzich, M. (1997). Immersion in desktop virtual reality. *Proceedings of UIST '97.*

Rogers, E. M. (1995). *Diffusion of innovations.* New York, NY: Free Press.

Rogers, E. M. (2003). *Diffusion of innovations*. New York, NY: Free Press.

Rogers, E. M. (1983). *Diffusion of innovation* (3rd ed.). New York, NY: Macmillan.

Rose, C., & Vega, Y. (2009). *Charlie Rose*. New York, NY: Public Broadcasting System.

Rose, A. Eckard, D., & Rubloff, G. (1998). *An application framework for creating simulation-based learning environments*. Human-Computer Interaction Laboratory, Institute for Systems Research. University of Maryland, North Carolina State University, (HCIL Technical Report No. 98-07).

Rose, H., & Billinghurst, M. (1996). *Zengo Sayu: An immersive educational environment for learning Japanese*. Final Report to The Washington Technology Center, University of Washington.

Rosenqvist, C. (2004). *Immersion, experience and understanding: Virtual theatres in drama teaching*. Retrieved from http://gupea.ub.gu.se/dspace/bitstream/2077/18100/1/gupea_2077_18100_1.pdf

Ross, J. A. (1996). *Computer communication skills and participation in a computer-mediated conferencing course*. Annual Conference of the American Educational Research Association.

Rourke, L., & Anderson, T. (2002). Exploring social communication in computer conferencing. *Journal of Interactive Learning Research*, *13*(3), 259–275.

Rovai, A. P., & Childress, M. D. (2002). Explaining and predicting resistance to computer anxiety reduction among teacher education students. *Journal of Research on Technology in Education*, *35*(2), 226–235.

Ruben, D. (1999). Simulations, games, and experience-based learning: The quest for a new paradigm for teaching and learning. *Health Education Research. Theory into Practice*, *30*(4), 498–505.

Russo, P. (2004). *What makes any school an urban school?* Retrieved June 2010 from http://www.oswego.edu/~prusso1/what_makes_any_school_an_urban_s.htm

Rymaszewski, M., Au, W. J., Winters, C., Ondrejka, C., & Batstone-Cunningham, B. (2007). *Second Life: The official guide*. Indianapolis, IN: Wiley.

Sadik, A. (2006). Factors influencing teachers' attitudes toward personal use and school use of computers: New evidence from a developing nation. *Evaluation Review*, *30*(1), 86–113. doi:10.1177/0193841X05276688

Sadler, R. (2009). Can you build this? Virtual construction for language learning in Second Life. In Stone, L., & Wilson-Duff, C. (Eds.), *Task-based III: Expanding the range of tasks with online resources*. International Association for Language Learning Technology.

Salen, K., & Zimmerman, E. (2004). *Rules of play*. Cambridge, MA: MIT Press.

Sanders, R. L., & Mckeown, L. (2007). Promoting reflection through action learning in a 3D virtual world. *International Journal of Social Sciences*, *2*(1), 50–55.

Savery, J., & Duffy, T. (1995). Problem based learning: An instructional model and its constructivist framework. *Educational Technology*, *35*(5), 31–38.

Scavenius Lopez, C. (2002). Le@rning in a digitised society. In Danielsen, O., Nielsen, J., & Sørensen, B. H. (Eds.), *Learning and narrativity in digital media*. Frederiksberg, Denmark: Samfundlitteratur.

Schaller, D., Goldman, K. H., Spickelmier, G., Allison-Bunnell, S., & Koepfler, J. (2009). *Learning in the wild: What Wolfquest taught developers and game players*. Museums and the Web.

Schiller, S. Z. (2009). Practicing learner-centered teaching: Pedological design and assessment of a Second Life project. *Journal of Information Systems Education*, *20*(3), 369–381.

Schrock, K. (n.d.). *Second Life: Interactive professional development*. Retrieved October 31, 2009, from http://www.hotchalk.com/mydesk/index.php/editorial/44-online-professional-development/86-second-life-interactive-professional-development-pt-1

Schutz, A., & Luckmann, T. (1971). *The structures of the life-world*. Evanston, IL: Northwestern University Press.

Schuurink, E., & Vries, M. D. (2009). Combining advanced learning technologies in an immigrant educational program. *Proceedings of the 13th International MindTrek Conference: Everyday Life in the Ubiquitous Era*.

Schwalbe, K. (2010). *Introduction to project management* (3rd ed.). Hamel, MN: Kathy Schwalbe LLC.

Schwienhorst, K. (2002). Why virtual, why environments? Implementing virtual reality concepts in computer-assisted language learning. *Simulation & Gaming, 33*, 196.

Sclater, N. (2008). *Large-scale open source e-learning systems at Open University UK.* Educause Centre for Applied Research. Retrieved from http://net.educause.edu/ir/library/pdf/ERB0812.pdf

Second Life in DH-Pisa Wiki. (2008). Retrieved June 2010 from http://iu.di.unipi.it/wiki/index.php/IU_Second_Life

Senges, M., & Alier, M. (2009). Virtual worlds as environment for learning communities. In Lytras, D., Tennyson, R., & Pablos, P. (Eds.), *Knowledge networks: The social software perspective.* Hershey, PA: IGI Global.

Senzaki. (2004). *101 Zen stories.* Whitefish, MT: Kessinger Publishing, LLC.

Shaffer, D. W. (2006). Epistemic frames for epistemic games. *Computers & Education, 46*(3), 223. doi:10.1016/j.compedu.2005.11.003

Shang, D. (2006). Caledon Oxbridge University. Retrieved May, 16, 2010, at http://slurl.com/secondlife/Caledon%20 Oxbridge /92/197/27

Sheehy, P. (2008). *The great leveller- Second Life in middle school.* Retrieved from http://olpglobalkids.org/rezed/

Sherman, W. R., & Craig, A. B. (2003). *Understanding virtual reality.* San Francisco, CA: Morgan Kauffman.

Shih, Y.-C., & Yang, M.-T. (2008). A collaborative virtual environment for situated language learning using VEC3D. *Journal of Educational Technology & Society, 11*(1), 56–68.

Shneiderman, B., & Plaisant, C. (2005). *Designing the user interface* (4th ed.). Reading, MA: Addison-Wesley.

Short, J. A., Williams, F., & Christie, B. (1976). *The social psychology of telecommunications.* New York, NY: Wiley.

Shulman, L. (1986). Those who understand: Knowledge growth in teaching. *Educational Researcher, 15*, 4–14.

Shuman, L. J., Atman, C. J., Eschenbach, E. A., Evans, D., Felder, R. M., & Imbrie, P. K. … Richard, L. G. (2002). The future of engineering education. *Proceedings of the 32nd Annual ASEE/IEEE Conference on Frontiers in Education.*

Siemens, G., & Downes, S. (2005). Connectivism: A learning theory for the digital age. *International Journal of Instructional Technology and Distance Learning, 2*(1).

Sigala, M. (2007). Integrating Web 2.0 in e-learning environments: A socio-technical approach. *International Journal of Knowledge and Learning, 3*(6), 628–648. doi:10.1504/IJKL.2007.016837

Silva, K., & Larsen, J. E. (2010). *Designing interactive speaking activities in Second Life.* Amherst, MA: Presentation at CALICO.

Simon, H. A. (1996). *The sciences of the artificial* (3rd ed.). Cambridge, MA: MIT Press.

Sinclair, B., & Ferguson, K. (2009). Integrating simulated teaching/learning strategies in undergraduate nursing education. *International Journal of Nursing Education Scholarship, 6*(1). doi:10.2202/1548-923X.1676

Slavin, R. E. (1997). *Research on cooperative learning and achievement: A quarter century of research.* Annual Meeting of Pedagogical Psychology.

Slone, D. J. (2009). A methodology for measuring usability evaluation skills using the constructivist theory and the Second Life virtual world. *Journal of Usability Studies, 4*, 178–188.

SLoodle 0.4 brochure. (2009). Retrieved December 2009 from http://www.scribd.com/doc/ 14996661/SLOODLE-Brochure

Smith, S., Salaway, G., Caruso, J., & Katz, R. (2009). The ECAR study of undergraduate students and Information Technology. *EDUCAUSE Center for Applied Research, 6*, 61.

Smith, M., & Berge, Z. (2009). Social learning theory in Second Life. *Merlot Journal of Online Learning and Teaching, 5*(2).

Smith, S. P., & Hart, J. (2006). *Evaluating distributed cognitive resources for wayfinding in a desktop virtual environment.* IEEE Symposium on 3D User Interfaces (3DUI 2006), (pp. 3-10).

Solimeno, A., Mebane, M., Tomai, M., & Francescato, D. (2008). The influence of students and teachers characteristics on the efficacy of face-to-face and computer supported collaborative learning. *Computers & Education, 51*(1), 109–128. doi:10.1016/j.compedu.2007.04.003

Soloway, E., Norris, C., Blumenfeld, P., Fishman, B., Krajcik, J., & Marx, R. (2000). Log on education: K-12 and the Internet. *Communications of the ACM, 43*(1). doi:10.1145/323830.323838

Springer, R. (2009). Speech in a virtual world. *Speech Technology, 14*(5), 42–43.

Squire, K. D. (2006). From content to context: Videogames as designed experiences. *Educational Researcher, 35*(8), 19–29. doi:10.3102/0013189X035008019

Squire, K. D., McKinster, J. G., Barnett, M., Leuhmann, A. L., & Barab, S. A. (2001). Designed curriculum and local culture: Acknowledging the primacy of classroom culture. *Science Education, 87*(4), 468–489. doi:10.1002/sce.10084

Squire, K. D. (2008). Video game–based learning: An emerging paradigm for instruction. *Performance Improvement Quarterly, 21*(2), 7–36. doi:10.1002/piq.20020

Stake, R. E. (2000). Case studies. In Denzin, N. K., & Lincoln, Y. S. (Eds.), *Handbook of qualitative research* (2nd ed., pp. 435–454). Thousand Oaks, CA: Sage Publications Ltd.

Stapleton, A. (2004). Serious games: Serious opportunities. *Proceedings of the 2004 Australian Game Developers Conference*, (pp. 1-6).

Steadman, R., Coates, W., Huang, Y., Matevosian, R., Larmon, B., McCullough, L., & Ariel, D. (2006). Simulation-based training is superior to problem-based learning for the acquisition of critical assessment and management skills. *Journal for the Society of Critical Care Medicine, 34*(1).

Steed, A., & Frecon, E. (2005). Construction of collaborative virtual environments. In Sanchez-Segura, M. I. (Ed.), *Developing future interactive systems* (pp. 235–268). Hershey, PA: IGI Global.

Steinkuehler, C. A. (2006). Massively multiplayer onine video gaming as participation in a discourse. *Mind, Culture, and Activity, 13*(1), 38–52. doi:10.1207/s15327884mca1301_4

Stephenson, N. (1992). *Snow crash.* New York, NY: Bantam Spectra Books.

Straub, E. T. (2009). Understanding technology adoption: Theory and future directions for informal learning. *Review of Educational Research, 79*(2), 625–649. doi:10.3102/0034654308325896

Strijbos, J. W., Kirschner, P. A., & Martens, R. L. (2004). *What we know about CSCL: And implementing it in higher education.* New York, NY: Kluwer Academic Publishers. doi:10.1007/1-4020-7921-4

Su, S., & Loftin, R. B. (2001). A shared virtual environment for exploring and designing molecules. *Communications of the ACM, 44*(12). doi:10.1145/501317.501344

Sulcic, A. (2010). *Taking Moodle out of the classroom: Making learning mobile, context-aware and fun.* Moodle. si 4th International Conference.

Sumner, M. (2004). *Enterprise resource planning.* Upper Saddle River, NJ: Prentice Hall.

Surry, D. W. (1997). *Presentation at the Annual Conference of the Association for Educational Communications and Technology* (AECT).

Svensson, P. (2002). Virtual weddings and a real wedding of linguistics, literature and cultural studies. Retrieved on June 16, 2010, from http://www.rhu.se/activities/projects/financed_projects/q-s/svensson_patrik_98_slut.pdf

Swain, M., & Lapkin, S. (1995). Problems in output and the cognitive processes they generate: A step towards second language learning. *Applied Linguistics, 16*, 371–391. doi:10.1093/applin/16.3.371

Syanum, S., & Bigatti, S. M. (2009). Academic course engagement during one semester forecasts college success: Engaged students are more likely to ear a degree, do it faster, and do it better. *Journal of College Student Development, 50*(1), 120–132. doi:10.1353/csd.0.0055

Syedain, H. (2008, April 17). Out of this world. *People Management.*

Teeler, D., & Gray, P. (2000). *How to use the Internet in ELT Harlow.* Upper Saddle River, NJ: Pearson Education Limited - Longman.

TheArketipo blog. (2009). Retrieved June 2010 from http://arketipo-sl.blogspot.com/

TheLondon Charter in Second Life project. (2009). Retrieved June 2010 from http://iu.di.unipi.it/sl/london/

The London Charter. (2006). Retrieved June 2010 from http://www.londoncharter.org/

The Schome Community. (2007). *The Schome-NAGTY teen Second Life pilot final report.* Retrieved from http://kn.open.ac.uk/public/ document.cfm?docid=9851

Thomas, S. (2008). Pervasive scale: A model of pervasive, ubiquitous, and ambient learning. *IEEE Pervasive Computing / IEEE Computer Society [and] IEEE Communications Society, 7*(1), 85–88.

Thomas, A. (n.d.) *Virtual Macbeth.* Retrieved on June 19, 2010, from http://www.virtualmacbeth.wikispaces.com.

Thompson, M., Tranvik, T., & Selle, P. (1999). *Doing technology (and democracy) the Pack-Domkey's way: The technomorphic approach to ICT policy.* Retrieved from http://www.sv.uio.no/mutr/ publikasjoner/rapp2000 /rapport9.htm

Ting, Y., Lin, S. D., Chen, C. H., Lee, S. S., & Chang, Y. F. (2003). Development of a virtual reality surgical platform for unicompartmental knee replacement. *Proceedings of the IEEE International Conference on Systems, Man and Cybernetics, 3,* (pp. 2932-2937).

Tobin, L. (2009, April 21). From video marking to Second Life, technology is transforming the options for online students. *The Guardian.* Retrieved October 22, 2009, from http://www.guardian.co.uk/education/2009/apr/21/ elearning-university-of-london/print

Todd, R. J. (1999). Transformational leadership and transformational learning: Information literacy and the World Wide Web. *NASSP Bulletin,* (March): 1999.

Trahan, M. (2004). *Online college students.* Unpublished research study.

Trasler, J. (2002). Effective learning depends on blend. *Industrial and Commercial Training, 34*(5), 191–193. doi:10.1108/00197850210437111

Triola, M. M., Campion, N., McGee, J. B., Albright, S., Greene, P., Smothers, V., & Ellaway, R. (2007). An XML standard for virtual patients: Exchanging case-based simulations in medical education. *AMIA Annual Symposium Proceedings,* (pp. 741-745).

Tromp, J. G., Steed, A., & Wilson, J. R. (2003). Systematic usability evaluation and design issues for collaborative virtual environments. *Presence (Cambridge, Mass.), 12*(3), 241–267. doi:10.1162/105474603765879512

Trotter, A. (2008). Educators get a Second Life. *Education Week, 27*(42), 1.

Tsitouridou, M., & Vryzas, K. (2003). Early childhood teachers' attitudes towards computer and Information Technology: The case of Greece. *Information Technology in Childhood Education Annual, 1,* 187–207.

Turbee, L. (1996). *MOOing in a foreign language: How, why, and who?* Retrieved on November 26, 2007, from http://web.syr.edu/~lmturbee/itechtm.html

Turkay, S. (2008). *Global Kids, Inc's Science Through Second Life curriculum evaluation.* Retrieved from http://www.webstrategies.com/ NPC/StSLEvaluation.pdf

Turkle, S. (1995). *Life on the screen: Identity in the age of the internet.* New York, NY: Simon & Schuster.

Turkle, S. (1995). *Life on the screen: Identity in the age of the Internet.* New York, NY: Simon & Schuster.

Twain, M. (1880). *A tramp abroad.* Des Moines, IA: Library of America.

Twining, P., & Footring, S. (2010). The Schome Park programme: Exploring educational alternatives. In Peachey, A., Gillen, J., Livingstone, D., & Smith-Robbins, S. (Eds.), *Researching learning in virtual worlds* (pp. 53–74). Lancaster, PA: Springer. doi:10.1007/978-1-84996-047-2_4

Tyberghein, J. (2002). *Crystal Space game engine*. Retrieved from http://crystal.sourceforge.net

University of Porto. (2009). *Erasmus statistic report - partnerships and mobility of students, teaching staff and staff training*. International Office.

Veen, W., & Vrakking, B. (2006). *Homo zappiens: Growing up in a digital age*. London, UK: Network Continuum Education.

Veerman, A., & Veldhuis-Diermanse, E. (2001). Collaborative learning through computer-mediated communication in academic education. *Proceedings of Euro-CSCL 2001*.

Veletsianos, G. (2009). The impact and implications of virtual character expressiveness on learning and agent-learner interactions. *Journal of Computer Assisted Learning, 25*(4), 345–357. doi:10.1111/j.1365-2729.2009.00317.x

Venkatesh, V., & Davis, F. D. (2000). A theoretical extension of the technology acceptance model: Four longitudinal field studies. *Management Science, 46*(2), 186–205. doi:10.1287/mnsc.46.2.186.11926

Virvou, M., & Katsionis, G. (2008). On the usability and likeability of virtual reality games for education: The case of VR-ENGAGE. *Computers & Education, 50*, 154–178. doi:10.1016/j.compedu.2006.04.004

Vygotsky, L. S. (1978). *Mind and society: The development of higher mental processes*. Cambridge, MA: Harvard University Press.

Vygotsky, L. S. (1962). *Thought and language*. Cambridge, MA: MIT Press. doi:10.1037/11193-000

Vygotsky, L. (1986). *Thought and language*. Cambridge, MA: MIT Press.

Vygotsky, L. S. (1967). Play and its role in the mental development of the child. *Social Psychology, 5*, 6–18.

Wang, S., & Hsu, H. (2009). Using the ADDIE model to design Second Life activities for online learners. *TechTrends: Linking Research and Practice to Improve Learning, 53*(6), 76–82.

Wang, C. X., Song, H., Stone, D. E., & Yan, Q. (2009). Integrating Second Life into an EFL program in China: Research collaborations across the continents. *Tech Trend, 53*(6).

Wang, Y. (2007). Chinese higher education on an overpass of fourfold transitions. *Journal of Higher Education Research in China, 8*.

Wankel, C., & Kingsley, J. (Eds.). (2009). *Higher education in virtual worlds: Teaching and learning in Second Life*. London, UK: Information Age Publishing.

Warkentin, M. E., Sayeed, L., & Hightower, R. (1997). Virtual teams versus face-to-face teams: An exploratory study of a Web-based conference system. *Decision Sciences, 28*(4), 975–996. doi:10.1111/j.1540-5915.1997.tb01338.x

Waters, J. (2009, January). A Second Life for educators. [from http://www.technteach.info/asecondlifeforeducators.pdf]. *T.H.E. Journal*, 1–6. Retrieved October 22, 2009.

Wearmouth, J., Smith, A. P., & Soler, J. (2004). Computer conferencing with access to a guest expert in the professional development of special educational needs coordinators. *British Journal of Educational Technology, 35*(1), 81–93. doi:10.1111/j.1467-8535.2004.00370.x

Wenger, E. (1998). *Communities of practice: Learning, meaning, and identity*. Cambridge, UK: Cambridge University Press.

Wertsch, J. V. (1984). The zone of proximal development: Some conceptual issues. *New Directions for Child and Adolescent Development, 1984*, 7–18..doi:10.1002/cd.23219842303

Wertsch, J. V. (1985). *Cultural, communication, and cognition: Vygotskian perspectives*. Cambridge, UK: Cambridge University Press.

Wheeler, S. (2001). Information and Communication Technologies and the changing role of the teacher. *Journal of Educational Media, 26*(1). doi:10.1080/135816500120069292

Wilhelm, W., Ross, S. C., & Love, E. (2009). *Opportunities and challenges for business education in Second Life. Higher Education in Virtual Worlds Teaching and Learning in Second Life*. Bingley, UK: Emerald Group Publishing Limited.

Willms, J. D., Friesen, S., & Miltion, P. (2009). *What did you do in school today: Transforming classrooms through social, academic, and intellectual engagement.* Toronto, ON, Canada: National Report, Canadian Education Association.

Wilson, W. (2002). *Lessons in reality: Teaching project management, professionalism and ethics to third year IT students. Informing Science, InSITE - Where Parallels Intersect.* Informing Science Institute.

Windeatt, S., Hardisty, D., & Eastment, D. (2000). *The Internet.* Oxford, UK: Oxford University Press.

Winn, W. (1993). *A conceptual basis for educational applications of virtual reality.* Human Interface Technology Laboratory, University of Washington. (Report No. TR-93-9).

Wittrock, M. C. (1978). The cognitive movement of instruction. *Educational Psychologist, 13*, 15–29. doi:10.1080/00461527809529192

Woolfolk, A. (2007). *Educational psychology* (10th ed.). Boston, MA: Allyn and Bacon.

Yankelovich, N., Walker, W., Roberts, P., Wessler, M., Kaplan, J., & Provino, J. (2004). Meeting central: Making distributed meetings more effective. *Proceedings of CSCW '04.*

Yellowlees, P. M., & Cook, J. N. (2006). Education about hallucinations using an Internet virtual reality system: A qualitative survey. *Academic Psychiatry, 30*(6), 534–539. doi:10.1176/appi.ap.30.6.534

Yellowless, P., & Cook, J. (2006). Education about hallucinations using an Internet virtual reality system: A qualitative study. *American Psychiatry, 30*, 534–539.

Yildirim, S. (2000). Effects of an educational computing course on pre-service and in-service teachers: A discussion and analysis of attitudes and use. *Journal of Research on Computing in Education, 32*(4), 479–495.

Youngblut, C. (1998). *Educational uses of virtual reality technology. (Technical report IDA Document D-2128).* Alexandria, Virginia: Institute for Defense Analyses.

Yuen, H. K., Law, N., & Chan, H. (1999). Improving IT training for serving teachers through evaluation. In Cumming, G., Okamoto, T., & Gomez, L. (Eds.), *Advanced research in computers and communications in education* (Vol. 2, pp. 441–448). Amsterdam, The Netherlands: IOS Press.

Zack, M. (1993). Interactivity and communication mode choice in ongoing management groups. *Information Systems Research, 4*(3), 207–261. doi:10.1287/isre.4.3.207

Zagami, J. (2010). *Second Life as an environment for education.* Paper presented at ISTE 2010 (International Society of Technology in Education (ISTE), Denver, CO.

Zaharias, P. (2004). Tutorial: Usability and e-learning: The road towards integration. *eLearn Magazine, 6*, 4.

Zaharias, P. (2006). A usability evaluation method for e-learning: Focus on motivation and learning. *Proceedings of CHI 2006.*

Zajtchuk, R., & Satava, R. M. (1997). Medical applications of virtual reality. *Communications of the ACM, 40*(9). doi:10.1145/260750.260768

Zhang, Y., & Espinoza, S. (1998). Relationships among computer self-efficacy, attitudes towards computers, and desirability of learning computer skills. *Journal of Research on Computing in Education, 30*(4), 420–431.

Zhou, G., Nocente, N., & Brouwer, W. (2008). Understanding student cognition through an analysis of their preconceptions in physics. *The Alberta Journal of Educational Research, 54*(1), 14–29.

About the Contributors

Giovanni Vincenti is a Lecturer for the Department of Computer and Information Sciences at Towson University, in Towson, MD. He received his Doctorate of Science in Applied Information Technology from Towson University in 2007. He has been teaching undergraduate and graduate courses for several years, letting him develop his interest in instructional technologies that range from simple learning objects as a supplement to in-person instruction, all the way to the utilization of Virtual Worlds in the classroom. He has been collaborating for years with James Braman, co-authoring several published works including the edited volume titled "Teaching through Multi-User Virtual Environments: Applying Dynamic Elements to the Modern Classroom." Vincenti and Braman are also leading e-learning projects of the Institute of Computer Sciences, Social Informatics, and Telecommunications Engineering (ICST). In addition, Dr. Vincenti also serves as a consultant to companies and universities that focus on online learning.

James Braman is a Lecturer in the Department of Computer and Information Sciences at Towson University. He earned a M.S. in Computer Science in 2006 and is currently pursuing a D.Sc. in Information Technology. James serves as joint editor-in-chief for the Institute for Computer Sciences, Social Informatics and Telecommunications Engineering (ICST) Transactions on e-education and e-learning along with Dr. Vincenti. He has published several edited books, the most recent, Teaching through Multi-User Virtual Environments: Adding Dynamic Elements to the Modern Classroom. He has been involved in virtual world research for several years, along with providing consulting and research services for businesses and organizations utilizing virtual worlds and augmented reality. As one of the four principle faculty members in the development of Towson University's Second Life initiative, he is actively promoting MUVEs for use in education. He has also published numerous articles related to affective computing, intelligent agents, computer ethics and education in virtual and immersive environments.

* * *

Nan B. Adams is an Associate Professor of Educational Leadership and Technology at Southeastern Louisiana University and currently serves as doctoral faculty. Her research interests center on the social aspects of technological change and currently focus on curriculum theory and the design of virtual learning environments, digital intelligence, and digital ethnicity.

Timothy Allen is IT Director, Web, for Wharton Research Data Services at The Wharton School at the University of Pennsylvania. Wharton Research Data Services provides academic financial research data to over 275 institutions across the world. In his previous role, Timothy was IT Director for Crompco, LLC, the largest independent environmental compliance tester in the petroleum industry. While at Crompco, Timothy spearheaded an effort in January, 2004 to build a virtual gas station, becoming the first corporate training simulation in Second Life. Known as FlipperPA Peregrine in the virtual realm, Timothy is one of the oldest Second Life users, joining in 2003. Timothy also started SLBoutique.com, a Web based marketplace for virtual products which was eventually sold to Linden Lab, and was a founding member of the yearly Second Life Community Convention.

Madelon Alpert has an MA in Reading from the University of Arizona, Tucson Arizona as well as an Educational Administration degree. She has been in education since 1961 as a teacher, reading specialist, school administrator, and college professor. The span of her career has provided rich experiences, which include diverse student populations and communities. She has taught all age levels from kindergarten to the adult learner, from traditional classrooms to the online platform. She has shared her knowledge and expertise by presenting at state, national, and international conferences on global issues dealing with teacher preparation programs, effective online teaching strategies, and staff development for adjunct instructors. She is currently the Lead Faculty for the student teaching program of National University in Costa Mesa, California.

David M. Antonacci is the Director of Teaching and Learning Technologies at the University of Kansas Medical Center (KUMC). In this role, he provides leadership in the use of technology-based teaching and learning strategies at KUMC. Dave is also a doctoral candidate in the School of Information Science and Learning Technologies (SISLT) at the University of Missouri-Columbia. Better known as Pietro Maracas in Second Life, Dave and Pietro have been exploring Second Life since its release from beta in 2004. Dave's other interests include case-based reasoning, computer-mediated communication, emerging technologies, online learning, technology integration, and educational simulations and games.

Raul Aquino-Santos graduated from the University of Colima with a BE in Electrical Engineering, and received his MS degree in Telecommunications from the Centre for Scientific Research and Higher Education in Ensenada, Mexico in 1990. He holds a PhD from the Department of Electrical and Electronic Engineering of the University of Sheffield, England. Since 2005, he has been with the College of Telematics at the University of Colima, where he is currently a Research Professor in telecommunications networks. His current research interests include wireless and sensor networks.

Cathy Arreguin has a Masters of Education, Educational Technology from San Diego State University. Formerly a K12 teacher, she is currently an online instructor for the SDSU EDTEC department–including a course for practicing K12 teachers on the use of MUVEs in the classroom. As an instructional designer, through her business, Instructional Muse, she regularly provides MUVE-related professional development, consultation, and MUVE design and development for both K12 and higher education educators and organizations wishing to incorporate effective MUVE practices into their designed instructional strategies. In addition to her writing, she regularly presents on K12 MUVE topics, most recently at the Digital Media and Learning, Immersive Education Day, and The Virtual Worlds Conferences. Recent projects include work with SDSU, Santa Barbara City, The Sloan Consortium, Global Kids, Inc., and individual educators. She is currently a co-designer/developer for Virtual Oaxaca, a mixed-reality project funded by the National Endowment for the Humanities.

Jacqueline Barnes is a Learning Sciences doctoral student at Indiana University. She received a B.S. in neuroscience from the University of Pittsburgh in 2009. Since arriving at IU, she has contributed extensively to both research and design on the Quest Atlantis project, and has been a lead designer on two math missions. Through continuing research on learning through games, her future research will pursue possibilities for metacognitive strategies, developing new technology for special education, creativity, and defining forms of intelligence. In particular, she is interested in finding ways to differentiate instruction for both mainstream and special education classrooms using new technologies such as immersive games.

Jim Barrett, B.A. in Journalism (USQ, Australia), M.A. in English Literature (Umeå University, Sweden), is a final stage PhD candidate at Umeå University, with a shared affiliation between the Department of Language Studies and HUMlab, a digital humanities computing lab. His research focuses on narrative and performative modes in digitally mediated literary works. Virtual and gaming worlds, interactive spatial narratives, augmented reality narratives, and the structures of narratives in indigenous and tribal societies are of particular interest to him. Other areas of activity for Barrett include performance, sound, and digital art. Barrett is Australian but has been living in Europe since the late 1990s.

Valerie Bartelt is currently a doctoral candidate in the Kelley School of Business at Indiana University. Her research interests include innovative technologies, group collaboration, and work-life balance issues. She received a M.S. in Immersive Mediated Environments. Bartelt has also worked as a consultant developing e-learning interactive media components for various companies.

Jan Baum is a design educator and consultant in Web 2.0 and immersive learning environments. With sixteen years of teaching at the university level, her current research initiatives include 3D immersive learning environments, interdisciplinary social design, and the integration of design, digital manufacturing, and new technologies. The Global Design Collaboration, an international collaborative project, engages a global dialogue focusing on communication technologies, multi-user virtual environments, and digital manufacturing. She is one of four Principal Investigators on the Towson Innovation Lab in Second Life grant. Baum writes and presents across disciplines. Her design work has been exhibited at the following international venues: The Museum of Decorative and Applied Arts (Moscow, Russia), International Design Center (Nagoya, Japan) Gallery Mukkumto (Seoul, South Korea). Her work is in the permanent collection of the Smithsonian American Art Museum. Currently Baum directs the Object Design and Metals + Jewelry programs at Towson University, Baltimore, Maryland.

Alberto Bucciero earned a PhD at the University of Lecce, Italy in 2006. Since 2003 he is a tutor in academic courses of Software Engineering and Computer Graphics, and since 2006 is a lecturer in Management of Business Information course. He carries on his research activities at the Innovation Engineering Innovation Dept. and his main interest are about the following topics: Enhanced Learning Management System based on 3D virtual environment to support the collaborative learning work on Internet, Service Oriented Architecture and middleware tools to support B2B e-commerce for the Supply

Chain Management, modeling and formalization of the requirements for the analysis of Information Systems, and formal declarative languages based on XML. He is member of ACM, IEEE Computer Society.

David Burden started his career in army communications before being "demobbed" in 1990, when he then worked for a variety of IT companies ending up as Marketing Director of Aseriti, a £70m B2B IT services company. During the Dot Com boom, David founded a wireless data company developing both WAP and Voice XML systems, as well as founding the Midlands chapter of the First Tuesday Networking organization. David has been involved in virtual worlds since the mid 1990s, having created early spaces using VRML and played in several early 3D communal worlds. David has been in Second Life since 2004, and has also had homes in There.com and Alpha World. David founded Daden, a Virtual Worlds and Virtual Character Consultancy in 2004 to help businesses and organizations explore the social, educational, and commercial potential of virtual worlds. David has a keen interest in artificial intelligence and Daden have an AI platform for use both in SL and on the Web. David is a Chartered Engineer and lives in Birmingham-where he is active in city and regional business, technology, and innovation initiatives.

Victor Callaghan is Professor of Computer Science, leader of the Inhabited Intelligent Environments Group at Essex University. He holds a BEng and PhD in Electronics and Computing from Sheffield University. His main expertise concerns embedded computing, especially applied to the creation of virtual environments, mixed-reality, digital homes, intelligent buildings, and other ubiquitous computing environments. He has authored over 100 papers in international journals, conferences, and books, and he holds 4 key patents on embedded agents and end-user programming techniques. He is on the organizational team of major intelligent environment and pervasive computing conferences (e.g. Pervasive Computing & Applications, Ubiquitous Intelligence & Computing, Intelligent Environments) and journals (e.g. Intelligent Buildings International, Pervasive Computing & Communications, Ubiquitous Computing & Intelligence).

Niccolo Capanni received a BSc (Hons) mathematics from Strathclyde University, UK; MSc (Eng) Information Systems & PhD Artificial Intelligence (Eng) from The Robert Gordon University, UK. He lectures the areas of Web Technologies, and publishes in the areas of artificial intelligence, hypersonics, and education.

Marc Conrad received a PhD in Mathematics (Algebraic Number Theory) at the Universität des Saarlandes (Germany) in 1998. After a period of research in Computer Security, his interests are now in the societal aspects of Information Technology. He teaches as a Senior Lecturer at the University of Bedfordshire in the subjects of Project Management and Software Systems. Recent work in the context of Second Life includes Project Management (as discussed in this book), a joint project with colleagues from media and social studies that tries to understand the relationship between avatars and identity, and the teaching of LSL (Linden Scripting Language) as part of a course Comparative Integrated Systems. He also supervises a PhD on customer satisfaction in virtual worlds. The name of his avatar in Second Life is Sanf Oh and she has her own Website at http://sl.sanfoh.com.

Ricardo Cruz is a Portuguese and English as a Foreign Language high school teacher with a degree in Portuguese and English Literature by the University of Porto. He has always been enthusiastic about distance education projects. During his teacher training year, he developed a Web-based blended-learning platform for English as a foreign language for his students. He has participated in conferences about language learning and teaching in Lisbon and Toronto. He is the responsible for the Social Communication Technological Course at the Development and Education Institute (INED) in Maia, Portugal, and he is a Portuguese teacher at INED Nevogilde, in Porto, Portugal. Currently he is taking a communication sciences Masters at the University of Porto. His main interests are virtual worlds as a learning and teaching platform and political communication through online social media.

Michael DeMers, OTLC (2007): New Mexico State University, (Ph.D. (1985), MPhil (1983): University of Kansas, MS (1980), BSEd (1974): University of North Dakota, is Associate Professor of geography at New Mexico State University. Dr. DeMers is the author of four GIS books including GIS for Dummies, and co-editor of the GIS&T Body of Knowledge, published jointly by the University Consortium for Geographic Information Science (UCGIS) and the Association of American Geographers (AAG). His first book, Fundamentals of Geographic Information Systems, now in its fourth edition, has been translated into both Russian and simple Chinese, and his GIS Modeling in Raster is currently being translated into Arabic. Mike's research involves GIS applications and design, GIS curriculum development, and online GIS education. DeMers is the Vice Chair of the Association of American Geographers (AAG) Geography Education Specialty Group, a member of the board of the (AAG) Applied Geography Specialty Group, and the Applied Geography Conferences, Inc. Besides his traditional university teaching duties, he is also a mentor and teaches Intermediate Second Life for Educators for Sloan-C.

Stavros Demetriadis is Assistant Professor of Technology-Enhanced Learning at CSD-AUTH. His main research interests include adaptive and collaborative systems for technology-enhanced learning, integration of ICT in education, blended learning, and didactics of informatics.

Hugh Denard BA (Dublin), MA, PhD (Exeter) is Associate Director of King's Visualization Lab (KVL) in the Centre for Computing in the Humanities, King's College London, where he convenes the MA Digital Culture and Technology. He is a specialist in ancient Greek, Roman and twentieth-century Irish theatre history and in the application of digital visualization technologies in the humanities. He proposed and edits the internationally-recognized London Charter for the Computer-based Visualization of Cultural Heritage and has jointly directed numerous projects funded by the AHRC, Arts Council England, British Council-Italian Ministry of Research, Eduserv Foundation, JISC, Leverhulme Trust, and the Metropolitan Museum of Art. In Second Life, he co-directed the Theatron 3 project, collaborates with artist Michael Takeo Magruder, and curates Digital Humanities Island, in which he teaches a postgraduate module on Applied Visualization in the Arts, Humanities, and Cultural Heritage.

Nicoletta Di Blas is assistant professor with the Department of Electronics and Information of Politecnico di Milano. She graduated in Classics and obtained a PhD in Linguistic Sciences from The Catholic University, Milan. She currently teaches Communication Theory for Politecnico di Milano (Como campus) and Communication for Cultural Heritage for the University of Lugano (Switzerland), at the TEC–CH (Technology-Enhanced Communication for Cultural Heritage) Master course. She works for the HOC-lab of Politecnico di Milano (http://hoc.elet.polimi.it) in projects related to the following areas: (1) multimedia, multi-channel applications (more than 40 developed so far, mainly in the Cultural Heritage domain); (2) serious games design (3D collaborative worlds, involving thousands of students from Europe and the USA, digital storytelling tools); (3) impact evaluation (on both fields of application).

Daniel C Doolan is a lecturer at the School of Computing, Robert Gordon University, UK. His research interests primarily lie in the areas of graphics, mobile, and parallel computing. He has published in excess of fifty articles covering these subject areas, with several focused on the pedagogical aspects of mobile computing.

Susan Vining Dupre is a National Board Certified Teacher in Adolescent and Young Adult English Language Arts who is pursuing a doctoral degree in Educational Leadership with an emphasis on Instructional Technology from the University of Louisiana at Lafayette. She is employed as the district technology facilitator for a rural school district in Louisiana and as an adjunct instructor in English Language Arts by the Louisiana Virtual Schools.

Arthur Edwards is a Senior Professor/Researcher at the College of Telematics of the University of Colima, Mexico, where his primary interest is Computer Assisted Language Learning, multimedia applications, collaborative learning environments, educational Information Systems, virtual reality applications, and wireless and mobile learning systems.

Jiuguang Feng was born in Inner Mongolia, China. In 2007, Jiuguang received his Master's degree from the College of Education at Towson University. He had been working as a teacher for seven years in China before he came to the U.S. in January 2009 for his doctoral study. He was the winner of the Marilyn Nicholas scholarship in 2009. Since coming to the U.S., he became very interested in MUVEs, and he believes that they are a wonderful tool to create immersive simulations in an educational setting. His interests include technology integration in education, especially MUVE learning environments, and technology integration in foreign language education.

Ricardo Fernandes is a social science researcher with a degree in Sociology from the University of Porto. He has always been interested in investigation projects, in the areas of Sociology and, more recently, Communication Sciences. He has participated in a conference about language learning and teaching in Toronto. He is a researcher at the company Dynargie, in Portugal, an enterprise whose core business is translating the strategies of companies into people's behavior, performance, and motivation. Nowadays he is taking a Communication Sciences Masters at the University of Porto. His interests are human resources investigation, virtual worlds as a learning and teaching environment, social networking, as well as political communication through online social media.

Beverly Forbes holds a Bachelor of Science in Business Education/Office Administration from Old Dominion University. She was employed as an Undergraduate Academic Advisor and Assistant to the Chairman of the Department of Electrical and Computer Engineering for 18 years. During that time, she completed her Master of Science in Guidance and Counseling with College Student Personnel including a practicum within the Career Management Center. Following a 6-year absence from the university, she returned in July 2003 to serve as the Career Management Center Liaison to the Batten College of Engineering and Technology where she manages the CMC engineering satellite office as the career specialist for engineering and engineering technology students and alumni. Beverly is also the Director of Experiential Education, providing oversight for internships and cooperative education experiences in all six university colleges. In addition, she teaches courses in career implementation and career engagement. Beverly serves as a co-advisor for the Golden Key International Honour Society and is currently the President-Elect of the ODU Association of University Administrators.

Paulo Frias is a teacher and researcher in Communication Sciences at University of Porto. He has a degree in Architecture at the University of Porto, a Master's degree in Interactive Apps at the University Pompeu Fabra in Barcelona, and a PhD in Communication Sciences at the New University of Lisbon. Paulo is currently managing the virtual space of the U. Porto in Second Life®. He is also responsible for a blog about virtual worlds, associated with the daily newspaper Público. He also has founded and edited a Portuguese Design magazine and worked in a private TV station as a reporter. In his PhD dissertation, Paulo studied the communication and spatial representation and appropriation in virtual worlds processes, especially among the Portuguese community in Second Life®. Currently, he is involved with an online project connecting the University of Porto and a private daily newspaper, where he co-leads the editorial and researching tasks.

Keysha I. Gamor earned her Ph.D. in Education, majoring in ISD and Organizational Learning from George Mason University in Fairfax, VA. Dr. Gamor is associated with the GMU Center for Online Workforce Development and is a Sr. ISD/Sr. Research Analyst at ICF International. She is recognized for research and publications in virtual worlds and immersive learning technologies. With 15+ yrs of experience in teaching, ISD, adult education, and training, she serves on the board of the United States Distance Learning Association (USDLA) and Association of Virtual Worlds (AVW), and participates in the IEEE VW Standard working group.

Adela Gánem-Gutiérrez is a Lecturer in the Department of Language and Linguistics at the University of Essex. Her research interests include: the impact of the computer in the L2 classroom and the potential of Virtual World Environments for L2 learning, task-based learning and the role of different CALL tasks in the learning process, as well as the significance of feedback and scaffolding in collaborative activity (through or at) the computer for L2 learning. More generally, in the area of SLA, she is interested in sociocultural theory, the role of interaction and collaborative activity in the second language learning process, and concept-based instruction.

Miguel A. Garcia-Ruiz graduated in Computer Systems engineering and obtained his MSc in Computer Science from the University of Colima, Mexico. He received his PhD in Computer Science and Artificial Intelligence at the University of Sussex, UK. He took a virtual reality course at Salford University, UK, and a graphics techniques internship at the Madrid Polytechnic University, Spain. Miguel is a professor of Computer Science with the College of Telematics of the University of Colima. He has published various scientific papers in major journals, book chapters and two books, and directed a video documentary on virtual reality. His research interests include virtual reality and usability of multimodal human-computer interfaces. Currently, Miguel is also a Visiting Professor at the University of Ontario Institute of Technology, Canada.

Michael Gardner, PhD, is a Research Fellow and Director of the Digital Lifestyles Centre at the University of Essex. This center explores future lifestyles based around the technical vision of ambient and pervasive computing. He has over 25 years of experience in knowledge media both within the industrial research environment and academia. During that time he has worked extensively in the areas of virtual reality, e-learning, collaborative working, social software and the Semantic Web. Over the years, he has worked closely with many industrial partners on innovative research projects, such as BT, Sun Microsystems, and Apple Computer. Many of his projects have been involved in developing and deploying innovative technologies in a range of concrete user contexts, such as within the home/school boundary, call-centers, and higher education settings. His current research interests are focused on the use of virtual reality environments for work, research, learning, and teaching.

Stefan Gelfgren, PhD in History of Science and Ideas (Umeå University, Sweden), MPhil in History of Christianity (University of Birmingham, UK), now works as associate professor and research coordinator at HUMlab, Umeå University. Gelfgren wrote his dissertation on secularization and revivalism in 19th century Sweden. He is interested in the relationship between social and religious transformation, and apart from the dissertation, has also done work on the relationship between revivalism and modernity, and revivalism and adult education. In the book "Christianity and The Modern World View: Northern Europe 1500-2000" (in Swedish) Gelfgren combines the history of ideas with church history. He is currently working in the research project "Pinocchio goes to Church: The Religious life of Avatars," studying how religious faith and practices are constructed and expressed in virtual worlds.

Melissa Gresalfi is an Assistant Professor in the Learning Sciences at Indiana University, and the Associate Director of the Center for Research on Learning and Technology. After receiving her PhD in Educational Psychology at Stanford University, she joined the faculty at IU in 2006. Her research considers cognition and social context by examining student learning as a function of participation in activity systems. Her current projects, funded by the National Science Foundation, the MacArthur Foundation, the Spencer Foundation, and the Department of Education, focus on investigating and designing innovative environments to support students' development of particular dispositions towards learning and engaging in mathematics, science, and beyond.

Berit Irene Helgheim is an Associate Professor with the Department of Economics, Informatics and Social Science at Molde University College in Norway. She has a MSc is in Logistics (2002) and PhD in Logistics (2007) from Molde University College. Dr. Helgheim teaches courses on Purchasing, Supply Chain Management and Enterprise Systems where Second Life has been used in various assignments for role playing activities.

Bernard Horan is a senior researcher in the School of Computer Science and Electronic Engineering at the University of Essex. Prior to joining the University, Horan was a Senior Staff Engineer for Sun Microsystems Laboratories, where he was the Principal Investigator and technical lead of the successful collaborative project that used Project Wonderland to create a mixed reality teaching & learning environment. Horan's earlier research has included work on the Semantic Web as part of Sun Labs' Advanced Search Technology project (he was a member of the W3C WebOnt WG) and the Sun SPOT project.

Bjørn Jæger is an Associate Professor with the Department of Economics, Informatics, and Social Science at Molde University College in Norway, and an Adjunct Research Fellow at School of Information Systems, Curtin University of Technology, Australia since 2009. His MSc is in Nuclear Physics (1989) and his PhD is in Informatics (2000) from the University of Bergen in Norway. Bjørn teaches courses on Information Assurance, Robust and Secure Systems, Enterprise Systems, and Supply Chain Management. He was project manager and co-founder of the Kamimo Virtual Campus in Second Life.

Andrew Jinman: Growing up on a steady diet of Ultima online, Warhammer, and Neverwinter Nights, he is no stranger to the MMORPGs scene. In 200,2 Andrew continued his interests in this genre and enrolled at Plymouth University to study digital art and technology. Then, in 2004, he experienced the sensational game of World of Warcraft, giving himself a greater insight into the community and behavior of online personas. In 2006, his interest for immersive environments grew as he began to further shape and broaden his area of study. The pivotal experience of WoW allowed him to comprehend and question gaming dynamics and player motivations, as defined in his dissertation. In 2007, he joined Twofour Learning, propelling the company into extremely new and groundbreaking markets, exploring virtual worlds and game based learning in education, and investigating their commercial potential throughout the company, overseeing the technical and creative developments across all Second Life and Teen Second Life projects for local schools and educational institutes. This, including The Open University, Plymouth City Council, Stoke Damerel and Estover Community Colleges. In 2010, Andrew joined Daden Limited as their PVIOTE product and community manager where he continues to investigate and write on the theme of v-learning to justify the importance of virtual worlds within education.

Regina Kaplan-Rakowski has a strong background in foreign languages, which allows her to combine expertise in applied linguistics with the research opportunities that are available using modern instructional technology. Kaplan-Rakowski's education includes B.Ed. in TESL, M.Ed. in European Studies, and M.A. in Foreign Languages and Literatures. Presently, she is pursuing a doctorate in Curriculum & Instruction (Instructional Technology & Design) at Southern Illinois University, Carbondale. Her current focus is research on the educational possibilities of teaching foreign languages in virtual environments, especially through virtual worlds and digital games. Nevertheless, she has also accumulated detailed research interests in second language acquisition, especially in bilingualism/multilingualism, code-switching, and the application of mnemonics in language acquisition and instruction.

Bill Kapralos is an Assistant Professor in the Game Development and Entrepreneurship Program at the University of Ontario Institute of Technology. Bill's current research interests include: real-time acoustical modeling and spatial sound generation for virtual environments and videogames, multi-modal virtual environments, perception of auditory events, and serious games development. He is currently involved in a number of serious games initiatives including those for training of accountants, community health nurses, critical care providers, and orthopaedic surgeons. Bill chaired ACM FuturePlay International Conference on the Future of Game Design and Technology in 2007 and 2008. He also chaired FuturePlay @GDC Canada 2009.

Andreas Konstantinidis holds a BSc in Computer Science and an MSc in Information and Communication Technology in Education (ICTE) from the Aristotle University of Thessaloniki and is currently studying for a PhD on 3D Virtual Environments for Collaborative Learning. Before joining SEERC (South-East European Research Centre) as a research associate in 2008, he worked on a number of academic and European projects and in the telecommunications industry. His research activities are in the areas of collaborative virtual environments, collaborative learning, and computer supported collaborative work. He is also interested in e-learning systems, which is the topic of the research project that he is involved in at SEERC. He has published his research in a number of international conferences and journals and has also written chapters in books and encyclopedias.

Tiffany A. Koszalka is an Associate Professor in the Instructional Design, Development and Evaluation Department at Syracuse University, New York, USA. Her research is in the exploration of relationships among learning, instructional design, and technologies. She has a long history of designing, developing, facilitating, evaluating, and researching face-to-face, distance, virtual, and blended instructional environments enhanced with different types of technologies for K-12, higher education, and business contexts.

Edward Lee Lamoureux (B.A. CSULB, Speech, 1975; M.A. WSU, Speech Communication, 1980; Ph.D. University of Oregon, Rhetoric and Communication, 1985). At Bradley University (PeoriaIL, USA) since 1985, Ed is co-appointed to the faculties in the Department of Interactive Media and the Department of Communication. Ed teaches Introduction to New Media Theory, Intellectual Property Law and New Media, Issues in New Media Theory—Privacy, Virtual World Building & Research, Field Research Methods (ethnography) in Virtual Worlds, and Theory and Literature of Rhetoric. His research interests include ethnography, rhetoric, religious communication, conversation, and teaching and learning in virtual worlds. Ed's creative production includes audio production and Web work as well as communication training via digital embellishments. He taught the first online course at Bradley and teaches the first Bradley course(s) in virtual worlds. Ed is Professor Beliveau in Second Life, where he also performs (guitar and voice) as "the Professor."

Luca Mainetti is an associate professor of Software Engineering and Computer Graphics in the Department of Innovation Engineering at the University of Salento (Italy). His research interests include Web design methodologies, notations and tools, Web and services oriented architectures and applications, and collaborative computer graphics. He is scientific coordinator of the GSA Lab – Graphics and Software Architectures Lab (www.gsalab.unisalento.it), and IDA Lab – Identification Atomation Lab (www.idalab.unisalento.it). He is Rector's delegate to ICT. Mainetti received a PhD in Computer Science from Politecnico di Milano (Italy), where he has been supply teacher of Hypermedia Applications and Human Computer Interaction, and he contributed to create the HOC (Hypermedia Open Center) laboratory. He is a member of the IEEE and ACM. He is author of more than 70 international scientific papers.

Anne P. Massey is Dean's Research Professor and Professor of Information Systems in the Kelley School of Business at Indiana University. She received her PhD in decision sciences and engineering systems from Rensselaer Polytechnic Institute. Her research interests include technology implementation, computer-mediated communication and collaboration, knowledge management, and related topics. Her publications have appeared in *Decision Sciences, MIS Quarterly, Journal of Management Information Systems, Academy of Management Journal,* and *IEEE Transactions on Engineering Education,* among others.

Mary Ann Mengel is a Multimedia Specialist and Webmaster in the Center for Learning and Teaching at the Berks Campus of the Pennsylvania State University, where she designs and develops online multimedia-based tutorials and interactive learning modules to support hybrid and Web-enhanced courses. Mary Ann has an extensive background in the area of graphic design and visual communication, which uniquely enables her to simplify and clarify the design, development, and presentation of online tutorials. Mary Ann holds a Master's degree in Instructional Technology and a B.F.A. in Communication Design. She has taught the online course, Technology Planning Across the Curriculum, for Bloomsburg University's graduate program. In addition, she has presented her instructional initiatives related to Second Life at conferences both in the "real world" and the "virtual world." At the Berks campus, she often presents on topics related to multimedia-based instructional technologies.

Erin Mills was born in the United States, but raised in the Dominican Republic. She earned a Bachelor of Arts degree in Communications and minor in Graphic Design from Longwood University, as well as a Master of Science in Education with a concentration in International Higher Education Leadership from Old Dominion University. Currently as Assistant Director and Liaison to the College of Science at the Career Management Center at Old Dominion University, Erin serves as a career consultant for college of science students. Additionally she overseas an international internship program for international students who are seeking an internship or co-op experiences in the United States and helps domestic students find international internships abroad. She has extensive experience living and traveling abroad and is fluent in Spanish. Erin also serves as the co-advisor for Golden Key International Honour Society at Old Dominion University.

Nellie Modaress graduated from Kansas State University with a Masters in Journalism and Mass Communications and Educational Technology. Soon thereafter, she landed a job at the University of Kansas Medical Center in the department of Educational Technology where she assisted faculty integrate classroom technology within their curriculum. Amazingly, it is fifteen years later, and she still loves being in this field. Currently, Nellie is the Liaison to the School of Medicine where she assists the integration of classroom technology with the Medical School's curriculum in all capacities (Years 1-4, Residencies, and Fellowship programs) as well as the Departments of Health, Policy, and Management, and Preventive Medicine (KUMC as well as the campus in Wichita, KS). Her research interests lie in the field of gaming and simulations and most recently, in e-portfolios.

Mitzi M. Montoya is the Executive Dean of the College of Technology & Innovation at Arizona State University. She received her PhD in Marketing and B.S. in Applied Engineering Sciences from Michigan State University. Her research focuses on innovation processes and strategies and the role of technology as an enabler of collaboration. Her publications have appeared in *Management Science, Journal of Marketing Research, Marketing Science, Academy of Management Journal, the Journal of the Academy of Marketing Science,* among others.

Paolo Paolini is full professor at Politecnico di Milano (Italy), adjunct professor at the School of Communication Sciences and scientific coordinator of the master TEC-CH (Technology Enhanced Communication for Cultural Heritage) at the University of Lugano (USI). He is the scientific coordinator of HOC-lab of Politecnico di Milano (http://hoc.elet.polimi.it), where, since 1998, he has managed several projects related to ICT-based communication for cultural heritage (websites, multimedia, multi-channel applications) and e-learning (from online courses to collaborative 3D environments for education). He has been involved in a number of European funded projects on cultural heritage communication, and for several of them, he has been scientific coordinator.

Patrick Pettyjohn is a Learning Science doctoral student at Indiana University. He is interested in developing a means of understanding how people perceive opportunities for action, which he seeks to apply to areas of education, leadership development, and philanthropy. His current work involves designing for and investigating how multi-user virtual learning environments can be used as reflective tools that communicate one's academic understanding while simultaneously allowing players to experience the consequences of their choices and ethical beliefs. His current research interests have been strongly influenced by his previous domestic and cross-cultural roles leading in various mentoring nonprofit organizations and as a personal and team consultant.

Caterina Poggi earned a PhD in Computer Science at Politecnico di Milano, Italy, in 2007. She graduated in Communication Science–with specialization in Communication Technologies-at the University of Italian Switzerland, Lugano, in 2002. Since 2003, she collaborates with the HOC-LAB of Politecnico di Milano on research projects concerning computer-enhanced education and edutainment, particularly blended-learning experiences based on collaborative 3D virtual environments, such as Learning@Europe. Her research interests focus on multimedia applications for edutainment, specifically 3D virtual worlds for education, virtual museums, educational games, and e-learning.

Andreas Pomportsis obtained his diploma and his Master's degree from the Physics Department of the Aristotle University of Thessaloniki (Greece) and his PhD from the Informatics Department of the same university. He is currently a professor at the Department of Informatics of the Aristotle University of Thessaloniki. His research interests include computer networks, multimedia systems, value added services, and environments on the Internet.

Enrica Salvatori was born in La Spezia (Italy) in 1963, earned her degree in History from the University of Pisa (1988), PhD in Medieval History at University of Milan (V cycle - 1990-1992), post-doctorate at University of Turin (1994-1996), research fellow in Medieval History at University of Pisa (1998), associate professor in Medieval History at University of Pisa (2006) and is a member of RetiMedievali (online network for medieval studies, http://www.retimedievali.it). She is also deputy director of Informatica Umanistica (Digital Humanities) degree http://infouma.di.unipi.it; visiting professor at the University P. Valéry (Montpellier, France) in 2006 and 2008; review committee member of "Informatica Umanistica" http://www.ledonline.it/informatica-umanistica/; founder and owner of Historycast (http://www.historycast.org).

John Scott obtained his first degree in Electrical and Electronic Engineering from Nottingham University and a Post-Graduate Certificate of Education from Cambridge University. In 2000, he was awarded an MSc in Telecommunications Engineering by UCL. John is a Chartered Engineer and a Member of the Chartered Institute of Personnel Development. For much of his early career, he was involved in training delivery and management. He then moved into learning related research with particular responsibility for system requirement definition and developing concept demonstrators and prototypes. His research topics have included the use of social networking and ontologies to share learning resources and the development of a mixed reality learning and teaching environment. His recent work was the investigation of virtual world technologies to create meaningful contexts for learning a foreign language. He is currently a Lecturer in the International Academy at the University of Essex.

Carol Shepherd has a Bachelor's in English and a Master's in Social Studies from Fairleigh Dickinson University in Teaneck, New Jersey, and a Doctorate in Educational Administration from Seton Hall University in South Orange, New Jersey. She is presently completing a second Master's degree in Psychology from National University, San Diego, California. She has taught in the middle school, high school, and community college, and on undergraduate and graduate levels in the university. She has shared her knowledge and expertise by presenting at state, national, and international conferences on global issues dealing with differentiated instruction and assessment, mentoring, utilizing divergent thinking, and greater efficacy and self-actualization for both faculty and students. With today's dependence on technology, the more recent emphasis of her research in these areas has been on supporting effective online teaching and learning in virtual environments. She is currently an Associate Professor at National University in Sacramento, California.

Maria Simi, graduated in Computer Science from the University of Pisa in 1974, and is Associate Professor at the University of Pisa, where she teaches Artificial Intelligence and Web design. She was visiting fellow at the MIT in Cambridge (Mass.) in the "Message Passing Semantics" group, directed by Prof. Carl Hewitt, and visiting scientist at the ICSI of Berkeley and the Computer Science Laboratory of Sony in Paris. She was Associate Professor in Udine, teaching Information Systems in a study program in cultural heritage. She was one of the promoters of the study program in Digital Humanities at the University of Pisa. Her main research interest are in the field of artificial intelligence (knowledge representation, machine learning), Information Systems and Web based applications, question answering, and language technologies.

Liyan Song, PhD, is an assistant professor in the Department of Educational Technology and Literacy at Towson University. Her research interests include technology integration in education, pre-service teachers' conceptual change learning experiences, and distance education.

Jay Shiro Tashiro is currently a Professor in the Faculty of Health Sciences at the University of Ontario Institute of Technology (UOIT). He also has helped build two research and development companies, Wolfsong Informatics LLC in the United States, and BeaconWall Limited in Hong Kong. Tashiro's research focuses on health education and adherence to disease self-management strategies, the relationships between evidence-based learning and evidence-based practice in healthcare, and assessment of complex competencies within clinical simulations. Beginning in the mid-1990s, Tashiro led research teams in the development and evaluations of virtual clinical simulations that monitor users' choices during treatment of complex patients within the simulations. The principal focus of these monitoring systems has been clinical judgment, with the software conducting automated analysis of choices made by the user while working within a simulation. Funding related to virtual learning environments has been over $10 million since 1990. At UOIT, Tashiro teaches in the Health Information Management Program and is currently building and evaluating simulation-rich courses that promote inter-professional collaborative patient-centered care. Tashiro also helped establish and now is part of the Management Team for the Health Education Technology Research Unit at UOIT.

David Thomas a videogame critic, researcher, teacher, and academic technology professional. Working with CU Online at the University of Colorado Denver, David helps faculty improve their online courses by matching technology to pedagogy. He teaches courses covering the history of digital media and games and learning. As a journalist, he writes for a wide variety of game magazines, enthusiast websites, and produces a nationally syndicated newspaper column covering the best in games. He is currently completing his PhD in the college of architecture and planning looking at the question: "What makes a place fun?"

Marc Thompson: Marc initially trained as a Geography and English as a Second Language (ESL) teacher before gaining qualifications in Special Educational Needs (SEN) support. He was Head of the English as an Additional Language (EAL) department in a large London comprehensive from 1995 to 2000. He became Deputy Head and just prior to his current post, Acting Head of Hertfordshire's West Area Ethnic Minority Achievement Centre, which employed 60 staff providing advice, training, and support to 40 primary and 12 secondary schools in the St Albans and Hemel area. He is currently employed by Cambridge Education @ Islington as a Senior Consultant, providing training and advice to schools as well as undertaking teaching placements to develop effective practice and pilot new initiatives. He qualified as an accredited office for standards in education (Ofsted) inspector in 2005 and completed a Masters Degree in Education (E-Learning) in 2010. In 2008, Marc organized the 'Education without Boundaries' conference in Second Life in collaboration with the Diplomacy team at the US state department.

Mitzi P. Trahan is an Assistant Professor in the Department of Foundations and Educational Leadership at the University of Louisiana at Lafayette. She has expertise in individual and community counseling, and currently serves as doctoral faculty in educational leadership. She is a state-level grant evaluator and primarily teaches classroom assessment and research methodology. Her research interests include virtual learning and computer assisted education with an emphasis on psychosocial and environmental factors impacting teaching and learning with technology.

Thrasyvoulos Tsiatsos obtained his diploma, his Master's degree and his PhD from the computer engineering and informatics department of Patras University (Greece). He is currently lecturer in the Department of Informatics of Aristotle University of Thessaloniki. His research interests include computer networks, telematics, networked virtual environments, multimedia, and hypermedia.

Elizabeth Wellman has an Ed.D. in Educational Psychology, Learning and Instruction from The University of California Los Angeles, an M.A. in Education from the Math/Science/Technology Education Project at the University of Massachusetts, Amherst, a B.S. in Meteorology from the Pennsylvania State University, University Park, and is a K-12 teacher certified in Earth Science. As the Director of an Apple Education grant, an AT&T Learning Initiatives Grant, the Associate Director of Technology Projects for the California History Social Science Projec,t and as an Associate Professor of Education at Bard College, she has researched and provided instructional design utilizing technology for learning. She has also designed, developed, and implemented courses and professional development in and with technology for teachers supporting their efforts to develop instruction for disciplinary expertise and thinking. Most recently, she has focused her efforts on immersive technologies and their promise for broadening methodological opportunities for K-16 classrooms and beyond.

YiYan Wu is a doctoral student working on her dissertation in the Instruction Design, Development and Evaluation Department at Syracuse University, New York, USA. Her research focuses on investigating and evaluating college science/engineering students' collaborative problem-solving, communication, and technology use within a technology-enhanced distributed educational environment.

Tom Wunderlich: Prior to appointment as the Assistant Dean of the Career Management Center, he supervised the Career Management Center's satellite office located in the College of Engineering and Technology. He directed the College's Cooperative Education and Internship programs and provided all career-related services to the students of the college for 14 years. He joined the University and the Career Management Center in 1989 after completing a 21 year career as a Marine Corps Lt. Colonel and fighter pilot. He received a bachelor's degree in Psychology and a Master's degree in College Student Personnel from Southern Illinois University, Carbondale, Illinois.

Index